JAMES E

TRAVELS

TO DISCOVER THE
SOURCE OF THE NILE,

IN THE YEARS 1768, 1769, 1770, 1771, 1772, AND 1773

Volume II

Elibron Classics
www.elibron.com

Elibron Classics series.

© 2005 Adamant Media Corporation.

ISBN 1-4021-6022-4 (paperback)
ISBN 1-4212-7901-0 (hardcover)

This Elibron Classics Replica Edition is an unabridged facsimile
of the edition published in 1790, Edinburgh.

TRAVELS

TO DISCOVER THE

SOURCE OF THE NILE.

TRAVELS

TO DISCOVER THE

SOURCE OF THE NILE,

In the Years 1768, 1769, 1770, 1771, 1772, and 1773.

IN FIVE VOLUMES.

BY JAMES BRUCE OF KINNAIRD, ESQ. F.R.S.

VOL. II.

Vixere fortes ante Agamemnona
Multi, fed omnes illachrymabiles
Urgentur ignotique longâ
Nocte, carent quia vate facro.   HORAT.

EDINBURGH:
PRINTED BY J. RUTHVEN,
FOR G. G. J. AND J. ROBINSON, PATERNOSTER-ROW,
LONDON.

M.DCC.XC.

CONTENTS

OF THE

SECOND VOLUME.

BOOK III.

ANNALS OF ABYSSINIA.
Tranſlated from the Original.

CONTAINING THE HISTORY OF THE ABYSSINIANS, FROM THE RESTORATION OF THE LINE OF SOLOMON TO THE DEATH OF SOCINIOS, AND THE DOWNFALL OF THE RO-MISH RELIGION.

ICON AMLAC.
From 1268 to 1283.

IGBA SION.
From 1283 to 1312.

AN-

CONTENTS. iii

DAVID

CONTENTS.

Z A

ZA DENGHEL.
From 1595 to 1604.

JACOB.
From 1604 to 1605.

SOCINIOS or MELEC SEGUED.
From 1605 to 1632.

BOOK IV.

CONTINUATION OF THE ANNALS, FROM THE DEATH OF SOCINIOS, TILL MY ARRIVAL IN ABYSSINIA.

FACILIDAS or SULTAN SEGUED.
From 1632 to 1665.

vi   CONTENTS.

                                                          DAVID

CONTENTS.

DAVID IV.
From 1714 to 1719.

Convocation of the Clergy—Catholic Priests executed—A Second Convocation—Clergy insult the King—His severe Punishment—King dies of Poison,

P. 577

BACUFFA.
From 1719 to 1729.

Bloody Reign—Exterminates the Conspirators—Counterfeits Death—Becomes very Popular, .

595

YASOUS II. or, ADIAM SEGUED.
From 1729 to 1753.

Rebellion in the Beginning of this Reign—King addicted to hunting—To building, and the Arts of Peace—Attacks Sennaar—Loses his Army.—Takes Samayat—Receives Baady King of Sennaar under his Protection,

608

JOAS.
From 1753 to 1769.

This Prince a favorer of the Galla his Relations—Great dissentions on bringing them to Court—War of Begemder—Ras Michael brought to Gondar—Defeats Ayo—Mariam Barea refuses to be accessary to his Death—King favours Waragna Fasil—Battle of Azazo—King Assassinated in his Palace, .

660

HANNES II.
1769.

Hannes, Brother to Bacuffa, chosen King—Is brought from Wechné—Crowned at Gondar—His horrid Behaviour—Refuses to march against Fasil—Is poisoned by Order of Ras Michael,

707

TECLA

TECLA HAIMANOUT II.
1769.

TRAVELS

TRAVELS

TO DISCOVER

THE SOURCE OF THE NILE.

BOOK III.

ANNALS OF ABYSSINIA,
TRANSLATED FROM THE ORIGINAL;

CONTAINING THE HISTORY OF THE ABYSSINIANS, FROM THE
RESTORATION OF THE LINE OF SOLOMON TO THE DEATH OF
SOCINIOS, AND THE DOWNFALL OF THE ROMISH RELIGION.

ICON AMLAC.
From 1258 to 1283.

Line of Solomon restored under this Prince—He continues the Royal Re-
sidence in Shoa—Tecla Haimanout dies—Reasons for the Fabrication
of the supposed Nicene Canon.

ALTHOUGH the multiplicity of names affumed by the
kings of Abyffinia, and the confufion occafioned by
this cuftom, has more than once been complained of in the
foregoing fheets, we have here a prince that is an exception

to this practice, otherwise almost general. Icon Amlac is the only name by which we know this first prince of the race of Solomon, restored now fully to his dominions, after a long exile his family had suffered by the treason of Judith. The signification of his name is, " Let him be made our sovereign," and is apparently that which he took upon his inauguration or accession to the throne ; and his name of baptism, and bye-name or popular name given him, are both therefore lost.

ALTHOUGH now restored to the complete possession of his ancient dominions, he was too wise all at once to leave his dutiful kingdom of Shoa and return to Tigré. He continued to make Tegular, the capital of Shoa, his seat of the empire, and there reigned fifteen years.

IN the 14th year of the reign of this prince, his great benefactor, Abuna Tecla Haimanout, founder of the Order of Monks of Debra Libanos, and restorer of the Royal family, died at that monastery in great reputation and very advanced age. He was the last Abyssinian ordained Abuna ; and this sufficiently shews the date of that canon I have already spoken of, falsely said to be a canon of the council of Nicea.

THOUGH Le Grande and some others have pretended to be in doubt at what time, and for what reason, this canon could have been made, I think the reason very plain, which fixes it to the time of Tecla Haimanout, as well as shews it to be a forgery of the church of Alexandria, no doubt with the council and advice of this great statesman Tecla Haimanout. Egypt was fallen under the dominion of the

4   Sara-

Saracens; the Coptic patriarch, and all the Chriftians of the church of Alexandria, were their flaves or fervants; but the Abyffinians were free and independent, both in church and ftate, and a mortal hatred had followed the conqueſt from variety of caufes, of which the perfecution of the Chriſtians in Egypt was not one of the leaft. As it was probable that thefe reafons would increafe daily, the confequence which promifed inevitably to follow was, that the Abyſſinians would not apply to Alexandria, or Cairo, for a metropolitan fent by the Mahometans, but would chooſe a head of their own, and fo become independent altogether of the chair of St Mark. As they were cut off from the reft of the world by feas and deferts almoft inacceffible, as they wanted books, and were every day relaxing in difcipline, total ignorance was likely to follow their feparation from their primitive church, and this could not end but in a relapfe into Pagan-ifm, or in their embracing the religion of Mahomet.

This prohibition of making any of their countrymen Abuna, fecured them always a foreigner, and a man of fo-reign education and attachments, to fill the place of Abuna, and by this means affured the dependence of the Abyffini-ans upon the patriarch of Alexandria. This is what I judge probable, for I have already invincibly fhewn, that it is im-poffible this canon could be one of the firft general Council; and its being in Arabic, and conceived in very barbarous er ms, fufficiently evinces that it was forged at this period.

A 2   IGBA

IGBA SION.

From 1295 to 1312.

Quick Succession of Princes—Memoirs of these Reigns deficient.

TO Icon Amlac succeeded Igba Sion, and after him five other princes, his brothers, Bahar Segued, Tzenaf Segued, Jan Segued, Hafeb Araad, and Kedem Segued, all in five years. So quick a succession in so few years seems to mark very unsettled times. Whether it was a civil war among themselves that brought these reigns to so speedy a conclusion, or whether it was that the Moorish states in Adel had grown in power, and fought successfully against them, we do not know. One thing only we are certain of, that no molestation was offered by the late royal family of Lasta, who continued in peace, and firm in the observation of their treaty. I therefore am inclined to think, that a civil war among the brothers was the occasion of the quick succession of so many princes; and that in the time when the kingdom was weakened by this calamity, the states of Adel, grown rich and powerful, had improved the occasion, and seized upon all that territory from Azab to Melinda, and cut off the Abyssinians entirely from the sea-coast, and from an opportunity of trading directly with India from the ports situated upon the ocean. And my reason is, that, in a reign which speedily follows, we find the kingdom of Adel

Adel increased greatly in power, and Moorish princes from Arabia establithed in little principalities, exactly correfponding with the fouthern limits of Abyffinia, and placed between them and the ocean; and we fee, at the fame time, a rancour and hatred firmly rooted in the breafts of both nations, one of the caufes of which is conftantly alledged by the Abyffinian princes to be, that the Moors of Adel were anciently their fubjects and vaffals, had withdrawn themfelves from their allegiance, and owed their prefent independence to rebellion only.

To thefe princes fucceeded Wedem Araad, their youngeft brother, who reigned fifteen years, probably in peace, for in this ftate we find the kingdom in the days of his fucceffor; but then it is fuch a peace that we fee it only wanted any fort of provocation from one party to the other, for both to break out into very cruel, long, and bloody wars.

A M D A   S I O N.

From 1312 to 1342.

Licentious beginning of this King's Reign—His rigorous Conduct with the Monks of Debra Libanos—His Mahometan Subjects rebel—Mara and Adel declare War—Are defeated in feveral Battles, and fubmit.

AMDA Sion fucceeded his father, Wedem Araad, who was youngeft brother of Icon Amlac, and came to the crown upon the death of his uncles. He is generally known by by this his inauguration name; his Chriftian name was Guebra Mafcal. His reign began with a fcene as difgraceful to the name of Chriftian as it was new in the annals of Ethiopia, and which promifed a character very different from what this prince preferved ever afterwards. He had for a time, it feems, privately loved a concubine of his father, but had now taken her to live with him publicly; and, not content with committing this fort of inceft, he, in a very little time after, had feduced his two fifters.

TEGULAT * (the capital of Shoa) was then the royal refidence; and near it the monaftery of Debra Libanos, founded by Tecla Haimanout reftorer of the line of Solomon. To this monaftery many men, eminent for learning and religion, had retired from the fcenes of war that defolated Paleftine and Egypt. Among the number of thefe was one Honorius, a Monk of the firft character for piety, who, fince, has been canonized as a faint. Honorius thought it his duty firft to admonifh, and then publicly excommunicate the king for thefe crimes.

It fhould feem that patience was as little among this prince's virtues as chaftity, as he immediately ordered Honorius to be apprehended, ftripped naked, and feverely whipped through every ftreet of his capital. That fame night the town took fire, and was entirely confumed, and the clergy loft no time to perfuade the people, that it was the blood of Honorius that turned to fire whenever it had dropt upon the ground, and fo had burnt the city. The

king,

---

* The city of Wolves, or Hyænas.

king, perhaps better informed, thought otherwife of this, and fuppofed the burning of his capital was owing to the Monks themfelves. He therefore banifhed thofe of Debra Libanos out of the province of Shoa. The mountain of Gefhen had been chofen for the prifon wherein to guard the princes of the male-line of the race of Solomon, after the maffacre by Efther *, upon the rock Damo in Tigré.

Geshen is a very fteep and high rock, in the kingdom of Amhara, adjoining to, and under the jurifdiction of Shoa. Hither the king fent Philip the Itchegué, chief of the monaftery of Debra Libanos, and he fcattered the reft through Dembea, Tigré, and Begemder, (whofe inhabitants were moftly Pagans and Jews), where they greatly propagated the knowledge of the Chriftian religion.

This inftance of feverity in the king had the effect to make all ranks of people return to their duty; and all talk of Honorius and his miracles was dropt. The town was rebuilt fpeedily, more magnificently than ever, and Amda Sion found time to turn his thoughts to correct thofe abufes, to efface the unfavourable impreffion which they had made upon the minds of his people at home, and which, befides, had gained confiderable ground abroad.

It has been before mentioned, and will be further inculcated in the courfe of this hiftory as a fact, without the remembrance of which the military expeditions of Abyffinia cannot be well underftood, that two oppofite feafons
prevail

---

* She had feveral names, as I have before faid, Judith in Tigré, and in Amhara Efther.

prevail in countries separated by a line almost imperceptible; that during our European winter months, that is, from October to March, the winter or rainy season prevails on the coast of the ocean and Red Sea, but that these rains do not fall in our summer, (the rainy season in Abyssinia', which was the reason why Amda Sion said to his mutinous troops, he would lead them to Adel or Aussa, where it did not rain, as we shall presently observe.

THE different nations that dwell along the coast, both of the Red Sea and of the ocean, live in fixed huts or houses. We shall begin at the northmost, or nearest Atbara. The first is Ageeg, so named from a small island on the coast, opposite to the mountains of the Habab, Agag, or Agaazi, the principal district of the noble or governing Shepherds, as is before fully explained, different in colour and hair from the Shepherds of the Thebaid living to the northward. Then follow the different tribes of these, Tora, Shiho, Taltal, Azimo, and Azabo, where the Red Sea turns eastward, towards the Straits, all woolly-headed, the primitive carriers of Saba, and the perfume and gold country. Then various nations inhabit along the ocean, all native blacks, remnants of the Cushite Troglodyte, but who do not change their habitations with the seasons, but live within land in caves, and some of them now in houses..

IN Adel and Aussa the inhabitants are tawny, and not black, and have long hair; they are called Gibbertis, which some French writers of voyages into this country say, mean Slaves, from Guebra, the Abyssinian word for slave or servant. But as it would be very particular that a nation like these, so rich and so powerful, who have made themselves inde-

2   inde-

independent of their ancient mafters the Abyffinians, have wrefted fo many provinces from them, and, from the difference of their faith, hold them in fuch utter contempt, fhould neverthelefs be content to call themfelves their flaves, fo nothing is more true, than that this name of Gibberti has a very different import. Jabber, in Arabic, the word from which it is derived, fignifies the *faith*, or the *true faith*; and Gibberti confequently means the *faithful*, or the *orthodox*, by which name of *honour* thefe moors, inhabiting the low country of Abyffinia, call each other, as being conftant in their faith amidft Chriftians with whom they are at perpetual war.

THERE is no current coin in Abyffinia. Gold is paid by weight; all the revenues are chiefly paid in kind, viz. oxen, fheep, and honey, which are the greateft neceffaries of life. As for luxuries, they are obtained by a barter of gold, myrrh, coffee, elephants teeth, and a variety of other articles which are carried over to Arabia; and in exchange for thefe is brought back whatever is commiffioned.

EVERY great man in Abyffinia has one of thefe Gibbertis for his factor. The king has many, who are commonly the fhrewdeft and moft intelligent of their profeffion. Thefe were the firft inhabitants of Abyffinia, whom commerce connected with the Arabians on the other fide of the Straits of Babelmandeb, with whom they intermarry, or with one another, which preferves their colour and features, refembling both the Abyffinians and Arabians. In Arabia, they are under the protection of fome of their own countrymen, who being fold when young as flaves, are brought up in the Mahometan religion, and enjoy all the principal pofts under the Sherriffe of Mecca and the Arabian princes. Thefe are the people who at particular times have appeared in Europe, and who have been ftraightway taken for, and treated as Ambaffadors.

More fouthward and weftward are the kingdoms of Mara, Worgla, and Pagoma, fmall principalities of fixed habitations by the fea, at times free, at others dependent upon Adel; and, to the fouth of thefe, in the fame flat country, is Hadea, whofe capital is Harar, and governed by a prince, who is a Gibberti likewife; and who, by marrying a Sherriffa, or female defcendant of Mahomet, is now reckoned a Sherriffe or noble of Mahomet's family, diftinguifhed by his wearing habits, for the moft part green, and above all a grafs-green turban, a mark of hatred to Chriftianity.

The Gibbertis, then, are the princes and merchants of this country, converted to the Mahometan faith foon after the death of Mahomet, when the Baharnagafh (as we have already ftated) revolted from the empire of the Abyffinians, in whofe hands all the riches of the country are centered. The black inhabitants are only their fubjects, hewers of wood and drawers of water, who ferve them in their families at home, take care of their camels when employed in caravans abroad, and who make the principal part of their forces in the field.

But there are other inhabitants ftill befides thefe Gibbertis and native blacks, whom we muft not confound with the indigenous of this country, how much foever they may refemble them. The firft of thefe are by the Portuguefe hiftorians called *Moors*, who are merchants from the weft of
Africa,

Africa. Many of thefe, expelled from Spain by Ferdinand and Ifabella, fixed their refidence here, and were afterwards joined by others of their Moorifh brethren, either exiles from Spain, or inhabitants of Morocco, whom the defire of commerce induced firft to fettle in Arabia, till the great oppreffions that followed the conqueft of Egypt and Arabia, under Selim and Soliman, interrupted their trade, and fcattered them here along the coaft. Thefe are the Moors that Vafques de Gama* met at Mombaza, Magadoxa, and Melinda; at all places, but the laft of which, they endeavoured to betray him. Thefe alfo were the Moors that he found in India, having no profeffion but trade, in every fpecies of which they excelled.

The fourth fort are Arabian merchants, who come over occafionally to recover their debts, and renew correfpondences with the merchants of this country. Thefe are the richeft of all, and are the bankers of the Gibbertis, who furnifh them funds and merchandife, with which they carry on a moft lucrative and extenfive trade into the heart of Africa, through all the mountains of Abyffinia to the weftern fea, and through countries which are inacceffible to camels, where the afs, the mule, and, in fome places, oxen, are the only beafts ufed in carriage.

There is a fifth fort, almoft below notice, unlefs it is for the mifchief they have conftantly done their country; they are the Abyffinian apoftates from Chriftianity, the moft inveterate enemies it has, and who are employed chiefly as foldiers. While in that country they are not much efteem-

ed,

---

* Conqueftes de Portugas por Laffiau, vol. 1. liv. ii. p. 90. Id. ibid. p. 124.

ed, though, when tranfported to India, they have conftantly
turned out men of confidence and truft, and the beft troops
thofe eaftern nations have.

THERE is a fixth, ftill lefs in number than even thefe, and
not known on this Continent till a few years before. Thefe
were the Turks who came from Greece and Syria, and who
were under Selim, and Soliman his fon, the inftruments of
the conqueft of Egypt and Arabia; fmall garrifons of whom
were everywhere left by the Turks in all the fortreffes and
confiderable towns they conquered. They are an hereditary kind of militia, who, marrying each others daughters,
or with the women of the country, continue from father
to fon to receive from Conftantinople the fame pay their
forefathers had from Selim. Thefe, though degenerate in
figure and manners into an exact refemblance to the natives of the countries in which they fince lived, do ftill continue to maintain their fuperiority by a conftant fkill and
attention to fire-arms, which were, at the time of their firft
appearance here, little known or in ufe among either Abyffinians or Arabians, and the means of firft eftablifhing this
preference.

IT has been already obferved, that the Mahometan Moors
and Arabs poffeffed all the low country on the Indian Ocean,
and oppofite to Arabia Felix; and being, by their religion,
obliged to go in pilgrimage to Mecca, as alfo by their fole
profeffion, which was trade, they became, by confequence,
the only carriers and directors of the commerce of Abyffinia. All the country to the eaft and north of Shoa was
poffeffed and commanded chiefly by Mahometan merchants
appointed.

appointed by the king; and they had eftablifhed a variety of marts or fairs from Ifat, all the way as far as Adel.

ADEL and Mara were two of the moft powerful kingdoms which lie on the Indian Ocean; and, being conftantly fupported by foldiers from Arabia, were the firft to withdraw themfelves from obedience to the king of Abyffinia, and feldom paid their tribute unlefs when the prince came to raife it there with an army. Ifat, Fatigar, and Dawaro, were indeed originally Chriftian provinces; but, in weak reigns, having been ceded to Moorifh governors for fums of money, they, by degrees, renounced both their religion and allegiance.

FROM what has been obferved, the reader will conceive, that where it is faid the king, from his capital in Shoa, marched down into Dawaro, Hadea, or Adel, that he then defcended from the higheft mountains down to the flat country on the level with the fea. That this country, from Hadea to Dawaro, having been the feat of war for ages, was, partly by the foldier for the ufe of the camp, partly by the hufbandman for the neceffaries of life, cleared of wood, where the water flood conftantly in pools throughout the year; and, being all compofed of fat black earth, which the torrents bring down from the rainy country of Abyffinia, was fown with millet and different kinds of grain in the drieft ground, while, nearer the mountains, they paftured numerous herds of cattle. Notwithstanding, however, the country was poffeffed of thefe advantages, the climate was intenfely hot, feverifh, and unhealthy, and, for the moft part, from thefe circumftances, fatal to ftrangers, and hated by the Abyffinians.

AGAIN,

AGAIN, when it is said that the king had marched to Samhar, it is meant that he had passed this fruitful country, and is come to that part of the zone, or belt, (nearest the sea) composed of gravel; which, though it enjoys neither the water nor the fruitfulness of the black earth, is in a great measure free from its attendant diseases, and here the cities and towns are placed, while the crop, oxen, and cattle, are in the cultivated part near the mountains, which in the language of the country is called *Mazaga*, signifying *black mould*.

LASTLY, when he hears the army murmuring at being kept during the rainy season in the Kolla below, he is to remember, that all was cool, pleasant, and safe in Upper A-byssinia. The soldiers, therefore, languished for the enjoyment of their own families, without any other occupation but merriment, festivity, and every species of gratification that wine, and the free and uncontrouled society of the female-sex, could produce.

HAVING now sufficiently explained and described the various names and inhabitants, the situation, soil, and climate of those provinces about to be the theatre of the war, I shall proceed to declare the occasion of it, which was nothing more than the fruit of those prejudices which, I have already said, the loose behaviour of the king in the beginning of his reign had produced among his neighbours, and the calamities which had enfeebled the kingdom in the preceding reigns.

IT happened that one of those Moorish factors, whom I have already described, having in charge the commercial

interests

interests of the king, had been affassinated and robbed in the province of Ifat, when the King was busied with Honorius and his Monks. Without complaining or expostulating, he suddenly assembled his troops, having ordered them to rendezvous at Shugura upon the frontiers, and, to shew his impatience for revenge, with seven* horsemen he fell upon the nearest Mahometan settlements, who were perfectly secure, and put all he found in his way to the sword without exception. Then placing himself at the head of his army, he marched, by a long day's journey, straight to Ifat, burning Hungura, Jadai, Kubat, Fadife, Calife, and Argai, towns that lye in the way, full of all sorts of valuable merchandise, and, finding no where a force assembled to oppose him, he divided his army into small detachments, sending them different ways, with orders to lay the whole countries, where they came, waste with fire and sword, while he himself remained in the camp to guard the spoil, the women, and the baggage.

The Moors, astonished at this torrent of desolation, which so suddenly had broken out under a prince whom they had considered as immersed in pleasure, flew all to arms; and being informed that the king was alone, and scarcely had soldiers to guard his camp, they assembled in numbers under the command of Hak-eddin, governor of Ifat, who had before plundered and murdered the king's servant. They then determined to attack Amda Sion early in the morning, but luckily two of his detachments had returned to the camp to his assistance, and joined him the very night before.

It

* It has been imagined that this number should be increased to seventy, but I have followed the text; there would be little difference in the rashness of the action.

It was fcarcely day when the Moors prefented themfelves; but, far from furprifing the Abyffinians buried in fleep, they found the king with his army ranged in battle, who, without giving them time to recover from their furprife, attacked them in perfon with great fury; and fingling out Derdar, brother to Hak-eddin, animating his men before the ranks, he ftruck him fo violently with his lance that he fell dead among his horfe's feet, in the fight of both armies; whilft the Abyffinian troops preffing every where brifkly forward, the Moors took to flight, and were purfued with great flaughter into the woods and faftneffes.

After this victory, the king ordered his troops to build huts for themfelves, at leaft fuch as could not find houfes ready built. He ordered, likewife, a great tract of land contiguous to be plowed and fown, meaning to intimate, that his intention was to ftay there with his army all the rainy feafon.

The Mahometans, from this meafure, if it fhould be carried into execution, faw nothing but total extirpation before their eyes; they, therefore, with one confent, fubmitted to the tribute impofed upon them; and the king having removed Hak-eddin, placed his brother Saber-eddin in his ftead, and the rainy feafon being now begun, difmiffed his army, and returned to Tegulat in Shoa.

Though the perfonal gallantry of the king was a quality fufficient of itfelf to make him a favourite of the foldiers, his liberality was not lefs; all the plunder got by his troops in the field was faithfully divided among thofe who had fought for him; nor did he ever pretend to a fhare him-

felf,

felf, unlefs on occafions when he was engaged in perfon, and then he fhared upon an equal footing with the principal officers.

WHEN returned to the capital, he fhewed the fame difinterestednefs and generofity which he had done in the field, and he diftributed all he had won for his fhare among the great men, whom the necefiary duties of government had obliged to remain at home, as alfo amongft the poor, and priefts for the maintenance of churches; and, as well by this, as by his zeal and activity againft the enemies of Chriftianity, he became the greateft favourite of all ranks of the clergy, notwithftanding the unpromifing appearances at the beginning of his reign.

THE rainy feafon in Abyflinia generally puts an end to the active part of war, as every one retires then to towns and villages to fcreen themfelves from the inclemency of the climate, deluged now with daily rain. The foldier, the hufbandman, and, above all, the women, dedicate this feafon to continued feftivity and riot. Thefe villages and towns are always placed upon the higheft mountains. The valleys that intervene are foon divided by large and rapid torrents. Every hollow foot-path becomes a ftream, and the valleys between the hills become fo miry as not to bear horfe; and the waters, both deep and violent, are too apt to fhift their direction to fuffer any one on foot to pafs fafely. All this feafon, and this alone, people fleep in their houfes in fafety; their lances and fhields are hung up on the fides of their hall, and their faddles and bridles taken off their horfes; for in Abyflinia, at other times, the horfes are always bridled, and are accuftomed to eat and drink with this

incumbrance.

incumbrance. It is not, indeed, the same sort of bridle they use in the field, but a small bit of iron like our hunting-bridles, on purpose merely to preserve them in this habit. The court, and the principal officers of government, retire to the capital, and there administer justice, make alliances, and prepare the necessary funds and armaments, which the present exigencies of the state require on the return of fair weather.

Amda Sion was no sooner returned to Tegulat, than the Moors again entered into a conspiracy against him. The principal were Amano king of Hadea, Saber-eddin, whom the king had made governor of Fatigar, and privately, without any open declaration, Gimmel-eddin governor in Dawaro. But this conspiracy could not be hid from a prince of Amda Sion's vigilance and penetration. He concealed, however, any knowledge of the matter, lest it should urge the Moors to commence hostilities too early. He continued, therefore, with diligence, and without ostentation of any particular design, to make the ordinary preparations to take the field on the approaching season. This, however, did not impose upon the enemy. Whether from intelligence, or impatience of being longer inactive, Saber-eddin began the first hostilities, by surprising some Christian villages, and plundering and setting fire to the churches before the rains had yet entirely ceased.

Those that have written accounts of Abyssinia seem to agree in extolling the people of that country for giving no belief to the existence or reality of witchcraft or sorcery. Why they have fixed on this particular nation is hard to determine. But, as for me, I have no doubt in asserting, that there is not a barbarous or ignorant people that I ever knew of which

this

this can be truly faid ; but certainly it never was lefs true than when faid of Abyffinians. There is fcarce a monk in any lonely monaftery, (fuch as thofe in the hot and un-wholefome valley of Waldubba), not a hermit of the many upon the mountains, not an old prieft who has lived any time fequeftered from fociety, that does not pretend to pof-fefs charms offenfive and defenfive, and feveral methods by which he can, at will, look into futurity. The Moors are all, to a man, perfuaded of this : their arms and necks are loaded with amulets againft witchcraft. Their women are believed to have all the mifchievous powers of faf-cination ; and both fexes a hundred fecrets of divina-tion. The Falafha are addicted to this in ftill a greater degree, if poffible. It is always believed by every indivi-dual Abyffinian, that the number of hyænas the fmell of carrion brings into the city of Gondar every night, are the Falafha from the neighbouring mountains, transformed by the effect and for the purpofes of inchantment. Even the Galla, a barbarous and ftranger nation, hoftile to the Abyf-finians, and differing in language and religion, ftill agree with them in a hearty belief of the poffibility of practifing witchcraft, fo as to occafion ficknefs and death at a very great diftance, to blaft the harvefts, poifon the waters, and render people incapable of propagating their fpecies.

Amano, king of Hadea, had one of thefe conjurers, who, by his knowledge of futurity, was famous among all the Mahometans of the low country. The king of Hadea him-felf had gone no further than to determine to rebel ; but whether he was to go up to fight with Amda Sion in Shoa, or whether greater fuccefs would attend his expect-ing him in Hadea, this was thought a doubt wholly with-

in

in the province of the conjurer, who affured Amano, his
mafter, that if he did remain below, and wait for Amda Sion
in Hadea, that prince would come down to him, and in one
battle lofe his kingdom and his life.

The king, whofe principal view was to prevent the conjunction of the confederates, and, if poffible, to fight them
feparately, did not flay till his whole army was affembled,
but, as foon as he got together a body of troops fufficient
to make head againft any one of the rebels, he fent that body
immediately on the fervice it was deftined for, in order to
difappoint the general combination.

A large number of horfe and foot (whofe poft was in
the van of the royal army when the king marched at the
head of it) was the firft ready, and, without delay, was fent
againft Amano into Hadea, under the command of the
general of the cavalry. This officer executed the fervice
on which he was fent with the greateft diligence poffible,
having the beft horfes, and ftrongeft and moft active men
in the army; by long marches, he came upon the king
of Hadea, furprifed him before his troops were all affembled, gave him an entire defeat, and made him prifoner.
However ill the conjurer had provided for the king's fafety,
he feems to have been more attentive to his own; great fearch
was made for him by order of Amda Sion, but he was not to
be found, having very early, upon the firft fight of the king's
troops, fled and hid himfelf in Ifat.

The next detachment was fent againft Saber-eddin in
Fatigar. The governor of Amhara commanded this, with
orders

orders to lay the whole country waste, and by all means provoke Saber-eddin to risk a battle, either before or after the junction of the troops which were to march thither from Hadea. But when the king was thus busy with the Moors, news were brought him that the Falasha had rebelled, and were in arms, in very great numbers. The king ordered Tzaga Christos, governor of Begemder, to assemble his troops with those of Gondar, Sacalta, and Damot, and march against these rebels before they had time to ruin the country; and having thus made provision against all his enemies, Amda Sion proceeded with the remainder of his army to Dawaro.

Hydar was governor in this province for the king, who, though he shewed outwardly every appearance of duty and fidelity, was, notwithstanding, deep in the conspiracy with Saber-eddin, and had close correspondence with the king of Adel, whose capital, Aussa, was not at a great distance from him.

The king kept his Easter at Gaza, immediately upon the verge of the desert; and, being willing to accustom his troops to action and hardship, he left his tents and baggage behind with the army; and, secretly taking with him but twenty-six horsemen, he made an incursion upon Samhar, destroying all before him, and staying all night, tho' he had no provisions, in the middle of his enemies, without so much as lying down to sleep, slacking his belt, or taking off any part of his armour.

The king was no sooner gone than the army missed him, and was all in the greatest uproar. But, having finished his expedition, he joined them in the morning, and encamped

camped again with them. On his arrival, he found waiting for him a meſſenger from Tzaga Chriſtos, with accounts that he had fought fucceſsfully with the Falaſha, entirely defeated them, ſlain many, and forced the reſt to hide themſelves in their inacceſſible mountains. Immediately after this intelligence, Tzaga Chriſtos, with his victorious army, joined the king alſo.

THESE good tidings were followed by others equally profperous from Hadea and Fatigar. They were, that the king's army in thoſe parts had forced Saber-eddin to a battle, and beaten him, taken and plundered his houſe, and brought his wife and children priſoners; and that the troops had found that country full of merchandiſe and riches of all kinds; that they were already laden and incumbered with the quantity to ſuch a degree, that they were all ſpeaking of diſbanding and retiring to their houſes with riches ſufficient for the reſt of their lives, although a great part of the country remained as yet untouched, and, therefore, it was requeſted of the king in all diligence to enter it on his ſide alſo, and march ſouthward till both armies met. Immediately upon this meſſage, the king, having refreſhed his troops, and informed them of the good profpects that were before them, decamped with his whole army, and entered the province of Ifat.

WHEN Saber-eddin ſaw the king's forces were joined, that he had no allies, and that it was, in the ſituation of his army, equally dangerous to ſtay or to fly, he took a reſolution of ſubmitting himſelf to the king's mercy; but, firſt, he endeavoured to ſoften his anger, and obtain ſome aſſurances

rances through the mediation of the queen. The king, however, having publicly reproved the queen for offering to intermeddle in such matters, and growing more violent and inflexible upon this application, there remained no alternative but that of surrendering himself at discretion. Whereupon Saber-eddin threw himself at the king's feet. The soldiers and by-standers, far from being moved at such a sight, with one voice earnestly besought the king, that the murderer of so many priests, and the profaner and destroyer of so many Christian churches, should instantly meet the death his crimes had merited. The king, however, whose mercy seems to have been equal to his bravery, after having reproved him with great asperity, and upbraided him with his cruelty, presumption, and ingratitude, ordered him only to be put in irons, and committed to a close prison. At the same time, he displaced Hydar, governor of the province of Dawaro, of whose treason he had been long informed ; and he invested Gimmel-eddin, Saber-eddin's brother, with the government of the Mahometan provinces, who, as he pretended, had not been present at the beginning of the war, but had preserved his allegiance to the king, and dissuaded his brother from the rebellion.

While the king was thus settling the government of the rebellious provinces, he received intelligence that the kings of Adel and Mara had resolved to march after him into Shoa when he returned, and give him battle.

At this time the king was encamped on the river Hawash, at the head of the whole army, now united. This news of the hostile intentions of the kings of Adel and Mara, so exasper-

4   ted

·ted him, that he determined to enlarge his scheme of vengeance beyond the limits he had first prescribed to it. With
this view, he called the principal officers of his army together, while he himself stood upon an eminence, the soldiers
surrounding him on all sides. Near him, on the same eminence, was a monk, noted for his holiness, in the habit in
which he celebrated divine service. The king, in a long
speech pronounced with unusual vehemence, described the
many offences committed against him by the Mahometan
states on the coast. The ringleaders of these commotions, he
declared, were the kings of Adel and Mara. He enumerated
various instances of cruelty, of murder, and sacrilege, of
which they had been guilty; the number of priests that they
had slain, the churches that they had burned, and the Christian women and children that they had carried into slavery,
which was now become a commerce, and a great motive of
war. They, and they only, had stirred up his Mahometan subjects to infest the frontiers both in peace and war. He said,
that, considering the immense booty which had been taken,
it might seem that avarice was the motive of his being
now in arms, but this, for his own part, he totally dis-
claimed. He neither had nor would apply the smallest portion of the plunder to his own use, but considered it as unlawful, as being purchased with the blood and liberty of his
subjects and brethren, the meanest of whom he valued more
than the blood and riches of all the infidels in Adel. He, therefore, called them together to be witnesses that he dedicated
himself a soldier to Jesus Christ; and he did now swear upon
the holy eucharist, that, though but twenty of his army
should join with him, he would not turn his back upon A-
del or Mara, till he had either forced them to tribute and
submission,

submiffion, or extirpated them, and annihilated their religion.

He then entered the tent-door, and took the facrament from the hands of the monk, in prefence of the whole army. All the principal officers did the fame, and every individual of the army, with repeated fhouts, declared, that they acceded to, and were bound by, the oath the king then had made. A violent fury fpread in this inftant through the whole army; they confidered that part of the king's fpeech as a reproach, which mentioned the fpoils they had taken to have been bought by the blood of Chriftians, their brethren. Every hand laid hold of a torch, and, whether the plunder was his own or his fellow-foldiers, each man fet fire, without interruption, to the merchandife that was next him. The whole riches of Ifat and Hadea, Fatigar and Dawaro, were confumed in an inftant by thefe fanatics, who, fatisfied now that they were purged from the impurity which the king had attributed to their plunder, returned poor to their ftandards, but convinced in their own confcience of having now, by their facrament and expiation, become the foldiers of Chrift, they thirfted no longer after any thing but the blood of the inhabitants of Adel and Mara.

Soon after, Amda Sion heard that the Moors had attacked his army in Ifat two feveral nights, and that his troops had fuffered greatly, and with difficulty been able to maintain themfelves in their camp. The king was then upon his march when he heard thefe difagreeable news ; he haftened, therefore, immediately to their relief, and encamped at night in an advantageous poft, fhort of his main army, with a view of taking advantage of this fituation, if the Moors, as he expected, renewed their attack that night for the third time.

The Abyssinians, to a man, are fearful of the night, unwilling to travel, and, above all, to fight in that season, when they imagine the world is in possession of certain genii, averse to intercourse with men, and very vindictive, if even by accident they are ruffled or put out of their way by their interference. This, indeed, is carried to so great a height, that no man will venture to throw water out of a bason upon the ground, for fear that, in ever so small a space the water should have to fall, the dignity of some elf, or fairy, might be violated. The Moors have none of these apprehensions, and are accustomed in the way of trade to travel at all hours, sometimes from necessity, but often from choice, to avoid the heat. They laugh, moreover, at the superstitions of the Abyssinians, and not unfrequently avail themselves of them. A verse of the Koran, sewed up in leather, and tied round their neck or their arms, secures them from all these incorporeal enemies; and, from this known advantage, if other circumstances are favourable, they never fail to fight the Abyssinians at or before the dawn of the morning, for in this country there is no twilight.

The Moors did not, in this instance, disappoint the king's expectation; as they, with all possible secrecy, marched to the attack of the camp, while the king, having refreshed his troops, put himself in motion to intercept them; and they were now arrived and engaged in several places with very great vigour. The camp was in apparent danger, though vigorously defended. At this moment the king, with his fresh troops, fell violently upon their rear; and, it

being

being known to the Moors that this was the king, they withdrew their army with all poſſible ſpeed, carrying with them a very conſiderable booty.

The ſucceſs which had followed theſe night expeditions, above all, the ſmall loſs that had attended the purſuit, even after they were defeated, from the perfect knowledge they had of the country, inſpired them with a reſolution to avoid pitched battles, but to diſtreſs and harraſs the king's army every night. They accordingly brought their camp nearer than uſual to the king's quarters. This began to be felt by the army, which was prevented from foraging at a great diſtance; but proviſions could not be diſpenſed with. The king, therefore, detached a large body of horſe and foot that had not been engaged or fatigued. The greateſt part of the foot he ordered to return with the cattle they ſhould have taken, but the horſe, with each a foot-ſoldier behind him, he directed to take poſt in a wood near a pool of water, where the Mooriſh troops, after an aſſault in the night, retired, and took refreſhments and ſleep by the time the ſun began to be hot. The Moors again appeared in the night, attacked the camp in ſeveral places, and alarmed the whole army; but, by the bravery and vigour of the king, who every where animated his troops by his own example, they were obliged to retreat a little before morning, more fatigued, and more roughly handled, than they had hitherto been in any ſuch expedition.

The king, as if equally tired, followed them no further than the precincts of his camp; and the Moors, ſcarcely comforted by this forbearance after ſo great a loſs, retreated to receive ſuccour of freſh troops as uſual, and enjoy their repoſe in the neighbourhood of ſhade and water. They had, however,

ever,

ever, fcarce thrown afide their arms, difpofed of their wounded in proper places, and begun to affuage their thirft after the toils of the affault, when the Abyffinian horfe, breaking through the covert, came fwiftly upon them, unable either to fight or to fly, and the whole body of them was cut, to pieces without one man efcaping.

THE king, upon return of his troops, began to confider; and, by combining various circumftances in his mind, to fufpect ftrongly, that, from the Moors attacking him, as they had for fome time lately done, always in the moft unfavourable circumftances, there muft be fome intelligence between his camp and that of the enemy. Upon examining more particularly into the grounds of this fufpicion, three men of Harar (who had long attended the army as fpies) were difcovered, and being convicted, were carried out, and their heads cut off at the entrance of the camp; after which the king, who now found himfelf without an enemy in thefe parts, ftruck his tents, and returned to Gaza in Dawaro.

THIS movement of Amda Sion's had more the appearance of opening a campaign than the clofing of one, and occafioned great difcontent among the foldiers, who had done their bufinefs, and were without an enemy, juft at that time that the rains fall fo heavy, and the country becomes fo unwholefome as to make it unadvifable to keep the field. They, therefore, remonftrated by their officers to the king, that they muft return to their houfes for the feveral months of winter which were to follow; and that, after the fatigues, dangers, and hardfhips they had undergone for fo many

3   months,

months, to perfift in ftaying longer at fuch a feafon in this country was equal to the condemning them to death.

GIMMEL-EDDIN, moreover, the new-appointed governor, infilled with Amda Sion, that he was able enough himfelf to keep all the tributary provinces in peace, and true allegiance to the king; but if, on the contrary, the king chofe to eat them up with a large army living conftantly among them, as well as upon every pretence laying them wafte with the fword in the manner he was now doing, he could not be anfwerable for, nor did he believe they would be able to pay him, the tribute he expected from them. But the king, who faw the motives both of his officers and of the Moorifh governor, continued firm in his refolutions. He fharply reproved both Gimmel-eddin and his army for their want of difcipline, and defire of idlenefs, and ordered the officers to acquaint their men, that, if they were afraid of rains, he would carry them to *Adel*, where there were *none*; that, for his part, he made a refolution, which he would keep moft fteadily, never to leave his camp and the field while there was one village in his own dominions that did not acknowledge him for its fovereign.

ACCORDINGLY on the 13th day of June 1316, immediately after this declaration, he ftruck his tents, and marched into Samhar, to difappoint, if poffible, the confederacy that fome of the principal Moorifh ftates had entered into againft him, which were agreed, one by one, to harrafs his camp by night, and, after having obliged him to retreat to Shoa in diforder, to give him battle there before he had time to refrefh his troops. The authors of this confpiracy were feven in number, Adel,

Mara,

Mara, Tico, Agwama, Bakla *, Murgar, and Gabula, and they had already collected a confiderable army. The king, who faw they perfifted in their nightly attacks, rode out, thinly accompanied, to choofe a poft for an encampment that was to give him the greateft advantage over his enemy; and, whilft thus occupied, he was fuddenly furrounded by a body of troops of Adel lying in ambufh for him. A foldier (in appearance an Abyffinian) came fo clofe to the king as to ftrike him with his fword on the back with fuch violence that it cut his belt in two, and, having wounded him thro' his armour, was ready to repeat the blow, when the king pierced him through the forehead with his lance, upon which his party fled.

But the Moors, for five fucceffive nights, did not fail in their attempts upon his camp, which wearied and greatly contributed to difcontent his men; and the more fo, becaufe the enemy declined coming to any general engagement, though the king frequently offered it to them. Amda Sion, therefore, decamped the 28th of June, and, leaving this dif-advantageous ftation, advanced a day's march nearer Mara, pointing, as it were, to the very center of that kingdom. But here, again, he was ftopt by the difcontent of his fol-diers, who abfolutely refufed to go farther, or fpend the whole feafon in arms, in this inclement climate, while the reft of his fubjects, in full enjoyment of health and plenty, were rioting at home.

This difpofition of his army was no fooner known to the king than he called the principal of them together, and,

* A tribe of the Shepherds; all the reft, but the two firft, unknown in Abyffinia at this day.

and, planting himſelf on a riſing ground, he began to ha-
rangue his ſoldiers with ſo much eloquence and force of
reaſoning, that they who before had only learned to admire
their king as a ſoldier, were obliged to confeſs that, as an
orator, he as much excelled every man in his ſtate, as he
did the loweſt man of his kingdom in dignity. He put his
ſoldiers in mind, " that this was not a common expedition,
" like thoſe of his predeceſſors, marching through the coun-
" try for the purpoſe of levying their revenue ; that the in-
" tention of the preſent war was to avenge the blood of ſo
" many innocent Chriſtians ſlain in ſecurity and full peace,
" from no provocation but hatred of their religion: that they
" were inſtruments in the hand of God to revenge the
" death of ſo many prieſts and monks who had been wan-
" tonly offered as ſacrifices upon their own altars : that
" they were not a common army, but one confederated up-
" on oath, having ſworn upon the ſacrament, at the paſſ-
" age of the river Hawaſh, that they would not return in-
" to Abyſſinia till they had beat down and ruined the
" ſtrength of the Mahometans in thoſe kingdoms ; ſo that
" now, when every thing had ſucceeded to their wiſhes,
" when every Mahometan army had been defeated as ſoon
" as it preſented itſelf, and the whole country lay open to
" the chaſtiſements they pleaſed to inflict, to talk of a re-
" treat or forbearance was to make a mockery at once of
" their oath, and the motive of their expedition. He ſhew-
" ed, by invincible reaſonings, the great hardſhips and dan-
" ger that would attend his retreat through a country al-
" ready waſted and unable to maintain his army ; what
" an alarm it would occaſion in Shoa, to find him return-
" ing with an enemy at his heels, following him to his
" very capital ; that ſuch, however, muſt be the conſe-
                                                " quence ;

" quence; for it was plain, that, though the enemy decli-
" ned fighting, yet there was no poffibility of hindering them
" from following him fo near as to give his retreat every
" appearance of flight, and to bring an expedition, begun
" with fuccefs, to an ignominious and a fatal end.

" He upbraided them with his own example, that early
" their prophets had foretold he was a prince fond of lux-
" ury and eafe, which, in the main, he did not deny, but
" confeffed that he was fo; and that they all fhould have
" an attachment to their pleafures and enjoyments, he
" thought but reafonable. He defired, however, in this,
" they would do as much as he did, and only fufpend their
" love of eafe and reft as long as their duty to God, to their
" country, and their murdered brethren, required; for, till
" thefe duties were fulfilled, eafe and enjoyment to a Chrif-
" tian, and efpecially to them bound by oath to accomplifh
" a certain purpofe, was, in his eyes, little fhort of apofta-
" cy." A loud acclamation now followed from the whole
army. They declared again, that they renewed their facrament taken at the paffage of the Hawafh, that they were
Chrift's foldiers, and would follow their fovereign unto death.

Though the great perfonal merit of the king, and
the grace, force, and dignity with which he fpoke, had, of
themfelves, produced a very fudden change in the mind
of the foldiers, yet, to the increafe of this good difpofition
it had very much contributed, that a monk, of great holinefs
and aufterity of manners, living in a cell on the point of a
fteep rock, had come down from Shoa to the camp, declaring that he had found it written in the Revelation of
St John, that this year the religion of Mahomet was to be
                                                    utterly

utterly extirpated throughout the world. Full of this idea, on the feaſt of Ras Werk, in the month of July, the army paſſed the Yafs, a large river of the kingdom of Mara, and encamped there. The troops were alarmed, the night after their arrival, by a piece of intelligence which proved a falſehood.

A woman, whoſe father had been a Chriſtian, ſaid, that ſhe had very lately left the Mooriſh camp; that the enemy were at no great diſtance, and only waited a night of ſtorm and rain to make a general attack upon the king's army; and the clouds threatening then a night of foul weather, it was not doubted but the engagement was thereupon immediately to follow. It blew, then, ſo violent a ſtorm, that the king's tent, and moſt of thoſe in the camp, were thrown down, and the ſoldiers were in very great confuſion, imagining, every moment, the Moors ready to fall on them. But whether the ſtory was a falſehood, or the ſtorm too great for the Moors to venture out, nothing happened that night, nor, indeed, during their ſtay in that ſtation.

At this time a number of prieſts and others came out of curioſity to ſee their king making conqueſts of provinces and people till then unknown to them even by name: ſeveral large detachments of freſh troops from Abyſſinia alſo arrived, and joined the army. Upon this, Amda Sion advanced a day's journey farther into Mara, and took a ſtrong poſt, reſolving to maintain himſelf there, and, by detachments, lay the whole country deſolate. This place is called *Daſſ*. There was neither river, however, nor ſpring near it, but only water procured by digging in the ſand, being what comes down from the ſides of the mountains in the rainy

ſeaſon,

feafon, and, having filtered through the loofe earth, has reached the fand and gravel, where it ftagnates, or finds flowly its level to the fea. Here the king was taken dangerouily ill with the fever of the Kolla.

The altercations between Amda Sion and his foldiers, and the refolutions taken in confequence of thefe, were faithfully carried to the king of Adel. The march of the king forward at fuch a feafon of the year, the flow pace with which he advanced towards the very heart of the country, the care he took of providing all neceffaries for his army, and his reinforcing it at fuch a feafon, all shewed this was no partial, fudden incurfion, but that it was meant as a decifive blow, fatal to the independence of thefe petty fovereigns and ftates. To this it may be added, that Gimmel-eddin, whom the king had releafed from prifon, and fet over the Moorifh provinces of Abyffinia, conveyed to them, in the moft direct manner, that fuch were the king's purpofes. He told them, moreover, this march into their country was not either to increafe their tribute, or for the fake of plunder, or to force them to be his fubjects; that Amda Sion's main defign was againft their religion, which he and his foldiers had vowed they were to deftroy; that it was not their time to think of peace or tribute upon any terms; for, were they even to fell their wives and children, the price would not be accepted, unlefs they forfook the religion of their fathers, and embraced Chriftianity. He further added, that *his* refolution was already taken, that he would die firm in the faith, a good Mahometan, as he had lived; not tamely, however, but in the middle of his enemies; and that he was now making every fort of preparation to refift to the lateft breath.

No.

No fooner was this intelligence from Gimmel-eddin publifhed, than a kind of frenzy feized the people of Adel; they ran tumukuoufly to arms, and, with fhrieks and adjurations, demanded to be led immediately a-gainft the Abyffinians, for they no longer defired to live upon fuch terms.

THERE was among the leading men of the Moors one Saleh, chief of a fmall diftrict called Caffi, by birth a Sher-riffe, *i. e.* one of the race of Mahomet, and who, to the nobi-lity of his birth, joined the holinefs of his character. He was *Imam*, as it is called, or *high prieft* of the Moors, and, for both thefe reafons, held in the greateft eftimation among them. This man undertook, by his perfonal influence, to unite all the Moorifh ftates in a common league. For it is to be ob-ferved, that, though religion was very powerful in uniting thefe Moors againft the Chriftians, yet the love of gain, and jealoufies of commerce, perpetually kept a party alive that favoured the king for their own intereft, in the very heart of the Moorifh confederacies and councils. To overcome this was the object of Saleh, and he fucceeded beyond expecta-tion, as fixteen kings brought 40,000 men into the field un-der their feveral leaders; but the chief command was given to the king of Adel.

I MUST put the reader in mind that I am tranflating an Abyffinian hiftorian. Thefe, then, whom this chronicle ftiles Kings, muft be confidered as being only hereditary and independent chiefs, not tributary to Abyffinia. Their names are Adel, Mara, Bakla, Haggara, Fadife, Gadai, Nagal, Zuba, Harlar, Hobal, Hangila, Tarfhith, Ain, Iibiro, Zeyla, and Effe. Now, when we confider that thefe fixteen kings brought

only

only 40,000 men, and that they were commanded under thefe fixteen by 2712 leaders, or governors of diftricts, all which are fet down by name, we muft have a very contemptible opinion of the extent and populoufnefs of thefe newly-erected kingdoms.

It appears to me unneceffary to repeat, after my hiftorian, the names of each of thefe villages, which probably do not now exift, and are, perhaps, utterly unknown. I fhall only obferve in paffing, that here we find Tarfhis, or Tarfhifh, a kingdom on the coaft of the ocean, directly in the way to Sofala; another ftrong prefumption that Sofala and Ophir were the fame, and that this is the Tarfhifh where Solomon's fleet ftopt when going to Ophir.

Amda Sion's fever hindering him to march forward, and being unwilling to rifk a battle where he was not able himfelf to command, he continued clofe in his ftrong camp at Dafii, waiting his recovery; but, in the mean time, he made confiderable detachments on all fides to lay the country wafte around him, till he fhould be able to advance farther into it.

Of all the royal army, as it ftood upon the eftablifhment, the king had only with him the troops from the provinces of Amhara, Shoa, Gojam, and Damot, and thefe were what compofed the rear, when the whole, called the royal army, was affembled; all his troops were regularly paid, well armed, and cloathed, and were not only provided with every neceffary, but were become exceedingly rich, and, therefore, the more carelefs of difcipline, and difficult to manage, on account of the repeated conquefts that had followed one

another

another ever fince the king had croffed the river Hawafh, and come into the defert kingdom of Mara, unfruitful in its foil, but flourifhing by trade, and rich in India commodities. The foldiers had here fo loaded themfelves with fpoils and merchandife, that they began rather to think of returning home, and enjoying what they had got, than of pufhing their conquefts ftill farther to the deftruction of Adel and Mara. The putrid ftate of the water, in this fultry and unwholefome climate, had afflicted the king with the fever of the country, which he thought not by any means to remedy or prevent. No confideration could keep him from expofing himfelf to the moft violent fun-beams, and to the more noxious vapours of the night; and it was now the feventh day his fever had been increafing, although he neither ate nor drank. The army expecting, from the king's illnefs, a fpeedy order to return, converfed of nothing elfe within their camp, with that kind of fecurity as if they had already received orders to return home.

The Mahometan army had affembled, and no news had been brought of it to the king. Saleh's influence had united them all; and the king's ficknefs had made this eafier than it otherwife would have been. It happened, then, that, the king's fever abating the ninth day, he fent out to procure himfelf venifon, with which this country ab unds, and which is believed, by people of all ranks in Abyflinia, to be the only proper food and reftorative after ficknefs. After having killed fufficiently for the king's immediate ufe, the huntfmen returned; two only remained, who continued the purfuit of the game through the woods, till they were four days journey diftant from their camp, when, being in fearch of water for their dogs, they met a Moor engaged

in

in the fame bufinefs with themfelves, who fhewed them his
army encamped at no confiderable diftance, and in very
great numbers. Upon this they returned in all hafte to the
king to apprize him of his danger, and he fent immediately
fome horfe to difcover the number, fituation, and defigns of
the enemy; above all, if poffible, to take a prifoner, for the
huntfmen had put theirs to death, that he might be no incumbrance to them upon their return.

The king's fever was now gone, but his ftrength was
not returned ; and, the neceffity of the cafe requiring it, he
attempted to rife from his bed and put on his armour, but,
fainting, fell upon his face with weaknefs, while his fervant was girding his fword.

The horfe now returned, and confirmed the tidings the
huntfmen had brought ; they had found the Moorifh army
in the fame place it was firft difcovered, by the water-fide ;
but the account of their number and appearance was fuch
that the whole army was ftruck with a panic. The king's
wives (as the hiftorian fays, by which it fhould appear he
had more than one) endeavoured to perfuade him not to
rifk a battle in the weak ftate of health he then was, but to
retire from this low, unwholefome country, and occupy the
paffes that lead into Upper Abyffinia, fo as to make it impoffible for the enemy to follow him into Shoa.

The king having wafhed and refrefhed himfelf, with a
countenance full of confidence, fat down at the door of his
tent: whilft officers and foldiers crowded about him, he calmly, in the way of converfation, told them,—" That, being
" men of experience as they were, he was furprifed they
2   " fhould

" should be liable, at every instant, to panic and despon-
" dency, totally unworthy the character of a veteran army.
" You know," said he, " that I came against the king of Adel,
" and to recover that province, one of the old dependencies
" of my crown. And though it has happened that, in
" our march, you have loaded yourselves with riches, which
" I have permitted, as well out of my love to you, as because
" it distresses the enemy, yet my object was not to plunder
" merchants. If in battle to-morrow I be beaten, for God
" forbid that I should decline it when offered, I shall be the
" first to set you the example how to die like men in the
" middle of your enemies. But while I am living, it never
" shall be said that I suffered the standard of Christ to fly
" before the profane ensigns of infidels. As to what regards
" our present circumstances, my sickness, and the number
" of the Moorish troops, these make no alteration in my good
" hopes that I shall tread upon the king of Adel's neck to-
" morrow. For as it was never my opinion that it was my
" own strength and valour, or their want of it, which has so
" often been the means of preserving me from their hands,
" so I do not fear at present that my accidental weakness
" will give them any advantage over me, as long as I trust
" in God's strength as much as ever I have done."

The army, hearing with what confidence and firmness
the king spake, began to look upon his recovery as a miracle. They all, therefore, with one accord, took to their
arms, and desired to be led forward to the enemy, without
waiting till they should come to them: They only beseech-
ed the king that he would not expose his person as usual,
but trust to the bravery of his troops, eager for action, without being lavish of that life, the loss of which would be to
the

the Mahometans a greater victory than the regaining all he had conquered. The king hereon, bidding his troops to be of good courage, take reft and refrefhment, fent away the women, children, and other incumbrances, to a fmall convent on the fide of the mountain, called *Debra Martel**; and, being informed of the fituation of the country in general, and the particular pofts where he could get water in greater plenty, he advanced with his army by a flow march towards the enemy.

The next day he received intelligence by a Moor, that the Mahometans had not only thrown poifon into all the wells, but had alfo corrupted all the water in the front of the army by various fpells and inchantments; that they were not advancing, but were waiting for troops from fome of the fmall diftricts of Adel that had not yet joined the army. Hereupon the king ordered his Fit-Auraris to advance a day before him, and fent a prieft, called *Teda Sion*, with him, that he might blefs and confecrate the water, and thereby free it from the inchantments of the Moors. He himfelf followed with his army, and fat down by a fmall river a fhort way diftant from the enemy.

The Fit-Auraris is an officer that commands a party of men, who go always advanced before the front of an Abyffinian army, at a greater or fmaller diftance, according as circumftances require. His office will be defcribed more at large in the fequel.

The king being arrived at the river, the army began to bathe themfelves, their mules, and their horfes, in the fame

4

manner

---

* Mountain of the Teftimony.

manner as is ufual throughout all Abyffinia on the feaft of the Epiphany. This luftration was in honour of Tecla Sion, who had confecrated the water, broken all the magic fpells, and changed its name to that of the river Jordan. But, while they were thus employed, the Fit-Auraris had come up with a large party of the enemy, and, with them, a number of women, provided with drugs to poifon and inchant the water; and this numerous body of fanatics had fallen fo rudely on the Fit-Auraris that it beat him back on the main body, to whom he brought the news of his own defeat.

A violent panic immediately feized the whole Abyffinian army, and they refufed to advance a ftep farther. The tents had been left ftanding on the fide of the river they firft came to, and they then paffed to the other fide. But, upon fight of the Fit-Auraris, they returned to the tents, that, having the river on their front, they might fight the enemy with more advantage if they came to attack them. They did not continue long in this refolution; the greateft part of them were for leaving their tents, and retiring to A-byffinia for affiftance, and, when the numbers fhould be more upon an equality, return to fight the enemy. The Moorifh army at this inftant coming in fight, increafed the number of converts to this opinion.

The king, in the utmoft agony, galloping through the ranks, continued to ufe all manner of arguments with his mutinous foldiers. He told them, that retiring to their camp was to put themfelves in prifon; that, being moftly compofed of horfe, their advantage was in a plain like that before them; that retreating to join the main body, at fuch a diftance, was a vain idea, as the enemy was fo clofe at their heels. Finally, all he defired of them was, that thofe who would not fight fhould only ſtand as ſpectators, but not leave their places. As no ſign of content conviction was returned, the king, feeing that all was loſt they diſbanded, the enemy being juſt ready to engage, ordered his maſter of the horſe, and five others, to attack the left wing of the enemy, while he, with a ſmall part of his fervants and houfe-hold, did the fame on the right.

THE Abyſſinian hiſtory, feldom juſt to the memory of indi-viduals, hath yet, in this inſtance, (almoſt a ſingle one), prefer-ved the names of thefe brave men. The firſt was Zana Asfe-ri; the fecond, Tecla; the third, Wanag Araad; the fourth, Saif Segued, (one of the king's fons;) the fifth, Badel Waliz; and the ſixth, Kedami. Thefe, as is fuppofed, with their at-tendants and fervants, (though hiſtory is filent but as to the ſix) fell furiouſly on the left of the Mahometan army.

THE king, at the firſt onſet, killed, with his own hand, the two leaders of the right wing; and his fon, Saif Segued, having alſo flain another confiderable officer on the left, a panic feized both thefe bodies of Moors, and the army ap-parently began, at one and the fame time, to waver: On which the Abyſſinians, now aſhamed of their conduct, and perceiving the king's danger, with a great ſhout fell furi-ouſly upon the enemy. The whole Moorith army having, by this time, joined, the battle was fought with great obſtinacy on both ſides, till firſt the center, then the left wing of the Moors, was broken and difperſed; but the right, confifting chiefly of ſtrangers from Arabia, kept together, and, not knowing the country, retired into a narrow deep valley surrounded

furrounded by fleep perpendicular rocks, covered thick with
wood.

THE Abyffinian army, thinking all at an end by the
flight of the Moors, began, after their ufual cuftom, to
plunder, by ftripping and mangling the bodies of the killed
and wounded. But the king, who, from the miftake of the
Arabians, faw the deftruction of this right wing certain, if
immediately purfued, ordered it every where to be proclaimed through the field, that the whole army fhould repair to the royal ftandard, which he had fet up on an eminence, and give over plundering, under pain of death. Finding this order, however, flackly obeyed, he himfelf, fcouring
the field at the head of a few horfe, with his own hand flew
two of his foldiers whom he found ftripping the dead without regard to his proclamation. This example from a
prince, exceedingly fparing of the blood of his foldiers, had
the effect to recal them all to the royal ftandard difplayed
on a rifing ground.

HE then feparated his army into two divifions; all the
foot, and thofe of his horfe that had principally fuffered in
the fevere engagement of the day, he led up to the mouth
of the valley where the right wing of the Arabians had fhut
themfelves up; and, having befet all accefs to the entrance
of it, he ordered the foot to climb up through the woods,
and on every fide furround the valley above the heads of
thofe unhappy people thus devoted to certain deftruction.

WHILE this was doing, the king ordered thofe of the
cavalry that had fuffered leaft in the fatigue of the day, to refrefh themfelves and their horfes. He knew no time was

F 2   left

loft by this, as the Moorifh army that efcaped from the engagement, worn out with fatigue, thirft, and hunger, would
only retire a fhort day's march to the water, where, finding
themfelves not purfued, and incumbered with the number
of their wounded, they would neceffarily reft themfelves ;
and this was precifely the fituation, in which his huntfmen
firft found them by the fide of a large pool of water.

The king gave the command of this part of his army to
the mafter of the horfe, with orders to purfue them one
day farther ; whilft he, having taken a fhort refrefhment,
began to attack the right wing of the Arabians fhut up
in the valley. The king, difmounting, led the attack a-
gainft the front of the Arabians, who, feeing their fituation
now defperate, began to make every effort to get from the
valley into the plain. But they did not know yet upon what
difadvantageous ground they were engaged, till the foldiers
from the rocks above, every way furrounding them, rolled
down immenfe ftones which paffed through them in all directions. Preffed, therefore, violently, by the king in their
front, and in the rear deftroyed by an enemy they neither
could fee nor refift, they fell immediately into confufion,
and were, to a man, flaughtered upon the fpot; upon which
the king, giving to his troops orders for a general plunder,
retired himfelf to his camp, and in his tent received from
the mafter of the horfe an account of his expedition.

This officer had proceeded flowly, fpreading his troops as
wide as poffible upon the tract of the retreating enemy, to
give a fmaller chance for any to efcape. All directed their
flight towards the pool of water, and were there deftroyed
without mercy, till a little after fun-fet. The purfuers had then
advanced

advanced to the ground where Saleh king of Mara had gathered the scattered remains of his once powerful army, but now overcome with heat, difpirited by their defeat, and worn out by the fatigues of a long and obstinate engagement, all that remained of thefe unfortunate troops were ftrowed upon the ground, lapping water like beafts, their only comfort that remained, equally incapable of fighting or flying. The mafter of the horfe, in great vigour and ftrength from his late refrefhments and recent victory, had no trouble with thefe unfortunate people but to direct their execution, and this was performed by the foldiers with all the rage and cruelty that a difference of religion could poffibly infpire. For, after the king's fpeech of the 9th of June, in which he upbraided them with breach of their oath, and that they were flow in avenging the blood of their brethren and priefts wantonly flain by the Moors, every man in the army meafured the exactnefs with which he acquitted himfelf of the facrament at the Hawafh, only by the quantity of blood that he could fhed. Weary at laft with butchery, a few were taken prifoners, and among thefe was Saleh king of Mara. It was evening before the king returned from the flaughter of the right wing; and it was night when the foldiers, as fatigued with plundering as with fighting, returned to the camp.

THE next morning, he heard of the fuccefs of his cavalry under the mafter of the horfe, who joined him before midday. The unfortunate Saleh was, in fight of the whole army, brought before the king, cloathed in the diftinguifhed habit and marks of his dignity in which he had fought the day before at the head of his troops; gold chains were about his arms, and a gold collar, enriched with precious

ftones

ftones about his neck. The king fcarcely deigned to fpeak to him, whilft the royal prifoner likewife obferved a profound filence. When the army had fatisfied their curiofity with the fight of this prince, (once the object of their fear), the king, by a motion of his hand, ordered him to be hanged upon a tree at the entrance of the camp, with all the ornaments he had upon him. After this the queen of Mara, concerning whom fo many furprifing ftories had been told of her poifoning the waters by drugs and inchantments, was, notwithftanding the known partiality of this king for the fair fex, ordered to be hewn in pieces by the foldiers, and her body given to the dogs.

Amda Sion then difpatched a meffenger with the news of his victory to the queens his wives, and the reft of the ladies he had left with the main army at Debra Martel, when the monks of the convent immediately began a folemn proceffion and thankfgiving, attended by the exercife of every fort of work of charity and piety.

It was now the end of July, when the rains in Abyffinia become both conftant and violent, that the king called a council of the principal nobility, officers, and priefts, to determine whether he fhould go ftraight home, or fend their wives, children, and baggage before them the direct road, when the light and unincumbered army fhould take a compafs, and lay wafte a part of the kingdom of Adel they had already invaded, and return in another direction. The majority of the army, and the priefts above all, were for the firft propofal; but the king and principal officers thought the advantages gained by fo much blood were to be followed, and not deferted, till they fhould either have reduced the

I   Mahometans

Mahometans to a ſtate of weakneſs that ſhould make them no longer formidable to Abyſſinia, or, if proſperous fortune ſtill attended them further, extirpate the people and religion together.—This opinion prevailed.

The king, therefore, diſmiſſed his baggage, his women, children, ſervants, and uſeleſs people. He retained an army of veteran ſoldiers only, more formidable than ſix times the number that could be brought againſt them; and, truſting now to the country into which he marched for ſupport, he advanced, and entered a town called Zeyla, and there took up his quarters. He had ſcarce taken poſſeſſion of the town, when that very night he ſent a detachment to ſurpriſe a large and rich village called Taraca, where he put all the men to the ſword, making the women ſlaves for the ſervice of the army, inſtead of thoſe whom he had ſent home.

The king's views, by ſuch ſmall expeditions, were to accuſtom his ſoldiers to fight out of his preſence, and wean them from a perſuaſion, now become general, that victory could not be obtained but where he commanded.

On the 10th of July, the king continued his march, without oppoſition, to Darbè, whence, the next morning, he ſent different parties to the right and left, to burn and deſtroy the country. They accordingly laid waſte all the province of Gaſſi, ſlaying Abdullah the Sherriffe, who was the governor and ſon of Saruch the Imam, author of the conſpiracy againſt him. From thence he fell ſuddenly upon Abalgé and Talab, a large diſtrict belonging to the king of Adel.

THE

THIS prince, hearing that Amda Sion, inſtead of returning, as was uſual in the rainy ſeaſon, into Abyſſinia, had determined to continue to ravage his whole country, had not, on his part, been remiſs in preparing means to reſiſt him; and he had aſſembled, from every province, all the forces they could raiſe, to make one laſt effort againſt their common enemy.

AMDA SION, therefore, had ſcarcely retired from the deſtruction of Talab, when the king of Adel (become now deſperate by being ſo long a ſpectator of the ruin of his kingdom) marched haſtily to meet him, with much leſs precaution than his own ſituation, and the character of his enemy, required. Amda Sion, whoſe whole wiſh was to bring the Moors to an engagement as often as occaſion preſented, left off his plundering upon the firſt news that the king of Adel had taken the field, and, allowing him to chooſe the ground on which he was to fight, the next day he marched againſt him, having (as ſure of victory) firſt detached bodies of horſe to intercept thoſe of the Moors that ſhould fly when defeated; For no general was more provident than this king for the deſtruction of his enemy. He then led his troops againſt the king of Adel, and, ſpurring his horſe, was already in the midſt of the Mooriſh army before the moſt active of his ſoldiers had time to follow him. The Abyſſinians, as uſual, threw themſelves like madmen upon the Moors, at the ſight of the king's danger. The king of Adel was defeated with little reſiſtance: that unfortunate prince himſelf was ſlain upon the ſpot, and the greateſt part of his army deſtroyed (after they thought themſelves ſafe) by the ambuſhes of freſh horſe the king had placed in their rear before the battle.

THE

THE three children of the king of Adel, and his brother, who had all been in the engagement, feeing the great inferiority of their troops, and terrified at the approaching fate of their country, loading themfelves with the moft valuable of their effects, (which, in token of humility, they carried upon their heads, fhoulders, and in their hands,) came with thefe prefents before the king, who was fitting armed at the door of his tent, and, without further apology, or affurance given, threw themfelves, as is the cuftom of Abyffinia, at his feet, with their foreheads in the duft, intreating pardon for what had hitherto been done amifs ; fubmiting to him as his fubjects, profeffing their readinefs to obey all his commands, provided only that he would proceed no further, nor wafte and deftroy their country, but fpare what ftill remained, which was, for the moft part, the property of Arabian merchants who had done him no injury.

BUT the king feemed little difpofed to credit thefe affurances. He told them plainly, " That they, and all Ethiopia, " knew the time was when they were under his dominion, " paid him the fame tribute, and owed him the fame alle- " giance with the reft of his fubjects ; that neither he, nor " his predeceffors, at that time, had ever oppreffed them, " but returned them prefent for prefent, gold for gold, ap- " parel for apparel, and difmiffed them contentedly home " whenever they came to pay their duty to them : That lately, " from fuppofed weaknefs in him, when he was young in " the beginning of his reign, and encouraged by the great " addition of their brethren, who flocked to them from A- " rabia, they had, without provocation, thrown off their al- " legiance to him, upbraiding him as a eunuch, fit only to " take care of the women of their feraglio, with many fuch

" taunting

" taunting messages, equally unworthy the majesty and me-
" mory of a prince like him: That, could this be passed over,
" still there was a crime that all the blood of Adel could not a-
" tone for: They had, without provocation, murdered his
" priests, burnt their churches, and destroyed his defenceless
" people in their villages, merely from a vain belief that they
" were too far to be under his protection: That, to punish them
" for this, he was now in the midst of their country, and, if
" his life was spared, never would he turn his back upon Adel
" while he had ten men with him capable of drawing their
" swords. He, therefore, ordered them to return, and ex-
" pect the approach of his army."

THE two eldest children and the brother were so struck
with the fierce manner and countenance with which the
king spoke, that they remained perfectly silent. But the
youngest son (a youth of great spirit, and who, with
the utmost difficulty, had been forced by his parents to
fly after the battle) answered the king with great resolution :—

" IT is a truth known to the whole kingdom, that Adel
" has never belonged to any sovereign on earth but to our-
" selves. Violence and power, which destroy and set up
" kingdoms, have at times done so with ours ; but that you
" are not otherwise, than by these means, king of our coun-
" try, our colour, stature*, and complexion sufficiently shew.
" We have been free, and were conquered ; we now have
" attempted to regain our freedom, and we have failed: We
                                                    have

---

* The Moors in general are much squarer, stouter-made men, than the Abyssinians.

" have not been inferior to you in every kind of civility, re-
" ceiving you and your predecessors when you came into
" our country, singing before you, and rejoicing, because
" we knew that you had always among you men of great
" worth and bravery.

" As to the accusation against us, that we robbed the
" Christians, you yourself see the riches of our country,
" which we get by our own industry and commerce,
" whilst the Abyssinians were naked shepherds and robbers.
" In the days of your predecessors, a handful of us would
" have chased an army of them, and it would be so now,
" were it not for the personal valour and conduct of you
" their prince. But you, better than any one, can be the
" judge of this; and I can appeal to you, how often they
" have been upon the point of deserting you, in return for
" all the victories and riches they have shared with you;
" while there is not a Moor in Adel but would have willing-
" ly died in the presence of such a prince as you. It is then
" you, not your army, that we fear; we know perfectly the
" value of both. You have already enjoyed all the merit
" and profit of conquest; but utterly destroying defenceless
" people is unworthy of any king, and still more of a prince
" of your character."

The king, without any sign of displeasure at the freedom
of this speech, answered him calmly : " Words and resolu-
" tions like these occasioned your father to lose his life in
" battle. I come not to argue with you what you are to do,
" nor did I send for you to preach to you; but if the queen
" your mother, the rest of your father's family, and the
" principal people who, after your father's death, are now

" to

" to govern Adel, do not, by to-morrow evening, furrender
" themfelves to me at my tent-door, as you have done, I will
" lay the province of Adel wafte, from the place where I
" now fit, to the borders of the ocean."

This unpromifing interview with the king was faithfully
communicated by the young princes to their mother, earneftly defiring her to truft the king's mercy, and to throw
herfelf at his feet the next morning without referve. But
thofe who had been the perfuaders of the war (for the
late king of Adel was but a weak prince) reckoned themfelves in much greater danger with Amda Sion than was
the royal family.   They, therefore, agreed to try their fortune again in battle, binding themfelves to live and die with
each other, by mutual oaths and promifes.   They alfo fent
to the princes this refolution, by an old enemy of Amda
Sion, perfuading them to make their efcape as foon as poffible, and come and head their forces that were then raifed,
and ready to conquer or die together, when the family
fhould be out of the enemy's hands.

The king, well informed of what had paffed, decamped
immediately from the ftation where he was, exceedingly
irritated; and, having paffed the great river called Aco, he
took poft in the town of Marmagab; and the next day, dividing his army, he fent two bodies by different routes into
the enemy's territories, with a ftrict command to leave nothing undeftroyed that had the breath of life; he himfelf,
with the third divifion, burning and laying wafte the whole
country before him, proceeded ftraight to the place where
he heard the chiefs of Adel were affembling an army.
There he found fome troops, moftly infantry, who kept a
                                                    good

good countenance, and seemed perfectly prepared and dif-
posed to engage him. But an immense multitude of useless
people covered the plain, old men, women, and children,
with the parents, wives, and families of those he had already slain ; and these were determined, with the remnant
of their countrymen, to conquer this invader, or to perish.

The king, upon perceiving this strange mixture, halted
for a time in great surprise and astonishment. He could not
penetrate into the motive of assembling such an army ; and
sending a party of horse, as it were, to disperse them, he
found everywhere a stout resistance ; soldiers well provided with swords and shields, and a multitude of archers, who
rained showers of arrows upon him, while the women, with
clubs, poles, stakes, and stones, damped the ardour of his
soldiers, who, when they first charged, scarcely expected resistance. The king, seeing the battle every minute become
more doubtful, and having but few troops, began to repent
that he had weakened his army by detachments ; he instantly dispatched orders to them to advance, and fall upon the
enemy in the nearest direction possible. At the same time,
he himself made an extraordinary effort with his horse, but
all in vain ; and he found, on every side, people who presented themselves willingly to death, but who would not quit
their station while they had power to defend themselves
in it.

Conspicuous above all these for his dress, his youth, his
many acts of valour, and his graceful figure, was the young
king of Wypo, who, encouraging his troops, presented himself wherever Amda Sion was in person. The remarkable
resistance that this young prince made, soon drew the attention

tention of the king of Abyssinia; who, sheathing his sword, took a bow in his hand, and, as my historian says, choosing the broadest arrow he could find, struck this young hero through the middle of his neck, so that, half being cut through, his head inclined to one shoulder, and soon after he fell dead among his horse's feet.

This fight was one just calculated to strike such an army as this with terror. They immediately turned their backs, and, unluckily falling in with the two detachments marching to the king's relief, they were all cut to pieces to the number of 5000; a great proportion of which were women and aged persons, unskilled in war, further than as they were prompted by a long sufferance of injuries, accumulated now to a mass, that made them weary of life. My historian further says, that three only of the Moorish army escaped. On the king's side many principal officers were killed; and there was scarce one horseman that was not wounded. Amda Sion, therefore, when speaking of this campaign, after his return, among his nobility at Shoa, used to say, " Deliver me from fighting with old women;" alluding to this battle, where he was in the greatest danger. The fate of the unfortunate king of Wypo was particularly hard. He had lately married the king of Adel's daughter; and it was the staying for him, and his marriage, that lost the favourable opportunity of fighting the Abyssinians, when the army was in despondency upon the king's being taken ill of the fever.

The next campaign the king began, by a march first to Saffogade, where he assisted at the celebration of the feast of St John the Baptist; and he gave orders, that day, to raze all

2   the

the Mahometan mosques to the ground, to destroy all the grain, burn the villages, and put the people to the sword, which was executed accordingly. The king then decamped the fourth of July; and, passing the great river (Zorat) came to the country of the Oritii, and took up his quarters there. The people of this province were in the very worst reputation for cruelty, and hatred of the Christian name. They were perpetually making incursions into the Christian villages, and those that fell alive into their hands, they either castrated, cut off their nose or ears, or otherwise mangled them.

THE king, to vindicate the severity he was about to exercise, ordered all those people, who had suffered in this manner, to be collected and brought before him. The number appeared very considerable; and, having inquired in what occupations they had been employed, they answered, that their business was to cut down wood, draw and fetch water, and some of them to take care of the Moorish women. Violently affected with this, he called his principal officers, and commanded them, that, when he decamped with his army the next day, small parties should remain in ambush on each side of the town. The king, early in the morning, marched out with sound of trumpet; and the Moors, thinking the army gone, returning to their houses, were set upon by the parties, and destroyed.

THE next place the king came to was Haggara, where he staid eight days, and celebrated there the feast of the Cross; surrounding his camp with palisades, as if he was to stay there a considerable time. Here he made his soldiers deposit all their plunder, leaving it under the care of a weak
guard,

guard, and marched out with found of trumpet, as if he was going upon some expedition. There was a large body of troops in ambuſh, and the Moors, concealed in woods, and hiding-places, attacked the intrenchment as ſoon as the king was gone, and had forced the paliſades, when they were every where ſurrounded by the parties left behind, and were all cut to pieces, excepting the old men and women, whoſe noſes and lips the king ordered to be cut off, by way of retaliation, and then diſmiſſed them. Great ſtore of bows, good arms and cloathing, were taken here, lately brought from Arabia for the uſe of the confederates.

The king now turned his face homewards, marched off in ſeven days to Begul in the Sahara, and thence ſent a meſſage to the governor of Ifat, commanding him to ſend to him all thoſe Chriſtians who had apoſtatized from their faith in his or his brother's time; with notice, that, if he did not comply, he would put him and all his family to death, and give his command to another family. The king ordered theſe apoſtates, when delivered, to be ſeverely whipped, and, fettering them with heavy irons, impriſoned them.

From Begul the army marched to Waz, thence to Gett, and from Gett to Harla, ſtill laying waſte the country. From Harla they marched five days to Delhoya, being determined to make a ſevere example of this place, becauſe the inhabitants had killed the governor the king had left with them, and, making large fires for the purpoſe, had burnt and tormented the Chriſtians reſiding there. He came, therefore, upon this town, and ſurrounded it in the night; and, after putting men, women, and children to the ſword, he razed it to the ground.

FROM

From Delhoya he proceeded to Degwa, from thence to Warga, which he treated in the same manner as Delhoya, and then entered the province of Dawaro, where he understood that Hydar, governor of that province, with Saber-eddin, and a very valuable convoy coming to him, under their conduct, from Shoa, were intercepted by Hydar's people, and their guard cut to pieces. Instead, therefore, of proceeding to Shoa, as his intention was, he encamped at Bahalla, and there kept the feast of Christmas, laying the whole province, by parties, under military execution; and hearing there that Joseph, governor of Serea, was in understanding with those of Dawaro, he put him in prison, carrying off all his horses, asses, mules, and a prodigious quantity of other cattle, which he drove before him, and ended his expedition by his entry into Shoa.

This is the Abyssinian account of the reign of their prince Amda Sion, a little abridged, and made more conformable to the manner of writing English history. The historian, contrary to the usual practice, gives no account of himself; but he seems to have lived in the time of Zara Jacob, the third reign after this. Though he wrote in Shoa, his book is in pure Geez, there being scarcely an Amharic word in it.

There are three things which I would now observe; not because they are single instances, but, on the contrary, because, though first mentioned here, they are uniformly confirmed throughout the whole Abyssinian history.

The first is, that the king of Abyssinia is, in all matters ecclesiastical and civil, supreme; that he punishes all offences committed by the clergy in as absolute and direct a manner as

if thefe offences were committed by a layman. Of this the
treatment of Honorius is an example, who made ufe only
of fpiritual weapons againft offences, that furely deferved the
cenfure of all churches.

WITH whatever propriety this fentence might have
been inflicted upon individuals, and, perhaps, without any
bad confequence to the public in general, the law of
the land, in Abyffinia, could not fuffer this to be inflicted on their king, becaufe very bad effects muft have
followed it towards the common-weal ; for excommunication there is really a capital punifhment if executed
with rigour. It is a kind of *interdictio aquæ et ignis*, for you
yourfelf are exprefsly prohibited from kindling a fire, and
every body elfe is laid under a prohibition from fupplying
either fire or water. No one can fpeak, eat, or drink with
you, enter your houfe, or fuffer you to enter theirs. You
cannot buy nor fell, nor recover debts. If under this fituation you fhould be violently flain by robbers, no inquifi-
tion is made into the caufe of your death, and your body is
not fuffered to be buried.

I WOULD fubmit now to the judgment of any one, what
fort of government there would be in Abyffinia, if a prieft
was fuffered to lay the king under fuch interdict or reftric-
tion. The kings of that country do not pretend to be faints ;
indeed, it may be faid, they are the very contrary, leading
very free lives. Pretences are never wanting, and it is only
neceffary to find a fanatic prieft (which, God knows, is not
a rarity in that country) to unhinge government perpetually,
and throw all into anarchy and confufion. But nothing of
this kind occurs in their hiftory, though the bigotted Le
                                                      Grande,

Grande, and fome of the Jefuits, lefs bigotted than him, have afferted, that fuch a practice prevailed in the Abyffinian church, to fhew its conformity with the church of Rome; which we fhall fee, however, contradicted almoft in every prince's reign.

THE fecond thing I fhall obferve is, that there is no ground for that prejudice, fo common in the writers concerning this country, who fay that thefe people are Nomades, perpetually roving about in tents. If they had ever fo little reflected upon it, there is not a country in the world where this is lefs poffible than in Abyffinia, a country abounding with mountains, where every flat piece of ground is, once a-day, during fix months rain, cut through by a number of torrents, fweeping cattle, trees, and every thing irrefiftibly before them; where no field, unlefs it has fome declivity, can be fown, nor even paffed over by a traveller, without fome danger of being fwept away, during the hours of the day when the rain is moft violent; in fuch a country it would be impoffible for 30 or 40,000 men to encamp from place to place, and to fubfift without fome permanent retreat. Accordingly they have towns and villages perched upon the pinnacles of fharp hills and rocks, and which are never thought fafe if commanded by any ground above them; in thefe they remain, as we do in cities, all the rainy feafon: Nor is there a private perfon (not a foldier) who hath a tent more than in Britain. In the fair feafon, the military encamp in all directions crofs the country, either to levy taxes, or in fearch of their enemy; but nothing in this is particular to Abyffinia; in moft parts of Africa and Afia they do the fame.

THE third particular to be observed here is, that, in this prince's reign, the king's sons were not imprisoned in the mountain. For Saif Araad was present with his father at the defeat of Saleh king of Mara, and yet the mountain of Geshen was then set apart as a prison. For the Itchegue of Debra Libanos was banished there; from which I infer, that after the massacre of the royal family by Judith, on the mountain of Damo, and the flight of the prince Del Naad, to Shoa, the king's children were not confined, nor yet till long after their restoration and return to Tigré, as will appear in the sequel.

AMDA SION died of a natural death at Tegulat in Shoa, after a reign of 30 years, which were but a continued series of victories, no instance being recorded of his having been once defeated.

SAIF ARAAD.

From 1342 to 1370.

This Prince enjoys a peaceable Reign—Protects the Patriarch of Cophts at Cairo from the Persecution of the Soldan.

SAIF ARAAD succeeded his father Amda Sion; and it should seem that, in his time, all was peaceable on the side of Adel, as nothing is mentioned relative to that war. Indeed,

Indeed, if the increase of trade and power in that corner of Abyssinia arose from the troubles and want of security which the merchants laboured under in Arabia, we cannot but suspect, from a parity of reasoning, that the violent manner in which war had been carried on by Amda Sion, must have occasioned a great many inhabitants to repass the Straits, and return to their own homes.

At this time, news were brought from Cairo, that the Soldan had thrown the Coptic patriarch, Marcus, into prison. There was then a constant trade carried on between Cairo and Abyssinia, through the desert; and also from Cairo and Suakem on the Red Sea. Besides, great caravans, formerly composed of Pagans, now of Mahometans, passed from west to east, in the same manner as in ancient times, to buy and disperse India goods through Africa. Saif Araad, not having it in his power to give the patriarch other assistance, seized all the merchants from Cairo, and sent horse to interrupt and terrify the caravans. As the cause of this was well known, and that the patriarch was in prison for the sake only of extorting money from him, people on all sides cried out upon the bad policy of the Soldan, who thereupon ordered Abuna Marcus to be set at liberty, without any other condition, than that he should make peace with Saif Araad on the part of Egypt, which was done through the mediation of that prelate.

VEDEM

WEDEM ASFERL

From 1370 to 1380.

Memoirs of this and the following Reign defective.

WE know nothing of this prince, only that he succeeded his father Saif Araad, and reigned ten years; yet
his name, which signifies *lever of war*, seems to indicate an active reign. It is remarkable, that in this reign is first mentioned an æra of Abyssinian chronology, which has very
much puzzled several learned writers, and the origin of
which is not, perhaps, yet fully known. This is that epoch,
called that of Maharat, or Mercy, which Scaliger and Ludolf
have called the æra of grace. Scaliger says, he has toiled
much before he found out what it was; and I doubt his
toil has not been blessed with all the success we could wish.
That it is not the æra of redemption, is plain upon a hundred trials, nor of the conversion, nor of Dioclesian. What
it alludes to we know not, but it is first quoted in the Abyssinian history in this reign, and answers to the year 1348
of Christ; but from what event it had its origin we cannot
positively say, nor further, than that all which Scaliger has
said concerning it is merely visionary.

       DAVID

D A V I D II.

From 1380 to 1409.

WEDEM ASFERI was succeeded by his brother David, Saïf Araad's second son. This prince's reign is remarkable in the annals of the church of Abyssinia, because, at this time, a piece of the true cross, on which our Saviour died, was brought hither from Jerusalem; and, in memory of this great event, the king ordered the sacerdotal vest, or capa, which was before plain, to be embroidered with flowers.

This king, after reigning twenty-nine years, one day viewing a favourite, but vicious horse, received so violent a kick upon his head that it fractured his skull, so that he died upon the spot, and was buried in the great island of Dek in the lake Dembea, or Tzana.

THEODORUS

THEODORUS.

From 1409 to 1412.

Memoirs of this Reign, though held in great Esteem in Abyssinia, defective; probably mutilated by the Ecclesiastics.

DAVID was succeeded by his eldest son Theodorus. He is called Son of the Lion, by the poet, in the Ethiopic encomium upon him, still extant in the liturgy. A miracle is mentioned to have happened, (which would lead us to suspect that he was a saint), during the celebration of his festival, by his mother, who is called Mogesa *. This lady had contented herself with providing great quantity of flesh for the feast; but, to make it more complete, the heavens in a shower supplied it with store of fine fish, ready roasted.

He was buried in the church of Tedba Mariam in Amhara, after having reigned three years. There must have been something very brilliant that happened under this prince, for though the reign is so short, it is before all others the most favourite epoch in Abyssinia. It is even confidently believed, that he is to rise again, and to reign in
Abyssinia

---

* Probably Magwas, or Berhan Magwas, the Glory of Grace; a name often used by queens; for Mogesa has no signification, that I know, in any of the languages of Ethiopia.

Abyſſinia for a thouſand years, and in this period all war is to ceaſe, and every one, in fulneſs, to enjoy happineſs, plenty, and peace. Fooliſh as theſe legends are, and diſtant the time, this one was the ſource of great trouble and perſonal danger to me, as will be ſeen in the ſequel. What we know certain in this prince's hiſtory is, that he abrogated the treaty of partition made by Icon Amlac in favour of the Abuna Teela Haimanout and his ſucceſſors, by which one third of the kingdom of Abyſſinia was for ever to be ſet apart as a revenue for the Abuna. This wiſe prince modiſied ſo exceſſive a proviſion, reſerving to the Abuna for his maintenance a ſufficient territory in every province of the kingdom. It is ſtill judged immoderate, and has ſuffered many defalcations under later princes, who, perhaps, not acting upon the principles of Theodorus, have not been commended by poſterity in the manner he has been.

I S A A C.

From 1412 to 1429.

No Annals of this nor the four following Reigns.

THEODORUS was ſucceeded by Iſaac his brother, ſecond ſon of David. In his reign the Falaſha, who, ſince their overthrow in the time of Amda Sion, had been quiet, broke out into rebellion. We do not know the particulars, but

apprehend fome injuftice was at that time done, or attempted, againſt the Jews ; for 24 Judges, 12 from Shoa and 12
from Tigré, (the number having been doubled when there
were two kings reigning *), were of a different opinion, and
would not comply with the king's will, who thereupon deprived them all of their office. The king, coming upon the
army of the Falaſha in Woggora, entirely defeated them at
Kollogué, and, in memory thereof, built a church on the
place, and called it Debra Ifaac, which remains there to this
day.

Isaac reigned near 17 years, was a prince of great piety
and courage. The annals of his reign, probably during the
troubleſome time that followed, have been loſt, and with
them great part of his atchievements

ANDREAS I. or AMDA SION.

Isaac was fucceeded by his fon Andreas, who reigned
only ſeven months, and they were both buried at Tedba
Mariam.

TECLA

* That is, while the family of Zague reigned in Tigré, and that of Solomon in Shoa, before the reſtoration.

TECLA MARIAM, or HASEB NANYA.

From 1429 to 1433.

THIS prince was third son of David, and succeeded his nephew. He reigned four years, and took for his inauguration name, Haseb Nanya.

SARWÉ YASOUS.

THIS prince was son of Tecla Mariam, he reigned only four months; his inauguration name was Maharak Nanya. He has been omitted in some of the lists of kings.

AMDA YASOUS.

SARWE YASOUS was succeeded by his brother Amda Yasous, whose inauguration name was Badel Nanya. He was second son of Tecla Mariam, and reigned nine months.

I 2   ZARA

ZARA JACOB.

From 1434 to 1468.

Sends Ambassadors from Jerusalem to the Council of Florence—First Entry of the Roman Catholics into Abyssinia, and Disputes about Religion—King persecutes the Remnants of Sabaism and Idolatry—Mahometan Provinces rebel, and are subdued—The King dies.

THESE very short reigns were followed by one of an extraordinary length. Zara Jacob, fourth son of David II. succeeded his nephew, and reigned 34 years, and, at his inauguration, took the name of Constantine. He is looked upon in Abyssinia to have been another Solomon; and a model of what the best of sovereigns should be. From what we know of him, he seems to have been a prince who had the best opportunity, and with that the greatest inclination to be instructed in the politics, manners, and religion of other countries.

A CONVENT had been long before this established at Jerusalem for the Abyssinians, which he in part endowed, as appears by his letters still extant *, written to monks of that convent.

---

* Vid. Ludolf. lib. 3. No. 29. I have this letter at length prefixed to the large volume of Canons and Councils, a copy of which was sent by Zara Jacob to the monks in Jerusalem.

convent. He also obtained from the Pope [*] a convent for the Abyssinians at Rome, which to this day is appropriated to them, though it is very seldom that either there, or even at Jerusalem, there are now any Abyssinians. By his desire, and in his name, ambassadors (i. e. priests from Jerusalem) were sent by Abba Nicodemus, the then Superior, who assisted at the council of Florence, where, however, they adhered to the opinion of the Greek church about the proceeding of the Holy Ghost, which created a schism between the Greek and Latin churches. This embassy was thought of consequence enough to be the subject of a painting in the Vatican, and to this picture we owe the knowledge of such an embassy having been sent.

The mild reign of the last Soldan of Egypt seems greatly to have favoured the disposition of Zara Jacob, in maintaining an intercourse with Europe and Asia. And it is for the first time now in this reign that we read of a dispute upon religion with the Franks, or Frangi, a name which afterwards became more odious and fatal to whomsoever it was applied. Abba George is said to have disputed before the king upon some point of his religion, and to have confuted his opponent even to conviction. We are not informed of the name of Abba George's antagonist, but he is thought to have been a Venetian painter [†], who lived many years after in Abyssinia, and, it is believed, died there. From this time, however, in almost every reign, there appear marks of a party formed in favour of the church of Rome, which probably had its first rise from the Abyssinian embassy to the council of Florence.

Although

---

[*] St Stefano in Rotundo.   [†] Francisco de Branca Leon.

ALTHOUGH the eſtabliſhed religion in Abyſſinia was that of the Greek church of Alexandria, yet many different ſuperſtitions prevailed in every part of the country. On the coaſt of the Red Sea, as well as the Ocean, that is in the low provinces adjoining to the kingdom of Adel, the greateſt part of the inhabitants were Mahometans; and the conveniencies of trade had occaſioned theſe to diſperſe themſelves through many villages in the high country, eſpecially in Woggora, and in the neighbourhood of Gondar. Dembea on the ſouth, and the rugged diſtrict of Samen on the eaſt, were crowded with many deformed ſects, while the people of the low valleys, towards Nubia, the Agows at the head of the Nile, and thoſe of the ſame name, though of a different nation and language, at the head of the Tacazzé, in Laſta, were, for the greateſt part, Pagans, i. e. of the old religion of Sabeans, worſhipping the planets, ſtars, the wind, trees, and ſuch like. But a more abominable worſhip than this ſeemed eſpecially predominant among ſome of the Agows at the ſource of the Nile, and the people bordering upon Nubia, as they adored the cow and ſerpents for their gods, and ſuppoſed that, by the latter, they could divine all that was to happen to them in futurity.

WHETHER it was that a long war had thrown a veil over theſe abuſes, or whether (which is more probable) a ſpirit of toleration had ſtill prevailed in this country, which had at firſt been converted to Chriſtianity without blood-ſhed, it is not eaſy at this time to ſay. Only their hiſtory does not mention, that, before the reign of this prince, idolatry had been conſidered as a capital crime, or judicially inquired into, and tried as ſuch. An accuſation, however, at this time, being brought againſt ſome families for worſhipping the

4　　　　　　　　　　　　　　　COW

cow and the ferpent, they were, by the king's orders, feized and brought before himfelf fitting in judgment, with the principal of his clergy, and with his officers of ftate, with whom he affociated fome ftrangers, lately come from Jerufalem; a cuftom which prevails to this day. Thefe criminals were all capitally convicted, and executed. A proclamation from the king followed, declaring, That any perfon who did not, upon his right hand, carry an amulet, with thefe words, *I renounce the devil for Chrif our Lord*, fhould forfeit his perfonal eftate, and be liable to corporal punifhment.

It has been the cuftom of all Pagan nations to wear amulets upon their arms, and different parts of their bodies. From the Gentiles this ufage was probably firft learned by the Jews. Amulets were adopted by the Mahometans, but, till now, not worn in Abyffinia by any Chriftians.

Thefe executions, which at firft confifted of feven people only, began to be repeated in different places, and at different times. The perfon employed as inquifitor, and the manner this examination was made, tended to make it ftill more odious. Anida Sion, the Acab Saat, was the man to whom this perfecution was committed. He was the king's principal confident; of very auftere manners: he neither fhaved his head nor changed his cloaths; had no connection with women, nor with any great man in court; never faw the king but alone, and, when he appeared abroad, was conftantly attended by a number of foldiers, with drums and trumpets, and other equipage, not at all common for a clergyman. He had under him a number of fpies, who brought him intelligence of any fteps taken in idolatry or treafon; and, after being, as he fuppofed, well informed, he went to the houfe of the delinquent, where he firft refreshed himfelf and his attendants, then ordered thofe of the houfe he came for, and all that were with them, to be executed in his prefence.

Among thofe that fuffered were the king's two fons-in-law, married to his daughters Medehan Zamidu, and Berhan Zamidu, having been accufed by their wives, the one of adultery, the other of inceft: they were both put to death in their own houfes, in a very private and fufpicious manner. This execution being afterwards declared by the king in an affembly of the clergy and ftates, certain priefts, or others, from Jerufalem, in public, condemned this procedure of the king, as contrary to law, found policy, and the firft principles of juftice, which feems to have had fuch an effect that we hear no more of thefe perfecutions, nor of Amda Sion the perfecutor, during the whole of this reign.

The king now turned his thoughts upon a nobler object, which was that of dividing his country into feparate governments, affigning to each the tax it fhould pay, at what time, and in what manner, according to the fituation and capacity of each province. The profperity of the Moorifh ftates, from the extenfive trade conftantly carried on there, the bad ufe they made of their riches by employing them in continual rebellions, made it neceffary that the king fhould fee and inquire into each perfon's circumftances, which he propofed to do, as was ufual, before the time of their feveral inveftitures.

The chief of the rich diftrict of Gadai, was the firft called on by the king, as it is on this occafion that confiderable
                                                    prefents

prefents (feldom lefs than two years rent of the province)
are given, about one half to the king, the other among his
courtiers. There was, at this period, a Moorifh woman of
quality in court, called the queen of Zeyla. She had been
brought to the palace with a view that the king fhould marry
her, but he difliking her for the length, as is faid, or fome
other defect, in her foreteeth, had married her to a nobleman.

THIS injury had funk very deep in the breaft of the
queen of Zeyla, though fhe was only nominally fo, having
been expelled from her kingdom before her coming into
Abyffinia. But it happened that fhe was fifter to Mihico
fon of Mahomet, chief of Gadai, whom fhe earneftly perfuaded to ftay at home, and fhe fucceeded fo far, as not only to prevail upon him to be abfent, but alfo to withdraw
himfelf entirely from his allegiance.

AT this very time, the king was informed by a faithful
fervant, a nobleman of Hadea, that the chief of Gadai had
long been meditating mifchief, and endeavouring to prevail
with the king of Adel to march with his army, while great
part of the principal people of Hadea, whom he had feduced, were to fall, on the oppofite fide, upon Dawaro and
Bali.

THE king, however, received certain accounts from A-
del, that all was quiet there; and inquiring who of his Moorifh fervants were of the confpiracy in Hadea, he found
them to be Goodalu, Alarea, Ditho, Hybo, Ganzè, Saag, Gi-
dibo, Kibben, Gugule, and Haleb. As there were ftill forces enough in the province to refift this confederacy, the

king, inftead of levying an army againft them, thought the proper way was to fend them a governor, who fhould divide the intereft and ftrength of the enemy. There was then an uncle of Mihico remaining in exile at Dejan *, whither he had been fent formerly into banifhment at the inftance of his nephew, but he ftill preferved the command of a fmall diftrict called Bomo, as well as the good inclinations of his own fubjects of Gadai, who held his memory in great veneration. The king, therefore, fent for this governor of Bomo, and, fetting before him the behaviour of his nephew, he gave him the inveftiture of his government, with many prefents both ufeful and honourable; and, having ordered fome troops from Amhara to attend him, he difmiffed him, to punifh and expel his nephew from the province of Gadai.

The fair of Adel was nigh, and thither all the inhabitants of Bali and Dawaro go. It was at this time the confpirators of Hadea had agreed to fall upon the provinces; while, probably, thofe at the fair had been likewife deftined to cut off the inhabitants which might be found there. To counteract thefe defigns, the king, by proclamation, exprefsly forbade any of the inhabitants of Bali or Dawaro to go to the fair, but all to join the governor of Bomo, who no fooner prefented himfelf in his diftrict, than the people of all ranks flocked to him and fubmitted.

Mihico faw himfelf undone by this addrefs of the king, of which he was quite uninformed. He fled immediately
with

---

* One of the fteep mountains ufed for prifons.

with his family, endeavouring, if possible, to reach Adel; and having come the length of Bawa Amba, a high mountain, where is one of the narrowest and most difficult passes between the high country and the Kolla, here he throwed about, in different places, all the riches that he had brought along with him, in hopes that his pursuers, wearied by the time they came there, should, by the difficulty of the ground, and the booty everywhere to be found, be induced to proceed no further. But this stratagem did not succeed; for he was so closely followed that he was overtaken and slain, his head, hands, and feet were cut off, and immediately sent to the king, who, after public rejoicings, gave the government of Gadai to the person who first informed him of Mihico's conspiracy, and confirmed the governor of Bomo in the province of Hadea likewise, which he made hereditary in his family. In order also to be more in readiness to suppress such insurrections for the future, he gave his Christian soldiers lands adjacent to each other, forming a line all along the frontiers of the Mahometan provinces of Bali, Fatigar, Wadge, and Hadea, that they might be ready at an instant to suppress any tumult in the provinces themselves, or resist any incursions from the kingdom of Adel.

THE king now set about fulfilling another duty of his reign, that of repairing the several churches in Abyssinia which had been destroyed in the late war by the Mahometans, and of building new ones, which it is their constant custom to vow and to erect where victories had been obtained over an infidel enemy. While thus employed, news were sent him from the patriarch of Alexandria, that the church of the Virgin had been destroyed at that city by fire. Full, therefore, of grief for this misfortune, he immediately

diately

diately founded another in Abyssinia, to repair that lofs
which Christianity had suffered in Egypt.

Being now advanced in life, he would willingly have
dedicated the remainder of it to these purposes, when he
was awakened from his religious employments by an a-
larm of war. The rebels of Hadea, by changing their
chief, had not altered their difpositions to rebel, and, feeing the king given to other purfuits, they began to affociate
and to arm. The governor, whom the king had created
after the death of Mihico, gave the king a very late notice
of this, which he diffembled, as he was the queen Helena's
father: but having, under pretence of confecrating the
church of St Cyriacos, affembled a fufficient number of
men whom he could truft, he made a fudden irruption into the rebel provinces before they had united their forces.
The firft that the king met to oppofe him was an officer of
the rebel governor of Fatigar, who imagined he was engaging only the van of a feparate body of Zara Jacob's troops,
not believing him to be yet come up in perfon with fo fmall
a number: But being undeceived, he beftirred himfelf fo
courageoufly, that he reached the king's perfon, and broke
his lance upon him; but, in return, received a blow from
the lance of the king which threw him to the ground; at
the fight of which his whole party took flight, but were o-
vertaken and put to the fword almoft to a man; nor was
the king's lofs confiderable, his number being fo fmall.

Upon this defeat, Hiradin, the governor's brother, declared his revolt, and advanced to fight the king at the paffage
of the river Hawafh. Zara Jacob, much offended at this
frefh delinquency, fent an officer, called Han Degna, who

3   found

found him at the watering-place unsuspecting an enemy; and, before he could put his army in order, he was surrounded, slain, and his head sent to the king, who rejoiced much at the sight, it being brought him on Chriftmas day.

AFTER this the king collected his dead, and buried them with great honour and shew of grief. He then summoned the governor of Hadea, who profeffed himself willing to submit his loyalty and conduct to the ftricteft inquiry. Above all the reasons which hindered him from attending the king, one was known to be, that the queen was not without reason fufpected to favour the Mahometans, being originally of that faith herfelf, and, therefore, for fear of revealing his secret to the enemy, the king did not choofe to make her father, the governor of Hadea, partaker in his expedition, but, from jealoufy to the queen, ordered him to ftay at home. Notwithftanding which it was found, that all in his government were in their allegiance, and ready to march upon the fhorteft notice had the king required it; therefore he extended his command over the conquered provinces, in room of the rebel governors whom he had removed.

BÆDA

BÆDA MARIAM.

From 1456 to 1478.

Revives the Banishment of Princes to the Mountain—War with Adel—Death of the King—Attempts by Portugal to discover Abyssinia and the Indies.

BÆDA MARIAM succeeded to the throne (as his historian says) against his father's inclination, after having received much ill usage during the earlier part of his life, of which this was the occasion. His mother took so violent and irregular a longing to see her son king, that she formed a scheme, by the strength of a party of her relations and friends, trusting to the weakness of an old man, to force him into a partnership with his father. Examples of two kings, at the same time, and even in this degree of relation, were more than once to be found in the Abyssinian annals, but those times were now no more. A strong jealousy had succeeded to an unreasonable confidence, and had thrown both the person and pretensions of the heirs-apparent of this age to as great a distance as was possible.

THE queen, whose name was Sion Magass, or the Grace of Sion, first began to tamper with the clergy, who, though they

1

they

they did not abſolutely join her in her views, ſhewed her, however, more encouragement than was ſtrictly conſiſtent with their allegiance. From theſe ſhe applied to ſome of the principal officers of ſtate, and to thoſe about the king, the beſt affected to her ſon and his ſucceſſion. Theſe, aware of the evil tendency of her ſcheme, firſt adviſed her, by every means, to lay it aſide; and afterwards, ſeeing ſhe ſtill perſiſted, and afraid of a diſcovery that would involve her accomplices in it, they diſcloſed the matter to the king himſelf, who reſented the intention ſo heinouſly, that he ordered the queen to be beaten with rods till ſhe expired. Her body afterwards was privately buried in a church dedicated to the Virgin Mary, not far from Debra Berhan [*].

Nothing had hitherto appeared to criminate the young prince. But it was ſoon told the king, that, after the death of the queen, her ſon Bæda Mariam had taken frankincenſe and wax-tapers from the churches, which he employed, at ſtated times, in the obſervation of the uſual ſolemnities over his mother's grave. The king, having called his ſon before him, began to queſtion him about what he had heard; while the prince, without heſitation, gave him a full account of every circumſtance, glorying in what, he ſaid, was his duty, and denying that he was accountable to any man on earth for the marks of affection which he ſhewed to his mother.

The king, conſidering his ſon's juſtification as a reproach made to himſelf for cruelty, ordered the prince, and, with him,

* Another church on a hill, one of the quarters of Gondar. It ſignifies the Hill of Glory, or Brightneſs.

him, his principal friend Meherata Chriſtos, to be loaded with irons, and baniſhed to the top of a mountain; and it is hard to ſay where this puniſhment would have ended, had not the monks of Debra Koſſo and Debra Libanos, and all thoſe of the deſert, (who thought themſelves in ſome meaſure accomplices with his mother), by exhortations, pretended prophecies, dreams and viſions, convinced the king, that Providence had decreed unalterably, that none but his ſon, Bæda Mariam, ſhould ſucceed him. To this ordinance the old king bowed, as it gave him a proſpect of the long continuance of his family on the throne of Abyſſinia.

ZARA JACOB was no ſooner dead, than his ſon, Bæda Mariam, who ſucceeded him, began to apply himſelf ſeriouſly to the affairs of government. From the reign of Judith, (in the tenth century), when ſo many of the princes of the royal family were maſſacred, the cuſtom of ſending the royal children to confinement on the top of a mountain had been diſcontinued. Theſe children all lived at home with their reſpective fathers and mothers, like private perſons; and the kings ſeemed to connive at aboliſhing their former practice, for no mountain had been yet choſen as a ſubſtitute to the unfortunate Damo. The diſagreement between Zara Jacob and his queen, with the cauſe of it, and the prince's franknefs and reſolution, ſeemed to point out the neceſſity of reviving the ſalutary ſeverity of the ancient laws. Bæda Mariam gave orders, therefore, to arreſt all his brethren, and ſend them priſoners for life to the high mountain of *Geſhen*, on the confines of Amhara and Begemder, which ever after continued the ſtate-priſon for the royal children, till a

slaughter,

ſlaughter, like to that made upon mount Damo, was the occaſion, as we ſhall ſee, of deſerting Geſhen likewiſe.

The king applied himſelf next to meaſures for the better government of his country. He ordered a general pardon to be proclaimed to all who, by the ſeverity of the late reign, lay under ſentence of death, baniſhment, or any other puniſhment; and, convoking the ſtates of the kingdom, he met them with a chearfulneſs and openneſs which inſpired confidence into every rank, while, at the ſame time, he filled all the places he found vacant, or that he thought proper to change, with men of the greateſt integrity. He then reviewed the whole cavalry that were in his ſervice, which he diſtributed into bodies, and ſtationed them in places where they could be readieſt called, to execute thoſe deſigns he had then in contemplation.

The next year the king went to Debra Libanos in Shoa. It was, however, obſerved, that his preparations were not ſuch as were uſual in theſe ſhort journies, nor ſuch as were made in peaceable times. On the contrary, orders were ſent to the borders of Tigré to receive the royal army, which was ſoon to arrive in thoſe parts. The rumour of this was quickly ſpread abroad, and affected all the neighbouring ſtates, according to their ſeveral intereſts. Mahomet king of Adel was the firſt that took the alarm. Tho' a kind of peace had ſubſiſted for ſeveral years between Adel and Abyſſinia, yet inroads had been made from each country into the other; and theſe might have ſerved them as pretexts for war, had that been the inclination of the times. Yet, as both countries happened to be diſpoſed for peace, theſe outrages paſſed unnoticed.

But, to prevent furprife upon this laft movement of the troops, the king of Adel thought he had a right to be informed of Bada Mariam's intentions, and, with this view, he fent fome of the principal people of his country as ambaffadors, under pretext of congratulating the king upon his acceffion to the throne. They met the king in Shoa, and had carried with them very confiderable prefents. They were received in a very diftinguifhed manner; and the prefents which Bæda Mariam returned to the king of Adel were nothing inferior to thofe he accepted. After having entertained the ambaffadors feveral days with feafting and diverfions, he confirmed a peace under the fame duties upon trade that had formerly fubfifted.

The king of Dancali alfo, old, infirm, yet conftant in his attachment to the Abyffinians, was not without his inquietudes, though he was not afraid they intended to attack his poor territory with an army. He dreaded left the army in its march fhould drink up that little quantity of water which remained to him in fummer, and, without which, his kingdom would become uninhabited. It is a low, fandy diftrict, lying on the Red Sea, juft where the coaft, after bearing a little to the eaft of north from Suez to Dancali, makes an elbow, and ftretches nearly eaft, as far as the Straits of Babelmandeb. It has the mines of foffilefalt immediately on the north and north-weft, a defert part of the province of Dawaro to the fouth, and the fea on the north. But it has no port, excepting a fpacious bay, with tolerable anchorage, called *the Bay of Behar* [*], in lat. 13° 3′,

and;

and, corruptly in vulgar maps and writings, the Bay of Bayloul.

THE kingdom of Dancali is bounded on the east at Azab by part of the kingdom of Adel, and the myrrh country. The king is a Mahometan, as are all his subjects. They are called Taltal, are all black, and only some of them woolly-headed; a circumstance which probably arises from a mixture with the Abyssinians, whose hair is long. There are but two small rivers of fresh water in the whole kingdom; and even these are not visible above ground in the hot season, but are swallowed up in the sand, so as to be dug for when water is wanted. In the rainy season, these are swelled by rain falling from the sides of the mountains and from the high lands of Abyssinia, and then only they run with a current into the sea. All the rest of the water in this country is salt, or brackish, and not fit for use, unless in absolute necessity and dry years. Even these sometimes fail, and they are obliged to seek, far off in the rainy frontiers of Abyssinia, water for themselves, and pasture for their miserable goats and sheep.

WHEN the Indian trade flourished, this prince's revenue arose chiefly from furnishing camels for the transport of merchandise to all parts of Africa. Their commerce is now confined to the carrying bricks of solid, or fossile salt, dug from pits in their own country, which, in Abyssinia, pass instead of silver currency; these they deliver at the nearest market in the high lands at a very moderate profit, after having carried them from the sea-side through the dry and burning deserts of their own country, at the great risk of being murdered by Galla.

THE

The prefents fent to Beda Mariam from Dancali did not make a great figure when compared with thofe of Adel. They confifted of one horfe, a mule, a fhield of elephant's hide, a poifoned lance, two fwords, and fome dates. Poor as thefe prefents were, they were much more refpected.than thofe of Adel, becaufe they came from a loyal heart; while the others were from a nation diftinguifhed every year by fome premeditated action of treachery and bloodfhed. The king, having firft fent for the Abuna, Imaranha Chrifdes, and called the ambaffadors of Dancali and Adel into his prefence, declared to them, that neither of thefe ftates was to be the fcene of war, but that he was inftantly to march againft the Dobas *, whofe conftant inroads into his country, and repeated cruelties, he was refolved no longer to fuffer. He required the ambaffadors to warn their mafters to keep a ftrict neutrality, otherwife they would be infallibly involved in the fame calamities with that nation.

Lent being now near, the king returned to Ifras, there to keep his faft, and diftributed his horfe on the fide of Amba-fanet, having fent orders to the governor of Amhara to join him immediately, who was then at Salamat befieging a party of rebels upon Mount Gehud, which fignifies the *Mountain of Manifeftation*. It was the intention of the king, that the troops of Amhara, Angot, and Tigré fhould prefs upon the enemy from the high country, while he with his own troops (chiefly horfe) fhould cut off their retreat to the plains of falt; and it was here that the king of Dancali was afraid that they would interfere with his frefh water.

THIS

* A race of very barbarous people, all fhepherds, having great fubftance, and much refembling the nations of Gaila. They are Pagans.

This prince kept ſtrictly his promiſe of ſecrecy made to Beda Mariam, while the king of Adel obſerved a very different line of conduct; for he not only diſcovered the king's intention, but he invited the Dobas to ſend their wives, children, and effects into Adel, while his troops ſhould cut off the king's proviſion, and fight him wherever they ſaw that it could be done with advantage. The plan was ſpeedily embraced. Twelve clans of Dobas marched with their cattle, as privately as poſſible, for Adel; but the king's intelligence was too good, and his motions too rapid, to allow their ſchemes to be carried into execution. With a large body of horſe, he took poſſeſſion of a ſtrong paſs, called Fendera; and when that unhappy people, fatigued with their march, and incumbered with baggage, arrived at this ſpot, they were cut to pieces without reſiſtance, and without diſtinction of age or ſex.

THE king, at the beginning of this campaign, declared, that his intention was not to carry on war with the Dobas as with an ordinary enemy, but totally to extirpate them as a nuiſance; and, to ſhew himſelf in earneſt in the declaration, he now made a vow never to depart from the country till he had plowed and ſown the fields, and ate the crop on the ſpot with his army. He, therefore, called the peaſants of two ſmall neighbouring diſtricts, Wadge and Ganz, and ordered them to plow and ſow that part; which having ſeen done, the king went to Axum, but returned again to the Dobas, by the feaſt of the Epiphany. That cruel, reſtleſs nation, ſaw now the king's real intent was their utter deſtruction, and that there was no poſſibility of avoiding it but by ſubmiſſion. This prudent conduct they immediately adopted; and, great part of them renouncing the Pagan religion,

2.

religion, they fo fatisfied Bæda Mariam that he decamped from their country, after having, at his own expence, re-ftored to them a number of cattle equal to that which he had taken away, having alfo given up, untouched, the crop which had been fown, and recompenfed the peafants of Wadge and Ganz for their corn and labour.

HAVING refolved to chaftife the king of Adel for his treacherous conduct, he retired fouthward into the provin-ces Dawaro and Ifat ; and, as if he had had no other views but thofe of peace, he croffed over to Begemder, where he directed the Abuna to meet him with his young fon Ifcan-der, of whom his queen, Romana Werk *, had been lately delivered. From this he proceeded to Gojam, everywhere leaving orders with the proper officers to have their troops in readinefs againft his return ; and having delivered the young prince to Ambafa David, governor of that province, he proceeded to Gimbota, a town lying on the banks of the Nile, which, in honour of his fon's governor, he changed to David Harafa ✝. Having thus fettled the prince to his mind, he fent orders to the army in Tigré and Dawaro to advance into the fouthernmoft frontier of Adel. He him-felf returned by the way he went to Gojam, and collecting the troops, and the nobility who flocked to him on that occafion, he marched ftraight for the fame country.

WHILST the king was occupied in thefe warlike prepara-tions, a violent commotion arofe among his clergy at home. In the reign of Zara Jacob, a number of ftrangers, after the

council

---

council of Florence, had come into Abyffinia with the Abuna Imaranha Chriftos. Among thefe were fome monks from Syria, or Egypt, who had propagated a herefy which had found many difciples. They denied the confubftantiality of Chrift, whom they admitted to be perfect God and likewife perfect man, but maintained that what we call his *humanity* was a precious fubftance, or nature, not compofed of flefh, blood, and arteries, (like ours), but infinitely more noble, perfect, peculiar to, and only exifting in himfelf. An affembly of the clergy was called, this herefy condemned, and thofe who had denied the perfect manhood of our Saviour were put to death by different kinds of torture. Some were fent to die in the Kolla, others expofed, without the neceffaries of life, to perifh with cold on the tops of the higheft mountains.

THERE was another motive of difcontent which appeared in that affembly, and which affected the king himfelf. A Venetian, whofe name was Branca Leon, was one of the ftrangers that arrived in Ethiopia at the time above mentioned. He was a limner by profeffion, and exceedingly favoured by the late king, for whom he had painted, with great applaufe, the pictures of Abyffinian faints for the decoration of the churches. It happened that this man was employed for an altar-piece of Atronfa Mariam ; the fubject was a common one in Italy, Chrift in his mother's arms ; where the child, according to the Italian mode, is held in his mother's left arm. This is directly contrary to the ufage of the Eaft, where the left hand is referved for the purpofe of wafhing the body when needful, and is therefore looked upon with difhonour, fo much, indeed, that at table the right hand only is put into the plate.

THE

THE fanatic and ignorant monks, heated with the laft difpute, were fired with rage at the indignity which they fuppofed was offered to our Saviour. But the king, ftruck with the beauty of the picture, and thinking blood enough had been already fhed upon religious fcruples, was refolved to humour the fpirit of perfecution no farther. Some of the ringleaders of thefe difturbances privately difappearing, the reft faw the neceffity of returning to their duty; and the picture was placed on the altar of Atronfa Mariam, and there preferved, notwithftanding the devaftation of the country by the Moors under the reigns of David III. and Claudius, till many years afterwards, together with the church, it was deftroyed by an inroad of the Galla.

IN the mean time, the army from Dawaro had entered the kingdom of Adel under Betwudet * Adber Yafous, and, expecting to find the Moors quite unprepared, they had begun to wafte every thing with fire and fword. But it was not long before they found the inhabitants of Adel ready to receive them, and perfectly inftructed of the king's intentions, from the moment he left Dawaro, to go to meet his fon in Gojam. Indeed, it could not be otherwife, from the multitude of Moors conftantly in his army, who, though they put on the appearance of loyalty, never ceafed to have a warm heart towards their own religion and countrymen. Advanced parties appeared as foon as the Abyffinian army entered the frontiers; and thefe were followed by the main body in good order, determined to fight their enemy before they had time to ravage the country.

A BATTLE

---

* Betwudet is an officer that has nearly the fame power as Ras; there were two of thefe, and both being flain at one battle, as we fhall fee in the fequel, the office grew into difufe as unfortunate.

A BATTLE immediately followed, very bloody, as might be expected from the mutual hatred of the soldiers, from the equality in numbers, and the long experience each had in the other's manner of fighting. The battle, often on the point of being lost, was as often retrieved by the personal exertion of the Moorish officers, upon whom the loss principally fell. Sidi Hamet, the king's son, the chiefs of Arar, Nagal, Telga, Adega, Hargai, Gadai, and Kumo, were slain, with several other principal men, who had either revolted from the king of Abyssinia, or whom friendship to the king of Adel had brought from the opposite coast of Arabia.

THE king was still advancing with diligence, when he was overtaken by an express, informing him that his queen Romana was delivered of another prince, christened by the name of Anquo Israel. Upon which good tidings he halted at once to rest and feast his army; and, in the middle of the festivity, an express from Adber Yasous brought him news of the complete victory over the Moors, and that there was now no army in Adel of consequence enough to keep the field. Hereupon the king detached a sufficient number of troops to reinforce Adber Yasous in Adel, and continued himself recruiting his army, and making greater preparations than before, that, during the first of the season, he might utterly lay waste the whole Moorish country, or so disable them that they might, for many years, be content to enjoy peace under the condition of becoming his tributaries.

WHILE planning these great enterprises, the king was seized with a pain in his bowels, whether from poison or otherwife is not known, which occasioned his death. Having, a few moments before he died, recollected that his face was turned on a different side from the kingdom of Adel, he ordered himself to be shifted in his bed, and placed so as to look directly towards it, (a token how much his heart was set upon its destruction) and in that posture he expired.

He was a prince of great bravery and conduct; very moderate in all his pleasures; of great devotion; zealous for the established church, but steady in resisting the monks and other clergy in all their attempts towards persecution, innovation, and independency. Many stories have been propagated of his inclination to the Catholic religion, and of his aversion to having an Abuna from Egypt; and it is said, that, during his whole reign, he obstinately persisted in refusing to suffer any Abuna in his kingdom. But these are fables invented by the Portuguese priests, who came into Abyssinia some time afterwards, and forged anecdotes to serve their own purposes; for, unless we except the story of the Venetian, Branca Leon, there is not a word said of any connection Bæda Mariam ever had with the few Catholics that then were in his country, and even that was a connection of his father's. And as to the other story, we find in history, that the Abuna had been in the country ever since his father Zara Jacob's time; and that, at his desire, the Abuna, Imaranha Christos, came and received, in the field of battle, large donations in gold, almost as often as the king gained a victory. Bada Mariam died at the age of forty, after reigning ten years, which were spent in continual war; during the whole course of which he was successful, and might (if he had lived) have very much weakened the Moorish states, and prevented the terrible retalia-

tion

tion that fell afterwards from that quarter upon his country.—It will be proper now to look back into the transactions in Europe, which are partly connected with the history of this kingdom.

THE conquest of the north part of Africa followed the reduction of Egypt, and the whole coast of Barbary was crowded with Mahometans, from Alexandria to the western ocean, and from the Mediterranean to the edge of the desert. Even the desert itself was filled with them; and trade, security, and good faith, were now everywhere disseminated in regions, a few years before the feat of murder and pillage.

TARIK and his Moors had invaded Spain; Mufa followed him, and conquered it. The history of Count Julian is in every one's hand; unfortunate in having had the provocation, still more so in having had the power to revenge it, by facrificing at once his fovereign, his country, religion, and life, to the private injuries done to his daughter. As often as I have read the hiftory of this cataftrophe, fo often have I regretted to fee with how little ceremony this young lady hath been treated by authors of all languages and nations. They call her *Caaba*, with the fame eafe and indifference as they would have called her Anne, or Margaret. This muft be from mere ignorance. Caaba could not be the name of the daughter of Count Julian before her feduction. Caaba means *Harlot*, in the broadeft way poffible to exprefs the term, and very cruelly and improperly, it feems to be given her, even after her misfortune; for fhe was a daughter of the firft family in Spain, of unexceptionable virtue.

She

She was not feduced, but *forced* by the king, while in the palace, and under protection of the queen.

A GREAT influx of trade followed the conqueſt ; and the religion, that contained little reſtraint and great indulgence, was every where embraced by the vanquiſhed, who long had been Chriſtians in name only. On the other ſide, the conquerors were now no longer that brutiſh ſet of madmen, ſuch as they were under the Khalifat of the fanatic Omar. They were now men eminent for their rank and attainments in every ſpecies of learning. This was a dangerous criſis for Chriſtianity, and nothing elſe was threatened than its total ſubverſion. The whole world, without the help of England, had not virtue enough to withſtand this torrent. That nation, the favourite weapon in the hand of Heaven for chaſtiſing tyranny and extirpating falſe religion, now lent its aſſiſtance, and the ſcale was quickly turned.

AT that time Europe ſaw with ſurpriſe an inconſiderable number of fiſhermen, very inconveniently placed at the fartheſt end of the Adriatic Gulf, applying themſelves with unwearied care and patience to cultivate, gather together, and improve the remnants and gleanings of the Indian trade by Alexandria, under all the cruelties and oppreſſions of thoſe ignorant and barbarous conquerors the Turks, whom no proſpect of gain, no change of place, no frequency of commerce, could ever civilize or ſubject to the rules of juſtice. Venice became at once the great market for ſpices and perfumes, and conſequently the moſt conſiderable maritime power that had appeared in Europe for ages.

GENOA.

Genoa followed, but funk, after great efforts, under the power of her rival; while Venice remained mistress of the sea, of a large dominion upon the continent, and of the Indian spice trade, the origin and support of all her greatness.

Rhodes, and the ships of the Military Order of St John of Jerusalem, to whom that island belonged, greatly harrassed the maritime trade carried on by the Moors in their own vessels from Alexandria, who were every day more discouraged by the unexpected progress of these once petty Christian states. Trade again began to be carried on by caravans in the desert. Large companies of merchants from Arabia, passed in safety to the western ocean, and were joined by other traders from the different parts of Barbary while passing to the southward of them, and that with such security and expedition, that the Moors began to set little value on their manner of trading by sea, content now again with the labours and conveniencies of their ancient, faithful friend, and servant, the camel.

Ormus, a small island in the Persian Gulf, had, by its convenient situation, become the market for the spice trade, after the discouragements it had received in the Mediterranean. All Asia was supplied from thence, and vessels, entering the Straits of Babelmandeb, had renewed the old resort to the temple of Mecca. From hence all Africa, too, was served by caravans, that never since have forsaken that trade, but continue to this day, and cross the continent, in various directions.

JOHN

JOHN I. king of Portugal, after many fuccefsful battles with the Moors, had at laft forced them to crofs the fea, and return vanquifhed to their native country. By this he had changed his former difhonourable name of *baftard* to the more noble and much more popular one of John the *avenger*. This did not fatisfy him. Affifted by fome Englifh navigators, he paffed over to Barbary, laid fiege to Ceuta, and fpeedily after made himfelf mafter of the city. This early connection with the Englifh arofe by his having married Philipina of Lancafter, fifter of Henry IV. king of England, by whom he had five fons, all of them heroes, and, at the taking of Ceuta, capable of commanding armies. Henry, the youngeft, fcarce twenty years of age, was the firft that mounted the walls of that city in his father's prefence, and was thereupon created Mafter of the Order of Chrift, a new inftitution, whofe fole end and view was the extirpation of the Mahometan religion.

ALTHOUGH every thing promifed fair to John in the war of Africa, yet it early occurred to prince Henry, that a fmall kingdom like Portugal never could promife to do any thing effectual againft the enormous power of the Mahometans, then in poffeffion of extenfive dominions in the richeft parts of the globe. The fudden rife of Venice was before his eyes, and almoft happened in his own time. By applying to trade alone, fhe had acquired a power fufficient to cope with the ftouteft of her enemies. Portugal, fmall as it was, merited quite another degree of refpect; but poverty, ignorance, pride, and idlenefs prevailed among the poor people; even agriculture itfelf was in a manner abandoned fince the expulfion of the Moors.

PRINCE HENRY, from his early years, had been paſſionately addicted to the ſtudy of what is generally known by the name of *mathematics*, that is, geometry, aſtronomy, and conſequently arithmetic. He was of a liberal turn of mind, devoid of ſuperſtition, haughtineſs, or paſſion; the Arab and the Jew were admitted to him with great freedom, as the only maſters who were capable of inſtructing him in thoſe ſciences. It was in vain to attempt to rival Venice in poſſeſſion of the Mediterranean trade: no other way remained but to open the commerce to India by the Atlantic Ocean, by ſailing round the point of Africa to the market of ſpices in India. Full of this thought, he retired to a country palace, and there dedicated the whole of his time to deliberate inquiry. The ignorance and prejudices of the age were altogether againſt him. The only geography then known was that of the poets. It was the opinion of the Portugueſe, that the regions within the tropics were totally uninhabited, ſcorched by eternal ſun-beams, while boiling oceans waſhed theſe burning coaſts; and, therefore, they concluded, that every attempt to explore them was little better than downright madneſs, and a braving, or tempting, of Providence.

BUT, on the other hand, he found great materials to comfort him, and to make him perſiſt in his reſolution. For Greek hiſtory, to which he then had acceſs, had recorded two inſtances, which ſhewed that the voyage was not only poſſible, but that it had been actually performed, firſt by the Phœnicians, under Necho king of Egypt, then by Eudoxus, during the time of Ptolemy Lathyrus, who, after doubling the ſouthern Cape of Africa, arrived in ſafety at Cadiz. Hanno, too, had ſailed from Carthage through the Straits, and

reached

reached to 25° of north latitude in the Atlantic Ocean. In more modern times, even in the preceding century, Macham, an Englishman, returning from a voyage on the west coast of Africa, was shipwrecked on the island of Madeira, together with a woman whom he tenderly loved. After her death he became weary of solitude; and having constructed a bark, or canoe, with which he paddled over to the opposite coast, he was taken by the natives, and presented to the Caliph as a curiosity. And the Normans of Dieppe had, as a company, traded in 1364, not fourscore years from prince Henry's time, as far as Sierra de Leona, only 7° from the Line.

THE prince's humanity to his Moorish prisoners had likewise been rewarded by substantial information; they reported that some of their countrymen of the kingdom of Sus had advanced far into the desert, carrying their water and provisions along with them on camels; that, after many days travel, they came to mines of salt, and, having loaded their cargoes, they proceeded till they came within the limits of the rains; there they found large and populous towns, inhabited by a people totally black and woolly-headed, who reported that there were many countries even beyond them, occupied by numerous and warlike tribes. To complete all, Don Pedro, Henry's brother, returning from Venice, brought along with him from that city a map, on which the whole coast of the Atlantic Ocean was distinctly traced, and the southern extremity of Africa was represented to be a cape surrounded with the sea, which joined with the Indian Ocean.

No sooner was the prince thus satisfied of the possibility of a passage to India round Africa, than he set about con-

structing

ftructing the neceffary inftruments for navigation. He cor-
rected the folar tables of the Arabs, and made fome alterations in the aftrolabe : For, ftrange to tell! the quadrant
was not then known in Portugal, though, a hundred years
before, Ulughbeg had meafured the fun's height at Sa-
marcand in Perfia, with a quadrant of about 400 feet radi-
us, the largeft ever conftructed, if, indeed, the fize of this
be not exaggerated.

Henry, who, by his liberality and affability, had drawn
together the moft learned mathematicians and ableft pilots
of the age, now propofed to reduce his fpeculations to practice. Many fhips had failed in the courfe of his difquifi-
tions, and ten years had now elapfed before the prince, after all his encouragement, could induce the captains to proceed farther than Cape Non, or, thirty leagues further, to
Cape Bojador. To this their courage held good; after which,
the fear of fiery oceans reviving in their minds, they returned
exceedingly fatisfied with their own perfeverance and abilities. Henry, though greatly hurt at this behaviour, diffembled the low opinion which he had formed of both. He
contented himfelf with propofing to them different reafons
and rewards; and urged them to repeat their voyages,
which, however, conftantly ended in the fame difappointment. And it is probable a much longer time might have
been fpent in their mifcarriages, had not accident, or rather
providence, ftept in to his affiftance.

John Gonsalez and Triftan Vaz, two gentlemen of his
bed-chamber, feeing the impreffion this behaviour had
made on the prince, and having obtained a fmall fhip from
him, refolved to double Cape Bojador, and difcover the coaft

yond it. Whether the fiery oceans might not have prefented
themfelves to thefe gentlemen, I know not; but a violent
ftorm forced them to fea. After being toffed about in perpetual fear of fhipwreck for feveral days, they at laft landed on
a fmall ifland, which they called Port Santo. Thefe two navigators poffeffed the true fpirit of difcovery. Far from giving
themfelves up for loft in a new world, or content with what
they had already done, they fet about making the moft diligent obfervation of every thing remarkable in this fmall
fpot. The ifland itfelf was barren; but, examining the horizon all around, they obferved a black fixed fpot there,
which never either changed its place or dimenfions. Satif-
fied, therefore, that this was land, they returned to the Infant with the news of this double difcovery.

Three veffels were fpeedily equipped by the prince; two
of them given to Vaz and Arco, and the third to Bartholomew Pereftrello, gentleman of the bed-chamber to Don John
his brother. Thefe adventurers were far from difappoint-
ing his expectations; they arrived at Port Santo, and proceeded to the fixed fpot, which they found to be the ifland
of Madeira, wholly covered with wood; an ifland that has
ever fince been of the greateft ufe to the trade of both Indies, and which has remained to the crown of Portugal,
after the greateft part of their other conquefts in the eaft
are loft. John I. was now dead, and Edward had fucceeded
him. The infant Henry, however, ftill continued the purfuit of his difcoveries with the greateft ardour.

Giles D'Anez, ftimulated by the fuccefs of the laft ad-
ventures, put to fea with a refolution to double Cape Bojador clofe in fhore, fo as to make his voyage a foundation

2   for

for pufhing farther the difcovery; and, being lucky in good
weather, he fairly doubled the Cape; and, continuing fome
leagues farther into the bay to the fouth of it, he returned
with the fame good fortune to Portugal, after having found
the ocean equally as navigable on the other fide as on this;
and that there was no foundation for thofe monftrous appearances or difficulties mariners till now had expected to
find there.

THE fuccefsful expedition round Cape Bojador being foon
fpread abroad through Europe, excited a fpirit of adventure
in all foreigners; the moft capable of whom reforted immediately to prince Henry, from their different countries,
which further increafed the fpirit of the Portuguefe, already
raifed to a very great height. But there ftill was a party of
men, who, not fufceptible of great actions themfelves, dedicated their time with fome fuccefs to criticifing the en-
terprifes of others. Thefe blamed prince Henry, becaufe,
when Portugal was exhaufted both of men and money by
a neceffary war in Africa, he fhould have chofen that very
time to launch out into expences and vain difcoveries of
countries, in an immenfe ocean, which muft be ufelefs, becaufe incapable of cultivation. And though they did not advance, as formerly, that the ocean was boiling among burning fands, they ftill thought themfelves authorifed to affert,
that thefe countries muft, from their fituation under the
fun, be fo hot as to turn all the difcoverers black, and alfo
to deftroy all vegetation. Futile as thefe reafons were, at
another time they would have been fufficient to have
blafted all the defigns of prince Henry, had they made half
the impreffion upon the king that they did upon the minds
of the people. Portugal was then only *growing* to the pitch

of heroifm to which it foon after arrived, their fpirit being continually foftered by a long fucceffion of wife, brave, and well-informed princes.

Edward, the reigning prince, difdained to give any anfwer to fuch objections, otherwife than by doubling his refpect and attention for his uncle Henry. To encourage him ftill further, he conferred upon him for life the fovereignty of Madeira, Port Santo, and all the difcoveries he fhould make on the coaft of Africa; and the fpiritual jurifdiction of the ifland of Madeira, upon his new Order of Chrift, for ever.

These voyages of difcovery were conftantly perfevered in. Nugno Triftan doubled Cape Blanco, and came to a fmall river, which, from their finding gold in the hands of the natives, was afterwards called *Rio del Oro;* and here a fort was afterwards built by the Portuguefe, called *Arguim.* I would not, however, have it fuppofed, that gold is the produce of any place in the latitude of Cape Blanco. It was brought here from the black nations, far to the fouthward, to purchafe falt from the mines which are in this defert near the Cape. The fight of gold, better than any argument, ferved to calm the fears, and overcome the fcruples, of thofe who hitherto had been adverfaries to thefe difcoveries.

In the year 1445, Denis Fernandes firft difcovered the great river Senega, the northern banks of which are inhabited by Afenagi Moors, whofe colour is tawny, while the fouthern, or oppofite banks, belong to the Jaloffes, or Negro nation, the chief market for the gum-arabic. Paffing this river he difcovered Cape Verde; and, to his inexpreffible fatisfaction,

fatisfaction, though now in the midft of the torrid zone, he found the country abounded with large rivers, and with the moft luxuriant verdure. He found a civil war in the nation of Jaloffes. Bemoy, a prince of that nation, had, in a minority, intruded himfelf into the throne of his brothers, (to whom he was but half blood), by the addrefs of his mother. The eldeft of the three brothers preferved the fhadow of government, and feemed to favour the ufurpation. Bemoy had improved that interval by cultivating the Portuguefe friendfhip to the uttermoft. He promifed every thing; a place to build their city on the continent, which the king very much defired ; and to be a convert to Chriftianity, the only thing the king wifhed ftill more. His eldeft brother dying, the king was brifkly preffed by the two younger, and fteadily fupported by the Portuguefe, from whom he had borrowed large fums; but ftill appearing to trifle with the day of his converfion, and the day of his payment, the king ordered the Portuguefe to withdraw from his country, and leave him to his fortune. The lofs of a battle with his brothers foon reduced him to the neceffity of flying acrofs the deferts to Arguim, and thence to Portugal, with a number of his followers. He was received by the king of Portugal with all the honours due to a fovereign prince, and baptifed at Lifbon, the king and queen being his fponfors.

Great feftivals and illuminations were made at this acquifition to Chriftianity ; and Bemoy appeared at thofe feftivals as the greateft ornament of them, performing feats of horfemanfhip never before practifed in Portugal. The modefty and propriety of his converfation and behaviour in private, and the great dignity and eloquence which he

I   difplayed

diſplayed in public, began to give the Portugueſe a very different idea of his clan from that which they had formerly entertained.

In the mean time the king went rapidly on with the preparations that were to eſtabliſh Bemoy in his kingdom; and the feſtivals were no ſooner terminated, than Bemoy found a large army and fleet ready to ſail with him, the command of which, unhappily for him and the expedition, was given to Triſtan d'Acugna, a ſoldier of great experience and courage, but proud, paſſionate, and cruel; the diſagreeable name of Biſagudo * had already been fixed upon him by his countrymen.

The fleet performed the voyage, and the troops landed happily. They were, by their number and valour, far from any apprehenſion of oppoſition. The general began immediately to lay the foundation of a fort, without having ſufficiently attended to its unhealthy ſituation. The ſpot which was choſen being low and marſhy, fevers began early to make havock among his men, and the work of courſe went on proportionably ſlower. The murmurs of the army againſt his obſtinacy in adhering to the choice of this place, and his fear that he himſelf ſhould be left alone governor of it, made D'Acugna deſperate; when one day, taking his pleaſure on board a ſhip, and having had ſome words with Bemoy, he ſtabbed him with his dagger to the heart, ſo that he fell dead without uttering a word. The fort was abandoned, and the army returned to Portugal, after

ter

* The literal tranſlation of this is, *doubly ſharp*, or *ſharp to a fault;* a character he had gained in Portugal.

ter having cost little less than all prince Henry's discoveries together had done.

But Heaven rewarded the wisdom of the king by a discovery, the consequences of which more than overpaid him, in his mind, for his loss. Prince Henry's principal view was to discover the way to India by the southern Cape of Africa; but this as yet was not known to be possible. In order to remedy a disappointment, if any such happened in this sea-voyage, another was attempted by land. We have seen that the common track for the Indian trade was from the east to the west sea, through the desert, the whole breadth of Africa. Prince Henry had projected a route parallel to this to the southward, through a Christian country: For it had been long reported by the Christians from Jerusalem, that a number of monks resorted thither, subjects of a Christian prince in the very heart of Africa, whose dominions were said to reach from the east to the west sea. Several of these monks had been met at Alexandria, whose patriarch had the sole right to send a metropolitan into that country. These facts, though often known, had been as often forgot by the western Christians. Marco Paulo*, a Venetian traveller, had much confuted the story, by saying he had met, in his travels through Tartary, with this prince, who they all agreed was a priest, and was called Joannes Presbyter Prete Janni, or Prester John.

The king of Portugal, therefore, chose Peter Covillan and Alphonso de Paiva for his ambassadors. Covillan was a man qualified

---

* See Marco Paulo's Travels into Tartary.

qualified for the undertaking. He had feveral times been employed by the late king in very delicate affairs, out of which he extricated himfelf with great credit by his addrefs and fecrecy. He was, befides this, in the vigour of his age, bold, active, and perfectly mafter of all forts of arms; modeft and chearful in converfation, and, what crowned all, had happily a great readinefs in acquiring languages, which enabled him to explain himfelf wherever he went, without an interpreter; an advantage to which, above all others, we are to afcribe the fuccefs of fuch a journey.

It was at the court of Bemoy that the firft certain account of the exiftence of this Chriftian prince was procured. This people, on the weft coaft of Africa, reported, that, inland to the eaftward, were many powerful nations and cities, governed by princes totally independent of each other; that the eaftermoft of thefe princes was called prince of the Mofaical people, who were neither Pagans nor Idolaters, but profeffed a religion compounded of the Chriftian and Jewifh.

It feems plain that this intelligence muft have been brought by the caravans; or, indeed, the cafe may have been that the language of the Negroes had, of old, been a dialect of Abyffinian. The black Ethiopians above Thebes are reported to have beftowed much care upon letters; and they certainly reformed the hieroglyphics, and probably invented the Syllabic alphabet, which we know is ufed in Abyffinia to this day, and which was probably the firft among the nations. Be that as it will, the various names which the Senega went by were all Abyffinian words. Senega comes from Afenagi, which is Abyffinian, and fignifies *car-*

riers,

ers, or *caravans*; Dengui, *a stone*, or *rock*; Angueah, a tree of
that name; Anzo, *a crocodile*; and, at the same time, all these
are names of Abyssinian rivers.

IT was at Benin, another Negro country, that the king
again received a confirmation of the existence of a Christian
prince, who was said to inhabit the heart of Africa to the
south-east of this state. The people of Benin reported him
to be a prince exceedingly powerful; that his name was
Ogané, and his kingdom about 250 leagues to the eastward.
They added, that the kings of Benin received from him a
brass cross and a staff as their investiture. It should seem
that this Ogané is but a corruption of Jan, or Janhoi, which
title the eastern Christians had given to the king of Abyssinia. But it is very difficult to account for the knowledge
of Abyssinia in the kingdom of Benin, not only on account
of the distance, but likewise, because several of the most savage nations of the world, the Galla and Shangalla, occupy
the intervening space.

THE court of Abyssinia, as we shall see afterwards, did,
indeed, then reside in Shoa, the south-east extremity of the
kingdom, and, by its power and influence, probably might
have pushed its dominion through these barbarians, down
to the neighbourhood of Benin on the western ocean. But
all this I must confess to be a simple conjecture of mine,
of which, in the country itself, I never found the smallest
confirmation.

AMHA YASOUS (prince of Shoa) being at court, on a visit
to the king at Gondar, in the years 1770 and 1771, and the
strictest friendship subsisting between us, every endeavour

VOL. II.   O   possible poffible was ufed on my part to examine this affair to the bottom. A number of letters were written, and meffengers fent; and, at this prince's defire, his father directed, that all the records of government fhould be confulted to fatisfy me. But never any thing occurred which gave room to imagine the prince of Shoa had ever been fovereign of Benin, nor was the weftern ocean, or that ftate, known to them in my time. Yet the country alluded to could be no other than Abyffinia; and, indeed, the crooked ftaff, as well as the crofs, corroborate this opinion, unlefs the whole was an invention of the Negroes, to flatter the king of Portugal.

THAT prince was refolved no longer to delay the difcovery of the markets of the fpice-trade in India, and the paffage over land, through Abyffinia, to the eaftern ocean. He, therefore, as has been before faid, difpatched Covillan and de Paiva to Alexandria, with the neceffary letters and credit. They had likewife a map, or chart, given them, made under the direction of prince Henry, which they were to correct, or to confirm, according as it needed. They were to enquire what were the principal markets for the fpice, and particularly the pepper-trade in India; and what were the different channels by which this was conveyed to Europe; whence came the gold and filver, the medium of this trade; and, above all, they were to inform themfelves diftinctly, whether it was poffible to arrive in India by failing round the fouthern promontory of Africa.

FROM Alexandria thefe two travellers proceeded to Cairo; thence to Suez, the port on the bottom of the Red Sea, where joining a caravan of weftern Moors, they continued their

I route.

route to Aden, a rich trading town, without the Straits of Babelmandeb. Here they separated: Covillan set sail for India, De Paiva for Suakem, a small trading town and island in Barbaria, or Barabra of the ancients. What other circumstances occurred we know not, only that De Paiva, attempting his journey this way, lost his life, and was never more heard of.

COVILLAN, more fortunate, passed over to Calicut and Goa in India; then crossed the Indian Ocean to Sofala, to inspect the mines; then he returned to Aden, and so to Cairo, where he expected to meet his companion De Paiva; but here he heard of his death. However, he was there met by two Jews with letters from the king of Abyssinia, the one called Abraham, the other Joseph. Abraham he sent back with letters, but took Joseph along with him again to Aden, and thence they both proceeded to Ormus in the Persian Gulf. Here they separated, and the Jew returned home by the caravans that pass along the desert to Aleppo. Covillan, now solely intent upon the discovery of Abyssinia, returned to Aden, and, crossing the Straits of Babelmandeb, landed in the dominions of that prince, whose name was Alexander, and whom he found at the head of his army, levying contributions upon his rebellious subjects. Alexander received him kindly, but rather from motives of curiosity than from any expectation of advantage which would result from his embassy. He took Covillan along with him to Shoa, where the court then resided.

COVILLAN returned no more to Europe. A cruel policy of Abyssinia makes this a favour constantly denied to strangers. He married, and obtained large possessions; conti-

O 2

nued greatly in the favour of feveral fucceeding princes, and was preferred to the principal offices, in which, there is no doubt, he appeared with all the advantage a polifhed and inftructed mind has over an ignorant and barbarous one. Frequent difpatches from him came to the king of Portugal, who, on his part, fpared no expence to keep open the correfpondence. In his journal, Covillan defcribed the feveral ports in India which he had feen; the temper and difpofition of the princes; the fituation and riches of the mines of Sofala: He reported that the country was very populous, full of cities both powerful and rich; and he exhorted the king to purfue, with unremitting vigour, the paffage round Africa, which he declared to be attended with very little danger; and that the Cape itfelf was well known in India. He accompanied this defcription with a chart, or map, which he had received from the hands of a Moor in India, where the Cape, and cities all around the coaft, were exactly reprefented.

Upon this intelligence the king fitted out three fhips under Bartholomew Dias, who had orders to inquire after the king of Abyffinia on the weftern ocean. Dias paffed on to lat. 24½ deg. fouth, and there fet up the arms of the king of Portugal in token of poffeffion. He then failed for the harbour of the Herdfmen, fo called from the multitude of cows feen on land; and, as it fhould feem, not knowing whither he was going, came to a river which he called *Del Infante*, from the captain's name that firft difcovered it, having, without dreaming of it, paffed that formidable Cape, the object fo much defired by the Portuguefe. Here he was toffed for many days by violent ftorms as he came near land, being more and more in the courfe of variable winds, but, obfti-

3   nately

mately perfiding to difcover the coaft, he at laft came within fight of the Cape, which he called the *Cape of Tempefts*, from the rough treatment his veffel had met in her paffage round it.

THE great end was now obtained.   Dias and his companions had really fuffered much, and, upon their return, they did not fail to do ample juftice to their own bravery and perfeverance; in doing this, they had conjured up fo many ftorms and dreadful fights, that, all the remaining life of king John, there was no more talk but of this Cape: Only the king, to hinder a bad omen, inftead of the Cape of Tempefts, ordered it to be called the Cape of Good Hope.

ALTHOUGH the difcovery now was made, there were not wanting a confiderable number of people of the greateft confequence who were for abandoning it altogether; one of their reafons was curious, and what, if their behaviour afterwards had not been beyond all inftance heroic, would have led us to imagine their fpirit of religion and conqueft had both cooled fince the days of prince Henry. They were afraid, left, after having difcovered a paffage to India, the depriving the Moorifh ftates of their revenues from the fpice-trade, fhould unite thefe powers to their deftruction.   Now, to deftroy their revenues effectually, and thereby ruin their power, was the very motive which fet prince Henry upon the difcovery, as worthy the Grand Mafter of the Order of Chrift; an order founded in the blood of unbelievers, and devoted particularly to the extirpation of the Mahometan religion.

DON

Don Emmanuel, then king, having no fuch apprehenfions, refolved to abide the confequences of a meafure the
moſt arduous ever undertaken by any nation, and which,
though it had coſt a great deal of time and expence, had yet
fucceeded beyond their utmoſt expectations. It was not till
after long deliberation that he fixed upon Vafques de Gama,
a man of the firſt diſtinction, remarkable for courage and
great prefence of mind. Before his departure, the king put
into his hands the journal of Peter Covillan, with his chart,
and letters of credit to all the princes in India of whom he
had obtained any knowledge.

The behaviour of Vafques de Gama, at parting, was far
from being characteriſtic of the foldier or great man : his
proceſſions and tapers favoured much more of the oftentatious devotion of a bigotted little-minded prieſt, and was
much more calculated to depreſs the fpirits of his foldiers,
than to encourage them to the fervice they were then about
to do for their country. It ferved only to revive in their
minds the hardſhips that Dias had met off the Terrible Cape,
and perfuade them there was in their expedition much
more danger than glory. I would not be underſtood as
meaning to condemn all acts of devotion before military
expeditions, but would have them always ſhort, ordinary,
and uniform. Every thing further infpires in weak minds
a fenfe of danger, and makes them defpond upon any ferious appearance of difficulty.

July 4th, 1497, Vafques, with his fmall fleet, failed from
Lifbon ; and, as the art of navigation was confiderably improved, he ſtood out to fea till he made the Canary Iſlands,
and then thofe of Cape de Verde, where he anchored, took

in

in water and other refreshments.   After which he was four months struggling with contrary winds and blowing weather, and at last obliged, through perfect fatigue, to run into a large bay called *St Helena**, in lat. 32° 32' south.   The inhabitants of this bay were black, of low stature, and their language not understood, though it afterwards was found to be the same with that of the Cape.   They were cloathed with skins of antelopes, which abounded in the country, since known to be that of the Hottentots ; their arms were the horns and bones of beasts and fishes, for they had no knowledge of iron.

The Portuguese were unacquainted with the trade-winds in those southern latitudes ; and Vasques had departed for India, in a most unfavourable season of the year.   The 16th of November they sailed for the Cape with a south-west wind ; but that very day, the weather changing, a violent storm came on, which continued increasing ; so, although on the 18th they discovered their long-desired Cape, they did not dare or attempt to pass it.   Then it was seen how much stronger the impressions were that Dias had left imprinted in their minds, than those of duty, obedience, and resignation, which they had so pompously vowed at the chapel, or hermitage.   All the crew mutinied, and refused to pass farther ; and it was not the common sailors only ; the pilots and masters were at their head.   Vasques, satisfied in his mind that there was nothing extraordinary in the danger, persevered to pass the Cape in spite of all difficulties ; and the officers, animated with the same ardour, seized the
most

* On the west side of the peninsula on the Atlantic.

moſt mutinous of their maſters and pilots, and confined them cloſe below in heavy irons.

VASQUES himſelf, taking hold of the rudder, continued to ſteer the ſhip with his own hand, and ſtood out to ſea, to the aſtoniſhment of the braveſt ſeaman on board. The ſtorm laſted two days, without having in the leaſt ſhaken the reſolution of the admiral, who, on the 20th of November, ſaw his conſtancy rewarded by doubling that Cape, which he did, as it were, in triumph, ſounding his trumpets, beating his drums, and permitting to his people all ſorts of paſtimes which might baniſh from their minds former apprehenſions, and induce them to agree with him, that the point had very aptly been called the Cape of Good Hope.

ON the 25th they anchored in a creek called *Aigua de Saint Blaze.* Soon after their arrival there appeared a number of the inhabitants on the mountains, and on the ſhore. The general, fearing ſome ſurpriſe, landed his men armed. But, firſt, he ordered ſmall braſs bells, and other trinkets, to be thrown out of the boats on ſhore, which the blacks greedily took up, and ventured ſo near as to take one of them out of the general's own hand. Upon his landing, he was welcomed with the ſound of flutes and ſinging. Vaſques, on his part, ordered his trumpets to ſound, and his men to dance round them.

ALL along from St Blaze, for more than ſixty leagues, they found the coaſt remarkably pleaſant, full of high and fair trees. On Chriſtmas day they made land, and entered a river which they called *the river of the kings;* and all the
distance

diſtance between this and St Blaze they named *Terra de Natal*. The weather being mild, they took to their boats to row along the ſhore, on which were obſerved both men and women of a large ſtature, but who ſeemed to be of quiet and civil behaviour. The general ordered Martin Alonzo, who ſpoke ſeveral languages of the Negroes, to land; and he was ſo well received by the chief, or king, that the admiral ſent him ſeveral trifles, with which he was wonderfully pleaſed, and offered, in return, any thing he wanted of the produce of his country.

On the 15th of January, in the year 1498, having taken in plenty of water, which the Negroes, of their own accord, helped them to put on board, they left this civil nation, ſteering paſt a length of coaſt terminated by a Cape called the *Cape of Currents*. There the coaſt of Natal ends, and that of Sofala begins, to the northward of the Cape. At this place, Gama from the ſouth joined Covilian's track from the north, and theſe two Portugueſe had completely made the circuit of Africa.

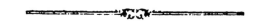

ISCANDER, or ALEXANDER.

From 1478 to 1495.

Iscander declares War with Adel—Good Conduct of the King—Betrayed and murdered by Za Saluce.

AS foon as the king Bæda Mariam was dead, the hiftory of Abyffinia informs us, that a tumultuous meeting of the nobles brought from the mountain of Gefhen the queen Romana, with her fon Ifcander, who upon his arrival was crowned without any oppofition.

It is to be obferved in the Abyffinian annals, that very frequent minorities happen. A queen-mother, or regent, with two or three of the greateft intereft at court, are, during the minority, in poffeffion of the king's perfon, and govern in his name. The tranfactions of this minority, too, are as carefully inferted in the annals of the kingdom as any other part of the fubfequent government, but as the whole of thefe minorities are but one continued chain of quarrels, plots, and treachery, as foon as the king comes of age, the greateft part of this reign of his minifters is cancelled, as being the acts of fubjects, and not worthy to be

inferted

inserted in their histories; which they entitle *Kibra Za Nagast*, the greatness or atchievements of their kings. This, however political in itself, is a great disadvantage to history, by concealing from posterity the first cause of the most important transactions.

For several years after Iscander ascended the throne, the queen his mother, together with the Acab Saat, Testo Georgis, and Betwudet Amdu, governed the kingdom despotically under the name of the young king. Accordingly, after some years sufferance, a conspiracy was formed, at the head of which were two men of great power, Abba Amda and Abba Hasabo, but the conspirators proving unsuccessful, some of them were imprisoned, some put to death, and others banished to unwholesome places, there to perish with hunger and fevers.

The king from his early age had shewn a passionate desire for a war with Adel, and that prince, whose country had been so often desolated by the Abyssinian armies, omitted no opportunity of creating an interest at that court, that should keep things in a quiet state. In this, however, he was much interrupted at present by a neighbouring chief of Arar, named Mafudi. This man, exceedingly brave, capable of enduring the greatest hardships, and a very great bigot to the Mahometan religion, had made a vow, that, every Lent, he would spend the whole forty days in some part of the Abyssinian kingdom; and to this purpose he had raised, at his own expence, a small body of veteran troops, whom he inspired with the same spirit and resolution. Sometimes he fell on one part of the frontier, sometimes upon another; slaying, without mercy, all that made

P 2   resistance,

refistance, and driving off whole villages of men, women, and children, whom he fent into Arabia, or India, to be fold as flaves.

It was a matter of great difficulty for the king of Adel to perfuade the Abyfiinians that Maffudi acted without his inftigation. The young king was one who could not diftinguifh Adel from Arar, or Mahomet's army from Maffudi's. He bore with very great impatience the exceffes every year committed by the latter; but he was over-ruled by his nobility at home, and his thoughts turned as much as poffible to hunting, to which he willingly gave himfelf up; and, tho' but fifteen years of age, was the perfon, in all Abyfinia, moft dexterous at managing his arms. At laft, being arrived at the age of feventeen, and returning from having obferved a very fuccefsful expedition made by Maffudi against his territories, he ordered Za Saluce, his firft minister, commander in chief, and governor of Amhara, to raife the whole forces to the fouthward, while he himfelf collected the nobility in Angot and Tigré. With thofe, as foon as the rainy feafon was over, he defcended into the kingdom of Adel.

The king of Adel had been forced into this war, yet, like a wife prince, he was not unprepared for it. He had advanced directly towards the king, but had not paffed his frontiers. Some inhabitants of a village called *Arno*, all Mahometans, but tributary to the king of Abyfiinia, had murdered the governor the king had fet over them. Ifcander marched directly to deftroy it, which he had no fooner accomplifhed, than the Moorifh army prefented itfelf. The battle was maintained obftinately on both fides, till the troops under

Za

Za Saluce withdrew in the heat of the engagement, leaving the king in the midst of his enemies. This treason, however, seemed to have inspired the small army that remained with new courage, so that the day was as yet dubious, when Iscander, being engaged in a narrow pass, and seeing himself close pressed by a Moor who bore in his hand the green standard of Mahomet, turned suddenly upon him, and slew him with a javelin; and, having wrested the colours from him as he was falling, he, with the point of the spear that bore the ensign, struck the king of Adel's son dead to the ground, which immediately caused the Moors to retreat.

The young prince was too prudent to follow this victory in the state the army then was; for that of Adel, though it had retreated, did not disperse. Za Saluce was returning by long marches to Amhara, exciting all those in his way to revolt; and it was high time, therefore, for the king to follow him. But, unequal as he was in strength to the Moors, he could not reconcile it with his own honour to leave their army masters of the field. He, therefore, first consulted the principal officers of his troops, then harangued his men, which, the historian says, he did in the most pathetic and masterly manner; so that, with one voice, they desired instantly to be led to the Moors. The king is said to have ranged his little army in a manner that astonished the oldest officers. He then sent a defiance to the Moors, by several prisoners whom he released. They, however, more desirous to keep him from ravaging the country than to fight another battle, continued quiet in their tents; and the king, after remaining on the field till near noon, drew off his troops in the presence of his enemy, making a retreat

treat which would not have been unworthy of the hero whofe name he bore.

The king, in his return to Shoa, left his troops, which was the northern army, in the northern provinces, as he paffed; fo that he came to Shoa with a very fmall retinue, hearing that Za Saluce had gone to Amhara. This traitor, however, had left his creatures behind him, after inftructing them what they were to do. Accordingly, the fecond day after Ifcander's arrival in Tegulat, the capital of Shoa, they fet upon him, during the night, in a fmall houfe in Aylo Meidan, and murdered him while he was fleeping. They concealed his body for fome days in a mill, but Taka Chriftos, and fome others of the king's friends, took up the corpfe and expofed it to the people, who, with one accord, proclaimed Andreas, fon of Ifcander, king; and Za Saluce and his adherents, traitors.

In the mean time, Za Saluce, far from finding the encouragement he expected in Amhara, was, upon his firft appearance, fet upon by the nobility of that province; and, being deferted by his troops, he was taken prifoner; his eyes were put out, and, being mounted on an afs, he was carried amidft the curfes of the people through the provinces of Amhara and Shoa.

Iscander was fucceeded by his fon Andreas, or Amda Sion, an infant, who reigned feven months only.

A wonderful confufion feems to be introduced at this time into hiftory, by the Portuguefe writers. Ifcander is faid to die in the 1495. He began, as they fay, to reign

4   in

in 1475, and this is confirmed by Ludolf; and, on all hands, it is allowed he reigned 17 years, which would have brought the laſt year of his reign to 1492. It ſeems alſo to be agreed by the generality of them, that Covillan ſaw and converſed with this prince, Iſcander, ſome time before his death: this he very well might have done, if that prince lived to the 1492, and Peter Covillan came into Abyſſinia in 1493, as Galvan ſays in his father's memoirs. But then Tellez informs us expreſsly, that Iſcander was dead 6 months before the arrival of Peter Covillan in that country: if Peter Covillan arrived 6 months after the death of Iſcander, it muſt have been in the end of his ſon's reign, Amda Sion, who was an infant, and reigned only 7 months.

ALVAREZ omits this king, Amda Sion, altogether, and ſo does Tellez; and there is a heap of miſtakes here that ſhew theſe Portugueſe hiſtorians paid very little attention to the chronology of theſe reigns. They call Alexander the father of Naod, when he was really but his brother; and Helena, they ſay, was David's mother, when, in fact, ſhe was his grandmother, or rather his grandfather's wife; for Helena, who was Iteghé in the time of David the III. had never either ſon or daughter. So that if I differ, as in fact I do, 4 years, or thereabout, in this account, I do not think in thoſe remote times, when the language and manner of accounting was ſo little known to theſe ſtrangers, that I, therefore, ſhould reject my own account and ſervilely adopt theirs, and the more ſo, becauſe, as we ſhall ſee in its proper place, by the examination and compariſon made by help of an eclipſe of the ſun in the 13th year of Claudius' reign in the 1553, and counting from that downwards to my arrival in Abyſſinia, and backwards to Iſcander, that that prince muſt have be-

gan

gun his reign in 1478, and reigning 17 years, did not die till the year 1495, and therefore muſt have ſeen Peter Co-villan, and converſed with him, if he had arrived in Abyſſi-nia ſo early as the 1490.

N   A   O   D.

From 1495 to 1508.

Wiſe Conduct of the King—Prepares for a War with the Moors—Con-cludes an honourable Peace with Adel.

AFTER the unfortunate death of the young king Alex-ander, the people in general, wearied of minorities, unanimouſly choſe Naod for their king. He was Alexan-der's younger brother, the difference of ages being but one year, though he was not by the ſame mother, but by the the king's ſecond wife Calliope. He was born at a town called Gabargué, the day the royal army was cut off in his father's time, when both the Betwudets periſhed. From this circumſtance, the Empreſs Helena and her party had uſed ſome underhand means to ſet him aſide as unfortu-nate, and in his place to put Anquo Iſrael, Bæda Mariam's youngeſt ſon, that they might govern him and the king-dom during his non-age. But Taka Chriſtos, their man of confidence, being, on his firſt declaration of ſuch inten-tions, cut off by the army in Dawaro, Naod was immedi-
2   ately

ately proclaimed, and brought from the mountain of Geſhen.

ALTHOUGH Naod was in the prime of life, and vigorous
both in body and mind, yet ſuch were the circumſtances of
the kingdom at his acceſſion, that it ſeemed a taſk too arduous for any one man. The continual intrigues of the
empreſs, the quantity of Mahometan gold which was cir-
culating on every occaſion throughout the court, the little
ſucceſs the army had in Adel, as alſo the treachery of Za
Saluce, and the untimely end of the young prince, who
ſeemed to promiſe a remedy to the misfortunes, had ſo diſ-
united the principal people in the government, that there
did not ſeem a ſufficient number of men worthy of truſt to
aſſiſt the king with their councils, or fill, with any degree
of dignity, the places that were vacant.

NAOD was no ſooner ſeated on the throne than he publiſhed a very general and comprehenſive amneſty. By proclamation he declared, " That any perſon who ſhould up-
" braid another with being a party in the misfortunes of
" paſt times, or ſay that he had been privy to this or to that
" conſpiracy, or had been a favourite of the empreſs, or a
" partizan of Za Saluce, or had received bribes from the
" Moors, ſhould, without delay, be put to death." This
proclamation had the very beſt effect, as it quieted the mind
of every guilty perſon when he ſaw the king, from whom
he feared an inquiry, cutting off all poſſible means by
which it could be procured againſt him. Andreas a monk,
a man of quality, and of very great conſequence in that
country, a relation of the king by his mother, having affected to talk lightly of the proclamation, the king ſent for
him.

him, and ordered the tip of his tongue to be cut off in his presence. This man, whose fault seems only to have been in his tongue, and of whom a very great character is given, lived in the succeeding reign to give the king a very distinguished proof of his attachment to his family, and love of his country.

Naod having thus prudently quieted disturbances at home, turned his thoughts to the war with Maffudi; for the king of Adel himself had made his peace through mediation of the emprefs Helena; and this king, more politic than Alexander his brother, was willing to diffemble with the king of Adel, that he might fight his two adverfaries fingly: He, therefore, prepared a fmaller army than was ufual for the king to head, without fuffering a Moor of any kind to ferve in it.

It was known to a day when Maffudi was to enter upon his expeditions againft Abyffinia. For near thirty years he had begun to burn the churches, and drive off the people and cattle on the firft day of Lent; and, as Lent advanced, he with his army penetrated farther up the country. The Abyffinians are the ftricteft people in the world in keeping fafts. They are fo auftere that they tafte no fort of animal food, nor butter, eggs, oil, or wine. They will not, though ever fo thirfty, drink a cup of water till fix o'clock in the evening, and then are contented, perhaps, with dry or four leaven bread, the beft of them only making ufe of honey; by which means they become fo weak as to be unable to bear any fatigue. This was Maffudi's reafon for invading the country in Lent, at which time fcarce a Chriftian, through fafting, was able to bear arms.

1

NAOD, like a wife prince who had gained the confidence of his army, would not carry with him any man who did not, for that time, live in the fame free and full manner he was ufed to do in feftivals. He himfelf fet the example; and Andreas the monk, after taking upon himfelf a vow of a whole year's fafting for the fuccefs of the army, declared to them, that there was more merit in faving one Chriftian village from flavery, and turning Mahometan, than in fafting their whole lives.

THE king then marched againft Maffudi; and having taken very ftrong ground, as if afraid of his army's weaknefs, the Moors, contrary to advice of their leader, attacked the king's camp in the moft carelefs and prefumptuous manner. They had no fooner entered, however, by ways left open on purpofe for them, than they found the king's army in order to receive them, and were fo rudely attacked, that moft of thofe who had penetrated into the camp were left dead upon the fpot. The king continued the purfuit with his troops, retook all the prifoners and cattle which Maffudi was driving away, and advanced towards the frontiers of Adel, where ambaffadors met him, hoping, on the part of the king, that his intention was not to violate the treaty of peace.

To this the king anfwered, That, fo far from it, he would confirm the peace with them, but with this condition, that they muft deliver up to him all the Abyffinians that were to be found in their country taken by Maffudi in his laft expedition, adding, that he would ftay fifteen days there to expect his anfwer. The king of Adel, defirous of peace, and

Q 2

not

not a little terrified at the difaster of Maffudi, hitherto reckoned invincible, gathered together all the flaves as foon as poffible, and returned them to the king.

NAOD having now, by his courage and prudence, freed himfelf from fear of a foreign war, returned home, and fet himfelf like a wife prince to the reforming of the abufes that prevailed everywhere among his people, and to the cultivation of the arts of peace. He died a natural death, after having reigned 13 years.

DAVID III.

From 1508 to 1540.

David, an Infant, fucceeds—Queen fends Matthew Ambaffador to Portugal—David takes the Field—Defeat of the Moors—Arrival of an Embaffy from Portugal—Difaftrous War with Adel.

THE vigorous reign of Naod had at leaft fufpended the fate of the whole empire; and, had it not been that they ftill perfifted in that ruinous and dangerous meafure of following minority with minority, by the election of children to the throne, it is probable this kingdom would have efcaped the greateft part of thofe difmal calamities that

that fell upon it in the fequel. But the Iteghé Helena, and the Abuna Marcos, (now become her creature) had intereſt enough, notwithſtanding the apparent neceſſities of the times, to place David ſon of Naod upon the throne, a child of eleven years old, that they might take upon themſelves the government of the kingdom; whereas Anquo Iſrael (third ſon of Bæda Mariam) was of an age proper to govern, and whom they would have preferred to Naod for the ſame reaſon, merely becauſe he was then a child.

Besides the deſire of governing, another motive operated, which, however good in itſelf, was very criminal from the preſent circumſtances. A peace with Adel was what the empreſs Helena conſtantly deſired; for ſhe could not ſee with indifference the deſtruction of her own country, far leſs contribute to it. She was herſelf by origin a Moor, daughter of Mahomet, governor for the king in Dawaro; had been ſuſpected, ſo early as her huſband's time, of preferring the welfare of her own country to that of the kingdom of Abyſſinia.

This princeſs, perfectly informed of the intereſts of both nations, ſeems, in her whole conduct, to have acted upon the moſt judicious and ſenſible principles. She knew the country of Adel to be, by ſituation and intereſt, perfectly commercial; that part of Africa, the oppoſite Arabia, and the peninſula of the Indies, were but three partners joined in one trade; they mutually conſumed each others produce; they mutually contributed to export the joint produce of the three countries to diſtant parts of Europe, Aſia, and Africa; which three continents then conſtituted the whole known world. When Adel was at peace with Abyſſinia,

then

then the latter became rich, from the gold, ivory, coffee, cattle, hides, and all manner of provifion, procured by the former from every part of the mountainous tract above it. Trade flourifhed and plenty followed it. The merchants carried every fpecies of goods to the moft diftant provinces in fafety, equally to the advantage of Abyffinia and Adel. Thefe advantages, fo fenfibly felt, were maintained by bribery, and a conftant circulation of Mahometan gold in the court of Abyffinia; the kingdom, however, thus profpered. A war with Adel, on the contrary, had its origin in a violent defire of a barbarous people, fuch as the Abyffinians were, to put themfelves in poffeffion of riches which their neighbours had gained by trade and induftry.

SHE faw that, even in this the worft of cafes, nothing utterly deftructive could poffibly happen to the Abyffinians; in their inroads into that country, they plundered the markets and got, at the rifk of their lives, India ftuffs of every kind, for which elfe they would have paid money. On the other hand, the people of Adel, when conquerors, acquired no ftuffs, no manufactures, but the perfons of the Abyffinians themfelves, whom they carried into flavery, and fold in Arabia, and all parts of Afia, at immenfe profits. Next to gold they are the moft agreeable and valuable merchandife in every part of the eaft; and thefe again, being chiefly the idle people who delighted in war, their abfence promoted the more defirable event of peace.

IN this ftate we fee that war was but another fpecies of commerce between the two countries, though peace was the moft eligible ftate for them both; and this the emprefs Helena had conftantly endeavoured to maintain, but could

not

not fucceed among a people fond of war, by any other means, but by giving them a minor for their king, who was by the law of the land under her direction, as the country was, during his minority, under her regency.

ALTHOUGH this, the ordinary ftate of the emprefs's politics, had hitherto anfwered well between the kingdoms, when no other parties were engaged, the introduction of a third power, and its influence, totally changed that fyftem. The Turks, an enemy not yet known in any formidable line by the fouthern part of Africa, or Afia, now appeared under a form that made all thofe fouthern ftates tremble.

SELIM, emperor of Conftantinople, had defeated Canfo el Gauri, Soldan of Egypt, and flain him in the field. After a fecond battle he had taken Cairo, the capital of that country; and, under the fpecious pretence of a violation of the law of nations, by Tomum Bey, the fucceffor, who was faid to have put his ambaffadors to death, he had hanged that prince upon one of the principal gates of his own capital; and, by this execution, had totally deftroyed the fucceffion of the Mamalukes. Sinan Batha, the great general and minifter of Selim, in a very few months over-ran all the peninfula of Arabia, to the verge of the Indian Ocean.

THESE people, trained to war, Mahomet had infpired with enthufiafm, and led them to the conqueft of the Eaft. Trade and luxury had, after that, difarmed and reduced them to much the fame fituation as, in a former age, they had been found by Auguftus Cæfar. Sinan Batha, with a troop of veterans, had, by degrees extirpated the native princes of the country; thofe that refifted, by force; and thofe that

submitted

submitted to him, by treachery; and in their place, in every principal town, he had substituted Turkish officers of confidence, strongly supported by troops of Janizaries, who knew no other government but martial law.

War had now changed its form entirely under these new conquerors. Muskets, and large trains of artillery, were introduced against javelins, lances, and arrows, the only arms then known in Arabia, and in the opposite continent of Abyssinia. A large fleet, crowded with soldiers, and filled with military stores, the very name of which, as well as their destructive qualities, were till now unknown in these southern regions, were employed by the Turks to extend their conquest to India, where, though by the superior valour of the Portuguese they were constantly disappointed in their principal object, they neverthelefs, in their paffage outward and homeward, reinforced their several posts in Arabia, from which they looked for affiftance and protection, had any enemy placed himself in their way, or a storm, or other unexpected misfortune, overtaken them in their return.

These Janizaries lived upon the very bowels of commerce. They had, indeed, for a shew of protecting it, established customhouses in their various ports ; but they soon made it appear, that the end proposed by these was only to give them a more distinct knowledge who were the subjects from whom they could levy the most enormous extortions. Jidda, Zibid, and Mocha, the places of confequence nearest to Abyssinia on the Arabian shore, Suakem, a sea-port town on the very barriers of Abyssinia, in the immediate way of their caravan to Cairo, on the African side, were each under

der

der the command of a Turkiſh baſha, and garriſoned by Turkiſh troops ſent thither from Conſtantinople by the emperors Selim and Soliman, his ſucceſſors.

THE peaceable Arabian merchants, full of that good faith which ſucceſsful commerce inſpires, fled everywhere from the violence and injuſtice of theſe Turkiſh tyrants, and landed in ſafety their riches and perſons on the oppoſite ſhore of the kingdom of Adel. The trade from India, flying from the ſame enemy, took refuge in Adel among its own correſpondents, the Mooriſh merchants, during the violent and impolitic tyranny that everywhere took place under this Turkiſh oppreſſion.

ZEYLA is a ſmall iſland, on the véry coaſt of Adel, oppoſite to Arabia Felix without the Straits of Babelmandeb, upon the entrance of the Indian Ocean. The Turks of Arabia, though they were blind to the cauſe, were ſenſible of the great influx of trade into the oppoſite kingdom. They took poſſeſſion, therefore, of Zeyla, where they eſtabliſhed what they called a Cuſtomhouſe, and by means of that poſt, and gallies cruiſing in the narrow Straits, they laid the Indian trade to Adel under heavy contributions, that might, in ſome meaſure, indemnify them for the great deſertion their violence and injuſtice had occaſioned in Arabia.

THIS ſtep threatened the very exiſtence both of Adel and Abyſſinia; and conſidering the vigorous government of the one, and the weak politics and prejudices of the other, it is more than probable the Turks would have ſubdued both Adel and Abyſſinia, had they not, in India their chief object, met the Portugueſe, ſtrongly eſtabliſhed, and governed

VOL. II.   R   by

by a fucceffion of kings who had not in any age their
equals, and feconded by officers and foldiers who, for difcipline, courage, love to their country, and affection to their
fovereign were, perhaps, fuperior to any troops, or any fet
of individuals, that, as far as we can judge from hiftory,
have ever yet appeared in the world.

It was not now a time for a woman to reign, nor, which
was the fame thing, to place a child upon the throne. The
emprefs Helena faw this diftinctly; but her ambition
made her prefer the love of reigning to the vifible necelli-
ties and welfare of her country. She knew the progrefs
and extent of the Portuguefe power in India; and faw plainly there was no profpect, but in their affiftance, at once to
fave both Abyffinia and Adel.

Peter Covillan, fent thither as ambaffador by John
king of Portugal, had, for two reigns, been detained in A-
byffinia, with a conftant refufal of leave to return. He was
now become an object of curiofity rather than ufe. However, except his liberty, he had wanted nothing. The emprefs had married him nobly in the country; had given
him large appointments, both as to profit and dignity. She
now began to be fenfible of the confequence of having with
her a man of his abilities, who could open to her the method
of corresponding effectually both with India and Portugal
in their own language, to which, as well as to the perfons
to whom her letters were to be addreffed, fhe was then an
utter ftranger.

She had about her court an Armenian merchant named
Matthew, a perfon of great truft and difcretion, who had

2.   been

been long accuftomed to go to the feveral kingdoms of the Eaft upon mercantile commiffions for the king and for his nobles. He had been at Cairo, Jerufalem, Ormus, Ifpahan, and in the Eaft Indies on the coaft of Malabar; both in places conquered by the Portuguefe, and in thofe that yet held out under their native Pagan princes. He was one of thofe factors which, as I have already faid, are employed by the king and great men in Abyffinia to fell or barter, in the places above mentioned, fuch part of their revenue as are paid them in kind.

These men are chiefly Greeks, or Armenians, but the preference is always given to the latter. Both nations pay caratch, or capitation, to the Grand Signior, (whofe fubjects they are) and both have, in confequence, paffports, protections, and liberty to trade wherever they pleafe throughout the empire, without being liable to thofe infults and extortions from the Turkifh officers that other ftrangers are.

The Armenians, of all the people in the Eaft, are thofe moft remarkable for their patience and fobriety. They are generally mafters of moft of the eaftern languages; are of ftrong, robuft conftitutions; of all people, the moft attentive to the beafts and merchandife they have in charge; exceedingly faithful, and content with little. This Matthew, queen Helena chofe for her ambaffador to Portugal, and joined a young Abyffinian with him, who died in the voyage. He was charged with letters to the king, which, with the other difpatches, as they are long, and abound with fiction and bombaft rather than truth and facts, I have not troubled myfelf to tranfcribe; they are, befides, in many printed collections *.

¹ᴛ

---

* Vide Hamed, tom. i. cap. 37.

It appears clearly from thefe letters, that they were the joint compofitions of Covillan, who knew perfectly the manner of correfponding with his court upon dangerous fubjects, and of the fimple Abyffinian confidents of the emprefs. Helena, who, unacquainted with embaffies or correfpondence with princes, or the ill confequence that thefe letters would be of to their ambaffador and his errand, if they happened to be intercepted by an enemy, told plainly all they defired and wifhed to execute by the affiftance of the Portuguefe. Thus, in the firft part of the letter, (which we fhall fuppofe dictated by Covillan) the emprefs remits the defcription of her wants, and what is the fubject of the embaffy, to Matthew her ambaffador, whom fhe qualifies as her confidential fervant, inftructed in her moft fecret intentions; defiring the king of Portugal to believe what he fhall report from her to him in private, as if they were her own words uttered immediately from her to him in perfon. So far was prudent; fuch a conduct as we fhould expect from a man like Covillan, long accuftomed to be trufted with the fecret negociations of his fovereign.

But the latter end of his difpatches (the work, we fuppofe, of Abyffinian ftatefmen) divulges the whole fecret. It explains the motives of this embaffy in the cleareft manner, defiring the king of Portugal to fend a fufficient force to deftroy Mecca and Medina; to affift them with a fufficient number of fhips, and to annihilate the Turkifh power by fea; while they, by land, fhould extirpate all the Mahometans on their borders; and it ftigmatizes thefe Mahometans, both Turks and Moors, with the moft opprobrious names it was poffible to devife.

With the firſt part of theſe diſpatches, it is plain, Matthew, as an envoy, might have paſſed unmoleſted; he had only to give to the ſecret wiſhes of the empreſs, with which he was charged, what kind of mercantile colour he pleaſed. But the laſt part of the letter brought home to him a charge of the deepeſt dye, both of ſacrilege and high-treaſon, that he meditated againſt the Ottoman empire, whoſe Raya* he was; and, there can be no doubt, had theſe letters been intercepted and read, Matthew's embaſſy and life would have ended together under ſome exquiſite ſpecies of torture. This, indeed, he ſeems to have apprehended; as, after his arrival in India, he conſtantly refuſed to ſhew his diſpatches, even to the Portugueſe viceroy himſelf, from whom, in the inſtant, he-had received very ſingular favour and protection.

The king, when of age, never could be brought to acknowledge this embaſſy by Matthew; but, as we ſhall ſee, did conſtantly deny it. If we believe the Portugueſe, the deſpair of the empreſs was ſo great, that ſhe offered onethird of the kingdom to the king of Portugal if he relieved her. Nothing of this kind appears in the letters; but, if this offer was part of Matthew's private diſpatches, we may ſee a reaſon why David did not with to own the commiſſion and offer as his.

Matthew had a fare paſſage to Dabul in India, but here his misfortunes began. The governor, taking him for a ſpy, confined him in cloſe priſon. But Albuquerque, then viceroy of India, reſiding at Goa, who had himſelf a deſign

4   upon

---

upon Abyssinia, hearing that such a person, in such a character, was arrived, sent and took him out of the hands of
the governor of Dabul, where his sufferings else would not
have so quickly ended. All the Portuguese cried out upon
seeing such an ambassador as Matthew sent to their master;
sometimes they pretended that he was a spy of the Sultan,
at other times he was an impostor, a cook, or some other
menial servant.

ALBUQUERQUE treated with him privately before he landed, to make his commissions known to him ; but he expressly refused shewing any letter unless to the king himself in
Portugal. This behaviour hurt him in the eyes of the viceroy, who was therefore disposed, with the rest of his officers,
to slight him when he should come ashore. But Matthew,
now out of danger, and knowing his person to be sacred,
would no longer be treated like a private person. He sent
to let the viceroy, bishop, and clergy know, that, besides his
consequence as an ambassador, which demanded their respect, he was the bearer of a piece of wood of the true cross,
which he carried as a present to the king of Portugal ; and,
therefore, he required them, as they would avoid an imputation of sacrilege, to shew to that precious relict the utmost respect, and celebrate its arrival as a festival. No more
was necessary after this. The whole streets of Goa were
filled with processions ; the troops were all under arms ; the
viceroy, and the principal officers, met Matthew at his landing, and conveyed him to the palace, where he was magnificently lodged and feasted. But nothing could long
overcome the prejudices the Portuguese had imbibed upon
the first sight of him ; and, notwithstanding he carried a piece
of the true cross, both he and it soon fell into perfect oblivion:

tion: Nor was it till 1513, after he had staid three years in India, that he got leave to proceed to Portugal by a fleet returning home loaded with spices.

Damianus Goez the historian, though apparently a man of good sense and candour, cannot conjecture why this Armenian was sent as an ambassador, and wishes to be resolved why not an Abyssinian nobleman. But it is obvious from the character I have already given of him, there could be nobody in the empress's power that had half his qualifications; and, besides, an Abyssinian nobleman would not have ventured to go, as knowing very well that everywhere beyond the limits of his own country he would have been without protection, and the first Turk in whose power he might have fallen would have sold him for a slave. In no other character is any of his nation seen, either in Arabia or India, and his master has no treaty with any state whatever. Add to this, that an Abyssinian speaks no language but his own, which is not understood out of his own country; and is absolutely ignorant even of the existence of other far distant nations.

But, besides, there was an Abyssinian sent with Matthew, who died; and here Damianus Goez's wonder should cease.

The same ill-fortune, which had attended Matthew in India, followed him in his voyage to Portugal. The Captains of the ships contended with each other who should behave worst to him; and, in the midst of all this ill-treatment, the ship which he was on board of arrived at Lisbon. The king, upon hearing the particulars of this ill usage, immediately put the offenders in irons, where they had,
                                                    probably,

probably, lain during their lives, had they not been freed by the interceffion of Matthew.

DAVID (as I have before observed) was only eleven years old * when he was placed upon the throne; and, at his inauguration, took the name of Lebna Denghel, or the Virgin's Frankincenfe; then that of Etana Denghel, or the Myrrh of the Virgin; and after that, of Wanag Segued, which fignifies Reverenced, or Feared, among the Lions, with whom, towards the laft of his reign, he refided in wilds and mountains more than with men.

DURING this minority, there was peace with Mahomet king of Adel. Maffudi ftill continued his depredations; and, by his liberality, had formed ftrong connections with the Turks in Arabia. In return for the number of flaves whom he had fent to Mecca, a green filk ftandard, (that of Mahomet and of the Faith), and a tent of black velvet, embroidered with gold, were fent him by the Sherriffe, the greateft honour a Mahometan could poffibly receive, and he was alfo made Shekh of the ifland of Zeyla, which was delivering the key of Abyffinia to him.

IT was not till David had arrived at fixteen years of age that the conftant fuccefs of Maffudi, the honours beftowed upon him, and the gain which accrued from all his expeditions, had at laft determined the king of Adel to break the peace with Abyffinia, and join him. Thefe princes, with the whole Mahometan force, had fallen together upon
Dawaro,

---

* Vid. David's letter to Emanuel, king of Portugal 1524.

Dawaro, Ifat, and Fatigar; and, in one year, had driven away, and flain, above nineteen thoufand Chriftians, fubjects to the king. A terror was now fpread over the whole kingdom, and great blame laid both upon the emprefs and the king, for fitting and looking timidly on, while the Turks and Moors, year after year, ravaged whole provinces without refiftance.

THESE murmurs at laft roufed David, who, for his own part, had not fuffered them willingly fo long. He determined immediately to raife an army, and to command it in perfon: In vain the emprefs admonifhed him of his danger, and his abfolute want of experience in matters of war; in vain fhe advifed him to employ fome of the old officers againft the veteran Moorifh troops.

THE king anfwered, That every officer of merit had been tried already, and baffled from beginning to end, fo that the army had no confidence in them; that he was refolved to take his trial as the others had done, and leave the event where it ought to be left. Though the diviners all prophefied ill from this refolution of the king, the generality of the kingdom, and young nobility, flocked to his ftandard, rejoicing in a leader fo near their own age. The middle-aged had great hopes of the vigour of that youth; and the old were not more backward, fatisfied of the weight their years and experience muft give them in the councils of a young king.

SELDOM a better army took the field; and the emprefs, from her own treafures, furnifhed every thing, even to fuperfluity, engaging all the people of confequence by giving them in the moft affable manner, prefents in hand, and magnificent promifes of recompence hereafter. Great as thefe preparations were, they had not made much impreffion among the confederates in Adel; and already the king had put himfelf at the head of his army, before the Moors feemed to think it worth their while to follow him. They were, indeed, at that very time, laying wafte a part of the kingdom of Abyffinia. The king, then, by quick marches, advanced through Fatigar, as if he was going to Auffa, the capital of Adel.

Between Fatigar and the plain country of Adel there is a deep large valley, through which it was neceffary the army fhould pafs. Very fteep mountains bound it on every fide, whilft two openings (each of them very narrow) were the only paffages by which it was poffible to enter or go out. The king divided his army into two; he kept the beft troops and largeft body with himfelf, and fent Betwudet with the reft, as if they intended to fight the enemy before they gained the defiles. The Moors, on the other hand, terrified at what muft happen if the king with his army marched into their defencelefs country, accounted it a great efcape to get into thefe very defiles before they were forced to an engagement. Betwudet, who defired no more, gave them their way, and, entering the valley behind them, encamped there. The king, at the other end, had done the fame, unfeen by the enemy, who thought he was advanced on his march to Auffa. The Moors were thus completely hemmed in, and the king's army vaftly fuperior. He had ordered his tents to be left ftanding, with a body of troops in them, and thefe completely covered the only outlet to the

I   valley,

valley, whilst Betwudet and his party had advanced confiderably, and made much the fame difpofition.

The king drew up his troops early in the morning, and offered the enemy battle, when the whole Abyffinian army was furprifed to difcover a backwardnefs in the Moors fo unlike their behaviour at former times; well they might, when they were informed from whom that panic among the Moors came. Maffudi, a fanatic from the beginning, whether really deceived by fuch a prophecy, or raifed to a pitch of pride and enthufiafm by the honours he had received, and defirous, by a remarkable death, to deferve the rank of martyr among thofe of his own religion, or from whatever caufe it arofe, came to the king of Adel, and told him, that his time was now come; that it had been prophefied to him long ago, that if, that year, he fought the king of Abyffinia in perfon, he was there to lofe his life: That he knew, for certain, David was then prefent, having, with his own eyes, feen the fcarlet tent, (a colour which is only ufed by the king); he defired, therefore, the king of Adel to make the beft of his way through a lefs fteep part of the mountain, which he fhewed him; to take his family and favourites along with him, and leave under his command the army to try their fortune with David. Mahomet, at no time very fond of fighting, never found himfelf lefs fo than upon this advice of Maffudi's. He refolved, therefore, to follow his council; and, before the battle began, withdrew himfelf through the place that was fhewn him, and was followed by a few of his friends.

It was now 9 o'clock, and the fun began to be hot, before which the Abyffinians never choofe to engage, when

Maffudi,

Maffudi, judging the king of Adel was beyond danger, fent a trumpet to the Abyffinian camp, with a challenge to any man of rank in the army to fight him in fingle combat, under condition that the victory fhould be accounted to belong to that army whofe champion was victorious, and that, thereupon, both parties fhould withdraw their troops without further bloodfhed. It does not appear whether the conditions were agreed to, but the challenge was accepted as foon as offered. Gabriel Andreas the monk, who, in the reign of Naod, had, by the king's order, loft a part of his tongue for giving it too much licence, offered himfelf firft to the king, befeeching him to truft to him that day, his own honour, and the fortune of the army. The king confented without hefitation, with the general applaufe of all the nobility; for Andreas, though a monk, was a man of great family and diftinction; the moft learned of the court; liberal, rich, affable, and remarkable for facetious converfation; he was, befides, a good foldier, of tried fkill and valour, and, in ftrength and activity, furpaffed by no man in the army.

Maffudi was not backward to prefent himfelf; nor was the combat longer than might be expected from two fuch willing champions. Gabriel Andreas, feeing his opportunity, with a two-handed fword ftruck Maffudi between the lower part of the neck and the fhoulder, fo violently, that he nearly divided his body into two, and felled him dead to the ground. He then cut his head off, and threw it at the king's feet, faying, " There is the Goliah of the Infidels."

This expreffion became inftantly the word of battle, or fignal to charge. The king, at the head of his troops, rufhed

upon

upon the Moorish army, and, throwing them into diforder, drove them back upon Betwudet, who, with his frefh troops, forced them again back to the king. Seeing no hopes of relief, they difperfed to the mountains, and were flaughtered, and hunted like wild beafts by the peafants, or driven to perifh with thirft and hunger. About 12,000 of the Mahometan army are faid to have been flain upon the field, with no very confiderable lofs on the fide of the conquerors. The green ftandard of Mahomet was taken, as alfo the black velvet tent embroidered with gold; which laft, we fhall fee, the king gave to the Portuguefe ambaffador fome time afterwards, to confecrate and fay mafs in. A vaft number of cattle was taken, and with them much rich merchandife of the Indies. Nor did the king content himfelf with what he had got in battle. He advanced and encamped at a place where was held the firft market of Adel*. The next day he proceeded to a town where was a houfe of the king, and, going up to the door, and finding it locked, he ftruck the door with his lance, and nobody anfwering, he prohibited the foldiers from plundering it, and retired with his army home, leaving his lance fticking in the door as a fign of his having been there, and having had it in his power.

Thereon the king was received on his return amidft the greateft acclamations of his fubjects, as the faviour of his country, the eyes of the whole nation and army were firft fixed on Andreas, whofe bravery had at laft delivered them from that conftant and inveterate fcourge, Maffudi. Every body preffed forward to throw flowers and green branches in his way; the women celebrating him with fongs, putting garlands on his head, and holding out the young children to fee him as he paffed. The battle was fought in the month

* Vide Map of Shoa.

month of July 1516; and, the fame day, the ifland of Zeyla, in the mouth of the Red Sea, was taken, and its town burned by the Portuguefe armament, under Lopez Suarez Alberguiera.

Neither the fufpicions tranfmitted from India, nor the mean perfon of Matthew the ambaffador, feem to have made any impreffion upon the king of Portugal. He received him with every fort of honour, and teftified the moft profound refpect for his mafter, and attention to the errand he came upon. Matthew was lodged and maintained with the utmoft fplendour; and, confidering the great ufe of fo powerful a friend on the African coaft of the Red Sea, where his fleets would meet with all fort of provifion and protection, while they purfued the Turkifh fquadrons, he prepared an embaffy on his part, and fent Matthew home on board the fleet commanded by Lopez Suarez for India.

Edward Galvan, a man of capacity and experience, who had filled the offices of fecretary of ftate and ambaffador in Spain, France, and Germany, arrived at that time of life when he might reafonably expect to pafs the reft of his days in eafe, wealth, and honour, found himfelf unexpectedly chofen, at the age of eighty-fix, to go ambaffador from his fovereign to Abyffinia. Goez had much more reafon to wonder at the ambaffador fixed upon by his mafter, than at that of Abyffinia fent by the emprefs Helena to Portugal. The fleet under Suarez entered the Red Sea, and anchored at the flat ifland of Camaran, clofe on the coaft of Arabia Felix, one of the moft unwholefome places he could have chofen. Here Edward Galvan died; and here Suarez, moft ignorantly, refolved to pafs the winter, which he did, fuffering

ing

ing much for want of every fort of provifion but water; whereas twenty-four hours of any wind would have carried him to Mafuah, to his journey's end; where, if he had loft the monfoon, he would ftill have had great abundance of neceffaries, and been in the way every moment of promoting the wifhes of his mafter.

Lopez de Segueyra fucceeded the ignorant Suarez, who had returned to India. He fitted out a ftrong fleet at Goa, with which he entered the Red Sea, and failed for the ifland of Mafuah, where he arrived the 16th of April 1520, having Matthew along with him. Upon the firft approach of the fleet, the inhabitants, both of the ifland and town, abandoned them, and fled to Arkeeko on the main land. Segueyra having remained before Mafuah a few days without committing any hoftilities, there came at laft to him a Chriftian and a Moor from the continent; who informed him that the main-land, then before him, was part of the kingdom of Abyffinia, governed by an officer called Baharnagafh: they added, that the reafon of their flying at the fight of the fleet was, that the Turks frequently made defcents, and ravaged the ifland; but that all the inhabitants of the continent were Chriftians. The Portuguefe general was very joyful on this intelligence, and began to treat Matthew more humanely, finding how truly and exactly he had defcribed thefe places. He gave, both to the Chriftian and Moor that came off to him, a rich veft; commended them for having fled to Arkeeko rather than expofe themfelves to an attack from the Turks, but directed them to affure the people on the continent, that they too were all Chriftians, and under the command of the king of Abyffinia; being arrived

there

there purpofely for his fervice, fo that they might return, whenever they fhould pleafe, in perfect fafety.

The next day, came down to the fhore the governor of Arkeeko, accompanied with thirty horfemen, and above two hundred foot. He was mounted on a fine horfe, and dreffed in a kind of fhirt refembling that of the Moors. The governor brought down four oxen, and received in return certain pieces of filk, with which he was well pleafed. A very familiar converfation followed ; the governor kindly inviting the Portuguefe general afhore, affuring him that the Baharnagafh, under whofe command he was, had already intelligence of his arrival.

In anfwer to his inquiries about the religion of the country, the governor told him, that in a mountain, then in fight, twenty-four miles diftant, there was a convent called *the Monaftery of Bifan*, (which Matthew had often defcribed in the voyage) whofe monks, being informed of his arrival, had deputed feven of their number to wait upon him, whom the Portuguefe general went to meet accordingly, and received them in the kindeft manner.

These monks, as foon as they faw Matthew, broke out into the warmeft expreffions of friendfhip and efteem, congratulating him with tears in their eyes upon his long voyage and abfence. The Portuguefe general then invited the monks on board his veffel, where he regaled them, and gave to each prefents that were moft fuitable to their auftere life. On his fide, Segueyra chofe feven Portuguefe, with Peter Gomez Teffera, auditor of the Eaft Indies, who underftood Arabic very well, to return the vifit of the monks, and fee the monaftery

naftery of Bifan.   This fhort journey they very happily performed.   Teffera brought back a parchment manuscript,
waich he received as a prefent from the monks, to be fent
to the king of Portugal.

It was on the 24th of April that the Baharnagafh arrived at Arkeeko, having before fent information of his intended vifit.   The Portuguefe general, who never doubted but that
he would come to thefea-fide, pitched his tents, andfpread his
carpets and cufhions on the ground to receive him.   But it
was fignified to him from the Baharnagafh, who was probably afraid of putting himfelf under the guns of the fleet,
that he did not intend to advance fo far, and that the governor fhould meet him half way.   This being agreed to on
both fides, they fat down on the grafs.

The Baharnagafh began the converfation, by telling the
Portuguefe, they had, in virtue of certain prophecies, been
long expected in this country; and that he, and all the officers of Abyffinia, were ready to do them every fervice and
kindnefs.   After the Portuguefe general had returned a
proper anfwer, the priefts and monks concluded the interview with certain religious fervices.   Segueyra then made
the Baharnagafh a prefent of a very fine fuit of complete
armour with fome pieces of filk; while the Baharnagafh,
on his fide, made the return with a very fine horfe and
mule.

All doubt concerning Matthew was removed at this
interview; he was acknowledged as a genuine ambaffador.   The Portuguefe now flocked to Segueyra, befeeching
him to choofe from among his men, who fhould accom-

pany him to the court. The first step was to name Roderigo de Lima ambaffador from the king of Portugal, inftead
of Galvan, who was dead; and, for his fuite, George de
Breu, Lopez de Gama, John Scolare fecretary to the ambaffador, John Gonfalvez his factor and interpreter, Emmanuel de Mare organift, Peter Lopez, Mafter John his phyfician, Gafpar Pereira, and Lazarus d'Andrad a painter. The
three chaplains were John Fernandes, Peter Alphonfo Mendez, and Francifco Alvarez. In this company alfo went
Matthew, the Abyffinian ambaffador returned from Portugal, and with him three Portuguefe, one called Magailanes,
the other Alvaremgo, and the third Diego Fernandes.

It feemed probable, the fevere blow which David had given
to the king of Adel, by the total deftruction of his army on
the death of his general Maffudi, would have procured a
ceffation of hoftilities to the Abyffinian frontiers, which they
had not experienced during the life of that general ; but it
appeared afterwards, that, increafed in riches and popula-
tion by the great acceffion of power which followed the interruption of the Indian trade in Arabia by the Turkifh
conqueft, far from entertaining thoughts of peace, they were
rather meditating a more formidable manner of attack, by
training themfelves to the ufe of fire-arms and artillery, of
which they had provided a quantity, and to which the A-
byffinians were as yet ftrangers.

The king was encamped in Shoa, covering and keeping
in awe his Mahometan provinces, Fatigar and Dawaro ; befides which he feemed to have no object but the conqueft
of the Dobas, that bordered equally upon the Moorifh and
Chriftian frontiers, and who (though generally gained by
the

the Mahometans) were, when occasion offered, enemies to both. The Shum * of Giannamora, a small district belonging to Abyssinia, full of brave soldiers, and considerably reinforced by David for the very purpose, had the charge of bringing these barbarians to subjection, as being their immediate neighbour.

The king had afterwards advanced eastward to the frontiers of Fatigar, but was still in the southern part of his dominions. The ambassador and his retinue were landed on the north. They were to cross the whole extent of the empire through woods and over mountains, the like of which are not known in Europe, full of savage beasts, and men more savage than the beasts themselves; intersected by large rivers, and what was the worst circumstance, swelling every day by the tropical rains. Frequently deserts of no considerable length, indeed, intervened, where no sustenance was to be found for man or beast, nor relief for accidental misfortunes. Yet such was the bravery of that small company, that they hesitated not a moment to undertake this enterprise. Every thing was thought easy which contributed to the glory of their king, and the honour of their country.

It was not long before this gallant company found need of all their constancy and courage; for in their short journey to the convent of St Michael (the first they attempted) they found the wood so thick that there was scarcely passage for either man or beast. Briers and thorns, too, of a

T 2   variety

* Or Governor.

variety of species, which they had never before seen, added
greatly to the fatigue which the thickness of the woods had
occasioned. Mountains presented themselves over mountains, broken into terrible precipices and ravines, by violent torrents and constant storms; their black and bare tops
seemed as it were calcined by the rays of a burning sun,
and by incessant lightnings and thunder. Great numbers of
wild beasts also presented themselves everywhere in these
dark forests, and seemed only to be hindered from devour-
ing them by their wonder at seeing so many men in so
lonely a situation. At last the woods began to grow thinner,
and some fields appeared where the people were sitting armed, guarding their small flocks of half-starved goats and
kine, and crops of millet, of which they saw a considerable
quantity sown. The men were black, their hair very grace-
fully plaited, and were altogether naked, excepting a small
piece of leather that covered their middle. At this place
they were met by twelve monks, four of whom were distinguished by their advanced years and the respect paid to
them by the others.

HAVING rested their mules and camels a short time, they
again began their journey by the side of a great lake, near
which was a very high mountain, and this they were too
weary to attempt to pass. Full of discontent and despondency, they halted at the foot of this mountain, where they
passed the night, having received a cow for supper, a present from the convent. Here Matthew (the ambassador) separated his baggage from that of the caravan, and left it to
the care of the monks. He had probably made some little
money in Portugal; and, distrusting his reception with the
king, wisely determined to place it out of danger. The precaution,

caution, however, proved fuperfluous ; for, a few days after, an epidemical fever began to manifeſt itſelf, which, in eight-and-forty hours, carried off Matthew, and foon after Pereira, the ſervant of Don Roderigo ; fo that no opportunity now offered for an explanation with the king about his or the emprefs's promiſe of ceding one-third of the kingdom to the Portuguefe in cafe the king would fend them fuccour. Terrified by the fever, and the bad profpect of the weather,. they refumed their journey.

THE monaſtery of Bifan (to which they were now going) is fo called from the great quantity of water which is eve-rywhere found about it. The fimilitude of found has made Poncet [*], and feveral other travellers, call it the Monaſtery of the Vifion ; but Bifan (water) is its true name, being plentifully fupplied with that moſt valuable element. A. number of lakes and rivers are interfperfed through its plains ; while abundant fprings, that are never dry, flow from the top of each rock, dafhing their rills againſt the rugged projections of the cliffs below.

THE monaſtery of Bifan, properly fo called, is the head of fix others in the compafs of 26 miles ; each convent placed like a tower on the top of its own rock. That upon which Bifan is fituated is very high, and almoſt perpendicular ; and from this rifes another ftill higher than it, which, un-lefs to its inhabitants, is perfectly inacceffible. It is, on every fide, furrounded with wood, interfperfed with fruit-trees of many different kinds, as well of thofe known as of thofe

unknown

---

[*] Vide Poncet's travels, in his return through Tigré, p. 116. London edit. 12mo. 1709.

unknown in Europe. Oranges, citrons, and limes are in
great abundance; wild peaches and small figs of a very indifferent quality; black grapes, on loaded branches, hang
down from the barren timber round which they are twined,
and afford plentiful supply to man and beast: The fields
are covered with myrtles and many species of jessamin; with
roses too of various colours; but fragrance is denied to them
all, except one sort, which is the white one, single-leafed *.

THE monks of these convents were said once to be about
a thousand in number. They have a large territory, and
pay a tribute in cows and horses to the Baharnagash, who
is their superior. Their horses are esteemed good, as coming
from the neighbourhood of the Arabs. However, though
I had the absolute choice of them all during the time I
commanded the king's guard, I never could draw from that
part of the country above a score of sufficient strength and
size to bear a man in complete armour.

I SHALL now leave Don Roderigo to pursue his journey
towards the king at Shoa. The history of it, and of his embassy, published at large by Alvarez his chaplain, has not
met, from the historians of his own country, with a reception which favours the authenticity of its narrative. There
are, indeed, in the whole of it, and especially where religion
is concerned, many things very difficult of belief, which
seem to be the work of the Jesuits some years posterior to
the time in which Alvarez was in Abyssinia. Tellez con-
demns him, though a writer of those times; and Damianus
Goez,

---

* In Barbary called *Melita*, in Abyssinia, *Kagga*.

Goez, one of the firſt hiſtorians, ſays, that he had ſeen a journal written in Alvarez's own name, very different from the journal that is gone forth to the public. For my part, I can only ſay, that what is related of the firſt audience with the king, and many of the following pages, ſeem to me to be fabrications of people that never have been in Abyſſinia; and, if this is the caſe, no imputation can be laid againſt Franciſco Alvarez, as, perhaps, he is not the author of the miſrepreſentation in queſtion. But, as to the cordiality with which the Catholic religion was received by the monks and people in general, during the long ſtay and bad reception Don Roderigo met with, I have no ſort of doubt that this is a falſehood, and this muſt be charged directly to his account.

We have already ſeen that, early as Zara Jacob's time, the religion of the Franks was held in the utmoſt deteſtation, and that in Bæda Mariam's reign the whole country was in rebellion, becauſe the king had directed the Virgin Mary to be painted by one Branca Leon, a Venetian painter, then alive, and in court, when Don Roderigo de Lima was with the king in Shoa. Iſcander and Naod were both ſtrict in the tenets of the church of Alexandria; and two Abunas, Imaranha Chriſtos, who lived till Iſcander's time, and Abuna Marcus, alive in Alvarez's, had given no allowance for ſtrange or foreign worſhip to be introduced. How the Catholic could be ſo favourably and generally received in the time of Alvarez is what I cannot conceive. Blood enough was ſpilt immediately afterwards, to ſhew that this affection to the Roman Catholic religion, if any ſuch there was in Alvarez's time, muſt have been merely tranſitory. When, therefore, I find any thing in this journal plainly miſunder

4 ſtood.

ftood, I explain and vindicate it; where I fee there is a fact deliberately mifreprefented, fuch as the celebration of the Epiphany, I refute it from ocular demonftration. The reft of the journal I leave *in medio* to the judgment of my reader, who will find it at his bookfeller's; only obferving, that there can be no doubt that the journey itfelf was made by Don Roderigo, and the perfons named with him.

I HAVE preferved the feveral ftations of thefe travellers in my map, though a great part of the countries through which they paffed is now in the hands of the Galla, and is as inacceffible to Abyffinians as it is to ftrangers.

THERE are two particulars in Alvarez's account of this journey which very much furprife me. The firft is, the daily and conftant danger this company was in from tigers, fo daring as to prefent themfelves within pike-length. Of this I have taken notice in the appendix when fpeaking of the hyæna.

THE other particular relates to the field of beans through which they paffed. I never yet faw this fort of grain, or pulfe, in Abyffinia. The lupine, a wild plant, fomewhat fimilar, chiefly infects thofe provinces from which the honey comes, and is regarded there with the utmoft averfion. The reafon of which will be feen in the fequel. But as thefe Mahometans, through whofe country Don Roderigo paffed, are not indigenous, and never had any connection with the ancient ftate of manners or religion of this country, it is more than probable the cultivation of the bean is no older than the fettlement of thefe Mahometans here, long after

the

the Pythagorean prejudices againſt that plant were forgotten.

It was on the 16th of April 1520 that Don Roderigo de Lima landed in Abyſſinia; and it was the 16th of October of the ſame year when he arrived within ſight of the king's camp, diſtant about three miles. The king had advanced, as hath been ſaid, into Fatigar, about twenty-five miles from the firſt fair in the kingdom of Adel, and ſomething leſs than two hundred from the port of Zeyla. The ambaſſador, after ſo painful a journey, expected an immediate admiſſion into the king's preſence. Inſtead of which, a great officer, called the Hadug Ras *, which is chief or commander of the aſſes, was ſent to carry him three miles farther diſtant, where they ordered him to pitch his tent, and five years paſſed in the embaſſy afterwards before he procured his diſmiſſion.

Alvarez accounts very lamely for this prodigious interval of time; and, excepting the celebration of the Epiphany, he does not mention one remarkable occurrence in the whole of this period. One would imagine their ſtay had not been above a month, and that one converſation only paſſed upon buſineſs, which I ſhall here ſet down as a ſpecimen of the humour the parties were in the one with the other.

The king carried the ambaſſador to ſee the church Mecana Selaſſé, the church of the Trinity, which was then repairing, where many of the kings had been buried while

Vol. II.   U   the

---

* This is a name of humility. He is a great officer, and has no care or charge of aſſes

the Royal family refided in Shoa. All the churches in A-byffinia are thatched. Some of Roderigo's own retinue, who bore him ill-will, had put it into the king's head how elegant this church would be if covered with lead, a thing he certainly could have no idea of. He afked Don Roderigo, whether the king of Portugal could not fend him as much fheet-lead as would ferve to cover that church? To which the ambaffador replied, That the king of Portugal, upon bare mentioning the thing, would fend him as much fheet-lead * as would cover not only that church, but all the other churches he fhould ever build in Abyffinia ; and, after all, the prefent would be but a trifling one.

IMMEDIATELY upon this the king changed his difcourfe ; and obferved to the ambaffador, in a very ferious tone of voice, " That, fince they were now upon the fubject of prefents, he could not help letting the king of Portugal know, that, if ever he fent an ambaffador again into that country, he fhould take care to accompany him with prefents of value, for otherwife ftranger ambaffadors that ventured to come before him without there were very ill received." To which the ambaffador returned warmly, " That it was very far from being the cuftom of the king of Portugal to fend prefents to any king upon earth ; that, having no fuperior, it was ufual for him, only to receive them from others, and to accept them or not, according to his royal pleafure ; for it was infinitely below him to confider what was the value of the prefent itfelf. He then defired the king of Abyffinia might be informed, that he, Don Roderigo, came ambaffador from the general of the Indies, and not from the king of Portugal ; neverthelefs, when the king of Portugal had lately difpatch-

ed

---

* Alvarez Hiftoire d'Ethiopie, p. 157.

ed Galvan, who had died upon the road, ambaſſador to his highneſs, he had ſent with him preſents to the value of 100,000 ducats, conſulting his own greatneſs, but not conſidering himſelf as under any obligation to ſend any preſents at all; and as to the many ſcandalous aſperſions that had been thrown upon him by mean people, which the king had given credit to, and were made conſtantly part of his diſcourſe, he wiſhed his highneſs, from the peruſal of the letters which he had brought from the general of the Indies, to learn, that the Portugueſe were not accuſtomed to uſe lying and diſſimulation in their converſations, but to tell the naked truth; to whichhe the ambaſſador had ſtrictly confined himſelf in every circumſtance he had related to his highneſs, if he pleaſed to believe him; if not, that he was very welcome to do juſt whatever he thought better in his own eyes. Yet he would, once for all, have his highneſs to know, that, though he came only as ambaſſador from the general of the Indies, he could, as ſuch, have preſented himſelf before the greateſt ſovereign upon earth, without being ſubjected to hear ſuch converſation as he had been daily expoſed to from his highneſs, which he, as a Portugueſe nobleman and a ſoldier, though he had been no ambaſſador at all, was not any way diſpoſed to ſuffer, and therefore he deſired his immediate diſmiſſion."

Upon this the king ſaid, "That the diſtinction he had ſhewn him was ſuch as he would never have met with from any of his predeceſſors, having brought no preſent of any value." To which the ambaſſador replied in great warmth, "That he had received no diſtinction in this country whatever, but only injuries and wrongs; that he ſhould think he became a martyr if he died in this country where

U 2   he

he had been robbed of every thing, except the clothes upon his back; that Matthew, who was but a pretended ambaſſador, had been much otherwiſe treated by the king of
Portugal; but for himſelf he deſired nothing but a ſpeedy
diſmiſſion, having delivered his letters and done his errand:
Till that time, he ſhould expect to be treated like a man of
honour, above lying or falſehood." To this the king anſwered, "That he believed him to be a man of honour, worth,
and veracity, but that Matthew was a liar: at the ſame time
he wiſhed Don Roderigo to know, that he was perfectly informed what degree of reſpect and good uſage Matthew had
met with from the king of Portugal's officers and captains,
but that he did not impute this to Don Roderigo."

THERE was a rumour at court which very much alarmed
the ambaſſador; it was, that the king intended to detain
him according to the invariable cuſtom and practice of his
country. Two Venetians, Nicholas Branca Leon and Tho-
mas Gradinego, had been forcibly detained ſince the reign
of Bæda Mariam. But what terrified Don Roderigo ſtill
more, as a caſe moſt ſimilar to his, was the fight of Peter
Covillan then in court, who had been ſent ambaſſador by
John king of Portugal to Iſcander, and ever ſince was detained without being able to get leave to return, but was
obliged to marry and ſettle in the country.

WHAT was the emperor's real intention is impoſſible now
to know; but, having reſolved to ſend an Abyſſinian ambaſſador to the king of Portugal, it was neceſſary to diſmiſs
Don Roderigo likewiſe. However, he did not entirely abandon the whole of his deſign, but forcibly detained Maſter
John the ſecretary, and Lazarus d'Andrad the painter, and
obliged

obliged Don Roderigo to depart without them.   Zaga Zaab, an Abyssinian monk, who had learned the Portuguese language by waiting on Don Roderigo during his stay in Abyssinia, was chosen for the function; and they set out together for Masuah, plentifully furnished with every thing necessary for the journey, and arrived safely there without any remarkable occurrence, where they found Don Hector de Silveyra, governor of the Indies, with his fleet, waiting to carry Don Roderigo de Lima home.   Whether the king had changed his mind or not is doubtful; but, on the 27th of April 1526, arrived four messengers from court with orders for Don Roderigo to return, and also to bring Don Hector along with him.   This was immediately and directly refused; but it was left in the power of Zaga Zaab to return if he pleased, who however declared, that, if he staid behind, he should be thrown to the lions. He, therefore, went on board with great readiness, and they all sailed from Masuah on the 28th of April of the year just mentioned, in their return to India.

THESE frequent intercourses with the Portuguese had given great alarm to the Mahometan powers, though neither the king of Abyssinia, nor the Portuguese themselves, had reaped any profit from them, or the several fleets that had arrived at Masuah, which had really no end but to seek the ambassador Don Roderigo. The six years spent in wrangling and childish behaviour, both on the part of the king and the ambassador, had an appearance of something serious between the two powers; and what still alarmed the Moors more was, that no part of the secret had transpired, because no scheme had really been concerted, only mere proposals of vain and idle enterprises, without either power or
                                                                  will

will to put them in execution. Such were the plans of a joint army, to attack Arabia, and to conquer it down to Jerufalem. The Turks* were on their progrefs fouthward in great force; they had conquered Arabia in lefs than half the time Don Roderigo had fpent quarrelling with the king about pepper and mules; and a ftorm was ready to break in a quarter leaft expected.

In the gentle reigns of the Mamalukes, before the conqueft of Egypt and Arabia by Selim †, a caravan conftantly fet out from Abyffinia directly for Jerufalem. They had then a treaty with the Arabs. This caravan rendezvoufed at Hamazen, a fmall territory abounding in provifions, about two days journey from Dobarwa, and nearly the fame from Mafuah; it amounted fometimes in number to a thoufand pilgrims, ecclefiaftics as well as laymen. They travelled by very eafy journies, not above fix miles a-day, halting to perform divine fervice, and fetting up their tents early, and never beginning to travel till towards nine in the morning. They had, hitherto, paffed in perfect fafety, with drums beating and colours flying, and, in this way, traverfed the defert by the road of Suakem.

The year after Selim had taken poffeffion of Cairo, Abba Azerata Chriftos, a monk famous for holinefs, had conducted fifteen hundred of thefe pilgrims with him to Jerufalem, and they had arrived without accident; but, on their return, they had fallen in with a body of Selim's troops, who flew a great part of them, and forced others to take refuge

---

* Cafo el Gucfi, and Tomum Bey.   † Selim I. emperor of the Ottomans.

refuge in the defert, where they perifhed with hunger and thirft. In the year 1525, another caravan affembled at Hamazen, confifting of 336 friars and priefts, and fifteen nuns. They fet out from Hamazen on the 12th day after leaving this place, travelling flowly; and, being loaded with provifions and water, they were attacked by the Moors of that diftrict, and utterly defeated and robbed. Of the pilgrims taken prifoners, all the old men were put to the fword, and the young were fold for flaves; fo that of 356 perfons fifteen only efcaped, but three of which lived to return to Shoa at the time the ambaffador was there. This was the firft vengeance the Moors to the northward had yet taken for the alliance made with the Portuguefe; and, from this time, the communication with Cairo through the defert ceafed as to the Chriftians, and was carried on by Mahometans only.

Since the time of Peter Covillan's arrival in Abyffinia, the views of all parties had very much changed. The Portuguefe at firft coveted the friendfhip of Abyffinia, for the fake of obtaining through it a communication with India. But they now became indifferent about that intercourfe, fince they had fettled in India itfelf, and found the convenience of the paffage of the Cape of Good Hope. David, freed from his fears of the Moors of Adel, whom he had defeated, and feeing the great power of the Turks, fo much apprehended after the conqueft of Egypt, difappointed in India in all their attempts againft the Portuguefe fettlements there; being, moreover, difpleafed with the abrupt behaviour of the ambaffador Don Roderigo, and the promifes the emprefs Helena had made by Matthew without his knowledge, he wifhed no further connection with the Portuguefe, for whofe affiftance, he thought, he fhould have no ufe.

Selim, whofe firft object was the conqueft of India, had met there fo rude a reception that he began to defpair of further fuccefs in his undertaking; but, having conquered A-rabia on one fide of the Red Sea, he was defirous of extending his dominions to the other alfo, and for three reafons : The firft was, that the fafety of the holy place of Mecca would be much endangered fhould a Portuguefe army and fleet rendezvous in Abyffinia, and be joined by an army there. The fecond, that his fhips and gallies could not be in fecu-rity at the bottom of the Gulf, fhould the Portuguefe ob-tain leave to fortify any ifland or harbour belonging to the Abyffinians. The third, that the king of Abyffinia being, as he was taught to believe, the prince whom the prophet Mahomet had honoured with his correfpondence, he thought it a duty incumbent upon him to convert this prince and kingdom to the Mahometan religion by the fword, a method allowable in no religion but that of Mahomet and of Rome.

The ancient and feeble arms of lances and bows, carried by half-naked peafants affembled in hafte and at random for an occafion, were now laid afide. In place of thefe, Se-lim had left garrifons of veteran troops in all the fea-coaft towns of Arabia, exercifed in fire-arms, and furnifhed with large trains of artillery, fupported by a large fleet which, though deftined againft the Portuguefe in India, and con-ftantly beat by them, never failed, both going and coming, to reinforce their pofts in Arabia with ftores and frefh fol-diers.

3

The

THE emprefs Helena died in 1525, the year before the Portuguefe embaffy ended, after having brought about an interview between the two nations, which, by the continual difavowal of Matthew's embaffy, it is plain that David knew not how to turn to his advantage. Soon after her death, the king prepared to renew the war with the Moors, without having received the leaft advantage from the Portuguefe. But very differently had the people of Adel employed this interval of peace. They had ftrengthened themfelves by the ftricteft friendfhip with the Turkifh officers in Arabia, efpecially with the bafha of Zibit, a large trading port nearly oppofite to Mafuah. A Turkifh garrifon was put into Zeyla; and a Turk, with a large train of artillery, commanded in it. All was ready againft the firft invafion the king was to make, and he was now marching directly towards their country.

THE firft retaliation, for the Portuguefe friendfhip, (as we have already obferved) had been the cutting off the caravan for Jerufalem. In revenge for this, the king had marched into Dawaro, and fent a body of troops from that province to fee what was the ftate of the Moorifh forces in Adel. Thefe were no fooner arrived on the frontiers of that kingdom, than they were met by a number of the enemy appointed to guard thofe confines, and, coming to blows, the Abyffinians defeated, and drove them into the defert parts of their own country. The king ftill advanced till he met the Mahometan army, and a battle was fought at Shimbra Coré, where the Abyffinian army was totally defeated; the Betwadet, Hadug Ras, the governor of Amhara, Robel, governor of the mountain of Gefhen, with the greateft part of the nobility, and four thoufand men, were all flain.

Mahomet, called Gragné, (which fignifies *left-handed*) commanded this army. He was governor of Zeyla, and had promoted the league with the Turkiſh baſhas on the coaſt of Arabia; and, having now given the king a check in his firſt enterpriſe, he reſolved to carry on the war with him in a way that ſhould produce ſomething deciſive. He remained then quiet two years at home, ſent all the priſoners he had made in the laſt expedition to Mecca, and to the Turkiſh powers on the coaſt, and required from them in return the number of troops ſtipulated, with a train of portable artillery, which was punctually furniſhed, while a large body of janizaries croſſed over and joined the Mooriſh army. Mahomet led theſe troops ſtraight into Fatigar, which he over-ran, as he did the two other neighbouring provinces Ifat and Dawaro, burning and laying waſte the whole country, and driving, as was his uſual manner, immenſe numbers of the inhabitants, whom the ſword had ſpared, back with him to Adel.

The next year, Mahomet marched from Adel directly into Dawaro, committing the ſame exceſſes. The king, who ſaw in deſpair that total ruin threatened his whole country, and that there were no hopes but in a battle, met the Mooriſh army at Ifras, very much inferior to them in every ſort of appointment. The battle was fought 1ſt May 1528; the king was defeated, and Iſlam Segued, his firſt miniſter, who commanded the army that day, with many of his principal officers, were ſlain upon the ſpot, and the Mooriſh army took poſſeſſion of Shoa. David retreated with his broken army into Amhara, and encamped at Hegu, thinking to procure reinforcements during the bad weather, but Gragné was too near to give him time for this. He entered Amhara,

deſtroying

deftroying all before him. The fecond of November he burnt the church of Mecana Selaffé of the holy fepulchre, and Atronfa Mariam; and, on the 8th of the fame month, Ganeta Georgis; on the 2d of December, Debra Agezia-beher; the 6th of the fame month, St Stephen's church; after which he returned to Adel with his booty.

The following year Gragné returned in April, plundered and burnt Warwar, and wintered there. In the year 1530 Gragné invaded the province of Tigré in the month of October, while the king, who had wintered in Dembea, marched up to Woggora; thence, in December, he went to Tfalamet, and returned to Tigré to keep the feaft of the Epiphany.

The king, next year, marched through Tzegadé, and Gragné clofe followed him, as if he had been hunting a wild beaft rather than making war. The 2d of January he burnt Abba Samuel, then went down into Mazaga the borders of Sennaar to a conference with Muchtar, one of his confederates, when it was refolved that they fhould fight the king wherever they could meet him, and attach themfelves to his perfon alone. Gragné by forced marches overtook the king upon the Nile at Delakus, the 6th of February, and offered him battle, knowing the proud fpirit of David, that he would not refufe, however great the difproportion was.

The event was fuch as might be expected. Fortune again declared againft the king. Negadé Yafous, Acab Saat, and many others of the nobility perifhed, fighting to the laft, in the fight of their fovereign. In this bat-

tle

tle the brave monk, Andreas *, much advanced in years, was
flain, behaving with the greateft gallantry, unwilling to furvive the ruin of his country.

The Moors now found it unneceffary to keep together
an army. They divided into fmall parties, that they might
more effectually and fpeedily ruin the country. Part of
Gragné's army was detached to burn Axum; the other under Simeon continued in Amhara to watch the king's motions; and, while he attempted to relieve Axum, difperfed
his army, on which the town was burnt, and with it many
of the richeft churches in Abyffinia, Hallelujah, Banquol,
Gafo, Debra Kerbé, and many others. And, on the 7th of
April, Saul, fon of Tesfo Yafous, fought another detachment
of the Moorifh army, and was cut to pieces.

The 28th year of his reign, 1536, the king croffed the
Tacazzé, and had many difaftrous encounters with the people of Siré and Serawé. Tesfo l'Oul, who commanded in
this latter province for the king, furprifed a Turkifh party
under Adli, whom he flew, and met with the fame fate
himfelf from Abbas, Moorifh governor of Serawé, when a
great many of the principal people of that province were there
flain. Galila, a large ifland in the lake Tzana, was plundered,
and the convent upon it burnt. It was one of the principal
places where the Abyffinians hid their treafure, and a great
booty was found there.

In the following year, Gragné, in a meffage reprefented
to him, that he might fee he was fighting againft God, exhorting

horting him to be wife, and make his peace in time, which he fhould have upon the condition of giving him his daughter in marriage, and he would then withdraw his army, otherwife he would never leave Abyffinia till he had reduced it to a condition of producing nothing but grafs. But the king, nothing daunted, returned him for anfwer, That he was an infidel, and a blafphemer, ufed as an inftrument to chaftife him and his people for their many fins ; that it was his duty to bear the correction patiently; but that it would foon happen, when this juft purpofe was anfwered, that he would be deftroyed, and all thofe with him, as fuch wicked inftruments had always been ; that he the king, and Abyffinia his kingdom, would be preferved as a monument of the mercy of God, who never entirely forfook his people, though he might chaftife them.

INDEED, the condition of the country was now fuch that a total deftruction feemed to be at hand; for a famine and plague, its conftant companion, raged in Abyffinia, carrying off thofe that the fword had fpared.

GIDEON and Judith, king and queen of the Jews, in the high country of Samen, after having fuffered much from Gragné, had at laft rebelled and joined him ; and the king, who it feems continued to fhew an inclination to the Catholic church, which he had imbibed during the embaffy of Don Roderigo, by this had occafioned many to fall off from him, he and the court obferving Eafter according to the Roman kalendar, whi e the reft of the clergy and kingdom continued firm to that of Alexandria.

At

AT this time Ofman of Dawaro, Jonadab, Kefla, Youfef, and other rebel Abyſſinians, part of Ammer's army, one of Gragné's generals, furprifed the king's eldeſt fon, Victor, going to join his father the 7th day of March; ſlew him, and difperfed his army. Three days after, the king himſelf came to action, with Ammer at Zaat in Waag, but he was there again beaten, and his youngeſt fon Menas was taken priſoner. The king had ſcarce now an attendant, and, being almoſt alone, he took refuge among the rocks and buſhes in a high mountain called *Tſalem*, in the diſtrict of Tſalamet. But he had not remained above a day there, when he was followed by Joram, (rebel-maſter of that diſtrict) and narrowly efcaped being taken as he was croſſing the Taçazzé on foot and alone; whence he took refuge on mount Tabor, a very high mountain in Siré, and there he paſſed the winter.

THE amazing ſpirit and conſtancy of the king, who alone ſeemed not to forſake the cauſe of his kingdom, who now, without children or army, ſtill ſingly, made war for the liberty of his country, aſtoniſhed all Abyſſinia as well friends as enemies. Every veteran ſoldier, therefore, that could efcape the ſmall parties of the Moors which furrounded the king, joined him at Tabor, and he was again at the head of a very ſmall, but brave body of troops, though it was ſcarcely known in what part of the kingdom he was hid. When Achmet-eddin, lieutenant of Ammer, paſſed through Siré, loaded with the ſpoils of the churches and towns he had plundered, the king, finding him within his reach, defcended from the mountain, and, by a ſudden march, furprifed and ſlew him with his own hand, leaving the greateſt part of his army dead on the field. After which he diſtributed the booty among his ſmall army.

AMMER,

AMMER, the king's mortal enemy, who had taken upon himself the destruction of the royal family, descended into the province of Siré, and neighbourhood of Tabor, and there indulged himself in the most wanton cruelties, torturing and murdering the priests, burning churches and villages, hoping by this the king would lose his temper, and leave his strong-hold in the mountain. But hearing at the same time, that a large quantity of plate, and other treasure, belonging to the church Debra Kerbé, had been carried into an island in the lake Tzana for safety, he left the king, and seized his booty in the lake to a very great amount.

HOWEVER, he there fell ill of a fever; but, on his return, was so far advanced in his recovery as to resume his schemes of destroying the king; when, the night of the 10th of February 1538, while he was sleeping in bed in his tent, a common soldier, from what quarrel or cause is not known, went secretly and stabbed him several times in the belly with a two-edged knife, so that he died instantly, to David's great relief, and much to the safety of the whole kingdom.

IT was now 12 years since Don Roderigo de Lima had failed from Masuah, carrying with him Zaga Zaab ambassador from the king of Abyssinia. This embassy arrived safe in Lisbon, and was received with great magnificence by king John; but, as the circumstances of the kingdom when he left Masuah were really flourishing, and as the treatment he met in Portugal was better than he had, probably, ever experienced at home, he seems to have been in no haste to put an end to this embassy. On the other side, the king of Portugal's affairs in India were arrived at that

2   degree

degree of profperity and power, that little ufe remained for fuch an ally as the king of Abyffinia.

The Moorifh trade and navigation to India had already received a fatal blow, as well from the Portuguefe them-felves, as from the fall of the Mamalukes in Egypt; and So-liman, and his fervant Sinan Bafha, by their conqueft, and introducing foldiers who had not any idea or talent for trade, but only plunder and rapine, had given a finifhing ftroke to what the difcovery of the Cape of Good Hope began. The filling Arabia with fire-arms and Turks was now of confe-quence to none but to David; and of fuch a confequence it had been, that, as we have feen, in the courfe of 12 years it had left him nothing in Abyffinia but the bare name of king, and a life fo precarious that it could not be counted upon from one day's end to the other.

David had detained in Abyffinia two Portuguefe, one call-ed Mafter John, the other Lazarus d'Andrad a painter, being two of Don Roderigo's train that came from the Indies with him. The Abuna (Mark) was become old and incapable, and, fince the Turkifh conqueft of Egypt, very indifferent to, and unconnected with, what paffed at Cairo. Before he died, at the king's defire he had appointed John his fuccef-for, and accordingly ordained him Abuna, as well as having firft given him all the inferior orders at once; for John was a layman and ftudent in phyfic; a very fimple creature, but a great bigot; and we fhall from henceforward call him John Bermudes.

John very willingly confented to his ordination, pro-vided the pope approved of it; and he fet out for Rome,

not

not by the ufual way of India, but through Arabia and E-
gypt ; and, arriving there without accident, was confirmed
by Paul III. the then pope, not only as patriarch of Abyffinia, but of Alexandria likewife ; to which he added, as Bermudes fays, the moft unintelligible and incomprehenfible title
of Patriarch of the Sea.   Bermudes, to this variety of charges, had this other added to him, of ambaffador from King
David to the court of Portugal ; and for this he was certainly very fit, however he might be for his ecclefiaftical dignities ; for he had been now 12 years in Abyffinia, knew the
country well, and had been witnefs of the variety of diftreff-
fes which, following clofe one upon another, had brought
this country to its then ftate of ruin.

WHILE thefe things paffed in the north of Abyffinia, a
terrible cataftrophe happened in the fouth.   A Mahometan
chief, called Vizir Mudgid, governor of Arar, having an opportunity from his fituation to hear of the riches which were
daily carried from churches, and other places, for fafety into the mountain of Gethen, took a refolution to attempt
that natural fortrefs, though in itfelf almoft impregnable,
and ftrengthened by an army conftantly encamped at the
foot of it.

WHEN Mudgid arrived near the mountain he found it
was forfaken by the troops deftined to guard it ; and led by
a Mahometan, who was a menial fervant to the princes a-
bove, he afcended with his troops without oppofition, putting all the royal family that were prifoners, and indeed every individual of either fex refident there, indifcriminately
to the fword.

THE meafure of David's misfortunes feems to have been now full, and he died accordingly this very year 1540.

IT will be neceffary here to remind the reader, that Alvarez, the chaplain and hiftorian of the firft Portuguefe embaffy, was (as he faid) on his return appointed by king David to make his fubmiffion to the pope. Leaving Zaga Zaab, therefore, in Portugal, he proceeded to Bologna, where the emperor Charles V. was then in perfon, before whom and the pope himfelf he delivered his credentials framed by Peter Covillan, and afterwards, in a long fpeech, the reafon's of his embaffy.

THE pope received this fubmiffion of David with infinite pleafure, at a time when fo many kingdoms in the weft were revolting from his fupremacy. He confidered it as a thing of the greateft moment to be courted before the emperor by fo powerful a prince in Africa. But as for the emperor himfelf, though he was then preparing for an expedition againft the Mahometans, and though it was his favourite war, he feems to have been perfectly indifferent either to the embaffy itfelf, or to the perfon that fent it; a great proof that he believed there was nothing real in it.

MANY other people have doubted whether this embaffy, or that of John Bermudes, actually came from the Abyffinian court, as the king would fcarcely have abandoned the form of the Alexandrian church in which he had been brought up by Abuna Mark, then alive. Abuna Mark, moreover, could fcarcely be believed to have promoted embaffies which were intended to ftrike at the root of his own religion,

3

religion, and the patriarchal power with which he was endowed.

But to this it is eaſily anſwered, That the Abyſſinian hiſtorian of David's reign, through the whole courſe of it, readily admits his conſtant attachment to the ſee of Rome. He
gives a ſtriking example of it during the war with Gragné,
when the king celebrated Eaſter after the manner of the
Roman Catholics, though it was to have this certain effect
of dividing his kingdom, and alienating the minds of his
ſubjects, of whoſe aſſiſtance he was then in the utmoſt need.
And as for the Abuna, we are to conſider that Cairo had
been taken, and the government, which Abuna Mark owned
for the lawful one, had been overturned by the Turks who
then poſſeſſed it, and were actually perſecuting the Alexandrian church.

The Abuna, then, and the king alſo, had the ſame reaſon
for not applying to Cairo, the ſeat of the Turks their enemies; and, therefore, they more readily accommodated matters with a people from whom only their aſſiſtance could
come; and without whom, it was probable, that both the
Chriſtian religion and civil government of Abyſſinia would
fall together.

It has been ſaid of this king by the European writers
who have touched upon the hiſtory of his reign, that he
was a prince who had began it in the moſt promiſing manner, but after the death of the empreſs Helena, he had abandoned himſelf to all ſort of debauchery, and eſpecially
that of women; inſomuch, as Mr Ludolf ſays, he ſuffered his concubines to have idols in his palace. This I take

to

to be a calumny copied from the Portuguese priests, who never forgave him the denial of his writing the letters by Matthew, in which it was said he gave the Portuguese, or rather king of Portugal, one-third of the kingdom; for he succeeded to the crown at 11 years of age, defeated and flew Maffudi when he was about sixteen; and, when Don Roderigo and the Portuguese embassy were with him, he was then something more than twenty, a very devout, prudent prince, according to the account Alvarez, an eye-witness, gives of him; and all this time empress Helena was alive.

Again, the very year after the Portuguese embassy left Abyssinia, that is, in the year 1526, the king was defeated by the Moors, and, from that time to his death, was hunted about the country like a wild beast, from rock to rock, very often alone, and at all times slenderly attended, till he died, in 1540, at the age of 46; so there is no period during his life in which this calumny can be justly fixed upon him.

As for the idolatry he is accused of suffering in his palace among his Pagan mistresses, I cannot recollect any place in the adjoining nations from which he could have brought these idolatrous rites or mistresses. The Pagan countries around him profess a remnant of ill-understood Sabaism, worshipping the stars, the moon, and the wind; but I do not, as I say, recollect any of these bordering on Abyssinia who worship idols.

CLAUDIUS,

CLAUDIUS, or ATZENAF SEGUED.

From 1540 to 1559.

Prosperous Beginning of Claudius's Reign—Christopher de Gama lands in Abyssinia—Prevented by the rainy Season from joining the King—Battle of Ainal—Battle of Offalo—Christopher de Gama slain—Battle of Isaac's Bet—Moors defeated, and their General slain—Abyssinian Army defeated—Claudius slain—Remarkable Behaviour of Nur, Governor of Zeyla, General of the Moors.

CLAUDIUS succeeded his father David III. being yet young, and found the empire in circumstances that would have required an old and experienced prince. But, though young, he possessed those graceful and affable manners which, at first sight, attached people of all sorts to him. He had been tutored with great care by the empress Helena, was expert in all warlike exercises, and brave beyond his years.—So say the Abyssinian annals; and though I have not thought myself warranted to depart from the letter of the context, yet it is my duty to the reader to shew him how this could not be.

CLAUDIUS was born about the 1522; the empress Helena died in 1525. From this it is plain, the first three years of

I   his

his life was all that he could be under the tutelege of the emprefs Helena; and, at fo early a period, it is not poffible he could receive much advantage. The princefs, to whom he was indebted for his education, was Sabel Wenghel, celebrated in the Abyffinian hiftory for wifdom and courage equal to the emprefs Helena herfelf. She was relict of David. We fhall hereafter fee her called Helena likewife upon another occafion; but the reader is defired to have in mind, that this confufion of perfons is owing only to that of names to be met with almoft in every reign in the Abyffinian hiftory.

CLAUDIUS is faid likewife in thefe annals to have been a child at the time of his acceffion; but, having been born in the 1522, and fucceeding to the throne in 1540, he muft have been eighteen years of age; and this cannot be called childhood, efpecially in Abyffinia, unlefs, as I have before faid, this obfervation of age was relative to the arduous tafk he had in hand, by fucceeding to a kingdom arrived at the very eve of perdition.

THE Moors, notwithftanding the conftant fuccefs they had againft David, ftill feared the confequences of his long experience and undaunted refolution in the moft adverfe fortune. They were happy, therefore, in the change of fuch an enemy, however unfortunate, for a young man fcarcely yet out of the influence of female government, which had always been favourable to them, and their religion.

A GENERAL league was formed without delay among all the Mahometan chiefs to furround Claudius, and fall upon
him

him before he was in a situation to defend himself, and by one stroke to put an end to the war. They accordingly set about collecting troops from all quarters, but with a degree of inattention and presumption that sufficiently shewed they thought themselves in no danger. But the young king having good intelligence that vizir Afa, Ofman, Debra Yafous, and Jeram, (who had fo nearly taken his father prifoner in the mountain Tfalem) had their quarters near him, and neglected a good look-out, fell upon them, without their knowing what his force was, entirely defeated them, difperfed their army, and ftruck a panic into the whole confederacy by the manner this victory was followed up; the king himfelf on horfeback continued the purfuit all that day and night, as alfo the next day, and did not return to his camp till the fecond evening after his victory, having flain without mercy every one that had fallen into his hands, either in the flight, or in the field of battle.

CLAUDIUS's behaviour, on this firft occafion, raifed the foldiers confidence to a degree of enthufiafm. Every man that had ferved under his father repaired to him with the greateft alacrity. Above all, the Agows of Lafta came down to him in great troops from their rugged and inacceffible mountains, the chief of that warlike nation being related to him by his mother.

THE king in perfon at the head of his army became now an object of fuch confideration as to make the Mahometan chiefs no longer retire as ufual to winter in Adel, but canton themfelves in the feveral diftricts they had conquered in Abyffinia, and lay afide the thoughts of farther wafting the country,

country, to defend themfelves againft fo active and fpirited
an affailant. They agreed then to join their whole forces
together, and march to force the king to a battle. Ofman
of Ganzé, vizir Mudgid who had fettled in Amhara, Saber-
eddin *, and all the leffer rebel officers of Siré and Serawé,
effected a junction about the fame time without oppofition.
Jonathan alone, a rebel of great experience, had not yet appeared with his troops. The king, on the other hand, did
not feem over anxious to come to an engagement, though
his army was every day ready for battle; and his ground
was always taken with advantage, fo that it was almoft defperate to pretend to force him.

JONATHAN at laft was on his way to join the confederates; but the king had as early intelligence of his motions
as his friends: and, while he was yet two days march diftant from the camp, the king, leaving his tents ftanding
and his fires lighted, by a forced march in the night came
upon him, (while he thought him blocked up by his rebel
affociates at a diftance) and, finding Jonathan without preparation or defence, cut his whole army to pieces, flew him,
and then returned to his own tents as rapidly as he went,
having ordered fmall detachments to continue in the way
between him and his camp, patroling left fome ambufh
fhould be laid for him by the enemy, who, if they had
been informed of his march, though they were too late to
prevent the fuccefs of it, might ftill have attempted to revenge it.

But

* Conftant in the faith.

But intelligence was now given to the Moors with much less punctuality and alacrity than formerly. So generally did the king possess the affections of the country-people, that no information came to the confederate army till the next day after his return, when, early in the morning, he dispatched one of the Moorish prisoners that he had taken three days before, and spared for the purpose, carrying with him the head of Jonathan, and a full account of the havock to which he had been a witness.

This messenger bore also the king's defiance to the Moors, whom he challenged, under the odious epithets they deserved, to meet him; and then actually to shew he was in earnest, marched towards them with his army, which he formed in order of battle. But tho' they stood under arms for a considerable time, whilst several invitations to single combat were sent from the Christian horsemen, as their custom is, before they engage, or when their camps are near each other, yet the Moors were so astonished at what had happened, and what they saw now before them, that not one officer would advise the risking a battle, nor any one soldier accept of the challenge offered. The king then returned to his camp, distributed the whole booty among his soldiers, and refreshed them, preserving a proper station to cover the wounded, whom he sent off to places of security.

The king was in the country of Samen in the neighbourhood of Laita. He then decamped and passed the river Tacazzé, that he might be nearer those districts of which the Turks had possessed themselves. In this march all sorts of people joined the victorious army. Those that had revolted, and many that had apostatized, came without fear and surrendered themselves, trusting to the clemency of the prince. Many of the Moors, natives of Abyssinia, did the same, after having experienced the difference between the mild Christian government, and that of their new masters, the Moors and Turks of Adel.

The king encamped at Sard, there to pass his Easter; and, as is usual in the great festivals, many of the nobility obtained leave to attend the religious offices of the season at home with their families. Ammer, governor of Ganzé, who knew the custom of the country, thought this was the time to surprise the king thinly attended; and it might have succeeded, if intelligence of the enemy's designs had not been received almost as soon as they were formed. Claudius, therefore, drawing together some of the best of his forces, placed himself in ambush in Ammers's way, who, not suspecting, fell into it with his army, which was totally destroyed on the 24th of April 1541. After which the king left his own quarter at Sard and came to Shume.

While things were taking this favourable turn in Abyssinia, the ambassador, John Bermudes, had passed from Rome to Lisbon, where he was acknowledged by the king as patriarch of Alexandria, Abyssinia, and, as he will have it, of the Sea. The first thing he did was to give the Portuguese a sample of Abyssinian discipline, by putting Zaga Zaab in irons for having wasted so much time without effecting any of the purposes of his embassy; but, by the interposition of the king, he was set at liberty in a few days. Bermudes then fell roundly to the subject of his embassy, and drew such a picture of the distresses of Abyssinia, and instilled in his own blunt way so violently with the king of

3   Portugal,

Portugal, and the nobility in general, that he procured an order from the king for Don Garcia de Noronha, who was then going out viceroy of the Indies, to send 400 Portuguese musqueteers from India to the relief of Abyssinia, and to land them at Masuah.

John Bermudes, to secure the assistance promised, resolved to embark in the same fleet with Don Garcia; but he fell sick, from poison given him, as he apprehends, by Zaga Zaab, and this delayed his embarkation a year. The next year, being recovered of his illness, he arrived safely at India. In the interim Don Garcia died, and Don Stephen de Gama, who succeeded him, did not embrace the scheme of the intended succour with such eagerness as Bermudes could have wished.

After some delay, however, it was resolved that Don Stephen should himself undertake an expedition from India, to burn the Turkish gallies that were at Suez. In this, however, Don Stephen was disappointed. Upon intelligence of the intended visit, the Turkish gallies had been all drawn ashore. He came after this to the port of Masuah, where the fleet intended to water; and, for that purpose, their boats were sent to Arkeeko, a small town and fortress upon the main-land, where good water may be found. But the Moors and Turks from Zeyla and Adel were now masters there, who took the 1000 webs of cotton-cloth the captain had sent to exchange for water and provisions, and sent him word back, that his master, the king of Adel, was now king of all Ethiopia, and would not suffer any further trade to be carried on, but through his subjects; if, therefore, the captain of the fleet would make peace with him, he should restore the cotton-

webs

webs which had been taken, supply him plentifully with provisions, and make amends for the sixty Portuguese slain on the coast near Zeyla: For, upon the fleet's entering the Red Sea, this number of Portuguese had run away with a boat; and, landing in the kingdom of Adel, where they could procure no water, they were decoyed to give up their arms, and were then all massacred.

The captain, Don Stephen, saw the trap laid for him by the Moors, and, resolving to pay them in their own coin, he returned this answer to their message, " That he was very willing to trade with the Moorish officer, but did not demand restitution of the clothes, as they were taken in fair war. As for the sixty Portuguese, they had met the death they deserved, as being traitors and deserters: That he now sent a thousand more clothes, desiring water and provisions, especially live cattle; and that, as it was now the time of their festival, he would treat with them for peace, and bring his goods ashore as soon as the holidays were over."

This being agreed to on both sides, with equal bad faith and intention towards each other, and Don Stephen having obtained his refreshments, he strictly forbade any further communication with the shore. He then selected a body of six hundred men, the command of whom he gave to Martin Correa, who, in light boats, without shewing any fire, landed undiscovered below Arkeeko, and took possession of the entrances to the town, putting all that they met to the sword. Nur, governor of the province for the king of Adel, fled as soon as he had heard the Portuguese were in the town: He was already in the fields, when Martin Correa shot him with a musquet, and cut off his head, which

which was fent before them to the queen, Sabel Wenghel, then in a ftrong-hold of the province of Tigré, and with her Degdeafmati (which, in common difcourfe, is called *Kefmati*) Robel. This was the perfon of that name who had met Don Roderigo in his journey to find the king, and who was now governor of the province. The queen received the Moorifh general's head with great demonftrations of joy, confidering it as an early pledge of future victories.

In the mean time, Don Stephen de Gama, captain of the fleet, began to inrol the men deftined to march to join Claudius. Four hundred and fifty mufqueteers was the number granted by the king to Bermudes; but an ardent defire of glory had feized all the Portuguefe, and every one ftrove to be in the nomination for that enterprife. All that Don Stephen could do was to choofe men of the firft rank for the officers; and thefe, of neceffity, having many fervants whom they carried with them, greatly, by this means, encreafed the number beyond the 450. Don Chriftopher de Gama, Don Stephen's youngeft brother, a nobleman of great hopes, was chofen to command this fmall army of heroes.

A very great murmuring, neverthelefs, prevailed among thofe that were refufed, which was fcarcely kept in due bounds by the prefence and authority of the governor Don Stephen himfelf. And from this honourable emulation, and the difcontent thefe brave foldiers who were left behind fhewed, the bay where the galley rode in the harbour of Mafuah, on board which this council was held, is called to this day *Bahia dos Agravados*, the Bay of Wronged, or Injured People, fometimes mifinterpreted the Bay *of the Sad*.

THE

THE army under Don Chriſtopher marched to Arkeeko, where the next day came the governor Don Stephen, and the principal officers of the fleet, and took leave of their countrymen; and, after receiving the bleſſing of Don John Bermudes, *Patriarch of the Sea*, the governor and reſt of the Portugueſe embarked, and returned to India.

DON CHRISTOPHER, with the greateſt intrepidity, began his march towards Dobarwa, the eaſieſt entrance into Abyſſinia, though ſtill over rugged and almoſt inacceſſible mountains. The Baharnagaſh had orders to attend him, and furniſh this little army with cattle both for their proviſion and carriages; and this he actually performed. But the carriages of the ſmall train of artillery giving way in this bad road, and there being nobody at hand to aſſiſt them with freſh ones in caſe the old failed, Gama made certain carriages of wood after the pattern of thoſe they had brought from Portugal; and, as iron was a very ſcarce commodity in Abyſſinia, he made them ſplit in pieces ſome barrels of old and uſeleſs firelocks for the wheels with which they were to draw their artillery.

THE queen, without delay, came forward to join Don Chriſtopher; who, hearing ſhe was at hand, went to meet her a league from the city with drums beating and colours flying, and ſaluted her with a general diſcharge of fire-arms, which terrified her much. Her two ſiſters accompanied her, and a number of attendants of both ſexes. Don Chriſtopher, at the head of his ſoldiers, paid his compliments with equal gallantry and reſpect. The queen was covered from head to foot, but lifted up her veil, ſo that her face could be ſeen by him; and he, on the other hand, appointed a hundred muſqueteers

musqueteers for her guard; and thus they returned to Dobarwa mutually satisfied with this their first interview.

Don Christopher marched from Dobarwa eight days through a very rugged country, endeavouring, if possible, to bring about a junction with the king. And it was in this place, while he was encamped, that he received a message from the Moorish general, full of opprobrious expressions, which was answered in much the same manner. Don Christopher continued his march as much as he could on account of the rains; and Gragnè, whose greatest desire was to prevent the junction, followed him into Tigrè. Neither army desired to avoid the other, and they were both marching to the same point; so that on the 25th of March 1542, they came in sight of each other at Ainal, a small village in the country of the Baharnagash.

The Moorish army consisted of 1000 horsemen, 5000 foot, 50 Turkish musqueteers, and a few pieces of artillery. Don Christopher, besides his 450 musqueteers, had about 12,000 Abyssinians, mostly foot, with a few bad horse commanded by the Baharnagash, and Robel governor of Tigrè. Don Christopher, whose principal view was a junction with the king, though he did not decline fighting, yet, like a good officer, he chose to do it as much as possible upon his own terms; and, therefore, as the enemy exceeded greatly in the number of horse, he posted himself so as to make the best of his fire-arms and artillery. And well it was that he did so, for the Abyssinians shewed the utmost terror when the firing began on both sides.

GRAGNE,

GRAGNE, mounted on a bay horse, advancing too near Don Christopher's line that he might see if in any part it was accessible to his cavalry, and being known by his dress to be an officer of distinction, he was shot at by Peter de Sa, a Portuguese markman, who killed his horse, and wounded the rider in the leg. This occasioned a great confusion, and would probably have ended in a defeat of the Moors, had not the Portuguese general also been wounded immediately after by a shot. Don Christopher, to shew his confidence of victory, ordered his men forthwith to pitch their tents, upon which the Moors retired with Gragnè (whom they had mounted on another horse) without being pursued, the Abyssinians having contented themselves with being spectators of the battle.

DON CHRISTOPHER, with his army and the empress, now entered into winter-quarters at Affalo; nor did Gragnè depart to any distance from him, but took up his quarters at Zabul, in hopes always to fight the Portuguese before it was possible for them to effect a junction with the king. The winter passed in a mutual intercourse of correspondence and confidence between the king and Don Christopher, and in determining upon the best scheme to pursue the war with success. Don Christopher and the queen were both of opinion, that, considering the small number of Portuguese first landed, and their diminution by fighting, and a strange climate, it was risking every thing to defer a junction till the winter was over.

THE Moorish general was perfectly of the same opinion; therefore, as soon as the king began his march from Dembea, Gragnè advanced to Don Christopher's camp, and placed him-

self

felf between the Portuguefe army and that of the king, drawing up his troops before the camp, and defying the Portuguefe to march out, and fight, in the moft opprobrious language. Don Chriftopher, in a long catalogue of virtues which he poffeffed to a very eminent degree, had not the fmalleft claim to that of patience, fo very neceffary to thofe that command armies. He was brave to a fault; rafh and vehement; jealous of what he thought military honour; and obftinate in his refolutions, which he formed in confequence. The defiance of this barbarian, at which an old general would have laughed, made him utterly forget the reafons he himfelf frequently alledged, and the arguments ufed by the queen, which the king's approach daily ftrengthened, that it was rifking every thing to come to a battle till the two armies had joined. He had, however, from no other motive but Gragnè's infolence, formed his refolution to fight, without waiting a junction; and accordingly the 30th of Auguft, early in the morning, having chofen his ground to the beft advantage, he offered battle to the Moorifh army.

GRAGNE, by prefents fent to the bafha of Zibid, had doubled his number of horfe, which now confifted of 2000. He had got likewife 100 Turkifh mufqueteers, an infinite number of foot, and a train of artillery more numerous and complete than ever had been feen before in Abyffinia. The queen, frightened at the preparation for the battle, fled, taking with her the Portuguefe patriarch, who feemed to have as little inclination as fhe had to fee the iffue of the day. But Don Chriftopher, who knew well the bad effects this example would have, both on Abyffinians and Portuguefe, fent twenty horfe, and brought them both back; telling the patriarch it was a breach of duty he would not fuffer, for him to withdraw until he had confeffed him, and given the army abfolution before the action with the Infidels.

THE battle was fought on the 30th of Auguft with great fury and obftinacy on both fides. The Portuguefe had ftrewed, early in the morning, all the front of their line with gun-powder, to which, on the approach of the Turks, they fet fire by trains, which burnt and difabled a great many of them; and things bore a profperous appearance, till the Moorifh general ordered fome artillery to be pointed againft the Abyffinians, who, upon hearing the firft explofion, and feeing the effect of fome balls that had lighted among them, fled, and left the Portuguefe to the number only of 400, who were immediately furrounded by the Moorifh army. Nor did Gragné purfue the fugitives, his affair being with the Portuguefe, the fmallnefs of whofe number promifed they would fall an eafy and certain facrifice. He therefore, attacked their camp upon every fide with very little fuccefs, having loft moft of his beft officers, till, unfortunately, Don Chriftopher, fighting and expofing himfelf everywhere, was fingled out by a Turkifh foldier, and fhot through the arm. Upon this all his men turned their thoughts from their own prefervation to that of their general, who obftinately refufed to fly, till he was by force put upon a litter, and fent off, together with the patriarch and queen.

NIGHT now coming on, Don Chriftopher had got into a wood in which there was a cave. There he ordered himfelf to be fet down to have his wounds dreffed; which, being done, he was urged by the queen and patriarch to continue
his

his flight. But he had formed his resolution, and, without deigning to give his reasons, he obstinately refused to retreat a step farther. In vain the queen, and those that knew the country, told him he was just in the tract of the Moorish horsemen, who would not fail soon to surround him. He repeated his resolution of staying there with such a degree of firmness, that the queen and patriarch, who had no great desire for martyrdom, left him to his fate, which presently overtook him.

In one of Don Christopher's expeditions to the mountains, he had taken a very beautiful woman, wife to a Turkish officer, whom he had slain. This lady had made a shew of conversion to Christianity; lived with him afterwards, and was treated by him with the utmost tenderness. It was said, that, after he was wounded and began to fly, this woman had given him his route, and promised to overtake him with friends that would carry him to a place of safety. Accordingly, some servants left by the queen, hidden among the rocks, to watch what might befal him, and assist him if possible, saw a woman, in the dawn of the morning, come to the cave, and return into the wood immediately, whence there rushed out a body of Moorish horse, who went straight to the cave and found Don Christopher lying upon the ground sorely wounded. Upon the first question that was asked him, he declared his name, which so overjoyed the Moors, that they gave over further pursuit, and returned with the prisoner they had taken. Don Christopher was brought into the presence of the Moorish general, Gragné, who loaded him with reproaches; to which he replied with such a share of invectives, that the Moor, in the violence of his passion, drew his sword and cut

A a 2

off

off his head with his own hand. His head was fent to Conſtantinople, and parts of his body to Zibid and other quarters of Arabia.

The Portugueſe camp was now taken, and all the wounded found in it were put to death. The women, from their fear, having retired all into Don Chriſtopher's tent, the Turks began to indulge themſelves in their uſual exceſſes towards their captives, when a noble Abyſſinian woman, who had been married to a Portugueſe, feeing the ſhocking treatment that was awaiting them, fet fire to feveral barrels of gunpowder that were in the tent, and at once deſtroyed herſelf, her companions, and thoſe that were about to abuſe them.

The queen and the patriarch, after travelling through moſt difficult ways, and being hoſpitably entertained whereever they paſſed, at laſt took up their reſidence in the Jews mountain, a place inacceſſible in point of ſtrength, having but one entrance, and that very difficult, being alſo defended by a multitude of inhabitants who dwell on a large plain on the top of that mountain, where there is plenty of ſpace to plow and ſow, and a large ſtream of water that runs through he whole of it. Here they ſtaid two months, as well to repoſe themſelves as to give the king time to relieve them. After hearing that he was in motion, they left the mountain of the Jews, and met him on his march towards them.

Claudius ſhewed great ſigns of ſorrow for the death of Don Chriſtopher, and mourned three days. He then ſent 1000 ounces of gold to be divided among the Portugueſe, who, in the place of Don Chriſtopher, had elected Alphonſo Caldevra

Caldeyra for their captain. Thefe all flocked about the king, demanding that he would lead them to battle, that they might revenge the death of Don Chriftopher. Soon after which, Alphonfo Caldcyra, exercifing a horfe in the field, was thrown off and died of the fall. In his place was elected Arius Dias, a Portuguefe, born at Coimbra, whofe mother was a black; he was very much favoured by the king, who now began to cultivate particular parties a-mong the Portuguefe, in order to divide them, and loo-fen their attachment for their patriarch, religion, and country.

THE king marched from Samen to Shawada, where the Moorifh army came in full force to meet him. They were not, however, thofe formidable troops that had defeated and taken Don Chriftopher: For the Turkifh foldiers, who were the ftrength of the army, expecting to have fhared a great fum each for Don Chriftopher's ranfom, thought themfelves exceedingly injured by the manner in which he was put to death; and they had accordingly all to a man returned into Arabia, leaving Gragné to fight his own batttles for his own profit. Nor was Claudius ignorant of this; and having collected all his army he gave the Moors battle on the 15th of November in a plain called Woggora, on the top of Lamalmon, in which the Moors, notwithftanding their recent victory, were not long in yielding to the fuperiority of the king's troops.

THE lofs of the day was not inconfiderable. Mahomet, Ofman, and Talil, three Moorifh leaders, famous for their
fuccefles

fucceffes againft David the king's father, were this day flain in the field.

CLAUDIUS now defcended into the low country of Derfe-guè, a very plentiful province, to which the Moors always retreated to ftrengthen themfelves after any misfortune. This the king utterly deftroyed; while Gragné did the fame with thofe countries in Dembea that had been recovered by the king. Claudius then returned to Sha-wada, and Gragnè to Derfeguè. After that the king march-ed to Wainadega, and Gragnè, leaving Derfeguè, advanced fo near the king's army, that the outpofts were nearly in fight of each other. In fuch a pofition of two fuch armies a battle became inevitable.

ACCORDINGLY, on the 10th of Feb. 1543, in the morning, the king, whofe quarters were at Ifaac's Bet, having well re-frefhed his army, marched out of his camp, and offered the enemy battle. The Portuguefe, ever mindful of Don Chrif-topher, fought with a bravery like to defperation, and the prefence of the king keeping the Abyffinians in their duty, the van of Gragné's army was pufhed back upon the center, and much confufion was like to follow, till Gragnè advanced alone before them, waving and beckoning with his hands to his men that they fhould follow; and he was already come fo near the Portuguefe line as to be eafily known and diftinguifhed by them.

PETER LYON, a man of low ftature, but very active and valiant, who had been valet-de chambre to Don Chriftopher, having crept unfeen along the courfe of a river a confider-able fpace nearer, to make his aim more certain, fhot Gragnè
with

with his mufquet, fo that the ball went through his body in the moment that both armies joined. Gragnè, finding that his wound was mortal, rode afide from the preffure
of the troops towards a fmall thicket, and was clofely followed by Peter Lyon, who faw him fall dead from his horfe;
and, defirous ftill to do further fervice in the battle, he
would not incumber himfelf with his head, but, cutting
off one of the ears, he put it in his pocket, and returned to
the action. The Moorifh army no fooner miffed the prefence
of their general, than concluding all loft, they fell into confufion, and were purfued by the Portuguefe and Abyffinians
with a great flaughter, till the evening.

The next morning, in furveying the dead, the body of
Gragnè was found by an Abyffinian officer, who cut his
head off, and brought it to the king, who received him with
great honour and promife of reward. Peter Lyon ftood a
filent fpectator of the impudence of his competitor; but A-
rius Dias, who knew the fact, defired the king's attention ;
faying, at the fame time, " That he believed his majefty
knew Gragnè well enough to fuppofe that he would not
fuffer any man to cut off his ear, without having it in his
power to fever his head alfo ; and confequently, that the ear
muft be in poffeffion of a better man than he that had
brought his head to the camp." Upon this, Peter Lyon pulled the ear out of his pocket, and laid it at the king's feet,
amidft the acclamations of all prefent, for his bravery in
revenging his old mafter's death, and his modefty in being
content with having done fo, without pretending to any
other reward.   2.

In

In this battle, a fon of Gragnè was taken prifoner, with many other confiderable officers; and Del Wumbarea, wife of Gragnè, with Nur fon of Mudgid, and a few troops, were obliged to throw themfelves, for fafety, among the wilds and woods of Atbara, thereby efcaping with great difficulty.

The king had now ample revenge of all the Moorifh leaders who had reduced his father to fuch extremities, excepting Joram, who had driven the king from his hiding-place on mount Tfalem, and forced him to crofs the Tacazzé on foot, with equal danger of being drowned or taken. This leader had, much againft his will, been detained from the laft battle, but, hoping to be ftill in time, was advancing by forced marches. The king, informed of his route, detached a party of his army to meet him before the news of the battle could reach him. They having placed them-felves in ambufh, he fell into it with his army, and was cut to pieces: this completed Claudius's account with his father's enemies.

During the late war with Gragné, the provinces of Tigrè and Sirè had been the principal feat of the war. They were immediately in the way between Dembea, Mafuah, and the other Moorifh pofts upon the Red Sea ; the enemy had croffed them in all directions, and a proportionable devaftation had been the confequence. Gragnè had burnt Axum, and deftroyed all the churches and convents in Tigrè. The king, now delivered from this enemy, had applied ferioufly to repair the ravages which had been made in the country. For this purpofe he marched with a fmall army towards Axum, intending afterwards an expedition againft the Galla.

It

IT was in the 13th year of the reign of Claudius, while he was at Sirè, that there happened a very remarkable eclipfe of the fun, which threw both court and army into great confternation. The prophets and diviners, ignorant monks of the defert, did not let flip fo favourable an opportunity of increafing their confequence by augmenting this panic, and declaring this eclipfe to portend nothing lefs than the renewal of the Moorifh war. The year, however, paffed in tranquillity and peace. Two old women, relations of the king, are faid to have died; and it was in this great calamity that thefe diviners were to look for the completion of their prophecies. It is from this, however, that I have taken an opportunity to compare and rectify the dates of the principal tranfactions in the Abyffinian hiftory. Sirè, where the king then refided, was a point very favourable for this application; for, in my journey from Mafuah to Gondar, I had fettled the latitude and longitude of that town by many obfervations.

ON the 22d of January 1770, at night, by a medium of different paffages of ftars over the meridian, and by an obfervation of the fun the noon of the following day, I found the latitude to be 14° 4' 35" north, and the evening of the 23d, I obferved an emerfion of the firft fatellite of Jupiter, and by this I concluded the longitude of Sirè to be 38° 0' 15" eaft of the meridian of Greenwich.

THE 13th year of the reign of Claudius falls to be in the 1553, and I find that there was a remarkable eclipfe of the fun that did happen that fame year on the 24th of January N. S. which anfwers to the 18th of the Ethiopic month Teir. The circumftances of this eclipfe were as follow:

	H.	M.	S.
Beginning,	7	21	0 A. M.
Middle,	8	40	0
End	10	1	0

The quantity of the fun's diſk obſcured was 10 digits; ſo that this was ſo near to a total eclipſe, it muſt have made an impreſſion on the ſpectators minds that ſufficiently accounts for the alarm and apprehenſions it occaſioned.

In the month of January, nothing can be more beautiful. than the ſky in Siré; not a cloud appears; the ſky is all of a pale azure, the colour lighter than an European ſky, and of inexpreſſible beauty. The manner of applying this eclipſe I ſhall mention hereafter.

Eclipses of the moon do not ſeem to be attended to in Abyſſinia. The people are very little out in the night, inſomuch that I do not find one of theſe recorded throughout their hiſtory. The circumſtances of the ſeaſon make even thoſe of the ſun ſeldomer viſible than in other climates, for in the rainy ſeaſon, from April to September, the heavens are conſtantly overcaſt with clouds, ſo that it is mere accident if they can catch the moment it happens. But in the month of Teir, that is December and January, the ſky is perfectly ſerene and clear, and at this time our eclipſe above mentioned happened.

The king now took into his conſideration the ſtate of the church. He had ſent for an Abuna from Cairo to ſucceed Abuna Marcus, and he was now in his way to Abyſſinia, while Bermudes, not able to bear this ſlight, on the other hand,

hand, publicly declared to the king, that, having been ambaffador from his father, and made his fubmiffion to the
Roman pontiff, for himfelf and for his kingdom, he now
expected that Claudius would make good his father's engagements, embrace the Roman Catholic religion himfelf, and, without delay, proclaim it as the eftablifhed religion in Abyffinia. This the king pofitively refufed to do,
and a converfation enfued, which is repeated by Bermudes
himfelf, and fufficiently fhews the moderation of the young
king, and the fiery, brutal zeal of that ignorant, bigotted,
ill-mannered prieft. Hitherto the Abyffinians heard the
Portuguefe mafs with reverence and attention; and the
Portuguefe frequented the Abyffinian churches with complacency. They intermarried with each other, and the children feem to have been chriftened indifferently by the
priefts of either church. And this might have long continued, had it not been for the impatience of Bermudes.

THE king, feeing the danger of connecting himfelf with
fuch a man, kept up every appearance of attachment to the
Alexandrian church. Yet, fays the Abyffinian hiftorian who
writes his life, it was well known that Claudius, in his heart,
was a private, but perfect convert, to the Romifh faith, and
kept only from embracing it by his hatred to Bermudes, the
conftant perfuafion of the emprefs Sabel Wenghel, and the
recollection of the misfortunes of his father. Upon being
required publicly to fubmit himfelf to the See of Rome, he
declared that he had made no fuch promife; that he confidered Bermudes as no patriarch, or, at beft, only patriarch of the
Franks; and that the Abuna of Abyffinia was the chief
prieft acknowledged by him. Bermudes told him, that he
was accurfed and excommunicated. Claudius anfwered, that

he,

he, Bermudes, was a neftorian heretic, and worfhipped four gods. Bermudes anfwered plainly, that he lied; that he would take every Portuguefe from him, and return to India whence he came. The king's anfwer was, that he wifhed he would return to India; but as for the Portuguefe, neither they, nor any other perfon, fhould leave his kingdom without his permiffion. Accordingly, having perfectly gained Arius Dias, he gave him the name of Marcus, with the command of the Portuguefe, and fent him a ftandard with his own arms, to ufe inftead of the king of Portugal's. But the Abyffinian page being met, on his return, with the Portuguefe ftandard in his hand, by James Brito, he wrefted it from him, felling him to the ground with a blow of his fword on the head.

From expoftulations with the king, the matter of religion turned into difputes among the priefts, at which the king always affifted in perfon. If we fuppofe they were no better fuftained on the part of the Abyffinians than they were by the patriarch Bermudes, who we know was no great divine, we cannot expect much that was edifying from the arguments that either of them ufed. The Portuguefe priefts fay *, that the king, ftruck with the ignorance of his own clergy, frequently took the difcuffion upon himfelf, which he managed with fuch force of reafoning as often to put the patriarch to a ftand. From verbal difputes, which terminated in nothing, Bermudes was refolved to appeal to arguments in writing; and, with the help of thofe that were with him of the fame faith, a fair ftate of the differences in queftion was made in a fmall book, and prefented to the king, who read it with fo much pleafure that he kept it conftantly by him. This gave very great offence to the

Abyffinian

---

* Tellez, lib. 2. cap. 27.

Abyffinian clergy; and the Abuna being now arrived, the king defired of him liberty to read that book, which he re-fufing, put the young king into fo violent a paffion that he called the Abuna Mahometan and Infidel to his face.

THINGS growing worfe and worfe between the Portu-guefe and Abyffinians, by the incendiary fpirit of the bru-tifh Bermudes, from reproaches they came to blows; and this proceeded fo far, that the Portuguefe one night affault-ed the king's tent, where they flew fome, and grievoufly wounded others. Upon this, the king, defirous to eftrange him a little from the Portuguefe, fent Bermudes to the coun-try of the Gafats, where he gave him large appointments, in hopes that the natural turbulence of his temper would involve him in fome difficulties. And there he ftaid feven months, oppreffing the poor ignorant people, and frighten-ing them with the noife of his fire-arms. During this period, the king went on an expedition againft the Galla; Bermu-des then returned to court, where he found that Arius Dias was dead, and a great many of the Portuguefe very well at-tached to the king. But he began his old work of diffen-tion, infomuch that the king determined to banifh him to a mountain for life.

GASPAR DE SUZA now commanded the Portuguefe inftead of Arius Dias, a man equally beloved by his own nation and the king. By his perfuafions, and that of Kafmati Robel, the banifhment to the mountain was laid afide; but Bermu-des was privately perfuaded to embark for India while it was yet time; and accordingly he repaired to Dobarwa, where he remained two years, as it fhould feem, perfectly quiet, neglected, and forlorn; faying daily mafs to ten Portuguefe

tuguefe who had fettled in that town after the defeat of Don Chriftopher. He then went to Mafuah, and the monfoon being favourable, he embarked on board a Portuguefe veffel, carrying with him the ten Portuguefe that were fettled at Dobarwa, who all arrived fafely at Goa.

St Ignatius, founder of the Order of Jefuits, was then at Rome in the dawn of his holinefs. The converfion of Abyffinia feemed of fuch confequence to him, that he refolved himfelf to go and be the apoftle of the kingdom. But the pope, who had conceived other hopes of him and his Order more important and nearer at hand, abfolutely refufed this offer. One of his fociety, Nugnez Baretto, was, however, fixed upon for patriarch, without any notice being taken of Don John Bermudes. By him Ignatius fent a letter addreffed to Claudius, which is to be found in the collections *. It does not, I think, give us any idea of the ingenuity or invention of that great faint. It feems moftly to beg the queftion, and to contain little elfe than texts of fcripture for his future miffionaries to preach and write on, relative to the difference of tenets of the two churches.

With this letter, and a number of priefts, Baretto came to Goa. But news being arrived there of king Claudius's fteady averfion to the Catholic church, it was then thought better, rather than rifk the patriarchal dignity, to fend Andrew Oviedo bifhop of Hierapolis, and Melchior Carneyro bifhop of Nice, with feveral other priefts, as ambaffadors from the governor of India to Claudius, with proper credentials. They arrived fafely at Mafuah in 1558, five days before the Turkifh bafha came with his fleet and army, and took poffeffion

of

---

* Dated at Rome 16th Feb. 1555.   See Tellez, lib. 2. cap. 22.

of Mafuah and Arkeeko, though thefe places had been occupied by the Turks two years before.

WHEN the arrival of thefe Portuguefe was intimated to
Claudius, he was exceedingly glad, as he confidered them as
an acceffion of ftrength. But when, on opening the letter,
he faw they were priefts, he was very much troubled, and
faid, that he wondered the king of Portugal fhould meddle
fo much with his affairs ; that he and his predeceffors knew
no obedience due but to the chair of St Mark, or acknowledged any other patriarch but that of Alexandria ; neverthelefs, continued he with his ufual goodnefs and moderation, fince they are come fo far out of an honeft concern
for me, I fhall not fail to fend proper perfons to receive and
conduct them. This he did, and the two bifhops and their
companions were immediately brought to court. It was at
this time that the difpute about the two natures began, in
which the king took fo confiderable a part. He was ftrenuous, eloquent, and vehement in the difcuffion ; when that
was ended, he ftill preferved his ufual moderation and kindnefs for the Portuguefe priefts.

NUGNEZ died in India, and Oviedo fucceeded him as patriarch to Abyffinia, it having been fo appointed by the pope
from the beginning of their miffion.

CLAUDIUS had no children ; a treaty was therefore fet on
foot, at the inftance of the emprefs Sabel Wenghel, for ran-
foming the prince Menas who had been taken prifoner in
his father David's time, and ever fince kept in confinement among the Moors, upon a high mountain in Adel.
The

The fame had happened to a fon of Gragné likewife, made prifoner at the battle of Wainadega, when his father was flain by Claudius. The Moors fettled in Abyffinia, as well as all the Abyffinian rebels who had forfaken their allegiance or religion during the war, were to a man violently againft fetting Menas at liberty, for he was the only brother Claudius had, and a difputed fucceffion was otherwife probable, which was what the Moors longed for. Befides this, Menas was exceedingly brave, of a fevere and cruel temper, a mortal enemy to the Mahometans, and at this time in the flower of his age, and perfectly fit to govern. It was not, then, by any means, an eligible meafure for thofe who were naturally the objects of his hatred, to provide fuch an affiftant and fucceffor to Claudius.

DEL WUMBAREA thought, that, having loft her hufband, to be deprived of her fon likewife, was more than fell to her fhare in the common caufe. She, too, had therefore applied to the bafha of Mafuah, who looked no farther than to a ranfom, and cared very little what prince reigned in Abyffinia. He, therefore, undertook the management of the matter, and declared that he would fend Menas to the Grand Signior, as foon as an anfwer fhould come from Conftantinople, while Claudius protefted, that he would give up Gragné's fon to the Portuguefe, if the ranfom for his brother was not immediately agreed on. This refolution, on both fides, quickly removed all objections. Four thoufand ounces of gold were paid to the Moors and the bafha ; Menas was releafed and fent home to Claudius, who thereupon, in his turn, fet Ali Gerad, fon of Gragné by Del Wumbarea, at liberty, and with him Waraba Guta brother of the king of Adel, and this finifhed the tranfaction.

1   I MUST

I must here obferve, that what Bermudes * fays, that Del Wumbarea was taken prifoner and given in marriage to Arius Dias, was but a fable, as appears both from the beginning and fequel of the narrative. Del Wumbarea having thus obtained her fon, took a very early opportunity of fhewing fhe had not yet forgot the father. Nur, governor of Zeyla, fon of Mudgid, who had flain the princes imprifoned upon the mountain of Gefhen, was deeply in love with this lady, and had deferved well of her, for he had affifted her in making her efcape into Atbara that day her hufband was flain. But this heroine had conftantly refufed to liften to any propofals; nay, had vowed fhe never would give her hand in marriage to any man till he fhould firft bring her the head of Claudius who had flain her hufband. Nur willingly accepted the condition, which gave him few rivals, but rather feemed to be referved for him, and out of the power of every one elfe.

Claudius, before this, had marched towards Adel, when he received a meffage from Nur, that, though Gragné was dead, there ftill remained a governor of Zeyla, whofe family was chofen as a particular inftrument for fhedding the blood of the Abyffinian princes; and defired him, therefore, to be prepared, for he was fpeedily to fet out to come to him. Claudius had been employed in various journies through different parts of his kingdom, repairing the churches which Gragné and the other Moors had burnt; and he was then rebuilding that of Debra Werk † when this meffage of

VOL. II.   C c   Nur

---

* See Bermudes's account of thefe times, printed at Lifbon by Francis Coirea, A. D. 1565.
† The Mountain of Gold.

Nur was brought to him. This prince was of a temper never to avoid a challenge; and if he did not march againſt
Nur immediately, he ſtaid no longer than to complete his
army as far as poſſible. He then began his march for Adel,
very much, as it is ſaid, againſt the advice of his friends.

THAT ſuch advice ſhould be given, at this particular time,
appears ſtrange; for till now he had been conſtantly victorious, and his kingdom was perfectly obedient, which was not
the caſe when any one of the former battles had been fought.
But many prophecies were current in the camp, that the
king was to be unfortunate this campaign, and was to loſe
his life in it. Theſe unfortunate rumours tended much to
diſcourage the army, at the ſame time that they ſeemed to
have a contrary effect on the king, and to confirm him in
his reſolution to fight. The truth is, the clergy, who had
ſeen the country delivered by him from the Mahometans
in a manner almoſt miraculous, and the conſtancy with
which he withſtood the Romiſh patriarch, and fruſtrated the
deſigns of his father againſt the Alexandrian church, and
who had experienced his extreme liberality in rebuilding
the churches, had wrought his young mind to ſuch a degree of enthuſiaſm that he was often heard to ſay, he preferred a death in the middle of an army of Infidels to the
longeſt and moſt proſperous life that ever fell to the lot of
man. It needed not a prophet to have foretold the likely
iſſue of a battle in theſe circumſtances, where the king,
careleſs of life, rather ſought death than victory; where
the number of Portugueſe was ſo ſmall as to be incapable,
of themſelves, to effect any thing; where, even of that number, thoſe that were attached to the king were looked upon
as traitors by thoſe of the party of the patriarch; and where

the

the Abyffinians, from their repeated quarrels and difputes, heartily hated them all.

THE armies were drawn up and ready to engage, when the chief prieft of Debra Libanos came to the king to tell him a dream, or vifion, which warned him not to fight; but the Moors were then advancing, and the king on horfeback made no reply, but marched brifkly forward to the enemy. The cowardly Abyffinians, upon the firft fire, fled, leaving the king engaged in the middle of the Moorifh army with twenty horfe and eighteen Portuguefe mufqueteers, who were all flain around his perfon; and he himfelf fell, after fighting manfully, and receiving twenty wounds. His head was cut off, and by Nur delivered to Del Wumbarea, who directed it to be tied by the hair to the branch of a tree before her door, that fhe might keep it conftantly in fight. Here it remained three years, till it was purchafed from her by an Armenian merchant, her firft grief, having, it is probable, fubfided upon the acquifition of a new hufband. The merchant carried the head to Antioch, and buried it there in the fepulchre of a faint of the fame name.

THUS died king Claudius in the 19th year of his reign, who, by his virtues and capacity, might hold a firft place among any feries of kings we have known, victorious in every action he fought, except in that one only in which he died. A great flaughter was made after this among the routed, and many of the firft nobility were flain in endeavouring to efcape; among the reft, the dreamer from Debra Lebanos, his vifion, by which he knew the king's death, not having extended fo far as to reveal his own.

The

The Abyffinians immediately transferred the name of this prince into their catalogue of Saints, and he is called St Claudius in that country to this day. Though endowed with every other virtue that entitled him to his place in the kalendar, he feems to have wanted one—that of dying in charity with his enemies.

This battle was fought on the 22d March 1559; and the victory gained by Nur was a complete one.. The king and moft of his principal officers were flain; great part of the army taken prifoners, the reft difperfed, and the camp plundered; fo that no Moorifh general had ever returned home with the glory that he did. But afterwards, in his behaviour, he exhibited a fpectacle more memorable, and that did him more honour than the victory itfelf; for, when he drew near to Adel, he clothed himfelf in poor attire like a common foldier, and bare-headed, mounted on an ordinary mule, with an old faddle and tattered accoutrements, he forbade the fongs and praife with which it is ufual to meet conquerors in that country when returning with victory from the field. He declined alfo all fhare in the fuccefs of that day, declaring that the whole of it was due to God alone, to whofe mercy and immediate interpofition he owed the deftruction of the Chriftian army..

The unworthy and unfortunate John Bermudes having arrived in Portugal from India, continued there till his death; and, in the infcription over his tomb, is called only *Patriarch of Alexandria.* Yet it is clear, from the hiftory of thefe times, that he was firft ordained by the old patriarch Marcus; and that the pope, Paul III. only confirmed the ordination of this heretical fchifmatical prelate, though we have

2

ftated

ftated that he was ordained by the pope, according to his own affertion, to be patriarch of Alexandria, Abyffinia, and the Sea. Bermudes lived many years after this, and never refigned any of his charges.

HOWEVER, on his arrival in Europe, feveral fuppofed well-meaning perfons at Rome began to difcourfe among them-felves, as if the converfion of Abyffinia had not had a fair trial when trufted in the hands of fuch a man as Bermudes. Scandalous ftories as to his moral character were propaga-ted at Rome to ftrengthen this. He was faid to have ftolen a golden cup in Abyffinia*; but this does not appear to me in any fhape probable, or like the manners of the man. He was a fimple, ill-bred zealot, exceedingly vain, but in no-wife coveting riches or gain of any fort. Sebaftian king of Portugal, hearing the bad pofture of the Catholic religion in Abyffinia, and the fmall hopes of the converfion of that country, befought the pope to fend all the miffionaries that were in that kingdom to preach the gofpel in Japan : but Oviedo ftated fuch ftrong reafons in his letter to Rome, that he was confirmed in the miffion of Ethiopia.

---

* Purch. vol. 2.

MENAS,

MENAS, or ADAMAS SEGUED.

From 1559 to 1563.

*Baharnagafh rebels, proclaims Tafcar King—Defeated by the King—
Cedes Dobarwa to the Turks, and makes a League with the Bafha of
Mafuah.*

MENAS fucceeded his brother Claudius, and found his
kingdom in almoft as great confufion as it had been
left by his father David.   His firft campaign was againft
Radaet the Jew.   The king attacked him at his ftrongeft
poft in Samen, where he fought him with various fuccefs;
and the enterprife did not feem much advanced, when a
hermit, refiding in thefe mountains, probably tired with the
neighbourhood of fuch troublefome people, came and told
the king, it had been revealed to him that the conqueft of
the Jews was not allotted to him, nor was their time yet
come.

WHILE the king feemed difpofed to avail himfelf cf the
hermit's warning, as a decent excufe to get rid of an affair
that did not fucceed to his mind, an accident happened
which determined him to quit his prefent undertaking.
Two men, fhepherds of Ebenaat in Beleffen, from what injury is not known, engaged two of the king's fervants, who
were

were their relations, to introduce them into Menas's tent while sleeping, with a design to murder him in his bed. While they were preparing to execute their intention, one of them stumbled over the lamp that was burning, and threw it down. The king awakening, and challenging him with a loud voice, the assassin struck at him with his knife, but so feebly, from the fright, that he dropt the weapon upon the king's cloak without hurting him. They fled immediately out of the tent, but were taken at Ebenaat the next day, and brought back to the king, who gave orders to the judges to try them: they were both condemned, the one to be thrust through with lances, the other to be stoned to death; after which, both their bodies were thrown to the dogs and to the beasts of the field, as is practised constantly in all cases of high-treason.

THE second year of the reign of Menas was ushered in by a conspiracy among the principal men of his court, at the head of which was Isaac Baharnagash, an old and tried servant of his brother Claudius. This officer had been treated ill by Menas in the beginning of his reign; and, knowing the prince's violent and cruel disposition, he could not persuade himself that he was yet in safety.

MENAS, to suppress this rebellion in its infancy, sent Zara Johannes, an old officer, before him, with what forces he could collect in the instant; but Isaac, informed of the bad state of that army, and consequently of his own superiority, left him no time to strengthen himself, but fell furiously upon him, and, with little resistance, dispersed his army. This loss did not discourage the king; he had assembled a very considerable force, and, desirous still to encrease it, it, he was advancing flowly that he might collect the fcattered remains of the army that had been defeated. The Baharnagafh, though victorious, faw with fome concern that he could not avoid the king, whofe courage and capacity, both as a foldier and a general, left him every thing to fear for his fuccefs.

Ever fince the maffacre of the princes upon mount Gefhen by vizir Mudgid, in the reign of David III. none of the remains of the royal family had been confined as heretofore. Tafcar, Menas's nephew, was then at liberty, and, to ftrengthen his caufe, was proclaimed king by the Baharnagafh, foon after the defeat of Menas's army under Zara Johannes. He was a prince very mild and affable in his manners, in all refpects very unlike his uncle then reigning.

It was on the 1ft of July 1561, that the king attacked the Baharnagafh in the plain of Woggora; and, having entirely routed his army, Tafcar was taken prifoner, and ordered by the king his uncle to be carried to the brink of the high rock of Lamalmon, and, having been thrown over the fteep precipice, he was dafhed to pieces. Ifaac himfelf efcaped very narrowly, flying to the frontier of his government in the neighbourhood of Mafuah. The Baharnagafh comprehended diftinctly to what a dangerous fituation he was now reduced. No hopes of fafety remained but in a peace with the bafha. This at firft appeared not eafily obtained; for, while Ifaac remained in his duty in the reign of Claudius, he had fought with the bafha, and loft his brother in the engagement. But prefent neceffity overcame the memory of paft injuries.

SAMUR

Samur Basha was a man of capacity and temper; he had been in possession of Masuah ever since the year 1558. He saw his own evident interest in the measure, and appeared full as forward as the Baharnagash to complete it. Isaac ceded Dobarwa to the basha, and put him into immediate possession of it, and all the low country between that and Masuah. By this acquisition, the Turks, before masters of the sea-coast, became possessed of the whole of the flat country corresponding thereto, as far as the mountains. Dobarwa is a large trading town, situated in a country abounding with provisions of all kinds which Masuah wanted, and it was the key of the province of Tigré and the high land of Abyssinia.

Menas, at his accession, had received kindly the compliments of congratulation made by the Portuguese patriarch, Oviedo. But hearing that he still continued to preach, and that the effect of this was frequent divisions and animosities among the people, he called him into his presence, and strictly commanded him to desist, which the patriarch positively refusing, the king lost all patience, and fell violently upon him, beating him without mercy, tearing his clothes and beard, and taking his chalice from him, that he might prevent him from saying mass. He then banished him to a desert mountain, together with Francis Lopez, where for seven months he endured all manner of hardships.

The king, in the mean time, published many rigorous proclamations against the Portuguese. He would not permit them to marry with Abyssinians. Those that were already married he forbade to go to the Catholic churches with their husbands; and, having again called the patriarch into his prefence, he ordered him forthwith to leave his kingdom upon pain of death. But Oviedo, who feems to have had an ambition to be the proto-martyr, refufed abfolutely to obey thefe commands. He declared that the orders of God were thofe he obeyed, not the finful ordinances of man; and, letting flip his cloak from his fhoulders, he offered his bare neck to the king to ftrike. This anfwer and gefture fo incenfed Menas, that, drawing his fword, he would have very foon put the patriarch in poffeffion of the martyrdom he coveted, had it not been for the interpofition of the queen and officers that ftood round him.

OVIEDO, after having been again foundly beaten, was banifhed a fecond time to the mountain; and in this fentence were included all the reft of the Portuguefe priefts, as well as others. But the bifhop would not fubmit to this punifhment, but with the Portuguefe, his countrymen, joined the Baharnagafh, who had already completed his treaty with Samur Bafha.

ISAAC, before the Portuguefe priefts, had fhewn a defire of becoming Catholic, and of protecting, or even embracing, their religion; and they, on their part, had affured him of a powerful and fpeedy fuccour from India, which was juft what he wanted; and with this view he had placed himfelf to the greateft advantage, avoiding a battle, and awaiting thofe auxiliaries, of the arrival of which the king was very apprehenfive. But the feafon of fhips coming from India had paffed without any appearance of Portuguefe, and the king was refolved to try his fortune without expecting what another feafon might produce. On the other hand, Ifaac, ftrengthened by his league with the bafha, thought himfelf

himfelf in a condition to take the field, rather than to leffen his reputation by conftantly declining battle.

In thefe difpofitions both armies met, and the confederates were again beaten by the king, with very little lofs or refiftance. This battle was fought on the 20th of April 1562. Immediately after this victory the king marched to Shoa, and fent feveral detachments of his army before him to furprife the robbers called Dobas, and drive off their cattle. What he intended by retiring fo far from his enemies, the Baharnagafh and Bafha, is what we do not know. Both of them were yet alive, but probably fo weakened by their laft defeat as to leave no apprehenfions of being able to moleft the country by any incurfions.

The king, being advanced into the province of Ogge, was taken ill of the Kolla, or low-country fever, and, after a few days illnefs, he died there on the 13th of January 1563, leaving three fons, Sertza Denghel, who fucceeded him, Tafcar, and Lefana Chriftos.

Some European hiftorians * have advanced that Menas was defeated and flain in this laft engagement juft now mentioned. This, however, is exprefsly contradicted in the annals of thefe times, which mention the death of the king in the terms I have here related; nor were either of the chiefs of the rebels, the Bafha or Baharnagafh, flain that day. The rebellion ftill continued, Ifaac having proclaimed a prince of the name of John to be king in place of Tafcar, his deceafed brother.

Menas

---

* Ludolf, lib. 2. cap. 6.

Menas was a prince of a very morose and violent dispo-sition, but very well adapted to the time in which he lived; brave in his person, active and attentive to the affairs of government. He was sober, and an enemy to all sorts of pleasure; frugal, and, in his dress or stile of living, little different from any soldier in his army.

These qualities made him feared by the great, without being beloved by the common soldiers accustomed to the liberality and magnificence of Claudius; and this want of popularity gave the Romish priests an opportunity to blacken his character beyond what in truth he deserved. Thus, they say, that he had changed his religion during his imprison-ment, and turned Mahometan, and that it was from the Moors he learned that ferocity of manners. But to this the answer is easy, That the manners of his own countrymen, that is of mountaineers without any profession but war and blood, in which they had been exercised for centuries, were, pro-bably of themselves, much more fierce and barbarous than any he could learn among the people of Adel, occupied from time immemorial in commerce and the pursuit of riches, and necessarily engaged in an honest intercourse, and practice of hospitality, with all the various nations that tra-ded with them. Besides, were this otherwise, he never had any society with these Moors. Banishment to the top of a mountain* would have been his fate in Abyssinia, had he lived a few years earlier or later than he did. Yet the mountain upon which the royal family was confined had not yet produced one of such savage manners; and it is not

probable

* To Geshen or Wechné.

probable that he was more ſtrictly guarded in Adel than he would have been in his own country.

As to his religion, we can only ſay that he abhorred the Romiſh faith, from the behaviour of thoſe that profeſſed it; and, that he had abundant reaſon ſo to do, we need only appeal to their conduct in the preceding reign, according to the accounts given by the Catholics themſelves. Let any man conſider a king ſuch as Claudius was; ſeated on his throne in the midſt of his courtiers and captains; curſed and excommunicated; called heretic and liar to his face by an ignorant peaſant and ſtranger, ſuch as John Bermudes; attacked in the night, and forced to fly for his life by·a body of ſtrangers who depended upon him for their daily bread: Next conſider Menas, at his firſt acceſſion, deſiring their patriarch to deſiſt from preaching a religion that was fatal to the quiet of his kingdom by ſowing diſſentions among it as it had done in the two preceding reigns; and then figure a fanatic prieſt, declaring that he would neither depart nor obey theſe orders; then ſay what would have been done to ſtrangers in France, Spain, or Portugal, that had behaved in this manner to the ſovereign or miniſters of theſe countries. Add to this, that all the Portugueſe to a man appeared in the army of a rebel ſubject in the laſt battle, ſupporting the cauſe of a pretender to his crown. If, upon a fair review of all this, it is any matter of ſurpriſe that he ſhould be averſe to ſuch people and behaviour, I am no judge of the fair feelings of man, and the duty a prince owes to himſelf or poſterity, his country or dignity.

As to his inclination to the Mahometan religion, the fact is, that he oppoſed it even with his ſword during his whole reign, and never fwerved from his attachment to the church of Alexandria, or his friendfhip and refpect to the Abuna Youfef, to the end of his life, as far as we can learn from hiftory. And leaft, of all people in the world, does it become the Roman Catholics to accufe him of being Mahometan, becaufe a letter is ftill extant to Menas from pope Paul III *, wherein the pope ftiles him beloved *fon in Chrift*, and the *moft holy of priefts*.

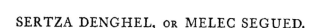

SERTZA DENGHEL, or MELEC SEGUED.

From 1563 to 1595.

King crowned at Axum—Abyffinia invaded by the Galla—Account of that People—The king defeats the Army of Adel—Beats the Falafha, and kills their King—Battle of the Mareb—Bafha flain, and Turks expelled from Dobarwa—King is poifoned—Names Za Denghel his Succeffor.

MENAS was fucceeded by his fon, Sertza Denghel, who took the name of Melec Segued. He was only twelve years old when he came to the throne, and was crowned at Axum with all the ancient ceremonies. The beginning of his

3

his reign was marked by a mutiny of his foldiers, who, joining themfelves to fome Mahometans, plundered the town, and then difbanded. A mifunderftanding alfo happened with Ayto Hamelmal, fon to Romana Werk, daughter of Hatzé Naod, which threatened many misfortunes in its confequences.

TECLA ASFADIN, governor of Tigré, was ordered by the king to march againft him; and the armies fought with equal advantage. But Hamelmal dying foon after, his party difperfed without further trouble. Fafil, too, his coufin, who had been appointed governor of Damot, rebelled foon after, and was defeated by the king, who this year (the fourth of his reign) commanded his army for the firft time in perfon, and greatly contributed to the victory, though he was but then fixteen years of age.

THE fixth year of his reign he marched againft a clan of Galla, called Azé, whom he often beat, ftaying in the country two whole years. Upon his return, he found the Baharnagafh, Ifaac and Harla, and other malcontents, when a fort of a pacification followed; and having received from the rebels confiderable prefents, he fat down at Dobi, a fmall town in Dembea, where he paffed the winter.

ALL this time Oviedo and the Portuguefe did not appear at court. The king, however, did not moleft the priefts in their baptifms, preachings, or any of their functions. He often fpake favourably of their moral characters, their fobriety, patience, and decency of their lives; but he condemned decifively the whole of their religious tenets, which he pronounced to be full of danger and contradiction, and deftructive ſtructive of civil order and monarchical government. At this period the Galla again made an irruption into Gojam.

It is now time we ſhould ſpeak of this nation, which has contributed more to weakening and reducing the Abyſſinian empire, than all their civil wars, and all the foreign enemies put together. When I ſpoke of the languages of the ſeveral nations in Abyſſinia, I took occaſion merely to mention the origin of theſe Galla, and their progreſs northward, till their firſt hoſtile appearance in Abyſſinia. I ſhall now proceed to lay before the reader what further I have collected concerning them. Many of them were in the king's ſervice while I was in Abyſſinia; and, from a multitude of converſations I had with all kinds of them, I flatter myſelf I have gathered the beſt accounts regarding theſe tribes.

The Galla are a very numerous nation of Shepherds, who probably lived under or beyond the Line. What the cauſe of their emigration was we do not pretend to ſay with certainty, but they have, for many years, been in an uniform progreſs northward. They were at firſt all infantry, and ſaid the country they came from would not permit horſes to breed in it, as is the caſe in 13° north of the Line round Sennaar. Upon coming northward, and conquering the Abyſſinian provinces, and the ſmall Mahometan diſtricts bordering on them, they have acquired a breed of horſes, which they have multiplied ſo induſtriouſly that they are become a nation of cavalry, and now hold their infantry in very little eſteem.

As

As under the Line, to the fouth of Abyffinia, the land is exceedingly high, and the fun feldom makes its appearance on account of the continual rains, the Galla are confequently of a brown complexion, with long black hair. Some, indeed, who live in the valleys of the low country, are perfectly black. Although the principal food of this people at firft was milk and butter, yet, when they advanced into drier climates, they learned of the Abyffinians to plow and fow the fields, and to make bread. They feem to affect the number feven, and have divided their immenfe multitude threefold by that number. They all agree, that, when the nation advanced to the Abyffinian frontiers, they were then in the centre of the continent. The ground beginning to rife before them, feven of their tribes or nations filed off to the eaft towards the Indian Ocean ; and, after making fettlements there, and multiplying exceedingly, they marched forward due fouth into Bali and Dawaro, which they firft wafted by conftant incurfions, then conquered and fettled there in the reign of David III. in 1537.

ANOTHER divifion of feven tribes went off to the weft about the fame time, and fpread themfelves in another femicircle round the fouth fide of the Nile, and all along its banks round Gojam, and to the eaft behind the country of the Agows, (which are on the eaft fide of the Nile) to that of the Gongas and Gafats. The high woody banks of this river have hitherto been their barrier to the fouthward ; not but that they have often fought for, and often conquered, and ftill oftener plundered, the countries on the Abyffinian fide of that river; and, from this reign downwards, the fcene of action with the Abyffinians has conftantly been on the eaft fide of the river. All I mean is, they have never made a fet-

tlement

tlement on the Abyffinian fide of the Nile, except fuch tribes of them as, from wars among themfelves, have gone over to the king of Abyffinia and obtained lands on the banks of that river, oppofite to the nation they have revolted from, a-gainft which they have ever after been the fecureft bulwark.

A THIRD divifion of feven tribes remained in the center,, due fouth of the low country of Shoa ; and thefe are the leaft known, as having made the feweft incurfions. They have, indeed, poffeffed Walaka, a fmall province between Amhara and Shoa ; but this has been permitted politically by the governor of Shoa, as a barrier between him and A-byffinia, on whofe fovereign he fcarcely acknowledges any dependence but for form's fake, his province being at pre-fent an hereditary government defcending from father to fon.

ALL thefe tribes of Galla gird Abyffinia round at all points from eaft to weft, making inroads, and burning and murdering all that fall into their hands. The privities of the men they cut off, dry, and hang them up in their houfes. They are fo mercilefs as to fpare not even women with child, whom they rip up in hopes of deftroying a male. The weftern part of thefe Galla, which furrounds the pe-ninfula of Gojam and Damot, are called the Boren Galla ; and thofe that are to the eaft are named Bertuma Galla, though this laft word is feldom ufed in hiftory, where the Galla to the weftward are called Boren ; and the others Galla merely, without any other addition. All thefe tribes, though the moft cruel that ever appeared in any country, are yet governed by the ftricteft difcipline at home, where the fmalleft broil or quarrel among individuals is taken. cognizance of, and receives immediate punifhment.

Each of the three divifions of Galla elect a king, that is, there is a king for every feven tribes. There is alfo a kind of nobility among them, from whofe families alone the fovereign can be chofen. But there are certain degrees of merit (all warlike) that raife, from time to time, their plebeian families to nobility, and the right of fuffrage. No one of thefe nobles can be elected till paft forty years of age, unlefs he has flain with his own hand a number of men which, added to his years, makes up forty.

The council of each of the feven tribes firft meets feparately in its own diftrict : Here it determines how many are neceffary to be left behind for the governing, guarding, and cultivating the territory, while thofe fixed upon by moft votes go as delegates to meet the reprefentatives of the other nations at the domicil, or head-quarters of the king, among the tribe from which the fovereign of the laft feven years was taken. Here they fit down under a tree which feems to be facred, and the god of all the nations. It is called Wanzey*; has a white flower, and great quantity of foliage, and is very common in Abyffinia. After a variety of votes, the number of candidates is reduced to four, and the fuffrage of fix of thefe nations go then no farther ; but the feventh, whofe turn it is to have a king out of their tribe, choofe, from among the four, one, whom they crown with a garland of Wanzey, and put a fceptre, or bludgeon, of that wood in his hands, which they call Buco.

The

---

* See the article Wanzey in the Appendix.

THE king of the weſtern Galla is ſtiled Lubo, the other Mooty. At this aſſembly, the king allots to each their ſcene of murder and rapine ; but limits them always to ſpeedy returns in caſe the body of the nation ſhould have occaſion for them. The Galla are reputed very good ſoldiers for ſurpriſe, and in the firſt attack, but have not conſtancy or perſeverance. They accompliſh incredible marches ; ſwim rivers holding by the horſes tail, (an exerciſe to which both they and their horſes are perfectly trained ;)·do the utmoſt miſchief poſſible in the ſhorteſt time ; and rarely return by the ſame way they came. They are excellent light horſe for a regular army in an enemy's country.

IRON is very ſcarce among them, ſo that their principal arms are poles ſharpened at the end, and hardened in the fire, which they uſe like lances. Their ſhields are made of bulls hides of a ſingle fold, ſo that they are very ſubject to warp in heat, or become too pliable and ſoft in wet weather. Notwithſtanding theſe diſadvantages, the report of their cruelty made ſuch an impreſſion upon the Abyſſinians, that, on their firſt engagements they rarely ſtood firmly the Galla's firſt onſet. Beſides this, the ſhrill and very barbarous noiſe they are always uſed to make at the moment they charge, uſed to terrify the horſes and riders, ſo that a flight generally followed the attack made by Galla horſe.

THESE melancholy and frantic howls I had occaſion to hear often in thoſe engagements that happened while I was in Abyſſinia. The Edjow, a body of Galla who had been in the late king Joas's ſervice, and were relations to him by his mother, who was of that clan of ſouthern Galla, were conſtantly in the rebel army, and always in the moſt diſ-

affected

affected part, who, with the troops of Begemder and Lasta, attacked the king's houfehold, where he was in perfon; and, though they behaved with a bravery even to rafhnefs, moft of them loft their lives, upon the long pikes of the king's black horfe, without ever doing any notable execution, as thefe horfes were too-well trained to be at all moved with their fhrieks, when they charged, though their bravery and fidelity merited a better fate.

THE women are faid to be very fruitful. They do not confine themfelves even a day after labour, but wafh and return to their work immediately. They plow, fow, and reap. The cattle tread out the corn, but the men are the herdfmen, and take charge of the cattle in the fields.

BOTH fexes are fomething lefs than the middle fize, exceedingly light and agile. Both, but efpecially the men, plait their hair with the bowels and guts of oxen, which they wear likewife, like belts, twifted round their middle; and thefe, as they putrify, occafion a terrible ftench. Both copioufly anoint their heads and bodies with butter, or melted greafe, which is continually raining from them, and which indicates that they came from a country hotter than that which they now poffefs. They greatly refemble the Hottentots in this filthy tafte of drefs. The reft of their body is naked; a piece of fkin only covers them before; and they wear a goat's fkin on their fhoulders, in fhape of a woman's handkerchief, or tippet.

IT has been faid *, that no religion was ever difcovered
among

---

* Jerome Lobo Hift. of Abyffinia ap. Le Grande.

among them. I imagine that the facts upon which this o-
pinion is founded have never been fufficiently inveftigated.
The Wanzey-tree, under which their kings are crowned, is
avowedly worfhipped for a god in every tribe. They have
certain ftones alfo, for an object of their devotion, which I
never could fufficiently underftand to give further defcription of them. But they certainly pay adoration to the moon;
efpecially the new moon, for of this I have frequently
been a witnefs. They likewife worfhip certain ftars in particular pofitions, and at different times of the year, and are,
in my opinion, ftill in the ancient religion of Sabaifm.   All
of them believe that, after death, they are to live again;
that they are to rife with their body, as they were on
earth, to enter into another life they know not where, but
they are to be in a ftate of body infinitely more perfect
than the prefent, and are to die no more, nor fuffer grief,
ficknefs, or trouble of any kind. They have very obfcure, or
no ideas at all of future punifhment; but their reward is to
be a moderate ftate of enjoyment with the fame family and
perfons with which they lived on earth.   And this is very
nearly the fame belief with the other Pagan nations in A-
frica with which I have converfed intimately; and this is
what writers generally call a belief of the immortality of
the foul.   Nor did I ever know one favage that had a more
diftinct idea of it, or ever feparated it from the immortality
of the body.

THE Galla to the fouth are moftly Mahometans; on the
eaft and weft chiefly Pagans. They intermarry with each
other, but fuffer no ftrangers to live among them. The
Moors, however, by courage, patience, and attention, have
found out the means of trading with them in a tolerable
degree

degree of safety. The goods they carry are coarse Surat blue cloaths, called *marowty*; also myrrh and salt. This last is the principal and most valuable article.

THE Galla sometimes marry the Abyssinian women, but the issue of those marriages are incapable of all employment. Their form of marriage is the following: The bridegroom, standing before the parents of the bride, holds grafs in his right hand and the dung of a cow in his left. He then says, "May this never enter, nor this ever come out, " if he does not do what he promises;" that is, may the grafs never enter the cow's mouth to feed it, or may she die before it is discharged. Matrimonial vows, moreover, are very simple; he swears to his bride that he shall give her meat and drink while living, and bury her when dead.

POLYGAMY is allowed among them, but the men are commonly content with one wife. Such, indeed, is their moderation in this respect, that it is the women that solicit the men to increase the number of their wives. The love of their children seems to get a speedy ascendency over passion and pleasure, and is a noble part of the character of these savages that ought not to be forgot. A young woman, having a child or two by her husband, intreats and solicits him that he would take another wife, when she names to him all the beautiful girls of her acquaintance, especially those that she thinks likeliest to have large families. After the husband has made his choice, she goes to the tent of the young woman, and fits behind it in a supplicant posture, till she has excited the attention of the family within. She then, with an audible voice, declares who she is; that she is daughter of such a one; that her husband.

has·

has all the qualifications for making a woman happy; that she has only two children by him; and, as her family is so small, she comes to solicit their daughter for her husband's wife, that their families may be joined together, and be strong; and that her children, from their being few in number, may not fall a prey to their enemies in the day of battle; for the Galla always fight in families, whether against one another, or against other enemies.

When she has thus obtained a wife for her husband, she carries her home, puts her to bed with her husband, where, having left her, she feasts with the bride's relations. There the children of the first marriage are produced, and the men of the bride's family put each their hands upon these children's heads, and afterwards take the oath in the usual manner, to live and die with them as their own offspring. The children, then, after this species of adoption, go to their relations, and visit them for the space of seven days. All that time the husband remains at home in possession of his new bride; at the end of which he gives a feast, when the first wife is seated by her husband, and the young one serves the whole company. The first wife from this day keeps her precedence; and the second is treated by the first wife like a grown up-daughter. I believe it would be very long before the love of their families would introduce this custom among the young women of Britain.

When a father dies and leaves many children, the eldest succeeds to the whole inheritance without division; nor is he obliged, at any time, or by any circumstance, to give his brothers a part afterwards. If the father is alive when the son first begins to shave his head, which is a declaration of
manhood,

manhood, he gives two or three milk-cows, or more, according to his rank and fortune. Thefe, and all their produce, remain the property of the child to whom they were given by his father; and thefe the brother is obliged to pay to him upon his father's death, in the fame number and kinds. The eldeft brother, is moreover, obliged to give the fifter, whenever fhe is marriageable, whatever other provifion the father may have made in his lifetime for her, with all its increafe from the day of the donation.

WHEN the father becomes old and unfit for war, he is obliged to furrender his whole effects to his eldeft fon, who is bound to give him aliment, and nothing elfe; and, when the eldeft brother dies, leaving younger brothers behind him, and a widow young enough to bear children, the youngeft brother of all is obliged to marry her; but the children of the marriage are always accounted as if they were the eldeft brother's; nor does this marriage of the youngeft brother to the widow entitle him to any part of the deceafed's fortune.

THE fouthern Galla are called Elma Kilelloo, Elma Gooderoo, Elma Robali, Elma Doolo, Elma Bodena, Elma Horreta, and Elma Michaeli; thefe are the feven fouthern nations which the Mahometan traders pafs through in their way to Narea, the fouthernmoft country the Abyffinians ever conquered.

THE weftern Galla for their principal clans have the Djawi, Edjow or Ayzo, and Toluma, and thefe were the clans we principally fought with when I was in Abyffinia. They are chiefly Pagans. Some of their children, who were left young in court, when their fathers fled, after the murder of the late king their mafter, were better Chriftians and better foldiers than any Abyffinians we had.

It is not a matter of fmall curiofity to know what is their food, that is fo eafy of carriage as to enable them to traverfe immenfe deferts, that they may, without warning, fall up-on the towns and villages in the cultivated country of Abyf-finia. This is nothing but coffee roafted, till it can be pul-verifed, and then mixed with butter to a confiftency that will fuffer it to be rolled up in balls, and put in a leather bag. A ball of this compofition, between the circumfer-ence of a fhilling and half-a-crown, about the fize of a billiard-ball, keeps them, they fay, in ftrength and fpirits during a whole day's fatigue, better than a loaf of bread, or a meal of meat. Its name in Arabia and Abyffinia is Bun, but I apprehend its true name is Caffé, from Caffa the fouth province of Narea, whence it is firft faid to have come; it is white in the bean. The coffee-tree is the wood of the country, produced fpontaneoufly everywhere in great a-bundance, from Caffa to the banks of the Nile.

Thus much for this remarkable nation, whofe language is perfectly different from any in Abyffinia, and is the fame throughout all the tribes, with very little variation of dia-lect. This is a nation that has conquered fome of the fineft provinces of Abyffinia, and of whofe inroads we fhall here-after have occafion to fpeak continually; and it is very dif-ficult to fay how far they might not have accomplifhed the conqueft of the whole, had not providence interpofed in a manner little expected, but more efficacious than a thoufand armies, and all the inventions of man.

THE

THE Galla, before their inroads into Abyffinia, had never in their own country feen or heard of the fmall-pox. This difeafe met them in the Abyffinian villages. It raged among them with fuch violence, that whole provinces conquered by them became half-defert; and, in many places, they were forced to become tributary to thofe whom before they kept in continual fear. But this did not happen till the reign of Yafous the Great, at the beginning of the prefent century, where we fhall take frefh notice of it, and now proceed with what remains of the reign of Sertza Denghel, whom we left with his army in the 9th year of his reign, refiding at Dobit, a fmall town in Dembea, watching the motion of the rebels, Ifaac Baharnagafh, and others, his confederates.

THE tenth year of his reign, as foon as the weather permitted him, the king went into Gojam to oppofe the inroads of the Djawi, a clan of the weftern or Boren Galla, who then were in poffeffion of the Buco, or royal dignity, among the feven nations. But they had repaffed the Nile upon the firft news of the king's march, without having time to wafte the country. The king then went to winter in Bizamo, which is fouth of the Nile, the native country of thefe Galla, the Djawi.

IF this nation, the Galla, has deferved ill of the Abyffinians by the frequent inroads made into their country, they muft, however, confefs one obligation, that in the end they entirely ruined their ancient enemy, the Mahometan king of Adel, and reduced him to a ftat eof perfect infignificance.

THE

· Sertza Denghel then returned with his army into Dembea, where, finding the militia of that province much difaffected by communication with the Moorifh foldiers fettled among them from Gragnè's time to this day, and that moft of them had in their hearts forfaken the Chriftian religion, and were all ready to fail in their allegiance, he affembled the greateft part of them without their arms, and, furrounding them with his foldiers, cut them to pieces, to the number of 3000 men.

In the 13th year of his reign, Mahomet king of Adel marched out of his own country with the view of joining the Bafha and Baharnagafh. But the king, ever watchful over the motions of his enemies, furprifed the Baharnagafh before his junction either with Mahomet or the bafha, and defeated or difperfed his army, obliging him to fly in difguife, with the utmoft danger of being taken prifoner, to hide himfelf with the bafha at Dobarwa. He then appointed Darguta, governor of Tigré, an old and experienced officer, giving him the charge of the province, and to watch the bafha; and, leaving with him his wounded, (and in their place taking fome frefh foldiers from Darguta) he, by forced marches, endeavoured to meet Mahomet, who had not heard of his victory over Ifaac; and being informed that the king of Adel was encamped on the hither fide of the river Wali, having paffed it to join Ifaac, the king, by a fudden movement, croffed the river, and came oppofite to Mahomet's quarters, who was then ftriking his tents, having juft heard of the fate of the Baharnagafh. Mahomet and his whole army were ftruck with a panic at this unexpected appearance of the king on the oppofite fide of the river, which had cut off his retreat to Adel. Fearing, however,

however, there might still be an enemy behind him, and that he should be hemmed in between both, he resolved to pass, but did it in so tumultuous a manner that the king's army had no trouble but to slaughter those who arrived at the opposite bank. Great part of the cavalry, seeing the fate of their companions at the ford, attempted to pass above and below by swimming: but, though the river was deep and smooth, the banks were high, and many were drowned, not being able to scramble up on the other side. Many were also destroyed by stones, and the lances of Sertza Denghel's men, from the banks above; some passed, however, joining Mahomet, and leaving the rest of the army to attempt a passage at the ford, crossed with the utmost speed lower down the river without being pursued, and carried the news of their own defeat to Adel.

THE whole Moorish army perished this day except the horse, either by the sword or in the river; nor had the Moors received so severe a blow since the defeat of Gragné by Claudius. The king then decamped, and took post at Zarroder, on the frontiers of Adel, with a design to winter there and lay waste the country, into which he intended to march as soon as the fair weather returned. But it was the misfortune of this great prince, that his enemies were situated at the two most distant extremities of the kingdom. For the Galla attacked Gojam on the west, at the very time he prepared to enter Adel on the east. Without loss of time, however, he traversed the whole kingdom of Abyssinia, and came up with the Boren Galla upon the river Madge, but no action of consequence followed. The Galla, attempting the king's camp in the night, and finding themselves too weak to carry it, retreated immediately into their own country.
While

While returning to Dembea, he met a party of the Falasha, called Al a i, at Wainadega, and entirely destroyed them, so that not one escaped.

The king was now so formidable that no army of the enemy dared to face him, and he obliged the Falasha to give up their king Radaet, whom he banished to Wadge; and the four following years he spent in ravaging the country of his enemies the Galla, in Shat and Bed, and that of the Falasha in Samen and Serkè, where he beat Caliph king of the Falasha, who had succeeded Radaet.

The Galla, in advancing towards Gojam and Damot, had over-run the whole low country between the mountains of Narea and the Nile. The king, desirous to open a communication with a country where there was a great trade, especially for gold, crossed the Nile in his way to that province, the Galla flying everywhere before him. He was received with very great joy by the prince of that country, who looked upon him as his deliverer from those cruel enemies. Here he received many rich presents; more particularly a large quantity of gold, and he wintered at Cutheny in that province, where Abba Hedar his brother died, having been blown up with gun-powder, with his wife and children. The Nareans desired, this year, to be admitted to the Christian faith; and they were converted and baptised by a mission of priests sent by the king for that purpose.

At the time he was rescuing the kingdom of Narea, Cadward Basha, a young officer of merit and reputation, lately come from Constantinople to Dawaro as basha of Masuah, had begun his command with making inroads into Tigrè,

i   and

and driving off a number of the inhabitants into flavery. The king, neceffarily engaged at a diftance, fuffered thefe injuries with a degree of impatience ; and, after having provided for the fecurity of the feveral countries immediately near him, he marched with his army directly for Woggora, committing every degree of excefs in his march, in order to provoke the Falafha to defcend from their heights and offer him battle.

A FRUGAL œconomical people, fuch as the Jews are, could not bear to fee their cattle and crops deftroyed in fo wanton a manner before their very faces. They came, therefore, down in immenfe numbers to attack the king, one of the moft excellent generals Abyffinia ever had, at the head of a fmall, but veteran army. Gefhen, brother of the famous Gideon, was then king of the Jews, and commanded the army of his countrymen. The battle was fought on the plain of Woggora on the 19th of January 1594, with the fuccefs that was to be expected. Four thoufand of the Jewifh army were flain upon the fpot ; and, among them, Gefhen, their unfortunate king and leader.

AFTER this victory, Sertza Denghel marched his army into Kuara, through the country where the Jews had many ftrong-holds, and received everywhere their fubmiffion. Then turning to the left, he came through the country of the Shangalla, called Woombarea, and fo to that of the Agows. There he heard that new troubles were meditating in Damot ; but the inhabitants of that province were not yet ripe enough to break out into open rebellion.

v. ii. f f   THAT

THAT he might not, therefore, have two enemies at such a diftance from each other upon his hands at once, this year, as foon as the rains were over, he determined to march and attack the bafha. The bafha was very foon informed of his defigns, and as foon prepared to meet them; fo that the king found him already in the field, encamped on his own fide of the Mareb, but without having committed, till then, any act of hoftility. He marched out of his camp, and formed, upon feeing the royal army approach; leaving a fufficient field for the king to draw up in, if he fhould incline to crofs the river, and attack him.

THIS confident, rather than prudent conduct of the bafha, did not intimidate the king, who being ufed to improve every advantage coolly, and without bravado, embraced this very opportunity his enemy chofe to give him. He formed, therefore, on his own fide of the March, and paffed it in as good order as poffible, confidering it is a fwift ftream, and very deep at that feafon of the year. He halted feveral times while his men were in the water, to put them again in order, as if he had expected to be attacked the moment he landed on the other fide. The bafha, a man of knowledge in his profeffion, who faw this cautious conduct of the king, is faid to have cried out, " How unlike he is to what I have " heard of his father!" alluding to the general rafh beha- viour of the late king Menas whilft at the head of his army.

SERTZA DENGHEL having left all his baggage on the other fide, and paffed the river, drew up his army in the fame deliberate manner in which he had croffed the Mareb, and formed oppofite to the bafha; as if he had been acting un-

2

der

der him, and by his orders, availing himfelf with great attention of all the advantages the ground could afford him. The bafha, confident in the fuperior valour of his troops, thought, now he had got the king betwcen him and the river, that he would eafily that day finifh Sertza Denghel's life and reign.

THE battle began with the moft determined refolution and vigour on both fides. The Abyffinian foot drove back the Turkifh infantry; and the king, difmounting from his horfe, with his lance and fhield in his hand, and charging at their head, animated them to preferve that advantage. On the other hand, the bafha, who had foon put to flight part of the Abyffinian horfe with whom he had engaged, fell furioufly upon the foot commanded by the king, the Turks making a great carnage among them with their fabres, and the affair became but doubtful, when Robel, gentleman of the bed-chamber to the king, who commanded the pike-men on horfeback, part of the king's houfehold troops, feeing his mafter's danger, charged the Turkifh horfe where he faw the bafha in perfon, and, clearing his way, broke his pike upon an officer of the bafha who carried the ftandard immediately before him, and threw him dead at his feet. Being without other arms, he then drew the fhort crooked knife which the Abyffinians always carry in their girdle, and, pufhing up his horfe clofe before the bafha could recover from his furprife, he plunged it in his throat, fo that he expired inftantly. So unlooked-for a fpectacle ftruck a panic into the troops. The Turkifh horfe firft turned their backs, and a general route followed.

The bafha's body was carried upon a mule out of the field, and ftruck a terror into all the Mahometans wherever it paffed. It no fooner entered Dobarwa than it was obliged to be carried out at the other end of the town. Sertza Denghel was not one that flumbered upon a victory. He entered Dobarwa fword in hand, putting all the Pagans and Mahometans that fell in his way to death, and, in this manner, purfued them to the frontiers of Mafuah, leaving many to die for want of water in that defert.

The king, in honour of this brave action performed by Robel, ordered what follows to be writ in letters of gold; and inferted in the records of the kingdom : " Robel, fer-
" vant to Sertza Denghel, and fon to Menetcheli, flew a Turk-
" ifh bafha on horfeback with a common knife."

Sertza Denghel, having thus delivered himfelf from the moft formidable of his enemies, marched through Gojam again into Narea, extirpating, all the way he went, the Galla that obftructed his way to that ftate. He left an additional number of priefts and monks to inftruct them in the Chriftian religion; though there are fome hiftorians of this reign who pretend that it was not till this fecond vifit that Narea was converted.

However this may be, victory had everywhere attended his fteps, and he was now preparing to chaftife the malcontents at Damot, when he was accofted by a prieft, famous for his holinefs and talent for divination, who warned him not to undertake that war. But the king, expreffing his contempt of both the meffage and meffenger, declared his fixed refolution to invade Damot without delay.
                                                                    The

The prieſt is ſaid to have limited his advice ſtill further, and to have only begged him to remember not to eat the fiſh of a certain river in the territory of Giba in the province of Shat. The king, however, fluſhed with his victory over the Boren Galla, forgot the name of the river and the injunction; and, having ate fiſh out of this river, was immediately after taken dangerouſly ill, and died on his return.

THE writer of his life ſays, that the fatal effects of this river were afterwards experienced in the reign of Yaſous the Great, at the time in which he wrote, when the king's whole army, encamped along the ſides of this river, were taken with violent ſickneſs after eating the fiſh caught in it, and that many of the ſoldiers died. Whether this be really fact or not, I will not take upon me to decide. Whether fiſh, or any other animal, living in water impregnated with poiſonous minerals, can preſerve its own life, and yet imbibe a quantity of poiſon ſufficient to deſtroy the men that ſhould eat it, ſeems to me very doubtful. Something like this is ſaid to happen in oyſters, which are found on copperas beds, or have preparations of copperas thrown upon them to tinge a part of them with green. I do not, however, think it likely, that the creature would live after this metallic doſe, or preſerve a taſte that would make it food for man till he accumulated a quantity ſufficient to deſtroy him.

SERTZA DENGHEL was of a very humane affable diſpoſition, very different from his father Menas. He was ſtedfaſt in his adherence to the church of Alexandria, and ſeemed perfectly indifferent as to the Romiſh church and clergy. In converſation, he frequently condemned their tenets, but always commended the ſobriety and ſanctity of their lives.

G g 2   He

He left no legitimate fons, but many daughters by his wife Mariam Sena ; and two natural fons, Za Mariam and Jacob. He had alfo a nephew called *Za Denghel*, fon of his brother Lefana Chriftos.

It is abfolutely contrary to truth, what is faid by Tellez and others, that the illegitimate fons have no right to fucceed to the crown. There is, indeed, no fort of difference, as may be feen by many examples in the courfe of this hiftory.

Sertza Denghel at firft feemed to have intended his nephew, Za Denghel, to fucceed him, a prince who had every good quality ; was arrived at an age fit for governing, and had attended him and diftinguifhed himfelf in great part of his wars. But, being upon his death-bed, he changed his mind, probably at the inftigation of the queen and the ambitious nobles, who defired to have the government in their own hands during a long minority. His fon Jacob, a boy of feven years old, was now brought into court, and treated as heir-apparent, which everybody thought was but natural and pardonable from the affection of a father.

At laft when he found that he was fick to death, the intereft and love of his country feemed to overcome even the ties of blood ; fo that, calling his council together around his bed, he defigned his fucceffor in this laft fpeech : ' As ' I am fenfible I am at the point of death, next to the care of ' my foul, I am anxious for the welfare of my kingdom. My ' firft idea was to appoint Jacob my fon to be fucceffor ; and ' I had done fo unlefs for his youth, and it is probable nei- ' ther you nor I could have caufe to repent it. Confidering,

2   ' however,

'however, the state of my kingdom, I prefer its interest to
' the private affection I bear my son ; and do, therefore, here-
' by appoint Za Denghel my nephew to succeed me, and be
' your king ; and recommend him to you as fit for war, ripe
' in years, exemplary in the practice of every virtue, and
' as deserving of the crown by his good qualities, as he is by
' his near relation to the royal family.' And with these words
the king expired in the end of August 1595, and was buried
in the island Roma.

As soon as Sertza Denghel died, the nobility resumed
their former resolutions. The very reasons the dying king
had given them, why Za Denghel was fitted to reign, were
those for the which they were determined to reject him ; as
they, after so long a reign as the last, were perfectly weary
at being kept in their duty, and desired nothing more than
an infant king and a long minority : this they found in
Jacob.

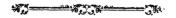

Z A

ZA DENGHEL.

From 1595 to 1604.

*Za Denghel dethroned—Jacob a Minor succeeds—Za Denghel is resto-
red—Banishes Jacob to Narea—Converted to the Romish Religion—
Battle of Bartcho, and Death of the King.*

SERTZA DENGHEL had several daughters, one of whom
was married to Kefla Wahad, governor of the province
of Tigrè, and another to Athanasius, governor of Amhara.
These two were the most powerful men then in the kingdom.
The empress and her two sons-in-law saw plainly, that the
succession of Za Denghel, a man of ripe years, possessed of
every requisite for reigning, was to exclude them from any
share in government but a subaltern one, for which they
were to stand candidates upon their own merits, in common
with the rest of the nobility.

ACCORDINGLY, no sooner was Sertza Denghel dead, perhaps
some time before, but a conspiracy was formed to change
the order of succession, and this was immediately executed
by order of this triumvirate, who sent a body of soldiers
and seized Za Denghel, and carried him close prisoner to

4   Dek,

Dek, a large ifland in the lake Tzana, belonging to the queen, where he was kept for fome time, till he efcaped and hid himfelf in the wild inacceffible mountains of Gojam, which there form the banks of the Nile. They carried their precautions ftill further; and fubfequent events after fhewed, that thefe were well-grounded. They fent a party of men at the fame time to furprife Socinios, but he, fufficiently upon his guard, no fooner faw the fate of his coufin, Za Denghel, than he withdrew himfelf, but in fuch a manner that fhewed plainly he knew the value of his own pretenfions, and was not to be an unconcerned fpectator if a revolution was to happen.

In order to underftand perfectly the claims of thofe princes, who were by turns placed on the throne in the bloody war that followed, it will be neceffary to know that the emperor David III. had three fons: The eldeft was Claudius, who fucceeded him in the empire; the hiftory of whofe reign we have already given: The fecond was Jacob, who died a minor before his brother, but left two fons, Tafcar and Facilidas: The third fon was Menas, called Adamas Segued, who fucceeded Claudius his brother in the empire; whofe reign we have likewife given in its proper place.

Menas had four fons; Sertza Denghel, called Melec Segued, who fucceeded his father in the empire, and whofe hiftory we have juft now finifhed; the fecond Aquieter; the third Abatè; and the fourth, Lefana Chriftos; whofe fon was that Za Denghel of whom we were laft fpeaking, appointed to fucceed to the throne by his uncle Sertza Denghel, when on his death-bed.

Tascar

Tascar, the fon of Jacob, died a minor; he rebelled a-
gainſt his uncle Menas, in confederacy with the Baharnagaſh, as we have already ſeen; and his army being beat by
his uncle and fovereign, he was, by his order, thrown over
the ſteep precipice of Lamalmon, and daſhed to pieces. Facilidas, the ſecond remaining fon of the fame minor Jacob,
lived many years, poſſeſſed great eſtates in Gojam, and died
afterwards in battle, fighting againſt the Galla, in defence
of theſe poſſeſſions.

This Facilidas had a natural fon named Socinios, who
inherited his father's poſſeſſions; was nephew to Sertza Denghel, and coufin-german to Za Denghel appointed to fucceed to the throne; fo that Za Denghel being once removed, as Jacob had been poſtponed, there could be no doubt
of Socinios's claim as the neareſt heir-male to David III.
commonly called Wanag Segued.

Socinios, from his infancy, had been trained to arms,
and had undergone a number of hardſhips in his uncle's
wars. Part of his eſtate had been feized, after his father's
death, by men in power, favourites of Sertza Denghel; and
he hoped for a complete reſtitution of them from Za Denghel his coufin, when he ſhould fucceed, for theſe two were
as much connected with each other by friendſhip and affection, as they were by blood. Nor would any ſtep, fays the
hiſtorian, have ever been taken by Socinios towards mounting the throne, had Za Denghel his coufin fucceeded, as by
right he ought.

In

In the mean time, he was at the head of a confiderable band of foldiers; had affifted Faïa Chriftos, governor of Go-jam, in defeating the Galla, who had over-run that province; and, by his courage and conduct that day, had left a ftrong impreffion upon the minds of the troops that he would foon become the moft capable and active foldier of his time.

The queen and her two fons-in-law being difappointed in their attempt upon Socinios, were obliged to take the on-ly ftep that remained in their choice, which was to appoint the infant Jacob * king, a child of feven years old, and put him under the tutelage of Ras Athanafius.

The emprefs Mariam Sena, and her two fons-in-law, had gained to their party Za Selaffé, a perfon of low birth, na-tive of an obfcure nation of Pagans, called Guraguè, a man efteemed for bravery and conduct, and beloved by the fol-diers; but turbulent and feditious, without honour, grati-tude, or regard, either to his word, to his fovereign, or the interefts of his country.

Jacob had fuffered patiently the direction of thofe that governed him, fo long as the excufe of his minority was a good one. But being now arrived at the age of 17, he began to put in, by degrees, for his fhare in the direction of affairs; and obferving fome fteps that tended to prolong the govern-ment of his tutors, by his own power he banifhed Za Selaf-fé, the author of them, into the diftant kingdom of Narea.

Vol. II.   H h   This

---

* The name of infant-king feems to have been given as a nick-name in Abyffinia, and is pre-ferved to this day.

This vigorous proceeding alarmed the emprefs and her party. They faw that the meafure taken by Jacob would prefently lead all good men and lovers of their country to fupport him, and to annihilate their power. They refolved not to wait till this took place, but inftantly to reftore Za Denghel, whom, with great difficulty, they found hid in the mountains between Gojam and Damot. And, to remove every fufpicion in Za Denghel's breaft, Ras Athanafius repaired to the palace, giving Jacob publicly, even on the throne, the moft abufive and fcurrilous language, calling him an obftinate, ftubborn, foolifh boy; declaring him degraded from being king, and announcing to his face the coming of Za Denghel to fupplant him. Jacob's behaviour on fo unexpected an occafion was not fuch as Athanafius's rafh fpeech led to expect. He gave a cool and mild reply to thefe invectives; but, finding himfelf entirely in his enemy's power, without lofing a moment, he left his palace in the night, taking the road to Samen, not doubting of fafety and protection if he could reach his mother's relations among thofe high, rocky mountains.

Fortune at firft feemed to favour his endeavours. He arrived at a fmall village immediately in the neighbourhood of the country to which he was going; but there he was difcovered and made prifoner; carried back and delivered to Za Denghel his rival, whom he found placed on his throne.

In all thefe cafes, it is the invariable, though barbarous practice of Abyffinia, to mutilate any fuch pretender to the throne, by cutting off his nofe, ear, hand, or foot, as they fhall be inclined the patient fhould die or live after the oper-

2   ation,

ation, it being an eftablifhed law, that no perfon can fucceed to the throne, as to the priefthood, without being perfect in all his limbs. Za Denghel, as he could not adopt fo
inhuman a procedure even with a rival, contented himfelf
with only banifhing Jacob to Narea.

EVER fince that period of Menas's reign, when Samur, bafha of Mafuah, had been put in poffeffion of Dobarwa in virtue of a treaty with Ifaac Baharnagafh, then in
rebellion, the Catholic religion was left deftitute of all fupport, the fathers that had remained in Abyffinia being dead,
and the entry into that kingdom fhut up by the violent animofity of the Turks, and the cruelties they exercifed upon all
miffionaries that fell into their hands. The few Catholics
that remained were abfolutely deprived of all affiftance,
when Melchior Sylvanus, an Indian vicar of the church of
St Anne at Goa, was pitched upon as a proper perfon to be
fent to their relief. His language, colour, eaftern air and
manners, feemed to promife that he would fucceed, and
baffle the vigilance of the Turks.

HE arrived at Mafuah in 1597, and entered Abyffinia un-
fufpected; but the power of the Turk being much leffened
by the great defeat given them by Sertza Denghel, who flew
Cadward Bafha, and retook Dobarwa and all its dependencies,
as has been already mentioned, a very confiderable part of
their former dangers, the miffionaries might now hope to
efcape. But there ftill remained others obftructing the communication with India, which, however, were furmount-
able, and gave way, as moft of the kind do, to prudence,
courage, and perfeverance.

ACCORDINGLY,

Accordingly, in the year 1600, Peter Paez, the moft capable, as well as moft fuccefsful miffionary that ever entered Ethiopia, arrived at Mafuah, after having fuffered a long imprifonment, and many other hardfhips, on his way to that ifland; and, taking upon him the charge of the Portuguefe, relieved Melchior Sylvanus, who returned to India.

Paez, however, did not prefs on to court as his predeceffors, and even his fucceffors conftantly did, but, confining himfelf to the convent of Fremona in Tigré, he firft fet himfelf by an invincible application to attain the knowledge of the Geez written language, in which he arrived to a degree of knowledge fuperior to that of the natives themfelves. He then applied to the inftruction of youth, keeping a fchool, where he taught equally the children of the Portuguefe, and thofe of the Abyffinians. The great progrefs made by the fcholars fpeedily fpread abroad the reputation of the mafter. Firft of all, John Gabriel, one of the moft diftinguifhed officers of the Portuguefe, fpoke of him in the warmeft terms of commendation to Jacob, then upon the throne, who fent to Paez, and ordered his attendance as foon as the rainy feafon fhould be over.

In the month of April 1604, Peter, attended only by two of his young difciples, prefented himfelf to the king, who then held his court at Dancaz, where he was received with the fame honours as are beftowed upon men of the firft rank, to the great difcontent of the Abyffinian monks, who eafily forefaw that their humiliation would certainly follow this exaltation of Petros; nor were they miftaken. In a difpute held before the king next day, Peter produced the two boys, as more than fufficient to filence all the theologians

in

in Abyffinia. Nor can it ever be doubted, by any who know the ignorance of thefe brutifh priefts, but that the victory, in thefe fcholaftic difputes, would be fairly, eafily, and completely on the fide of the children.

Mass was then faid according to the ufage of the church of Rome, which was followed by a fermon (among the firft ever preached in Abyffinia,) but fo far furpaffing, in elegance and purity of diction, any thing yet extant in the learned language, Geez, that all the hearers began to look upon this as the firft miracle on the part of the preacher.

Za Denghel was fo taken with it, that, from that inftant, he not only refolved to embrace the Catholic religion, but declared this his refolution to feveral friends, and foon after to Paez himfelf, under an oath of fecrecy that he fhould conceal it for a time. This oath, prudently exacted from Peter, was as imprudently rendered ufelefs by the zeal of the king himfelf, who being of too fanguine a difpofition to temporize after he was convinced, publifhed a proclamation, forbidding the religious obfervation of Saturday, or the Jewifh fabbath, for ever after. He likewife ordered letters to be wrote to the pope Clement VIII. and to Philip III. king of Spain and Portugal, wherein he offered them his friendfhip, whilft he requefted mechanics to affift, and Jefuits to inftruct his people.

These fudden and violent meafures were prefently known; and every wretch that had, from other caufes, the feeds of rebellion fown in his heart, began now to pretend they were only nourifhed there by a love and attachment to the true religion.

Many

MANY of the courtiers followed the king's example; fome as courtiers for the fake of the king's favour, and meaning to adhere to the religion of Rome no longer than it was a fafhion at court, promoted their intereft, and expofed them to no danger; others, from their firm attachment to the king, the refolution to fupport him as their rightful fovereign, and a confidence in his fuperior judgment, and that he beft knew what was moft for the kingdom's advantage in its prefent diftracted ftate, and for the confirmation of his own power, fo intimately connected with the welfare of his people. Few, very few it is believed, adopted the Catholic faith, from that one difcourfe only, however pure the language, however eloquent the preacher. A hundred years and more had paffed without convincing the Abyffinians in general, or without any material proof that they were prepared to be fo.

HOWEVER, the Jefuits have quoted an inftance of this inftantaneous converfion by the fermon, which, for their credit, I will not omit, though no notice is taken of it in the annals of thofe times, where it is not indeed to be expected, nor do I mean that it is lefs credible on this account.

AN Abyffinian monk, of very advanced years, came forward to Peter Paez, and faid in a loud voice before the king, " Although I have lived to a very great age, without a doubt of the Alexandrian faith, I blefs God that he has fpared me to this day, and thereby given me an opportunity of choofing a better. The things we knew before, you have fo well explained, that they become ftill more intelligible; and we are thereby confirmed in our belief. Thofe things that were difficult, and which we could hardly underftand, you have

have made so clear, that we now wonder at our own blindness in not having seen them plainly before. For these benefits which I now confess to have received, I here make my declaration, that it is my stedfaft purpose, with the affistance of Almighty God, to live and die in the faith you profess, and have now preached."

Among those of the court most attached to the king was Laeca Mariam, the inseparable companion of his good and bad fortune, who had followed his master from principles of duty and affection, without designing to throw away a confideration upon what were likely to be the confequences to himself. He was reputed, in his character and abilities as a foldier, to be equal to Za Selaffé, but a very different man, compared to him in his qualities of civil life; for he was fober in his general behaviour, fparing in difcourfe, and much more ready to do a good office than to promife one; very affable and courteous in his manner, and of fo humble and unaffuming a deportment, that it was thought impoffible to be real in a man, who had fo often proved his fuperiority over others upon trial.

This man, a true royalist, was one of thofe that embraced the Catholic religion that day, probably following the example of the king; and this, in the hands of wicked men their enemies, became very foon a pretence for the murder of both; for Za Selaffé, impatient of a rival in any thing, more efpecially in military knowledge, began to hold feditious affemblies, and efpecially with the monks, whom he taught to believe what the king's conduct daily confirmed, that the Alexandrian faith was totally reprobated, and no
religion

religion would be tolerated but that of the church of Rome.

Gojam, a province always inveterate againft any thing that bore the fmalleft inclination to the church of Rome, declared againft the king; and, before he went to join his affociates, the traitor, Za Selaffé, in a conference he had with the Abuna Petros, propofed to him to abfolve Za Denghel's fubjects and foldiers from their oaths of allegiance to their fovereign.   The Abuna, a man of very corrupt and bad life, very hearty in the caufe, and an enemy to the king, was ftaggered at this propofal; not that he was averfe to it, be-caufe it might do mifchief, but becaufe he doubted whether any fuch effect would follow it as Za Selaffé expected; and he, therefore, afked what good he expected from fuch a novelty? when this traitor affured him, that it would be moft efficacious for that very reafon, becaufe it was then firft introduced: the Abuna forthwith abfolved the foldiers and fubjects of Za Denghel from their allegiance, declaring the king excommunicated and accurfed, together with all thofe that fhould fupport him, or favour his caufe.

I must here obferve, that, though we are now writing the hiftory of the 17th century, this was the firft example of any prieft excommunicating his fovereign in Abyffinia, ex-cept that of Honorius, who excommunicated Amda Sion for the repeated commiffion of inceft.   And the doubt the zea-lot Abuna Petros had of its effect as being a novelty, which fact the Jefuits themfelves atteft, fhews it was a practice that had not its origin in the church of Alexandria. Neither had thefe curfes of the Abuna any vifible effect, till Za Selaffé had put himfelf at the head of an army raifed in Gojam.

The

The king was prepared to meet him, and ready to march from Dancaz.

Za Denghel immediately marched out into the plain of Bartcho, and in the way was deserted, first by Ras Athanasius, then by many of his troops; and, by this great desertion in his army, found the first effects of the Abuna's curses, insomuch, that John Gabriel, a Portuguese officer of the first distinction, advised the king to retire in time, and avoid a battle, by flying to strong-holds for a season, till the present delusion among his subjects should cease. But the king, thinking himself dishonoured by avoiding the defiance of a rebel, resolved upon giving Za Selassè battle, who, being an able general, knew well the danger he would incur by delay.

It was October 13th 1704 that the king, after drawing up his army in order of battle, placing 200 Portuguese, with a number of Abyssinian troops, on the right, took to himself the charge of the left, and called for Peter Paez to give him absolution; but that Jesuit was occupied at a convenient distance in Tigré, by his exorcisms destroying ants, butterflies, mice, locusts, and various other enemies, of much more importance, in his opinion, than the life of a king who had been blindly, but directly conducted to slaughter by his fanatical preachings.

The battle began with great appearance of success. On the right, the Portuguese, led by old and veteran officers, destroyed and overturned every thing before them with their fire-arms: but on the left, where the king commanded, things went otherwise, for the whole of this division fled, excepting a body of nobility, his own officers and companions, who remained with him, and fought manfully in his defence. Above all, the king himself, trained to a degree of excellence in the use of arms, strong and agile in body, in the flower of his age, and an excellent horseman, performed feats of valour that seemed above the power of man : but he and his attendants being surrounded by the whole army of Za Selaffé, and decreasing in number, were unable to support any longer such difadvantage.

L'AECA MARIAM, folicitous only for the king's fafety, charging furioufly every one that approached, was thruft through with a lance by a common foldier who had approached him unobferved. The king, defirous only to avenge his death, threw himfelf like lightning into the oppofite fquadron, and received a ftroke with a lance in his breaft, which threw him from his horfe on the ground. Grievous as the wound was, he inftantly recovered himfelf, and, drawing his fword, continued to fight with as much vigour as ever. He was now hemmed in by a ring of foldiers, part of whom, afraid of encountering him, remained at a diftance, throwing miffile weapons without good direction or ftrength, as if they had been hunting fome fierce wild beaft. Others, wifhing to take him prifoner, abftained from ftriking him, out of regard to his character and dignity; but the traitor, Za Selaffé, coming up at that inftant, and feeing the king almoft fainting with fatigue, and covered with wounds, pointed his lance, and, fpurring his horfe, furioufly ftruck him in the middle of the forehead, which blow threw the king fenfelefs to the ground, where he was afterwards flain with many wounds.

THE

THE battle ended with the death of Za Denghel; many saw him fall, and more his body after the defeat; but no one chose to be the first that should in any way difpofe of it, or care to own that they knew it. It lay in this abject ftate for three days, till it was buried by three peafants in a corner of the plain, in a little building like a chapel (which I have feen) not above fix feet high, under the fhade of a very fine tree, in Abyffinia called *faffa*: there it lay till ten years after, when Socinios removed it from that humble maufoleum, and buried it in a monaftery called Daga, in the lake Dembea, with great pomp and magnificence.

THE grief which the death of Za Denghel occafioned was fo univerfal, and the odium it brought upon the authors of it fo great, that neither Za Selaffé nor Ras Athanafius dared for a time take one ftep towards naming a fucceffor, which the fear of Za Denghel, and the uncertainty of victory, had prevented them from doing by common confent before the battle.   There was no doubt but that the election would fall upon Jacob, but he was far off, confined in the mountainous country of Caffa in Narea.   The diftance was great; the particular place uncertain; the way to it lay through deferts, always dangerous on account of the Galla, and often im-paffable.

JACOB.

JACOB.

From 1604 to 1605.

Makes Proposals to Socinios, which are rejected—Takes the Field—Bad Conduct and Defeat of Za Selassé—Battle of Debra Zeit—Jacob defeated and slain.

DURING the interim, Socinios appeared in Amhara, not as one offering himself as a candidate to be supported by the strength and interest of others, but like a conqueror at the head of a small but well-disciplined army of veteran troops, ready to compel by force those who should refuse to swear allegiance to him from conviction of his right.

THE first step he took was to send Bela Christos, a nobleman of known worth, to Ras Athanasius then in Gojam, stating to him his pretensions to succeeding Za Denghel in the kingdom, desiring his assistance with his army, and declaring that he would acknowledge the service done him as soon as it was in his power. Without waiting for an answer, at the head of his little army he passed the Nile, and entered Gojam. He then sent a second message to Ras Athanasius, acquainting him that he was at hand, and ordering him to prepare to receive him as his sovereign.

THIS

This abrupt and confident conduct of Socinios very much disconcerted Ras Athanasius. He had as yet concerted nothing with his friend Za Selaffé, and it was now late to do it. There was no person then within the bounds of the empire that solicited the crown but Socinios, and he was now at hand, and very much favoured by the soldiers. For these reasons, he thought it best to put a good face upon the matter in his present situation. He, therefore, met Socinios as required, and joined his army, as if it had been his free choice, and saluted him king in the midst of repeated chearful congratulations of both armies now united.

Having succeeded in this to his wish, Socinios lost no time to try the same experiment with Za Selaffé, who was then in Dembea, the province of which he was governor. To him he sent this message, " That God by his grace having called him to the throne of his anceftors, he was now on his march to Dembea, where he requested him to prepare his troops to receive him, and dispose them to deserve the favours that he was ready to confer upon all of them." Za Selaffé remained for a while as if thunder-struck by so peremptory an intimation. Of all masters he most wished for Jacob, because, from experience, he thought he could govern him. Of all masters he most feared Socinios, because he knew he possessed capacity and qualities that would naturally determine him to govern alone. After having concerted with his friends, he sent Socinios answer, " That not having till now known any thing of his claims or intentions, he had sent an invitation to Jacob into Narea, whose answer he expected ; but that, in case Jacob did not appear, he then would receive Socinios with every mark of duty and affection, and hoped he would grant him the

i   short

short delay to which he had inadvertently, though innocently, engaged himself."

This answer did in no shape please Socinios, who dispatched the messenger immediately with this declaration,
" That he was already king, and would never cede his right
to Jacob, who was deposed and judged unworthy to reign;
no nor even to his father Melec Segued, though he should
rise again from the grave, and claim the throne he had so
long sat upon."

Za Selasse, easily penetrating that there was no peace in
Socinios's intentions, first imprisoned the messenger, and, instead of another answer, marched instantly with his whole
army to surprise him before he had time to take his measures. And in this he succeeded. For Socinios being at
that instant overtaken by sickness, and not knowing what
trust to put in Athanasius's army, retired in haste to the
mountains of Amhara; while Athanasius also withdrew his
troops till he should know upon what terms he stood both
with Za Selassé and the king.

Still no return came from Jacob. The winter was nearly past, and not only the soldiers, but people of all ranks
began to be weary of this interregnum, and heartily wished
for their ancient form of government. They said, That
since Jacob did not appear, there could be no reason for ex-
cluding Socinios, whose title was undoubted, and who had
all the qualities necessary to make a good king.

Za Selasse seeing this opinion gained ground among his
troops, and fearing they might mutiny and leave him alone,

made

made a virtue of neceffity : he difpatched an ambaffador to acknowledge Socinios as his fovereign, and declare that he was ready to fwear allegiance to him. Socinios received this embaffy with great apparent complacency. He fent in return a monk, in whom he confided, a perfon of great worth and dignity, to be his reprefentative, and receive the homage of Za Selaffé and his army. On the news of this monk's approach, Za Selaffé fent on his part ten men, the moft refpectable in his camp, to meet this reprefentative of the king, and conduct him into the camp, where Za Saleffé, and all his troops, did homage, and fwore allegiance to Socinios. Feafts and prefents were now given in the camp, as is ufual at the acceffion of a new king to the throne, and all the army abandoned themfelves to joy.

THESE good tidings were immediately communicated both to Socinios and Ras Athanafius. But, in the midft of this rejoicing, a meffenger came from Jacob, informing Za Selaffé that he was then in Dembea ; that he had conferred upon him the title of Ras and Betwudet, that is, had made him the king's lieutenant-general throughout the whole empire. Za Selaffé, in poffeffion of the height of his wifhes, and making an ample diftribution among his troops, deter-mined immediately to march and join Jacob in Dembea ; but firft he wrote privately to the ten men that had accompa-nied the monk to Socinios, that they fhould withdraw them-felves as fuddenly and privately as poffible before the co-ming of Jacob was known. Eight of thefe were lucky e-nough to do fo ; two of them were overtaken in the flight and brought back to Socinios, who ordered them to imme-diate execution, .

RAS

Ras Athanasius, feeing the profperous turn that Jacob's affairs had taken, renounced his oath to Socinios, and repaired to Jacob at Coga, while Socinios retired into Amhara at the head of a very refpectable army, waiting an opportunity to repay Jacob for his ambition, and Athanafius and Za Selaffé for their treafon and perjury towards him.

Although Jacob was now again feated on the throne, furrounded by the army and great officers of the empire, his mind was always difturbed with the apprehenfion of Socinios. In order to free himfelf from this anxiety, he employed Socinios's mother in an application to her fon, with an offer of peace and friendfhip ; promifing, befides, that he would give him in property the kingdoms of Amhara, Walaka, and Shoa, and all the lands which his father had ever poffeffed in any other part of Abyffinia. Socinios fhortly anfwered, " That what God had given him, no man could take from him ; that the whole kingdom belonged to him, nor would he ever relinquifh any part of it but with his life. He advifed Jacob to confider this, and peaceably refign a crown which did not belong to him ; and the attempting to keep which, would involve him and his country in a fpeedy deftruction."

Upon this defiance, feeing Socinios implacable, Jacob took the field, and was followed by Za Selaffé. But this proud and infolent traitor, who never could confine himfelf within the line of his duty, even under a king of his own choofing, would not join his forces with Jacob, but vain-glorioufly led a feparate army, fubject to his orders alone. In this manner, having feparate camps, choofing different ground, and fometimes at a confiderable diftance from each other, they

they came up with Socinios in Begemder. Jacob advanced
so near him that his tent could be distinctly seen from that
of Socinios, and, on the morrow, Jacob and Za Selaffé, drawing up their armies, offered Socinios battle.

THAT wise prince saw too well that he was overmatched ;
and, though he defired a battle as much as Jacob, it was not
upon such terms as the present. He declined it, and kept
hovering about them as near as poffible on the heights and
uneven ground, where he could not be forced to fight till
it perfectly fuited his own intereft.

THIS refufal on the part of Socinios did but increafe Za
Selaffé's pride. He defpifed Jacob as a general, and thought
that Socinios declining battle was owing only to the apprehenfion he had of his prefence, courage, and abilities.
He continued parading with the feparate army, perfectly
intoxicated with confidence and an imaginary fuperiority,
neglecting all the wholefome rules of war rigidly adhered
to by great generals for the fake of difcipline, however diftant they may be from their enemy.

IT was not long before this was told Socinios, who foon
faw his advantage in it, and thereupon refolved to fight Za
Selaffé fingly, and watch attentively till he fhould find him
as far as poffible from Jacob. Nor did he long wait for the
occafion ; for Za Selaffé, attempting to lead his army through
very uneven and ftony ground, called *the Pafs of Mount De-*
fer, and at a confiderable diftance from Jacob, Socinios attacked him while in the pafs fo rudely, that his army, entangled in broken and unknown ground, was furrounded
and almoft cut to pieces. Za Selaffé, with a few followers,

faved

faved themfelves by the goodnefs of their horfes, and joined the king, being the firft meffengers of their own defeat.

Jacob received the news of this misfortune without
any apparent concern. On the contrary, he took Za Selaffé roundly to tafk for having loft fuch an army by his
mifconduct; and from that time put on a coolnefs of carriage towards him that could not be bruiked by fuch a character. He made direct propofals to Socinios to join him, if
he could be affured that his fervices would be well received.
Socinios, though he repofed no confidence in one that had
changed fides fo often, was yet, for his own fake, defirous to
deprive his rival of an officer of fuch credit and reputation
with the foldiers. He therefore promifed him a favourable
reception; and, a treaty being concluded, Socinios marched
into Gojam, followed by Jacob, and there was joined by Za
Selaffé whom Jacob had made governor of that province.

Jacob, not knowing how far this defertion might extend, and
to fhew Socinios the little value he fet upon his new acquifition,
immediately advanced towards him, and offered him battle..
This was what Socinios very earneftly wifhed for; but, as his
army was much inferior to Jacob's, he feemed to decline it
from motives of fear, till he had found ground proper for
his army to engage in with advantage.

Jacob, fenfible of the great fuperiority he had, (hiftorians
fay it was nearly thirty to one) grew every day more impatient to bring Socinios to an engagement, fearing he might
retreat, and thereby prolong the war, which he had no
doubt would be finifhed by the firft action. Therefore he

was

was anxious to keep him always in fight, without regarding the ground through which his eagerness led him. Several days the two armies marched fide by fide in fight of each other, till they came to Debra Tzait, or the Mountain of Olives. There Jacob halted; he then advanced a little further, and feeing Socinios encamped, he did the fame in a low and very difadvantageous poft on the banks of the river Lebart.

Socinios having now obtained his defire, early in the morning of the 10th of March 1607 fell fuddenly upon Jacob cooped up in a low and narrow place, which gave him no opportunity of availing himfelf of his numbers. Jacob foon found that he was over-reached by the fuperior generalfhip of his enemy. Socinios's troops were fo ftrongly pofted, that Jacob's foldiers found themfelves in a number of ambufhes they had not forefeen, fo that, fighting or flying being equally dangerous to them, his whole army was nearly deftroyed in the field, or in the flight, which was moft ardently and vigoroufly followed till night, with little lofs on the part of Socinios.

This battle, decifive enough by the route and difperfion of the enemy, became ftill more fo from two circum 'ances attending it: The firft was the death of his competitor, who fell unknown among a herd of common foldiers in the beginning of the action, without having performed, in his own perfon, any thing worthy of the character he had to fuftain, or that could enable any fpectator to give an account in what place he fell; the confequence of which was, that he was thought to be alive many years afterwards. The fecond was the death of the ALuna Petros. This prieft

K k 2   ha!

had diftinguifhed himfelf in Za Denghel's reign, by abfol-
ving the king's fubjects and foldiers from their oaths of allegiance, which was followed by the unfortunate death of
Za Denghel in the plain of Bartcho. Vain of the importance he had acquired by the fuccefs of his treafon, he had
purfued the fame conduct with regard to Socinios, and followed Jacob to battle, where, trufting to his character and
habit for the fafety of his perfon, he neglected the danger
that he ran amidft a flying army. While occupied in uttering
vain curfes and excommunications againft the conquerors,
he was known, by the crucifix he held in his hand, by a
Moorifh foldier of Socinios, who thruft him through with
a lance, then cut his head off, and carried it to the king.

THE Abyffinian annals ftate, that, immediately after feeing the head of Abuna Peter, Socinios ordered a retreat to
be founded, and that no more of his enemies fhould be
flain. On the contrary, the Jefuits have faid, that the purfuit was continued even after night; for that a body of
horfe, among whom were many Portuguefe belonging to
the army of Jacob, flying from Socinios's troops, fell over
a very high precipice, it being fo dark that they did not
difcover it; and that one foldier, called Manuel Gonfalez,
finding his horfe leave him, as it were flying, lighted luckily on a tree, where, in the utmoft trepidation, he fat all
night, not knowing where he was. This fear was greatly
encreafed in the morning, when he beheld the horfes, and
the men who were his companions, lying dead and dafhed
to pieces in the plain below.

RAS ATHANASIUS, who had followed the party of Jacob,
narrowly efcaped by the fwiftnefs of his horfe, and hid
himfelf in the monaftery of Dima, at no great diftance from
the

the field of battle; and Peter Paez, from remembrance of his former good offices, having recommended him to Sela Chriftos, Socinios's brother-in-law, he was pardoned; but lofing favour every day, his effects and lands having been taken from him on different occafions, he is faid at laft to have died for want, juftly defpifed by all men for unfteadinefs in allegiance to his fovereigns, by which he had been the occafion of the death of two excellent princes, had frequently endangered the life and ftate of the third, and had been the means of the flaughter of many thoufands of their fubjects, worthier men than himfelf, as they fell in the difcharge of their duty. But before his death he had ftill this further mortification, that his wife, daughter of Sertza Denghel, called Melec Segued, voluntarily forfook his bed and retired to a fingle life.

SOCINIOS,

SOCINIOS, or MELEC SEGUED.

From 1605 to 1632.

Socinios embraces the Romiſh Religion—War with Sennaar—With the Shepherds—Violent Conduct of the Romiſh Patriarch—Laſta rebels —Defeated at Wainadega—Socinios reſtores the Alexandrian Religion—Reſigns his Crown to his eldeſt Son.

SOCINIOS, now univerſally acknowledged as king, began his reign with a degree of moderation which there was no reaſon to expect of him. Often as he had been betrayed, many and inveterate as his enemies were, now he had them in his power, he ſought no vengeance for injuries which he had ſuffered, but freely pardoned every one, receiving all men gracioufly without reproach or reflections, or even depriving them of their employments.

BEING informed, however, that one Mahardin, a Moor, had been the firſt to break through that reſpect due to a king, by wounding Za Denghel at the battle of Bartcho, he ordered him to be brought at noon-day before the gate of

his

his palace, and his head to be there ftruck off with an ax, as a juft atonement for violated majefty.

THE king, now retired to Coga, gave his whole attention to regulate thofe abufes, and repair thofe loffes, which this long and bloody war had occafioned. He had two brothers by the mother's fide, men of great merit, Sela Chriftos, and Emana Chriftos, deftined to fhare the principal part in the king's confidence and councils.

BELA CHRISTOS, a man of great family, who had been attached to him fince he formed his firft pretenfions to the crown, was called to court to take his fhare in the glory and dangers of this reign, which it was eafy to fee would be a very active one; for every province around was full of rebels and independents, who had fhaken off the yoke of government, paid no taxes, nor fhewed other refpect to the king than juft what at the moment confifted with their own intereft or inclination.

THE Portuguefe foldiers, remnants of the army which came into Abyffinia under Chriftopher de Gama, had multiplied exceedingly, and their children had been trained by their parents in the ufe of fire-arms. They were at this time incorporated in one body under John Gabriel a veteran officer, who feems to have conftantly remained with the king, while his foldiers (at leaft great part of them) had followed the fortune they thought moft likely to prevail ever fince the time of Claudius.

MENAS did not efteem them enough to keep them in his army at the expence of enduring the feditious converfations

of

of their priefts reviling and undervaluing his religion and government. He therefore banifhed them the kingdom; but, inftead of obeying, they joined the Baharnagafh, then confederated with the Turks and in rebellion againft his fovereign, as we have already mentioned. Sertza Denghel feems to have fcarcely fet any value upon them after this, and made very little ufe of them during his long reign. Upon the infant Jacob's being put upon the throne they all adhered to him; and, after Jacob's banifhment, part of them had attached themfelves to Za Denghel, and behaved with great fpirit in the battle of Bartcho.

Upon Jacob's reftoration they had joined him, and with him were defeated at the decifive battle of Lebart, being all united againft Socinios; fo that, on whatever fide they declared themfelves, they were conftantly beaten by the cowardice of the Abyffinians with whom they were joined. Yet, tho' they had been fo often on the fide that was unfortunate, their particular lofs had been always inconfiderable; becaufe, whatever was the fate of the reft of the army, none of the country troops would ever ftand before them, and they made their retreat from amidft a routed army in nearly the fame fafety as if they had been conquerors; becaufe it was not, for feveral reafons, the intereft of the conquerors to attack them, nor was the experiment ever likely to be an eligible one to the affailants.

Socinios followed a conduct oppofite to that of Menas. He determined to attach the Portuguefe wholly to himfelf, and to make them depend upon him entirely. For this reafon he made great advances to their priefts, and fent for Peter Paez to court, where, after the ufual difputes upon the

4   pope's

pope's fupremacy, and the two natures in Chrift, mafs was
faid, and a fermon preached, much with the fame fuccefs
as it had been in the time of Za Denghel, and with full as
great offence to the Abyffinian clergy.

THE province of Dembea, lying round the lake Tzana,
is the moft fertile and the moft cultivated country in Abyffinia. It is entirely flat, and feems to have been produced
by the decreafe of water in the lake, which, from very vifible marks, appears to have formerly been of four
times the extent of what it is at prefent. Dembea, however fruitful, has one inconvenience to which all level
countries in this climate are fubject: A mortal fever rages
in the whole extent of it, from March to Heder Michael,
the eighth day of November, when there are always gentle
fhowers. This dangerous fever ftops immediately upon the
falling of thefe rains, as fuddenly as the plague does upon
the firft falling of the nucta, or dew, in Egypt.

ON the fouth fide of this lake the country rifes into a
rocky promontory, which forms a peninfula and runs far
into the lake. Nothing can be more beautiful than this
fmall territory, elevated, but not to an inconvenient height,
above the water which furrounds it on all fides, except the
fouth. The climate is delightful, and no fevers or other
difeafes rage here. The profpect of the lake and diftant
mountains is magnificent beyond European conception, and
Nature feems to have pointed this place out for pleafure,
health, and retirement. Paez had afked and obtained this
territory from the king, who, he fays, gave him a grant of
it in perpetuity. The manner of this he defcribes: "A civil
officer is fent on the part of the king, who calls together

all the proprietors of the neighbouring lands, and vifits the bounds with them ; they kill a goat at particular diftances, and bury the heads under ground upon the boundary line of this regality; which heads, Paez fays, it is felony to dig up or remove; and this is a mark or gift of land in perpetuity."

Without contradicting the form of burying the goats heads, I fhall only fay, I never faw or heard of it, nor is there fuch a thing as a gift of land in *perpetuum* known in Abyffinia. All the land is the king's; he gives it to whom he pleafes during pleafure, and refumes it when it is his will. As foon as he dies the whole land in the kingdom (that of the Abuna excepted) is in the difpofal of the crown; and not only fo, but, by the death of every prefent owner, his poffeffions, however long enjoyed, revert to the king, and do not fall to the eldeft fon. It is by proclamation the poffeffion and property is reconveyed to the heir, who thereby becomes abfolute mafter of the land for his own life or pleafure of the king, under obligation of military and other fervices; and that exception, on the part of the Abuna, is not in refpect to the fanctity of his perfon, or charge, but becaufe it is founded upon treaty*, and is become part of the conftitution.

The Abyffinians faw, with the utmoft aftonifhment, the erection of a convent ftrongly built with ftone and lime, of which before they had no knowledge, and their wonder was ftill increafed, when, at defire of the king, Paez undertook

* We have mentioned this treaty in the reign of Icon Amlac.

took, of the fame materials, to build a palace for him at the
fouthmoft end of this peninfula, which is called Gorgora.
It was with amazement mixed with terror that they faw a
houfe rife upon houfe, for fo they call the different ftoreys.

PAEZ here difplayed his whole ingenuity, and the extent
of his abilities. He alone was architect, mafon, fmith, and
carpenter, and with equal dexterity managed all the inftruments ufed by each profeffion in the feveral ftages of the
work. The palace was what we fhall call wainfcoted with
cedar, divided into ftate-rooms, and private apartments
likewife for the queen and nobility of both fexes that formed the court, with accommodations and lodgings for guards
and fervants.

As the king had at that time a view to attack the rebels,
the Agows and Damots, and to check the inroads of the
Galla into Gojam, he faw with pleafure a work going on
that provided the moft commodious refidence where his occupation in all probability was chiefly to lie. His principal
aim was to bring into his kingdom a number of Portuguefe
troops, which, joined to thofe already there, and the converts he propofed to make after embracing the Catholic
religion, might enable him to extirpate that rebellious fpirit which feemed now univerfally to have taken poffeffion
of the hearts of his fubjects, and efpecially of the clergy, of
late taught, he did not feem to know how, that moft dangerous privilege of curfing and excommunicating kings.
He had not feen in Peter Paez and his fellow-priefts any
thing but fubmiffion, and a love of monarchy ; their lives
and manners were truly apoftolical ; and he never thought,
till he came afterwards to be convinced upon proof, that

the

the patriarch from Rome, and the Abuna from Cairo, tho' they differed in their opinion as to the two natures in Chrift, did both heartily agree in the defire of erecting ecclefiaftical dominion and tyranny upon the ruins of monarchy and civil power, and of effecting a total fubordination of the civil government, either to the chairs of St Mark or St Peter.

In the winter, during the ceffation from work, Socinios called Paez from Gorgora to Coga, where he enlarged the territory the Jefuits then had at Fremona. After which he declared to him his refolution · to embrace the Catholic religion ; and, as Paez fays, prefented him with two letters, one to the king of Portugal, the other to the pope : the firft dated the 10th of December 1607, the latter the 14th of October of the fame year. Thefe letters fay not a word of his intended converfion, nor of fubmiffion to the fee of Rome ; but complain only of the diforderly ftate of his kingdom, and the conftant inroads of the Galla, carneftly requefting a number of Portuguefe foldiers to free them from their yoke, as formerly, under the conduct of Chriftopher de Gama, they had delivered Abyffinia from that of the Moors.

While thefe things paffed at Coga, two pieces of intelligence were brought to the king, both very material in themfelves, but which affected him very differently. The firft was, that the traitor Za Selaffé, while making one of his incurfions into Gojam, had fallen into an ambufh laid for him by the Toluma Galla, guardians of that province on the banks of the Nile, and that thefe Pagans had flain him and cut off his head, which they then prefented to the

3   king,

king, who ordered it to be expofed on the lance whereon it was fixed, in the moft confpicuous place in the front of his palace.

This was the end of Ras Za Selaffé, a name held in deteftation to this day throughout all Abyffinia. Though his death was juft fuch as it ought to have been, yet, as it was in an advanced time of life, he ftill became a hurtful example, by fhewing that it was poffible for a man to live to old age in the continual practice of murder and treafon.

He was of low birth, as I have already obferved, of a Pagan nation of Troglodytes, of the loweft efteem in Abyffinia, employed always in the meaneft and moft fervile occupations, in which capacity he ferved firft in a private family. Being obferved to have an active, quick turn of mind, he was preferred to the fervice of Melec Segued, upon whofe death he was fo much efteemed by his fon Jacob, for the expertnefs and capacity he fhewed in bufinefs, that he gave him large poffeffions, and appointed him afterwards to feveral ranks in the army; having regularly advanced through the fubordinate degrees of military command, always with great fuccefs, he was made at laft general; and being now of importance fufficient to be able to ruin his benefactor, he joined Ras Athanafius, who had rebelled againft Jacob, by whom he was taken prifoner, and, being mercifully dealt with, only banifhed to Narea. From this difgraceful fituation he was freed by Za Denghel, who conferred upon him the moft lucrative important employment in the ftate. In return, he rebelled againft Za Denghel; and at Bartcho deprived him of his kingdom and life. Upon Jacob's acceffion he was appointed Betwudet, the firft

place

place in Ethiopia, after the king, and governor of Go-
jam, one of the largeſt and richeſt provinces in Abyſſinia.
But he ſoon after again forſook Jacob, ſwore allegiance to
Socinios, and joined him.

Not content with all this, he began to form ſome new
deſigns while with the court at Coga; and, having ſaid to
ſome of the king's ſervants, over wine, that it was prophe-
ſied to him he ſhould kill three kings, which he had veri-
fied in two, and was waiting for the third, this ſpeech was
repeated to Socinios, who ordered Za Selaſſè to be apprehended; and, though he moſt juſtly deſerved death, the king
mercifully commuted his puniſhment to baniſhment to the
top of Oureé Amba, which ſignifies the Great Mountain upon
the high ridge, called *Guſman*, near the banks of the Nile;
and, though cloſe confined in the caves on the top of that
mountain, after a year's impriſonment he eſcaped to Walaka, and there declared himſelf captain of a band of robbers, with which he infeſted the province of Gojam, when
he was ſlain by a peaſant, and his head cut off and ſent to
Socinios, who very much rejoiced in the preſent, and diſpoſed of it as we have mentioned.

The ſecond piece of intelligence the emperor received
was that in the mountains of Habab, contiguous to Maſuah,
where is the famous monaſtery of the monks of St Euſtathius, called *Biſen;* a perſon appeared calling himſelf Jacob, ſon
of Sertza Denghel, and pretending to have eſcaped from the
battle of Lebart; thus, taking advantage of the circumſtance
of Jacob's body not having been found in the field among
the dead after that engagement, he pretended he had been
ſo grievouſly wounded in the teeth and face that it was
not

not poffible to fuffer the deformity to appear ; for which reafon, as he faid, but, as it appeared afterwards, to conceal the
little refemblance he bore to Jacob, he wrapped about his
head the corner of his upper cloth, and fo concealed one
fide of his face entirely.

ALL Tigrè haftened to join this impoftor as their true
fovereign ; who, finding himfelf now at the head of an army, came down from the mountains of Bifan, and encamped in the neighbourhood of Dobarwa upon the Mareb,
where he had a new acceffion of ftrength.

THE fhape of the crown in Abyffinia is that of the hood,
or capa, which the priefts wear when faying mafs. It is
compofed of filver, fometimes of gold, fometimes of both
metals, mixed and lined with blue filk. It is made to cover
part of the forehead, both cheeks, and the hind-part of the
neck likewife to the joining of the fhoulders. A crown of
this fhape could not but be of great fervice in hiding the
terrible fcars with which the impoftor's face was fuppofed
to be deformed. He had accordingly got one made at Mafuah, beat very thin out of a few ounces of gold which he
had taken from a caravan that he had robbed. He wore it
conftantly upon his head as a token that he was not a candidate for the crown, but real fovereign, who had worn that
mark of power from his infancy.

THE news of this impoftor, with the ufual exaggeration
of followers, foon came to Sela Chriftos, governor of Tigré,
who, feeing that the affair became more ferious every day,
refolved to attempt to check it. He conceived, however, he
had little truft to put in the troops of his province, who all

I   of

of them were wavering whether they fhould not join the rebel. His fole dependence, then, was upon the troops of his own houfehold, veteran foldiers, well paid and cloathed, and firmly attached to his perfon, and likewife upon the Portuguefe. Above all, being himfelf a man of confummate courage and prudence, he was far from judging of the power of his enemy by the multitude of rabble which compofed it.

As foon as the armies came in prefence of each other, Jacob offered the governor battle. But no fooner did the impoftor's troops fee the eagernefs with which the fmall but chofen band rufhed upon them, than they fled and difperfed; and though Sela Chriftos had taken every precaution to cut off the pretended Jacob from his ufual fculking places, it was not poffible to overtake or apprehend him; for he arrived in fafety in one of the higheft and moft inacceffible mountains of the diftrict, whence he looked down on Sela Chriftos and his army without apprehenfion, having behind him a retreat to the more diftant and lefs known mountains of Hamazen, fhould his enemies prefs him further.

As long as Sela Chriftos remained with his little army in that country, the impoftor Jacob continued on the higheft part of the mountains, accompanied only by two or three of his moft intimate friends, who being people whofe families dwelt in the plain below, brought him conftant intelligence of what paffed there.

Sela Christos, wifhing by all means to engage the enemy, marched into a confiderable plain called *Mai-aquel;* but, feeing on every fide the top of each mountain guarded by

troops

troops of foldiers, he was afraid he had advanced too far ; and, apprehenfive left he fhould be inclofed in the midft of a multitude fo pofted, he began to think how he could beft make his retreat before he was furrounded by fo numerous enemies. But they no fooner faw his intention by the movement of his army, than, leaving their leader as a fpectator above, they fell on all fides upon Sela Chriftos's troops, who, having no longer any fafety but in their arms, began to attack the hill that was next them, which they ftormed as they would do a caftle. Finding the fmall refiftance that each of thefe pofts made, the governor divided his fmall army into fo many feparate bodies, leaving his cavalry in the plain below, who, without fighting, were only employed in flaughtering thofe his troops had diflodged from their feparate pofts.

THE day after, the impoftor affembling his fcattered troops, retreated towards the fea into the territory of Hamazen, between the country of the Baharnagafh and the mountains of the Habab.

SELA CHRISTOS, finding that, while he purfued his victory in thefe diftant parts, the fpirit of rebellion increafed nearer home, refolved to inform the king his brother of the unpromifing ftate of his affairs in Tigrè, and the great neceffity there was of his prefence there. Nor did Socinios lofe a moment after receiving this intelligence from Sela Chriftos, although it had found him, in one refpect, very ill prepared for fuch an undertaking ; for he had fent all his horfe from Coga upon an expedition againft the Shangalla and Gongas, nations on the north-weft border of this kingdom ; fo that, when he marched from Wainadega, his cavalry amounted to 530 men only, befides a fmall reinforce-ment brought by Emana Chriftos, governor of Amhara.

It was at Aibo the king turned off the road to Tigrè to-wards Begemder, and that day encamped at Wainadega. From Wainadega he advanced to Davada ; and, croffing the Reb, he turned off by the way of Zang, and encamped at Kattamè. He then proceeded to Tzamè, and arrived at Ha-der. At this place fome fpies informed him that an advan-ced party of the Galla Marawa were ftrongly lodged in a hill not far off. Upon receiving this notice, Socinios order-ed his army to refrefh themfelves, to extinguifh all lights, and march with as little noife as poffible.

While it was fcarce dawn of day, a ftrong detachment of the king's army furrounded the hill where the Galla were, and found there a fmall number of thefe savages placed like piquets to give the alarm and prevent furprife. Ele-ven Galla-were flain, and their heads cut off and carried to the king, the firft fruits of his expedition.

Resolving to profit by this early advantage, Socinios fol-lowed with all diligence, and came in fight of the army of the enemy, without their having taken the fmalleft alarm. They were lying clofely and fecurely in their huts that they had made. A large ravine full of trees and ftumps divided the two armies, and in part concealed them from each o-ther. The king ordered Emana Chriftos, and Abeton Wel-leta Chriftos, to pafs the ravine with the horfe, and fall up-on the Galla fuddenly, throwing the heads of thofe of the advanced guard they had cut off on the ground towards them.

Before

BEFORE the king's horfe had paffed the ravine, the Galla were alarmed, and mounted on horfeback. As they never fight in order, it required no time to form; but they received the king's cavalry fo rudely, that, though Emana Chriftos and the young prince behaved with the utmoft courage, they were beat back, and obliged to fly with confiderable lofs, being entangled in the bufhes. No fooner did the king obferve that his horfe were engaged, than he ordered his troops to pafs the ravine to fupport them, and was defirous to bring on a general engagement. But a panic had feized his troops. They would not ftir, but feemed benumbed and overcome by the cold of the morning, fpectators of the ruin of the cavalry.

EMANA CHRISTOS, and thofe of the cavalry that had efcaped the maffacre, had repaffed the ravine, and difperfed themfelves in the front of the foot; while the victorious Marawa, like ignorant favages, pufhed their victory to the very front of the king's line. Socinios, ordering all the drums of the army to beat and trumpets to found, to excite fome fpirit in his troops, advanced himfelf before any of his foldiers, and flew the firft Galla within his reach with his own hands. The example and danger the king expofed himfelf to, raifed the indignation of the troops. They poured in crowds, without regarding order, upon the Marawa, great part of whom had already paffed the ravine, and all that had paffed it were cut to pieces.

THE Galla, unable to ftand this lofs, fled from the field, and immediately after left Begemder. The want of horfe on the king's part faved their whole army from the deftruction which would infallibly have been the confequence of

M m 2

a vi-a vigorous purfuit, through a country where every inhabitant was an enemy. The king after this returned to his palace at Coga to finifh the bufinefs he had in hand.

In the mean time, a report was fpread through all Ti-grè, that the king had been defeated by the Galla, and that Ras Sela Chriftos had repaired to Gondar in confequence of that difafter. The impoftor Jacob loft no time in taking advantage of this report. He defcended from his natural fortrefs, and, in conjunction with the governor of Axum, flew feveral people, and committed many ravages in Sirè. The Ras no fooner learned that he was encamped on plain ground, than he prefented himfelf with the little army he had before; and, though the odds againft him were exceffive, yet by his prefence and conduct, the rebels, though they fought this time with more than ordinary obftinacy, were defeated with great lofs, and their leader, the fuppofed Jacob, forced again to his inacceffible mountains.

Socinios having now finifhed the affairs which detained him at Coga, and being informed that the fouthern Galla, refenting the defeat of the Marawa, had entered into a league to invade Abyffinia with united forces, and a complete army to burn and lay wafte the whole country between the Tacazzé and Tzana, and to attack the emperor in his capital of Coga, which they were determined to deftroy, fent orders to Kafmati Julius, his fon-in-law, to join him immediately with what forces he had, as alfo to Kefla Chriftos; and, being joined by both thefe officers and their troops, he marched and took poft at Ebenaat in the diftrict of Beleffen, in the way by which the Galla intended to pafs to the capital, and he refolved to await them there.

3   The

THE Galla advanced in their usual manner, burning and destroying churches and villages, and murdering without mercy all that were so unfortunate as to fall into their hands. The king bore these excesses of his enemy with the patience of a good general, who saw they contributed to his advantage. He therefore did not offer to check any of their disorders, but by not resisting rather hoped to encourage them. He had an army in number superior, and this was seldom the case; but in quality there was no comparison, five of the king's troops being equal to twenty of the enemy, and this was the general proportion in which they fought. He, therefore, contented himself with choosing proper ground to engage, and improving it by ambushes such as the nature of the field permitted or suggested.

. IT was the 7th of January 1608, early in the morning, that the Galla presented themselves to Socinios in battle, in a plain below Ebenaat, surrounded with small hills covered with wood. The Galla filled the whole plain, as if voluntarily devoting themselves to destruction, and from the hills and bushes were destroyed by fire-arms from enemies they did not see, who with a strong body took possession of the place through which they entered, and by which they were to return no more.

SOCINIOS that day, for what particular reason does not appear, distinguished himself among the midst of the Galla, by fighting like a common soldier. It is thought by the historians of those times, that he had received advice while at Coga, that his son-in-law Julius intended to rebel, and therefore he meant to discourage him by comparison of their personal abilities. This, however, is not probable; the
king's

king's character was established, and nothing more could be added to it. However that may be, all turned to the disadvantage of the Galla. No general or other officer thought himself entitled to spare his person more than the king; all fought like common soldiers; and, being the men best armed and mounted, and most experienced in the field, they contributed in proportion to the slaughter of the day. About 12,000 men on the part of the Galla were killed upon the spot; the very few that remained were destroyed by the peasants, whilst 400 men only fell on the part of the king, so it was a massacre rather than a battle.

Socinios now resolved to try his fortune against the impostor Jacob, and with that resolution he crossed Lamalmon, descending to the Tacazzè in his way to Sirè. Here, as on the frontiers of his province, he was met by Sela Christos, who brought Peter Paez along with them. Both were kindly received by the king, who encamped in the large plain before Axum, in consequence of a resolution he had long taken of being crowned with all the ancient ceremonies used on this occasion by former kings, while the royal residence was in the province of Tigrè.

It was on the 18th of March, according to their account, the day of our Saviour's first coming to Jerusalem, that this festival began. His army consisted of about 30,000 men. All the great officers, all the officers of state, and the court then present, were every man dressed in the richest and gayest manner. Nor was the other sex behind-hand in the splendour of their appearance. The king, dressed in crimson damask, with a great chain of gold round his neck, his head bare, mounted upon a horse richly caparisoned, advanced

1   at

at the head of his nobility, paffed the outer court, and came to the paved way before the church. Here he was met by a number of young girls, daughters of the umbares, or fupreme judges, together with many noble virgins ftanding on the right and left of the court.

Two of the nobleft of thefe held in their hands a crimfon cord of filk, fomewhat thicker than common whip-cord, but of a loofer texture, ftretched acrofs from one company to another, as if to fhut up the road by which the king was approaching the church. When this cord was prepared and drawn tight about breaft-high by the girls, the king entered, advancing at a moderate pace, curvetting and fhewing the management of his horfe. He was ftopped by the tenfion of this ftring, while the damfels on each fide afking who he was, were anfwered, " I am your king, the king of " Ethiopia." To which they replied with one voice, " You " fhall not pafs ; you are not our king."

The king then retires fome paces, and then prefents himfelf as to pafs, and the cord is again drawn acrofs his way by the young women fo as to prevent him, and the queftion repeated, "Who are you ?" The king anfwered, " I am your " king, the king of Ifrael." But the damfels refolved, even on this fecond attack, not to furrender but upon their own terms ; they again anfwer, " You fhall not pafs ; you are not " our king."

The third time, after retiring, the king advances with a pace and air more determined; and the cruel virgins, again prefenting the cord and afking who he is, he anfwers, " I am your king, the king of Sion ;" and, drawing his

his fword, cuts the filk cord afunder. Immediately upon
this the young women cry, " It is a truth, you are our king;
" truly you are the king of Sion." Upon which they begin
to fing Hallelujah, and in this they are joined by the court
and army upon the plain ; fire-arms are difcharged, drums
and trumpets found ; and the king, amidft thefe acclamations and rejoicings, advances to the foot of the ftair of the
church, where he difmounts, and there fits down upon a
ftone, which, by its remains, apparently was an altar of Anu-
bis, or the dog-ftar : At his feet there is a large flab of free-
ftone, on which is the infcription mentioned by Poncet, and
which fhall be quoted hereafter, when I come to fpeak of
the ruins of Axum.

After the king comes the nebrit, or keeper of the book
of the law in Axum, fuppofed to reprefent Azarias the fon
of Zadock ; then the twelve umbares, or fupreme judges,
who with Azarias accompanied Menilck, the fon of Solomon, when he brought the book of the law from Jerufalem,
and thefe are fuppofed to reprefent the twelve tribes. After
thefe follow the Abuna at the head of the priefts, and the
Itcheguè at the head of the monks ; then the court, who
all pafs through the aperture made by the divifion of the
filk cord, which remains ftill upon the ground.

The king is firft anointed, then crowned, and is accompanied half up the fteps by the finging priefts, called Dep-
teras, chanting pfalms and hymns. Here he ftops at a hole
made for the purpofe in one of the fteps, and is there fu-
migated with incenfe and myrrh, aloes and caffia. Divine
fervice is then celebrated; and, after receiving the facrament,
he returns to the camp, where fourteen days fhould regularly

larly be fpent in feafting, and all manner of rejoicing and military exercife.

The king is, by the old cuftom, obliged to give a number of prefents, the particulars of which are ftated in the deftar, or treafury-book, the value, the perfon to whom they are due, and the time of giving; but a great part of thefe are gone into defuetude fince the removal of the court from Tigrè, as alfo many of the offices are now fuppreffed, and with them the prefents due to them.

The nobles and the court were likewife obliged to give prefents to the king upon that occafion.   The prefent from the governor of Axum is two lions and a fillet of filk, upon which is wrote, " *Mo Anbafa am Nizilet Solomon am Negadé* " *Jude*—The lion of the tribe of Judah and race of Solomon " hath overcome ;" this ferves as a form of inveftiture of lands that the king grants, a ribband bearing this infcription being tied round the head of the perfon to whom the lands are given.

This governor was then in rebellion, fo did not affift at the ceremony. Notwithftanding the difference of expence which I have mentioned, by fuppreffing places, prefents, and dues, the king Tecla Haimanout told me at Gondar, that when he was in Tigrè, driven there by the late rebellion, Ras Michael had fome thoughts of having him crowned there in contempt of his enemies ; but, by the moft moderate calculation that could be made, not to turn the ceremony into ridicule by parfimony, it would have coft 20,000 ounces of gold, or L. 50,000 Sterling ; upon which he laid afide the thoughts of it, faying to the king, " Sir, truſt to me, 20,000 ounces of Tigrè iron ſhall crown you better; if more is wanted, I will beſtow it upon your enemies with pleaſure till they are ſatisfied;" meaning the iron balls with which his ſoldiers loaded their muſquets.

AFTER the coronation was over, the king paſſed the Mareb, deſiring to finiſh his campaign by the death of his competitor Jacob; but that impoſtor knew too well the ſuperiority of his rival, and hid himſelf in the inmoſt receſſes, without other attendants than a few goats, who furniſhed him with their milk, as well as their ſociety.

SOCINIOS left the affair of the rebel Jacob to be ended by Amſala Chriſtos, an officer of great prudence, whom he made governor of Tigré; and, taking his brother Ras Sela Chriſtos along with him, returned to Coga*. Amſala Chriſtos being ſeized with a grievous ſickneſs, ſaw how vain it was for him to purſue the ſuppreſſion of a rebellion conducted by ſuch a head as this impoſtor Jacob, and therefore ſecretly applied to two young men, Zara Johannes and Amha Georgis, brothers, and ſons of the Shum Welled Georgis, who had committed murder, and were outlawed by Socinios, and, keeping hid in the mountains, had joined in fellowſhip with the impoſtor Jacob.

THESE, gained by the promiſe of pardon given them by Amſala Chriſtos, choſe an opportunity which their intimacy gave them, and, falling upon Jacob unawares in his retirement,

---

* Then the metropolis upon the Lake Tzana.

ment, they flew him, cut his head off, and fent it to the king at Coga, who received it very thankfully, and returned it to Tigrè to Amfala Chriftos, to be expofed publicly in all the province to undeceive the people; for it now appeared, that he had neither fcars in his face, broken jaw, nor lofs of teeth, but that the covering was intended only to conceal the little refemblance he bore to king Jacob, flain, as we have feen, at the battle of Lebart; and he was now found to have been a herdfman, in thofe very mountains of Bifan to which he had fo often fled for refuge while his rebellion lafted.

The king, in his return from Tigrè, paffing by Fremona, fent to the Jefuits there thirty ounces of gold, about L. 75 Sterling, for their immediate exigency; teftifying, in the moft gracious manner, his regret, " That the many affairs in which he was engaged had prevented him from hearing mafs in their convent, as he very fincerely wifhed to do; but he left with them the Abuna Simon, to whom he had recommended to ftudy their religion, and be a friend to it."

In this he fhewed his want of penetration and experience; for though he had feen wars between foldier and foldier, who, after having been in the moft violent ftate of enmity, had died in defence of each other as friends, he was not aware of that degree of enmity which reigns upon difference of opinion, not to fay religion, between prieft and prieft. It was not long, however, before he faw it, and the example was in the perfon of his prefent friend the Abuna Simon.

WHILE

WHILE Socinios was yet in Tigré, news were brought to Coga from Woggora to Sanuda Tzef Leham * of Dembea, who could not accompany the king to Tigré on account of ficknefs, but was left with the charge of the capital and palace during the king's abfence, that Melchizedec, one of the meaneft and loweft fervants of the late king Melec Segued, had rebelled, and was collecting troops, confifting of foldiers, fervants, and dependents of that prince, and had flain fome of Socinios's fervants. Sanuda was a brave and active officer; but, being without troops, (the king having carried the whole army to Tigrè) immediately fet out from Maitfha to the town of Tchelga, one of the frontiers of Abyffinia, poffeffed by Wed Ageeb prince of the Arabs.

IT is here to be obferved, that though the territorial right of Tchelga did then, and does ftill appertain to the kingdom of Abyffinia, yet the poffeffion of it is ceded by agreement to Wed Ageeb, under whofe protection the caravans from Egypt and Sennaar, and thofe from Abyffinia to Sennaar and Egypt, were underftood to be ever fince they were cut off in the laft century by the bafha of Suakem, for this purpofe, that a cuftomhoufe might be erected, and the duties divided between the two kingdoms equally. The fame is the cafe with Serké, a town belonging to Sennaar, ceded for the fame purpofe to the king of Abyffinia.

IT happened that Abdelcader †, fon of Ounfa, late king of Sennaar, or of Funge, as he is called in the Abyffinian annals, had been depofed by his fubjects in the 4th year of his

---

* Regifter of the cattle; fo the governor of Dembea is called.

† See the Hiftory of the rife of this monarchy in my return through Sennaar.

his reign, and remained at Tchelga under the mutual protection of Wed Ageeb and the emperor of Abyssinia, a kind of prisoner to them both; and had brought with him a number of soldiers and dependents, the partakers of his former good fortune, who, finding safety and good usage at Tchelga, were naturally well-affected to the king. These, ready mounted and armed, joined Sanuda immediately upon his declaring the exigency; and with these he marched straight to Coga, to the defence of the palace with which he had been intrusted.

Melchizedec, whose design was against Coga, no sooner heard Sanuda was arrived there than he marched to surprise him, and a very bloody and obstinate engagement followed. The Funge, piqued in honour to render this service to their protector, fought so obstinately that they were all slain, and Sanuda, mounted that day upon a fleet horse belonging to Socinios, escaped with difficulty, much wounded.

As soon as Socinios heard of this misfortune, he sent Ras Emana Christos, who marched straight to Woggora, creating Zenobius, son of Imael, governor of that district; and there he found Sanuda Zenobius and Ligaba Za Denghel together, in a place called Deberaffo.

As soon as the rebel Melchizedec heard Emana Christos was come, and with him the fore-mentioned noblemen, he set himself to exert the utmost of his power to draw together forces of all kinds from every part he could get them, and his army was soon increased to such a degree as,

4   notwith-

notwithftanding the prefence of Emana Chriftos, to ftrike
terror into all the territory and towns of Dembea. Nothing
was wanted but a king of the royal race for whom to fight.
Without a chief of this kind, it was evident that the army,
however often fuccefsful, would at laft difperfe.   They,
therefore, brought one Arzo, a prince of the royal blood,
from his hiding-place in Begemder.   Arzo, in return for a
throne, conferred the place of Ras upon Melchizedec.   Za
Chriftos, fon of Hatzir Abib, was appointed to the command
of the army under him; and, having finifhed this and many
fuch neceffary preparatives, they marched ftraight to meet
Emana Chriftos, with a better countenance than rebel armies generally bear.

It was the 9th of March 1611, at 9 in the morning, when
the two armies were firft in fight of each other, nor did
they long delay coming to an engagement.   The battle was
very obftinate and bloody; Melchizedec re-eftablifhed his character for worth, at leaft as a foldier; the fame did Za Chriftos.
Of the competitor Arzo, hiftory makes no mention; his
blood, probably, was too precious to rifk the fpilling of it,
being fo far-fetched as from king Solomon.   After a moft
obftinate refiftance, part of Za Chriftos's army was broken
and put to flight; but it rallied fo often, and fold the ground
it yielded fo dear, that it gave time to Emana Chriftos to
come up to his army's affiftance.

The Ras, who was as brave a foldier as he was a wife
and prudent general, faw it was a time when all fhould
be rifked, and threw himfelf into the midft of his enemies;
and he was now arrived near the place where Melchizedec
fought, when that rebel, feeing him advancing fo faft a-

2   mong

mong his flaughtered followers, guefling his intention, declined the combat, turned his horfe and fled, while affairs
even yet appeared in his favour. This panic of the general
had the effect it ordinarily has in barbarous armies. Nobody
confidered how the profpect of the general iffue ftood ; they
fled with Melchizedec, and loft more men than would have
fecured them victory had they ftood in their ranks..

A BODY of troops, joined by fome peafants of Begemder,
purfued Melchizedec fo clofely that they came up with him
and took him prifoner, together with Tenfa Chriftos, a very active partizan, and enemy to Emana Chriftos. Having brought
them to the camp, before the Ras returned to Coga, they
were tried and condemned to die for rebellion, as traitors,
and the fentence immediately executed, after which their
heads were fent to the king. Very foon after this, Arzo,
and his general Za Chriftos, were taken and fent to the
king, who ordered them to be tried by the judges in common form, and they underwent the fame fate.

THE king was employed in the winter feafon while he refided at Coga, in building a new church, called St Gabriel.
But the feafon of taking the field being come, he marched
out with his army and halted at Gogora, fending Emana
Chriftos and Sela Chriftos againft the rebels ; thefe were not
in a particular clan, or province, for all the country was
in rebellion, from the head of the Nile round, eaftward, to
the frontiers of Tigré. Part of them indeed were not in
arms, but refufed to pay their quota of the revenue ; part of
them were in arms, and would neither pay, nor admit a governor from the king among them ; others willingly fubmitted.

mitted to Socinios, and were armed, only thereby to exempt
themfelves from payment.

SELA CHRISTOS fell upon the inhabitants of the mountainous diftrict of Gufman, on the Nile, whofe principal
ftrong-hold, Oureé Amba, he forced, killing many, and carrying away their children as flaves, which, upon the interceffion of Peter Paez, were given to the Jefuits to be educated as Catholics.

THE next attempt was upon the Gongas, a black Pagan
nation, with which he had the fame fuccefs ; the reft were
the Agows, a very numerous people, all confederates and
in arms, and not willing to hear of any compofition.   The
king ordered one of thefe tribes, the Zalabaffa, to be extirpated as far as poffible, and their country laid wafte.   But
notwithftanding this example, which met with great interruption in the execution, the Agows continued in rebellion
for feveral years afterwards, but much impoverifhed and
leffened in number by variety of victories obtained over
them.

THE two next years were fpent in unimportant fkirmifhes with the Agows of Damot, and with the Galla, invaders
of Gojam. In 1615, the year after, Tecla Geòrgis made governor of Samen, and Welled Hawaryat, fhum of Tfalemat*,
were both fent againft a rebel who declared himfelf competitor for the crown.   His name was Amdo.   He pretended
to be the late king Jacob, fon of Melec Segued ; and this
character he gave himfelf, without the fmalleft communication

* A low territory at the foot of Lamalmon.

cation with the relations or connections of that prince. As soon as Aſſera Chriſtos and Tecla Garima, ſervants of Welled Hawaryat, heard of this adventurer, they ſurpriſed him in Tſalemat, and, putting him in irons, confined him in the houſe of Aſſera Chriſtos.

GIDEON, king of the Jews, whoſe reſidence was on the high mountain of Samen, upon hearing that Amdo was priſoner, ſent a body of armed men who ſurpriſed Aſſera Chriſtos in his own houſe in the night, and killed him, bringing with them his priſoner Amdo to Samen, and delivered him to Gideon there; who not only took him into protection, but aſſiſted him in raiſing an army by every means in his power. There were not wanting there idle vagabonds and lawleſs people enough, who fled to the ſtandard of a prince whoſe ſole view ſeemed to be murder, robbery, and all ſort of licentiouſneſs. It was not long till Amdo, by the aſſiſtance of Gideon, found himſelf at the head of an army, ſtrong enough to leave the mountain, and try his fortune in the plain below, where he laid waſte Shawada, Tſalemat, and all the countries about Samen which perſevered in their duty to the king.

SOCINIOS, upon this, appointed Julius his ſon-in-law governor of Woggora, Samen, Waag, and Abbergalé, that is, of all the low countries from the borders of the Tacazzè to Dembea. Abram, an old officer of the king, deſirous to ſtop the progreſs of the rebel, marched towards him, and offered him battle; but that brave officer had not the ſucceſs his intention deſerved, for he was defeated and ſlain; which had ſuch an effect upon Julius, that, without hazarding his fortune farther, he ſent to beſeech the king to march againſt Amdo with all poſſible expedition, as his affairs were become deſperate in that part of his dominions.

The king hereupon marched ſtraight to Woggora, and joined Julius at Shimbra-Zuggan; thence he deſcended from Samen, and encamped upon Tocur-Ohha, (the black river) thence he proceeded to Debil, and then to Sobra; and from this laſt ſtation he ſent a detachment of his army to attack a ſtrong mountain called Meſſiraba, one of the natural fortreſſes of Gideon, which was forced by the king's troops after ſome reſiſtance, and the whole inhabitants, without diſtinction of age or ſex, put to the ſword, for ſuch were the orders of the king.

This firſt ſuccefs very much diſheartened the rebels, for Meſſiraba was, by nature, one of the ſtrongeſt mountains, and it, beſides, had been fortified by art, furniſhed with plenty of proviſions, and a number of good troops. The next mountain Socinios attacked was Hotchi, and the third Amba Za Hancaſſé, where he had the like ſuccefs, and treated the inhabitants in the ſame manner; thence he removed his army to Seganat, where he met with a very ſtout reſiſtance; but this mountain, too, was at laſt taken, Gideon himſelf eſcaping narrowly by the bravery of his principal general, who, fighting deſperately, was ſlain by a muſqueteer.

The conſtant ſuccefs of the king, and the bloody manner in which he purſued his victory, began to alarm Gideon, leſt the end ſhould be the extirpation of his whole nation. He, therefore, made an overture to the king, that, if he would pardon him and grant him peace, he would deliver the rebel Amdo bound into his hands.

THE

THE king affented to this, and Amdo was accordingly de-livered up; and, being convicted of rebellion and murder, he was fentenced to be nailed to a crofs, and to remain there till he died. But the terrible cries and groans which he made while they were fixing him to the crofs, fo much fhocked the ears of the king, that he ordered him to be taken down, and his head ftruck off with an ax, which was executed in the midft of the camp.

SOCINIOS after this retired to Dancaz, and ordered Kefla governor of Gojam, and Jonael his mafter of the houfehold, to march fuddenly and furprife Belaya, a country belonging to the Gongas and Guba, Pagan nations, on whom, every year, he made war for the fake of taking flaves for the ufe of the palace. Thefe two officers, with a large body, moft-ly horfe, fell unawares upon the favages at Belaya, flaying part, and bringing away their children. But not content with doing this, they likewife attacked the two diftricts of Agows, Dengui and Sankara, then in peace with the king, and drove away an immenfe number of cattle, which the king no fooner heard, than he ordered a ftrict fearch to be made, and the whole cattle belonging to the Agows to be gathered together, and reftored to their refpective owners; a piece of juftice which foftened the hearts of this people more than all the feverities that had been hitherto ufed; and the good effects of which were foon after feen upon the Agows, though it produced fomething very different in the conduct of Jonael.

THE king this year, 1616, left his capital at the ufual time, in the month of November, and ordered his whole houfehold to attend him. His intention was againft the Galla on the weſt of Gojam, eſpecially the tribe called Libo. But this campaign was rendered fruitleſs by the death of the king's eldeſt ſon, Kennaffer Chriſtos, a young prince of great hopes, eſteemed both by the king and the people. He had an excellent underſtanding, and the moſt affable manners poſſible, to thoſe even whom he did not like; was very fond of the ſoldiers; merciful, generous, and liberal; and was thought to be the favourite of the king his father, who buried him with great pomp in the church of Debra Roma, built by king Iſaac, in the lake Tzana.

In the midſt of this mourning, there came a very bloody order* from the king. Hiſtory barely tells us the fact, but does not aſſign any other reaſon than the wanton manner in which Gideon king of the Jews had endeavoured to diſturb his reign and kingdom, which was thought a ſufficient excuſe for it. However this may be, the king gave orders to Kaſmati Július, Kaſmati Welled Hawaryat, Billetana Gueta Jonael, and Fit-Auraris Hoſannah, to extirpate all the Falaſha that were in Foggora, Janfakara, and Bagenarwè, to the borders of Samen ; alſo all that were in Bagla, and in all the diſtricts under their command, wherever they could find them ; and very few of them eſcaped, excepting ſome who fled with Phineas.

In this maſſacre, which was a very general one, and executed very ſuddenly, fell Gideon king of that people ; a man of great reputation, not only among his ſubjects, but throughout all Abyſſinia, reputed alſo immenſely rich. His treaſures,

---

* It was probably part of the fruits of the new religion, and the work of his new religious adviſers.

futes, fuppofed to be concealed in the mountains, are the objects of the fearch of the Abyffinians to this day.

The children of thofe that were flain were fold for flaves by the king; and all the Falafha in Dembea, in the low countries immediately in the king's power, were ordered upon pain of death to renounce their religion, and be baptifed. To this they confented, feeing there was no remedy ; and the king unwifely imagined, that he had extinguifhed, by one blow, the religion which was that of his country long beforeChriftianity,by the unwarrantable butchery of a number of people whom he had furprifed living in fecurity under the affurance of peace. Many of them were baptifed accordingly, and they were all ordered to plow and harrow upon the fabbath-day.

The king next fent orders to Sela Chriftos, and Kefla governor of Gojam, that, affembling their troops, they fhould transfer the war into Bizamo, a province on the fouth fide of the Nile, called alfo in the books a kingdom. Through this lies the road of the merchants leading to Narea. It is inhabited by feveral clans of Pagans, which together make the great divifion of thefe nations into Boren, and Bertuma Galla *.

The army paffed the Nile, laying wafte the whole country, driving off the cattle, collecting the women and children as flaves, and putting all the men to the fword; without thefe people, though they make conftant inroads into

3   Gojam,

---

* The words, Boren, and Bertuma Galla, have no meaning in the Ethiopic.

Gojam, appearing anywhere in force to ftop the defolation of their country. The whole tract between Narea and the Nile was now cleared of enemies, and a number of priefts at that time fent to revive drooping Chriftianity in thofe parts.

IN the year 1617, a league was again made among the Boren Galla, that part of them fhould invade Gojam, while the others (namely the Marawa) fhould enter Begemder. Upon hearing this, the king in hafte marched to Begemder, that he might be ready in cafe of need to affift Tigré. He then fixed his head-quarters at Shima, but from this he fpeedily removed; and, paffing Emfras, came to Dobit, a favourite refidence of the emperor Jacob, where he held a council to determine which of the two provinces he fhould firft affift.

IT was the general opinion of his officers, that to march at that time of the year into Tigré by Begemder, was to de-ftroy the army, and diftrefs both provinces; that an army, well provided with horfe, was neceffary for acting with fuc-cefs againft the Galla, and that, in effect, though the royal army at prefent was fo appointed, yet there was no grafs at that time of the year in all that march for the fubfiftence of the cavalry, and very little water for the ufe of man or beaft, an inconvenience the Galla themfelves muft experi-ence if they attempted an invafion that way. It was, more-over, urged, that, if the king fhould march through Wog-gora and Lamalmon, they might get more food for their beafts, and water too; but then they would throw them-felves far from the place where the Galla had entered, and would be obliged to fall into the former road, with the in-conveniencies already ftated. The confequence of this deliberation

liberation was, that it was with very great regret the good
of the commonweal obliged them to leave Tigré to the protection of Providence alone for a time, and haften to meet
the enemy that were then laying Gojam waite.

With this view the king left Dobit, and came to the river Gomara in Foggora. He then paffed the Nile near Dara, and came to Selalo, where he heard that the Djawi had
paffed the Nile from Bizamo, and entered Gojam at the oppofite fide to where he then was. He there left his baggage, and, by a forced march, advancing three days journey
in one, he came to Bed, upon the river Sadi; but, inftead of
finding the enemy there, he received intelligence from Sela
Chriftos, that he had met the Galla immediately after their
paffing the Nile; had fought them, and cut their army to
pieces, without allowing them time to ravage the country.

Upon this good news the king turned off on the road to
Tchegal and Wainadaffa, and ordered Bela Chriftos to affemble as great an army as he could, and fall upon the
Djawi and Galla in Walaka and Shoa, as alfo Ras Sela Chriftos, to pafs the Nile and join him there.

That general loft no time, but marched ftraight to Amca Ohha, or the river Amca, where he found the Edjow,
who fled upon his coming, without giving him any opportunity of bringing them to an engagement, abandoning
their wives, children, and fubftance, to the mercy of the
enemy. Sela Chriftos, having finifhed this expedition as he
intended, returned to join the king, whom he found encamped upon the river Suqua, near Debra Werk, guarding
thofe provinces in the abfence of Sela Chriftos. From this

z

the

the king, retreating towards Dembea, paſſed the Nile near Dara, and encamped at Zinzenam, whence he marched round the lake into Dembea to his palace at Gorgora.

THIS village, whoſe name ſignifies *rain upon rain*, affords us a proof of what I have ſaid in ſpeaking of the cauſe of the overflowing of the Nile, in contradiction to the Adulitic inſcription, that no ſnow falls in Abyſſinia, or rather, that though ſnow may have fallen in the courſe of centuries, it is a phænomenon ſo rare as not to have a name or word to expreſs it in the whole language, and is entirely unknown to the people in general, at leaſt to the weſt of the Tacazzé.

THE Abyſſinian hiſtorian, from whom theſe memoirs are ·compoſed, ſays, " That this village, called Zinzenam, has its name from an extraordinary circumſtance that once hap-pened in theſe parts, for a ſhower of rain fell, which was not properly of the nature of rain, as it did not run upon ·the ground, but remained very light, having ſcarce the weight of feathers, of a beautiful white colour like flour ; it fell in ſhowers, and occaſioned a darkneſs in the air more than rain, and liker to miſt. It covered the face of the whole country for ſeveral days, retaining its whiteneſs the whole time, then went away like dew, without leaving any ſmell or unwholeſome effect behind it.

THIS was certainly the accidental phænomenon of a day; for, notwithſtanding the height of the mountains Taranta and Lamalmon, ſnow never was ſeen there, at leaſt for ages paſt; and Laſta, in whoſe mountains armies have periſhed by cold, as far as a very particular inquiry could go, never yet had ſnow upon them ; and Zinzenam is not in theſe mountains,

tains, or in any elevated fituation. On the contrary, it is
adjoining to the plain country of Foggora, near where it
borders upon Begemder, not above 20 miles from the fecond cataract, or 40 miles from Gondar; fo that this muft
have been a fhort and accidental change of the atmofphere,
of which there are examples of many different kinds, in the
hiftories of all countries.

As foon as the weather permitted, the king left his palace at Gorgora in the way to Tocuffa, where he ftaid feveral days; removed thence to Tenkel, where he continued alfo four days, and proceeded to Gunkè, where he halted. From his head-quarters at Gunkè, the king, meditating
an expedition againft Atbara, fent a meffenger to Nile Wed
Ageeb, prince of the Arabs, defiring a meeting with him before he attacked the Funge, for fo they call the fubjects of
the new monarchy, lately eftablifhed at Sennaar by the conqueft of the Arabs, under Wed Ageeb, a very confiderable
part of whofe territory they had taken by force, and now
enjoyed as their own poffeffions.

ABDELCADER, fon of Ounfa, was the ninth prince of the
race of Funge then reigning; a weak, and ill-inclined man,
but with whom Socinios had hitherto lived in friendfhip,
and, in a late treaty, had fent him as a prefent, a nagareet, or
kettle-drum, richly ornamented with gold, with a gold chain
to hang it by. Abdelcader, on his part, returned to Socinios
a trained falcon, of an excellent kind, very much efteemed
among the Arabs.

SOON after this, Abdelcader was depofed by his brother
Adelan, fon of Ounfa, and fled to Tchelga, under protection

of the king of Abyffinia, who allowed him an honourable maintenance; a cuftom always obferved in fuch cafes in the Eaft, by princes towards their unfortunate neighbours.

BAADY, fon of Abdelcader, an active and violent young prince, although he depofed his uncle Adelan, took this protection of his father in bad part. It was likewife fuggefted to him, that the prefent fent by Socinios, a nagareet, or kettle-drum, imported, that Socinios confidered him as his vaffal, the drum being the fign of inveftiture fent by the king to any one of his fubjects whom he appoints to govern a province, and that the return of the falcon was likely to be confidered as the acknowledgement of a vaffal to his fuperior. Baady, upon his acceffion to the throne, was refolved to rectify this too great refpect fhewn on the part govern father, by an affront he refolved to offer. With this blind he fent to Socinios two old, blind, and lame horfes.

SOCINIOS took this amifs, as it was intended he fhould, and the flight was immediately followed by the troops of Atbara, under Nile Wed Ageeb, fent by Baady to make an inroad into Abyffinia, to lay wafte the country, and drive off the people, with orders to fell them as flaves.

AMONG the moft active in this expedition, were thofe of the town of Serké. When Baady complained that his father and rival was protected in his own town of Tchelga, it had been anfwered, That true it was, Tchelga had been ceded and did belong to Sennaar, for every purpofe of revenue, but that the fovereignty of the place had never been alienated or furrendered to the king of Sennaar, but remained now, as ever, vefted in the king of Abyffinia. Serkè ftood precifely

in

in the fame fituation with refpect to Abyffinia, as Tchelga did to Sennaar, when Socinios demanded fatisfaction for the violence committed againft him by his own town of Serkè. The fame anfwer was given him, That for all fifcal purpofes Serkè was his, but owed him no allegiance; for, being part of the kingdom of Sennaar, it was bound to affift its fovereign in all wars againft his enemies.

Socinios, deeply engaged in the troubles that attended the beginning of his reign, paffed over for a time both the affront and injury, but fent into Atbara to Nile Wed Ageeb, propofing a treaty with him independent of the king of Sennaar.

There were, at this time, three forts of people that inhabited the whole country from lat. 13° (the mountains of Abyffinia) to the tropic of Cancer (the frontiers of Egypt.) The firft was the Funge, or negroes, eftablifhed in Atbara fince the year 1504, by conqueft. The fecond, the old inhabitants of that country, known in very early ages by the name of Shepherds, which continues with them to this day; and thefe lived under a female government. The third, the Arabs, who came hither after the conqueft of Egypt, in an army under Caled Ibn el Waalid, or Saif Ullah, *the Sword of God*, during the Khalifat of Omar, deftined to fubdue Nubia, and, ftill later, in the time of Salidan and his brother.

These Arabs had affociated with the firft inhabitants, the Shepherds, from a fimilarity of life and manners, and, by treaty, the Funge had eftablifhed a tribute to be paid them from both; after which, thefe were to enjoy their former habitations without further moleftation.

P p 2 This

THIS prince of the Arabs, Nile Wed Ageeb, embraced the offer of the king of Abyſſinia very readily; and a treaty was accordingly made between Socinios and him, and a territory in Abyſſinia granted him on the frontiers, to which he could retire in ſafety, as often as his affairs were embroiled with the ſtate of Sennaar.

IT happened ſoon after this, that Alico, a Mahometan, governor of the Mazaga for Socinios, that is, of Nara and Ras el Feel, a low country, as the name imports, of black earth, revolted from his maſter, and fled to Sennaar, carrying with him a number of the king's horſes. Socinios made his complaint to the king of Sennaar, who took no notice of it, neither returned any anſwer, which exaſperated Socinios ſo much that it produced the preſent expedition, and was a cauſe of much bloodſhed, and of a war which, at leaſt in intention, laſts to this day between the two kingdoms.

WED AGEEB, upon Socinios's firſt ſummons, came to Gunkè, his head-quarters, attended by a number of troops, and ſome of the beſt horſe in Atbara. Upon his entering the king's tent, he proſtrated himſelf, (as is the Abyſſinian cuſtom) acknowledged himſelf the king's vaſſal, and brought preſents with him to a very conſiderable value. Socinios received him with great marks of diſtinction and kindneſs. He decorated him with a chain and bracelets of gold, and gave him a dagger of exquiſite workmanſhip, mounted with the ſame metal; clothed him in ſilk and damaſk after the Abyſſinian faſhion, and confirmed the ancient treaty with him. The fruit of all this was preſently ſeen; the king and his new ally fell ſuddenly upon Serké, put all the male inhabitants to the ſword, ſold the women and children as

ſlaves,

flaves, and burned the town to the ground. The fame they did to every inhabited place on that fide of the frontier, weſt to Fazuclo. After which, the king, having ſent a ſarcaſtic compliment to Baady, returned to Dancaz, taking Wed Ageeb with him.

Socinios had only ravaged the frontier of the kingdom of Sennaar to the weſtward, from Serkè towards Fazuclo. This was but a part of the large ſcheme of vengeance he had reſolved to execute progreſſively from Serkè, in reparation of the affront he had received from the king of the Funge. But he delegated what remained to the two princes his ſons, and to the governor of Tigrè.

Welled Hawaryat, at the head of the Koccob horſe, and another body of cavalry reckoned equal in valour, called _Maia_, and the greateſt part of the king's houſehold troops, were ordered to fall upon that part of the frontier of Sennaar which the king had left from Serkè eaſtward. Melca Chriſtos, with the horſe of Siré and Samen, was appointed to attack the frontier ſtill farther eaſt, oppoſite to the province of Sirè. Tecla Georgis, governor of Tigrè, was directed to lay waſte that part of the kingdom of Sennaar bordering upon the frontiers of his province.

The whole of this expedition ſucceeded to a wiſh; only Melea Chriſtos, in paſſing through the country of Shangalla, was met by a large army of that people, who, thinking the expedition intended againſt them, had attacked him in his paſſage, with ſome appearance of advantage; but by his own exertions, and thoſe of his troops alarmed at their prince's danger, he not only extricated himſelf from

the

the bad fituation he was in, but gave the Shangalla fo entire an overthrow, that one of their tribes was nearly exterminated by that day's flaughter, and crowds of women and children fent flaves to the king at Dancaz.

The delay that this occafioned had no bad effect upon the expedition. The victorious troops poured immediately into Atbara under Melca Chriftos, and completed the deftruction made by Welled Hawaryat, and the governor of Tigré. All Sennaar was filled with people flying from the conquerors, and an immenfe number of cattle was driven away by the three armies. Baady feems to have been an idle fpectator of this havock made in his kingdom ; and the armies returned without lofs to Dancaz, loaded with plunder.

Still the vengeance of Socinios was not fatisfied. The Baharnagafh, Guebra Mariam, was commanded to march againft Fatima queen of the Shepherds, called at that time Negufta Errum, queen of the Greeks. This was a princefs who governed the remnant of that ancient race of people, once the fovereigns of the whole country, who, for feveral dynafties, were mafters of Egypt, and who ftill, among their ancient cuftoms, preferved that known one, of always placing a woman upon the throne. Her refidence was at Mendera*, on the N. E. of Atbara, one of the largeft and moft populous towns in it; a town, indeed, built like the reft, of clay, ftraw, and reeds, but not lefs populous or flourifhing on that account. It was in the way of the caravans from Suakem, both to Abyffinia and Sennaar, as alfo of thofe large caravans to and from Sudan, the Negro country upon the Niger, which then came, and ftill ufe that road in their way to Mecca. Its female fovereign was confidered as
                                                    guardian

---

* See the Map.

guardian of that communication, and the caravans paffing it.

The Baharnagafh had in orders from Socinios to purfue this queen till he had taken her prifoner, and to bring her in that condition into his prefence. The enterprife was by no means an eafy one. Great part of the road was without water; but Guebra Mariam, the Baharnagafh, was an active and prudent officer, and perfectly acquainted with the feveral parts of the country. With a fmall, but veteran army, he marched down the Mareb, between that river and the mountains, deftroying all the places through which he paffed, putting the inhabitants unmercifully to the fword, that no one might approach him, nor any report be made of his numbers, which were everywhere magnified by thofe that efcaped, and who computed them from the greatnefs of the defolation they had occafioned.

On the 13th day he came before Mendera, and fent a fummons to the queen Fatima to furrender. Being told that fhe had fled on his approach, he anfwered, That he cared not where fhe was; but that, unlefs fhe furrendered herfelf prifoner before he entered Mendera, he would firft fet the town on fire, and then quench the flames by the blood of its inhabitants..

Fatima, though old and infirm, was too great a lover of her people to rifk the fulfilling this threat from any confideration of what might happen to her. She furrendered herfelf to Guebra Mariam, with two attendants; and he, without lofs of time, marched back to his own country, abftaining from every fort of violence or excefs in his way,.

2

from respect to his female prisoner, whom he brought in triumph before Socinios to Dancaz, and was the first messenger of his own victory.

Socinios received this queen of the Greeks on his throne; but, in consideration of her infirmities, dispensed with the ceremony of prostration, constantly observed in Abyssinia on being introduced to the presence of the king: seeing that she was unable to stand during the time of her interrogation, he ordered a low stool to be set for her on the ground; a piece of consideration very rarely shewn to any stranger in Abyssinia, however great their dignity and quality.

Socinios sternly demanded of his prisoner, " Why she and her predecessors, being vassals to the crown of Abyssinia, had not only omitted the payment of their tribute, but had not even sent the customary presents to him upon his accession to the throne ?"

To this the queen answered with great frankness and candour, " That it was true, such tributes and presents were due, and were also punctually paid from old times by her ancestors to his, as long as protection was afforded them and their people, and this was the principal cause of paying that tribute ; but the Abyssinians having first suffered the country to be in great part conquered by the Arabs, and then again by the Funge, without ever interfering, she had concluded a peace with the Funge of Sennaar, and paid the tribute to them, in consequence of which they defended her from the Arabs : That she had had no soldiers but such as were employed in keeping a strict watch over the road through the desert to Suakem, which was anciently trusted

to

to her; that the other part of her fubjects was occupied in keeping and rearing great herds of cattle for the markets of Sennaar and other towns, as well as camels for the caravans of Mecca, Cairo, and Sudan, both employments being of public benefit; and, therefore, as fhe did harm to none, fhe had a greater reafon to wonder what could be his motive of fending fo far from home to feek her, and her harmlefs fubjects, in the defert, with fuch effufion of innocent blood."

THE king hearing this fagacious anfwer, which was followed by many others of the kind, was extremely pleafed; but affured her, " That he intended to maintain his ancient right both over her fubjects, and the Arabs under Wed Ageeb, who was now his vaffal, in all the country from Fazuclo to Suakem; that he confidered the Funge as ufurpers, and would certainly treat them as fuch." ·After this Socinios difmiffed the queen, and gave her affurances of protection, having firft cloathed her as his vaffal in filk and damafk, after the fafhion of women in her own country.

BUT it was not long before this train of fuccefs met with a confiderable check. Very foon afterwards, the king being in Gojam, a meffage was brought to him from the principal people of Narea, informing him plainly, " That Benero, having become cruel and avaricious, put many people to death wantonly, and many more for the fake of their money; having taken from them their wives and daughters, either for his own pleafure, or to fell them as flaves to the Galla—they had at laft murdered him, and chofen a man in his room diftinguifhed for his virtue and goodnefs."

THE king was very much exafperated at this meffage. He told them, however bad Benero might have been, he confidered his murder as an infult done to himfelf, and had, therefore, difpatched Muftapha Bafha with fome troops, and given command to all the Mahometans in Narea to affift him, and to inquire into the death of Benero, and the merit of his fucceffor.

AT the fame time, the Galla made an inroad into Begemder; and Welled Hawaryat, affembling what troops he could, in hafte, to ftop the defolation of that province, and having come in fight of the enemy, he was forfaken by his army, and flain, together with the Cantiba of Dembea, Amdo, and Nile Wed Ageeb prince of the Arabs, after fighting manfully for the king. Socinios, upon the arrival of this news, gave himfelf up to immoderate forrow ; not fo much for the lofs of his army which had mifbehaved, as for the death of Welled Hawaryat his favourite fon, and Amdo and Nile, the two beft officers in his army.

IT will now be neceffary that we look back a little to the ftate of religious affairs in Abyffinia, which began from this time to have influence in every meafure, and greatly to promote the troubles of that empire; though they were by no means their only caufe, as fome have faid, with a view to throw greater odium upon the Jefuits, who furely have enough to anfwer for, without inflaming the account by any exaggeration.

PAEZ, in the courfe of building the palace at Gorgora, had defervedly aftonifhed the whole kingdom by a difplay of his univerfal genius and capacity. If he was affiduous

and

and diligent in raiſing this fabric, he had not neglected the advancing of another, the converſion of Abyſſinia to the obedience of the ſee of Rome.

Ras Sela Christos (if we believe theſe miſſionaries) had converted himſelf, by reading with attention the Abyſſinian books only. Being about to depart from Gojam to fight a-gainſt the Galla, he wanted very much to have made his renunciation and confeſſion in the preſence of Peter Paez. But, as he was buſied at Gorgora building a convent and palace there, he contented himſelf with another Jeſuit, Fran-ciſco Antonio d'Angelis; and, being victorious in his expe-dition, he gave the fathers ground and a ſum of money to build a monaſtery at Collela, which was now the third in Abyſſinia belonging to the Jeſuits.

As for the king, though probably already determined in his own mind, he had not taken any ſtep ſo deciſive as could induce the compliance of others. Diſputes were con-ſtantly maintained, for the moſt part in his preſence, be-tween the miſſionaries and the Abyſſinian monks, chiefly concerning the long-agitated queſtion, the two natures in Chriſt, in which, although the victory declared always in favour of the Jeſuits, if we may credit their repreſentations, no conviction followed on the part of the adverſaries. At laſt Abuna Simon complained to the king, that unuſual and irregular things had been permitted without his knowledge; that diſputes upon articles of faith had been held without calling him, or his being permitted to give his clergy the advantage of his ſupport in theſe controverſies.

The

THE king, who did not believe that the Abuna's eloquence or learning would make any great alteration, ordered the difputations to be held a-new in the Abuna's prefence. That prieft's ignorance made the matter worfe ; and the king, holding this point as now fettled, made his firft public declaration, that there were two natures in Chrift, perfect God and perfect man, really diftinct between themfelves, but united in one divine perfon, which is the Chrift.

AT this time, letters came by way of India, both from the king of Spain, Philip II. dated in Madrid the 15th of March 1609, and from the pope Paul V. of the 4th of January 1611. Thefe letters contain nothing but general declamatory exhortations to Socinios to perfevere in the Chriftian faith, affuring him of the affiftance of the Holy Spirit, inftead of thofe Portuguefe regiments which he had folicited. However, the affair of the converfion being altogether fettled between the king and Paez, it was thought proper to make the renunciation firft, and then depend upon the king of Spain and the pope for fending the foldiers, if their prayers were not effectual.

IT was neceffary that Socinios fhould write to the pope, notifying his fubmiffion to the fee of Rome. But letters on fuch a fubject were thought of too great confequence to be fent, as former difpatches to Europe had been, without being accompanied by proper perfons, who, upon occafion, might affume the character of ambaffadors, and give any affurance or explanation needful.

IT was at the fame time confidered, that the way by Mafuah was fo liable to accidents, the intermediate province of
Tigré

Tigré being ftill as it were in a ftate of rebellion, that it would be eafy for the enemies of the Catholic faith to intercept thefe meffengers and letters by the way, fo that their contents might be publifhed amongft the king's enemies in Abyffinia, without ever being made known in Europe. Some propofed the longer, but, as they apprehended, the more fecure way, by paffing Narea and the provinces fouth of the frontiers of that kingdom, partly inhabited by Gentiles, partly by Mahometans, to Melinda, on the Indian Ocean, where they might embark for Goa.

Lots were caft among the miffionaries who of their number fhould undertake this long and dangerous journey. The lot fell upon Antonio Fernandes, a man of great prudence, much efteemed by the king, and by the general voice allowed to be the propereft of all the fociety for this undertaking. He, on his part, named Fecur Egzie *(beloved of the Lord)* as his companion, to be ambaffador to the king of Spain and the pope. This man had been one of the firft of the Abyffinians converted to the Catholic faith by the Jefuits, and he continued in it fteadily to his death. He was a perfon of tried courage and prudence, and of a pleafant and agreeable converfation.

It was the beginning of March 1613 Antonio Fernandes * fet out for Gojam, where was Ras Sela Chriftos. Fecur Egzie had fet out before, that he might adjuft his family affairs, and took with him ten Portuguefe, fix of whom were to go

3

no

---

* See the provincial letters of the Jefuits in Tellez, lib. iv. cap. 5..

no farther than Narea, and return, the other four to embark with him for India.

The governor detained the fmall company till he procured guides from among the Shats and Gallas, barbarous nations near Narea, and eaftward of it, from whom he took hoftages for properly protecting this caravan in their way, paying them well, as an encouragement for behaving honeftly and faithfully.

On the 15th of April they had fet out from Umbarma, then the head-quarters of Sela Chriftos, who gave them for guards forty men armed with fhields and javelins. Nor was it long before their difficulties began. Travelling about two days to the weft, they came to Senaffé, the principal village or habitation of the Pagan Gongas, very recently in rebellion, and nearly deftroyed, rather than fubdued. To the firft demand of fafe conduct, they anfwered in a manner which fhewed that, far from defending the travellers from others, they were refolved themfelves to fall upon them, and rob or murder them in the way. One Portuguefe offered himfelf to return with Fernandes to complain of thefe favages to Sela Chriftos; who, upon their arrival, difpatched three officers with troops to chaftife thefe Pagans, and convey the ambaffador and his attendants out of their territory and reach.

The Gongas, being informed that a complaint was fent to Sela Chriftos, which would infallibly be followed by a detachment of troops, gave the ambaffador the fafeguard he demanded, which carried him in three days to Minè*.

This

* Which fignifies the Paffage.

This is the name of fome miferable villages, often rebuilt, and as often deftroyed, upon a ford of the Nile, over which is the ordinary paffage for the Mahometan merchants into Bizamo, the way to the mountainous country of Narea and Caffa. As the rains had begun to fall here with violence, when Fernandes and his companions arrived, they were obliged to pafs the river on fkins blown full of wind.

The diftance from Minè to Narea is 50 leagues due fouth, with little inclination to weft. The road to it, and the places through which you pafs, are very diftinctly fet down in my map, and, I believe, without any material error; it is the only place where the reader can find this route, which, till now, has never been publifhed.

The next day our travellers entered the kingdom of Bizamo, inhabited by Pagan Galla. Thefe people came in crowds with arms in their hands, infifting upon being paid for liberty of paffing through their country; but, feeing the company of the ambaffador take to their arms likewife, they compounded for a few bricks of falt and coarfe cotton cloaths, and thereupon fuffered them to pafs. The fame day, the guide, fent from Narea to conduct them by crooked and unfrequented paths out of the way of the Pagan Galla, made them to enter into a large thicket through which they could fcarcely force themfelves; after which they came to a river called *Maleg*, when it was nearly night. Next day they could find no ford where they could pafs. They now entertained a fufpicion, that the guard from Narea had betrayed them, and intended to leave them in thefe woods to meet their death from the Galla.

THE day after, they found the ford, and paffed it without difficulty; and, being on the other fide, they began to be a little more compofed, as being far from the Pagans, and now near entering the territory of Narea. After afcending a high mountain, they came to Gonea, where they found a garrifon under one of the principal officers of that kingdom, who received them with great marks of honour and joy, on account of the warm recommendation Sela Chriftos had given them, and perhaps as much for a confiderable prefent they had brought along with them.

NAREA, the fouthmoft province of the Abyffinian empire, is ftill governed by its native princes, who are called *the Beneros;* its territory reached formerly to Bizamo.

THE Galla have quite furrounded them, efpecially on the fouth-eaft and north. What is to the weft is a part of Africa, the moft unknown. The people of Narea have a fmall trade with Melinda on the Indian Ocean, and with Angola on the weftern, by means of intermediate nations. Narea is abundantly fupplied with gold from the Negro country that is neareft them. Some have, indeed, faid there is gold in Narea; but, after a very diligent inveftigation, I find it comes chiefly from towards the Atlantic.

THE kingdom of Narea ftands like a fortified place in the middle of a plain. Many rivers, rifing in the fourth and fifth degrees of latitude, fpread themfelves, for want of level, over this flat country, and ftagnate in very extenfive marfhes from fouth by eaft, to the point of north, or north-weft.

THE

THE foot of the mountains, or edge of thefe marfhes neareft Narea, is thick overgrown with coffee-trees, which, if not the *only*, is the *largeft* tree known there. Then comes the mountainous country of Narea Proper, which is interfperfed with fmall, unwholefome, but very fertile valleys. Immediately adjoining is the more mountainous country of Caffa, without any level ground whatever. It is faid to be governed by a feparate prince: they were converted to Chriftianity in the time of Melec Segued, fome time after the converfion of Narea. The Galla, having fettled themfelves in all the flat ground to the very edge of the marfhes, have, in great meafure, cut off the communication with Abyffinia for many years together; fo that their continuance in the Chriftian faith feems very precarious and uncertain, for want of books and priefts to inftruct them.

THE Nareans of the high country are the lighteft in colour of any people in Abyffinia; but thofe that live by the borders of the marfhes below are perfect blacks, and have the features and wool of negroes: whereas all thofe in the high country of Narea, and ftill more fo in the ftupendous mountains of Caffa, are not fo dark as Neopolitans or Sicilians. Indeed it is faid that fnow has been feen to lie on the mountains of Caffa, as alfo in that high ridge called Dyre and Tegla; but this I do not believe. Hail has probably been feen to lie there; but I doubt much whether this can be faid of a fubftance of fo loofe a texture as fnow.

THERE is great abundance both of cattle, grain, and all forts of provifions in Narea, as well in the high as in the low country. Gold, which they fell by weight, is the medium of commerce within the country itfelf; but coarfe cotton cloths, ſtibium, beads, and incenſe, are the articles with which their foreign trade to Angola, and the kingdoms on the Atlantic, is carried on.

The Nareans are exceedingly brave. Though they have been conquered, and driven out of the low country, it has been by multitudes—nation after nation pouring in upon them with a number of horſe to which they are perfect ſtrangers : But now, confined to the mountains, and ſurrounded by their marſhes and woods, they deſpiſe all further attempts of the Galla, and drive them from their frontiers whenever they approach too near.

In theſe ſkirmiſhes, or in ſmall robbing parties, thoſe Nareans are taken, whom the Mahometan merchants ſell at Gondar. At Conſtantinople, India, or Cairo, the women are more eſteemed as ſlaves than thoſe of any other part of the world, and the men are reckoned faithful, active, and intelligent. Both ſexes are remarkable for a chearful, kind diſpoſition, and, if properly treated, ſoon attach themſelves inviolably to their maſters. The language of Narea and Caffa is peculiar to that country, and is not a dialect of any neighbouring nation.

Antonio Fernandes in this journey, ſeeking to go to India by Melinda in company with Fecur Egzie ambaſſador, paſſed through this country ; but none of the Jeſuits ever went to Narea with a view of converting the people, at which I have been often ſurpriſed. There was enough of gold and ignorance to have allured them. That ſoftneſs and ſimplicity of manners for which the Nareans are remarkable, their affection for their maſters and ſuperiors, and firm attachment

4

tachment to them, would have been great advantages in the hands of the fathers. Every Abyſſinian would have encouraged them at the beginning of this miſſion ; and, if once they had firmly eſtabliſhed themſelves in a country of ſo difficult acceſs, they might have bid defiance to prince Facilidas, and the perſecution that deſtroyed the progreſs of the Catholic faith in that reign.

From Gonea, in ſix days they came to the reſidence of Benero, the ſovereign of the country ; ſince the conqueſt and converſion under Melec Segued, he is called Shum. The ambaſſador and Fernandes were received by the Benero with an air of conſtraint and coolneſs, though with civility. They found afterwards the cauſe of this was the inſinuation of a ſchiſmatic Abyſſinian monk, then at the court of that prince, who had told him that the errand of the ambaſſador and miſſionary to India was to bring Portugueſe troops that way into Abyſſinia, which would end in the deſtruction of Narea, if it did not begin with it.

Terrified at a danger ſo near, the Benero called a council, in which it was reſolved that the ambaſſador ſhould be turned from the direct road into the kingdom of Bali, to a much more inconvenient, longer, and dangerous one ; and, the ambaſſador heſitating a little when this was propoſed, the Benero told him plainly, that he would not ſuffer him to paſs further by any other way than that of Bali.

Bali was once a province belonging to Abyſſinia, and was the firſt taken from them by the Galla. It is to the north-eaſt of Narea, to the weſt of the kingdom of Adel,

R r 2

which

which feparates it from the fea; of which ample mention has been already made in the beginning of this hiftory.

This was to turn them to Cape Gardefan, the longeft journey they could poffibly make by land, and in the middle of their enemies; whereas the direction of the coaft of the Indian Ocean running greatly to the weftward, and towards Melinda, was the fhorteft journey they could make by land. Melinda, too, had many rich merchants, who, though Moors, did yet traffic in the Portuguefe fettlements on the coaft of Malabar, and had little intelligence or con-cern with the religious difputes which raged in Abyffinia.

However, I very much doubt whether this neareft route could be accomplifhed, at leaft by travellers, fuch as Fecur Egzie, Fernandes, and their companions, all ignorant of the language, and, therefore, conftantly at the difcretion of interpreters, and the malice or private views of different people through whofe hands they muft have paffed.

The Benero, having thus provided againft the dangers with which his ftate was threatened, if our travellers went by Melinda, made them a prefent of fifty crufades of gold for the neceffaries of their journey; and, as their way lay through the fmall ftate of Gingiro, and an ambaffador from the fovereign of that ftate was then at Narea, he difpatched that minifter in great hafte, recommending the Portuguefe to his protection fo long as they fhould be in his territory.

Fecur Egzie and his company fet out with the ambaffador of Gingiro in a direction due eaft; and the firft day they arrived at a poft of Narea, where was the officer who was to give them a guard to the frontiers; and who, after some delay, in order to see what he could extort from them, at last gave them a party of eighty soldiers to conduct them to the frontiers.

After four long days journey through countries totally laid waste by the Galla, keeping scouts constantly before them to give advice of the first appearance of any enemy, that they might hide themselves in thickets and bushes; at mid-day they began to descend a very steep craggy ridge of mountains, when the ambassador of Gingiro, now their conductor, warned them, that, before they got to the foot of the mountain, they should enter into a very thick wood to hide themselves till night, that they might not be discovered by the Galla shepherds feeding their flocks in the plain below; for only at night, when they had retired, could those plains be passed in safety.

At four o'clock in the afternoon they began to enter the wood, and were lucky in getting a violent shower of rain, which dislodged the Galla sooner than ordinary, and sent them and their cattle home to their huts. But it was, at the same time, very disagreeable to our travellers on account of its excessive coldness. Next day, in the evening, descending another very rugged chain of mountains, they came to the banks of the large river Zebeé, as the Portuguese call it; but its true name is Kibbeé, a name given it by the Mahometan merchants, (the only travellers in this country) from its whiteness, approaching to the colour of melted butter, which that word signifies.

THE

THE river Zebeé, or Kibbeé, furrounds a great part of the kingdom of Gingiro. It has been miftaken for the river El Aice, which runs into Egypt in a courfe parallel to the Nile, but to the weft of it.

NAREA feems to be the higheft land in the peninfula of Africa, fo that here the rivers begin to run alternately towards the Cape of Good Hope and Mediterranean; but the defcent at firft is very fmall on either fide. In the adjoining latitudes, that is 4° on each fide of the Line, it rains perpetually, fo that thefe rivers, though not rapid, are yet kept continually full.

THIS of Zebeé, is univerfally allowed by the merchants of this country to be the head of the river Quilimancy, which, pafling through fuch a tract of land from Narea to near Melinda, muft have opened a very confiderable communication with the inland country.

THIS territory, called Zindero, or Gingiro, is a very fmall one. The father and Fecur Egzie refted the fixth day from their fetting out from Narea. The river Zebeè, by the defcription of Fernandes, feems to incline from its fource in a greater angle than any river on the north of that partition. He fays it carries more water with it than the Nile, and is infinitely more rapid, fo that it would be abfolutely impaffable in the feafon of rains, were it not for large rocks which abound in its channel.

THE paffage was truly tremendous; trees were laid from the fhore to the next immediate rock; from that rock to the next another tree was laid; then another that reached

to

to the fhore. Thefe trees were fo elaftic as to bend with the weight of a fingle perfon. At a great diftance below ran the foaming current of the river, fo deep an abyfs that it turned the heads of thofe who were paffing on the moveable elaftic fupport or bridge above.

Yet upon this feeming inconvenience the exiftence of that country depended. The Galla that furrounded it would have over-run it in a month, but for this river, always rapid and always full, whofe ordinary communication by a bridge could be deftroyed in a moment; and which, though it had one ford, yet this was ufelefs, unlefs paffengers had affiftance from both fides of the river, and confequently could never be of fervice to an enemy.

The terrible appearance of this tottering bridge for a time ftopped the ambaffador and miffionary. They looked upon the paffing upon thefe trembling beams as certainly incurring inevitable deftruction. But the reflection of dangers that preffed them behind overcame thefe fears, and they preferred the refolution to run the rifk of being drowned in the river Zebeé, rather than, by ftaying on the other fide all night, to ftand the chance of being murdered by the Galla. But, after all the men only could pafs the bridge, they were obliged to leave the mules on the other fide till the next morning, with inftructions to their people, that, upon the firft appearance of the Galla, they fhould leave them, and make their beft way over the bridge, throwing down one of the trees after them. The next morning, two peafants, fubjects of Gingiro, fhewed them the ford, where their beafts paffed over with great difficulty and danger, but without lofs.

IT was neceffary now to acquaint the king of Gingiro of their arrival in his kingdom, and to beg to be honoured with an audience. But he happened at that time to be employed in the more important bufinefs of conjuration and witchcraft, without which this fovereign does nothing.

THIS kingdom of Gingiro may be fixed upon as the firft on this fide of Africa where we meet with the ftrange practice of divining from the apparition of fpirits, and from a direct communication with the devil: A fuperftition this which likewife reaches down all along the weftern fide of this continent on the Atlantic Ocean, in the countries of Congo, Angola, and Benin. In fpite of the firmeft foundation in true philofophy, a traveller, who decides from the information and inveftigation of facts, will find it very difficult to treat thefe appearances as abfolute fiction, or as owing to a fuperiority of cunning of one man in over-reaching another. For my own part, I confefs I am equally at a lofs to affign reafons for difbelieving the fiction on which their pretenfions to fome preternatural information are founded, as to account for them by the operation of ordinary caufes. The king of Gingiro found eight days neceffary before he could admit the ambaffador and Fernandes into his prefence. On the ninth, they received a permiffion to go to court, and they arrived there the fame day.

WHEN they came into the prefence of the king he was feated in a large gallery, open before, like what we call a balcony, which had fteps from below on the outfide, by which he afcended and defcended at pleafure. When the letter which the ambaffador carried was intimated to him, he came down from the gallery to receive it, a piece of refpect

fpect which he fhewed to the king of Abyffinia, though he was neither his fubject nor vaffal. He inquired much after the king's health, and ftood a little by the ambaffador and Fernandes, fpeaking by an interpreter. Afterwards he a-gain returned to his balcony, fat down there, read his letter, and then correfponded with the ambaffador by mef-ages fent from above to them below.

It is impoffible to conceive from this, or any thing that Fernandes fays, whether the language of Gingiro is pecu-liar to that country or not. The king of Gingiro read So-cinios's letter, which was either in the Tigrè or Arabic lan-guage. Fernandes underftood the Arabic, and Fecur Egzie the Tigrè and Amharic. It is not poffible, then, to know what was the language of the king of Gingiro, who read and underftood Socinios's letter, but fpoke to Fecur Egzie by an interpreter.

At laft the king of Gingiro told them, that all contained in the king of Abyffinia's letter was, that he fhould ufe them well, give them good guard and protection while they were in his country, and further them on their journey; which he faid he would execute with the greateft pleafure and punctuality.

The next day, as is ufual, the ambaffador and miffionary carried the king's prefent, chints, calicoe, and other manufac-tures of India, things that the king efteemed moft. In re-turn to Fernandes he fent a young girl, whom the father returned, it not being cuftomary, as he faid, for a Chriftian prieft to have girls in his company. In exchange for the girl, the good-natured king of Gingiro fent him a flave of the other fex, and a beautiful mule. With all refpect to the fcruples of the father, I think it would have been fair to have kept the beautiful mule, and given the young female Gingerite to his companion in the journey, Fecur Egzie, who could have had no fcruples.

FERNANDES fays he received the boy from the only view of faving his foul by baptifm. I wonder, fince Providence had thrown the girl firft in his way, by what rule of charity it was he configned her foul to perdition by returning her, as he was not certain at the time that he might not have got a mule or camel in exchange for the girl; and then, upon his own principles, he certainly was author of the perdition of that foul which Providence feemed to have conducted by an extraordinary way to the enjoyment of all the advantages of Chriftianity ; furely the care of Neophytes of the female fex was not a new charge to the Jefuits in Abyffinia.

IT feems to be ridiculous for Fernandes to imagine that the fovereign of this little ftate called himfelf Gingiro, knowing that this word fignified a monkey. His enemies might give him that name ; but it is not likely he would adopt it himfelf. And the reafon of that name is ftill more ridiculous; for he fays it is becaufe the gallery is like a monkey's cage. If that was the cafe, all the princes in Congo and Angola give their audiences in fuch places. Indeed, it feems to me that it is here the cuftoms, ufed in thefe laft-mentioned parts of Africa, begin, although Gingiro is nearer the coaft of the Indian Ocean than that of the Atlantic. The colour of the people at Gingiro is nearly black, ftill it

is

is not the black of a negro; the features are fmall and
ftraight as in Europe or Abyffinia.

ALL matters in this ftate are conducted by magic; and
we may fee to what point the human underftanding is debafed in the diftance of a few leagues. Let no man fay that
ignorance is the caufe, or heat of climate, which is the unintelligible obfervation generally made on thefe occafions.
For why fhould heat of climate addict a people to magic
more than cold? or, why fhould ignorance enlarge a man's
powers, fo that, overleaping the bounds of common intelligence, it fhould extend his faculty of converfing with a new
fet of beings in another world? The Ethiopians, who nearly furround Abyffinia, are blacker than thofe of Gingiro,
their country hotter, and are, like them, an indigenous
people that have been, from the beginning, in the fame part
where they now inhabit. Yet the former neither adore the
devil, nor pretend to have a communication with him: they
have no human facrifices, nor are there any traces of fuch
enormities having prevailed among them. A communication with the fea has been always open, and the flave-trade
prevalent from the earlieft times; while the king of Gingiro, fhut up in the heart of the continent, facrifices thofe
flaves to the devil which he has no opportunity to fell to
man. For at Gingiro begins that accurfed cuftom of making the fhedding of human blood a neceffary part in all
folemnities. How far to the fouthward this reaches I do
not know; but I look upon this to be the geographical
bounds of the reign of the devil on the north fide of the
equator in the peninfula of Africa.

THIS

THIS kingdom is hereditary in one family, but does not descend in course to the eldest son, the election of the particular prince being in the nobles ; and thus far, indeed, it seems to resemble that of their neighbours in Abyssinia.

WHEN the king of Gingiro dies, the body of the deceased is wrapped in a fine cloth, and a cow is killed. They then put the body so wrapped up into the cow's skin. As soon as this is over, all the princes of the royal family fly and hide themselves in the bushes; while others, intrusted with the election, enter into the thickets, beating everywhere about as if looking for game. At last a bird of prey, called in their country Liber, appears, and hovers over the person destined to be king, crying and making a great noise without quitting his station. By this means the person destined to be elected is found, surrounded, as is reported, by tigers, lions, panthers, and suchlike wild beasts. This is imagined to be done by magic, or the devil, else there are everywhere enough of these beasts lying in the cover to furnish materials for such a tale, without having recourse to the power of magic to assemble them.

As they find their king, then, like a wild beast, so his behaviour continues the same after he is found. He flies upon them with great rage, resisting to the last, wounding and killing all he can reach without any consideration, till, overcome by force, he is dragged to a throne, which he fills in a manner perfectly corresponding to the rationality of the ceremonies of his instalment.

ALTHOUGH there are many that have a right to seek after this king, yet, when he is discovered, it does not follow,

4   that

that the fame perfon who finds him fhould carry him to his coronation; for there is a family who have a right to difpute this honour with the firſt poſſeſſor; and, therefore, in his way from the wood, they fet upon the people in whofe hands he is, and a battle enfues, where feveral are killed or wounded; and if thefe laſt, by force, can take him out of the hands of the firſt finder, they enjoy all the honours due to him that made him king.

BEFORE he enters his palace two men are to be flain; one at the foot of the tree by which his houfe is chiefly fupported; the other at the threfhold of his door, which is befmeared with the blood of the victim. And, it is faid, (I have heard this often in Abyſſinia from people coming from that country) that the particular family, whofe priviledge it is to be flaughtered, fo far from avoiding it, glory in the occafion, and offer themfelves willingly to meet it.— To return to our travellers—

THE father and the ambaſſador, leaving the kingdom of Gingiro, proceeded in a direction due eaſt, and entered the kingdom of Cambat, depending ſtill on the empire of Abyſſinia, and there halted at Sangara, which feems to be the principal place of the province, governed at that time by a Moor called *Amelmal.*

ON the left of Cambat are the Guragués, who live in fome beggarly villages, but moſtly in caves and holes in the mountains. The father was detained two days at Sangara, at the perfuafion of the inhabitants there, who told him there was a fair in the neighbourhood, and people would pafs in numbers to accompany him, fo that there
would

would be no danger. But, after ſtaying that time at Sangara, he found that the intention of this delay was only to
give time to ſome horſemen of the Guragués to aſſemble,
in order to attack the caravan on the road, which they did
ſoon after; and, though they were repulſed, yet it was
with loſs of one of the company, a young man related to
Socinios, who, being wounded with a poiſoned arrow, died
ſome days after.

In the mean time, an Abyſſinian, called *Manquer*, overtook
their caravan. As he was a ſchiſmatic, his intention was
very well known to be that of diſappointing their journey ;
and he prevailed with Amelmal ſo far as to make him
ſuſpect that the recommendations which the ambaſſador
brought were falſe. He, therefore, inſiſted on the ambaſſador's ſtaying there till he ſhould get news from court. Amelmal, Manquer, and the ambaſſador, each diſpatched a meſſenger, who tarried three months on the road, and at laſt
brought orders from the king to diſpatch them immediately.

As Amelmal now ſaw the bad inclination of Manquer,
he detained him at Cambat that he might occaſion no more
difficulties in their way. He gave the ambaſſador likewiſe
ſeven horſes, which were ſaid to be the beſt preſents to the
princes or governors that were in his road, and diſpatched
the travellers with another companion, Baharo, who had
brought the letters from the king.

From Cambat they entered the ſmall territory of Alaba,
independent of the king of Abyſſinia, whoſe governor was
called *Aliko*, a Moor. This man, already prejudiced againſt
the

the miffionary and the ambaffador, was ftill hefitating whether to allow them to procced, when Manquer, who fled from Amelmal, arrived. Aliko, hearing from this incendiary, that the father's errand was to bring Portuguefe that way from India to deftroy the Mahometan faith, as in former times, burft into fuch violent rage as to threaten the father, and all with him, with death, which nothing but the reality of the king's letters, of which he had got affurance from Baharo, and fome regard to the law of nations, on account of the ambaffador Fecur Egzie, could have prevented. In the mean time, he put them all in clofe prifon, where feveral of the Portuguefe died. At laft, after a council held, in which Manquer gave his voice for putting them to death, a man of fuperior character in that country advifed the fending them back to Amelmal, the way that they came; and this meafure was accordingly adopted.

THEY returned, therefore, from Cambat, and thence to Gorgora, without any fort of advantage to themfelves or to us, only what arifes from that opportunity of rectifying the geography of the country through which they paffed; and even for this they have furnifhed but very fcanty materials, in comparifon of what we might reafonably have expected, without having occafioned any additional fatigue to themfelves.

WE have already faid, that though Socinios had not openly declared his refolution of embracing the Catholic faith, yet he had gone fo far as to declare, upon the difpute held between the Catholic and fchifmatic clergy, in his own prefence and that of the Abuna, that the Abyffinian

2   difputants

difputants were vanquifhed, and ought to have been convinced from the authority of their own books, efpecially
that of Haimanout Abou, the faith of the ancient fathers
and doctors of their church received by them from the beginning as the undoubted rule of faith : That the doctrine
of the Catholic church being only what was taught in the
Haimanout Abou concerning the two natures in Chrift, this
point was to all intents and purpofes fettled ; and, therefore,
he fignified it as his will, that, for the future, no one fhould
deny that there are two natures in Chrift, diftinct in themfelves, but divinely united in one perfon, which was Chrift ;
declaring at the fame time, that in cafe any perfon fhould
hereafter deny, or call this in doubt, he would chaftife him
for feven years.

THE Abuna, on the contrary, fupported by the half-bro-
ther of the king, Emana Chriftos, (brother to Ras Sela Chriftos) publifhed a fentence of excommunication, by affixing
it to the door of one of the churches belonging to the palace, in which he declared all perfons accurfed who fhould
maintain two natures in Chrift, or embrace or vindicate
any of the errors of the church of Rome.

THE king had received various complaints of the Agows,
who had abufed his officers, and refufed payment of tribute. He had fet out upon an expedition againft them, intending to winter in that country ; but, hearing of the rafh
conduct of the Abuna, and the leagues that were in confequence everywhere forming againft him, he returned to
Gorgora, and fent to the Abuna, that unlefs, without delay,
he recalled the excommunication he had publifhed, he fhould
be forthwith punifhed with lofs of his head. This language
was

was too clear and explicit to admit a doubt of its meaning; and the Abuna, giving way for the time, recalled his excommunication.

A conspiracy was next formed by Emana Chriftos, the eunuch Kèfla Wahad mafter of the houfehold to the king, and Julius governor of Tigrè, to murder Socinios in his palace; for which purpofe they defired an audience upon weighty affairs, which being granted by the king, the three confpirators were admitted into his prefence.

It was concerted that Julius fhould prefent a petition of fuch a nature as probably to produce a refufal; and, in the time of the altercation that would enfue, when the king might be off his guard, the other two were to ftab him.

Just before the converfation began, he was advifed of his danger by a page, and Julius prefenting his petition, the king granted it immediately, before Emana Chriftos could come up to affift in the difpute which they expected; and this confpirator appearing in the inftant, the king, who had got up to walk, invited them all three up to the terrace. This was the moft favourable opportunity they could have wifhed. They, therefore, deferred affaulting him till they fhould have got up to the terrace: The king entered the door of the private ftair, and drew it haftily after him. It had a fpring-lock made by Peter Paez, which was fixed in the infide, and could not be opened from without, fo that the king was left fecure upon the terrace. Upon this the confpirators, fearing themfelves difcovered, retired, and from that time refolved to keep out of the king's power.

At that period, Socinios had determined upon an expedition againſt the Funge, that is, againſt the blacks of Sennaar, who had entered his country in a violent manner, deſtroying his people, and carrying them off as ſlaves. It was, therefore, concerted, that while the king was buſied far off with the Funge, Emana Chriſtos, Julius, and the eunuch Kèfla, at once ſhould attack Sela Chriſtos, at whom, next to the king, the conſpirators chiefly aimed; and the cauſe was, that the king had taken the poſts of Ras and the government of Gojam from Emana Chriſtos, who was a ſchiſmatic, and had given them to his younger brother, Sela Chriſtos, a violent Catholic.

Julius began by a proclamation in Woggora, in which he commanded, that thoſe who believed two natures in Chriſt ſhould immediately leave the province, and that all thoſe who were friends to the Alexandrian faith ſhould forthwith repair to him, and fight in defence of it. He then ordered the goods of all the Catholics in Tigrè to be confiſcated, and ſtraightway marched to ſurpriſe Sela Chriſtos then in Gojam. But the king received intelligence of his deſigns, and returned into Dembea before it was well known that he had left it. This, at firſt, very much diſconcerted Julius ; and the rather, that Emana Chriſtos and Kéfla Wahad kept aloof, nor had they declared themſelves openly yet, nor did they ſeem inclined to do it till Julius had firſt tried his fortune with the king.

This rebel, now full of preſumption, advanced with his army to where the Nile iſſues out of the great lake Tzana ; and there he found the Abuna Simon, who had ſtaid for ſome weeks in one of the iſlands upon pretence of devotion. Simon,

Simon, after having confirmed Julius in his refolution of murdering the king, his father-in-law, or of dying in defence of the Alexandrian faith, if neceffary, perfuaded him to lay afide his defign of marching againft Sela Chriftos, but rather immediately to return back and furprife the king before thefe two joined.

Julius readily adopted this advice of the Abuna; while that prieft, to fhew he was fincere, offered to accompany him in perfon, and fhare his fortune. This was accepted with pleafure by Julius, who next morning received the Abuna's benediction at the head of his army, and affifted at a folemn excommunication pronounced againft the king, Sela Chriftos, the fathers, and all the Catholics at court.

The king's firft thought, upon hearing thefe proceedings, was to fend fome troops to the affiftance of Sela Chriftos, warning him of his danger; but, upon hearing meafures were changed, and that the firft defign was againft himfelf, he marched to meet Julius, and fent a meffage to Sela Chriftos to join him with all poffible fpeed; and, as he was an excellent general, he took his poft fo judicioufly that he could not be forced to fight againft his will till fuccour was brought him, without great difadvantage to the enemy.

Julius, fearing the junction of Sela Chriftos, endeavoured to fight the two armies feparately. For which purpofe he advanced and pitched his camp clofe within fight of that of Socinios, refolving to force him to an engagement. This was thought a very dangerous meafure, and was contrary to the advice of all his friends, who faw how judicioufly Socinios had chofen his ground; and it was known to the meaneft

foldier

foldier on both fides, how confummate the king was in the art of war.

But the Abuna having perfuaded him, that, as foon as the foldiers fhould fee him, they would abandon the king and join his colours, early in the morning he put on his coat of mail, and, mounted on a ftrong and fiery horfe, was proceeding to the king's camp, when Malacotawit, his wife, (daughter to Socinios) perfuaded him at leaft to take fome food to enable him to bear the fatigues of the day. But difdaining fuch advice, he only anfwered furioufly, "That he had fworn not to tafte meat till he had brought her her father's head;" and, without longer waiting for the reft of his troops, he leaped over the enemy's lines in a quarter where the Abuna had promifed he fhould be well received.

Indeed, on his firft appearance, no one there oppofed his paffage, but feemed rather inclined to favour him as the Abuna had promifed: And he had now advanced near to a body of Tigrè foldiers that were the guard of the king's tent, loudly crying, " Where is your emperor?" when one of thefe with a ftone ftruck him fo rudely upon the forehead that it felled him to the ground; and, being now known, another foldier (called Amda) thruft him through with a fword, and thereafter killed him with many wounds. His head was cut off and carried to Socinios.

The few that attended him perifhed likewife among the foldiers. Nor did any of Julius's army think of a battle, but all fought their fafety by a flight. The king's troops being all frefh, purfued the fcattered rebels with great vigour,

gour, and many were slain, without any loss on the part of the royalists.

The Abuna Simon had, for a considerable time, stood as an ecclesiastic, unhurt and unheeded, among the flying troops. Being at last distinguished by his violent vociferation, and repeated imprecations upon the king and the conquerors, he was slain by a common soldier, who cut his head off and carried it to Socinios, who ordered it, with the body, to be taken from the field of battle and buried in a church-yard.

Socinios gave the spoil of the camp to his soldiers. It was said, that no time, since the Turks were defeated under Mahomet Gragné, was there ever so much treasure found in a camp. The pride of Julius induced him to carry all his riches with him. They were the fruits of avarice and oppression in all the principal posts of the empire, and which in their turn he had enjoyed. They were likewise the spoils of the Catholics, newly acquired by the confiscations made since his rebellion. A great number of cattle was likewise taken, which the king distributed among the priests of the several churches, the judges, and other lay-officers. Very great rejoicings were made everywhere, in the midst of which arrived Ras Sela Christos with his army from Gojam, and was struck with astonishment on seeing the small number of troops with which the king had been exposed to fight Julius, and how complete a victory he had gained with them.

In the mean time, Emana Christos had retired to a high mountain in Gojam, called *Melca Amba*, where he continued

I   to

to excite the people of that province to rebel and join Julius, whofe arrival he daily expected, that, together, they might fight Sela Chriftos. But the rafhnefs of Julius, and the march of Sela Chriftos to the king's affiftance, had very much difconcerted their whole fcheme.

AF CHRISTOS, who commanded in Gojam after the depar- ture of Ras Sela Chriftos, fent to Melca Amba, "reproaching Emana Chriftos with feditious practices; upbraiding him with the unnatural part he acted, being a brother-german to Sela Chriftos, and brother to Socinios by the fame mo- ther, while Julius was married to his daughter, and had conftantly enjoyed the great places of the empire. He afked him, What they could be more? Kings they could not be, neither he nor Julius. Ras, the next place in the empire, they both had enjoyed; and, if the king had taken that office lately from Emana Chriftos, he had not given it to a ftranger, but to his brother Sela Chriftos, who, it was but fair, fhould have his turn; and that the importance of his family was not the lefs increafed by it. Laftly, he re- prefented the danger he ran, if Julius made his peace, of falling a facrifice as the advifer of the rebellion."

EMANA CHRISTOS anfwered, "That though he rebelled with Julius, and at the fame time, yet it was not as a fol- lower of Julius, nor againft the king; but that he took up arms in defence of the ancient faith of his country, which was now, without reafon, trodden under foot in favour of a religion, which was a falfe one if they underftood it, and an ufelefs one if they did not. He faid he was fatisfied of his own danger; but neither his connection with the king, nor his being related to Sela Chriftos, could weigh with him

.3   againft againſt his duty to God and his country. The king and his brother might be right in embracing the Romiſh religion, becauſe they were convinced of the truth of it: he had uſed, however, the ſame means, and the ſame application, had heard the arguments of the ſame fathers, which, unluckily for him, had convinced him their religion was not a true, but a falſe one. For the ſame reaſons he continued to be an Alexandrian, which his brother alledged had made him a Roman. He, therefore, begged Af Chriſtos to conſider, by a review of things ſince David III.'s time, how much blood the change would coſt to the kingdom by the attempt, whether it ſucceeded or not; and whether, after that conſideration, it was worth trying the experiment."

THIS artful and ſenſible meſſage, ſent by a man of the capacity and experience of Emana Chriſtos, eaſily convinced Af Chriſtos that it was not by argument Emana Chriſtos was to be brought to his duty; but, like a good officer, he kept up correſpondence with him, that he might be maſter of the intelligence to what place he retired.

SOON after Sela Chriſtos had left Gojam to join the king, by forced marches he ſurrounded Melca Amba, where Emana Chriſtos was, and had aſſembled a number of troops to deſcend into the plain and create a diverſion in favour of Julius. The mountain had neither water in it nor food for ſuch a number of men, nor had Emana Chriſtos forces enough to riſk a battle with an officer of the known experience of Af Chriſtos, who had choſen the ground at his full leiſure, and with complete knowledge of it.

THRE

THREE days the army within the mountain held out without complaining; but, in the evening of the third day, some monks and hermits (*holy men*, the abettors of this rebellion) came to Af Chriftos to remonftrate, that there were feveral convents and villages in the mountain, alfo fmall fprings, and barley enough to anfwer the neceffities of the ordinary inhabitants, but were not enough for fuch an additional number which had taken forcible poffeffion of the wells, and drank up all the water, to the immediate danger of the whole inhabitants perifhing with thirft.

To this Af Chriftos anfwered, That the reducing the mountain, and the taking Emana Chriftos, was what was given him in commiffion by the king, to attain which end he would carefully improve all the means in his power. He was forry, indeed, for the diftrefs of the convents in the mountain, but could not help it; nor would he fuffer one of them to remove or come down into the plain, nor would he difcontinue blockading the mountain while Emana Chriftos was there and alive. No other alternative, therefore, remained but the delivering up Emana Chriftos. His army would have fought for him againft a common enemy, but againft thirft their fhields and fwords were ufelefs.

AF CHRISTOS, with his prifoner, forthwith proceeded to join the king, and paffed the Nile into Begemder. At croffing the river Bafhilo, they were informed of the defeat and death of Julius and the Abuna. The meffenger had alfo letters for Emana Chriftos, whom the king did not know to be yet prifoner: among thefe was one from Sela Chriftos, in which he upbraided his brother with his unnatural treafon, and affured him fpeedily of a fate like that of Julius.

Emana

Emana Chriftos received this intelligence almoft dead with fear, for never was a prophecy made which feemed to have needed lefs time to accomplifh than this of his brother's.

Af Christos furrendered his prifoner to the king at Dancaz, who immediately affembled a full convocation of judges of all degrees ; and the prifoner being ordered to anfwer to his charge concerning the rebellion of Julius and his confpiracy againft the king's life, he took the part he had been advifed, and palliated the whole of his actions, without pofitively denying any one of them, and fubmitted to the king's mercy. The judges, confidering the defence, unanimoufly found him guilty of death ; but the king, whofe laft vote, when fitting in judgment, fuperfedes and overturns all the reft, reprieved, and fent him prifoner to Amhara.

Hitherto the king had contented himfelf with fixing two points in favour of the Roman church, in contradiction to that of Alexandria. The firft denounced punifhment to every one who did not believe that there are two natures in Chrift, and that he is perfect God and perfect man, without confufion of perfons. The fecond was rather a point of difcipline than of faith ; yet it was urged as fuch, by declaring it to be unlawful to obferve Saturday, the ancient Jewifh fabbath. The firft of thefe, if it was not the caufe, had been affumed as the pretext for the rebellion of Julius. The fecond produced that of Jonael governor of Begemder, of which we are now to fpeak. But thus far only the king had gone. He had not openly joined the church of Rome, nor as yet renounced that of Alexandria, nor forced any one elfe to do fo.

The firſt prelude to Jonael's rebellion was an anonymous letter written to the king, in which all the ſtale and lame arguments of the Alexandrians were raked together, and ſtated with a degree of preſumption worthy of the ignorance and obſtinacy of thoſe from whom they came. This, though ridiculous, and below notice in point of argument, offended greatly both the king and the Jeſuits, by the aſperity of its terms, and the perſonal applications contained in it. The king was treated as another Diocleſian, thirſting after Chriſtian blood, and for this devoted to hell; as were alſo the Jeſuits, whom they called relations of Pilate, in alluſion to their origin from Rome.

The king, grievouſly offended, added this injunction to the former proclamation, " That all out-door work, ſuch as plowing and ſowing, ſhould be publicly followed by the huſbandman on the Saturday, under penalty of paying a web of cotton cloth, for the firſt omiſſion, which cloth was to be of five ſhillings value ; and the ſecond offence, was to be puniſhed by a confiſcation of moveables, and the crime not to be pardoned for ſeven years;"—the greateſt puniſhment for miſdemeanors in Abyſſinia. To this Socinios added, *vivâ voce*, from his throne, that he never *aboliſhed*, but *explained* and eſtabliſhed their religion, which always taught, as their own books could teſtify, that Chriſt was perfect God and perfect man, two diſtinct natures united in one hypoſtaſis of the eternal word ; neither was it in compliance with the Jeſuits that he abrogated the obſervation of the Jewiſh ſabbath, but in obedience to the council of Chalcedon, which was founded in the holy ſcriptures, for which he was ready at all times to loſe his life, though he ſhould endea-

2.   vour

vour firſt to inflict that puniſhment on ſuch as were its enemies."

In order to ſhew that he did not mean to trifle, he ordered the tongue of a monk (called Abba Af Chriſtòs) to be
cut out, for denying the two natures in Chriſt; and Buco,
one of the principal generals of his court (who afterwards
died a zealous Catholic) he ordered to be beaten with rods,
and degraded from his employment, for obſerving the Jewiſh ſabbath.

The king, having given theſe public, unequivocal teſti-
monies of his reſolution, put himſelf at the head of his
army, and marched againſt Jonael; but that rebel, not daring to meet his offended ſovereign, retired into the mountains; whereupon the king laid waſte the country of the
Galla, who had protected him. This occaſioned a diviſion
among the Galla themſelves. One party declaring for the
king, apprehended Jonael with intention to deliver him up;
but he was ſoon reſcued out of their hands by the contrary
party, enemies to Socinios. His protectors being once known,
the manner of working his deſtruction was ſoon known
likewiſe. The king's preſents made their way to that
faithleſs people, the only barbarians with whom the right
of hoſpitality is not eſtabliſhed. Upon receiving the king's
bribe, they murdered Jonael, cut his head off, and ſent it to
the king.

The rebellion in Damot was not ſo eaſily quelled. Sela
Chriſtos, a zealous Catholic, was ſent againſt the rebels to
inforce the proclamation with regard to the ſabbath. But
as his connections were very conſiderable among them, he

U u 2 choſe

chofe firft to endeavour, by fair means, to induce the ignorant favages to return to reafon and obedience. With this
view, he fent to expoftulate with them ; and to beg that, in
articles of faith, they would fuffer themfelves to be examined and inftructed by men of learning and good life; not
by thofe monks, ignorant like themfelves, from whom
they only could learn vice, blafphemy, and rebellion. To
this the Damots anfwered, as one man, That, if his friendfhip for them and good intentions were real, he fhould give
them, for proof, the immediate burning of all the Latin
books which had been tranflated into the Ethiopian language, and that, then, he fhould hang thofe Jefuits who
were with him upon a high tree.

We are not, however, to confider this was really from a
conviction or perfuafion of the Damots, who inhabit a province bordering upon the Agows and Gongas, and their
chriftianity much upon a par with that of either of thefe
nations. But the fact was, that the fanatics and zealots for
the Alexandrian faith had retired in great numbers to Damot, as to a province the worft affected to the king, from
the recent violence of Julius, who, in an expedition againft
the Shangalla, by order of the king had driven off the cattle of the peaceable Damots, who had been then guilty of
no offence. And as thefe were ready to rebel for a quarrel
merely their own, it was very eafy for the fchifmatical
monks to add this religious grievance to the fum of the
preceding.

Sela Christos had with him about 7000 men, moft of
them Catholics and veteran foldiers ; and among thefe 40
Portuguefe, partly on foot, armed with mufquets, the others

I on

on horfeback, clad in coats of mail.   Very different was the
army of Damots. They were fuperior in number for they
exceeded 12000 men, and among thefe were 400 monks, well
armed with fwords, lances, and fhields, earneftly bent upon
the obtaining a crown of martyrdom in defence of their religion, from the innovation propofed by Socinios. At the
head of thefe was a fanatical monk (one Batacu) who promifed them armies of angels, with flaming fwords, who
fhould flay their enemies, but render them invulnerable,
as he declared himfelf to be, either by fword or lance.

THE battle was fought at the foot of the mountains of
Amid Amid, on the 6th of October 1620. Sela Chriftos,
fure of victory, and unwilling to flaughter a people he had
been ufed to protect, began firft to fhew his fuperiority in
flight fkirmifhes. After which, defiring a parley, he fent
meffengers to them, begging them to confider their own
danger, and offering them a general amnefty upon their
fubmiffion. Thefe meffengers were not allowed to approach,
for fhowers of arrows that were poured upon them ; fo the
battle began with great animofity on both fides. The Damots were foon broken and put to flight by the fuperiority
of Sela Chriftos's foldiers. But the 400 monks, already mentioned, fought moft defperately in defiance of numbers, nor
did they feek their fafety by a flight. One hundred and
eighty of them were killed on the place they occupied, valiantly fighting to the very laft. A rare example, and feldom
found in hiftory, that fanatics like thefe, always ready to
rebel, fhould perfift and facrifice their lives to the follies of
their own preaching.

As

As for their celestial auxiliaries, whose assistance they were promised as far as could be discovered, they neither did harm nor good. We may suppose they stood neuter. But Batacu the hermit, ringleader of this sedition, whose body was so miraculously armed, that neither sword nor spear could make any impression upon it, was unfortunately thrust through with a lance in the very beginning of the engagement, which greatly served to discredit these supernatural aids.

It was in this year 1620, that Socinios marched into Begemder against Jonael. At which time Peter Paez was employed at Gorgora in building the church there. The king returned immediately to Dancaz after the defeat of Jonael, and passed his winter at that place.

It was on the 16th of January 1621, that the dedication of the church of Gorgora was made by Peter Paez; and at that time the king was in Begemder. Upon his return to Dancaz he met Paez at Gorgora for the first time. He remained at Gorgora till the 3d of October of that year, when the news of the defeat of the Damots by Sela Christos arrived, which he received in presence of that priest at Gorgora. In this, both the Jesuits and Abyssinian annals agree. It is not then possible that Peter Paez could have been with the king at Sacala, or Geesh, in the country of the Agows on the 21st of March 1621[*]; for both Peter Paez and Socinios were at that time in Gorgora.

AT

---

[*] This will be more enlarged upon hereafter.

At this time the Ethiopic memoirs of Socinios's reign interrupted their continual topics of rebellion and bloodshed, to record a very trifling anecdote; which, however, I insert, as it serves to give some idea of the simplicity and ignorance of those times.

The historian says, that this year there was brought into Abyssinia, a bird called *Para*, which was about the bigness of a hen, and spoke all languages; Indian, Portuguese, and Arabic. It named the king's name: although its voice was that of a man, it could likewise neigh like a horse, and mew like a cat, but did not sing like a bird. It was produced before the assembly of judges, of the priests, and the azages of court, and there it spoke with great gravity. The assembly, after considering circumstances well, were unanimously of opinion, that the evil spirit had no part in endowing it with these talents. But to be certain of this, it was thought most prudent to take the advice of Ras Sela Christos, then in Gojam, who might, if he thought fit, consult the superior of Mahebar Selaffé; to them it was sent, but it died on the road. The historian closes his narrative by this wise reflection on the parrot's death; " Such is the lot of all " flesh."

The king, immediately after his victory over Jonael, had resolved to throw off the mask, and openly to profess the Catholic religion. The success of Sela Christos against the Damots had confirmed him. He had passed the rainy season, as I have before observed, between Gorgora and Dancaz; and, in the usual time, in the month of November, marched to Foggora, a narrow stripe of plain country, reaching from Emfras to Dara, bounded on one side by the lake

Dem-

Dembea, and on the other by the mountains of Begemder.

For this purpose he sent to Peter Paez, his ordinary confeffor, to come to him; and, having told him his refolution,
he declared, that, in proof of the fincerity of his converfion,
he had put away all his wives (of whom he had feveral of
the firft quality, and many children by them) and retained
only his firft, by whom he had the eldeft of his fons, deftined to fucceed him in the empire.

Paez, having received his confeffion, and public renunciation of the Alexandrian faith, returned to Gorgora finging his *nunc dimittis*, as if the great end of his miffion was now
completed; nor was he deceived in his prognoftication. For,
having too much heated himfelf with zeal in travelling, he
was, upon his arrival, taken with a violent fever; and, tho'
every fort of remedy was adminiftered to him by Antonio
Fernandes, yet he died on the third of May 1623, with great
demonftrations of piety and refignation, and firm conviction,
that he had done his duty in an active, innocent, and well-
fpent life.

He had been feven years a captive in Arabia in the hands
of the Moors, and nineteen years miffionary in Abyffinia,
in the worft of times, and had always extricated himfelf
from the moft perilous fituations, with honour to himfelf
and advantage to his religion. In perfon, he was very tall
and ftrong; but lean from continual labour and abftinence.
He was red faced; which, Tellez fays, proceeded from the
religious *warmth* of his heart. He had a very good underftanding,

Collela of which he had cultivated, every hour of his life, by convents practice.

Besides poffefling univerfal knowledge in fcholaftic divinier, and the books belonging to his profeffion, he underftood never, Latin, and Arabic well, was a good mathematician, an careillent mechanic, wrought always with his own hands, and in building was at once a careful, active labourer, and an architect of refined tafte and judgment. He was, by his own ftudy and induftry, painter, mafon, carver, carpenter, fmith, farrier, quarrier, and was able to build convents and palaces, and furnifh them without calling one workman to his affiftance; and in this manner he is faid to have furnifhed the convent at Collela, as alfo the palace and convent at Gorgora.

With all thefe accomplifhments, he was fo affable, compaffionate, and humble in his nature, that he never had opportunity of converfing, even with heretics, without leaving them his friends. He was remarkably chearful in his temper; and the moft forward always in promoting innocent mirth, of that puerile fpecies which we in England call *fun*, in great requeft among the young men in Abyffinia, who fpend much of their time in this fort of converfation, whether in the city or the camp. Above all, he was a patient, diligent inftructor of youth; and the greateft part of his difciples died in the perfecution that foon followed, refolutely maintaining the truths of that religion their preceptor firft had taught them. In a word, he was the hinge upon which the Catholic religion turned. He had found the feeds of it fown in the country for a hundred years before his time, which had borne little fruit, and was then apparently on

the decline.   Nineteen years of this moſt active miſſionary,.
and the death of three kings, had advanced it only ſo far,
as to be embraced publicly by one of them ; after Paez's
death, in ſix years it fell, though ſupported moſt ſtrenuouſly
by a king prodigal of the blood of his ſubjects in this cauſe;
by a patriarch ſent from Rome, and by above 20 very zealous and active miſſionaries ; and, as far as my foreſight can
carry me, it is ſo entirely fallen, that, unleſs by a ſpecial miracle of Providence wrought for that purpoſe, it never will,
riſe again.

THE king's renunciation of the Alexandrian faith was.
followed by a very ſtrong, or rather violent manifeſto, and.
we need not be at a loſs to gueſs whom he employed to,
draw it up.   It begins by aſſerting the ſupremacy of the
church of Rome, as the ſee of St Peter; it mentions the
three firſt general councils, which condemned Arius, Mace-
donius, and Neſtorius ; next quotes the council of Chal-.
cedon, as the fourth general council, as having juſtly condemned Dioſcurus ; but ſays not a word of the council of
Epheſus, which the Abyſſinians receive inſtead of that of
Chalcedon ; inſiſts largely upon the two natures in Chriſt ;
then, leaving the patriarchs of Alexandria, it attacks not the,
doctrine, but the morals of the Abunas, ſent from Alexandria.
into Abyſſinia, accuſes the eccleſiaſtics in general of ſimony and.
paying money to the Abuna for their ordination, (a well-.
founded part of the charge) which I fear continues to this day.

THE Abuna Marcus was, it is there ſaid, convicted by So-.
cinios, or Melec Segued, of a crime of ſuch turpitude that
the name of it ſhould never ſtain paper.   He was degraded
and baniſhed to the iſland of Dek. His ſucceſſor Chriſtodulus,
                                                        had

had many concubines. Abuna Petros, who fucceeded, took the wife of a poor Egyptian, and lived with her; he then excommunicated his fovereign Jacob, after he had reigned feven years, and died in battle in the actual commiffion of treafon, fighting againft the prince.

Simon, the laft Abuna, befides living in adultery with the wife of an Egyptian called Matti, kept feveral young women with him as concubines; and being detected in having a daughter by one of them, with a view to conceal it, he caufed the child to be expofed to be devoured by the hyæna. After living in conftant difobedience to God's law, he joined the crime of rebellion to the repeated breach of every command in the decalogue; and appearing in battle, and excommunicating his fovereign, God (fays the manifefto) delivered him, into our victorious hands, and he was flain by a common foldier in the very commiffion of his crime.

It muft be owned, we cannot have a worfe picture of any Chriftian church than that here given of the bifhop's church of Alexandria. Charity fhould induce us to hope fome exaggeration had crept into it. Yet when we confider that the facts mentioned were all within the fpace of forty years, and confequently muft have been within the knowledge, not only of Socinios, but of many people then alive and at court, we cannot, with the impartiality of an hiftorian, deny our apprehenfions, that thefe charges were but too-well founded.

However this may be, neither the king's example, nor his manifefto, had the effect he defired. A rebel, whom the annals call the fon of Gabriel, declared himfelf againft the king in Amhara, juft at the time that Socinios, mifled by

X x 2   the

the enemies of Sela Chriftos, had begun to entertain fufpicion of his loyalty, and had deprived him of the government of Gojam and the Agows. Finding, after an examination, there was no perfon that was qualified to bring this affair to a happy iffue but Sela Chriftos, he replaced him in his government of Gojam, giving him, at the fame time, orders to march againft the fon of Gabriel into Amhara.

This command of the king, Ras Sela Chriftos foon complied with, and, upon his firft appearance in that province, the rebel retired to a high mountain which he made his place of arms, the top producing both provifions and water fufficent to maintain a large garrifon.

The Ras, feeing that force availed nothing, had recourfe to the ufual trap thefe rebels fall into. Weary of confinement on the mountain, fenfible that he was by himfelf too weak to leave it, while fuch an enemy expected him below, he accepted the friendfhip of the neighbouring Galla, who offered to join him in fuch numbers as to enable him to defcend from the mountain, and try his fortune in a battle. The treaty was concluded, and the junction no fooner effected, than the faithlefs Galla, before gained by the Ras, fell upon the fon of Gabriel with their clubs, and killed him on the fpot, having fo mangled his body that fcarce a piece was referved to fend to his enemy.

The joy this victory occafioned at court met with a great addition by the arrival of the Romifh patriarch. It has been before obferved, that the king had himfelf wrote letters to the pope and king of Spain, declaring his intentions to turn Catholic. Peter Paez, Antonio Fernandes, and the other priefts,

priefts, had given a much more favourable profpect of religious affairs than had as yet been conveyed to Rome; the
wifer part of the conclave, however, had doubted. But now,
the king had voluntarily made his recantation, it was no
longer thought time for delay, and accordingly Alphonfo
Mendez, a Jefuit doctor of divinity, a man of great learning, by birth a Portuguefe, was ordained at Lifbon the 25th
of May 1624.

From thence he proceeded to India by the way of Goa,
attended by feveral frefh miffionaries; and finding there
letters from Socinios, and a paffport from the king of Dancali, a Mahometan prince in alliance with the Abyffinians,
he arrived at Bilur, an open bay in the fmall and barren
ftate of Dancali, on the fecond of May 1625, and was received, by the brother of the reigning prince, with every token of friendfhip that fo poor a ftate and fovereign could afford; the king of Dancali himfelf was at the diftance of fix
days journey, in a place where there was greater plenty of
water and provifions. The following day the king fent four
mules for the fathers to join him, and received them in a
room of a round figure, furrounded and covered with bun-
dles of ftraw, but fo low they fcarce could raife themfelves
after having made their bows.

In this miferable kingdom, which I fhall not defcribe, as,
fince that period, it has been conquered by the Galla, the patriarch and fathers ftaid almoft in want of neceffaries for
fixteen days. At laft they fet out, having, with much difficulty, muftered fufficient beafts of burden to carry their
baggage. The road lay through part of the country wherein are the mines of foffile-falt, hot, barren, and abfolutely
                                                        without

without water, and expofed greatly to the incurfions of the Galla. After two days journey, they arrived in the morning of the third, at the foot of Senaffé, where there was water. It is the frontier (as the name imports) of the province of Enderta, now united to the government of Tigré. It is part of that ridge of mountains which feparates the feafons, occafioning fummer on the one fide, while rain and cold prevail on the other.

On the night before they came to the mountain, while dubious of their way, a ftar of more than ordinary magnitude, and of furprifing brightnefs, appeared over the patriarch, giving fo ftrong a light that it illuminated the heavens down to the horizon. It was not, in its place or manner of appearing, like a common ftar, but ftood ftationary, in the way leading to Senaffé, for above fix minutes, and difappeared *. This ftar, the patriarch and his followers modeftly fay, was probably the fame that conducted the Magi to the cradle of Chrift, and was now fent to fhew them the way into Abyffinia.

While they were at the foot of this mountain, the Muleteers, all Mahometans, thought the occafion a proper one to plunder them, by obliging them to pay an additional hire for their beafts, which they pretended were not able to afcend fo fteep a mountain. The camels certainly could not pafs; but mules and affes have a more practicable road, for the fake of carrying the falt. They infifted to leave the company till they fhould bring them frefh mules. The caravan confifted of the patriarch and fix ecclefiaftics, priefts, and friars, and thirteen laymen, three of whom were muficians.

* Tellez, lib. iv. cap. 38.

cians. It was very probably their intention to have fent to them people who would very foon have put a fatal period to the miffion, had not Emanuel Baradas, with a number of Abyffinians, and officers, and plenty of all things necef-fary, joined the patriarch on the 16th of June 1625; while their late conductors, confcious of mifbehaviour, fled with-out feeking their hire.

In five days they came to Fremona, where they ftaid till November; and, in December, arrived at Gorgora, where they were introduced to the king in his palace. Socinios ordered the patriarch to be placed on a feat equal in height to his own, on his right hand; and at that very audience, which was on the 11th of February 1626, it was fettled that the king fhould take an oath of fubmiffion to the fee of Rome.

This ufelefs, vain, ridiculous ceremony, was accordingly. celebrated on the 11th of February, with all the pageantry of a heathen feftival or triumph. The palace was adorned with all the pomp and vanity that the church of Rome, and efpecially that part of it, the Order of the Jefuits, had-folemnly abjured. The patriarch, as a mark of his fuperi-ority over the Abunas, preached a fermon in the Portu-guefe language upon the primacy of the chair of St Peter, full of Latin quotations, which is faid to have had a won-derful effect upon the king and Sela Chriftos, neither of whom underftood one word either of Latin or Portuguefe.

That part of the patriarch's difcourfe, which was appli-cable to Socinios's converfion, was anfwered by Melca Chri-ftos, governor of Samen, (himfelf a fchifmatic) in the lan-guage of Amhara, which neither the patriarch nor his re-

tinue .

tinue underflood, and concluded with thefe words, " That
as the king thought himfelf obliged to fulfil thofe promifes
of fubmitting himfelf to the fee of Rome which his predeceffors had made, the time was now come in which he
fhould do that, if fuch was his pleafure. Thefe laft words
of the orator feem not to have fatisfied the zeal of Socinios.
He interrupted Melca Chriftos by faying, that it was not
now, but a long time fince, that he had fubmitted to the
church of Rome, as true fucceffor of St Peter; and the prefent occafion was only a confirmation of what he had formerly profeffed."

THE patriarch anfwered by a few words, prudently and
fenfibly, I fuppofe to fave time, feeing that, fhort or long,
his difcourfe would not be underflood. But proceeding to
facts, he opened a new teftament, while Socinios, upon his
knees, took the following oath : " We, fultan Segued, em-
perör of Ethiopia, do believe and confefs that St Peter, prince
of the apoftles, was conftituted, by Chrift our Lord, head of
the whole Chriftian church, and that he gave him the principality and dominion over the whole world, by faying to
him, *You are Peter, and upon this rock will I build my church ; and I
will give you the keys of the kingdom of heaven.* And again when
he faid, *Keep my fheep.* Alfo we believe and confefs, that
the pope of Rome, lawfully elected, is the true fucceffor of St Peter the apoflle, in government ; that he holdeth
the fame power, dignity, and primacy, in the whole Chriftian church: and to the holy father Urban VIII. of that name,
by the mercy of God, pope, and our lord, and to his fucceffor in the government of the church, we do promife, offer,
and fwear true obedience, and fubject, with humility at his
feet, our perfon and empire : fo help us God and thefe holy
gofpels

gofpels before us."—After this, each man fwore perfonal o-
bedience, officers, priefts, and monks, according to their feveral orders or conditions.

THE prince royal Facilidas, purely and fimply in the
form prefcribed, took this oath, without any addition or alteration. But Ras Sela Chriftos, heated with zeal, after repeating the formula, drawing his fword in violent paffion,
uttered thefe words, "What has paffed let it be paft; but,
from this day forward, he that falls from his duty this fhall
be his judge*."

THIS hafty fpeech, not well underftood, was thought by
fome to reflect on thofe he had difcovered to be in the confederacy with the rebel fon of Gabriel. As the court was
full of parties and difcontent, every one applied the threat
to himfelf, and all joined in a league to undo Sela Chriftos,
who had fo wantonly declared himfelf the leader and champion of perfecution.

To this oath of obedience to the pope, he likewife added
one to the king, and to the prince his fucceffor, Facilidas,
with a ftrange claufe, or qualification, which made what he
faid formerly ftill worfe:—"I likewife fwear to the prince,
as heir of his father in this empire, as long as he fhall hold
favour, and defend the holy Catholic faith; and if he fhall
fail in this, I hereby fwear to be his greateft enemy." This
extravagant addition he infifted fhould be impofed upon all
the officers of ftate, and of the army then at court, and

VOL. II.   Y y   therefore

---

* It is apparently a fpeech in a paffion, for this Sela Chriftos was one of the moft learned of
the Abyffinians; yet the words themfelves, if literally tranflated, are fcarcely intelligible.

therefore did moſt deſervedly ſeal his own condemnation and puniſhment, which overtook him in the end, though it did not follow till long afterwards.

To theſe violent proceedings were added others ſtill more violent. A ſolemn excommunication was pronounced a-gainſt all ſuch as did not keep that oath, and a proclamation was forthwith made, " That all people, in the line of being ordained prieſts, ſhould firſt embrace the Catholic re-ligion upon pain of death ; that all ſhould obſerve the form of the church of Rome in the celebration of Eaſter and Lent, under the ſame penalty ; and with that the ceremonies of the day ended.

Tempus erit cum magno optaverit emptum,
Intaɛtum Pallanta.

It was a day ever to be marked with black, not only in the annals of Ethiopia, but in thoſe of Rome.

ALTHOUGH the arrival of the patriarch at Bilur had been happily effected, both as to himſelf and thoſe that attended him, it was not ſo with ſome of his brethren ſent to aſſiſt him in that miſſion. Two Jeſuits, Franciſco Machado and Bernard Pereira, had received the king's letters in India for their ſafe conduct to Bilur in Dancali. Whether by malice, or inadvertency, the king's ſecretary, inſtead of Bilur, had mentioned Zeyla in the letter.

ZEYLA, an iſland belonging to the king of Adel, was of all other places that where the people were moſt inveterate againſt the Catholic religion. No ſooner did the Shekh know

3

the

the quality and errand of thefe miffionaries, than he confined them to clofe prifon, where, after great fuffering, they were both put to death; and, to aggravate this, a letter was written to Socinios ftigmatizing him with the name of apoftate from the religion of his forefathers, and applying to him many opprobrious names.

THIS letter, at another time, would not have failed to have been followed by the chaftifement it deferved. But Adel, formerly a flourifhing and commercial kingdom, was now fallen, and reduced to a multitude of banditti. Trade had left it. A garrifon of nominal janizaries, fince the reign of Sultan Selim, had kept the little ifland of Zeyla for the pretended purpofe of a cuftomhoufe; but, in fact, it was a poft of robbers, who only maintained themfelves there for the fake of plundering merchants who came by fea; while the Galla poured in numbers upon the prince from the continent, and of the ancient kingdom of Adel, had left him nothing but Auffa the capital, a town fituated upon a rock, on the banks of the river Hawafh, Azab, and Raheeta, and a few other miferable villages upon the fea; and even part of thefe were daily falling into the hands of that enemy, deftined very foon to over-run them all. This abject ftate to which they had been reduced, we may fuppofe, was the only reafon that protected them from the vengeance of a high-fpirited prince, fuch as Socinios certainly was.

THIS violent conduct of Socinios in his abjuration was followed by that of the patriarch Alphonfo Mendes, perfectly in the fame fpirit. The clergy were re-ordained, their churches confecrated anew, grown men as well as children again baptifed, the moveable feafts and feftivals reduced to

the

the forms and times of the church of Rome; circumcifion, polygamy, and divorce were abrogated for ever; and the many queftions that thereupon arofe, and which were underftood to belong to the civil judge, the patriarch called to his own tribunal exclufively.

ALL the tenets of the church of Alexandria, whether of faith or difcipline, were rejected; and it was not known how far the patriarch intended to fubject the civil jurifdiction of the judges to the ecclefiaftical power. Two fteps that he took, the one immediately after the other, feemed to give great reafon of fear upon this head.

IN order to underftand the firft of thefe cafes, it will be neceffary to know, that it is a fundamental conftitution of the monarchy of Ethiopia, that all lands belong to the king; and that there is no fuch thing as church-lands in this country. Thofe that the king has given for the maintenance of churches or monafteries are refumed every day, at the inftance of, and for the convenience of individuals, and new ones granted in their ftead fometimes of a greater value, fometimes of a lefs. Nor have the priefts or monks any property in thefe lands. A lay-officer, appointed by the king, divides to each monk or prieft, his quota of the revenue, applying any overplus to other ufes, which is, we may fuppofe, often putting it into his own pocket.

THERE was a nobleman of great diftinction for his family and rank at court, for his age, and the merit of his fervice; he had occupied fome of the lands belonging to a monk who happened to be a Catholic. This man, had he been an Alexandr.a.., could have had no recourfe to the Abuna his
patri-

patriarch, and the caufe muft have been tried before the civil judge. But Mendes was of another opinion. He ordered the nobleman to make his defence before the ecclefiaftical tribunal; and, upon his refufing this as a novelty to which he was not bound, he condemned him immediately to reftore the lands to the monk. This, too, was refufed on the part of the prefent poffeffor, who being one day attending the king at church, the patriarch, without preamble, pronounced againft him a formal fentence of excommunication, by which he gave him over, foul and body, to the devil.

Such procedure was, till then, unknown in Abyffinia. The nobleman, though otherwife brave, was fo much affected with the terms of his fentence as to faint, imagining himfelf already in the clutches of Satan, and it was with difficulty he was recovered, the king making interceffion with the patriarch to take off this cenfure, or rather this curfe.

Sudden as it was, however, in the inflicting, and eafy in the removal, it made very lafting and ferious impreffions on the minds of men of all ranks, greatly to the difadvantage of the patriarch and the profeffors of his new religion, in the exercife of which they did not difcover that degree of charity, meeknefs, mercy, and long-fuffering, that they had been taught were the very effentials of it.

The next inftance was this: There had been an Itchegué, that is, the fuperior of the monks of Debra Libanos, an Order inftituted by Abba Tecla Haimanout, the laft Abyffinian Abuna, not more celebrated by the church than the ftate,

3

as being the reftorer of the line of Solomon, for many years baniſhed to Shoa; and this fuperior, befides the dignity of his office, was remarkable for an innocent, pious, and holy life. It happened that a Catholic monk officiated in a church where this Itcheguè had been buried under the altar; the patriarch declared the church defiled by the burial of that heretic and ſchiſmatic, and ſuſpended the celebration of divine ſervice till the body was raiſed and thrown out of the church in a moſt indecent manner. Univerſal diſcontent ſeized the minds of all men; and, from that time, it ſeemed the friends of the old religion began again to recover ſtrength, and the Catholics to be looked upon, if not with hatred, yet with terror. And every trifle now contributed towards the one or the other.

THE Jeſuits, following practices or cuſtoms of their own, had thought fit to exhibit a kind of religious plays or farces. The devil in theſe pieces is always the buffoon; he plays harlequin and ſlight-of-hand tricks, fires ſquibs and gun-powder, very little confiſtent with the decency of the other perſons who compoſe the drama. This continued to be practiſed in ſeveral Catholic countries in Europe, while that learned company exiſted*. It happened to be neceſſary to introduce figures of this kind blacked all over, and in maſks, with cloven feet, &c. The firſt exhibition of theſe figures ſo ſurpriſed and terrified the Abyſſinian audience, that they fled immediately upon their appearance, crying out, Alas! alas! theſe Franks have brought devils into our country with them!

THIS

---

* I have ſeen them often at Madrid.

THIS great extenfion of civil jurifdiction, and the large ftrides it took to annihilate the civil power, the encroachments it made upon the prerogative of the king, till now fupreme in all caufes ecclefiaftical and civil, the more than regal, the mcre, if poffible, than papal pride of the patriarch, began to be felt univerfally, and it was feen to be intended to leffen every order of government, from the king to the loweft officer in the province. From this time, therefore, we date the decline of the Catholic intereft in Abyffinia. The firft blow was given it by the king himfelf, not with a view to deftroy it, for he was a fincere Catholic upon principle, but to controul and keep it within fome bounds, as he found there was no order could otherwife be maintained.

HE defired the patriarch to permit the ufe of the ancient liturgies of Ethiopia, altered by himfelf in every thing where they did not agree with that of the church of Rome. With this the patriarch was obliged to comply, becaufe there was in it an appearance of reafon that men fhould pray to God in a language that they underftood, and which was their own, rather than a foreign tongue of which they did not underftand one word. This was thought fo obvious in Ethiopia as not to admit any doubt. But the order and practice of the church of Rome was juft the contrary; and this wound was a mortal one; for no fooner was the permiffion given to ufe their own liturgies, than all the Abyffinians embraced them to a man, and went on in their old prayers and fervices without any of the patriarch's alterations.

To

To thefe events, not important in themfelves, but only from the effect they had upon the minds of mankind, fucceeded tragedies of a more ferious nature. I have already obferved, in fpeaking of the Galla, that they were divided into three principal divifions, thofe on the eaft of Abyffinia were called Bertuma Galla, thofe on the fouth called Toluma, and thofe on the weft Boren Galla; each of thefe were divided into feven, and thefe again fubdivided into a number of tribes. Each of thefe feven nations choofe a king once in feven years called Lubo; and it is ufually the firft act of the new king's reign to over-run the neighbouring provinces of Abyffinia, laying every thing wafte with fire and fword for this year, even if they had no provocation, but had been at peace for feveral years before.

The Abyffinians remained long in ignorance of this caufe of thefe invafions, and, while that was the cafe, they could take no meafures to be prepared againft, and refift them. But after, when the cuftoms of the Galla were better known, their periodical invafions were watched and provided againft, fo that though they were ftill continued, they were generally repelled with the flaughter and defeat of the invaders.

It happened that the prefent year, 1627, was the feafon of electing the king, and of the invafion. Though the time of the expedition was known, no intelligence had been given of the manner in which it was to be executed. In paft times, the nations, or tribes of Galla, affaulted each the oppofite province in whofe frontiers they were fettled; but this year it was agreed among them to choofe one province. Gojam, which, by uniting their whole force, they
were

were to devote to deſtruction, or, if poſſible, keep poſſeſſion of it.

Buco was governor of Gojam; the king had ſent Sela Chriſtos to his aſſiſtance, and was intending to follow with another army himſelf. In the mean time, the paſſes through which the Galla uſed to enter were all lined with men, and every preparation made to receive them.

These barbarians advanced to the Nile in multitudes never ſeen before; and, finding the province perfectly on its guard, they feigned a panic, or diſagreement among themſelves, retired in ſeeming confuſion, and diſperſed, ſome, as it was ſaid, to their own homes, and ſome to an expedition againſt Narea. This in reality had often happened; but now it was only a ſtratagem; for they all aſſembled in their own country Bizamo, of which the Abyſſinians had no intelligence. Buco, thinking he was free of them for that year, diſbanded his troops, or detached them to other ſervices; Sela Chriſtos did the ſame; neither did Socinios advance with his army.

In that interval of weakneſs, news were ſent to Buco that the Galla had paſſed the Nile. Upon which he advanced with 1000 foot and 200 horſe, believing that it was ſome ſmall part of that army which he thought had ſome time before been diſperſed. After hearing maſs with great devotion, and receiving the ſacrament, in paſſing through a thick wood he was aſſaulted by the Galla. Being a man, brave in his own perſon, and exceedingly well-trained to arms, he fought ſo ſucceſsfully, and ſo encouraged his men by his example, that he cut that body of Galla entirely to pieces; and, as he thought the whole matter then at an end, he ordered his drums to beat, and his trumpets to found, in token of victory.

THE reft of the Galla, who were now difperfed through the province, but at no great diftance, burning and deftroying, as their cuftom is, and who left this body behind them only to fecure their retreat acrofs the river, returned all to their colours, upon hearing the drums and trumpets of Kafmati Buco, whom they did not know to be fo near; and, as foon as he came in fight, defpifing his fmall number, they furrounded them on every fide. Buco immediately faw that he was a loft man; but, confidering the multitude of the enemy, and the unprepared ftate of the province, he thought his own life and thofe of his followers could not be better employed than by obftinately fighting to difable the enemy, fo as to put it out of their power to purfue the ruin of the country further; throwing himfelf furioufly into the thickeft of the Galla, he, at firft onfet, killed four of the moft forward of their leaders, and made himfelf a lane through the troops oppofing him; and he was now got without their circle, when fome of his officers feeing him, cried to him to make the beft of his way, as affairs were defperate, and not to add by his death to the misfortunes of that day.

UPON this he paufed, as recollecting himfelf for a moment; but, difdaining to furvive the lofs of his army, he threw himfelf again among the Galla, where his men were ftill fighting, carrying victory wherever he went. His horfe was at laft wounded, and, being otherwife young and untrained, became ungovernable. It was neceffary to quit him, when, drawing his fword, and leaping upon the ground, he
continued

continued the fight with the fame degree of courage, till the Galla, who did not dare to approach him near, killed him by a number of javelins thrown at a diſtance.

The news of the defeat and death of Buco reached Sela Chriſtos, then in march to join him; nor did the misfortune that had already happened, nor the bad profpect of his own fituation, alter his refolution of attacking the enemy: But he firſt wrote to the king his brother, telling him his fituation, and the probable confequences of doing his duty as he had determined, laying all the blame upon the malice of his enemies, who, to gratify their own private malice, had left him without affiftance, and occafioned misfortunes fo detrimental to the common-weal.

Sela Christos paffed this night upon a rifing ground, and in the morning early defcended into the plain, with a view of attacking the Galla, when, to his great furprife, that barbarous people, content with the flaughter of Kafmati Buco and his army, and not willing to rifk a large quantity of plunder with which their whole army was loaded, had repaffed the Nile, and returned home.

Tecla Georgis was fon-in-law to Socinios, and then governor of Tigré, but at variance with his father-in-law upon fome quarrel with his wife. Determined on this account to rebel, he affociated with fome noblemen of the firſt rank and power in Tigré, particularly Guebra Mariam and John Akayo, declaring to them, that he would no longer fuffer the Roman religion, but defend the ancient chuich of Alexandria to the utmoſt of his power.   And, to convince all the Abyffinians of his fincerity, he tore off the figures of

Z z 2   crucifixes

crucifixes, and all church-ornaments and images of faints that were in relief, and burned them publicly, to make his reconciliation with the king impoffible. He then called before him Abba Jacob his Catholic chaplain, and, having ftripped him of his pontificals, killed him with his own hand. There was no method he could devife of bringing his quarrel fooner to an iffue than this which he had adopted. But he did not feem to have taken equal pains to provide for his defence, as he had done to give provocation.

Socinios, upon the firft intelligence of this murder and treafon, ordered Keba Chriftos to march againft him with the troops that he had at hand. This general, equally a good foldier, fubject, and Catholic, being convinced of the neceffity of punifhing fpeedily fo monftrous a crime, paffed by forced marches through Siré to Axum, thence to Fremona; and, having appointed Gafpar Paez to meet him there, he confeffed himfelf, and received the facrament from that Jefuit's hands. From Fremona he continued with the fame fpeed, making three ordinary days marches in one, being defirous of preventing the poffibility of Tecla Georgis's collecting troops, and taking refuge on a mountain called *Mafba*, which he heard to be his defign.

It was the 12th of December 1628 that news were brought him of the fituation of the enemy; upon which he ordered his baggage to be left behind, and every foldier to carry two loaves, and to march without refting till he came up with Tecla Georgis.

In the morning of the day following, two horfemen, on the fcout before him, difcovered five of the rebel foldiers.
upon

upon the look-out likewife. Thefe, upon feeing Keba Chri-ftos's horfemen, returned immediately to their mafter, and told him that they had feen armed men, and concei-ved them to be the foldiers of Keba Chriftos. To this in-telligence Tecla Georgis anfwered, That Keba Chriftos was in the king's palace at Dancaz the 15th of November, and that it was impoffible he then could be fo near with an ar-my, if he had even wings to fly; but that the men they had feen were probably reinforcements that he expected.

KEBA CHRISTOS, on the contrary, hearing that the enemy was at hand, drew up his army in three divifions. The firft confifted of his own houfehold, the fecond of a body of horfe of the king's houfehold, called *the Koccob Horfe*, or *Star Cavalry*, from a filver ftar which each of them wears on the front of his helmet; and the third, of the people of Tigré who had joined him. In this order he came in fight of his enemy pofted upon a fmall height, divided only from him by a narrow plain. Tecla Georgis, convinced now that it was. Keba Chriftos, formed his army into two divifions; the one compofed of a body called *Tcheraguas*, the other of a body called *Sultan ba Chriftos;* with thefe was a large corps of Galla which had lately joined them.

KEBA CHRISTOS, now turning to his troops, briefly faid, " My children, I will not wafte my time nor yours in dif-courfe, or in telling you what you are to do. You have all arms in your hands ; you are good Chriftians; and I can po-fitively affure you there is not before you one of your ene-mies that is not alfo an enemy to Chrift." Then, placing himfelf before the Koccob horfe, he pulled off his helmet and gave it to his fervant, faying, " By my naked face you fhall shall know me to-day, that I am not going in the midst of you as general or commander, but foot for foot along with you like a common soldier."

Upon having uncovered his head, he was quickly known by Tecla Georgis, from whose troops a number of muskets was fired at him. But this had so little effect upon this gallant officer, that, changing his place, (which then was at the head of the second division) he placed himself still nearer the enemy in the front of his own household troops, which were the first; and the Galla charging them in that instant, he slew their leader with his own hand. Upon the death of their commander, these barbarians immediately fled, as is their custom, while Keba Christos endeavoured to make his way to where Tecla Georgis was employed keeping his troops from following so bad an example. But so soon as that rebel saw his enemy approach him, he and his whole army joined the Galla in their flight; tho' he narrowly escaped, by the swiftness of his horse, a light javelin, thrown by Keba Christos, which struck him behind, but so feebly, by reason of the distance, that it did not pierce his armour.

The king's troops pursued vigorously, and soon brought to their general the mule, the sword, and helmet of Tecla Georgis, with the heads of 300 slain in the battle, most of them Gallas, and with them 12 heads of the most turbulent rebellious monks of Tigré. With these they also brought Adera, sister to Tecla Georgis, wounded in the throat, who had instigated him very strongly to commit the violences against the professors of the Catholic religion. Tafa, too, his master of the household, was taken prisoner; and it being made known to Keba Christos that this man had af-

fisted

fifted at the murder of Abba Jacob, he ordered him directly to be put to death.

TECLA GEORGIS, aided by the ftrength of his horfe and knowledge of the country, efcaped and concealed himfelf from his purfuers for four days ; but, on the Saturday that followed the victory, he was found in a cavern with his great confidents, Woldo Mariam, and a fchifmatic monk whofe name was Sebo Amlac.   Tecla Georgis was carried alive to Keba Chriftos, who fent him to the king, his two companions being flain as foon as found, and their heads accompanied their living mafter, which, on their arrival at Dancaz, the king ordered to be hung upon a tree.

TECLA GEORGIS being convicted of facrilege as well as murder, having burnt the crucifixes and images of the faints, was condemned to be burnt alive, and a lime-kiln was immediately prepared in which he was to fuffer. Upon hearing this, he defired a Catholic confeffor, as wifhing to be reconciled to the church of Rome, and for this purpofe he fent a requeft to the patriarch, who was at three leagues diftance, and who difpatched Antonio Fernandes with full powers to abfolve from all manner of fins, and at the fame time gave him orders to intercede ftrongly with the king to pardon the criminal.   Tecla Georgis confeffed publicly at the door of the church, and abjured the errors of the church of Alexandria.

AFTER this, the father Fernandes applied to the king, pleading ftrongly for his pardon.   To which the king anfwered, " Many reafons there are why I fhould defire to pardon Tecla Georgis. To fay no more, he has been married.

ried to two of my daughters, and he has by them two fons, both good foldiers and horfemen, who actually ride before me, and accompany me in battle. I have therefore pardoned him all the affronts and injuries he has done to me. But, were I to take upon myfelf to pardon the affronts and infults he has offered the Divine Majefty, I fhould turn the punifhment of his fins upon myfelf, my family, and kingdom ; and, therefore, I refufe your petition, and order you to return forthwith to Gorgora."

AFTER the departure of the father, in confideration that Tecla Georgis had again embraced the Catholic religion, the king altered his fentence of being burnt, into that of being hanged privately in the houfe where he was then in prifon ; and, for that purpofe, the executioner had brought with him the cord with which Tecla had ordered the feet of Abba Jacob to be tied. No fooner did he perceive that there were no hopes of pardon, by their beginning to tie his hands, than he again, with a loud voice, renounced his confeffion, declaring that he died an Alexandrian, and that there was but one nature in Chrift. The executioner endeavoured to ftop his further blafphemies, by drawing him up on the beam in the room ; but he refifted fo ftrongly, that there was time to inform Socinios of his abjuration : upon which the king ordered that he fhould be hanged publicly upon a pine-tree ; and he was accordingly taken down, half-ftrangled, from the beam in the houfe, and hung upon the tree before the palace.

ADERA, his fifter, was next examined ; and it being clearly proved that fhe had been a very active agent in the murder of Abba Jacob, fhe likewife was condemned to be hang-

4   ed

ed upon the fame tree with her brother, fifteen days afterwards.

ALL that interval, the queen and ladies at court employed their utmoft intereft with the king to pardon Adera, for
they looked upon it as a difgraceful thing, both to their fex
and quality, that a woman of her family fhould be thus
publicly executed. All the ladies of the court having joined, therefore, in a public petition to the king while on his
throne, he is faid to have anfwered them by the following
fhort parable.:—

" THERE was once an old woman, who being told of the
death of an infant, faid, with great indifference, Children
are but tender; it is no wonder that they die, for any
thing will kill a child. Being told of a youth dying, fhe
obferved, Young people are forward and rafh; they are always in the way of fome difafter; no wonder they die; it is
impoffible it fhould be otherwife. But being told an old
woman was dead, fhe began to tear her hair, and lament,
crying, Now the world is at an end if old women begin
to die, fearing that her turn might be the next. In this manner all of you have feen Tecla Georgis die, and alfo feveral
of his companions, and you have not faid a word. But
now it is come to the hanging of one woman, you are all
alarmed, and the world is at an end. Do not then deceive
yourfelves, but be affured that the fame cord which tied
the feet of Abba Jacob, ftill remains fufficient to hang that
fow Adera, and all thofe that fhall be fo wicked as to behave like her, to the difgrace of your fex, and their own
rank and quality."

THE effects of thefe oftentatious acts of reformation foon produced confequences which troubled their joy. The A-gows of Lafta, called Tcheratz Agow, who live at the head of the Tacazzè, rebelled. The country they occupy is not extenfive, but exceedingly populous, and was fuppofed at that time to be able to bring into the field above 50,000 fighting men, befides leaving behind a fufficient number to defend the paffes and ftrong-holds of their country, which are by much the moft difficult and inacceffible of any in Abyffinia. They are divided into five clans, Waag, Tettera, Dehaanah, Gouliou, and Louta, each having an independent chief. They are exceedingly warlike; and, though the country be fo rude and rocky, they have a confiderable number of good horfes; and are in general reckoned among the braveft and moft barbarous foldiers in Abyffinia. Their province abounds with all forts of provifions, and they rarely can be forced to pay any thing to government in the name of tax, or tribute.

TECLA GEORGIS was now dead, but the caufe of the rebellion ftill fubfifted. While governor of Begemder, he had connived at many abufes of his officers who occupied the pofts neareft to Lafta. Thefe being young men, from wantonnefs only, without provocation, had made many different inroads, driving away cattle, and committing many other exceffes. The Agows carried their complaints to the governor, who, far from hearing or redreffing their wrongs, juftified the conduct of his officers, by making inroads himfelf immediately after; but coming to an action in perfon with that people, he was fhamefully beat, and a great part of his army left dead upon the field.

THIS

THIS misfortune very much affected Socinios. Nor did the Agows themselves doubt, but that a speedy chastisement was to follow this victory over Tecla Georgis.

THERE was a youth descended of the royal family, who, to preserve the freedom of his person, lived among the Galla, in expectation of better times. His name was Melca Christos. To him the Agows applied, that, with this prince of the house of Solomon at their head, they might wipe off the odium of being reputed rebels, and appear as fighting under a lawful sovereign for reformation of abuses. The renunciation of the Alexandrian faith, forcibly obtruded upon them by Socinios, served as cause of complaint. The Roman Catholic writers in the history of this mission, say this was but a pretext, in which I conceive they are right. I have lived among the Agows of Lasta, and in intimacy with many of them, who are not, to this day, so anxious about Christianity as to ascend one of their hills for the difference between that and Paganism; and I am satisfied, for these 300 years last past there has been scarcely a common layman in Lasta that has known the distinction between the Alexandrian and the Roman church.

IN the beginning of February 1629 the king marched from Dancaz towards Gojam, where he collected an army of 30,000 men, which, with the baggage, servants, and attendants, at that time very great and numerous, amounted to above 80,000 men.

SOCINIOS detached a number of small parties to enter Lasta at different places. On the other hand, Melca Christos assembled his troops on the most inaccessible rocks; whence,

when

when he fpied occafion, he came fuddenly down and furprifed the enemy below.　Among all the rude, high, and
tremendous mountains of which this country confifts,
there is one efpecially, called by the name of *Lafta*.　It is in
the territory of Waag, ftrongly furrounded with inacceffible
precipices, having a large plain on the top, abounding with
every thing neceffary, and watered by a fine ftream that
never fails.

THE manner in which the Agows remained fecure in
this ftrong poft was mifconftrued into fear by the king's army, which, in two divifions, advanced to the attack of the
mountain.　That on the right had with fome difficulty
fcrambled up without oppofition; but, being now arrived to
the fteep part of the rock, fuch a number of large ftones
was rolled down upon them from above, that this divifion
of the army was entirely deftroyed.　The number of ftones
on the brink of the precipices. was inexhauftible; and, once
put in motion, purfued the fcattered troops with unavoidable
fpeed, even down to the plains below.　Among the flain was
Guebra Chriftos, the king's fon-in-law, dafhed to pieces by
the fragment of a rock.　The left divifion was upon the
point of fuffering the fame misfortune, had not Keba Chriftos come to their relief and drawn them off, juft before the
enemy had begun to difcharge this irrefiftible artillery a-
gainft them.

THE king, thus fhamefully beaten, retired to Dancaz, leaving the entrances from Lafta ftrongly defended, left thefe
mountaineers fhould, by way of retaliation, fall upon the
province of Begemder.　But the late ill-fortune had difpirited the troops, and caufed an indifference about duty, a
want

want of obedience, and a relaxation in difcipline in the whole army. Each of the detachments, therefore, one after the other, left their poft from different excufes, and returned home. The bad confequence of this was now experienced. The Agows entered Begemder fpreading defolation everywhere. Melca Chriftos, no longer fculking among the rocks of Lafta, planted his ftandard upon the plain, within five days march of the capital where the king was refiding.

The jealoufies that had arifen between Socinios and his brother-in-law Sela Chriftos, had been fo much aggravated fince the oath adminiftered by the patriarch, that the king had again deprived him of Gojam, fuffering him to live in obfcurity in Damot, and among the Agows, occupied, as the Jefuits fay, in the converfion of that Pagan people, by deftroying their idols, which they reprefent to be a fpecies of cane or bamboo *, and in forbidding the ceremonies of adoration and devotion, which at ftated times they paid to the river.

No remedy could be propofed, but the prefence of Sela Chriftos, who, upon the firft warning, joined the king, and coming fuddenly upon the army of Lafta occupied in laying wafte the low country of Begemder, gave them fuch an overthrow that fufficiently compenfated the firft lofs of the king, and forced them again to take refuge among their ftrong-holds in Lafta.

A MIS-

---

* Called by the Agows, Krihaha.

A MISFORTUNE of another kind followed this victory: Laeca Mariam, a near relation to the king, was appointed governor of Begemder; but no sooner did he see himself vested with that government, than he meditated shaking off his allegiance to Socinios.

THE king, after his last battle with the Agows, had named his son Facilidas commander in chief of his forces; and, to secure him a powerful and able assistant, he had first restored Sela Christos to his government of Gojam, then sent him with an army to join Facilidas, and command under him.

THE success was answerable to the prudence of the measure; for, immediately upon their arrival, they obliged Laeca Mariam to seek for refuge in the mountains of Amhara, and, without giving him time to recollect himself there, forced their way to the mountain to which he had retired, and from which he and his followers had no way to escape, but by venturing down a steep precipice; in attempting this, Laeca Mariam fell, and was dashed to pieces, as were many others of his followers; the rest were slain by the army that pursued them.

AT this time, Facilidas began to attract the eyes of the nation in general. Besides personal bravery, he had shewn great military talents in the former campaign of Lasta. Though young, he was in capacity and resolution equal to his father, but less warm, more reserved in his temper and discourse. He was thought to be an enemy to the Catholic religion, because he did not promote it, and neither exceeded nor fell short of what his father commanded him. Yet,

3   he

he lived with the Jesuits on such an even footing, that they confess they did not know whether he was their friend or enemy: he kept one of their number, called Father Angelis, constantly in his household, where he was much favoured, and constantly in his presence. He was thought to be an enemy to Sela Christos, though he never had shewn it.

Facilidas received a flattering message from Urban VIII. but did not answer it; nor does it appear his father ever desired him; for, through the whole course of the life of Sonios, as his enemies are forced to confess, he paid to his father's will, the most passive obedience in every thing. The tyranny, however, of church-government began to appear unmasked; and it is probable that the king, though resolved to die a Roman Catholic from principles of conscience, was indifferent about forging for his son the chains he had himself worn with pain.

However this may be, the last step of placing Facilidas at the head of the army was construed as another stroke of humiliation to the Catholics, especially as it was followed with the removal of Keba Christos (the support of that religion) from court, where he had been appointed Billetana Gueta. It is true he was removed by what, in other times, would have been called preferment; but things had now changed their qualities, and places were not estimated, as formerly, by the consequence they gave in the empire, but by the opportunities they afforded of constant access to the king, and occasion of joining in councils with him, and defeating those of their enemies.

KEBA

KEBA CHRISTOS being fent governor to Tigré, was to enter Lafta from that quarter on the N. E.   He is faid to have
received his appointment with a great degree of concern, and
to have told his friends, that he forefaw he never was to return from that expedition, which he did not regret, becaufe
he was convinced, by living much longer, it would be made
his duty to affift at the fall of the Catholic religion.

AFTER having performed his devotions at Fremona, this
general advanced through Gouliou, a territory moftly inhabited by Galla, and deftitute of any fort of provifions; after which he took poffeffion of the mountains of Lafta, with
a view to cover the march of the young prince Facilidas,
whom he every day expected.   But that prince not appearing in time, and provifions becoming fcarce, no meafure remained but making his retreat to Tigré ; and, although he
formed the beft difpofition for that purpofe, the people of
Lafta obferving his intention in time, on his firft movement
attacked his rear-guard while he was defcending the mountain, and put it to flight : being thereby mafters of the
higher ground, they had the command of the cowardly
foldiers below them, who could not infure their deftruction more certainly than by the indecent manner in which
they were flying.

KEBA CHRISTOS, deferted by all except a few fervants,
continued courageoufly fighting ; and, although it was very poffible for him to have efcaped, he difdained to furvive
the lofs of his army.   Receiving at that time a wound from
a javelin, which paffed through his belly, and judging the
ftroke to be mortal, he gave up all further refiftance, fell
upon his knees to prayer, and was again wounded by a

3   ftone,

stone, which struck him to the ground. Two of the mountaineers immediately came up to him, one of whom did not know him, and contented himself with stripping the body; but the other remembering his face, cut his head off, and carried it to the rebel Melca Chriftos.

THE misfortune was followed by another in Gojam, great to the nation in general, and greater still to the Catholic caufe in particular. At the time that Sela Chriftos was in Begemder with prince Facilidas, the Galla from Bizamo, fuppofing the province of Damot without defence, paffed the Nile, laying the whole province wafte before them. Fecur Egzie, lieutenant-general under Sela Chriftos, although he had with him only a fmall number of troops, did not hefitate to march againft thofe favages, to endeavour, if poffible, to ftop their ravages. The Galla, furprifed at this, thought it was Sela Chriftos, and fled before him. He had now purfued them almoft alone, and lighted in a low meadow to give grafs to his horfe, when he was furrounded and flain by a number of the enemy that lay hid among the bufhes, and difcovered how ill he was attended.

HE was reputed a man of the beft underftanding, and the moft liberal fentiments of any in Ethiopia; a great orator, excelling both in the gracefulnefs of manner and copioufnefs and purity of his language. He was among the firft that embraced the Catholic religion, even before the king or Sela Chriftos, and was the principal promoter of the tranflations of the Portuguefe books into Ethiopic, affifted by the Jefuit Antonio de Angelis. We have feen, in the year 1613, the great efforts he made in the embaffy to India by the coaft of Melinda. He was an excellent horfeman, but more violent and rafh in battle than could have been expected from a man of fuch mild manners.

THERE happened at this time another novelty. The king brought the patriarch from Gorgora to Dancaz this year, at Eafter, to hear that feaft celebrated, with the Ethiopic fervice amended, of which we have already fpoken abundantly. This countenance, fo unneceffarily given to an innovation that produced every day fuch very bad effects to the Catholic intereft, joined to many other circumftances, feemed clearly to indicate a change in that prince's mind.

THE patriarch having made but a fhort ftay at Dancaz, it was currently reported a difagreement had happened, and that the king had fent him prifoner to Gorgora; and this falfe report affected greatly the weight the Catholics were fuppofed before to have had at court. But the tranfaction that followed was of a nature to promife much more confequences.

SOCINIOS had a daughter called *Ozoro Wengelawit*, which means the Evangelical, a name fhe certainly deferved not from her manners. This lady was firft married to Bela Chriftos, a man of rank at court, from whom fhe had been divorced. She was next married to another, and then (her two former hufbands being ftill alive) to Tecla Georgis, who had before married her fifter, another of the king's daughters. During this marriage fhe had openly lived in adultery with Za Chriftos, who had been married to her fifter, a third daughter of the king. Za Chriftos had been happy enough in preferving this lady's efteem longer than any other of her hufbands, and nothing would content her now but a marriage

riage with her lover folemnly and publicly. For which purpofe fhe applied to the patriarch to difpenfe with the affinity between her and Za Chriftos, arifing from his having been married before to her fifter.

It is not to be fuppofed that the patriarch would have refifted, if nothing had ftood in the way except the affinity: but weighty impediments prefented themfelves befides; for either the firft marriage was valid, or it was not. If it was valid, then Wengelawit could not marry Za Chriftos or any one elfe, becaufe her hufband was alive; nor could fhe marry her fecond, nor Tecla Georgis, her third. If the firft marriage was not valid, then the fecond was, which hufband was ftill alive; and, in this cafe, a licence to marry was giving her liberty of having three hufbands at one time. The patriarch, for thefe reafons, refufed his authority to this manifold adultery and inceft; nor could he, notwithftanding the interceffion of the whole court, ever be brought to comply. His firmnefs (however commendable) greatly increafed the hatred to his perfon, and averfion to the church of Rome.

One day when the king was fitting in his apartment, a monk entered the room, crying with a loud voice, " Hear " the ambaffador of God and of the Virgin Mary!" The king, upon firft fight of the man, expecting fome improper liberty might be taken, ordered his attendants to turn him out at the door, and, being removed from his prefence, to bring word what he had to fay, which was to this effect: " It is three days fince I rofe from the dead. One day when I was ftanding in paradife, God called me, and fent me with this meffage to you:—O emperor! fays God, it is now many years that I hoped you would amend of the great fin, the having forfaken the faith of your anceftors. All this time the Virgin Mary was kneeling before her blefled Son, befeeching him to pardon you ; and, upon the whole, it was agreed, that, unlefs you repent in a fortnight's time, you fhould be punifhed in fuch a manner that you will not forget it prefently."

Socinios defired them to afk the man, " How it was poffible that, having fo lately left the grave, his body fhould have fo little of the emaciated appearance of one long buried, and be now in fuch good cafe, fat and fair ?" To this he anfwered, " That, in paradife, he thanked God there was abundance of every thing; and people were very well ufed there, for he had lived upon good bread, and plenty of good wine, bifkets, and fweetmeats." To which Socinios anfwered, " Tell him, after the pains he had taken, it would be wrong in me to keep him long from fo good a place as this his paradife. Let him go and acquaint the perfon who fent him, I fhall live and die in the Roman Catholic faith ; and, in order that he may deliver the meffage quickly in the other world, fpeed him inftantly out of this, by hanging him upon the tree before the palace-gate."

The love of the wine, fweetmeats, and other celeftial food, feemed to have forfaken the ambaffador. Upon hearing this meffage he recanted, and was pardoned at the joint petition of thofe of the court that were prefent, who concurred with the monk in thinking, that the meffage of the emperor was an indecent one, and ought not to be delivered; that having been in paradife once, was as much as fell to the lot of any one man, and that he fhould therefore remain upon earth.

earth. The intended cataftrophe, then, of this fingular ambaffador was remitted; but the truth of his miffion was believed by the populace, and raifed great fcruples in every
weak mind.

THE many misfortunes that had lately befallen the troops
of the king were accounted as fo much increafe of power
to the rebel Melca Chriftos, who, encouraged by the correfpondence he held with the chiefs of the Alexandrian religion, began now to take upon him the ftate and office of a
king. His firft effay was to fend, as governor to the province
of Tigrè, a fon of that great rebel Za Selaffé, whofe manifold
treafons, we have already feen, occafioned the death of two
kings, Za Denghel and Jacob. .

ASCA GEORGIS was then governor of Tigrè for Socinios,
a man of merit and valour, but poor, and though related to
the king himfelf, had very few foldiers to be depended on,
excepting his own fervants, and two bodies of troops which
the king had fent him to maintain his authority, and to keep
his province in order.

THE new governor, fent by the rebel Melca Chriftos, had
with him a confiderable army ; and, knowing the weaknefs
of Afca Georgis, he paraded through the province in the
utmoft fecurity.

ONE Saturday which, in defiance of the king's edict, he
was to folemnize as a feftival equal to Sunday, he had refolved on a party of pleafure in a valley, where, much at
his eafe, he was preparing an entertainment for his troops
and friends, and fuch of the province as came to offer their

2. obedience.

obedience.   Intelligence of this party came to three Shum's, commanders of fmall diftricts, two of them fons-in-law of the king, the third a very loyal fubject.   Thefe three fent to Afca Georgis, to propofe that, at a ftated time, they fhould, each with his own men, fall feparately upon the fon of Za Selaffé, and interrupt his entertainment.

THIS was executed with great order and punctuality.   In the height of the feftival, the rebels were furrounded by an unexpected enemy.   To think of fighting was too late, nor was there time for flight.   The greateft part of the army was cut to pieces with little refiftance.   The new governor faved himfelf among the reft by the goodnefs of his horfe, leaving Billetana Gueta, or chief mafter of the houfehold of the rebel Melca Chriftos, dead upon the fpot, with about 4000 of his men.   Among the plunder were taken 32 kettle-drums, which alone were evidence fufficient of the greatnefs of the flaughter.

ALTHOUGH the happy turn Socinios's affairs had taken had given him leifure to pafs this winter at home, and in greater quiet than he had done in former ones, yet the calm which it had produced was of very fhort duration. The people of Lafta, perceiving fome of the prince's army bufy in deftroying their harveft when almoft ripe, came down fuddenly upon them from the mountain, and put them to flight with very great flaughter.   The blame of this was laid upon Sela Chriftos, who might have prevented the calamity; and this accufation, with many others, were brought againft him to the king by Lefana Chriftos.

This man had been condemned to die for an offence, fome time before, by Ras Sela Chriftos; but having fled to the king, who heard his caufe, the fentence was reverfed. Some time after this he fell into the hands of the Ras, who put him to death upon his former fentence, without regarding the late pardon of the king. This violent act became the foundation upon which his enemies built many accufations, moftly void of truth.

The king upon this took from him the government of Gojam, and gave it to a young nobleman whofe name was Serca Chriftos, fuppofed to be a friend and dependent upon the prince Facilidas. Serca Chriftos was no fooner arrived in his government than he refolved to rebel, and privately folicited the young prince Facilidas to take up arms and make a common caufe againft the king his father, in favour of the Alexandrian church. At the time that the young man departed to his government, Socinios had earneftly recommended to him, and he had moft folemnly promifed, to protect the Catholic religion in his province, and feemingly for this purpofe he had taken with him a Jefuit named Francifco de Carvalho.

Another affair which the king particularly charged him with was, the care of a caravan which once a-year came from Narea. This, befides many other valuable articles for the merchant, brought 1000 wakeas of gold as tribute to the king, equal to about 10,000 dollars, or crowns of our money: its whole way was through barbarous and lawlefs nations of Galla till they arrived at the Nile; then through Gafats and Gongas, immediately after having paffed it.

SERCA CHRISTOS, in his march, was come to a settlement of those last-mentioned savages, where Gafats, Agows, and Damots, all in peace, pastured immense flocks of cattle together. There are no where, I believe, in the world, cattle so beautiful as those of the Gafats, nor in such numbers. Large plains, for many days journey, are filled so full of them that they appear as one market.

SERCA CHRISTOS halted here to give grass to his horses; and, while this was doing, it entered into his young head, that making prize of the cattle was of much greater consequence than protecting the caravan of Narea. Assembling then his cavalry, he fell upon the poor Gafats and Damots, who feared no harm; and, having soon put them all to flight, he drove off their cattle in such numbers, that, at Dancaz, it was said, above 100,000 had reached that market.

THE king, much shocked at this violent robbery, ordered Serca Christos to give up the cattle, and surrender himself as prisoner. This message of the king he answered in terms of duty and obedience; but, in the mean time, went to the prince, and proposed to him to declare himself king and champion of the church of Alexandria. Facilidas received him with sharp reproofs, and he returned home much discontented. However, as he had now declared himself, he resolved to put the best face upon the matter; and, in order to make it generally believed that the prince and he understood each other, he sent him publicly word, " I have done what your highness ordered me; come and take possession of your kingdom." Upon which the prince ordered his messenger to be put in irons, and sent to Dancaz to the king his father.

AFTER

AFTER this, Serca Chriſtos ordered proclamation to be made that prince Facilidas was king, at the palace of the governor of Gojam, which Sela Chriſtos had built near the convent of Collela. As one article of it was the aboliſhing the Roman faith, the fathers ran precipitately into the convent, and ſhut the doors upon themſelves, fearing they ſhould be inſulted by the army of ſchiſmatics: but a number of the Portugueſe, who lived in the neighbourhood, being brought into the church with them, and there having been loop-holes made in the walls, and abundance of fire-arms left there in depoſit by Sela Chriſtos, the rebel governor did not chooſe to attempt any thing againſt them at that time. On the contrary, he ſent them word that he was in his heart a Roman Catholic, and only, for the preſent, obliged to diſſemble; but he would protect them to the utmoſt, deſiring them to ſend him the fire-arms left there by Sela Chriſtos, which they abſolutely refuſed to do.

SERCA CHRISTOS, apprehending that his army (if not acting under ſome chief of the royal family) would forſake him on the firſt appearance of the prince, had recourſe to a child of the blood-royal, then living in obſcurity among his female relations, and this infant he made king, in hopes, if he ſucceeded, to govern during his minority. There were many who expected the prince would reconcile him to the king, eſpecially as he had yet preſerved a ſhadow of reſpect for the Jeſuits, and this he imagined was one cauſe why the ſchiſmatics had not joined him in the numbers neceſſary. In order to ſhew them that he deſigned no reconciliation with the king, and to make ſuch agreement impoſſible, he adopted the ſame ſacrilegious example that had ſo ill ſucceeded with Tecla Georgis.

Za Selasse, a prieft of Selalo, had been heard to fay, when Serca Chriftos was appointed to the government of Gojam, " There is an end of the Catholic faith in this province." Being now called before the governor, he was forbid to fay mafs according to the forms of the church of Rome. This the prieft fubmitted to ; but, being ordered to deny the two natures in Chrift, he declared this was a point of faith which he would never give up, but always confefs Chrift was perfect God and perfect man. Upon this Serca Chriftos ordered him to be flain ; and he was accordingly thruft through with many lances, repeating thefe words, God and man ! God and man ! till his laft breath.

Serca Christos had now drawn the fword; and thrown away the fcabbard. Upon receiving the news, the king ordered the prince, who waited but his command, to march againft him. The murder of Za Selaffé had procured an acceffion of fanatics and monks, but very few foldiers ; fo that as foon as he heard with what diligence the prince was advancing, he left his whole baggage, and fled into thofe high and craggy mountains that form the banks of the Nile in Damot.

The prince preffed clofely upon him, notwithftanding the difficulty of the ground ; fo that no fafety remained for him but to pafs the Nile into the country of the Galla, where he thought himfelf in fafety. In this, however, he was miftaken. He had to do with a general of the moft active kind, in the perfon of Facilidas, who croffed the Nile after him, and, the third day, forced him to a battle on fuch ground as the prince had chofen, who was likewife much his fuperior in number of troops. But there was no longer

any

any remedy ; Serca Chriftos made the beft that he could of
this neceffity, and fought with great obftinacy, till his men
being for the moft part flain, he was forced, with the few
that remained, to take refuge on a high hill, whence the
prince obliged him to deliver himfelf up to his mercy without condition.

FACILIDAS immediately difpatched news of his victory to
court, and fifteen days after, he followed himfelf, bringing
Serca Chriftos, with fix of his principal officers and counfellors, loaded with heavy chains. Being interrogated by the
judges, What he had to anfwer for his treafons ? the prifoner
denied that he had any occafion to anfwer, becaufe he had
already received pardon from the prince.   This excufe was
not admitted, the prince having difowned it abfolutely. Upon which he was fentenced to death ; and, though he appealed to the king, his fentence was confirmed.

IT was too late to execute the fentence that night,
but next morning the feven prifoners were put to death.
One of the principal fervants of Serca Chriftos being afked
to confefs and turn Catholic, abandoned himfelf to great
rage, uttering many curfes and blafphemies againft the
king, who, therefore, ordered him to be faftened upon a
hook of iron, where he continued his curfes till at laft he
was flain by lances.

SERCA CHRISTOS, coufin to Socinios, was treated with more
refpect. He, with feeming candour, declared, that he would
die a Catholic ; and the king, very defirous of this, gave orders to Diego de Mattos, a prieft, to attend him conftantly
in prifon.   After which, one night he fent five of his confidential

fidential fervants, who killed him privately, to prevent his recantation.

SOCINIOS had again taken Gojam from Sela Chriftos;
which laft difgrace fo affected him, that he defired to retire
and live as a private man in that province.

THE king, having now no other enemy, all his attention
was employed in preparing for a campaign againft Melca
Chriftos of Lafta. But, as he found his army full of difaffec-
ion, it was propofed to him, before he took the field, to content them fo far as to indulge the Alexandrians in fome
rites of the old church ; and a proclamation was accordingly made by the king, " That thofe who chofe to obferve
" the Wednefday as a faft, inftead of Saturday, might do it;"
and fome other fuch indulgences as thefe were granted,
which were underftood to affect the faith..

As foon as this came to the ears of the patriarch, he
wrote a very fharp letter to the king, reproving him for the
proclamation that he had made ; adding, that it was an encroachment upon the office of the priefthood, that he, a
layman, fhould take upon him to direct in matters merely
ecclefiaftical. He warned the king, moreover, that God
would call him to the very ftricteft account for this prefumption, and reminded him of the words of Azarias the chief
prieft to king Uzziah, and of the punifhment of leprofy that
followed the king's encroachment on the ecclefiaftical function ; and infifted upon Socinios contradicting his proclamation by another..

SOCINIOS

Socinios fo far complied, that the alteration made by the laft proclamation was confined to three articles. Firft, that no liturgy, unlefs amended by the patriarch, was to be ufed in divine fervice. Secondly, that all feafts, excepting Eafter and thofe that depended upon it, fhould be kept according to the ancient computation of time. And, thirdly, that, whoever chofe, might faft on Wednefday, rather than on the Saturday.

At the fame time, the king expreffed himfelf as greatly offended at the freedom of the application of the ftory of Azarias and Uzziah to him. He told the patriarch plainly, that it was not by his fermons, nor thofe of the fathers, nor by the miracles they wrought, nor by the defire of the people, but by his edicts alone, that the Roman religion was introduced into Ethiopia; and, therefore, that the patriarch had not the leaft reafon to complain of any thing being altered by the authority that firft eftablifhed it. But, from this time, it plainly appears, that Socinios began to entertain ideas, at leaft of the church difcipline and government, very oppofite to thofe he had when he firft embraced the Romifh religion.

The king now fet out in his campaign for Lafta with a large army, which he commanded himfelf, and under him his fon, the prince Facilidas. Upon entering the mountain, he divided his army into three divifions. The firft commanded by the prince, and under him Za Mariam Adebo his mafter of the houfehold, was ordered to attack, fcale, and lodge themfelves on the higheft part of the mountain. The fecond he gave to Guebra Chriftos, governor of Begemder; and in this he placed the regiment, or body of troops, called

3   Inaches,

Inaches, veteran foldiers of Sela Chriftos, and a fmall, but brave body of troops containing the fons of Portuguefe: Thefe he directed to occupy the valleys and low ground. In the center the king commanded in perfon.

THE rebel chief and his mountaineers remained in a ftate of fecurity; for they neither thought to be fo fpeedily attacked, nor that Socinios could have raifed fo large an army. They abandoned, therefore, the lower ground, and all took pofts upon the heights. The prince advanced to the firft entrance, and ordered Damo, his Billetana Gueta, to force it with four companies of good foldiers, who afcended the mountain with great perfeverance; and, notwithftanding the obftinate defence of the rebels, made themfelves mafter of that poft, having killed two of the braveft officers Melca Chriftos had, the one named Billene, the other Tecla Mariam, firnamed *defender of the faith*, becaufe he was the firft that brought Galla to the affiftance of Melca Chriftos.

THERE were likewife flain, at the fame time, four priefts and five monks, after a defperate refiftance; one of whom, calling the king's troops Moors, forbade them to approach for fear of defiling him, and then, with a book in his hand, threw himfelf over the rock, and was dafhed to pieces in the plain below. Here the prince met with an enemy he did not expect: The cold was fo exceffive, that above fifty perfons were frozen to death.

THE top of the mountain, which was the fecond entry into Lafta, was occupied by a ftill larger body of rebels, and, therefore, neceffary to be immediately ftormed, elfe thofe

I   below

below were in imminent danger of being dafhed to pieces by the large ftones rolled down upon them. The prince divided his army into two parties, exhorting them, without lofs of time, to attack that poft; but the rebels, feeing the good countenance with which they afcended, forfook their ftation and fled; fo that this fecond mountain was gained with much lefs lofs and difficulty than the firft.

BEHIND this, and higher than all the reft, appeared the third, which ftruck the affailants at firft with terror and defpair. This was carried with ftill lefs lofs on the part of the prince, becaufe he was affifted by the Inaches and Portuguefe, who cut off the communication below, and hindered one mountain from fuccouring the other. Here they found great ftore of arms, offenfive and defenfive; coats of mail, mules, and kettle drums; and they penetrated to the head-quarters of Melca Chriftos, which was a fmall mountain, but very ftrong in fituation, where a Portuguefe captain feized the feat which ferved as a throne to the rebel; and, had not they loft time by falling to plunder, they would have taken Melca Chriftos himfelf, who with difficulty efcaped, accompanied by ten horfe.

To this laft mountain Socinios repaired with the prince, and they were joined by the governors of Amhara and Tigré, who had forced their way in from the oppofite fide.

HITHERTO all had gone well with the king; but when he had detached Guebra Chriftos, governor of Begemder, with the Inaches and Portuguefe, who were at fome diftance, to deftroy the crop, the mountaineers, again affembled on a high hill

hill above them, faw their opportunity, and fell fuddenly upon the fpoilers, and cut all the foldiers of Begemder to pieces. A confiderable part of the Inaches fell alfo; but the reft, joining themfelves with the Portuguefe in one body, made good their retreat to the head-quarters.

The deftruction of the corn everywhere around them, and the impoffibility of bringing provifions there, as they were fituated in the midft of their enemies, obliged the king to think of returning before the rebels fhould collect themfelves, and cut off his retreat. And it was with great difficulty, and ftill greater lofs, he accomplifhed this, and retired to Dancaz, abandoning Lafta as foon as he had fubdued it, but leaving Begemder almoft a prey to the rebels whom he had conquered in Lafta.

Socinios being now determined upon another campaign againft Lafta, and for the relief of Begemder, ordered his troops to hold themfelves in readinefs to march as foon as the weather fhould permit. But an univerfal difcontent had feized the whole army. They faw no end to this war, nor any repofe from its victories obtained with great bloodfhed, without fpoil, riches, or reward; no territory acquired to the king, nor nation fubdued; but the time, when they were not actually in the field, filled up with executions and the conftant effufion of civil blood, that feemed to be more horrid than war itfelf. They, therefore, pofitively refufed to march againft Lafta; and the prince was deputed by them to inform the king, that they did not fay the Roman faith was a bad one, as they did not underftand it, nor defire to be inftructed; that this was an affair which entirely regarded themfelves, and no one would pretend to fay there was

any

any merit in profeffing a religion they did not underftand or believe: that they were ready, however, to march and lay down their lives for the king and common-weal, provided he reftored them their ancient religion, without which they would have no concern in the quarrel, nor even wifh to be conquerors. Whether the king was really in the fecret or not, I fhall not fay; but it is exprefsly mentioned in the annals of his reign, that Socinios did promife by his fon to the army, that he would reftore the Alexandrian faith if he fhould return victorious over Lafta; and the fudden manner in which he executed this muft convince every other perfon that it was fo.

THE army now marched from Dancaz, upon intelligence arriving that the rebels had left their ftrong-holds in Lafta, and were in their way to the capital to give the king battle there. It was the 26th of July 1631 the king difcovered, by his fcouts, that the rebel Melca Chriftos was at hand, having with him an army of about 25,000 men. Upon this intelligence he ordered his troops to halt, and hear mafs from Diego de Mattos; and, having chofen his ground, he halted again at mid-day, and confeffed, according to the rite of the church of Rome, and then formed his troops in order of battle.

IT was not long till the enemy came in fight, but without fhewing that alacrity and defire of engaging they ufed to do when in their native mountains. The king, at the head of the cavalry, fell fo fuddenly and fo violently upon them, that he broke through the van-guard commanded by Melca Chriftos, and put them to flight before his foot could come up. The reft of the army followed the example of the leader, and the enemy were everywhere trodden down and de-ſtroyed by the victorious horſe, till night put an end to the purſuit.

Melca Christos, in the beginning of the engagement, ſaved himſelf by the ſwiftneſs of his horſe; but 8000 of the mountaineers were ſlain upon the ſpot, among whom was Bicané, general to Melca Chriſtos, an excellent officer both for council and the field, and ſeveral other conſiderable perſons, as well inhabitants of Laſta as others, who had ta-ken that ſide from diſlike to the king and his meaſures.

Next morning the king went out with his ſon to ſee the field of battle, where the prince Facilidas is ſaid to have ſpoke to this effect in name of the army: " Theſe men, whom you ſee ſlaughtered on the ground, were neither Pa-gans nor Mahometans at whoſe death we ſhould rejoice— they were Chriſtians, lately your ſubjects and your coun-trymen, ſome of them your relations. This is not victory which is gained over ourſelves. In killing theſe you drive the ſword into your own entrails. How many men have you ſlaughtered? How many more have you to kill? We are become a proverb even among the Pagans and Moors for carrying on this war, and for apoſtatizing, as they ſay, from the faith of our anceſtors."—The king heard this ſpeech without reply, and returned manifeſtly diſconſolate to Dan-caz; though many times before he had feaſted and trium-phed for the gaining of a leſſer victory.

After his arrival at Dancaz, he had a conference with the patriarch Alphonſo Mendes, who, in a long ſpeech, up-braided him with having deſerted the Catholic faith at the time

time when the victory obtained by their prayers gave him an opportunity of eftablifhing it. The king anfwered, with feeming indifference, that he had done every thing for the Catholic faith in his power; that he had fhed the blood of thoufands, and as much more was to be fhed; and ftill he was uncertain if it would produce any effect; but that he fhould think of it, and fend him his refolutions to-morrow.

THE next day Socinios made a declaration by Za Mariam to the patriarch, to this purport: "When we embraced the faith of Rome, we laboured for it with great diligence, but the people fhewed no affection for it. Julius rebelled out of his laboured Sela Chriftos, under pretence of being defender of the ancient faith, and was flain, together with many of his followers. Gabriel did the fame. Tecla Georgis, likewife, made a league to die for the Alexandrian faith, which he did, and many people with him. The fame did Serca Chriftos the preceding year; and thofe peafants of Lafta fight for the fame caufe at this day. The faith of Rome is not a bad one; but the men of this country do not underftand it. Let thofe that like it remain in that faith, in the fame way as the Portuguefe did in the time of Atzenaf Segued; let them eat and drink together, and let them marry the daughters of Abyffinians. As for thofe that are not inclined to the Roman faith, let them follow their ancient one as received from the church of Alexandria."

UPON this declaration, delivered by Za Mariam, the patriarch inquired if it came from the king. Being anfwered that it did; after a little paufe, he returned this anfwer by Emanuel Almeyda, "That the patriarch underftood that both religions fhould be permitted in the kingdom, and that the Alexandrians were to have every indulgence that could be wished by them, without violating the purity of the Catholic faith; that, therefore, he had no difficulty of allowing the people of Lasta to live in the faith of their anceftors without alteration, as they had never embraced any other; but as for thofe that had fworn to perfift in the Catholic faith, and had received the communion in that church, by no means, without a grievous fin, could it be granted to them to renounce that faith in which they had deliberately fworn to live and die."

The king, upon this anfwer, which he underftood well, and expected, only replied, " What is to be done? I have no longer the power of government in my own kingdom;"— and immediately ordered a herald to make the following proclamation:—

" Hear us! hear us! hear us! Firft of all we gave you the Roman Catholic faith, as thinking it a good one; but many people have died fighting againft it, as Julius, Gabriel, Tecla Georgis, Serca Chriftos, and, laftly, thefe rude peafants of Lafta. Now, therefore, we reftore to you the faith of your anceftors; let your own priefts fay their mafs in their own churches; let the people have their own altars for the facrament, and their own liturgy, and be happy. As for myfelf, I am now old and worn out with war and infirmities, and no longer capable of governing; I name my fon Facilidas to reign in my place."

Thus, in one day, fell the whole fabric of the Roman Catholic faith, and hierarchy of the church of Rome, in Abyffinia; firft regularly eftablifhed, as I muft always think, by Pe-

ter

ter Paez, in moderation, charity, perfeverance, long-fuffering, and peace; extended and maintained afterwards
by blood and violence beyond what could be expected from
heathens, and thrown down by an exertion of the civil power
in its own defence, againft the encroachments of priefthood and ecclefiaftical tyranny, which plainly had no other
view than, by annihilating the conftitution under its native
prince, to reduce Abyffinia to a Portuguefe government, as
had been the cafe with fo many independent ftates in India already.

THIS proclamation was made on the 14th of June 1632.
After this Socinios took no care of public affairs. He had
been for a long time afflicted with various complaints, e-
fpecially fince the laft campaign in Lafta; and affairs were
now managed by prince Facilidas in his father's place,
though he did not take upon him the title of King. E-
mana Chriftos, brother of Sela Chriftos, a fteady Alexandrian, and Guebra Chriftos, were then made governors of
Lafta and Begemder; but no fteps were taken in this interval againft the Jefuits.

ON the 7th of September the king died, and was buried
with great pomp, by his fon Facilidas, in the church of Ganeta Jefus, which he himfelf had built, profeffing himfelf
a Roman Catholic to the laft. The Portuguefe hiftorians
deny both his refignation of the crown, and his perfeverance
in the Roman Catholic faith to his death, but this apparently
for their own purpofes.

HE was a prince remarkable for his ftrength of body; of
great courage and elevation of mind; had early learned the
4 exercife

exercife of arms, patience, perfeverance, and every military virtue that could be acquired; and had paffed the firft of his life
as a private perfon, in the midft of hardfhips and dangers.

He is celebrated to this day in Abyffinia for a talent,
which feems to be the gift of nature, that of choofing upon
the firft view the proper ground for the camp or battle, and
embracing, in his own mind in a moment, all the advantages
and difadvantages that could refult from any particular part
of it.   This talent is particularly recorded in feveral fhort
proverbs, or military adages, fuch as the following: " Blind
him firft, or you fhall never beat him." This moft material
qualification feemed to have been in part tranfmitted to Ras
Michael, the great general in my time, defcended from Socinios by his mother; and, by this fuperiority alone over the
other commanders oppofed to him, he is faid to have been
victorious in forty-three pitched battles.

Socinios embraced the Catholic religion from conviction,
and ftudied it with great application, as far as his narrow
means of inftruction would allow him; and there can be no
doubt that, under the moderate conduct of Peter Paez, who
converted him, he would have died a martyr for that religion ; and there feems as little reafon to doubt, confcienti-
ous as he was, if he had been a young man he would
have quitted it for the good of his country, and from his
inability to fuffer the tyranny of the patriarch Alphonfo
Mendes, and his continual encroachment upon civil government.   Being, in the laft years of his life, left without
one foldier to draw his fword for the Catholic caufe, he kept
his religion, and abandoned his crown ; and having been, it
fhould feem, for fome time convinced that the government
                         2   of

of the church of Rome, in fuch hands as he left it, was incompatible with monarchy, he took no pains to change Facilidas's known fentiments, or to render him favourable to the Roman faith, or to name another of his fons to fucceed him whom he found to be more fo..

THE Jefuits, confidering only the cataftrophe, and unmindful of the ftrenuous efforts made to eftablifh their religion during his whole reign, have traduced his character as that of an apoftate, for giving way to the univerfal demand of his people to have their ancient form of worfhip reftored when his army had deferted him, and he himfelf was dying of old age. But every impartial man will admit, that the ftep he took, of abdicating his fovereignty over a people who had abjured the religion he had introduced among them, was, in his circumftances, the nobleft action of his life, and juft the reverfe of apoftacy.

THIS refignation of the crown, and his tenacious perfevering in the Catholic faith, together with the moderation of his fon, the prince Facilidas, in appointing a regency to govern, rather than to mount the throne himfelf during his father's life, are three facts which we know to be true from the Abyffinian annals, and which the Jefuits have endeavoured to fupprefs, that they might the more eafily blacken the character both of the father and the fon.

THEY have pretended that it was the queen, and other ladies at court, who by their influence feduced the king from the Catholic religion. But Socinios was then paft feventy, and the queen near fixty, and he had no other wives or miftreffes. To judge, moreover, by his behaviour in the affair of Adera, fifter to Tecla Georgis, the voice of the women at court feems to have had no extraordinary weight with him. In a word, he never varied in his religion after he embraced that of Rome, but ftedfaftly adhered to it, when the pride and bad conduct of the Jefuits, its profeffors, had fcarcely left another friend to it in the whole kingdom; and, therefore, the charge of apoftacy is certainly an unmerited falfehood.

As it is plain the Portuguefe, from the beginning, believed their religion could only be eftablifhed by force, and were perfuaded fuch means were lawful, the blame of fo much bloodfhed for fo many years, and the total mifcarriage of the whole fcheme at laft, lay at the door of their fovereign, the king of Spain and Portugal; who, having fucceeded to his wifh in his conqueft of India, feems not to have had the fame anxiety the patriarch had for the converfion of Abyffinia, nor even to have thought further of fending a body of troops with his priefts to the fuccour of Socinios, whom he left to the prayers of Urban VIII. the merit of Ignatius Loyola, and the labours of his furious and fanatic difciples.

TRAVELS

TRAVELS

TO DISCOVER

THE SOURCE OF THE NILE.

BOOK IV.

ANNALS OF ABYSSINIA,
TRANSLATED FROM THE ORIGINAL.

CONTINUATION OF THE ANNALS, FROM THE DEATH OF SOCI-
NIOS TILL MY ARRIVAL IN ABYSSINIA.

FACILIDAS, OR SULTAN SEGUED.

From 1632 to 1665.

*The Patriarch and Miffionaries are banifhed—Seek the Protection of a
Rebel—Delivered up to the King, and fent to Mafuah—Prince Claudius rebels—Sent to Wechné—Death and Character of the King.*

A S foon as the prince Facilidas had paid the laft honours
to his father, he fet about compofing thofe diforders
which had fo long diftracted the kingdom by reafon of the
difference of religion. Accordingly he wrote to the patri-

arch, that, the Alexandrian faith being now reſtored, his leaving the kingdom had become indiſpenſible : that he had
lately underſtood, that an Abuna, ſent for by his predeceſſor
and by himſelf, was now actually on the way, and only deferred his arrival from a reſolution not to enter the kingdom till the Romiſh patriarch and his prieſts ſhould have
left it ; and, therefore, he commanded the patriarch and fathers, aſſembled from their ſeveral convents in Gojam and
Dembea, to retire immediately to Fremona, there to wait
his further pleaſure.

THE patriarch endeavoured to parry this, with offering
new conceſſions and indulgencies ; but the king informed
him that he was too late; and that he wiſhed him to be
adviſed, and fly, while it was time, from greater harm that
would otherwiſe fall upon him.

IT was not long before the patriarch had revenge of Facilidas for this intimation of the expectation of a ſucceſſor
in the perſon of the Abuna.   For on that very Eaſter there
did arrive one, whoſe name was Sela Chriſtos, calling himſelf Abuna, who performed all the functions of his office,
dedicated churches, adminiſtered the ſacrament, and ordained prieſts.   After continuing in office ſome months, he was
detected by a former companion of his, and found to be a
man of very bad character, from Nara, the frontier of Abyſſinia, and that by profeſſion he had been a dealer in horſes.

FACILIDAS then ordered his uncle, Sela Chriſtos, to be
brought before him, received him kindly, and offered him
again his riches and employments.   That brave man, Chriſtian in every thing but in his hatred and jealouſy againſt
                                                              his

his fovereign and nephew, refufed abfolutely to barter his faith to obtain the greateft good, or avoid the greateft punifhment, it was in the power of the king to inflict. After repeated trials, all to no purpofe, the king, overcome by the inftigation of his enemies, banifhed him to Anabra in Shawada, a low, unwholefome diftrict amidft the mountains of Samen. But hearing that he ftill kept correfpondence with the Jefuits, and that their common refolution was to folicit Portuguefe troops from India, and remembering his former oath, he fent orders to his place of exile to put him to death, and he was in confequence hanged upon a cedar-tree.

TELLEZ, the Portuguefe hiftorian, in his collection of martyrs that died for the faith in Abyffinia, has defervedly inferted the name of Sela Chriftos; but profeffes that he is ignorant of the time of his death, and under what fpecies of torment he fuffered. The only information that I can give is what I have juft now written. It was in the beginning of the year 1634 he was carried to Shawada in chains, and confined upon the mountain Anabra; but no mention is made of any other hardfhip being put upon him than his being in irons, nor is more ufual in that kind of banifhment. It was at the end of that year, however, that he was executed in the manner above mentioned, being fufpected of having correfponded with the patriarch and Jefuits, and afterwards of inciting his nephew Claudius to rebel, as, it appears, he had meditated long before, and actually did very foon after.

THE 9th of March 1633, the king ordered the patriarch to leave Dancaz, and, with the reft of the fathers, to proceed im-

mediately

mediately to Fremona, under the conduct of four people of the firft confideration, Tecla Georgis, brother of Keba Chriftos, Tecla Saluce, one of the principal perfons in Tigré, and two Azages, men of great dignity at court. Thefe were joined by a party of foldiers belonging to Claudius, brother of the king, fuppofed to have been in the confpiracy with Sela Chriftos his uncle, to fupplant his brother Facilidas by the help of the Jefuits and Portuguefe troops from India. But as foon as the patriarch had fallen into difgrace, and Sela Chriftos loft his life, that prince returned to the church of Alexandria, as did all the other fons of Socinios; after which, Claudius feized to his own ufe all the lands and effects that he found in Gojam, and was now by the king made governor of Begemder. Under this efcort the patriarch and his company arrived at Fremona in the end of April 1633, after having been often robbed and ill-treated by the way, the guards that were given to defend them conniving with the banditti that came to rob them.

However ftrictly the fathers obferved the precepts of fcripture on other occafions, in this they did not follow the line of conduct prefcribed by our Saviour—" And whofo-" ever fhall not receive you, nor hear your words, when you " depart out of that houfe or city, fhake off the duft of your " feet." They were not fheep that went patiently and dumb to the flaughter; and, if their hearts, as they fay, were full of love and charity to Abyffinia, it was ftrangely accompanied with the refolution they had taken to fend Jerome Lobo, the moft famous, becaufe the moft bigotted Jefuit of the whole band, firft to the viceroy of India, and then to Spain, to folicit an army and fleet which were to lay all this kingdom in blood.

The

The king was perfectly advised of all that paffed. As he faw that the patriarch endeavoured to gain time, and knew the reafon of it; and, as the fathers among them had a confiderable quantity of fire-arms, he fent an officer to the patriarch at Fremona, commanding him to deliver up the whole of thefe, with gun-powder and other ammunition, and to prepare, at the fame time, to fet out for Mafuah. This at firft the patriarch refufed to do. Nor did Facilidas punifh this difobedience by any harfher method than convincing him mildly of the imprudence and inutility of fuch refufal, and the bad confequences to themfelves. Upon which the patriarch at laft furrendered the articles required to the officer fent by the king, but he refolved very differently as to the other injunction of carrying all his brethren to Mafuah. On the contrary, he determined by every means to fcatter them about the kingdom of Abyffinia, and leave them behind if he was forced to embark at Mafuah, which he, however, refolved to avoid and refift to the utmoft of his power.

In order to do this, it was refolved that he fhould folicit the Baharnagafh (John Akay, then in rebellion) to take them under his protection, and for that purpofe to fend a number of armed men, on a night appointed, to meet them near Fremona, and carry them in fafety from any purfuit of the governor of Tigré. This project, extraordinary as it was, fucceeded. Akay promifed them his protection. The patriarch and priefts, deceiving the guard the king had fet upon them, efcaped in the night, and joined the foldiers of John Akay, commanded by Tecla Emanuel, who was ready to receive them: They took refuge at Addicota, the foldiers of the guard, though alarmed, not daring to purfue them in the night, as

not

not knowing the number and power of their protectors, and fearing they might fall into fome ambufh.

It may not be amifs here to take notice, that this John Akay was the very man with whom Tecla Georgis had affociated for the murder of Abba Jacob. He was a fhrewd man, and had great power by living in the neighbourhood of Sennaar, to which country he could retreat when occafion required. He received the patriarch with great kindnefs.

Addicota is an inacceffible rock, perpendicular on all fides, excepting where there is a narrow path by which was the entrance. Here the patriarch thought he could continue in Abyffinia, in defiance of Facilidas, till he fhould procure fuccours from India.

It was not, however, long before he found how little dependence there was upon this new protector ; for, in the midft of all his fchemes, he received orders to remove from Addicota, under pretence that they were not there enough in fafety ; and Akay transferred them vexatioufly from place to place, into hot and unwholefome fituations, always under the fame pretence, till he had deftroyed their healths, and exhaufted their ftrength and patience.

There is but one way of difpofing fuch people to grant a favour, and it was furprifing the patriarch did not find this out fooner. Jerome Lobo was fent with a fmall prefent in gold, defiring they might have leave to continue in their old habitation, Addicota. Lobo found John Akay very much taken up in a purfuit that fome ignorant monks had put

into

into his head. They had made him believe that there was a treafure hid under a certain mountain which they had fhewn him, but that the devil who guarded it had conftantly hindered his predeceffors from acquiring it. At prefent they had found out, that this devil had gone a journey far off, was become blind and lame, and was, befides, in very great affliction for the death of a fon, the only hopes of his devilfhip's family, having now only a daughter remaining, very ugly, lame, fquinting, and fickly, and that all thefe reafons would hinder him from being very anxious about his treafure. But, even fuppofing he did come, they had an old monk that would exorcife him, a man as eminent for wifdom as for fanctity.

In fhort, they produced a monk, one of their brethren, above a hundred years old, whom they mounted upon a horfe, then tied him to the animal, wrapping him round with black wool, which, it feems, was the conjuring habit. He was followed by a black cow and fome monks, who carried beer, hydromel, and roafted wheat, which was neceffary, it feemed, to refrefh the devil after his long journey and great affliction, and put him in good humour, if he fhould appear.

The old monk fung without ceafing, the workmen wrought vigoroufly, and much earth and ftones were removed; at laft they difcovered fome rat, mice, or moleholes, at the fight of which a cry of joy was heard from all the parties prefent.

The old monk fings again; the cow is brought in great hurry, and facrificed, and pieces of it thrown to the rats and mice;

mice: again they fall to work with double keennefs, the mole-holes vanifh, and a hard rock appears. This being the laft obftacle, they fall keenly upon the rock, and the old monk chants till he is hoarfe with finging; the heat of the fun is exceffive; no gold appears; John Akay lofes his patience, and afks when it may be feen? The monks lay the whole blame upon him, becaufe, they fay, he had not enough of faith. They give over work; with one confent fall to eating the cow, and then difperfe.

FATHER Jerome, takes the opportunity of this difappointment to abufe the monks. He prefents the Baharnagafh with two ounces of gold, and fome other trifles, inftead of the treafure which he was to get in the mountain: he obtains the requeft he came to folicit, and the patriarch and fathers return to Addicota.

FACILIDAS, informed of the afylum afforded to the Jefuits who had fled from Fremona, applied to John Akay, promifing him forgivennefs of what was paft if he would deliver the priefts under his protection. This John Akay declined to do from motives of delicacy. It was breaking his word to deliver his guefts into the hands of the king; but, by a very ftrange refinement, he agreed to fell them to the Turks. Accordingly they were delivered for a fum to the bafha of Mafuah, who received them with much greater kindnefs than they had experienced in the Chriftian country from which they fled.

Two Jefuits were purpofely left behind, with the confent of John Akay, unknown to Facilidas, in fervent hopes that fome occafion would foon offer of fuffering martyrdom for

i   the

the true faith; and in this expectation they were not long difappointed, all thofe who were left in Abyffinia having loft their lives by violent deaths, moft of them on a gibbet, by order of Facilidas, the laft of whom was Bernard Nogeyra.

FACILIDAS, weary of the obftinacy of thefe miffionaries, uneafy alfo at the fufpicions they created, that a number of Portuguefe troops would be poured in upon his country by the viceroy of India, concluded a treaty with the bafhas of Mafuah and Suakem, for preventing any Portuguefe paffing into Abyffinia, by fhutting thefe ports againft them. Not above eight years before, that is, in the year 1624, Socinios had fent a zebra, and feveral other curious articles, as prefents to the bafha of Suakem, with a requeft to him not to obftruct, as the Turks had ufed to do, the entrance of any Portuguefe into his dominions. But thofe times were now fo changed, that both nations, Turks and Abyffinians, had refolved, with one confent, to exclude them all, for their mutual fafety, peace, and advantage.

THIS treaty with the Turks, made by Facilidas, probably gave rife to that calumny of the Jefuits, that, for fear of a return of the Portuguefe, that prince had embraced the Mahometan religion, and fent for preceptors from Mocha to inftruct him in their tenets. This, I fay, if not founded upon the treaty I mention, was deftitute of the leaft fhadow of truth; but, like other calumnies then propagated in great number, arofe folely from the rage, malice, and heated imaginations of defperate fanatics.

AMIDST the general regret this revolution in the church of Ethiopia occafioned at Rome, there were fome who thought the pride, obftinacy, and violence of the Jefuits, the hardnefs and cruelty of their hearts in inftigating Socinios to that perpetual effufion of blood, and their independence, their encroachments upon, and refiftance of the civil power, were faults refulting from the inftitutions of that particular fociety, and that thefe occafioned the mifcarriage; that a well-grounded averfion to the teachers had created a repugnance to the doctrines preached, and was the reafon of the expulfion of the fathers, and the relapfe of Abyffinia to the Alexandrian faith. From this perfuafion, fix capuchins, all of them Frenchmen of the reformed Order of St Francis, were fent from Rome after the death of Nogeyra, by the congregation *De Propagandâ Fide*, and thefe had protections from the grand fignior.

Two attempted the entering Abyffinia by way of the Indian Ocean, that is, from Magadoxa, and were flain by the Galla, after advancing a very fhort way into the country. Two of them penetrated into Abyffinia, and were ftoned to death. The remaining two, hearing the fate of their companions at Mafuah, and not being fo violently bent upon a crown of martyrdom as were the Portuguefe miffionaries, prudently returned home, carrying with them the account of this bad fuccefs.

THREE other capuchins were fent after this. It is impoffible to judge from their conduct what idea they had formed ; for they themfelves gave the firft information of their intended coming to Facilidas, who thereupon recommended it to the bafha to receive them according to their merits;

and

and thereupon, on their arrival at Suakem, their heads were cut off by his order; the skins of their heads and faces stripped off and sent to the king of Abyssinia, that, by their colour, he might know them to be franks, and by their tonsure to be priests. Nor was it possible afterwards to introduce any Catholic missionaries, either during this or the following reign.

FACILIDAS having thus provided against being further disturbed by missionaries, and having reduced all his subjects to the obedience of the Alexandrian church, sent again messengers to bring an Abuna from Cairo, while he took the field against Melca Christos his rival, who continued in arms at the head of the peasants of Lasta, though there was now no longer any pretence that the Alexandrian faith was in danger. Both armies met in Libo, a country of the Galla, where a panic seized the king's troops, his horse flying at the first onset. The royal army being entirely dispersed, Melca Christos pursued his good fortune, and entered the king's palace, took possession of the throne, and was crowned; he appointed to all the great places in government, and distributed a largess, or bounty, to his soldiers.

THE Portuguese historians say, that this happened at Dancaz, not at Libo. But they should have remembered what they before have said, that an epidemic fever raged in all Dembea, so that the king was not at Dancaz that year. He passed the winter of the preceding one at Dobit, near Begemder.

THE memoirs of these missionaries, even when they were in the country, are to be read with great caution, being

3 F 2   full

full of mifreprefentations of the manners and characters of men, magnifying fome actions, flighting others, and attributing to their favourites fervices that were really performed by their adverfaries; and, from the coming of Alphonfo Mendes, till they were banifhed to Mafuah, great part of their account is untrue, and the reft very fufpicious. After their retiring to India, which is the time we are now fpeaking of, the whole that they have publifhed is one continued tiffue of falfehood and calumny, either hear-fay ftories communicated to them, as they fay, by the remnants of zealots ftill alive in Abyffinia, or fabrications of their own, invented for particular purpofes. In continuing this hiftory, I fhall take notice of fome of thefe, though for facts I rely entirely upon the annals of the country, treating, however, the Abyffinian account of the Jefuits doctrines and behaviour with the fame degree of caution.

THIS forwardnefs of his rival Melca Chriftos did not difcourage Facilidas. Without lofing a moment, he fent expreffes to Kafmati Dimmo, governor of Samen, to Ras Sela Chriftos, of Damot, and to his brother Claudius, governor of Begemder, ordering them to march and attack Melca Chriftos, then acting as fovereign in the king's palace at Libo.

THESE three generals were not flack in obeying the commands of Facilidas. They furrounded Melca Chriftos before he expected them, and forced him to a battle, in which he was defeated and loft his whole army. He himfelf, fighting manfully at the head of his troops, was flain hand to hand by Cofmas, a foldier of Kafmati Claudius, the king's brother.

JEROME

Jerome Lobo mentions Facilidas's bad fuccefs againft the Gallas and Agows as an inftance of divine vengeance which purfued him.   But if the approbation or difapprobation of heaven is to be appealed to in this reign as a proof of the juftnefs of the meafures taken, we muft be obliged to fay the caufe of the Jefuits was not the caufe of heaven.   If we except the temporary advantage·gained over Facilidas, and the accident that happened to his army at Lafta, perpetual victory had attended the wars in which this prince was engaged; for fo far was he from being unfortunate this campaign againft the Agows, that, on the 9th of February 1636, he marched from Libo into Gojam, and totally defeated the two great tribes Azena and Zeegam.   After which he fent his army with Kafmati Melca Bahar, who coming up with the Galla, a great body of whom had made an incurfion into Gojam, he totally overthrew them, and paffing the Nile into their country, laid it wafte, and returned with a great number of cattle, and multitudes of women and children to be fold as flaves.

The king then returned to Begemder, and took up his head-quarters at Gonfala ; but, foon hearing that the Abuna Marcus was arrived, he quitted that place, and came to meet him in Gondar.

The next year, which was the fifth of his reign, and the firft of the coming of Abuna Marcus, he again fought with the Agows, and beat the Denguis, Hancafha, and the Zeegam, and paffed that winter in Gafat ; nor was he ever unfortunate with the Agows or Galla.   But a misfortune happened this year (the 6th of his reign) which very much affected the whole kingdom.   The people of Lafta feemed to

grow

grow more inveterate after the defeat they had received under Melca Chriftos.   In the ftead of that prince flain in battle, they appointed his fon, a young man of good hopes.

FACILIDAS, trufting to his former reputation acquired in thefe mountains in his father's time, on the 3d of March 1638 advanced with a large army into Lafta, with a defign to bring thefe peafants to a battle. But the rebels, growing wife by their loffes, no longer chofe to truft themfelves on the plain, but, retiring to the ftrongeft pofts, fortified them fo judicioufly, that, without rifking any lofs themfelves, they cut off all fupplies or provifions coming to the king's army.

IT happened at that time the cold was fo exceffive that almoft the whole army perifhed amidft the mountains; great part from famine, but a greater ftill from cold, a very remarkable circumftance in thefe latitudes.   Lafta is barely 12° from the Line, and it was now the equinox in March, fo that the fun was but 12° from being in the zenith of Lafta, and there was in the day twelve hours of fun.   Yet here is an example of an army, not of foreigners, but natives, perifhing with cold in their own country, when the fun is no farther than 12° from being vertical, or from being directly over their heads ; a ftrong proof this, as I have often remarked, that there is no way of judging by the degrees of heat in the thermometer, what effect that degree of heat or cold is to have upon the human body.

THE eighth year of the reign of Facilidas, Claudius, gornor of Begemder, his brother, revolted and joined the rebels

I

bels of Lasta. It seems, that this prince had been long encouraged by the Jesuits, and his uncle Sela Christos, in expectation of succeeding his father Socinios, and supplanting Facilidas, his brother, in the kingdom. But, after the banishment of the Jesuits, and the death of Sela Christos, Facilidas thinking, these bad counsellors being removed, he would continue firm in his duty, and willing to disbelieve the whole that had been reported of his designs, made him governor of Begemder.

It happened, however, that this very year two Abunas arrived from Egypt, one by way of Sennaar, the other by Dancali. Upon inquiry it was found, that Abba Michael, the latter of these Abunas, had been sent for by Kasmati Claudius, in expectation that he was to be on the throne by the time of his Abuna's arrival. This implied clearly that the king's death was agreed on. Claudius, without attempting a vindication, or awaiting the discussion of this step, fled to Lasta, and joined Laeca, son of Melca Christos, a youth then at the head of the rebels..

Facilidas banished Abba Michael to Serké, a Mahometan town in the way to Sennaar, and admitted Abba Johannes, whom he himself had sent for from Cairo, into the office of Abuna.

Soon after this, Claudius was surprised and taken prisoner, and brought to the king, and, though stained in a high degree with ingratitude, treason, and intended fratricide, he could not be brought to order his execution, but, like a wise and merciful prince, reflecting on the ancient usages of the empire, and how much royal blood might be daily

saved

faved by fequeftering the defcendents of the imperial family upon the mountain, he chofe that of Wechné in Beleffen, which ferved ever after for this purpofe.

This is the third mountain within the reach of written hiftory, firft chofen, and then reprobated, as a ftate-prifon for all the males of the royal family, excepting the one feated upon the throne.

This interruption of the imprifonment of the princes for a time, and the refuming it again for another period, have led the Portuguefe writers, very little acquainted with the hiftory or conftitution of this country, into various difputes and difficulties, which I fhall fully explain and reconcile in their proper place. It is fufficient for the prefent to obferve, that Claudius was fent into exile to the mountain of Wechnè, and that he was the firft prince banifhed thither, where he lived for many years.

The king, finding that nothing material preffed at home, marched into Gojam to Enzagedem, whence he fent Ras Bela Chriftos againft the Shangalla, N. W. of the country of the Agows. Thefe people being put upon their guard by their neighbours, all difaffected to the king, contrived to place themfelves in ambufh fo judicioufly, that Bela Chriftos, marching in fecurity into their country, was furrounded by the Shangalla, whom he thought yet at a diftance. Great part of his troops was flain by the arrows of the enemy, who, from their caves and holes in the mountain, poured their miffile weapons, ftones, and arrows on the troops, at fo fmall a diftance that every one took place, though above the reach of fwords, and lances, or fuch common wea-

3   pons ;

pons; others were overpowered by large bodies of men fallying from the thickets, and fighting them firmly foot to foot. Many officers were that day flain, among the reft Alzaguè and Petros, two perfons of great diftinction in the palace. But the king, however afflicted for the lofs of his men, well knew that this defeat would have no other confequences; fo returned to his capital, with refolution to make another vigorous effort againft Lafta.

THE manner in which this expedition was prevented cannot but give us a high idea of Facilidas: Laeca, at the head of an army of veteran troops, whofe affection he never had occafion to doubt, thought it fafer to truft to the generofity of a king, who had flain his father in battle, than to the acquiring a crown that was not his, by perfevering any longer in rebellion. Accordingly he furrendered himfelf, without condition, to Facilidas, who immediately committed him to prifon, which feeming feverity, however, meant nothing further, than to fhew him the lenity which followed was entirely his own, and not fuggefted to him by the officioufnefs of courtiers; for no fooner was he arrived at Gondar, than he fent for Laeca from prifon, received him not only kindly, but with great marks of diftinction; and, inftead of banifhing him to Wechné, as he did his own brother Claudius, and which, as being of the blood-royal, fhould have been his deftination likewife, the king entered into a kind of treaty with Laeca, by which he gave him large poffeffions in Begemder near Lafta, and married him to his daughter Theoclea, by whom, however, he had no children, but lived long in conftant friendfhip and confidence with Facilidas.

EXCEPT

Except the events which I have already recorded, there is nothing farther in this long reign worthy of being infifted upon; the early inroads of the Galla, in plundering parties, and the feditions and revolts of the Agows from the oppreffion and extortion of their governors, were fuch as we find in every reign; and in all thefe Facilidas was victorious, whilft the Hancafha and Zeegam were greatly weakened in thefe campaigns.

Facilidas was taken ill at Gondar, in the end of October, of a difeafe which, from its firft appearance, he thought would prove mortal. He, therefore, fent to his eldeft fon Hannes, whom he had conftantly kept with him, and who was now of age to govern, and recommended to him his kingdom, and the perfevering in the ancient religion. He died the 30th of September 1665, in great peace and compofure of mind, and they buried him at Azazo.

If we are obliged to give his father the preference, from the greater variety of trials which he underwent, we muft in juftice allow, that, after his father, Facilidas was the greateft king that ever fat upon the Abyffinian throne. He had every good quality neceffary to conftitute a great prince, without any alloy or mixture, that, upon fo much provocation as he had, might have mifled him to be a bad one. He was calm, difpaffionate, and courteous in his behaviour. In the very difficult part he had to act between his father and the nation, the neceffities of the times had taught him a degree of referve, which, if it was not natural, was not therefore the lefs ufeful to him. He was in his own perfon the braveft foldier of his time, and always expofed himfelf in proportion as the occafion was important.

To

To this were added all the qualities of a good general, in which character he feems to have equalled his father Socinios, who elfe was univerfally allowed to be the firft of his time. Fierce and violent in battle, he was backward in fhedding blood after it. Though an enemy to the Catholic religion, yet, from duty to his father, he lived with the patriarch and Jefuits upon fo familiar a footing, that they confefs themfelves it was not from any part of his behaviour to them they ever could judge him an enemy. He was moft remarkable for an implicit fubmiffion to his father's commands ; and, upon this principle, fought in favour of the Catholic religion againft his own friends and perfuafion, becaufe fuch were the orders of his fovereign. He was of a very mild and pleafant temper, as appeared by his behaviour to Melca Chriftos, to his brother Claudius, to his uncle Sela Chriftos, and to the patriarch and Jefuits.

It is true, that, of thefe laft, Sela Chriftos, and many of the Jefuits, were put to death in his reign ; but this was not till they had experienced repeated acts of mercy and forgivennefs ; ftill, perfifting in conftant rebellion againft government, they were juftly cut off as traitors and rebels by the civil power, in the very act of their confpiracy againft the life of the king and conftitution of the country.

There is publifhed by Tellez a letter of Alphonfo Mendes, written, as is falfely faid, from Mafuah, where it is dated, but truly from Goa. If, as the patriarch pretends, he wrote it from Mafuah, it is another proof of this prince's clemency, that he ever fuffered the author of fuch an indecent libel to return to India in peace. It is well known, that, on the firft requifition of Facilidas, the Turks would

3 G 2   have

have delivered the patriarch into his hands; and, every one that reads it muft allow, fuch language from a low-born prieft to a king, deferved every exemplary punifhment offended royalty could inflict: It would not have been mild, had fuch liberty been taken by a ftranger in his native country, Portugal.

THE patriarch accufes Facilidas with the crime committed by Abfalom, which is, I fuppofe, debauching his father's wives and concubines. But, unluckily for the truth of this ftory, we have the Jefuit's own teftimony, that Socinios had put away his wives and concubines before he embraced the Catholic religion, fo at his father's death this was impoffible, unlefs he could commit inceft with his own mother, who was at that time a woman near fixty. But we fhall fuppofe that they exifted, were never married, and, at the time of their being put away, they were 18 years of age at an average. The king put them away in the year 1621; and, therefore, in the year 1634, they would be 30 years of age; and any body that has feen the effects that number of years has upon Abyffinian beauty, muft confefs they could be no great temptation to a prince.

THE next calumny mentioned in this libel is, the murder of his brother Claudius, nay, of all his brothers. Now we have feen, in the hiftory of his reign, that Claudius had fairly forfeited his life by a meditated fratricide, and by an overt act of rebellion in which he was taken prifoner. Yet fo mild and placable was Facilidas, that he refufed to put him to death, but fent him prifoner to the mountain of Wechnè, and mercifully revived the ancient ufage of banifhing the princes of the blood-royal to the mountain, inftead of executing
them,

them, which had been the practice to his time, and had occasioned the death of above sixty of these unfortunate princes within the last hundred years.

To mount Wechné he also sent his own son David, and with him all his brothers; and, so far from being murdered, we shall find them mostly alive attending an extraordinary festival made for their sakes by Facilidas's grandson; an accident so rare, that it seems Providence had permitted it in favour and vindication of truth and innocence, and to stamp the lie upon the patriarch's scandalous aspersions.

The third falsehood is, that Facilidas turned Mahometan, and got doctors from Mocha to instruct him in the Koran. We have already seen what gave rise to this, if it indeed had any foundation at all; but it is a well-known fact, that, though he governed the church, during a whole reign, mildly and judiciously, without any mark of bigotry, never were two princes better affected to the Alexandrian church than Facilidas and his son; and never were two that had better reason, having both seen the disorders that other religions had occasioned.

We see throughout all this piece of the patriarchs, a self-sufficient mind, gratifying itself by disgorging its passion and malice. If Alphonso Mendes had no regard, as it seems indeed he had not; if he had no reverence to higher powers, such as scripture had taught him to have; if he was too enlightened, or too infatuated, to take our Saviour's precepts for his rule, and, shaking the dust of Abyssinia from his feet, remit them to a Judge who will, at his own time, separate good from evil, still he should have had, at least, a brotherly

love

love and charity for thofe unfortunate people who were to fall into Facilidas's hands; and we cannot reafonably fuppofe but that the conftant butcheries committed by the Turks afterwards upon the Catholic priefts, wild enough to enter at Mafuah and Suakem, were the fruits of the calumnious, intemperate libel of the patriarch.

AFTER the death of the laft miffionary, Bernard Nogeyra, no intelligence arrived of what was doing in Abyffinia, excepting from the Dutch fettlements of Batavia, where Abyffinian factors, or merchants, had arrived; and where the induftrious Mr Ludolf, very much engaged in the hiftory of this country, and who fpared no pains, maintained a correfpondence, and thence he was informed that Facilidas had died after a long and profperous reign, and had left his kingdom in peace to his fon.

THIS intelligence alarmed the zeal of two great champions of the Jefuits; the one M. le Grande, late fecretary to the French embaffy to Portugal; and the other M. Piques, a member of the Sorbonne, a very confufed, dull difputant upon the difference of religion.

THESE two worthies, without any proof or intelligence but their own warm and weak imaginations, fell violently upon poor Ludolf, accufing him of falfehood, partiality, and prevarication; and, right or wrong, they would have Facilidas plunged up to the neck in troubles, wading through labyrinths of misfortunes, confpiracies, and defeats, certainly dead, or about to die fome terrible death by the vengeance of heaven; and this ridiculous report is unjuftly fpread abroad by all the zealots of thofe times. *Fata obftant;*—truth

4   will

will out. The annals of the country, written without a regard to either party, ſtate, that, in the long reign of Facilidas, notwithſtanding the calamitous ſtate in which his
father left him the empire, very few misfortunes only
are reported to have happened either to himſelf or lieute-
nants.

HANNES I. or ŒLAFE SEGUED,

From 1665 to 1680.

Bigotry of the King—Diſguſts his Son Yaſous, who flies from Gondar.

IF this prince ſucceeded to his kingdom in peace, he had
the addreſs ſtill to keep it ſo. He was not in his nature
averſe to war, though, beſides two feeble attempts he made
upon Laſta, and one againſt the Shangalla, all without material conſequences, no military expedition was undertaken
in his time; and no rebellion or competitor (ſo frequent in
other reigns) at all diſturbed his.

HANNES ſeems to have had the ſeeds of bigotry in his
temper; from the beginning of his reign he commanded
the

the Mahometans to eat no other flefh but what had been killed by Chriftians; and gathered together the Catholic books, which the Jefuits had tranflated into the Ethiopic language, and burned them in a heap. Much of his attention was given to church matters, and, in regulating thefe, he feems to have employed moft of his time. He depofed the Abuna Chriftadulus, appointed by his father, and in his place put the Abuna Sanuda.

THIS laft meafure feems to have difpleafed his eldeft fon Yafous, who fled from the palace one night, and paffed t e Nile; and, though he was followed by Kafmati Aferaьa Chriftos, he was not overtaken, but ftaid fome time in his fifter's houfe, and then returned to Gondar at the requeft of his father.

A CONVOCATION of the clergy, the fecond in this reign, was now held, and great heats and divifions followed among two orders of monks, thofe of Euftathius and thofe of Debra Libanos. The king feems to have affifted at all thefe debates, and to have contented himfelf with holding the balance in his hands without declaring for either party. But thefe altercations and difputes could not fatisfy the active fpirit of the prince his fon, who again fled from his father and from Gondar, but was overtaken at the river Bafhilo, and brought back to the palace, where he found his father ill.

HANNES died the 19th of July, and was buried at Tedda, after having reigned 15 years. He feems, from the fcanty memorials of his long reign, to have been a weak prince;

2   but,

but, perhaps, if the circumſtances of the times were known, he may have been a wiſe one.

YASOUS I.

From 1680 to 1704.

Brilliant Expedition of the King to Wechnè—Various Campaigns againſt the Agows and Galla—Comet appears—Expedition againſt Zeegam and the Eaſtern Shangalla—Poncet's Journey—Murat's Embaſſy— Du Roule's Embaſſy—Du Roule aſſaſſinated at Sennaar—The King is aſſaſſinated.

YASOUS ſucceeded his father Hannes with the approbation of the whole kingdom. He had, as we have ſeen, twice in Hannes's life-time abſconded from the palace; and this was interpreted as implying an impatience to reign. But I rather think the cauſe was a difference of manners, his father being extremely bigotted, ſordid, and covetous; for he never, in thoſe elopements, pretended to make a party contrary to his father's intereſt, nor ſhewed the leaſt inclination to give either the army or the people a favourable impreſſion of himſelf, to the diſadvantage of the king. There was, beſides, a difference in religious principles. Yaſous had a great predilection for the monks of Debra Libanos,

banos, or the high church; while Hannes, his father, had done every thing in his power to inftil into his fon a pre-poffeffion in favour of thofe of Abba Euftathius.

To thefe opinions, therefore, fo widely different, as well in religion as the things of the world, I attribute the young prince's difinclination to live with his father. This feems confirmed by the firft ftep he took upon his mounting the throne, which was to make an alteration in the church government from what his father had left it at his death.

It was on the 7th of July 1680 he was proclaimed king; the next day he depofed the Acab Saat Conftantius, and gave his place to Afera Chriftos. He then called a council of the clergy on the 27th of September, when he depofed Itchegué Tzaga Chriftos, and in his room named Cyriacus.

It was now the time that, according to cuftom, he was to make his profeffion in regard to the difference I have formerly mentioned that fubfifted between the two parties about the incarnation of Chrift. But this he refufed to do in the prefent ftate of the church, as there was then no certain Abuna in Abyffinia. For Hannes, before he died, had written to the patriarch of Alexandria to depofe both Abuna Chriftodulus and Marcus, who, in cafe of death, was to have fucceeded him, and this under pretence that he had varied in his faith between the two contending parties.

HANNES, therefore, defired the patriarch to appoint Abuna
Sanuda, a man known to be devoted to the monks of St
Euftathius and their tenets; whereas the other two priefts
were fuppofed to be inclined to the monks of Debra Libanos. Yafous told his clergy that he would not fuffer Sanuda to be elected; and the affembly, with little oppofition, con-
formed to the fentiments of the king, who fent immediately thereupon to Cairo, demanding peremptorily that Marcus might be appointed Abuna, and declaring his refolution to admit no other. He then ordered the church of Tecla Haimanout to be confecrated with great folemnity; he
repaired and adorned it with much magnificence, and endowed it with lands, which increafed its revenue very confiderably.

THESE two circumftances (efpecially the laft) fhewed diftinctly to the whole kingdom his affection for the high
church, as explicitly as any proclamation could have done.
And in this he continued fteady during his whole life, notwithftanding the many provocations he met with from that
reftlefs body of men.

HAVING thus fettled the affairs of the church, he proceeded to thofe of the ftate, and appointed Anaftafius (then
governor of Amhara) to be Ras, or lieutenant-general, in his
whole kingdom, allowing him alfo to keep his province of
Amhara. In this he fhewed a wifdom and penetration that
gained him the good opinion of every one; for Anaftafius
was a man advanced in years, of great capacity and experience, and of a moft unblemifhed character among his
neighbours, who, in all their own affairs, had recourfe to,
and were determined by, his counfels.

3 H 2 THE

THE king then took a journey of a very extraordinary nature, and such as Abyssinia had never before seen. Attended only by his nobility, of whom a great number had flocked to him, he sat down at the foot of the mountain of Wechné, and ordered all the princes of the royal family who were banished, and confined there, to be brought to him.

DURING the last reign, the mountain of Wechné, and those forlorn princes that lived upon it, had been, as it were, totally forgotten. Hannes having sons of an age fit to govern, and his eldest son Yasous living below with his father, no room seemed to remain for attempting a revolution, by the young candidates escaping from the mountain. This oblivion to which they were consigned, melancholy as it was, proved the best state these unhappy prisoners could have wished ; for to be much known for either good or bad qualities, did always at some period become fatal to the individuals. Punishment always followed inquiries after a particular prince ; and all messages, questions, or visits, at the instance of the king, were constantly forerunners of the loss of life, or amputation of limbs, to these unhappy exiles. To be forgotten, then, was to be safe ; but this safety carried very heavy distress along with it. Their revenues were embezzled by their officers or keepers, and ill paid by the king; and the sordid temper of Hannes had often reduced them all to the danger of perishing with hunger and cold.

YASOUS, as he was well acquainted with all these circumstances, so he was, in his nature and disposition, as perfectly willing to repair the injuries that were past, and prevent
                                                                    the

the like in future. Nothing tended fo much to conciliate the minds of the people to their fovereign as this behaviour of Yafous.

In the midft of his relations there now appeared (as rifen from the dead) Claudius, fon of Socinios, the firft exile who was fent to the mountain of Wechnè by his brother Facilidas, grandfather of Yafous. This was the prince who, as we have already ftated, was fixed upon by the Jefuits to fucceed his father, and govern that country when converted to the Romifh religion by their intrigues, and conquered by the arms of the Portuguefe: This was the prince who, to make their enemies appear more odious, thefe Jefuits have afferted was flain by his brother Facilidas, one inftance by which we may judge of the juftice of the other charges laid againft that humane, wife, and virtuous prince, whofe only crime was an inviolable attachment to the religion and conftitution of his country, and the juft abhorrence he moft reafonably had, as an independent prince, to fubmit the prerogatives of his crown, and the rights of his people to the blind controul of a foreign prelate.

There came from the mountain alfo the fons of Facilidas, with their families; and likewife his own brothers, Ayto Theophilus, and Ayto Claudius, fons of his father Hatzè Hannes. The fight of fo many noble relations, fome advanced in years, fome in the flower of their youth, and fome yet children; all, however, in tatters, and almoft naked, made fuch an impreffion on the young king that he burft into tears. Nor was his behaviour to the refpective degrees of them lefs proper or engaging. To the old he paid that reverence and refpect due to parents; to thofe about his

2   own

own age, a kind and liberal familiarity; while he beſtowed upon the young ones careſſes and commendations, ſweetened with the hopes that they might ſee better times.

His firſt care was to provide them all plentifully with apparel and every neceſſary. His brothers he dreſſed like himſelf, and his uncles ſtill more richly. He then divided a large ſum of money among them all.

In the month of December, which is the pleaſanteſt ſeaſon of the whole year, the ſun being moderately hot, the ſky conſtantly clear and without a cloud, all the court was encamped under the mountain, and the inferior ſort ſtrewed along the graſs. All were treated at the expence of the king, paſſing the day and night in continual feſtivals. It is but right, ſaid the king, that I ſhould pay for a pleaſure ſo great that none of my predeceſſors ever dared to taſte it; and of all that noble aſſembly none ſeemed to enjoy it more ſincerely than the king. All pardons ſolicited for criminals at this time were granted. In this manner having ſpent a whole month, before his departure the king called for the deftar, (*i. e.* the treaſury book) in which the account of the ſum allowed for the maintenance of theſe priſoners is ſtated; and having inquired ſtrictly into the expenditure, and cancelled all grants that had been made of any part of that ſum to others, and provided in future for the full, as well as yearly payment of it, he, for his laſt act, gave to the governor of the mountain a large acceſſion of territory, to make him ample amends for the loſs of the dues he was underſtood to be intitled to from that revenue. After this, he embraced them all, aſſuring them of his conſtant protection; and, mounting his horſe, he took the keep-

er

er along with him, leaving all the royal family at their liberty at the foot of the mountain.

THIS laſt mark of confidence, more than all the reſt,
touched the minds of that noble troop, who hurried every
man with his utmoſt ſpeed to reſtore themſelves voluntarily to their melancholy priſon, imputing every moment of delay as a ſtep towards treaſon and ingratitude to
their munificent, compaſſionate, and magnanimous benefactor. All their way was moiſtened with tears flowing
from ſenſible and thankful hearts; and all the mountain
reſounded with prayers for the long life and proſperity of
the king, and that the crown might never leave the lineal
deſcendents of his family. It was very remarkable, that,
during this long reign, though he was conſtantly involved
in war, no competitor from the mountain ever appeared in
breach of thoſe vows they had ſo voluntarily undertaken.

THERE was another great advantage the king reaped by
this generous conduct. All the moſt powerful and conſiderable people in the kingdom had an opportunity, at one
view, to ſee each individual of the royal family that was
capable of wearing the crown, and all with one voice agreed,
upon the compariſon made, that, if they had been then aſſembled to elect a king, the choice would not have fallen
upon any but the preſent.

THOUGH the country of the Agows of Damot is generally
plain and laid out in paſture, each tribe has ſome mountain
to which, upon the alarm of an enemy, they retire with
their flocks. The Galla, being their neighbours on the
other ſide of the Nile to the ſouth, and the Shangalla in the

4.   low

low country immediately to the weſt, theſe natural fortreſſes are frequently of the greateſt uſe during the incurſions of both.

THEY alone, of all the nations of Abyſſinia, have found
it their intereſt ſo far to cultivate their neighbours the Shangalla, that there are places ſet apart in which both nations
can trade with each other in ſafety; where the Agows ſell
copper, iron, beads, ſkins, or hides, and receive an immenſe
profit in gold; for, below theſe to the ſouth and weſt, is the
gold country neareſt Abyſſinia, none of that metal being
anywhere found in Abyſſinia itſelf.

YASOUS, from this country of the Agows, deſcended into
that of the Shangalla; where, conforming to the ancient
cuſtom of Abyſſinia, he hunted the elephant and rhinoceros,
the ordinary firſt expedition in the kings his predeceſſors
reigns, but the ſecond in his; the firſt having been (as before ſtated) ſpent in charity and mercy, much more nobly,
at the foot of the mountain of Wechné.

YASOUS is reported to have been the moſt graceful and
dexterous horſeman of his time. He diſtinguiſhed himſelf
in this hunting as much for his addreſs and courage againſt
the beaſts, as he had, for a ſhort while before, done by his
affability, generoſity, and benevolence, amidſt his own
family. All was praiſe, all was enthuſiaſm, wherever the
young king preſented himſelf; the ill-boding monks and
hermits had not yet dared to foretel evil, but every common mouth predicted this was to be an active, vigorous,
and glorious reign, without being thought by this to have
laid any pretenſion to the gift of prophecy.

IT

It was now the fecond year of his reign when the king took the field with a fmall, but very well chofen army. The Edjow and Woolo, two of the moft powerful tribes of fouthern Galla, taking advantage of the abfence of Ras Anaftafius, had entered Amhara by a pafs, on the fide of which is fituated Melec Shimfa, one of the principal towns of the province.

The king, leaving old Anaftafius to the government of Gondar, took upon himfelf the relief of Amhara; and, being oined by all the troops in his way, he arrived at Melec Shimfa before the Galla had any intelligence of him. The Galla always chofe for their refidence a very level country, becaufe they are now become all horfemen. The country of Amhara, on the contrary, is full of high mountains, and only acceffible by certain narrow paffes. The king, therefore, inftead of marching directly to the enemy, paffed above them, and left them ftill advancing, burning the villages and churches in the country below. He then took poffeffion of the pafs (through which he knew they muft retreat) with a ftrong body of troops ; and filled the entrance of the defile, which was very rugged ground, with fufileers, and his beft foot armed with lances : after this, he feparated his horfe into two divifions, and, referving one half to himfelf, gave the other to Kafmati Demetrius. He then placed the troops conducted by himfelf in a wood, about half a mile from the entrance of the pafs, and ordered Demetrius to fall upon the Galla brifkly on the plain, but to retreat as if terrified by their numbers, and to make the beft of his way then to the pafs in the mountains.

DEMETRIUS, finding the enemy's parties fcattered wide wafting the country, fell upon them, and flew many, till he had
arrived near the middle of their body, when the Galla, ufed
to fuch expeditions, poured in from all fides, and prefently
united. Demetrius, furrounded on every fide, was flain,
fighting to the laft in the moft defperate manner, and his
party, much diminifhed in number, fled in a manner that
could not be miftaken for ftratagem. They were clofely
purfued, and followed into the pafs by the Galla, who
thought they had thus entirely cut them off from Amhara.
But they were foon received by a clofe fire from the foot a-
mong the bufhes, and by the lances that mingled with
them from every fide of the mountain.

THE king, upon the firft noife of the mufquetry, advanced quickly with his horfe, and met the Galla, in the height
of their confufion, flying back again into the plain. Here
they fell an eafy facrifice to the frefh troops led by Yafous,
and to the peafants, exafperated by the havoc they before
had made in the country. Of the enemy, about 6000 men
fell this day on the field; a few were brought to Gondar,
and, in contempt, fold for flaves. Few on the king's fide
were flain, excepting thofe that fell with Demetrius, the account of whofe death the king heard without any figns of
regret:—"I told the man (fays the king) that he fhould fhew
" himfelf and retire; if I wanted a victory I would have led
" the army in perfon; I march againft the Galla, not as a
" king, but as an executioner, becaufe my aim is to extir-
" pate them."

ALTHOUGH Yafous was ftedfaft in his own opinion as to
his religion, or, as it may be more properly called, the dif-

2   putes

putes and quibbles with the monks concerning it, yet he
fuffered each fect to enjoy its own, and, probably, in his
heart he perfectly defpifed botl .

THE monks, however, were far from poffeffing any fuch
fpirit of toleration. They confidered the depofing of Acab
Saat, Conftantius, and the Itchegué Tzaga Chriftos, as a declaration of diflike the king entertained towards their party.
They bore with great impatience and indignation, that A-
buna Sanuda, who was once their zealous partizan in the
time of Hannes, fhould now fuddenly change his fentiments,
and declare implicitly for thofe of the king, and thereby increafe both the number and the confequence of their adverfaries. They declared that they would fuffer every thing
rather than live under a king who fhewed himfelf fo openly a favourer of Debra Libanos, though it was now but their
turn, having in the laft reign had a king more partial, and
more attached to St Euftathius, than ever Yafous was to any
fet of monks whatever.

THE ringleaders in all thefe feditious declarations were
Abba Tebedin, fuperior of the monaftery of Gondga, and
Kafmati Wali of Damot, by origin a Galla. Thefe two turbulent men, having firft drawn over to their party the Agows
and province of Damot, paffed over the Nile to Goodero and
Baffo, whom they joined, and then proclaimed king one
Ifaac, grandfon of Socinios a prince, who was never fent to
the mountain, but whofe predeceffors, being at liberty when
Facilidas firft banifhed his brothers and children to Wechné,
had fled to the Galla, and there remained in obfcurity, waiting the juncture which now happened to declare his royal
defcent, and offer himfelf for king.

THE

THE Galla, who fought but a pretence for invading Abyffinia, readily embraced this opportunity, and fwarmed to him on all fides. His army, in a very fhort time, was exceedingly numerous, and the Agows and all Damot were ready to join him when he fhould repafs the Nile. This revolt was indeed likely to have proved general, but for the activity and diligence of the king, who, on the firft intelligence, put himfelf fo fuddenly in motion that he was on the banks of the Nile before the Galla on the one fide were ready for their junction with the confederates on the other.

THE king's prefence impofed upon the Agows and the rebels of Damot, fo that they let him pafs quietly over the Nile into the country of the Galla, hoping that, as their defigns were not difcovered, he might again return through their country in peace if victorious over the Galla; but, if he was beaten, they then were ready to intercept him.

But the Galla, who expected that they would have had to fight with an army already fatigued and half-ruined by an action with the Agows on the other fide of the river, no fooner faw it pafs the Nile unmolefted in full force, than they began to think how far it was from their intereft to make their country a feat of war, when fo little profit was to be expected. On the approach, therefore, of the king's army, many of them deferted to it, and made their peace with him. The few that remained faithful to Ifaac were difperfed after very little refiftance; and he himfelf being taken prifoner, and brought before the king, was given up to the foldiers, who put him to death in his prefence. On

4.   the

the king's fide, no perfon of confideration was flain but Kafmati Maziré, and very few on the part of the enemy.

THIS year 1685, the 5th of Yafous's reign, there was no military expedition. He had pardoned Abba Tebedin, and Kafmati Wali, and the monks again defired an affembly of the clergy, which was granted. But the king feeing, at its firft meeting, that it was to produce nothing but wrangling and invectives; with great calmnefs and refolution told the affembly, "That their difputes were of a nature fo confufed and unedifying, that he queftioned much their being really founded in fcripture; and the rather fo, becaufe the patriarch of Alexandria feemed neither to know, nor concern himfelf about them, nor was the A- buna, at his firft coming, ever inftructed on any one of thefe points. If they were, however, founded in fcripture, one of them was confeffedly in the wrong ; and, if fo, he doubted it might be the cafe with both; that he had, therefore, come to a refolution to name feveral of the beft-qualified perfons of both parties, who, in the prefence of the Itche- gué and Abuna, might infpect the books, and from them fettle fome premifes that might be hereafter accepted and admitted as *deta* by both."

THIS being affented to, the very next year he ordered two of the priefts of Debra Libanos then at Gondar, together with Abba Tebedin, Cofmas of Aruana, the Abuna Sanuda, and the Itcheguè, forthwith to repair to Debra Mariam, an ifland in the lake Tzana, where, fequeftered from the world, they might difcufs their feveral opinions, and fettle fome points admiffible by both fides. After which, with out giving any opportunity for reply, he diffolved the affembly, and took the field with his army.

THE

THE king, though perfectly informed of the part that the whole province of Damot had taken in the rebellion of Ifaac, as alfo great part of the Agows, but moft of all that tribe called Zeegam, yet had fo well diffembled, that moft of them believed he was ignorant of their fault, and all of them, that he had no thoughts of punifhing them, for he had returned through Damot, after the defeat of Ifaac, without fhewing any mark of anger, or fuffering his troops to commit the fmalleft hoftility. He now paffed in the fame peaceable manner through the country of Zeegam, intending to attack the Shangalla of Geefa and Wumbarea.

THESE two tribes are little known. Like the other Shangalla they are Pagans, but worfhip the Nile and a certain tree, and have a language peculiar to themfelves. They are woolly-headed, and of the deepeft black ; very tall and ftrong, ftraighter and better-made about the legs and joints than the other blacks ; their foreheads narrow, their cheekbones high, their nofes flat, with wide mouths, and very fmall eyes. With all this they have an air of chearfulnefs and gaiety which renders them more agreeable than other blacks. Their women are very amorous, and fell at a much greater price than other blacks of the fex.

THIS country is bounded on the fouth by Metchakel; on the weft by the Nile; the eaft by Serako, part of Guefgué and Kuara; and, on the north, by Belay, Guba, and the Hamidge * of Sennaar. They make very frequent inroads, and

* A name of the black Pagans bordering on Sennaar to the fouth-weft.

and furprife the Agows, whofe children they fell at Guba to the Mahometans, who traffic there for gold and flaves, and get iron and coarfe cotton-cloths in return. Their country is full of woods, and their manner of life the fame as has been already defcribed in fpeaking of the other tribes.

THE Geefa live clofe upon the Nile, to which river they give their own name. It is alfo called Geefa by the Agows, in the fmall diftrict of Geefh, where it rifes from its fource. They never have yet made peace with Abyffinia, are governed by the heads of families, and live feparately for the fake of hunting, and, for this reafon, are eafily conquered. The men are naked, having a cotton rag only about their middle. The nights are very cold, and they lie round great fires; but the fly is not fo dangerous here as to the eaftward, fo that goats, in a fmall number, live here. Their arms are bows, lances, and arrows; large wooden clubs, with knobs, nearly as big as a man's head, at the end of them; their fhields are oval. They worfhip the Nile, but no other river, as I have faid before; it is called Geefa, which, in their language, fignifies the firft Maker, or Creator. They imagine its water is a cure for moft difeafes.

EAST of the Geefa is Wumbarea, which reaches to Belay. The king fell firft on the Geefa, part of whom he took, and the reft he difperfed. He then turned to the right through Wumbarea, and met with fome refiftance in the narrow paffes in the mountains, in one of which Kafmati Kofté, (one of his principal officers) a man of low birth, but raifed by his merit to his prefent rank, was flain by an arrow.

THE

THE king then repaſſed the Agows of Zeegam, in the ſame peaceable manner in which he came, and then marched on without giving any cauſe of ſuſpicion, taking up his quarters at Ibaba. It was here he had appointed an aſſembly of the clergy to meet, before whom the ſeveral delegates, choſen to conſider the controverted points, and find ſome ground for a reconciliation, were to make their report. The Abuna, Itchegué, and all thoſe who, for this purpoſe, were ſhut up in Debra Mariam, appeared before the king. But, however amicably things had been carried on while they were ſhut up in the iſland, the uſual warmth and violence prevailed before the aſſembly. Ayto Chriſtos, Abba Welled Chriſtos of Debra Libanos, on one ſide, and Tebedin and Coſmas on the other, fell roundly, and without preface, upon a diſpute about the incarnation, ſo that the affair from argument was likely to turn to ſedition.

THE turbulent Tebedin, leaving the matter of religion wholly apart, inveighed vehemently againſt the retirement to Debra Mariam, which he loudly complained of as baniſhment. Ras Anaſtaſius and Abuna Sanuda reproved him ſharply for the freedom with which he taxed this meaſure of the king, and in this they were followed by many of the wiſer ſort on both ſides. Immediately after the aſſembly, the king ordered Tebedin to be put in irons, and ſent to a mountainous priſon. He then returned to Gondar.

THIS year, the 9th of Yaſous reign, there appeared a comet, remarkable for its ſize and fiery brightneſs of its body, and for the prodigious length and diſtinctneſs of its tail. It

was

was firſt taken notice of at Gondar, two days before the feaſt of St Michael, on which day the army takes the field. A fight ſo uncommon alarmed all ſorts of people; and the prophets, who had kept themſelves within very moderate bounds during this whole reign, now thought that it was incumbent upon them to diſtinguiſh themſelves, and be ſilent no longer. Accordingly they foretold, from this phænomenon, and publiſhed everywhere as a truth infallibly and immutably pre-ordained, that the preſent campaign was to exhibit a ſcene of carnage and bloodſhed, more terrible and more extenſive than any thing that ever had appeared in the annals of Ethiopia. That theſe torrents of blood, which were everywhere to follow the footſteps of the king, were to be ſtopped by his death, which was to happen before he ever returned again to Gondar; and, as the object of the king's expedition was ſtill a ſecret, theſe alarming preſages gained a great deal of credit.

But it was not ſo with Yaſous, who, notwithſtanding he was importuned, by learned men of all ſorts, to put off his departure for ſome days, abſolutely refuſed, anſwering always ſuch requeſts by irony and deriſion: "Pho! Pho! "ſays he, you are not in the right; we muſt give the co "met fair play; uſe him well, or he will never appear again, "and then idle people and old women will have nothing "to amuſe themſelves with."

He accordingly left Gondar at the time he had appointed; and he was already arrived at Amdaber, a few days diſtance from the capital, when an expreſs brought him word of his mother's death, on which he immediately marched back to Gondar, and buried her in the iſland of Mitraha with all poffible magnificence, and with every mark of fincere grief.

Though the prophets had not juft fucceeded in what they foretold, they kept neverthelefs a good countenance. It is true that no blood was fhed, nor did the king die before he returned to Gondar; but his mother died when he was away, and that was much the fame thing, for they contended that it was not a great miftake, from the bare authority of a comet, to err only in the fex of the perfon that was to die; a queen for a king was very near calculation. As for the bloody ftory, and the king's death, they faid they had miftaken the year in computing, but that it ftill was to happen (when it pleafed God) *fome other time.*

Every body agreed that thefe explanations were the beft poffible, excepting the king, who perceived a degree of malice in the foretelling his death and certain lofs of his army juft at the inftant he was taking the field. But he difguifed his refentment under ftrong irony, with which he attacked thefe diviners inceffantly. He had inquired accurately the day of his mother's death : " How is it, fays he to his chaplain, (or kees hatzé) that this comet fhould come to *foretel* my mother's death, when fhe was dead four days before it appeared ?" Another day, to the fame perfon he faid, " I fear you do my mother too much honour at the expence of religion. Is it decent to fuppofe that fuch a ftar, the moft remarkable appearance at the birth of Chrift, fhould now be employed on no greater errand than to foretel the death of the daughter of Guebra Mafcal ?" Thefe, and many more fuch railleries, accounted by thefe vifion-

aries,

aries, as little fhort of impiety, fo mortified Koftè (the kees hatzé,) a great believer in, and protector of the dreamers, that he refigned all his employments, and retired among the hermits into the defert of Werk-leva towards Sennaar, to ftudy the afpects of the ftars more accurately, and more at leifure.

THOUGH we neither pay this comet the fuperftitious re- verence the idle fanatics of Abyffinia fhewed it, nor yet treat it with that contempt which this great king's good fenfe prompted him to do, we fhall make fome ufe of it, ac- knowledging our gratitude to the hiftorian who has re- corded it. We fhall hereby endeavour to eftablifh our chronology in oppofition to that of the catholic writers, re- lating to the date of fome tranfactions with which they were not cotemporaries, and only relate from hearfay, as happening before the arrival of the miffionaries in this country.

YASOUS the Great, of whom we are now writing, came to the throne upon the death of his father Hannes in 1680 ; the 9th year of this reign then was 1689.

HEDAR is the 3d month of the Abyffinians, and anfwers to part of our November; and the 12th of that month, Hedar, is the feaft of St Michael the archangel, or 8th day of our month November, N. S.

GONDAR is in lat. 12° 34′ 30″ N. and in long. 37° 33′ 0″ E. from the meridian of Greenwich. By the fiery appearance of the nucleus, or body of the comet, it certainly then was very near the fun, and either was going down upon it to its
3 K 2   perihelion,

perihelion, or had already paffed it, and was receding to its aphelion; but by its increafing tail, already at a great length, we may conjecture it was only then going down to its conjunction, and was then near approaching to the fun.

From this we fhould conclude that this comet muft have been feen, however rapidly it did move, fome time before the 6th of November, or two days before the feaft of St Michael. But this depends on the circumftances of the climate; for though the tropical rains ceafe the firft of September, the cloudy weather continues all the month of October; at the end of thefe fall the latter rains in gentle fhowers, which allay the fevers in Dembea, and make the country wholefome for the march of the army, and thefe rains fall moftly in the night. From this it is probable that the comet, having at firft little light and no tail, as yet at a diftance from the fun, was not very apparent to the naked eye, till by its increafed motion and heat it had acquired both tail and brightnefs, as it approached its perihelion.

Now we find by our European accounts *, that, in the year 1689, there did appear a comet, the orbit of which was calculated by M. Pingrè. And this comet arrived at its perihelion on the 1ft day of December 1689, fo was going down much inflamed, and with a violent motion to the fun, the 6th of November, when it was obferved at Gondar, being but 25 days then from its perihelion.

As thefe circumftances are more than fufficient to conftitute the identity of the comet, a phænomenon too rare to

rifk

---

* Aftronom. de M. de La Lande, liv. 19. p. 366.

rifk being confounded with another, we may hardly conclude the 9th year of Yafous the Firft to be the year 1689 of
Chrift, fuch as our chronology, drawn from the Abyffinian
annals, ftates it to be ; or, at leaft, if there is any error, it muft
be fo fmall as to be of no fort of confequence to any fort
of readers, or influence upon the narrative of any tranfactions.

THE 10th year began with a fudden and violent alarm,
which fpread itfelf in an inftant all over the kingdom
without any certain authority. The Galla with an innumerable army were faid to have entered Gojam, at feveral
places, and laid wafte the whole province, and this was the
more extraordinary, as the Nile was now in the height of
its inundation. On his march, the king learned that this
ftory arofe merely from a panic; and this formidable army
turned out no more than a fmall band of robbers of that
nation, who had paffed the river in their ufual way, part
on horfeback, while the foot were dragged over, hanging at
the horfes tails, or riding on goats fkins blown up with
wind. This fmall party had furprifed fome weak villages,
killed the inhabitants, and immediately returned acrofs the
river. But the alarm continued, and there were people at
Gondar who were ready to fwear they faw the villages and
churches on fire, and a large army of Galla in their march
to Ibaba, at the fame time that there was not one Galla on
the Gojam fide of the river.

THE king, however, either confidering this fmall body of
Galla coming at this unfeafonable time, and the panic that
was fo artificially fpread, as a feint to throw him off his
guard when a real invafion might be intended, or with a

3   view

view to cover his own defigns, fummoned all the men of the province of Gojam to meet him in arms at Ibaba the 7th day of January, being the proper feafon for preparing an expedition into the country of the Galla. He himfelf in the mean time retired to Dek, an ifland in the lake Tzana, there to ftay till his army fhould be collected.

WHILE the king was in the ifland, a number of the malcontents among the monks, who had, in the feveral affemblies, been banifhed for fedition with Tebedin, came to him there, defiring to be heard before an affembly; and they brought with them Arca Denghel, of Debra Samayat, to fupport their petition. The king anfwered, that he was ready to call an affembly, provided the Abuna defired, or would promife to be prefent; but that the Abuna was then at Debra Mariam, where they might go and know his mind.

THE Abuna, who forefaw little good could be expected from fuch meetings, and knew how difagreeable they were to the king, abfolutely refufed to attend. On this they returned again to the king, defiring that, of his own mere prerogative, he would call their affembly without confulting further the Abuna. To this the king anfwered boldly, That he knew it was his right to call his fubjects together, without any other reafon for fo doing but his will; yet, when the avowed caufe of the meeting was to canvafs matters of faith, he had made it a rule to himfelf, that the Abuna fhould always be prefent, or at leaft confent to the meeting. And with this anfwer he ordered them all to depart immediately.

MANY

MANY of the principal people about the king advifed him to put thefe turbulent people in irons, for daring to come into his prefence without leave. But Yafous was contented to remand each to the place of his banifhment from whence he came. He then removed from Dek to Ibaba, on the 10th of January, the journey being no more than two eafy days; but, whether it was that the Galla did not intend another invafion, or whether they were overawed by the king's preparations and prefence, and did not think themfelves fafe even in their own country, none of them this year paffed the Nile, or gave any uneafinefs either to Gojam or Damot.

THOUGH the whole nation believed that the king's attention was entirely engaged in the various expeditions againft the Galla and Shangalla, which he executed with fo much diligence and fuccefs, yet there was ftill a principal object fuperior to all thefe, which remained a fecret in his own breaft, after the parties concerned had abfolutely forgot it. All his campaigns againft the Shangalla were only defigned to lull afleep thofe he confidered as his principal enemies, that he might make the blow he aimed at them more certain and effectual.

SIX years had now paffed fince the Agows, and particularly the moft powerful tribe of them, the Zeegam, had, with thofe of Damot and the Galla, confpired to put the crown upon the head of the rebel prince Ifaac, who had loft his life in the engagement which followed on the other fide of the Nile. It will be remembered alfo, that the country of the Agows is in general open, full of rich plains, abundantly watered by variety of fine ftreams; in other parts, gentle

r   rifings

rifings and defcents, but without mountains, faving that, almoft in every tribe, Nature had placed one rugged mountain to which thefe people retired upon the approach of their neighbouring enemies the Galla and Shangalla. This defcription does, in a more extenfive manner, belong to the country of the Zeegam, the moft powerful, rich, and trading tribe of the whole nation.

Not one fingle mountain, but a confiderable ridge, divides the country nearly in the middle, the bottom of which, and nearly one-third up, is covered with brufh-wood, full of ftiff bamboos and canes, bearing prickly fruit, with aloes, acacia very thorny, and of feveral dwarf fhrubby kinds, interfperfed with the kantuffa *, a beautiful thorn, which alone is confidered, where it grows thick and in abundance, as a fufficient impediment for the march of a royal army. Through thefe are paths known only to the inhabitants themfelves, which lead you to the middle of the mountain, where are large caves, probably begun by Nature, and afterwards enlarged by the induftry of man. The mouths of thefe are covered with bufhes, canes, and wild oats, that grow fo as to conceal both man and horfe, while the tops of thefe mountains are flat and well-watered, and there they fow their grain out of the reach of the enemy. Upon the firft alarm they drive the cattle to the top, lodge their wives and children in the caves, and, when the enemy approaches near, they hide the cattle in the caves likewife, fome of which cavities are fo large as to hold 500 oxen, and all the people to which they belong. The men then go down to the

---

* See the article *kantuffa* in the Appendix.

the loweft part of the mountain, from whofe thickets they fally, upon every opportunity that prefents itfelf, to attack the enemy whom they find marauding in the plains.

The king had often affembled his army at Ibaba, only four days march from Zeegam. He had done more; he had paffed below the country, and returned by the other fide of it, in his attack upon Geefa and Wumbarea; but he had never committed any act of hoftility, nor fhewn himfelf difcontented with them. To deceive them ftill farther, he ordered now his army to meet him at Efté in Begemder; and fent to Kafmati Claudius, governor of Tigrè, to join him with all his forces as foon as he fhould hear he was arrived at Lama, a large plain before we defcend the fteep mountain of Lamalmon, which ftands not far from the banks of the river Tacazzé. He privately gave orders alfo to Kafmati Claudius, Kafmati Dimmo Chriftos of Tigrè, and to Adera and Quaquera Za Menfus Kedus, to inform themfelves where the water lay below, and whether there was enough for his army in Betcoom, for fo they call the territory of the eaftern branch of Shangalla adjoining to Siré and Tigré. By this manœuvre the enemy was deceived, as the moft intelligent thought he was to attack Lafta, and the others, that knew the fecret of the water, were fure his march was againft the Shangalla.

The king began his march from Ibaba, and croffed the Nile at the fecond cataract below Dara, where there is a bridge; and, entering Begemder, he joined his army at Efté, which was going in a route directly from Agow and Damot towards Lafta. But no fooner was he arrived at Efté, than, that very night, he fuddenly turned back the way he came, and, marching through Maitſha, he croſſed the Nile, for the ſecond time, at Coutto, above the firſt cataract.

THE morning of the 3d of May, the ſixth day of forced marches, without having encamped the whole way, he entered Zeegam at the head of his army. He found the country in perfect ſecurity, both people and cattle below on the plains and in the villages; and having put all to the ſword who firſt offered themſelves, and the principal of the conſpirators being taken priſoners, he ſold their wives and children at a public auction for ſlaves to the higheſt bidder. He then took the principal men among them along with him for ſecurity for paying ſix years tribute which they were in arrears, fined them 6000 oxen, which he ordered to be delivered upon the ſpot; and then collecting his army, he ſent to the chiefs of Damot to meet him before he entered their territory, and to bring ſecurity with them for the fine he intended to lay upon them, otherwiſe he would deſtroy their country with fire and ſword; and he advanced the ſame day to Aſſoa, ſouth of the ſources of the Nile, divided only from Damot by the ridge of mountains of Amid Amid.

THE people of Damot, inhabiting an open level country without defence, had no choice but to throw themſelves on the king's mercy, who fined them 500 ounces of gold and 100 oxen, and took the principal people with him in irons as hoſtages.

HE then returned, leaving the ſources of the Nile on his right, through Dengui, Fagitta, and Arooſi; croſſed the river Kelti, having the Agow and Atcheffer on his left, and returned

turned to Gondar by Dinglebcr. He then gave 2000 cattle to the churches of Tecla Haimanout and Yafous, being near-eft the king's palace, to the Itchegué Hannes, the judges and principal fervants of his houfehold, to all a fhare, without referving one to himfelf. And the rains being now very conftant, (for it was the 25th of June) he refolved to continue the reft of the winter in Gondar to regulate the affairs of the church.

This year the king refumed his expedition againft the Shangalla, towards which he had taken feveral preparatory fteps, while he was projecting the furprife of the Zeegam. Thefe are the Troglodytes on the eaftern part of Abyffinia, towards the Red Sea, fouth of Walkayt, Sire, Tigré, and Baharnagafh, till they are there cut off by the mountains of the Habab. Thefe, the moft powerful of all their tribes, are comprehended under the general name of *Dobenah*; the tribe Baafa, which we have already fpoken of as occupying the banks of the Tacazzé, are the only partners they have in the peninfula formed by that river and the Mareb. Their country and manner of life have been already abundantly defcribed. It is all called Kolla, in oppofition to Daga, which is the general name of the mountainous parts of Abyffinia.

The king, being informed by Kafmati Claudius that there was water in great plenty at Betcoom, marched from Gondar the 29th of October to Deba, thence to Koffogue, after to Tamama. He then turned to the left to a village called Sidrè, nearer to the Shangalla. From this ftation he forbade the lighting fires in the camp, and took the road leading to the Mareb; then turning to the left, the 1ft of December he furprifed a village called Kunya. The king

3 L 2   was

was the firſt who began the attack, and was in great danger, as Mazmur, captain of his guard, was killed by a lance
at his ſide. But the ſoldiers ruſhing in upon ſight of the
king's ſituation, who had already ſlain two with his own
hand, the village was carried, and the inhabitants put to
the ſword, refuſing all to fly, and fighting obſtinately to the
laſt gaſp.

From Kunya the king proceeded rapidly to Tzaada Amba*, the largeſt and moſt powerful ſettlement of theſe ſava-
ges. They have no water but what they get from the river
Mareb, which, as I have elſewhere obſerved, riſes above
Dobarwa, and, after making the circle of that town, loſes
itſelf ſoon after in the ſand for a ſpace, then appears again,
and, after a ſhort courſe, hides itſelf a ſecond time to the
N. E. near the Taka, whoſe wells it ſupplies with freſh water. But in the rainy months it runs with a full ſtream, in
a wide and deep bed, and unites itſelf to the Tacazzé, with
it making the northmoſt point of the ancient iſland of Me-
roë.

The king met the ſame ſucceſs at Tzaada Amba that he
had before experienced at Kunya, at which laſt village he
paſſed the feaſt of the epiphany and benediction of the waters; a ceremony annually obſerved both by the Greek and
Abyſſinian church, the intent of which has been ſtrangely
miſtaken by foreigners.

From

---

*-The white mountain.

From Kunya, his head-quarters, Yafous attacked the feveral nations of which this is, as it were, the capital, Zacoba, Fadè, Qualquou, and Sahalé, and he returned again to Tzaada Amba, refolving to complete their deftruction. The remains of thefe miferable people, finding refiftance vain, had hid themfelves in inacceffible caves in the mountains, and the thickeft parts of the woods, where they lay perfectly concealed in the day-time, and only ftole out when thirft obliged them at night. The king, who knew this, and that they had no other water but what they brought from the Mareb, formed a ftrong line of troops along the banks of that river, till the greateft part of the Shangalla of Tzaada Amba died with thirft, or were taken or flain by the army.

His next enterprize was to attempt Betcoom, a large habitation of Shangalla eaft of the Mareb, whofe number, ftrength, and reputation for courage, had hitherto prevented the Abyffinians from molefting them, never having touched, unlefs the fartheft fkirts of their country. The names of their tribes inhabiting Betcoom are, Baigada, Dadé, Ketfè, Kicklada, Moleraga, Megaerbé, Gana, Selé, Hamta, Shalada, Elmfi, and Lentè. The fmall river of Lidda falling from a high precipice, when fwelled with the winter rains, hollows out deep and large refervoirs below, which it leaves full of water when the rains ceafe, fo that thefe people are here as well fupplied with water as thofe that dwell on the large rivers the Mareb and Tacazzè. This was a circumftance unknown, till this fagacious and provident king ordered the place to be reconnoitred by Kafmati. Claudius, then marched and encamped on the river

4   Lidda

Lidda, which, after a fhort but violent courfe, falls into the Mareb.

The Shangalla of Betcoom did nothing worthy of their reputation or numbers. They had already procured intelligence of the fate of great part of their nation, and had difperfed themfelves in unknown and defolate places. The king, however, made a confiderable number of flaves of the younger fort, and killed as many of the reft as fell into his hands.

Leaving Betcoom, the army proceeded ftill eaftward; paffed through the mountains of the Habab, into the low level country which runs parallel to the Red Sea, at the bafe of thefe mountains, where he fpent feveral days hunting the elephant, fome of which he flew with his own hand, and turned then to the left to Amba Tchou * and Taka.

The Taka are a nation of Shepherds living near the extremity of the rains. They are not Arabs, but live in villages, and were part formerly of the Bagla, or Habab; they fpeak the language of Tigré, and are now reputed part of the kingdom of Sennaar.

While the king was at Taka, he received the difagreeable news, that, after he had left the Shangalla on the Mareb, Muftapha Gibberti, a Mahometan foldier in the fervice of Kafmati Fafa Chriftos of Dedgin, had, with a fmall number of men, ventured down, thinking that he fhould furprife

---

* The mountain of falt.

prife the Shangalla of Muftapha and   entered inhabitants
from their late misfortun Chriftos cut fmall army   that
or three Shangalla with fire-arms; and at firt they flood
aloof as fearing the king.   But finding foon that it was no
part of his army, and only a fmall body of adventurers, the
Shangalla 'now collected in numbers, furrounded Muftapha
and his party, whom they cut off to a man; and, purfuing
their advantage, they entered and took Dedgin, wounded
Kafmati Fafa Chriftos, and put the inhabitants of the town
to the fword.

News of this misfortune were carried fpeedily to Kafmati
Claudius, governor of Tigré: Caffem, a Mahometan, led the
Gibbertis, the people of that religion in the province; and,
as he was an advanced party, came fpeedily to blows with
the Shangalla, and was clofely engaged, with great appearance of fuccefs, when Claudius came up with an army that
would foon have put an end to the conteft.   But no fooner
was his army engaged with the Shangalla, than a panic
feized him, and he founded a retreat; which, in an inftant,
became a moft fhameful flight.   Caffem and his gibbertis
fell, fighting to the laft man in the middle of their enemies.
The Shangalla followed their advantage, and great part of
the Abyffinian army perifhed in the flight; Claudius, tho'
he efcaped, left his ftandard, kettle-drums, and his whole
province in poffeffion of the enemy.

The king, upon hearing this, returned haftily into Siré;
and his prefence eftablifhed order and tranquillity in that
province, already half abandoned for fear of the Shangalla.
From Sirè the king proceeded to Axum, where he celebrated

2.   his

his victories over the Shangalla, by feveral days of feafting and thankfgiving.

In the midft of this rejoicing, news were brought that Murat, a fervant of the king, whom he had difpatched to India with merchandife, to bring fuch commiffions as he flood in need of, was arrived at Mafuah, where Mufa the Naybe, or Turkifh governor of the ifland, had detained him, and feized his goods, under fome vexatious pretences. There is not indeed a more mercilefs, thievifh fet of mifcreants, than in that government of Mafuah. But the king knew too well the few refources that ifland had, to be long in applying a remedy, without moving from Axum; after being fully informed of the affair, in all its circumftances, by Murat, he fent to Abba Saluce, Guebra Chriftos, and Zarabrook of Hamazen, the governors of the diftricts, that as it were furround Mafuah, prohibiting all, upon pain of death, to fuffer·any provifions to be carried by any perfon whatever into the ifland of Mafuah.

A severe famine inftantly followed, which was to terminate in certain death, before any relief could come to them, unlefs from Abyffinia. The Naybe Mufa, therefore, found into what a terrible fcrape he had got; but hunger did not leave him a moment to deliberate. No third way remained, but either he muft fee the king, or die; and without hefitation he chofe the former. He, therefore, fet out for Axum, bringing with him Murat and all the merchandifes he had feized, as alfo feveral very confiderable prefents for Yafous himfelf, who accepted them, received his fubmiffion, and ordered the communication with Abyffinia to be open

as

as before. This done, he difmiffed the Naybe, who returned to Mafuah in peace.

The next affair that came before the king was that of
Kafmati Claudius, (governor of Tigré) who was accufed and
found guilty of having fled while the battle with the Shangalla was yet undecided, leaving his ftandard and kettle-
drums in the power of the enemy. Befides his prefent
mifbehaviour, ftrong prejudice exifted againft him, drawn
from his former character; for it was averred, from ,very
credible authority, that on one occafion, upon a very flender
appearance of fedition, he ordered his troops to fire upon
feveral priefts of Axum, fome of whom were killed on the
fpot. Befides which, in the reign of Hatzè Hannes, he was
found guilty of capital crimes committed at Emfras, condemned to die, and was already hanging upon the tree,
when a very feafonable reprieve arrived from the king, and
he was thereupon cut down whilft yet alive. Yafous contented himfelf with depriving him of his employment, and
afterwards fending him to perpetual banifhment.

The next brought to their trial were Za Woldo, and A-
dera and his fons. Thefe laft were very near relations to
the king, for they were fons of Ozoro Kedufet Chriftos,
daughter of Facilidas. They were accufed of having deferted their country and left it wafte to be over-run by wild
beafts, and a rendezvous for the Shangalla, who thence extended their incurfions as far as Waldubba. Of this there
was ample proof againft them, and they were therefore fentenced to die, but the king commuted their punifhment in-

to that of being imprifoned for life in a cave in the ifland of Dek.

As for the province of Sirè itfelf, he declared all the inhabitants and nobility, degraded from their rank, and all lands, whether feus from the king, or held by any other tenure, were confifcated, refumed by, and re-united to the crown. He then reduced the whole province from a royal government to a private one, and annexed it to the province of Tigrè, whofe governor was to place over it a fhum, or petty officer, without any enfigns of power. And, laft of all, he gave the government of Tigrè to the Ras Feres, or mafter of the horfe, in room of Kafmati Claudius degraded and banifhed.

THE many ftriking examples which the king had lately given, one clofe upon the other, of his own perfonal bravery, his impartial juftice, his fecrecy in his expeditions, and the certain vengeance that followed where it was deferved, his punifhment of the Zeegam, his expedition againft the Shangalla, his affair with the Naybe Mufa, and his behaviour to the cowardly Claudius and daftardly nobility of Sirè, fully convinced his fubjects of all degrees, that neither family, nor being related to the crown, nor the ftrength of their country, nor length of time fince they offended, nor indeed any thing but a return to and continuance in their duty, could give them fecurity under fuch a prince. Thus ended the campaign of the Dobenah, fpoke of to this day in Abyffinia as the greateft warlike atchievement of any of their kings. Twenty-fix thoufand men are faid to have perifhed by thirft when the king took poffeffion of the water at Tzaada Amba. And yet, notwithftanding the fmall-pox which,

which, in fome places, exterminated whole tribes, the Dobe-nah have not loft an inch of territory, but feem rather to be gaining upon Sirè.

Yasous arrived at Dancaz on the 8th of March 1692, having difmiffed his army as he paffed Gondar. From Dancaz he went to Lafta, and after a fhort ftay there, came to Arringo in Begemder. At this place the king received accounts that far exceeded his expectations, and gratified his warmeft wifhes. He had long endeavoured to gain a party among the Galla to divide them; and, though no marks of fuccefs had yet followed, he ftill had continued to ufe his endeavours.

On his arrival at Arringo, he was met by a chief of the fouthern Galla, called Kal-kend, who brought him advice that, while he was bufy with the Shangalla, an irruption had been made into Amhara by the Galla tribes of Liban and Toluma; that they, the king's friends, had come up with them at Halka, fought with them, and beat them, and freed Amhara entirely from all apprehenfion. The king, exceedingly rejoiced to fee his moft inveterate enemies be-come the defenders of his country, ordered the governor of Amhara to pay the Kal-kend 500 webs of cotton-cloth, 500 loads of corn, and efcort both the men and the prefent till they were fafely delivered in their own country.

The 30th of June the king arrived at Gondar from Ar-ringo, and immediately fummoned an affembly of the clergy to meet and receive a letter from the patriarch of Alexan-dria, brought by Abba Mafmur of Agde, and Abba Diof-curos of Maguena, who were formerly fent to Egypt to

afk

afk the patriarch why he difplaced Abuna Chriftodulus, and appointed Abba Sanuda in his room, and defiring that Abba Marcus fhould be made Abuna, and Sanuda depofed. The clergy met very punctually, and the patriarch's letter was produced in the affembly, the feal examined, and declared to be the patriarch's, and unbroken. The letter being opened by the king's order, it contained the patriarch's mandate to depofe Abba Sanuda, and to put Marcus Abuna in his place, which was immediately done by command of the king.

While Yafous was thus bufied in directing the affairs of his kingdom with great wifdom and fuccefs, both in church and ftate, a matter was in agitation, unknown to him, at a diftance from his dominions, which had a tendency to throw them again into confufion.

Towards the end of the laft century, there was fettled at Cairo a number of Italian miffionaries of the reformed Order of St Francis, who, though they lived in the fame convent, and were maintained at the expence of the fathers of the Holy Land, yet did they ftill pretend to be independent of the guardian of Jerufalem, the fuperior of thefe latter.

The expence of their maintenance, joined with their pretenfions to independence, gave great offence to thofe religious of the Holy Land, who thereupon carried their complaints to Rome, offering to be at the whole charge of the miffion of Egypt, and to furnifh from their own fociety fubjects capable of attending to, and extending the Chriftian faith. This offer met with the defired fuccefs at Rome. The miffion of Egypt, to the exclufion of every

other

other Order, was given to the fathers of Jerusalem, or the Holy Land, whom we shall henceforth call Capuchin friars. These capuchins lost no time, but immediately dismissed the reformed Francifcans, whom we shall hereafter distinguish by the name of Francifcans, suffering only two of that Order to remain at Cairo.

The Francifcans, thus banished, returned all to Rome, and there, for several years together, openly defended their own cause, insisting upon the justice of their being replaced in the exercise of their ancient functions. This, however, they found absolutely impossible. They were a poor Order, and the interest of the capuchins had stopped every avenue of the sacred college against them. Finding, therefore, that fair and direct means could not accomplish their ends, they had recourse to others not so commendable, and by these they succeeded, and obtained their purpose. They pretended that, when the Jesuits were chased out of Abyssinia, a great number of Catholics, avoiding the persecution, had fled into the neighbouring countries of Sennaar and Nubia; that they still remained, most meritoriously preserving their faith amidst the very great hardships inflicted upon them by the infidels; but that, under these hardships, they must soon turn Mahometans, unless spiritual assistance was speedily sent them.

This representation, as totally void of truth as ever fable was, was confirmed by the two Francifcans, who still remained at Cairo by permission of the capuchins, or fathers of the Holy Land; and, when afterwards published at Rome, it excited the zeal of every bigot in Italy. All interested themselves in behalf of these imaginary Christians of Nubia;

bia; and pope Innocent XII. was fo convinced of the truth of the ftory, as to eftablifh a confiderable fund to fupport the expence of this, now called the Ethiopic miffion, the fole conduct of which remains ftill with the reformed Francif-cans.

To take care of thefe fugitive Chriftians of Nubia, though it was the principal, yet it was not the only charge commit-ted to the fathers of his miffion. They were to penetrate into Abyffinia, and keep the feeds of the Romifh faith alive there until a proper time fhould prefent itfelf for convert-ing the whole kingdom.

In order to this, a large convent was bought for them at Achmim, the ancient Panopolis in Upper Egypt, that here they might be able to afford a refrefhment to fuch of their brethren as fhould return weary and exhaufted by their preaching among the Nubian confeffors; and, for further affiftance, they had permiffion to fettle two of their Order at Cairo, independent of the fathers of the Holy Land, not-withftanding the former exclufion.

Such is the ftate of this miffion at the prefent time. No Nubian Chriftians ever exifted at the time of their eftablifh-ment, nor is there one in being at this day. But if their profelytes have not increafed, their convents have. Ach-mim, Furfhout, Badjoura, and Negadè are all religious houfes belonging to this miffion, although I never yet was able to learn, that either Heretic, or Pagan, or Mahometan, was fo converted as to die in the Chriftian faith at any one of thefe places; nor have they been much troubled with relieving their brethren, worn out with the toils of

Abyffinian

Abyffinian journies, none of them, as far as I know, having ever made one ftep towards that country; nor is this indeed to be regretted by the republic of letters, becaufe, befides a poor ftock of fcholaftic divinity, not one of them that I faw had either learning or abilities to be of the fmalleft ufe either in religion or difcovery.

It was now the moft brilliant period of the reign of Louis XIV. almoft an Auguftan age, and generally allowed fo, both in France and among foreigners. Men of merit, of all countries and profeffions, felt the effects of the liberality of this great encourager of learning; public works were undertaken, and executed fuperior to the boafted ones of Greece or Rome, and a great number and variety of noble events conftituted a magnificent hiftory of his reign, in a feries of medals. Religion alone had yet afforded no hint for thefe. His conduct in this matter, inftead of that of a hero, fhewed him to be a blind, bloody, mercilefs tyrant, madly throwing down in a moment, with one hand, what he had, with the affiftance of great minifters, been an age in building with the other. The Jefuits, zealous for the honour of the king, their great protector, thought this a time to ftep in and wipe away the ftain. With this view they fet upon forwarding a fcheme, which might have furnifhed a medal fuperior to all the reft, had its infcription been, " The Kings of Arabia and Saba fhall bring gifts."

Father Fleuriau, a friend of father de la Chaife, the king's confeffor, was employed to direct the conful of Cairo, that he fhould, in co-operation with the Jefuits privately, fend a fit perfon into Abyffinia, who might infpire the king of that country with a defire of fending an embaffy into

France,

France, and, upon the management of this political affair, they founded their hopes of getting themfelves replaced in the miffion they formerly enjoyed, and of again fuperfeding their rivals the Francifcans, in directing all the meafures to be taken for that country's converfion.   But this required the utmoft delicacy, for it was well known, that the court of Rome was very much indifpofed towards them, imputing to their haughtinefs, implacability, and imprudence, the lofs of Abyffinia.   Their conduct in China, where they tolerated idolatrous rites to be blended with Chriftian worfhip, began alfo now to be known, and to give the greateft fcandal to the whole church.   It was, therefore, neceffary to make the king declare firft in their favour before they began to attempt to conciliate the pope.

Louis took upon him the protection of this miffion with all the readinefs the Jefuits defired ; and the Jefuit Verfeau was fent immediately to Rome, with ftrong letters to cardinal Janfen, protector of France, who introduced him to the pope.

Verseau knew well the confequence of the protection with which he was honoured.   At his firft audience he declared, in a very firm voice and manner, to the pope, that the king had refolved to take upon himfelf the conduct of the Ethiopic miffion, and that he had caft his eyes upon them (the Jefuits) as the fitteft perfons to be entrufted with the care of it, for *reafons beft known to himfelf.*   The pope diffembled ; he extolled, in the moft magnificent terms, the king's great zeal for the advancement of religion, approved of the choice he had made of the Jefuits, and praifed their refolution as highly acceptable to him, immediate-

ly

ly confenting that Verfeau, and five other Jefuits, fhould without delay pafs into Abyffinia.

But it very foon appeared, that, however this might be the language of the pope, nothing could be more remote from his intentions; for, without the knowledge of the Jefuits, or any way confulting them, he appointed the fuperior of the Francifcans to be his legate a latere to the king of Abyffinia, and provided him with prefents to that prince, and the chief noblemen of his court.

Some time afterwards, when, to prevent ftrife or concurrence, the Jefuits applied to the pope to receive his directions which of the two fhould firft attempt to enter Abyffinia, the Francifcans, or their own Order, the pope anfwered fhortly, That it fhould be thofe who were moft expert. Whether this apparent indifpofition of his Holinefs intimidated Verfeau is not known; but, inftead of going to Cairo, he went to Conftantinople, thence to Syria, to a convent of his Order of which he was fuperior, and there he ftaid. So that the Ethiopic miffion at Cairo remained in the hands of two perfons of different Orders, the one Pafchal, an Italian Francifcan friar, the other a Jefuit and Frenchman, whofe name was Brevedent.

Brevedent was a perfon of the moft diftinguifhed piety and probity, zealous in promoting his religion, but neither imprudent nor rafh in his demonftrations of it; affable in his carriage, chearful in his difpofition, of the moft profound humility and exemplary patience. Befides this, he was reputed a man of good tafte and knowledge in profane learning, and, what crowned all, an excellent mathe-

matician. He feems indeed to me to have been a copy of
the famous Peter Paez, who firft gave an appearance of fta-
bility to the Portuguefe converfion of Abyffinia; like him
he was a Jefuit, but of a better nation, and born in a better
age.

I must here likewife take notice of what I have already·
hinted, that in Abyffinia the character of ambaffador is not
known.   They have no treaties of peace or commerce with
any nation in the world: But, for purpofes already mentioned, factors are employed; and, Abyffinia being everywhere furrounded by Mahometans, thefe of courfe have the
preference; and, as they carry letters from their mafters, the
cuftom of the Eaft obliges them to accompany thefe with
prefents to the fovereigns of the refpective kingdoms
through which they pafs, and this circumftance dignifies
them with the title of ambaffador in the feveral courts at
which they have bufinefs.   Such was Mufa, a factor of the
king, whom we have feen detained, and afterwards delivered by the Naybe of Mafuah, not many years before, in this
king's reign; and fuch alfo was Hagi Ali, then upon his
mafter's bufinefs at Cairo, when M. de Maillet was conful
there, and had received his inftructions from father Fleuriau
at Paris, to bring about this embaffy from Abyffinia.

Besides his other bufinefs, Hagi Ali had orders to bring
with him a phyfician, if poffible, from Cairo; for Yafous
and his eldeft fon were both of a fcorbutic habit, which
threatened to turn into a leprofy.   Hagi Ali, in former
voyages, had been acquainted with a capuchin friar Pafchal;
and, having received medicines from him before, he now
applied to Pafchal to return with him into Abyffinia,
                                                         and

and undertake the cure of the king. Paschal very readily complied with this, upon condition that he should be allowed to take for his companion a monk of his own Order, friar Anthony; to which Hagi Ali readily confented, happy in being enabled to carry two phyficians to his mafter inftead of one.

THE French conful was foon informed of this treaty with the friar Pafchal; and, having very eafy means to bring Hagi Ali to his houfe, he informed him, that neither Pafchal nor Anthony were phyficians, but that he himfelf had a man of his own nation, whofe merit he extolled beyond any thing that had hitherto been faid of Hippocrates or Galen. Hagi Ali very willingly accepted of the condition, and it was agreed that, as Verfeau had not appeared, Brevedent above mentioned fhould attend the phyfician as his fervant.

THIS phyfician was Charles Poncet, a Frenchman, fettled in Cairo, who was (as Mr Maillet fays) bred a chymift and apothecary, and, if fo, was neceffarily better fkilled in the effects and nature of medicine than thofe are who call themfelves phyficians, and practife in the eaft. Nothing againft his private character was intimated by the conful at this time; and, with all deference to better judgment, I muft ftill think, that if Poncet did deferve the epithets of drunkard, liar, babbler, and thief, which Maillet abundantly beftows upon him towards the end of this adventure, the conful could not have chofen a more improper perfon as the reprefentative of his mafter, nor a more probable one to make the defign he had in hand mifcarry; nor could he, in this cafe, ever vindicate the preventing Pafchal's journey, who muft have been much fitter for all the em-

ployments

ployments intended than fuch a man as Poncet was, if one half is true of that which the conful faid of him after, wards.

Maillet, having fo far fucceeded, prevailed upon one Ibrahim Hanna, a Syrian, to write five letters, according to his own ideas, in the Arabic language, one of which was to the king, the four others to the principal officers at the court of Abyffinia: doubting, however, whether Ibrahim's expref, fions were equal to the fublimity of his fentiments, he directed him to fubmit the letters to the confideration of one Francis, a monk, capuchin, or friar of the Holy Land. Ibrahim knew not this capuchin; but he was intimate with another Francis of the reformed Francifcan Order, and to him by miftake he carried the letters.

These Francifcans were the very men from whom Mr de Maillet would have wifhed to conceal the fending Poncet with the Jefuit Brevedent; but the fecret being now revealed, Ibrahim Hanna was difcharged the French fervice for this miftake; and Hagi Ali departing immediately after with Poncet and Brevedent, no time remained for the Francifcans to take the fteps they afterwards did to bring about the tragedy in the perfon of Poncet, which they completely effected in that of Mr Noir du Roule.

Mr Poncet, furnifhed with a cheft of medicines at the expence of the factory, accompanied by father Brevedent, who, in quality of his fervant, now took the name of Jofeph, joined Hagi Ali, and the caravan deftined in the firft place, to Sennaar the capital of Nubia.

PONCET

Poncet set out from Cairo on the 10th of June of the year 1698, and, fifteen days after, they came to Monfalout, a considerable town upon the banks of the Nile, the rendezvous of the caravan being at Ibnah, half a league above Monfalout. Here they tarried for above three months, waiting the coming of the merchants from the neighbouring towns.

In the afternoon of the 24th of September, they advanced above a league and a half distance, and took up their lodging at Elcantara, or the bridge, on the eastern bank of the Nile. A large calish, or cut, from the Nile stretches here to the east, and, at that season, was full of water, the inundation being at its height.

Poncet believes he was on the eastern banks of the Nile; but this is a mistake. Siout and Monfalout, the cities he speaks of, are both on the western banks of that river; nor had the caravan any thing to do with the eastern banks, when their course was for many days to the west, and to the southward of west. Nor was the bridge he passed a bridge over the Nile. There are no bridges upon that river from the Mediterranean till we arrive at the second cataract near the lake Tzana in Abyssinia. The amphitheatre and ruins he speaks of are the remains of the ancient city Isiu; and what he took for the Nile was a calish from the river to supply that city with water.

The 2d of October the caravan set out in earnest, and passed, as he says, into a frightful desert of sand, having first gone through a narrow passage, which he does not mention

tion, amidſt thoſe barren, bare, and ſtony mountains which border the valley of Egypt on the weſt.

THE 6th of October they came to El-Vah, a large village, or town, thick-planted with palm-trees, the Oaſis Parva of the ancients, the laſt inhabited place to the weſt that is under the juriſdiction of Egypt. By ſoftening the original name, Poncet calls this Helaoue, which, as he ſays, ſignifies *ſweetneſs*. But ſurely this was never given it from the productions he mentions to abound there, *viz.* ſenna and coloquintida. The Arabs call El-Vah a ſhrub or tree, not unlike our hawthorn either in form or flower. It was of this wood, they ſay, Moſes's rod was made when he ſweetened the waters of Marah. With a rod of this wood, too, Kaleb Ibn el Waalid, the great deſtroyer of Chriſtians, ſweetened theſe waters at El-Vah, once very bitter, and gave it the name from this miracle. A number of very fine ſprings burſt from the earth at El-Vah, which renders this ſmall ſpot verdant and beautiful, though ſurrounded with dreary deſerts on every quarter; it is ſituated like an iſland in the midſt of the ocean.

THE caravan reſted four days at El-Vah to procure water and proviſions for the continuation of the journey thro' the deſert. Poncet's deſcription of the unpleaſantneſs of this, is perfectly exact, and without exaggeration. In two days they came to Cheb, where there is water, but ſtrongly impregnated with alum, as the name itſelf ſignifies; and, three days after, they reached Selima, where they found the water good, riſing from an excellent ſpring, which gives its name to a large deſert extending weſtward forty-five days journey to Dar Fowr, Dar Sclè, and Bagirma, three ſmall

2   principalities

principalities of Negroes that live within the reach of the tropical rains.

At Selima they provided water for five days; and, on the 26th of October, having turned their courfe a little to the eaftward, came to Mofcho, or Machou, a large village on the weftern banks of the Nile, which Poncet ftill mif-takes for the eaftern, and which is the only inhabited place fince the leaving El-Vah, and the frontiers of the kingdom of Dongola, dependent upon that of Sennaar. The Nile here takes the fartheft turn to the weftward, and is rightly delineated in the French maps.

Poncet very rightly fays, this is the beginning of the country of the Barabra, or Berberians, (I fuppofe it is a mif-take of the printer when called in the narrative Barauras). The true fignification of the term is *the land of the Shepherds*, a name more common and better known in the firft dynafties of Egypt than in more modern hiftories. The Erbab (or governor) of this province received him hofpitably, and kindly invited him to Argos, his place of refidence, on the eaftern or oppofite fide of the Nile, and entertained him there, upon hearing from Poncet that he was fent for by the king of Abyffinia.

After refrefhing themfelves eight days at Mofcho, they left it on the 4th of November 1698, and arrived at Dongola on the 13th of the fame month. The country month paffed along the Nile is very pleafant, and pleafant its him very properly. It does not owe its November is overflowing of the Nile, the bank days Nile refrefhing confiderably too high. It is themfelves Mofcho 4th too duftry of the inhabitants, who, by different machines, raife water from the ftream.

We are not to attribute to Poncet, but to thofe who pub-lifhed, the ftory here put into father Brevedent's mouth about the fugitive Chriftians in Nubia, which fable gave rife to the firft inftitution of the Ethiopic miffion. " It drew tears, " fays he, from the eyes of father Brevedent, my dear com- " panion, when he reflected that it was not long fince this " was a Chriftian country; and that it had not loft the faith " but only for want of fome perfon who had zeal enough " to confecrate himfelf to the inftruction of this abandoned " nation." He adds, that upon their way they found a great number of hermitages and churches half ruined; a fiction derived from the fame fource.

Dongola was taken, and apoftatized early, and the ftones of hermitages and churches had long before this been car-ried off, and applied to the building of mofques. Father Brevedent, therefore, if he wept for any fociety of Chriftians at Dongola, muft have wept for thofe that had perifhed there 500 years before.

Poncet was much careffed at Dongola for the cures he made there. The Mek, or king, of that city wifhed him much to ftay and fettle there; but defifted out of refpect, when he heard he was going to the emperor of Ethiopia. Dongola, Poncet has placed rightly on the eaftern bank of the Nile, about lat. 20° 22′.

The caravan departed from Dongola on the 6th of January 1699; four days after which they entered into the kingdom

4   of

of Sennaar, where they met Erbab Ibrahim, brother of the prime minister, and were received civilly by him. He defrayed their expences also as far as Korti, where they arrived the 13th of January.

Our travellers from Korti were obliged to enter the great desert of Bahiouda, and cross it in a S. E. direction till they came to Derreira, where they rested two days, which, Poncet says, was done to avoid the Arabs upon the Nile. These Arabs are called Chaigie; they inhabit the banks of that river to the N. E. of Korti, and never pay the king his revenue without being compelled and very ill-treated.

The country about Derreira is called Belled Ullah, from the cause of its plenty rather than the plenty itself. This small district is upon the very edge of the tropical rains, which it enjoys in part; and, by that, is more fruitful than those countries which are watered only by the industry of man. The Arabs of these deserts figuratively call rain Rahamet Ullah, 'the mercy of God', and Belled Ullah, 'the country which enjoys that mercy.'

Some days after the caravan came to Gerri. Poncet says, the use of this station was to examine caravans coming from the northward, whether they had the small-pox or not. This usage is now discontinued by the decay of trade. It must always have served little purpose, as the infection oftener comes in merchandise than by passengers. At Gerri great respect was shewn to Poncet, as going to Ethiopia.

I cannot conceive why Poncet says, that, to avoid the

great windings of the Nile, he fhould have been obliged to travel to the north-eaft. This would have plainly carried him back to the defert of Bahiouda, and the Arabs: his courfe muft have been S. W. to avoid the windings of the Nile, becaufe he came to Herbagi, which he defcribes very properly as a delicious fituation. The next day they came to Sennaar.

THE reader, I hope, will eafily perceive that my intention is not to criticife Mr Poncet's journey. That has been done already fo illiberally and unjuftly that it has nearly brought it into difrepute and oblivion. My intention is to illuftrate it; to examine the facts, the places, and diftances it contains; to correct the miftakes where it has any, and reftore it to the place it ought to hold in geography and difcovery. It was the firft intelligible itinerary made through thefe deferts; and I conceive it will be long before we have another; at any rate, to reftore and eftablifh the old one will, in all fenfible minds, be the next thing to having made a fecond experiment.

HE furely is in fome degree of miftake about the fituation of Sennaar when he fays it is upon an eminence. It is on a plain clofe on the weftern banks of the Nile. A fmall error, too, has been made about its latitude. By an obfervation faid to have been made by father Brevedent, the 21ft of March 1699, he found the latitude of Sennaar to be 13° 4' north. The French maps, the moft correct we have in all that regards the eaft, place this capital of Nubia in lat. 15° and a few minutes. But the public may reft affured, that the correct latitude of Sennaar, by a mean of very fmall differences

ences of near fifty obfervations, made with a three-feet brafs quadrant, in the courfe of feveral months I ftaid in that town, is lat 13° 34′ 36″ north.

WHAT I have to fay further concerning Sennaar will come more naturally in my own travels; and I fhall only fo far confider the reft of Poncet's route, as to explain and clear it from miftakes, Sennaar being the only point in which our two tracts unite.

I SHALL beg the reader to remark, that, from the time of Poncet's fetting out of Egypt till his arrival at Sennaar, fo far was he from being ill-looked upon, or any bad conftruction being put upon his errand, that he was, on the contrary, refpected everywhere, as going to the king of Abyffinia. It never was then imagined he was to dry up the Nile, nor that he was a conjurer to change its courfe, nor that he was to teach the Abyffinians to caft cannon and make war, nor that he was loaded with immenfe fums of money. Thefe were all *piæ fraudes*, lies invented by the priefts and friars to incite thefe ignorant barbarians to a crime which, though it paffed unrevenged, will juftly make thefe brethren in iniquity the deteftation of men of every religion in all ages.

PONCET left Sennaar the 12th of May 1699, and croffed the Nile at Bafboch, about four miles above the town, where he ftopped for three days. This he calls a fair village; but it is a very miferable one, confifting of fcarce 100 huts, built of mud and reeds.

HE

He departed the 15th in the evening, and travelled all the night as far as Bacras, and arrived the day after at A-bec; then at Baha, a long day's journey of about ten hours. He is miſtaken, however, when he ſays Baha is ſituated upon the banks of the Nile, for it is upon a ſmall river that runs into it. But, at the ſeaſon he paſſed it, moſt of thoſe rivers were dried up.

On the 19th he came to Dodar, a place as inconſiderable as Baha; then to Abra, a large village; then to Debarke and Enbulbul. On the 25th they came to Giefim. Giefim is a large village ſituated upon the banks of the Nile, in the middle of a foreſt of trees of a prodigious height and ſize, all of which are loaded with fruit or flowers, and crowded with paroquets, and variety of other birds, of a thouſand different colours. They made a long ſtay at this place, not leſs than nineteen days.

In this interval, father Brevedent is ſaid to have made an obſervation of the latitude of the place, which, if admitted, would throw all the geography of this journey into confuſion. Poncet ſays, that Giefim is half-way between Sennaar and the frontiers of Ethiopia, and that a ſmall brook, a little beyond Serké, is the boundary between thoſe ſtates. Now, from Sennaar to Giefim are nine ſtages, and one of them we may call a double one, but between Giefim and Serkè, only four; Giefim then cannot be half way between Sennaar and Serkè.—Again, the latitude of Sennaar is 13° 4′ north, according to Brevedent, or rather 13° 34′. Now, if the latitude of Giefim be 10°, then the diſtance between Sennaar and it muſt be about 250 miles which they

I   had

had travelled in eight days, or more than thirty miles a-day, which, in that country, is abfolutely impoffible.

But what muſt make this evident is, that we know certainly that Gondar, the metropolis to which they were then going, is in lat. 12° 34′ north. Giefim then would be ſouth of Gondar, and the caravan muſt have paſſed it when the obſervation was made. But they were not yet arrived at the confines of Sennaar, much leſs to the capital of Abyſſinia, to which they were indeed advancing, but were ſtill far to the northward of it. There is a miſtake then in this obſervation which is very pardonable, Brevedent being then ill of a mortal dyſentery, which terminated in death ſoon after. We ſhall, therefore, correct this error, making the latitude of Giefim 14° 12′ north, about 110 Engliſh miles from Sennaar, and 203 from Gondar.

The 11th of June they ſet out from Giefim for Deleb, then to Chow, and next to Abotkna. They reſted all night, the 14th, in the delightful valley of Sonnone, and, two days after, they came to Serkè, a large town of trade, where there are many cotton weavers. Here ends the kingdom of Sennaar, the brook without this town being the boundary of the two ſtates.

Arrived now in Abyſſinia, they halted at Tambiſſo, a village which belongs to the Abuna; next at Abiad, a village upon the mountain. On the 23d they ſtopped in a valley full of canes and ebony-trees, where a lion carried away one of their camels. On the 24th they paſſed the Gandova, a large, violent, and dangerous river. The country being prodigiouſly woody, one of their beaſts of carriage,
ſtraggling

ftraggling from the caravan, was bit on the hip by a bear, as Mr Poncet apprehends. But we are now in the country correfponding to that inhabited by the Shangalla, that is one of the hotteft in the world, where the thermometer ri- fes to 100° in the fhade. Bears are not found in climates like this ; and moft affuredly there are none even in the higher and colder mountains above. Poncet does not fay he faw the bear, but judged only by the bite, which might have been that of a lion, leopard, or many other animals, but more probably that of the hyæna.

THE 27th they arrived at Girana, a village on the top of a mountain. Here they left their camels, and began to af- cend from the Kolla into the more temperate climate in the mountains of Abyffinia. From Girana they came to Barangoa, and the next day to Tchelga, where anciently was the cuftomhoufe of Sennaar while peace and com- merce fubfifted between the two kingdoms. The 3d of July they arrived at Barcos, or Bartcho, about half a day's journey from Gondar; and on the 9th of Auguft father Brevedent died. Poncet was himfelf detained by indifpo- fition at this village of Barcos till the 21ft of July, on which day he fet out for Gondar and arrived in the evening, where he fucceeded to his wifhes, performing a complete cure up- on his royal patient in a very fhort time ; and fo fulfilled this part of his miffion as perfectly as the ableft phyfician could have done.

As for the other part with which he was charged, I doubt very much if it was in his power to perform it in another manner than he did. It required a mind full of ignorance and prefumption, fuch as was that of Mr de Maillet and all

3   the

the miffionaries at the head of whom he was, to believe
that it was poffible for a private man, fuch as Poncet, without language, without funds, without prefents, or without
power or poffibility of giving them any fort of protection
in the way, to prevail upon 26 or 28 perfons, on the word
of an adventurer only, to attempt the traverfing countries
where they ran a very great rifk of falling into flavery—to
do what? why, to go to France, a nation of Franks whofe
very name they abhorred, that they might be inftructed in
a religion they equally abhorred, to meet with certain death
if ever they returned to their own country; and, unlefs
they did return, they were of no fort of utility whatever.

M. de Maillet fhould have informed himfelf well in the
beginning, if it was poffible that the nobility in Abyffinia
could be fo contemptible as to fuffer twelve of their children to go to countries unknown, upon the word of a ftranger, at leaft of fuch a doubtful character as Poncet. I fay
doubtful, becaufe, if he was fuch a man as M. de Maillet re-
prefents him, a drunkard, a liar, a thief, a man without religion, a perpetual talker, and a fuperficial practitioner of
what he called his own trade, furely the Abyffinians muft
have been very fond of emigration, to have left their homes
under the care of fuch a patron as this. When did M. de
Maillet ever hear of an Abyffinian who was willing to leave
his own country and travel to Cairo, unlefs the very few
priefts who go for duty's fake, for penances or vows, to Jerufalem? When did he ever hear of an Abyffinian layman,
noble, or plebeian, attending even the Abuna though the firft
dignitary of the church? We fhall fee prefently a poor flave,
a Chriftian Abyffinian boy, immediately under the protection
of M. de Maillet, and going directly from him into the prefence

fence of his king, taken forcibly from the chancellor of the nation *, and made a Mahometan before their eyes.

The Abyſſinian embaſſy then demanded from France, and recommended to M. de Maillet, was a preſumptuous, vain, impracticable chimera, which muſt have ended in diſappointment, and which never could have cloſed more innocently than it did.

I shall paſs over all that happened during Poncet's ſtay at Gondar, as he did not underſtand the language, and muſt therefore have been very liable to miſtake. But as for what he ſays of armies of 300,000 men ; of the king's dreſs at his audience; of his mourning in purple; of the quantity of jewels he had, and wore; of his having but one wife; and of large ſtone-croſſes being erected on the corners of the palace at Gondar; theſe, and ſeveral other things, ſeem to me to have been ſuperadded afterwards. Nor do I think what is ſaid of the churches and Chriſtians remaining in the kingdom of Dongola, nor the monſtrous lie about the golden rod ſuſpended in the air in the convent of Bifan †, is at all the narrative of Poncet, but of ſome fanatic, lying friar, into whoſe poſſeſſion Poncet's manuſcript might have fallen. The journey itſelf, ſuch as I have reſtored it, is certainly genuine; and, as I believe it deſcribes the beſt and ſafeſt way into Abyſſinia, I have rectified ſome of the few errors it had, and now recommend it to all future travellers, and to the public.

This

---

* By Chancellor of the Nation is meant the officer immediately next the conſul, who keeps the records, and has a department abſolutely independent of the Conſul.

† Vid. Poncet.

Th:s is to be underſtood of his travels to Abyſſinia, his journey in returning being much more inaccurate and in-returning the reaſon of which we have in his own words: "ſays he not, ſays he, exactly noted down the places through "road little paſſed, the great weakneſs I then lay under not " ſupplied me to write as I could have wiſhed." I ſhall, ſupplied ſay little upon his return, as the deficiency will bexactly by ſupplied by the hiſtory of my own journey from Maſuah, the road by which he left the country being very nearly the ſame as that by which I entered.

It was on the 2d of May of the year 1700 that Pon-cet left Gondar and took his journey to the town of Em-fras. Here there is a miſtake in the very beginning. Em-fras *, at which place I ſtaid for ſeveral weeks, is in lat. 12° 12' 38", and long. 37° 38' 30", conſequently about 22 miles from Gondar, almoſt under the ſame meridian, or ſouth from it; ſo that, as he was going to the eaſt, and northward of eaſt, this muſt have been ſo many miles out of his way; for, going towards Maſuah, his firſt ſtation muſt have been upon the river Angrab.

The ſame may be ſaid of his next to Coga. It was a royal reſidence indeed, but very much out of his way. He has forgot likewiſe, when he ſays, that, in the way from Gondar to Emfras, you muſt go over a very high mountain. The way from Gondar to Emfras is the beaten way to Be-gemder, Foggora, and Dara, and ſo on to the ſecond cataract of the Nile. It is on that plain the armies were encamped

Vol. II.   3 P   before

---

* It is plain Poncet had no inſtruments for obſervation with him, nor was he probably ac-quainted with the uſe of them.

before the battle of Serbraxos *, whence the road paffes by
Correva, which is indeed upon a rifing ground, floping
gently to the lake Tzana, but is not either mountain or
hill.

Seven or eight days are a fpace of time juft enough for
the paffing through Woggora, where he juftly remarks
the heats are not fo exceffive as in the places he came from.
He takes no notice of the paffage of Lamalmon, which ought
to have been very fenfible to a man in a decayed ftate of
health, the lefs fo as he was only defcending it. Every thing
which relates to the paffage of the Tacazzé is juft and proper, only he calls the river itfelf the Tekefel, inftead of the
true name, the *Tacazzé*.   It was the Siris of the ancients; and
it is doing juftice to both countries, when he compares the
province of Siré with the moft delicious parts of his own
country of France.   This province is that alfo where he
might very probably receive the young elephant, which he
fays awaited him there as a prefent to the king of France,
and which died a few days after.

He paffed afterwards to Adowa.   It is the capital of Tigré, is ftill the feat of its governor, and was that of Ras
Michael in my time.   All that he fays of the intermediate
country and its productions, fhew plainly that his work is
genuine, and his remarks to be thofe of an eye-witnefs..

From this province of Tigré he enters the country of the
Baharnagafh, and arrives at Dobarwa, which he erroneouf-
ly

ly calls Duvarna, and fays it is the capital of the province of Tigrè, whereas it is that of the Baharnagafh. Ifaac Baharnagafh, when in rebellion againft his fovereign, furrendered this town to the Turks in the year 1558, as may be feen at large in my hiftory of the tranfactions of thofe times.

As the authenticity of this journey, and the reality of Poncet's having been in Abyffinia, has been queftioned by a fet of vain, ignorant, fanatic people, and that from malice only, not from fpirit of inveftigation, of which they were incapable, I have examined every part of it, and compared it with what I myfelf faw, and fhall now give one other inftance to prove it genuine, from an obfervation Poncent has made, and which has efcaped all the miffionaries, though it was entire and vifible in my time.

AMONG the ruins of Axum * there is a very high obelifk, flat on both fides, and fronting the fouth. It has upon it no hieroglyphic, but feveral decorations, or ornaments, the fancy of the architect. Upon a large block of granite, into which the bottom of it is fixed, and which ftands before it like a table, is the figure of a Greek patera, and on one fide of the obelifk, fronting the fouth, is the reprefentation of a wooden door, lock, and a latch to it, which firft feems defigned to draw back and then lift up, exactly in the manner thofe kind of locks are fafhioned in Egypt at this very day. Poncet obferved very juftly, there are no fuch locks made ufe of

3 P 2   in

---

* See an elevation of this in my account of Axum

in Abyſſinia, and wonders how they ſhould have repreſent-
ed a thing they had neveꝛ ſeen, and, having done ſo, remained ſtill incapable to make or uſe it. Poncet was no
man of reading out of his own profeſſion ; he nowhere
pretends it; he recorded this faƈt becauſe he ſaw it, as a
traveller ſhould do, and left others to give the reaſon
which he could not. Poncet calls this place Heleni, from
a ſmall village of that name in the neighbourhood. Had he
been a ſcholar he would have known that the ruins he was
obſerving were thoſe of the city of Axum, the ancient metropolis of this part of Ethiopia.

PTOLEMY EVERGETES, the third Grecian king of Egypt,
conquered this city and the neighbouring kingdom ; reſi-
ded ſome time there ; and, being abſolutely ignorant of
hieroglyphics, then long diſuſed, he left the obeliſk he had
ereƈted for aſcertaining his latitudes ornamented with figures of his own chooſing, and the inventions of his ſubjeƈts the Egyptians, and particularly the door for a convenience of private life, to be imitated by his new-acquired
ſubjeƈts the Ethiopians, to whom it had hitherto been unknown.

FROM Dobarwa he arrived at Arcouva, which, he ſays,
geographers miſcal Arequies. M. Poncet might have ſpared this criticiſm upon geographers till he himſelf had been
better informed, for both are equally miſcalled, whether Arcouva or Arequies. The true and only name of the place,
known either to Mahometans or Chriſtians, is Arkeeko, as
the iſland to which he paſſed, croſſing an arm of the ſea, is
called Maſuah, not Meſſoua, as he everywhere ſpells it.

FROM

From Mafuah, Poncet croffed the Red Sea to Jidda, paffing the ifland Dahalac and Kotumbal, a high rock, the name of which is not known to many navigators.

Had old Murat, Mufa, and Hagi Ali, happened at that time to have been upon fome mercantile errand to Cairo, there is no doubt but they would have been preferred and become ambaffadors to France. They would have gone there, perplexed the minifter and the conful with a thoufand lies and contrivances, which the French never would have been able to unravel; they would have promifed every thing; obtained from the king fome confiderable fum of money, on which they would have undertaken to fend the embaffy in any form that was prefcribed, and, after their return home, never been heard of more. But thofe worthies were, probably, all employed at this time; therefore the only thing Poncet could do was to bring Murat, fince he was to procure at all events an ambaffador.

He had been a cook to a French merchant at Aleppo; was a maker of brandy at Mafuah; and probably his uncle old Murat's fervant at the time. But he was not the worfe ambaffador for this. Old Murat, Hagi Ali, and Mufa, had perhaps been alfo cooks and fervants in their time. Prudence, fobriety, and good conduct, fkill in languages, and acquaintance, with countries recommended them afterwards to higher trufts. Old Murat probably meant that his nephew fhould begin his apprenticefhip with that embaffy to France; and M. Poncet, to increafe his confequence, and fulfil the commiffion the conful gave him, allowed him to invent all the reft.

PONCET;

Poncet, from Jidda, went to Tor, and thence to Mount Sinai, where, after fome ftay, being overtaken by Murat, they both made their entry into Cairo.

M. de Maillet, the conful, was an old Norman gentleman, exceedingly fond of nobility, confequently very haughty and overbearing to thofe he reckoned his inferiors, among which he accounted thofe of his own nation eftablifhed at Cairo, though a very amiable and valuable fet of men.   He was exceedingly tefty, choleric, obftinate, and covetous, though fagacious enough in every thing concerning his own intereft.   He lived for the moft part in his clofet, feldom went out of his houfe, and, as far as I could learn, never out of the city.   There, however, he wrote a defcription of all Egypt, which fince has had a confiderable degree of reputation *.

Maillet had received advice of the miferable ftate of this embaffy from Jidda, that the Sherriffe of Mecca had taken from Poncet, by force, two female Abyffinian flaves, and that the elephant was dead ; which particulars being written to France, he was advifed in a letter from father Fleuriau by no means to promote any embaffy to the court of Verfailles ; that a proper place for it was Rome ; but that in France they looked upon it in the fame light as they did upon an embaffy from Algiers or Tunis, which did no honour to thofe who fent it, and as little to thofe that received it ; this, however, was a new light.

M. de

---

* And there he wrote his Teliamede which fuppofes men were firft created fifhes, for which he was excommunicated.   It was an opinion perfectly worthy of alarming the Sorbonne.

M. DE MAILLET, by this letter, becoming mafter of the ambaffador's deftiny, began firft to quarrel with him upon etiquette, or who fhould pay the firft vifit; and, after a variety of ill-ufage, infifted upon feeing his difpatches. This Murat refufed to permit, upon which the conful fent privately to the bafha, defiring him to take the difpatches or letters from Murat, fending him at the fame time a confiderable prefent.

THE bafha on this did not fail to extort a letter from Murat by threats of death. He then opened it. It was in Arabic, in very general and indifferent terms, probably the performance of fome Moor at Mafuah, written at Murat's inftance. And well was it for all concerned that it was fo; for had the letter been a genuine Abyffinian letter, like thofe of the emprefs Helena and king David III. propofing the deftruction of Mecca, Medina, and the Turkifh fhips on the Red Sea, the whole French nation at Cairo would have been maffacred, and the conful and ambaffador probably impaled.

THE Jefuits, ignorant of this manœvure of M. de Maillet, but alarmed and fcandalized at this breach of the law of nations, for fuch the bafha's having opened a letter, addreffed to the king of France, was juftly confidered, complained to M. Feriol the French ambaffador at Conftantinople, who thereupon fent a capigi from the port, to inquire of the bafha what he meant by thus violating the law of nations, and affronting a friendly power of fuch confequence as France.   3

THESE

THESE capigis are very unwelcome guefts to people in office to whom they are fent. They are always paid by thofe they are fent to. Befides this, the report they carry back very often cofts that perfon his life. The bafha, accufed by the capigi at the inftance of the French ambaffador at Conftantinople, anfwered like an innocent man, That he had done it by defire of the French conful, from a wifh to ferve him and the nation, otherwife he fhould never have meddled in the matter. The confequence was, M. de Maillet was obliged to pay the bafha the expence of the capigi; and, having fome time afterwards brought it in account with the merchants, the French nation at Cairo, by deliberation of the 6th of July of the year 1702, refufed to pay 1515 livres, the demand of the bafha, and 518 livres for thofe of his officers.

THE conful, however, had gained a complete victory over Murat, and thereupon determined to fend Monhenaut, chancellor of France at Cairo, with letters, which, though written and invented by himfelf, he pretended to be tranflations from the Ethiopian original.

BUT father Verfeau, the Jefuit, now returned to Cairo, who had entered into a great diftruft of the conful fince the difcovery of his intrigue with the bafha about Murat's letter, refolved to be of the party. Poncet, who was likewife on bad terms with the conful, neither inclined to lofe the merits of his travels into Abyffinia, nor truft the recital of it to Monhenaut, or to the manner in which it might be reprefented in the conful's letters. Thefe three, Monhenaut, Poncet, and Verfeau, fet out therefore for Paris with very different views and defigns. They embarked at Bulac, the

I   fhipping-

fhipping-place of Cairo upon the Nile, taking with them the ears of the dead elephant.

The remaining part of the prefent brought for the king of France by this illuftrious embaffy, was an Abyffinian boy, a flave bought by Murat, and who had been hid from the fearch of the Sheriffe, when he forcibly took from him the two Abyffinian girls, part of the intended prefent alfo. This boy no fooner embarked on board the veffel at Bulac than a great tumult arofe. The janizaries took the boy out of the veffel by force, and delivered him to Muftapha Cazdagli, their kaya; nor could all the intereft of M. de Maillet and the French nation, or all the manœuvres of the Jefuits, ever recover him.

As for Monhenaut, Poncet, and Verfeau, his protectors, they were obliged to hide themfelves from the violence of he mob, nor dared they again to appear till the veffel failed. And happy was it for them that this fell out at Cairo, for, had they offered to embark him at Alexandria, in all probability it would have coft all of them their lives.

I must beg leave here to fuggeft to the reader, how dangerous, as well as how abfurd, was the plan of this embaffy. It was to confift of twenty-eight Abyffinians, twelve of whom were to be fons of noble families, all to be embarked to France. What a pleafant day would the embarkation have been to M. de Maillet! What an honourable appearance for his king, in the eyes of other Chriftian princes, to have feen twenty-eight Chriftians under his immediate protection, twelve of whom we might fay were princes, (as all the nobility in Abyffinia are directly of the family of the

king),

king), from motives of vanity only, by the pride of the Jefuits, and the ignorance of the conful, hurried in one day
into apoftacy and flavery! Whatever Maillet thought of Poncet's conduct, his bringing Murat, and him only, cook as
he was, was the very luckieft accident of his life.

I know French flatterers will fay this would not have
happened, or, if it had, a vengeance would have followed;
worthy the occafion and the refentment of fo great a king,
and would have prevented all fuch violations of the law of
nations for the future. To this I anfwer; The mifchief
would have been irreparable, and the revenge taken, however complete, would not have reftored them their religion,
and, without their religion, they themfelves would not have
returned into their own country, but would have remained
neceffary facrifices, which the pride and rafhnefs of the Jefuits had made to the faith of Mahomet.

Besides, where is the threatened revenge for the affaffination of M. du Roule, then actual ambaffador from the king
of France, of which I am now to fpeak ? Was not the law of
nations violated in the ftrongeft manner poffible by his
murder, and without the fmalleft provocation ? What vengeance was taken for this ?—Juft the fame as would have
been for the other injury ; for the Jefuits and conful
would have concealed the one, as tendernefs for the Fran-
cifan Friars had made them cover the other, left their a-
bominable wickednefs fhould be expofed. If the court of
France did not, their conful in Cairo fhould have known
what the confequence would be of decoying twenty-eight
Abyffinians from their own country, to be perverted from
their

their own religion, and remain flaves and Mahometans at Cairo, a nuifance to all European nations eftablifhed there.

Upon the arrival of the triumvirate at Paris, Monhenaut immediately repaired to the minifter; Verfeau was introduced to the king, and Poncet, foon after, had the fame honour. He was then led as a kind of fhow, through all Paris, cloathed in the Abyffinian drefs, and decorated with his gold chain. But while he was vainly amufing himfelf with this filly pageantry, the conful's letters, and the comments made upon them by Monhenaut, went directly to deftroy the credit of his ever having been in Abyffinia, and of the reality of Murat's embaffy.

The Francifcan friars, authors of the murder of M. du Roule, enemies to the miffion, as being the work of the Jefuits; M. Piques, member of the Sorbonne, a body never much diftinguifhed for promoting difcoveries, or encouraging liberal and free inquiry; Abbé Renaudot, M. le Grande, and fome ancient linguifts, who, with great difficulty, by the induftry of M. Ludolf, had attained to a very fuperficial knowledge of the Abyffinian tongue, all fell furioufly upon Poncet's narrative of his journey. One found fault with the account he gave of the religion of the country, becaufe it was not fo conformable to the rites of the church of Rome, as they had from their own imagination and prejudice, and for their own ends conceived it to be. Others attacked the truth of the travels, from improbabilities found, or fuppofed to be found, in the defcription of the countries through which he had paffed; while others difcovered the forgery of his letters, by faults found in the orthography of

that

that language, not one book of which, at that day, they had ever feen.

ALL thefe empty criticifms have been kept alive by the merit of the book, by this alone they have any further chance of reaching pofterity ; while, by all candid readers, this itinerary, fhort and incomplete as it is, will not fail to be received as a valuable acquifition to the geography of thefe unknown countries of which it treats.

I THINK it but a piece of duty to the memory of a fellow-traveller, to the lovers of truth and the public in general, to ftate the principal objections upon which this outcry againft Poncet was raifed; that, by the anfwers they admit of, the world may judge whether they are or are not founded in candour, and that before they are utterly fwallowed up in oblivion.

THE firft is, that of the learned Renaudot, who fays he does not conceive how an Ethiopian could be called by the name of Murat. To this I anfwer, Poncet, de Maillet, and the Turkifh Bafha, fay Murat was an Armenian, a hundred times over; but M. Renaudot, upon his own authority, makes him an Ethiopian, and then lays the blame upon others, who are not fo ignorant as himfelf.

SECONDLY, Poncet afferts Gondar was the capital of Ethiopia ; whereas the Jefuits have made no mention of it, and this is fuppofed a ftrong proof of Poncet's forgery. I anfwer, The Jefuits were banifhed in the end of Socinios's reign, and the beginning of that of his fon Facilidas, that is about the year 1632 ; they were finally extirpated in the end of this laft prince's reign, that is before the year 1666, by
his

his ordering the laft Jefuit Bernard Nogueyra, to be publicly hanged. Now Gondar was not built till the end of the
reign of Hannes I. who was grandfon to Socinios, that is
about the year 1680.   Unlefs, then, thefe holy Jefuits, who,
if we believe the miffionaries, had all of them a fight into
futurity before their martyrdom, had, from thefe their *laſt
vifions*, defcribed Gondar as capital of Abyffinia, it does not
occur to me how they fhould be hiftorians of a fact that
had not exiftence till 50 years after they were dead.

THIRDLY, Poncet fpeaks of towns and villages in Ethiopia ; whereas it is known there are no towns, villages, or cities, but Axum.—I believe that if the Abyffinians, who built
the large and magnificent city of Axum, never had other
cities, towns, and villages, they were in this the moft fingular people upon earth ; or, if places where 6000 inhabitants live together in contiguous houfes, feparated with
broad ftreets where there are churches and markets, be not
towns and villages, I do not know the meaning of the term ;
but if thefe are towns, Poncet hath faid truth ; and many
more fuch towns, which he never did fee nor defcribe, are
in Abyffinia at this day.

FOURTHLY, The Abyffinians live, and always have lived,
in tents, not in houfes.—It would have been a very extraordinary idea in people living in tents to have built fuch a city as Axum, whofe ruins are as large as thofe of Alexandria ;
and it would be ftill more extraordinary, that people, in fuch
a climate as Abyffinia, in the whole of which there is fcorching
weather for fix months, deluges of rain, ftorms of wind, thunder, lightning, and hurricanes, fuch as are unknown in
Europe, for the other fix, fhould choofe to live in tents, after

3   knowing

knowing how to build fuch cities as Axum. I wonder a man's underftanding does not revolt againft fuch abfurdities in the moment he is ftating them.

The Abyffinians, while at war, ufe tents and encampments, to fecure the liberty of movements and changing of ground, and defend themfelves, when ftationary, from the inclemency of the weather. But no tent has, I believe, yet been invented that could ftand in the fields in that country from June to September; and they have not yet formed an idea of Abyffinia who can fuppofe this.

I conceive it is *ignorance* of the language which has led thefe *learned* men into this miftake. The Abyffinians call a houfe, ftanding by itfelf, allotted to any particular purpofe, Bet. So Bet Negus is a palace, or the houfe of a king; Bet Chriftian is a church, or a houfe for Chriftian worfhip; whilft Bet Mocha is a prifon, or houfe under ground. But houfes in towns or villages are called Taintes, from the Abyffinian word Tain, to fleep, lie down, reft, or repofe. I fuppofe the fimilitude of this word to tents has drawn thefe *learned* critics to believe, that, inftead of towns, thefe were only collections of tents. But ftill I think, no one acquainted with the Abyffinian language, or without being fo, would be fo void of underftanding as to believe, a people that had built Axum of ftone, fhould endure, for ages after, a tropical winter in bare tents.

The fifth thing that fixes falfehood upon Poncet is, that he defcribes delicious valleys beyond European ideas; beautiful plains, covered with odoriferous trees and fhrubs, to be everywhere in his way on the entrance of Abyffinia;

whereas, when Salidan's brother conquered this country, the Arabian books fay they found it deftitute of all this fruitfulnefs. But, with all fubmiffion to the Arabian books, to Abbé Renaudot and his immenfe reading, I will maintain, that neither Salidan, nor his brother, nor any of his tribe, ever conquered the country Poncet defcribes, nor were in it, or ever faw it at a diftance.

THE province where Poncet found thefe beautiful fcenes' lies between lat. 12 and 13°. The foil is rich, black mould, which fix months tropical rain are needed to water fufficiently, where the fun is vertical to it twice a-year, and ftationary, with refpect to it, for feveral days, at the diftance of 10°, and at a leffer diftance ftill for feveral months; where the fun, though fo near, is never feen, but a thick fcreen of watery clouds is conftantly interpofed, and yet the heat is fuch, that Fahrenheit's thermometer rifes to 100° in the fhade. Can any one be fo ignorant in natural hiftory, as to doubt that, under thefe circumftances, a luxuriant, florid, odoriferous vegetation muft be the confequence? Is not this the cafe in every continent or ifland within thefe limits all round the globe?

BUT Poncet contradicts the Arabian books, and all travellers, modern and ancient; for they unanimoufly agree that this country is a dreary miferable defert, producing nothing but Dora, which is millet, and fuch like things of little or no value. I wifh fincerely that M. Renaudot, when he was attacking a man's reputation, had been fo good as to name the author whofe authority he relied on. I fhall take upon me to deny there ever was an Arabian book which treated of this country. And with regard to the an-

cient

cient and modern travellers, his quotations from them are, if poffible, ftill more vifionary and ridiculous. The only ancient travellers, who, as I believe, ever vifited that country, were Cambyfes's ambaffadors; who, probably, paffed this part of Poncet's track when they went to the Macrobii, and the moft modern authors (if they can be called modern) that came neareft to it, were the men fent by Nero* to difcover the country, whofe journey is very doubtful; and they, when they approached the parts defcribed by Poncet, fay " the country began to be green and beautiful." Now I wifh M. Renaudot had named any traveller more modern than thefe meffengers of Nero, or more ancient than thofe ambaffadors of Cambyfes, who have travelled through and defcribed the country of the Shangalla.

I, THAT have lived months in that province, and am the only traveller that ever did fo, muft corroborate every word Poncet has faid upon this occafion. To dwell on landfcapes and picturefque views, is a matter more proper for a poet than a hiftorian. Thofe countries which are defcribed by Poncet, merit a pen much more able to do them juftice, than either his or mine.

It will be remembered when I fay this, it is of the country of the Shangalla, between lat. 12° and 13° north, that this is the people who inhabit a hot woody ftripe called Kolla, about 40 or 50 miles broad, that is from north to fouth, bounded by the mountainous country of Abyffinia, till they join the Nile at Fazuclo, on the Weft.

I HAVE

* Plin. vol. 1. lib. 6. cap. 30. p. 376.

I HAVE alſo ſaid, that, for the ſake of commerce, theſe Shangalla have been extirpated in two places, which are like two gaps, or chaſms, in which are built towns and villages, and through which caravans paſs between Sennaar and Abyſſinia. All the reſt of this country is impervious and inacceſſible, unleſs by an armed force. Many armies have periſhed here. It is a tract totally unknown, unleſs from the ſmall detail that I have entered into concerning it in my travels.

AND here I muſt ſet the critic right alſo, as to what he ſays of the produce of theſe parts. There is no grain called Dara, at leaſt that I know of. If he meant millet, he ſhould have called it Dora. It is not a mark of barrenneſs in the ground where this grows : part of the fineſt land in Egypt is ſown with it. The banks of the Nile which produce Dora would alſo produce wheat ; but the inhabitants of the deſert like this better ; it goes farther, and does not ſubject them to the violent labour of the plough, to which all inhabitants of extreme hot countries are averſe.

THE ſame I ſay of what he remarks with regard to cotton. The fineſt valleys in Syria, watered by the cool refreſhing ſprings that fall from Mount Libanus, are planted with this ſhrub ; and, in the ſame grounds alternately, the tree which produces its ſiſter in manufactures, ſilk, whoſe value is greatly inhanced by the addition. Cotton clothes all Ethiopia ; cotton is the baſis of its commerce with India, and of the commerce between England, France, and the Levant ; and, were it not for ſome ſuch ignorant, ſuperficial reaſoners as Abbè Renaudot, cotton, after wool, ſhould be the favourite manufacture of Britain. It will in time take place of that ungrateful culture, flax; will employ more hands, and be a more ample field for diftinguifhing the ingenuity of our manufacturers.

WE fee, then, how the leaft confideration poffible · deftroys thefe ill-founded objections, upon which thefe very ignorant enemies of Poncet attempted to deftroy his credit, and rob him of the merit of his journey. At laft they ventured to throw off the mafk entirely, by producing a letter fuppofed to be written from Nubia by an Italian friar, who afferts roundly, that he hears Poncet was never at the capital of Ethiopia, nor ever had audience of Yafous; but ftole the clothes and money of father Brevedent, then married, and foon after forfook his wife and Ethiopia together.

MAILLET could have eafily contradicted this, had he acted honeftly; for Hagi Ali had brought him the king of Abyffinia's letter, who thanked him for his having fent Poncet, and fignified to him his recovery. But without appealing to M. Maillet upon the fubject, I conceive nobody will doubt, that Hagi Ali had a commiffion to bring a phyfician from Cairo to cure his mafter, and that Poncet was propofed as that phyfician, with confent of the conful. Now, after having carried Poncet the length of Bartcho, where it is agreed he was when Brevedent died, (for he was fuppofed there to have robbed that father of his money) what could be Hagi Ali's reafon for not permitting him to proceed half a day's journey farther to the capital, and prefenting him to the king, who had been at the pains and expence of fending for him from Egypt? What excufe could Hagi Ali make for not producing him, when he muft have delivered the

conful's

conful's letters, telling him that Poncet was come with the caravan for the purpofe of curing him?

BESIDES this, M. de Maillet faw Hagi Ali afterwards at Cairo, where he reproached him with his cruel behaviour, both to Poncet and to friar Juftin, another monk that had come along with him from Ethiopia. Maillet then muft have been fully inftructed of Poncet's whole life and converfation in Ethiopia, and needed not the Italian's fuppofed communication to know whether or not he had been in Ethiopia. Befides, Maillet makes ufe of him as the forerunner of the other embaffy he was then preparing to Gondar, and to that fame king Yafous, which would have been a very ftrange ftep had he doubted of his having been there before.

SUPPOSING all this not enough, ftill we know he returned by Jidda, and the conful correfponded with him there. Now, how did he get from Bartcho to the Red Sea without paffing the capital, and without the king's orders or knowledge? Who franked him at thofe number of dangerous barriers at Woggora, Lamalmon, the Tacazzé, Kella, and Adowa, where, though I had the authority of the king, I could not fometimes pafs without calling force to my affiftance? Who freed him from the avarice of the Baharnagafh, and the much more formidable rapacity of that murderer the Naybe, who, we have feen in the hiftory of this reign, attempted to plunder the king's own factor Mufa, though his mafter was within three days journcy at the head of an army that in a few hours could have effaced every veftigc of where Mafuah had ftood? All this, then, is a ridiculous fabrication of lies; the work, as I have before

3 R 2

faid,

said, of those who were concerned in the affair of the unhappy Du Roule.

Poncet, having lost all credit, retired from Paris in disgrace, without any further gratification than that which he at first received. He carried to Cairo with him, however, a gold watch and a mirror, which he was to deliver to the consul as a present to his companion Murat, whose subsistence was immediately stopped, and liberty given him to return to Ethiopia.

Nor did Maillet's folly stop here. After giving poor Murat all the ill-usage a man could possibly suffer, he entrusted him with a Jesuit * whom he was to introduce into Ethiopia, where he would certainly have lost his life had not the bad-treatment he received by the way made him return before he arrived at Masuah.

This first miscarriage seemed only to have confirmed the Jesuits more in their resolution of producing an embassy. But it now took another form. Politicians and statesmen became the actors in it, without a thought having been bestowed to diminish the enemies of the scheme, or render their endeavours useless, by a superior knowledge of the manners and customs of the country through which this embassy was to pass.

No adventurer, or vagrant physician, (like Poncet) was to be employed in this second embassy. A minister versed

in

---

* Father Bernat, a Frenchman.

in languages, negociations, and treaties, accompanied with proper drugomans and officers, was to be fent to Abyffinia to cement a perpetual friendfhip and commerce between two nations that had not a national article to exchange with each other, nor way to communicate by fea or land. The minifter, who muft have known this, very wifely, at giving his fiat, pitched upon the conful M. de Maillet to be the amabaffador, as a man who was acquainted with the caufes of Poncet's failure, and, by following an oppofite courfe, could bring this embaffy to a happy conclufion for both nations.

MAILLET confidered himfelf as a general whofe bufinefs was to direct and not to execute. A tedious and trouble-fome journey through dangerous deferts was out of the fphere of his clofet, beyond the limits of which he did not choofe to go. Beyond the limits of this, all was defert to him. He excufed himfelf from the embaffy, but gave in a memorial to ferve as a rule for the conduct of his fucceffor in the nomination in a country he had never feen ; but this, being afterwards adopted as a well-confidered regulation, proved one of the principal caufes of the mifcarriage and tragedy that followed..

M. NOIR DU ROULE, vice-conful at Damiata, was pitched upon as the ambaffador to go to Abyffinia. He was a young man of fome merit, had a confiderable degree of ambition, and a moderate fkill in the common languages fpoken in the eaft, but was abfolutely ignorant of that of the country to which he was going, and, what was worfe, of the cuftoms and prejudices of the nations through which he was to pafs. Like moft of his countrymen, he had a violent predilection

4   for

for the drefs, carriage, and manners of France, and a hearty contempt for thofe of all other nations; this he had not addrefs enough to difguife, and this endangered his life. The whole French nation at Cairo were very ill-difpofed towards him, in confequence of fome perfonal flight, or imprudences, he had been guilty of; as alfo towards any repetition of projects which brought them, their commerce, and even their lives into danger, as the laft had done.

THE merchants, therefore, were averfe to this embaffy; but the Jefuits and Maillet were the avowed fupporters of it, and they had with them the authority of the king. But each aimed to be principal, and had very little confidence or communication with his affociate.

As for the capuchins and Francifcans, they were mortally offended with M. de Maillet for having, by the introduction of the Jefuits, and the power of the king of France, forcibly wrefted the Ethiopic miffion from them which the pope had granted, and which the facred congregation of cardinals had confirmed. Thefe, by their continual communication with the Cophts, the Chriftians of Egypt, had fo far brought them to adopt their defigns as, one and all, to regard the mifcarriage of du Roule and his embaffy, as what they were bound to procure from honour and mutual intereft.

THINGS being in thefe circumftances, M. du Roule arrived at Cairo, and took upon him the charge of this embaffy, and from that moment the intrigues began.

THE conful had perfuaded du Roule, that the proper prefents he fhould take with him to Sennaar were prints of the king and queen of France, with crowns upon their heads; mirrors, magnifying and multiplying objects, and deforming them; when brocade, fattin, and trinkets of gold or filver, iron or fteel, would have been infinitely more acceptable.

ELIAS, an Armenian, a confidential fervant of the French nation, was firft fent by way of the Red Sea into Abyffinia, by Mafuah, to proceed to Gondar, and prepare Yafous for the reception of that ambaffador, to whom he, Elias, was to be the interpreter. So far it was well concerted; but, in preparing for the end, the middle was neglected. A number of friars were already at Sennaar, and had poifoned the minds of that people, naturally barbarous, brutal, and jealous. Money, in prefents, had gained the great; while lies, calculated to terrify and enrage the lower clafs of people, had been told fo openly and avowedly, and gained fuch root, that the ambaffador, when he arrived at Sennaar, found it, in the firft place, neceffary to make a *procez verbal*, or what we call a precognition, in which the names of the authors, and fubftance of thefe reports, were mentioned, and of this he gave advice to M. de Maillet, but the names and thefe papers perifhed with him.

IT was on the 9th of July 1704 that M. du Roule fet out from Cairo, attended by a number of people who, with tears in their eyes, forefaw the pit into which he was failing. He embarked on the Nile; and, in his paffage to Siout, he found at every halting-place fome new and dangerous

gerous

gerous lie propagated, which could have no other end but his deftruction.

BELAC, a Moor, and factor for the king of Sennaar, was chief of the caravan which he then joined. Du Roule had employed, while at Cairo, all the ufual means to gain this man to his intereft, and had every reafon to fuppofe he had fucceeded. But, on his meeting him at Siout, he had the mortification to find that he was fo far changed that it coft him 250 dollars to prevent his declaring himfelf an abettor of his enemies. And this, perhaps, would not have fufficed, had it not been for the arrival of Fornetti, drugo- man to the French nation at Cairo, at Siout, and with him a capigi and chiaoux from Ifmael Bey, the port of janizaries, and from the bafha of Cairo, exprefsly commanding the governor of Siout, and Belac chief of the caravan, to look to the fafety of du Roule, and protect him at the hazard of their lives, and as they fhould anfwer to them.

ALL the parties concerned were then called together; and the fedtah, or prayer of peace, ufed in long and dan- gerous journies, was folemnly recited and affented to by them all; in confequence of which, every individual be- came bound to ftand by his companion even to death, and not feparate himfelf from him, nor fee him wronged, though it was for his own gain or fafety. This teft brought all the fecret to light; for Ali Chelebi, governor of Siout, informed the ambaffador, that the Chriftian merchants and Francif- can friars were in a confpiracy, and had fworn to defeat and difappoint his embaffy even by the lofs of his life, and that, by prefents, they had gained him to be a partner in that confpiracy.

BELAC,

BELAC, moreover, told him, that the patriarch of the Cophts had affured the principal people of which that caravan confifted, that the Franks then travelling with him were not merchants, but forcerers, who were going to Ethiopia, to obftruct, or cut off the courfe of the Nile, that it might no longer flow into Egypt, and that the general refolution was to drive the Franks from the caravan at fome place in the defert which fuited their defigns, which were to reduce them to perifh by hunger or thirft, or elfe to be otherwife flain, and no more heard of.

THE caravan left Siout the 12th of September. In twelve days they paffed the leffer defert, and came to Khargué, where they were detained fix days by a young man, governor of that place, who obliged M. du Roule to pay him 120 dollars, before he would fuffer him to pafs further; and at the fame time forced him to fign a certificate, that he had been permitted to pafs without paying any thing. This was the firft fample of the ufage he was to expect in the further profecution of his journey.

ON the 3d of October they entered the great defert of Selima, and on the 18th of fame month they arrived at Machou, or Mofcho, on the Nile, where their caravan ftaid a confiderable time, till the merchants had tranfacted their bufinefs. It was at this place the ambaffador learned, that feveral Francifcan friars had paffed the caravan while it remained at Siout, and advanced to Sennaar, where they had ftaid fome time, but had lately left that capital upon news of the caravan's approaching, and had retired, nobody knew whether.

A REPORT was foon after fpread abroad at Cairo, but no one could ever learn whence it came, that the ambaſſador, arriving at Dongola, had been aſſaſſinated there. This, indeed, proved falſe, but was, in the mean time, a mournful preſage of the melancholy cataſtrophe that happened fooa afterwards.

M. DU ROULE arrived at Sennaar towards the end of May, and wrote at that time; but a packet of letters was after brought to the conſul at Cairo, bearing date the 18th of June. The ambaſſador there mentions, that he had been well received by the king of Sennaar, who was a young man, fond of ſtrangers; that particular attention had been ſhewn him by Sid Achmet-el-coom; or, as he ſhould have called him, Achmet Sid-el-coom, i. e. Achmet maſter of the houſehold. This officer, ſent by the king to viſit the baggage of the ambaſſador, could not help teſtifying his ſurpriſe to find it ſo inconſiderable, both in bulk and value..

HE ſaid the king had received letters from Cairo, informing him that he had twenty cheſts of ſilver along with him. Achmet likewiſe told him, that he himſelf had received information, by a letter under the hand and ſeal of the moſt reſpectable people of Cairo, warning him not to let M. du Roule paſs; for the intention of his journey into Abyſſinia was to prevail on Yaſous to attack Maſuah and Suakem, and take them from the Turks. Achmet would not ſuffer the bales intended for the king of Abyſſinia to be opened or viſited, but left them in the hands of the ambaſſador.

M. DU ROULE, however, in writing this account to the conful, intimated to him that he thought himſelf in danger,

ger, and declares that he did not believe there was on earth fo barbarous, brutal, and treacherous a people, as were the Nubians.

It happened that the king's troops had gained fome advantage over the rebellious Arabs, on which account there was a feftival at court, and M. du Roule thought himfelf obliged to exert himfelf in every thing which could add to the magnificence of the occafion. With this intention he fhaved his beard, and dreft himfelf like a European, and in this manner he received the vifit of the minifter Achmet. M. Macé, in a letter to the conful of the above date, complains of this novelty. He fays it fhocked every body; and that the * mirrors which multiplied and deformed the objects, made the lower forts of the people look upon the ambaffador and his company as forcerers.

Upon great feftivals, in moft Mahometan kingdoms, the king's wives have a privilege to go out of their apartments, and vifit any thing new that is to be feen. Thefe of the king of Sennaar are very ignorant, brutifh, fantaftic, and eafily offended. Had M. du Roule known the manners of the country, he would have treated thefe black majefties with ftrong fpirits, fweetmeats, or fcented waters; and he might then have fhewed them with impunity any thing that he pleafed.

But being terrified with the glaffes, and difgufted by his inattention, they joined in the common cry, that the ambaffador was a magician, and contributed all in their power to

ruin

---

* We have feen thefe were recommended by M. Maillet, the conful.

ruin him with the king; which, after all, they did prince complish, without the utmost repugnance and this was The fartheft length at firft they could get this prince to go was, to demand 3000 dollars of the ambaffador. This was exprefsly refufed, and private difguft followed.

M. du Roule being now alarmed for his own fafety, infifted upon liberty to fet out forthwith for Abyffinia. Leave was accordingly granted him, and after his baggage was loaded, and every thing prepared, he was countermanded by the king, and ordered to return to his own houfe. A few days after this he again procured leave to depart; which a fhort time after was again countermanded. At laft, on the 10th of November, a meffenger from the king brought him final leave to depart, which, having every thing ready for that purpofe, he immediately did.

The ambaffador walked on foot, with two country Chriftians on one hand, and Gentil his French fervant on the other. He refufed to mount on horfeback, but gave his horfe to a Nubian fervant to lead. M. Lipi, and M. Macé, the two drugomans, were both on horfeback. The whole company being now arrived in the middle of the large fquare before the king's houfe, the common place of execution for criminals, four blacks attacked the ambaffador, and murdered him with four ftrokes of fabres. Gentil fell next by the fame hands, at his mafter's fide. After him M. Lipi and the two Chriftians; the two latter protefting that they did not belong to the ambaffador's family.

M. du Roule died with the greateft magnanimity, fortitude, and refignation. Knowing his perfon was facred by

3   the

the law of nations, he difdained to defend it by any other means, remitting his revenge to the guardians of that law, and he exhorted all his attendants to do the fame. But M. Macè the Drugoman, young and brave, and a good horfeman, was not of the fheep kind, to go quietly to the flaughter. With his piftols he fhot two of the affaffins that attacked him, one after the other, dead upon the fpot; and was continuing to defend himfelf with his fword, when a horfeman, coming behind him, thruft him through the back with a lance, and threw him dead upon the ground.

Thus ended the fecond attempt of converting Abyffinia by an embaffy. A fcheme, if we believe M. de Maillet, which had coft government a confiderable expence, for in a memorial, of the 1ft of October 1706, concerning the death of M. du Roule, he makes the money and effects which he had along with him, when murdered, to amount to 200 purfes, or L.25,000 Sterling. This, however, is not probable; becaufe, in another place he fpeaks of M. du Roule's having demanded of him a fmall fupply of money while at Sennaar, which friar Jofeph, a capuchin, refufed to carry for him. Such a fupply would not have been neceffary if the ambaffador had with him fuch a fum as that already mentioned; therefore I imagine it was exaggerated, with a view to make the Turkifh bafha of Suakem quarrel with the king of Sennaar about the recovering it.

The friars, who were in numbers at Sennaar, left it immediately before the coming of M. du Roule. This they might have done without any bad intention towards him; they returned, however, immediately after his murder. This, I think, very clearly conftitutes them the authors of it.

it. For had they not been privy and promoters of the assassination, they would have fled with fear and abhorrence from a place where six of their brethren had been lately so treacherously slain, and were not yet buried, but their carcases abandoned to the fowls of the air, and the beasts of the field, and where they themselves, therefore, could have no assurance of safety.

THEY however pretended, first to lay the blame upon the king of Abyssinia, then upon the king of Sennaar, and then they divided it between them both. But Elias, arrived at Gondar, vindicated that prince, as we shall presently see, and the list of names taken at Sennaar; and a long series of correspondence, which afterwards came out, and a chain of evidence which was made public, incontestibly prove that the king of Sennaar was but an agent, and indeed an unwilling one, who two several times repented of his bloody design, and made M. du Roule return to his own house, to evade the execution of it.

THE blood then of this gallant and unfortunate gentleman undoubtedly lies upon the heads of the reformed Franciscan friars, and their brethren, the friars of the Holy Land. The interest of these two bodies, and a bigotted prince, such as Louis XIV then was, was more than sufficient to stop all inquiry, and hinder any vengeance to be taken on those holy assassins. But he who, unperceived, follows deliberate murther through all its concealments and darkness of its ways, in a few years required satisfaction for the blood of du Roule, at a time and place unforeseen, and unexpected.

WE

WE fhall now return to Gondar to king Yafous, who being recovered of his difeafe, and having difmiffed his phyfician, was preparing to fet out on a campaign againft the Galla.

YASOUS, for his firft wife, had married Ozoro Malacotawit, a lady of great family and connections in the province of Gojam. By her he had a fon, Tecla Haimanout, who was grown to manhood, and had hitherto lived in the moft dutiful affection and fubmiffion to his father, who, on his part, feemed to place unlimited confidence in his fon. He now gave a proof of this, not very common in the annals of Abyffinia, by leaving Tecla Haimanout behind him, at an age when he was fit to reign, appointing him Betwudet, with abfolute power to govern in his abfence. Yafous had a miftrefs whom he tenderly loved, a woman of great quality likewife, whofe name was Ozoro Keduftè. She was fifter to his Fit-Auraris, Agné, a very diftinguifhed and capable officer, and by her he had three children, David, Hannes, and Jonathan.

IT happened, while he was watching the motions of the Galla, news were brought that Ozoro Keduftè had been taken ill of a fever; and though, upon this intelligence, he difpofed his affairs fo as to return with all poffible expedition, yet when he came to Bercanté, the lady's houfe, he found that fhe was not only dead, but had been for fome time buried. All his prefence of mind now left him; he fell into the moft violent tranfport of wild defpair, and, ordering her tomb to be opened, he went down into it, taking his three fons along with him, and became fo frantic at the fight of the corpfe, that it was with the utmoft difficulty

culty he could be forced again to leave the fepulchre. He returned firft to Gondar, then he retired to an ifland in the lake Tzana, there to mourn his loft miftrefs.

But before this, Elias, ignorant of what had paffed at Sennaar, prefented M. de Maillet's letter to him, befeeching his leave for M. du Roule to enter Abyffinia, and come into his prefence. This he eafily procured : Yafous was fond of ftrangers ; and not only granted the requeft, but fent a man of his own to Sennaar with letters to the king to protect and defray the expences of the ambaffador to Gondar. This man, who had affairs of his own, loitered away a great deal of time in the journey, fo that Elias, upon firft hearing of the arrival of the ambaffador, fet out himfelf to meet him at Sennaar. The king, in the mean time, having finifhed his mourning, difpatched Badjerund Ouftas to his fon the Betwudet, at Gondar, ordering him forthwith to fend him a body of his houfehold troops to rendezvous on the banks of the lake, oppofite to the ifland Tchekla Wunze, where he then had his refidence.

It has been faid, contrary to all truth, by thofe who have wrote travels into this country, that fons born in marriage had the fame preference in fucceffion as they have in other countries.   But this, as I have faid, is entirely without foundation : For, in the firft place, there is no fuch thing as a regular marriage in Abyffinia ; all confifts in mere confent of parties.   But, allowing this to be regular, not only natural children, that is, thofe born in concubinage where no marriage was in contemplation; and adulterous baftards, that is, the fons of unmarried women by married men; and all manner of fons whatever, fucceed equally as well to the

crown

crown as to private inheritance; and there cannot be a more clear example of this than in the present king, who, although he had a son, Tecla Haimanout, born of the queen Malacotawit in wedlock, was yet succeeded by three baftard brothers, all sons of Yafous, born in adultery, that is, in the life of the queen. David and Hannes were sons of the king by his favourite Ozoro Keduftè; Bacuffa, by another lady of quality.

ALTHOUGH the queen, Malacotawit, had paffed over with feeming indifference the preference the king had given his miftrefs, Ozoro Keduftè, during her lifetime, yet, from a very unaccountable kind of jealoufy, fhe could not forgive thofe violent tokens of affection the king had fhewn fter her death, by going down with his fons and remaining with the body in the grave. Full of refentment for this, fhe her perfuaded her fon, Tecla Haimanout, that Yafous very perfuaded to deprive him of his fucceffion, to fend him and her, his mother, both to Wechnè, and place h·s baftard brother, David, fon of Ozoro Kedufié, upon the throne.

THe een had been very diligent in attaching to her the people people about the court. By her own friends, and the affiftance of the difcontented and banifhed monks, for had raifed a great army in Gojam under her brothers, Dermin and Paulus. Tecla Haimanout had fhewn great figns of wifdom and talents fdifcontented, and very much governingo himfclf fome of his father's oldeft and ableft father's

It was, therefore, agreed, in return to Yafous's meffage by Ouftas, to anfwer, That, after fo long a reign, and fo much bloodfhed, the king would do well to retire to fome convent for the reft of his life, and atone for the many great fins he had committed; and that he fhould leave the kingdom in the hands of his fon Tecla Haimanout, as the ancient king Caleb had refigned his crown into the hands of St Pantaleon in favour of his fon Guebra Mafcal. As it was not very fafe to deliver fuch a meffage to a king fuch as Yafous, it was therefore fent to him by a common foot-foldier, who could not be an object of refentment.

The king received it at Tchekla Wunze, the ifland in the lake Tzana, where he was then refiding. He anfwered with great fharpnefs, by the fame meffenger, " That he had been long informed who thefe were that had feduced his fon, Tecla Haimanout, at once from his duty to him as his father, and his allegiance as his fovereign; that though he did not hold them to be equal in fanctity to St Pantaleon, yet, fuch as they were, he propofed immediately to meet them at Gondar, and fettle there his fon's coronation."

This ironical meffage was perfectly underftood. Thofe of the court that were with Tecla Haimanout, and the inhabitants of the capital, met together, and bound themfelves by a folemn oath to live and die with their king Tecla Haimanout. The feverity of Yafous was well known; his provocation now was a juft one; and the meafure of vengeance that awaited them, every one concerned knew to be fuch that there was no alternative but death or victory.

NEITHER

Neither party were flack in preparations. Kafmati Honorius, governor of Damot, a veteran officer and old fervant of Yafous, collected a large body of troops and marched them down the weft fide of the lake. Yafous having there joined them, and putting himfelf at the head of his army, began his march, rounding the lake on its fouth fide towards Dingleber.

Neither did Tecla Haimanout delay a moment after hearing his father was in motion, but marched with his army from Gondar, attended with all the enfigns of royalty. He encamped at Bartcho, in that very field where Za Denghel was defeated and flain by his rebellious fubjects. Thinking this a poft ominous to kings, he refolved to wait for his father there, and give him battle.

The king, in his march through the low country of Dembea, was attacked by a putrid fever, very common in thofe parts, which fo increafed upon him that he was obliged to be carried back to Tchekla-Wunze. This accident difcouraged his whole party. His army, with Honorius, took the road to Gojam, but did not difperfe, awaiting the recovery of the king.

But the queen, Malacotawit, no fooner heard that Yafous her hufband was fick at Tchekla Wunze, than fhe fent to her fon Tecla Haimanout to leave his unwholefome ftation, and march back immediately to Gondar; and, as foon as he was returned, fhe difpatched her two brothers, Dermin and Paulus, with a body of foldiers and two Mahometan mufqueteers, who, entering the ifland Tchekla Wunze by furprife, fhot and difabled the king while fitting on a couch;

3 T 2   immediately

immediately after which, Dermin thruft him through with a fword. They attempted afterwards to burn the body, in order to avoid the ill-will the fight of it muft occafion: In this, however, they were prevented by the priefts of the ifland and the neighbouring nobility, who took poffeffion of the body, wafhed it, and performed all the rites of fepulture, then carried it in a kind of triumph, with every mark of magnificence due to the burial of a king, interring it in the fmall ifland of Mitraha, where lay the body of all his anceftors, and where I have feen the body of this king ftill entire.

Nor did the prince his fon, Tecla Haimanout, now king, difcourage the people in the refpect they voluntarily paid to his father. On the contrary, that parricide himfelf fhewed every outward mark of duty, to the which inwardly his heart had been long a ftranger.

Poncet, who faw this king, gives this character of him: He fays he was a man very fond of war, but averfe to the fhedding of blood. However this may appear a contradiction, or faid for the fake of the antithefis, it really was the true character of this prince, who, fond of war, and in the perpetual career of victory, did, by pufhing his conquefts as far as they could go, inevitably occafion the fpilling of much blood. Yet, when his army was not in the field, though he detected a multitude of confpiracies among priefts and other people at home, whofe lives in confequence were forfeited to the law, he very rarely, either from his own motives, or the perfuafion of others, could be induced to inflict capital punifhments though often ftrongly provoked to it.

Upon

Upon his death the people unanimoufly gave to him the name of Tallac, which fignifies *the Great*, a name he has ever fince enjoyed unimpeached in the Abyffinian annals, or hiftory of his country, from the which this his reign is taken.

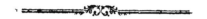

TECLA HAIMANOUT I.

From 1704 to 1706.

Writes in Favour of Du Roule—Defeats the Rebels—Is affaffinated while hunting.

ELIAS the Armenian, of whom we have already fpoken, and who was charged with letters of protection from Yafous to meet M. du Roule at Sennaar, had reached within three days journey of that capital when he heard that king Yafous was affaffinated. Terrified at the news, he returned in the utmoft hafte to Gondar; and prefented the letters, which had been written by Yafous, to be renewed by his fon, king Tecla Haimanout. Tecla Haimanout read his father's letters, and approved of their contents, ordering them to be copied in his own name; and Elias without delay fet out with them. I have inferted a tranflation of thefe letters, which were originally written in Arabic, and feem to

me

me to be of the few that are authentic among thofe many which have been publifhed as coming from Abyffinia.

" The king Tecla Haimanout, fon of the king of the
" church of Ethiopia, king of a thoufand churches,

" On the part of the powerful auguft king, arbiter of
" nations, fhadow of God upon earth, the guide of kings
" who profefs the religion of the Meffiah, the moft power-
" ful of Chriftian kings, he that maintains order between
" Mahometans and Chriftians, protector of the boundaries
" of Alexandria, obferver of the commandments of the go-
" fpel, defcended of the line of the prophets David and Solo-
" mon,—may the bleffing of Ifrael be upon our prophet and
" upon them.—To the king Baady, fon of the king Ounfa,
" may his reign be full of happinefs, being a prince endow-
" ed with thefe rare qualities that deferve the higheft
" praifes as governing his kingdom with diftinguifhed wif-
" dom, and by an order full of equity.—The king of France,

4   " who

* This is not the king's feal. It is the invention of fome Mahometan employed to write the letters.

" who is a Chriftian, wrote a letter feven or eight years ago,
" by which he fignified to me, that he wifhed to open a
" trade for the advantage of his fubjects and of mine, which
" requeft we have granted. We come at prefent to under-
" ftand, that he has fent us prefents by a man whofe name
" is du Roule, who has likewife feveral others along with
" him, and that thefe people have been arrefted at your
" town of Sennaar. We require of you, therefore, to fet
" them immediately at liberty, and to fuffer them to come
" to us with all the marks of honour, and that you fhould
" pay regard to the ancient friendfhip which has always
" fubfifted between our predeceffors, fince the time of the
" *king of Sedgid* and the *king of Kim*, to the prefent day. We
" alfo demand of you to fuffer all the fubjects of the king of
" France to pafs, and all thofe that come with letters of his
" conful who is at Cairo, as all fuch Frenchmen come for
" trade only, being of the fame religion with us. We likewife
" recommend to you, that you permit to pafs freely, all
" French Chriftians, Cophts, and Syrians who follow our
" rites, obferving our religion, and who intend coming into
" our country; and that you do not fuffer any of thofe
" who are contrary to our religion to pafs, fuch as the monk
" Jofeph, and his companions, whom you may keep at Sen-
" naar, it being in no fhape our intention to fuffer them to
" come into our dominions, where they would occafion
" troubles, as being enemies to our faith. God grant you
" your defires."—Wrote the 10th of Zulkadè, Anno 1118, *i. e.*,
the 21ft of January 1706.

☞ THE direction is—" To king Baady, fon of king
" Ounfa, may God favour him with his grace."

THE

THE firſt thing I remark upon this letter is, the mention of the ancient peace and friendſhip which ſubſiſted between the predeceſſors of theſe two princes now correſponding. It was a friendſhip, he ſays, that had endured from the time of the king of *Sedgid*, and the king of *Kim*, to the preſent day.

THE kingdom of Sennaar, as we ſhall ſee, was but a modern one, and recently eſtabliſhed by conqueſt over the Arabs. Therefore the kingdoms of *Sedgid* and of *Kim* were, before that conqueſt, places whence this black nation came that had eſtabliſhed their ſovereignty at Sennaar by conqueſt : from which, therefore, I again infer, there never was any war, conqueſt, or tribute between Abyſſinia and that ſtate.

THE Arabs, who fed their flocks near the frontiers of the two countries, were often plundered by the kings of Abyſſinia making deſcents into Atbara; but this was never reckoned a violation of peace between the two ſovereigns. On the contrary, as the motive of the Arabs, for coming ſouth into the frontiers of Abyſſinia, was to keep themſelves independent, and out of the reach of Sennaar, whe the king of Abyſſinia fell upon them there, he was underſtood to do that monarch ſervice, by driving them down farther within his reach. The Baharnagaſh has been always at war with them ; they are tributary to him for eating his graſs and drinking his water, and nothing that he ever does to them gives any trouble or inquietude to Sennaar. It is interpreted as maintaining his ancient dominion over the Shepherds, thoſe of Sennaar being a new power, and accounted as uſurpers.

    M. DE

M. DE MAILLET, nor M. le Grande his hiſtorian, have not thought fit to explain who the monk Joſeph was mentioned in this letter. Now it is certain, that, when Murat and Poncet were returned from Abyſſinia, there was a miſſionary of the minor friars, who arrived in Ethiopia, had an audience of the king, and wrote a letter in his name to the pope, wherein he has foiſted many improbabilities and falſehoods; and concludes with declaring on the part of Yaſous, that he ſubmits to the ſee of Rome in the ſame manner the kings his predeceſſors had ſubmitted. He makes Yaſous ſpeak Latin, too; and it is perfectly plain from the * whole letter, that, though he writes it himſelf, he cannot conceal that the king Yaſous wanted him very much away, and was very uneaſy at his ſtay at Gondar. Who this was we know not, but ſuppoſe it was one of thoſe aſſaſſins of M. du Roule, carrying on a private intrigue without participation of the conſul, ſome of whom were afterwards detected in Walkayt in the reign of David IV.

As for Elias, the forerunner of the French embaſſy, now become the only remains of it, he continued in Abyſſinia (to judge by his letter) in great poverty, till the year 1718, immediately after which he went over to Arabia Felix, and firſt wrote from Mocha to M. de Maillet conſul at Çairo, as it will appear in the reign of David IV. where I have inſerted his letter; that written to M. du Roule in the name of Yaſous, that of Tecla Haimanout to the Baſha and Divan of Cairo, I have now here inſerted, becauſe I have advanced facts founded upon them.

* See the letter itſelf, it is the laſt in Le Grande's book, and in Latin, if I remember rightly.

TRANSLATION *of an* ARABIC LETTER *from the* KING *of* ABYSSI-
NIA *to* M. DU ROULE.

" THE king Tecla Haimanout, king of the eſtabliſhed
" church, ſon of the king of a thouſand churches.

" THIS letter cometh forth from the venerable, auguſt
" king, who is the ſhadow of God, guide of Chriſtian prin-
" ces that are in the world, the moſt powerful of the Naza-
" rean kings, obſerver of the commandments of the goſpel,
" protector of the confines of Alexandria, he that maintain-
" eth order between Mahometans and Chriſtians, deſcended
" from the family of the prophets David and Solomon, up-
" on whom being the bleſſings of Iſrael, may God make his
" happineſs eternal, and his power perpetual, and protect his
" arms—So be it.—To his excellence the moſt virtuous and
" moſt prudent man du Roule, a Frenchman ſent to us,
" may God preſerve him, and make him arrive at a degree
" of eminence—So be it.—Elias, your interpreter whom you
" ſent before you, being arrived here, has been well receiv-
" ed. We have underſtood that you are ſent to us on the
" part of the king of France our brother, and are ſurpriſed
" that you have been detained at Sennaar. We ſend to you
" at preſent a letter for king Baady, in order that he may
" ſet you at liberty, and not do you any injury, nor to thoſe
" that are with you, but may behave in a manner that is
" proper both for you and to us, according to the religion
" of Elias that you ſent, who is a Syrian ; and all thoſe that
" may come after you from the king of France our brother,
" or his conſul at Cairo, ſhall be well received, whether they
" be

" be ambaffadors or private merchants, becaufe we love
" thofe that are of our religion. We receive with pleafure
" thofe who do not oppofe our laws, and we fend away thofe
" that do oppofe them. For this reafon we did not receive
" immediately Jofeph * with all his companions, not choo-
" fing that fuch fort of people fhould appear in our prefence,
" nor intending that they fhould pafs Sennaar, in order to
" avoid troubles which may occafion the death of many;
" but with refpect to you, have nothing to fear, you may
" come in all fafety, and you fhall be received with ho-
" nour."—Written the 10th of the month Zulkadé, Anno
1118, *i. e.* the 21ft of January of the year 1706.

    ☞ THE addrefs is—" Let the prefent be delivered to M.
" du Roule at the town of Sennaar."

I SHALL only obferve upon this letter, that all the priefts,
who had flocked to Sennaar before M. du Roule arrived
there, difappeared upon his near approach to that city, after
having prepared the mifchief which directly followed. And,
no fooner was the murder, which they before concerted, committed, than they all flocked back again as if invited to a
feftival. M. de Maillet fpeaks of feveral of them in his letters, where he complains of the murder of du Roule, and
fays that they were then on their way to enter Abyffinia.
Of thefe probably was this Jofeph, whom Tecla Haimanout
ftrictly prohibits to come farther than Sennaar, having feen
what his father had written concerning him in the firft letters Elias was charged with.

3 U 2

OTHERS

---

* Vid. the letter as quoted above.

OTHERS are mentioned in Elias's letter to the conful as having been in Abyffinia. He calls them thofe of the league of Michael and Samuel, of whom we fhall fpeak afterwards. But, even though the French conful had ordered his nation to drive all the fubjects of Sennaar from their houfes and fervice, none of thefe miffionaries were afraid to return and abide at Sennaar, becaufe they knew the murder of the ambaffador was the work of their own hands, and, without their inftigation, would never have been committed.

THE unlucky meffenger, Elias, was again about to enter Sennaar, when he received information that du Roule was affaffinated. If he had fled haftily from this inaufpicious place upon the murder of Yafous, his hafte was now ten-fold, as he confidered himfelf engaged in the fame circum-ftances that had involved M. du Roule's attendants in his misfortunes.

THE king, upon hearing the account given by Elias of the melancholy fate of the ambaffador at Sennaar, was fo exafperated, that he gave immediate orders for recalling fuch of his troops as he had permitted to go to any confi-derable diftance ; and, in a council held for that purpofe, he declared, that he confidered the death of M. du Roule as an affront that immediately affected his crown and dignity. He was, therefore, determined not to pafs it over, but to make the king of Sennaar fenfible that he, as well as all the other kings upon earth, knew the neceffity of obferving the law of nations, and the bad confequence of perpetual retaliations that muft follow the violation of it. In the mean time, thinking that the bafha of Cairo was the caufe of this, he wrote the following letter to him.

TRANSLATION

Translation *of an* Arabic Letter *from the* King *of* Abyssinia *to the* Basha *and* Divan *of* Cairo.

" To the Pacha, and Lords of the Militia of Cairo.

" On the part of the king of Abyssinia, the king Tecla Haimanout, son of the king of the church of Abyssinia.

" On the part of the august king, the powerful arbiter of
" nations, shadow of God upon earth, the guide of kings
" who profess the religion of the Messiah, the most power-
" ful of all Christian kings, he who maintains order between
" Mahometans and Christians, protector of the confines of
" Alexandria, observer of the commandments of the gospel,
" heir from father to son of a most powerful kingdom, de-
" scended of the family of David and Solomon,—may the
" blessing of Israel be upon our prophet, and upon them!
" may his happiness be durable, and his greatness lasting,
" and may his powerful army be always feared.—To the
" most powerful lord, elevated by his dignity, venerable by
" his merits, distinguished by his strength and riches among
" all Mahometans, the refuge of all those that reverence
" him, who by his prudence governs and directs the armies
" of the noble empire, and commands his confines; victori-
" ous viceroy of Egypt, the four corners of which shall be
" always respected and defended:—so be it.—And to all the
" distinguished princes, judges, men of learning, and other
" officers whose business it is to maintain order and good
" government and to all commanders in general, may God
" preserve them all in their dignities, in the noblenefs of

I   their

" their health. You are to know that our anceſtors never
" bore any envy to other kings, nor did they ever occaſion
" them any trouble, or ſhew them any mark of hatred. On the
" contrary, they have, upon all occaſions, given them proofs of
" their friendſhips, aſſiſting them generouſly, relieving them
" in their neceſſities, as well in what concerns the caravan
" and pilgrims of Mecca in Arabia Felix, as in the Indies, in
" *Perſia*, and other diſtant and out-of-the-way places, alſo by
" protecting diſtinguiſhed perſons in every urgent neceſſity.

    " NEVERTHELESS, the king of France our brother, who
" profeſſes our religion and our law, having been induced
" thereto, by ſome advances of friendſhip on our part ſuch
" as are proper, ſent an ambaſſador to us ; I under-
" ſtand that you cauſed arreſt him at Sennaar, and alſo ano-
" ther by name Murat, the Syrian, whom you did put in
" priſon alſo, though he was ſent to that ambaſſador on
" our part, and by thus doing, you have violated the law of
" nations, as ambaſſadors of kings ought to be at liberty to
" go wherever they will ; and it is a general obligation to
" treat them with honour, and not to moleſt or detain them,
" nor ſhould they be ſubject to pay cuſtoms, or any ſort of
" preſents. We could very ſoon repay you in kind, if we
" were inclined to revenge the inſult you have offered to
" the man Murat ſent on our part; the Nile would be ſuffi-
" cient to puniſh you, ſince God hath put into our power
" his fountain, his outlet, and his increaſe, and that we can
" diſpoſe of the ſame to do you harm ; for the preſent we
" demand of, and exhort you to deſiſt from any future vex-
" ations towards our envoys, and not diſturb us by detain-
" ing thoſe who ſhall be ſent towards you, but you ſhall
" let them paſs and continue their route without delay,

3   " coming

" coming and going wherever they will freely for their
" own advantage, whether they are our fubjects or French-
" men, and whatever you fhall do to or for them, we fhall
" regard as done to or for ourfelves."

  ☞ THE addrefs is—" To the bafha, princes, and lords
 " governing the town of great Cairo, may God favour
 " them with his goodnefs."

THERE are feveral things very remarkable in this letter.
The king of Abyffinia values himfelf, and his predeceffors,
upon never having molefted or troubled any of his neighbours who were kings, nor borne any envy towards them.
We are not then to believe what we fee often in hiftory,
that there was frequent war between Sennaar and Abyffinia,
or that Sennaar was tributary to Abyffinia. That ftripe of
country, inhabited by the Shangalla, would, in this cafe,
have been firft conquered. But it is more probable, that
the great difference of climate which immediately takes
place between the two kingdoms, the great want of water
on the frontiers, barriers placed there by the hand of Nature, have been the means of keeping thefe kingdoms from
having any mutual concerns ; and fo, indeed, we may guefs
by the utter filence of the books, which never mention any
war at Sennaar till the beginning of the reign of Socinios.

I APPREHEND, that protecting diftinguifhed perfons upon
great occafions, alludes to the children of the king of Sennaar, who frequently fly after the death of their father to
Abyffinia for protection, it being the cuftom of that ftate

               to

' Abdelcader, fon of Ounfa, retired here.

to murder all the brothers of the prince that fucceeds, inftead of fending them to a mountain, as they do in Abyffinia.

THE next thing remarkable is his protection of the pilgrims who go to Mecca, and the merchants that go to India. Several caravans of both fet out yearly from his kingdom, all Mahometans, fome of whom go to Mecca for religion, the others to India, by Mocha, to trade. But it is not poffible to underftand how he is to protect the trade in Perfia, with which country he certainly has had no fort of concern thefe 800 years, nor has it been in that time poffible for him either to moleft or protect a Perfian. What, therefore, I would fuppofe, is, that the king has made ufe of the common phrafe which univerfally obtains here both in writing and converfation, calling Ber el Ajam the Weft, and Ber el Arab the Eaft coaft of the Red Sea.—Ber el Ajam, in the language of the country, is the coaft where there is water or rain, in oppofition to the Tehama, or oppofite fhore of Arabia, where there is no water. The Greeks and Latins tranflated this word into their own language, but did not underftand it; only from the found they called it Azamia, from Ajam. Now Ajam, or Ber el Ajam, is the name of Perfia alfo ; and the French interpreter fays, the king of Abyffinia protects the caravans of Perfia; when he fhould fay, the caravans, going through Ber el Ajam, the Azamia of the ancients, to embark at the two ports Suakem and Mafuah, both in the country of that name.

THE next thing to remark here is, that the king acknowledges Murat to be his ambaffador; and it is the arrefting him, which we have feen was done at the inftance of M. de
Maillet

Maillet collusively, that the king says was a violation of the law of nations; and it was this insult, done to Murat his ambassador, that he all along complains of, not that offered to du Roule, which he leaves to the king of France; for he says expressly, if he was to starve, or destroy them all, by stopping the Nile from coming into Egypt, it would be on account of the insult offered to Murat, the envoy, or man, sent on his part to France. It is plain, therefore, that M. de Maillet persecuted the poor Syrian very wrongfully, and that in no one instance, from first to last, was he ever in the right concerning that embassy.

This step, which justice dictated, was not without its reward; for Tecla Haimanout, who had assembled his army on this account sooner than he otherwise intended, found immediately after, that a rival and rebel prince, Amda Sion, was set up against him by the friends of his father Yasous, and that he had been privately collecting troops, intending to take him by surprise, when he was, however, at the head of his army ready to give him battle.

The first thing the king did was to dispatch a large body of troops to reinforce Dermin, governor of Gojam, and to him he sent positive orders to force Amda Sion to fight wherever he should find him, while he, with the royal army, came forward with all expedition to keep the people in awe, and prevent them from joining his rival.

Amda Sion, on the other hand, lost no time. From Ibaba, through Maitsha, he marched straight to Gondar. Being arrived at the king's house at Dingleber, he sat down on the throne with the ensigns of royalty about him, and there appointed feveral officers that were moft needed, in the army, the provinces, and about his perfon. During his ftay here, news were brought that Dermin had followed him ftep by ftep in the very track he had marched, and laid the whole country wafte that had fhewn him any countenance or favour. Amda Sion's heart feemed to fail him upon this; for he left Dingleber, croffed the ford at Delakus, and endeavoured to pafs Dermin, by keeping on the weft fide of the Nile, and on the low road by which he returned to Ibaba.

DERMIN, well-informed as to his motions, and perfectly inftructed in the fituation of the country, inftead of paffing him, turned fhort upon his front, croffing the Nile at Fagitta, and forced him to an engagement in the plain country of Maitfha. The battle, though it was obftinately fought by the rebels, ended in a complete victory in favour of the king. Thofe among the rebels who moft diftinguifhed themfelves were the banifhed monks, the greateft part of whom were flain fighting defperately. Among thefe, were Abba Welleta Chriftos, Tobias and his brother Abba Nicolaus, who had been ringleaders in the late religious difputes in the time of Yafous, and were now chiefs of the rebellion againft his fon.

THE greateft part of the lofs fell upon the common men of Gojam, of the clans Elmana and Denfa. No man of note among them was loft; only Amda Sion, who fell at their head in the beginning of the engagement, fighting with all the bravery that could be expected from a man in his circumftances. The rebel army was entirely difperfed,

On

On the king's fide no man of confideration was flain, but Anaftè, fon of Ozoro Sabel Wenghel.

After having reinforced Dermin, the firft thing the king did was to fend three of his brothers, David, Hannes, and Jonathan, to be imprifoned on the mountain of Wechnè. He then marched with his army from Gondar ; and, being ignorant of what had happened, he difpatched his mafter of the horfe, by way of Dingleber, to join Kafmati Dermin, in cafe he had not ftill been ftrong enough to fight the rebels. With his main army he took the road to Tedda, intending to proceed to Gojam ; but, by the way, was informed that Dermin had defeated and flain his rival Amda Sion : and he had fcarce croffed the Nile at Dara, when another meffenger arrived with news that Dermin had alfo come up with Kafmati Honorius and his army on the banks of the Nile, at Goutto, had entirely defeated and flain him, together with his principal officers, and difperfed the whole army. Upon this the king marched towards Ibaba, and was there joined by Dermin, when great rejoicing and feafting enfued for feveral days.

On this occafion the king crowned his mother Malacotawit, conferring upon her the dignity and title of Iteghè ; the confequence of which ftation I have often defcribed. Having now no longer enemies to fear, he was perfuaded, by fome of his favourites, firft to difmifs Dermin and his army, then all the troops that had joined him, and go with a few of his attendants, or court, to hunt the buffalo in the neighbouring country, Idi ; which council the young prince too rafhly adopted, fufpecting no treafon.

WHILE

WHILE the hunting-match lasted, a conspiracy was formed by Gueber Mo, his two brothers, Palambaras, Hannes, and several others, old officers belonging to the late king Yasous, who saw that he intended, one by one, to weed them out of the way as soon as safely he could, and that the whole power and favour was at last to fall into the hands of the Iteghé, and her brothers Dermin and Paulus. Accordingly one morning, the conspirators having surrounded him while riding, one of them thrust him through the body with a sword, and threw him from his mule upon the earth. They then laid his body upon a horse, and, with all possible expedition, carried him to the house of Azena Michael, where he arrived yet alive, but died immediately upon being taken from the horse. Badjerund Oustas, and some others of his father's old officers, who had attached themselves to him after his father's death, took the body of the king and buried it in Quebran.

As soon as this assassination was known, the master of the horse, with the few troops that he could gather together, came to the palace, and took a young son of Tecla Haimanout, aged only four years, whom he proclaimed king, and the Iteghé, Malacotawit, regent of the kingdom. But Badjerund Oustas, and those who had not been concerned in the murder of either king, went straight to the mountain of Wechné, and brought thence Tifilis, that is Theophilus, son to Hannes, and brother to the late king Yasous, whom they crowned at Emfras, and called him, by his inauguration name, Atserar Segued.

TIFILIS,

T I F I L I S.

From 1706 to 1709.

Diffembles with his Brother's Affaffins—Execution of the Regicides—Re-
bellion and. Death of Tigi.

THEOPHILUS, a few days after his coronation, having called the whole court and clergy together, declared to them, that his faith upon the difputable point con-
ce: ning our Saviour's incarnation was different from that of
his brother Yafous, or that of his nephew Tecla Haimanout;
but in every refpect conformable to that of the monks of Gojam, followers of Abba Euftathius, and that of the Iteghè,
Malacotawit, Dermin, and Paulus. A violent clamour was inftantly raifed againft the king.by the priefts of Debra Libanos, as having forfaken the religious principles of his predeceffors. But the king was inflexible; and this ingratiated
him more with the inhabitants of Gojam. . Not many days
after, the king arrefted the mafter of the horfe, Johannes Palambaras, the Betwudet Tigi, and feveral others, all fuppofed to be concerned in the murder of the late king, and
confined.them in feveral places and prifons.

THIS

THIS laſt action of the king entirely relieved the minds of all the friends of Tecla Haimanout from any further fear of being called to account for the murder of Yaſous; and, in conſequence of this, the queen Malocotawit, with her brothers Dermin and Paulus, and all the murderers of the laᵗe king Yaſous, came to Gondar that ſame winter to do homage to Theophilus, whom they now thought their greateſt protector.

BUT the wiſe and ſagacious king had kept his ſecret in his own boſom. All his behaviour hitherto had been on-ly diſſimulation, to induce his brother's murderers to come within his power. And no ſooner did he ſee that he had ſucceeded in this, than the very firſt day, while they were yet at audience, he ordered an officer, in his own preſence, to arreſt firſt the queen, and then her two brothers Dermin and Paulus. He gave the ſame directions concerning the reſt of the conſpirators, who were all ſcattered about Gon-dar, eating, drinking, and fearing nothing, but rejoicing at the happy days they had promiſed themſelves, and were now to ſee: he ordered the whole of them, amounting to 37 perſons, many of theſe of the firſt rank, to be all execu-ted that ſame forenoon.

HE began with the queen, who was taken immediately from his preſence and hanged by the common hangman on the tree before the palace gate; the firſt of her rank, it is believed, that ever died ſo vile a death, either in Abyſ-ſinia or any other country, the hiſtory of which has come down to our hands. Dermin and Paulus were firſt carried to the tree to ſee their ſiſter's execution; after which, one after the other, they were thruſt through with ſwords, the

4   weapon

weapon with which they had wounded the late king Yafous. But the two Mahometans were fhot with mufkets, it
having been in that manner they had ended the late king's
life, after Dermin had wounded him with a fword. As they
had committed high treafon, none of the bodies of thefe
traitors were allowed to be buried; they were hewn in fmall
pieces with knives, and ftrewed about the ftreets, to be eat
by the hyænas and dogs; a moft barbarous and offenfive
cuftom, to which they ftrictly adhere to this very day.

AFTER having thus taken ample vengeance for the murder of his brother Yafous, Theophilus did not ftop here.
Tecla Haimanout was, it is true, a parricide, but he was
likewife a king, and his nephew; nor did it feem juft to
Theophilus that it fhould be left in the will of private fubjects, after having acknowledged Tecla Haimanout as their
fovereign, to choofe a time afterwards, in which they were
to cut him off for a crime which, however great, had not
hindered them from fwearing allegiance to him at his acceffion, and entering into his fervice at the time when it
was recently committed. He, therefore, ordered all the regicides in cuftody to be put to death; and fent circular letters to the feveral governors, that they fhould obferve the
fame rule as to all thofe directly concerned in the murder
of his nephew Tecla Haimanout, who fhould be found in
places under their command.

TIGI, formerly Betwudet, had been imprifoned in Hamazen, a fmall diftrict near the Red Sea, under the government
of Abba Saluce. This man, by birth a Galla, had efcaped
from Hamazen, and collected a confiderable army of the different tribes of his nation, Liban, Kalkend, and Baffo; and,
having

having found one that pretended to be of the royal blood, he proclaimed him king, and put his army in motion.

Upon the first news of this revolt, the king, though attended with few troops, immediately left Gondar, ordering all those whose duty it was to join him at Ibaba. Having there collected a little army, he marched immediately for the country of the Baffo, destroying every thing with fire and sword. Tigi, in the mean time, by forced marches came to Ibaba, where he committed all sorts of cruelties without distinction of age or sex. The cries of the sufferers reached the king, who turned immediately back to the relief of Ibaba; and, not discouraged by his enemy's great superiority of number, offered battle to them as soon as he arrived. Nor did Tigi and his Galla refuse it; but, on the 28th day of March 1709, a very obstinate engagement ensued; where, though the king was inferior in forces, yet being himself warlike and active, he was so well seconded by his troops that Baffo and Liban were almost entirely cut off.

In the field of battle there was a church, built by the late king Yasous after a victory gained there over the Pagans, whence it had the name it then bore, Debra Mawea, or the *Mountain of Victory*. A large body of these Galla, seeing that all went against them in the field, fled to the church for a sanctuary, trusting to be protected from the fury of the soldiers by the holiness of the place, and they so far judged well; for the king's troops, though they surrounded the church on every side, did not offer to break into it, or molest the enemy that had sheltered themselves within. Theophilus, informed of this scruple of his soldiers, immediately rode up to them, crying out, "That the church was

2   " defiled

" defiled by the entrance of so many Pagans, and no long-
" er fit for Christian worship, that they should therefore im-
" mediately put fire to it, and he would build a nobler one
" in its place." The soldiers obeyed without further hesi-
tation; and, with cotton wads wrapt about the balls of their
guns, they set fire to the thatch, with which every church
in Abyssinia is covered. The whole was instantly consumed,
and every creature within it perished. Many principal officers and men of the best families on the king's side, Billetana Gueta, Sana Denghel, and Billetana Gueta Kirubel,
Ayto Stephenous, son of Ozoro Salla of Nara, all men of
great consideration, were slain that day. What came of the
rebel prince was never known. Tigi, with his two sons, fled
from the field; but they were met by a peasant, who took
them prisoners first; and, after discovering who they were,
put them all three to death, and brought their heads to the
king.

AFTER so severe a rebuke, the Galla, on both sides of the
Nile, seemed disposed to be quiet, and the king thereupon
returned to Gondar amidst the acclamations of his soldiers
and subjects; but scarce had he arrived in the capital when
he was taken ill of a fever, and died on the 2d of September,
and was buried at Tedda, after a reign of three years and
three months.

O U S T A S.

From 1709 to 1714.

Ufurps the Crown—Addicted to hunting—Account of the Shangalla—
Active and bloody Reign—Entertains Catholic Priests privately—Falls
fick and dies; but how, uncertain.

IT has been already obferved in the courfe of this hiftory, that the Abyffinians, from a very ancient tradition, attribute the foundation of their monarchy to Menilek fon of Solomon, by the queen of Saba, or Azab, rendered in the Vulgate, the Queen of the fouth. The annals of this country mention but two interruptions to have happened, in the lineal fucceffion of the heirs-male of Solomon. The firft about the year 960, in the reign of Del Naad, by Judith queen of the Falafha, of which revolution we have already fpoken fufficiently. The fecond interruption happened at the period to which we have now arrived in this hiftory, and owed its origin, not to any misfortune that befel the royal family as in the maffacre of Judith, but feemed to be brought about by the peculiar circumftances of the times, from a well-founded attention to felf-prefervation.

YASOUS

YASOUS the Great, after a long and glorious reign, had been murdered by his son Tecla Haimanout. Two years after, this parricide fell in the same manner. The affaffination of two princes, so nearly related, and in so short a time, had involved, from different motives, the greatest part of the noble families of the kingdom, either in the crime itself, or in the suspicion of aiding and abetting it.

UPON the death of Tecla Haimanout, Tifilis, or Theophilus, brother of Yasous, had been brought from the mountain, and placed on the throne as successor to his nephew ; this prince was scarcely crowned when he made some very severe examples of the murderers of his brother, and he seemed privately taking informations that would have reached the whole of them, had not death put an end to his inquiries and to his justice.

THE family of king Yasous was very numerous on the mountain. It was the favourite store whence both the soldiery and the citizens chose to bring their princes. There were, at the very instant, many of his sons princes of great hopes and of proper ages. Nothing then was more probable than that the prince, now to succeed, would be of that family, and, as such, interested in pursuing the same measures of vengeance on the murderers of his father and of his brother as the late king Theophilus had done ; and how far, or to whom this might extend, was neither certain nor safe to trust to.

THE time was now past when the nobles vied with each other who should be the first to steal away privately, or go with open force, to take the new king from the mountain,

and

and bring him to Gondar, his capital: A backwardnefs was vifible in the behaviour of each of them, becaufe in each one's breaft the fear was the fame.

In fo uncommon a conjuncture and difpofition of men's minds, a fubject had the ambition and boldnefs to offer himfelf for king, and he was accordingly elected.   This was Ouftas *, fon of Delba Yafous, by a daughter of the late king of that name; and Abyffinia now faw, for the fecond time, a ftranger feated on the throne of Solomon.   Ouftas was a man of undifputed merit, and had filled the greateft offices in the ftate.   He had been Badjerund, or mafter of the houfehold, to the late king Yafous.   Tecla Haimanout, who fucceeded, had made him governor of Samen; and though, in the next reign, he had fallen into difgrace with Theophilus, this ferved but to aggrandize him more, as he was very foon after reftored to favour, and by this very prince raifed to the dignity of Ras, the firft place under the king, and invefted at once with the government of two provinces, Samen and Tigré. He was, at the death of Theophilus, the greateft fubject in Abyffinia; one ftep higher fet him on the throne, and the circumftances of the time invited him to take it.   He had every quality of body and mind requifite for a king; but the conftitution of his country had made it unlawful for him to reign.   He took, upon his inauguration, the name of Tzai Segued.

Oustas, though a new king, followed the cuftoms of the ancient monarchs of Abyffinia; for that very reafon was
                                                              unwilling

---

* It fignifies Juftus,

unwilling to add novelty to novelty, and it has been a con
ftant practice with thefe to make a public hunting-match
the firft expedition of their reign. On thefe occafions the
king, attended by all the great officers of ftate, whofe merit
and capacity are already acknowledged, reviews his young
nobility, who all appear to the beft advantage as to arms,
horfes, and equipage, with the greateft number of fervants
and attendants. The fcene of this hunting is always in the
Kolla, crowded with an immenfe number of the largeft
and fierceft wild beafts, elephants, rhinoceros, lions, leopards,
panthers, and buffaloes fiercer than them all, wild boaɪs,
wild affes, and many varieties of the deer kind.

As foon as the game is roufed, and forced out of the
wood by the footmen and dogs, they all fingly, or feveral together, according to the fize of the beaft, or as ftrength and
ability in managing their horfes admit, attack the animal
upon the plain with long pikes or fpears, or two javelins
in their hands. The king, unlefs very young, fits on horfeback on a rifing ground, furrounded by the graver fort,
who point out to him the names of thofe of the nobility
that are happy enough to diftinguifh themfelves in his
fight. The merit of others is known by report.

EACH young man brings before the king's tent, as a tro-
phy, a part of the beaft he has flain; the head and fkin of
a lion or leopard; the fcalp or horns of a deer; the private
parts of an elephant; the tail of a buffalo, or the horn of a
rhinoceros. The great trouble, force, and time necceffary
to take out the teeth of the elephant, feldom make them
ready to be prefented with the reft of the fpoils; fire, too, is
neceffary for loofing them from the jaw. The head of a

ɪ   boar

boar is brought ftuck upon a lance; but is not touched, as being unclean.

THE elephant's teeth are the king's perquifites. Of thefe round ivory rings are turned for bracelets, and a quantity of them always brought by him to be diftributed among the moft deferving in the field, and kept ever after as certificates of gallant behaviour. Nor is this mark attended with honour alone. Any man who fhall from the king, queen-regent, or governor of a province, receive fo many of thefe rings as fhall cover his arm down to his wrift, appears before the twelve judges on a certain day, and there, laying down his arm with thefe rings upon it, the king's cook breaks every one in its turn with a kind of kitchen-cleaver, whereupon the judges give him a certificate, which proves that he is entitled to a territory, whofe revenue muft exceed 20 ounces of gold, and this is never either refufed or delayed. All the different fpecies of game, however, are not equally rated. He that flays a Galla, or Shangalla, man to man, is entitled to two rings; he that flays an elephant to two; a rhinoceros, two; a giraffa, on account of its fpeed, and to encourage horfemanfhip, two; a buffalo, two; a lion, two; a leopard, one; two boars, whofe tufks are grown, one; and one for every four of the deer kind.

GREAT difputes conftantly arife about the killing of thefe beafts; to determine which, and prevent feuds and quarrels, a council fits every evening, in which is an officer called *Dimfhafha*, or *Red Cap*, from a piece of red filk he wears upon his forehead, leaving the top of his head bare, for no perfon is allowed to cover his head entirely except the king, the twelve judges, and dignified priefts. This of-

3

ficer

ficer regulates the precedence of one nobleman over another, and is poffeffed of the hiftory of all pedigrees, the nobleft of which are always accounted thofe neareft to the king reigning.

Every man pleads his own caufe before the council, and receives immediate fentence. It is a fettled rule, that thofe who ftrike the animal firft, if the lance remain upright, or in the fame direction in which it enters the beaft, are underftood to be the flayers of the beaft, whatever number combat with him afterwards. There is one exception, however, that if the beaft, after receiving the firft wound, tho' the lance is in him, fhould lay hold of a horfe or man, fo that it is evident he would prevail againft them ; a buffalo, for example, that fhould tofs a man with his horns, or an elephant that fhould take a horfe with his trunk, the man who fhall then flay the beaft, and prevent or revenge the death of the man or horfe attacked, fhall be accounted the flayer of the beaft, and entitled to the premium.

This was the ancient employment of thefe councils. In my time they kept up this cuftom in point of form ; the council fat late upon moft ferious affairs of the nation ; and the death, banifhment, and degradation of the firft men in the kingdom were agitated and determined here under the pretence of fitting to judge the prizes of paftimes. This hunting is feldom prolonged beyond a fortnight.

The king, from ocular infpection, is prefumed to be able to choofe among the young nobility thofe that are ready for taking the neceffary charges in the army ; and it is from his judgment in this that the priefts foretel whether
his

his reign is to be a fuccefsful one, or to end in misfortune and difappointment.

Oustas, having taken a view of his nobility, and attached fuch to him as were moft neceffary for his fupport, fet out for this hunting with great preparations. The high country of Abyffinia is deftitute of wood; the whole lower part of the mountains is fown with different forts of grain; the upper part perfectly covered with grafs and all forts of verdure. There are no plains, or very fmall ones. Such a country, therefore, is unfit for hunting, as it is incapable of either fheltering or nourifhing any number of wild beafts.

The lower country, however, called Kolla, is full of wood, confequently thinly inhabited. The mountains, not joined in chains or ridges, run in one upon the other, but, ftanding each upon its particular bafe, are acceffible all round, and interfperfed with plains. Great rivers falling from the high country with prodigious violence, during the tropical rains, have in the plains wafhed away the foil down to the folid rock, and formed large bafons of great capacity, where, though the water becomes ftagnant in pools when the currents fail above, yet, from their great depth and quantity, they refift being confumed by evaporation, being alfo thick covered with large fhady trees whofe leaves never fall. Thefe large trees, which, in their growth, and vegetation of their branches, exceed any thing that our imagination can figure, are as neceffary for food, as the pools of water are for cifterns to contain drink for thofe monftrous beafts, fuch as the elephant and rhinoceros, who there make their conftant refidence, and who would die with
                                                            hunger

hunger and with thirft unlefs they were thus copioufly fupplied both with food and water.

THIS country, flat as the deferts on which it borders,
has fat black earth for its foil. It is generally about 40
miles broad, though in many places broader and narrower.
It reaches from the mountains of the Habab, or Bagla,
which run in a ridge, as I have already faid, from the fouth
of Abyffinia * north down into Egypt, parallel to the Red Sea,
dividing the rainy feafons, and it ftretches like a belt from
eaft to weft to the banks of the Nile, encircling all the
mountainous, or high land part of Abyffinia ; which latter
country is, at all times, temperate, and often cold, while the
other is unwholefome, hazy, clofe, and intolerably hot.

MANY nations of perfect blacks inhabit this low country,
all Pagans, and mortal enemies to the Abyffinian government. Hunting thefe miferable wretches is the next expedition undertaken by a new king. The feafon of this is
juft before the rains, while the poor favage is yet lodged
under the trees preparing his food for the approaching
winter, before he retires into his caves in the mountain,
where he paffes that inclement feafon in conftant confinement, but as conftant fecurity; for thefe nations are all
Troglodytes, and by the Abyffinians are called Shangalla.

HOWEVER Ouftas fucceeded in attaching to him thofe of
the nobility that partook of his fports, his good fortune in

* Vid general map.

the capital was not equal to it. A dangerous confpiracy was already forming at Gondar by thofe very people who had perfuaded him to mount the throne, and whom he had left at home, from a perfuafion that they only were to be trufted with the fupport of his intereft and the government in his abfence.

Upon the firft intelligence, the king, with a chofen body of troops, entered Gondar in the night, and furprifed the confpirators while actually fitting in council. Ras Hezekias, his prime minifter, and Heraclides, mafter of his houfehold, and five others of the principal confederates, loft their ears and nofes, and were thrown into prifon in fuch circumftances that they could not live. Benaia Bafilé, one of the principal traitors, and the moft obnoxious to the king, efcaped for a time, having had already intelligence of Ouftas's coming.

The king having quieted every thing at Gondar, being at peace with all his neighbours, and having no other way to amufe his troops and keep them employed, fet out to join the remainder of his young nobility whom he had left in the Kolla to attack the Shangalla.

The Shangalla were formerly a very numerous people, divided into diftinct tribes, or, as it is called, different nations, living each feparately in diftinct territories, each under the government of the chief of its own name, and each family of that name under the jurifdiction of its own chief, or head.

THESE

THESE Shangalla, during the fair half of the year, live under the fhade of trees, the loweft branches of which they cut near the ftem on the upper part, and then bend, or break them down, planting the ends of the branches in the earth. Thefe branches they cover with the fkins of wild beafts. After this they cut away all the fmall or fuperfluous branches in the infide, and fo form a fpacious pavilion, which at a diftance appears like a tent, the tree ferving for the pole in the middle of it, and the large top overfhadowing it fo as to make a very picturefque appearance.

EVERY tree then is a houfe, under which live a multitude of black inhabitants until the tropical rains begin. It is then they hunt the elephant, which they kill by many various devices, as they do the rhinoceros and the other large creatures. Thofe who refide where water abounds, with the fame induftry kill the hippopotami, or river-horfes, which are exceedingly numerous in the pools of the ftagnant rivers. Where this flat belt, or country, is broadeft, the trees thickeft, and the water in the largeft pools, there the moft powerful nations live, who have often defeated the royal army of Abyffinia, and conftantly laid wafte, and fometimes nearly conquered, the provinces of Tigré and Siré, the moft warlike and moft populous part in Abyffinia.

THE moft confiderable fettlement of this nation is at Amba Tzaada, between the Mareb and Tacazzè, but nearer by one-third to the Mareb, and almoft N. W. from Dobarwa. Thefe people, who have a variety of venifon, kill it in the fair months, and hang it up, cut into thongs as thick as a man's thumb, like fo many ropes, on the trees around them. The fun dries and hardens it to a confiftence almoft like

3 Z 2   leather,

leather, or the hardeft fifh fent from Newfoundland. This
is their provifion for the winter months : They firft beat it
with a wooden mallet, then boil it, after which they roaft
it upon the embers ; and it is hard enough after it has undergone all thofe operations.

THE Dobenah, the moft powerful of all the Shangalla,
who have a fpecies of fupremacy or command over all the
reft of the nations, live altogether upon the elephant or rhinoceros.. In other countries, where there is lefs water, fewer
trees, and more grafs, the Shangalla feed chiefly upon more
promifcuous kinds of food, as buffaloes, deer, boars, lions,
and ferpents. Thefe are the nations nearer the Tacazzé,
Ras el Feel, and the plains of Siré in Abyffinia, the chief of
which nations is called Baafa. And ftill farther weft of the
Tacazzè, and the valley of Waldubba, is a tribe of thefe,
who live chiefly upon the crocodile, hippopotamus, and
other fifh ; and, in the fummer, upon locufts, which they
boil firft, and afterwards keep dry in bafkets, moft curiouf-
ly made with fplit branches of trees, fo clofely woven together as to contain water almoft as well as a wooden veffel.

THIS nation borders nearly upon the Abyffinian hunting-
ground; but, not venturing to extend themfelves in the chace
of wild beafts, they are confined to the neighbourhood of
the Tacazzé, and rivers falling into it, where they fifh in
fafety : the banks of that river are deep, interrupted by fteep
precipices inacceffible to cavalry, and, from the thicknefs of
the woods, full of thorny trees of innumerable fpecies, almoft as impervious to foot. Thefe ftreams, poffeffed only by
themfelves, afford the Baafa the moft excellent kinds of fifh
in the moft prodigious plenty.

IN

In that part of the Shangalla country more to the eaft-ward, about N. N. E. of Amba Tzaada, in the northern extremities of the woody part, where the river Mareb, leaving Dobarwa, flows through thick bufhes till it lofes itfelf in the fands, there is a nation of thefe blacks, who being near the country of the Baharnagafh, an officer whofe province produces a number of horfe, dare not, for that reafon, venture to make an extenfive ufe of the variety of wild beafts which throng in the woods to the fouthward, for fear of being intercepted by their enemy, conftantly upon the watch for them, part of his tribute being paid in black flaves. Thefe, therefore, confine themfelves to the fouthern part of their territory, near the Barabra.

The extraordinary courfe of this river under the fand, allures to it multitudes of oftriches, which, too, are the food of the Shangalla, as is a beautiful lizard, never, that I know, yet defcribed. Thefe are the food of the eaftern Shangalla; and I muft here obferve, that this country and people were much better known to the ancients than to us. The Egyptians traded with them, and caravans of thefe people were conftantly in Alexandria in the reigns of the firft Ptolemies. Moft of the productions of thefe parts, and the people themfelves, are mentioned in the remarkable proceffion made by Ptolemy Philadelphus on his acceffion to the throne of Egypt, as already obferved, though a confufion often arifes therein by this country being called by the name of India.

Ptolemy, the geographer, claffes thefe people exactly enough, and diftinguifhes them very accurately by their particular food, or dietetique regimen, though he errs, indeed

deed, a little in the particular fituation he gives to the different nations. His Rhizophagi, Elephantophagi, Acridophagi, Struthiophagi, and Agriophagi, are all the clans I have juft defcribed, exifting under the fame habits to this day.

This foil, called by the Abyffinians *Mazaga*, when wet by the tropical rains, and diffolving into mire, forces thefe favages to feek for winter-quarters. Their tents under the trees being no longer tenable, they retire with their refpective foods, all dried in the fun, into caves dug into the heart of the mountains, which are not in this country bafaltes, marble, or alabafter, as is all that ridge which runs down into Egypt along the fide of the Red Sea, but are of a foft, gritty, fandy ftone, eafily excavated and formed into different apartments. Into thefe, made generally in the fteepeft part of the mountain, do thefe favages retire to fhun the rains, living upon the flefh they have already prepared in the fair weather.

I cannot give over the account of the Shangalla without delivering them again out of their caves, becaufe this return includes the hiftory of an operation never heard of perhaps in Europe, and by which confiderable light is thrown upon ancient hiftory. No fooner does the fun pafs the zenith, going fouthward, than the rains inftantly ceafe; and the thick canopy of clouds, which had obfcured the fky during their continuance, being removed, the fun appears in a beautiful fky of pale blue, dappled with fmall thin clouds, which foon after difappear, and leave the heavens of a moft beautiful azure. A very few days of the intenfe heat then dries the ground fo perfectly, that it gapes

4   in

in chafms; the grafs, ftruck at the roots by the rays, fupports itfelf no more, but droops and becomes parched. To clear this away, the Shangalla fet fire to it, which runs with incredible violence the whole breadth of Africa, paffing under the trees, and following the dry grafs among the branches with fuch velocity as not to hurt the trees, but to occafion every leaf to fall.

A PROPER diftance is preferved between each habitation, and round the principal watering-places; and here the Shangalla again fix their tents in the manner before defcribed. Nothing can be more beautiful than thefe fhady habitations; but they have this fatal effect, that they are difcernible from the high grounds, and guide their enemies to the places inhabited.

THE country now cleared, the hunting begins, and, with the hunting, the danger of the Shangalla. All the governors bordering upon the country, from the Baharnagafh to the Nile on the weft, are obliged to pay a certain number of flaves. Ras el Feel (my government) was alone excepted, for a reafon which, had I ftaid much longer in the country, would probably have been found more advantageous to Abyffinia than all the flaves they procure by the barbarous and prodigal effufion of the blood of thefe unhappy favages; for, when a fettlement of thefe is furprifed, the men are all flaughtered; the women, alfo, are many of them flain, many throw themfelves down precipices, run mad, hang themfelves, or ftarve, obftinately refufing food.

THE boys and girls under 17 and 18 years of age, (the younger the better) are taken and educated by the king.

and

and are fervants in all the great houfes of Abyffinia. They are inftructed early in the Chriftian religion, and the talleft, handfomeft, and beft inclined, are the only fervants that attend the royal perfon in his palace. The number of the men was 300 that had horfes in my time. They were once 280, and, before my time, lefs than 200. Thefe are all cloathed in coats of mail, and mounted on black horfes; always commanded by foreigners devoted entirely to the king's will. By ftrict attention to their morals, removing all bad examples from among them, giving premiums to thofe that read moft and beft, (for they had all time enough upon their hands, efpecially in winter) and, above all, by the great delight and pleafure the king ufed to take in converfing with them while alone, countenancing and rewarding them in the line he knew I followed, this body became, as to firmnefs and coolnefs in action, equal perhaps to any of the fame number in the world ; and the greateft difficulty was keeping them together, for all the great men ufed to wifh one of them for the charge of his door, which is a very great truft among the Abyffinians. The king's eafinefs was conftantly prevailed upon to promife fuch, and great inconvenience always followed this, till Ras Michael difcharged this practice by proclamation, and fet the example, by returning four that he himfelf had kept for the purpofe before mentioned.

WHILE what I have faid is ftill in memory, I muft apply a part of it to explain a paffage in Hanno's Periplus. We faw, fays that bold navigator, when rowing clofe along the coaft of Africa, rivers of fire, which ran down from the higheft mountains, and poured themfelves into the fea; this

2   alarmed

alarmed him fo much, that he ordered his gallies to keep a confiderable offing.

After the fire has confumed all the dry grafs on the plain, and, from it, done the fame up to the top of the higheft mountain, the large ravines, or gullies, made by the torrents falling from the higher ground, being fhaded by their depth, and their being in poffeffion of the laft water that runs, are the lateft to take fire, though full of every fort of herbage. The large bamboos, hollow canes, and fuch like plants, growing as thickas they can ftand, retain their greennefs, and are not dried enough for burning till the fire has cleared the grafs from all the reft of the country. At laft, when no other fuel remains, the herdfmen on the top of the mountains fet fire to thefe, and the fire runs down in the very path in which, fome months before, the water ran, filling the whole gully with flame, which does not end till it is checked by the ocean below where the torrent of water entered, and where the fuel of courfe ceafes. This I have often feen myfelf, and been often nearly inclofed in it, and can bear witnefs, that, at a diftance, and by a ftranger ignorant of the caufe, it would very hardly be diftinguifhed from a river of fire.

The Shangalla go all nakeu ; they have feveral wives, and thefe very prolific. They bring forth children with the utmoft eafe, and never reft or confine themfelves after delivery, but wafhing themfelves and the child with cold water, they wrap it up in a foft cloth made of the bark of trees, and hang it upon a branch, that the large ants, with which they are infefted, and the ferpents, may not devour it. After a few days, when it has gathered ftrength, the mother carries it in the fame cloth upon her back, and gives it fuck with the breast, which she throws over her shoulder, this part being of such a length as, in some, to reach almost to their knees.

The Shangalla have but one language, and of a very guttural pronunciation. They worship various trees, serpents, the moon, planets, and stars in certain positions, which I never could so perfectly understand as to give any account of them. A star passing near the horns of the moon denotes the coming of an enemy. They have priests, or rather diviners; but it should seem that these were looked upon as servants of the evil-being, rather than of the good. They prophecy bad events, and think they can afflict their enemies with sickness, even at a distance. They generally wear copper bracelets upon their wrists and arms.

I have said the Shangalla have each several wives. This, however, is not owing to any inordinate propensity of the men to this gratification, but to a much nobler cause, which should make European writers, who object this to them, ashamed at the injustice they do the savage, who all his life, quite the reverse of what is supposed, shews an example of continence and chastity, which the purest and most refined European, with all the advantages of education, cannot pretend to imitate.

It is not the men that seek to avail themselves of the liberty they have by their usages of marrying as often and as many wives as they please. Hemmed in on every side by active and powerful enemies, who consider them as a species of wild beasts, and hunt them precisely as they do

the

the elephant and rhinoceros, placed in a small territory, where they never are removed above 20 miles from these powerful invaders furnished with horses and fire-arms, to both of which they are strangers, they live for part of the fair season in continual apprehension. The other part of the season, when the Abyssinian armies are all collected and abroad with the king, these unhappy savages are constantly employed in a most laborious hunting of large animals, such as the rhinoceros, the elephant, and giraffa; and afterwards, in the no less laborious preparation of the flesh of these quadrupeds, which is to serve them for food during the six months rains, when each family retires to its separate cave in the mountain, and has no intercourse with any of its neighbours, but leaves the country below immersed in a continual deluge of rain. In none of these circumstances, one should imagine, the savage, full of apprehension and care, could have much desire to multiply a race of such wretched beings as he feels himself to be. It is the wife, not the man, that is the cause of this polygamy; and this is surely a strong presumption against what is commonly said of the violence of their inclinations.

Although the Shangalla live in separate tribes, or nations, yet these nations are again subdivided into families, who are governed by their own head, or chief, and of a number of these the nation is composed, who concur in all that regards the measures of defence and offence against their common enemy the Abyssinian and Arab. Whenever an expedition is undertaken by a nation of Shangalla, either against their enemies, the Arabs on the north, or those who are equally their enemies, the Abyssinians on the south, suppose the nation or tribe to be the Baasa, each family attacks

4 A 2   and

and defends by itfelf, and theirs is the fpoil or plunder who take it.

THE mothers, fenfible of the difadvantage of a fmall family, therefore feek to multiply and increafe it by the only means in their power; and it is by their importunity that the hufband fuffers himfelf to be overcome. A fecond wife is courted for him by the firft, in nearly the fame manner as among the Galla.

I WILL not fear to aver, as far as concerns thefe Shangalla, or negroes, of Abyffinia, (and, I believe, moft others of the fame complexion, though of different nations), that the various accounts we have of them are very unfairly ftated. To defcribe them juftly, we fhould fee them in their native purity of manners, among their native woods, living on the produce of their own daily labours, without other liquor than that of their own pools and fprings, the drinking of which is followed by no intoxication or other pleafure than that of affuaging thirft. After having been torn from their own country and connections, reduced to the condition of brutes, to labour for a being they never before knew; after lying, ftealing, and all the long lift of European crimes, have been made, as it were, neceffary to them, and the delufion oecafioned by drinking fpirits is found, however fhort, to be the only remedy that relieves them from reflecting on their prefent wretched fituation, to which, for that reafon, they moft naturally attach themfelves; then, after we have made them monfters, we defcribe them as fuch, forgetful that they are now not as their Maker created them, but fuch as, by teaching them our vices, we have transformed them into, for ends which, I fear, one day will

not

not be found a fufficient excufe for the enormities they have occafioned.

I would not, by any means, have my readers fo far miftake what I have now faid as to think it contains either cenfure upon, or difapprobation of, the flave-trade. I would be underftood to mean juft the contrary; that the abufes and neglect of manners, fo frequent in our plantations, is what the legiflature fhould direct their coercion againft, not againft the trade in general, which laft meafure, executed fo fuddenly, cannot but contain a degree of injuftice towards individuals. It is a fhame for any government to fay, that enormous cruelties towards any fet of men are fo evident, and have arrived to fuch excefs, without once having been under confideration of the legiflature to correct them. It is a greater fhame ftill for that government to fay, that thefe crimes and abufes are now grown to fuch a height that wholefome feverity cannot eradicate them ; and it cannot be any thing but an indication of effeminacy and weaknefs at once to fall to the deftruction of an object of that importance, without having firft tried a reformation of thofe abufes which alone, in the minds of fober men, can make the trade exceptionable.

The incontinence of thefe people has been a favourite topic with which blacks have been branded ; but, throughout the whole of this hiftory, I have fet down only what I have obferved, without confulting or troubling myfelf with the fyftems or authorities of others, only fo far, as having thefe relations in my recollection, I have compared them with the fact, and found them erroneous. As late as two

centuries

centuries ago, Chriſtian prieſts were. the only hiſtorians of heathen manners.

In the number of theſe Shangalla, or negroes, of which every department of Gondar was full, I never ſaw any proof of unbridled deſires in either ſex, but very much the contrary; and I muſt remark, that every reaſon in phyſics ſtrongly militates againſt the preſumption.

The Shangalla of both ſexes, while ſingle, go entirely naked: the married men, indeed, have a very ſlender covering about their waiſt, and married women the ſame. Young men and young women, till long paſt the age of puberty, are totally uncovered, and in conſtant converſation and habits with each other, in woods and ſolitudes, free from conſtraint, and without any puniſhment annexed to the tranſgreſſion. Yet criminal commerce is much leſs frequent among them than in the ſame number choſen among Chriſtian nations, where the powerful prejudices of education give great advantage to one ſex in ſubduing their paſſions, and where the conſequences of gratification, which always involve ſome kind of puniſhment, keep within bounds the deſires of the other.

No one can doubt, but that the conſtant habit of ſeeing people of all ages naked at all times, in the ordinary tranſactions and neceſſities of life, muſt greatly check unchaſte propenſities. But there are ſtill further reaſons why, in the nature of things an extraordinary vehemence of paſſion ſhould not fall to be a diſtinguiſhing characteriſtic among the Shangalla. Fahrenheit's thermometer riſes there beyond 100°. A violent relaxation from profuſe perſpiration muſt greatly

3   debili-

debilitate the favage. In Arabia and Turkey, where the whole bufinefs of man's life is the devoting himfelf to do-meftic pleafure, men remain conftantly in a fedentary life, eat heartily, avoiding every manner of exercife, or expence of animal fpirits by fweats. Their countries, too, are cold-er than that of the Shangalla, who, living fparingly under a burning fun, and obliged to procure food by laborious hunting, of confequence deprive themfelves of that quantity of animal fpirits neceffary to lead them to any extreme of voluptuoufnefs. And that this is the cafe is feen in the conftitution of the Shangalla women, even though they are without fatigue.

A woman, upon bearing a child or two, at 10 or 11 years old, fees her breaft fall immediately down to near her knees *. Her common manner of fuckling her children is by carrying them upon her back, as our beggars do, and giving the infant the breaft over her fhoulders. They rare-ly are mothers after 22, or begin child-bearing before they are 10; fo that the time of child-bearing is but 12 years. In Europe, very many examples there are of wo-men bearing children at 14, the civil law fixes puberty at 12, but by an inuendo † feems to allow it may be fomething earlier. Women fometimes in Europe bear children at 50. The fcale of years of child-bearing between the favage and the European is, therefore, as 12 is to 38. There can be little doubt but their defires are equal to their ftrength and conftitution; but a Shangalla at 22 is more wrinkled and

deformed,

---

* Juvenal, fat. 13. l. 163. † Nifi malitia fuppleat ætatem.

deformed, apparently by old age, than is a European woman
of 60.

To come ftill nearer; it is a fact known to naturalifts, and
which the application of the thermometer fufficiently indicates, that there is a great and fenfible difference in the
degree of animal heat in both fexes of different nations at
the fame ages or time of life. The voluptuous Turk eftran-
ges himfelf from the faireft and fineft of his Circaffian and
Georgian women in his feraglio, and, during the warm
months in fummer, addicts himfelf only to negro flaves
brought from the very latitudes we are now fpeaking of;
the fenfible difference of the coolnefs of their fkins leading
him to give them the preference at that feafon. On the
other hand, one brown Abyffinian girl, a companion for
the winter months, is fold at ten times the price of the
faireft Georgian or Circaffian beauty, for oppofite reafons.

The very great regard I fhall conftantly pay my fair
readers has made me, as they may perceive, enter as tenderly as poffible into thefe difcuffions, which, as a philofo-
pher and a hiftorian, I could not, however, wholly omit: the
moft ufeful ftudy of mankind is man; and not the leaft in-
terefting view of him is when, ftripped of his vain-glory and
the pageantry of palaces, he wanders naked and uncorrupt-
ed among his native woods and rivers.

I must mention, greatly to the credit of two of the firft
geniufes of this age, M. de Buffon and Lord Kaimes, that they
were both fo convinced by the arguments above mentioned,
ftated in greater detail and with more freedom, that they
immediately ordered their bookfeller to ftrike out from the

subfequent editions of their work all that had been advanced againft the negroes on this head, which they had before drawn from the herd of prejudiced and ignorant compilers, ftrangers to the manners and language of the people they were difhonouring by their defcriptions, after having before abufed them by their tyranny.

The Shangalla have no bread: No grain or pulfe will grow in the country. Some of the Arabs, fettled at Ras el Feel, have attempted to make bread of the feed of the Guinea grafs; but it is very taftelefs and bad, of the colour of cow-dung, and quickly producing worms.

They are all archers from their infancy. Their bows are all made of wild fennel, thicker than the common proportion, and about feven feet long, and very elaftic. The children ufe the fame bow in their infancy that they do when grown up; and are, by reafon of its length, for the firft years, obliged to hold it parallel, inftead of perpendicular to the horizon. Their arrows are full a yard and a half long, with large heads of very bad iron rudely fhaped. They are, indeed, the only favages I ever knew that take no pains in the make or ornament of this weapon. A branch of a palm, ftript from the tree and made ftraight, becomes an arrow; and none of them have wings to them. They have this remarkable cuftom, which is a religious one, that they fix upon their bows a ring, or thong, of the fkin of every beaft flain by it, while it is yet raw, from the lizard and ferpent up to the elephant. This gradually ftiffens the bow, till, being all covered over, it can be no longer bent even by its mafter. That bow is then hung upon a tree,

and a new one is made in its place, till the fame circumftance again happens ; and one of thefe bows, that which its
mafter liked beft, is buried with him in the hopes of its rifing again materially with his body, when he fhall be endowed with a greater degree of ftrength, without fear of
death, or being fubjected to pain, with a capacity to enjoy
in excefs every human pleafure. There is nothing, however, fpiritual in this refurrection, nor what concerns the
foul, but it is wholly corporeal and material; although
fome writers have plumed themfelves upon their fancied
difcovery of what they call the favages belief of the immortality of the foul.

BEFORE I take leave of this fubject, I muft again explain,
from what I have already faid, a difficult paffage in claffical
hiftory. Herodotus * fays, that, in the country we have been
juft now defcribing, there was a nation called Macrobii, which
was certainly not the real name of the Shangalla, but one
the Greeks had given them, from a fuppofed circumftance
of their being remarkable long livers, as that name imports.
Thefe were the weftern Shangalla, fituated below Guba and
Nuba, the gold country, on both fides of the Nile north of
Fazuclo.

THE Guba and the Nuba, and various black nations that
inhabits the foot of that large chain of mountains called
Dyre and Tegla†, are thofe in whofe countries the fineft gold
is found, which is wafhed from the mountains in the time of
violent

Herod. lib. 3. par. 17. & feq.   † Suppofed to be the Garamantica Vallis of Ptolemy.

violent rains, and lodged in holes, and roots of trees and grafs, by the torrents, and there picked up by the natives; it is called Tibbar, or, corruptly, gold-duft. The greateft part finds its way to Sennaar by the different merchants, Pagan and Mahometan, from Fazuclo and Sudan. The Agows and Gibbertis alfo bring a fmall quantity of it to Gondar, moftly debafed by alloy; but there is no gold in Abyffinia, nor even in Nubia, weft of Tchelga, among the Shangalla them-felves.

Cambyses marched from Egypt exprefsly with a view of conquering the gold country, and fent meffengers before him to the king, or chief of it, requiring his immediate fubmiffion. I omit romantic and fabulous circumftances; but the anfwer of the king of Macrobii to Cambyfes was, Take this bow, and till you can bring me a man that can bend it, you are not to talk to us of fubmiffion. The bow was accordingly carried back with the defiance, but none of the Perfian army could bend it. Yet it was their own wea-pon with which they practifed from their infancy; and we are not to think, had it been poffible to bend this bow, but that fome of their numerous archers would have done it, for there is no fuch difproportion in the ftrength of men. But it was a bow which had loft its elaftic force from the circumftance above mentioned, and had been long given up as impoffible to be bent by the Macrobii themfelves, and was now taken down from the tree where it had probably fome time hung, and grown fo much the lefs flexible, and in-tended to be buried, as thefe bows are, in the grave with their mafter, who is to ufe it, after his refurrection, in an-other world, where he is to be endowed with ftrength infi-

4 B 2

nitely

nitely more than human : it is probable this bow would have broke, rather than have bent.

If the fituation of thefe Macrobii· in Ptolemy did not put it paft difpute that they were Shangalla, we fhould hefitate much at the characteriftic of the nation; that they were long livers; none of thefe nations are fo; I fcarcely remember an example fairly vouched of a man paft fixty. But there is one circumftance that I think might have fairly led Herodotus into this miftake; fome of the Shangalla kill their fick, weak, and aged people; there are others that honour old age, and protect it. The Macrobii, I fuppofe, were of this laft kind, who certainly, therefore, had many old men, more than the others.

I shall now juft mention one other obfervation tending to illuftrate a paffage of ancient hiftory.

Hanno, in his Periplus, remarks, that, while failing along the coaft of Africa, clofe by the fhore, and probably near the low country called Kolla, inhabited by the kind of people we have been juft defcribing, he found an univerfal filence to prevail the whole day, without any appearance of man or beaft : on the contrary, at night, he faw a number of fires, and heard the found of mufic and dancing. This has been laughed at as a fairy tale by people who affect to treat Hanno's fragment as fpurious ; for my own part, I. will not enter into the controverfy.

A very great genius, (in fome matters, perhaps, the greateft that ever wrote, and in every thing that he writes highly refpectable) M. de Montefqieu, is perfectly fatisfied that
this

this Periplus * of Hanno is genuine; and it is a great pleasure again to endeavour to obviate any doubt concerning the authenticity of the work in this second paſſage, as I have before done in another.

In countries, ſuch as thoſe that we have been now deſcribing, and ſuch as Hanno was then ſailing by, when he made the remark, there is no twilight. The ſtars, in their full brightneſs, are in poſſeſſion of the whole heavens, when in an inſtant the ſun appears without a harbinger, and they all diſappear together. We ſhall ſay, at ſun-riſing the thermometer is from 48° to 60°; at 3 o'clock in the afternoon it is from 100° to 115°; an univerſal relaxation, a kind of irreſiſtible languor and averſion to all action takes poſſeſſion of both man and beaſt; the appetite fails, and ſleep and quiet are the only things the mind is capable of deſiring, or the body of enduring: cattle, birds, and beaſts all flock to the ſhade, and to the neighbourhood of running ſtreams, or deep ſtagnant pools, and there, avoiding the effects of the ſcorching ſun, pant in quiet and inaction. From the ſame motive, the wild beaſt ſtirs not from his cave; and for this, too, he has an additional reaſon, becauſe the cattle he depends upon for his prey do not ſtroll abroad to feed; they are aſleep and in ſafety, for with them are their dogs and their ſhepherds.

But no ſooner does the ſun ſet, than a cold night inſtantly ſucceeds a burning day; the appetite immediately returns; the cattle ſpread themſelves abroad to feed, and
paſs

---

* Dodſwell's diſſertation of Hanno's Periplus—Monteſquieu, tom. I. lib. 21, cap. 11.

pafs quickly out of the fhepherds fight into the reach of a multitude of beafts feeking for their prey. Fires, the only remedy, are everywhere lighted by the fhepherds to keep thefe at a refpectful diftance; and dancing, finging, and mufic at once exhilarate the mind, and contribute, by alarming the beafts of prey, to keep their flocks in fafety, and prevent the bad effects of fevere cold *. This was the caufe of the obfervation Hanno made in failing along the coaft, and it was true when he made it: juft the fame may be obferved ftill, and will be, fo long as the climate and inhabitants are the fame.

I HAVE been more particular in the hiftory of this extraordinary nation, becaufe I had, by mere accident, an opportunity of informing myfelf fully and with certainty concerning it; and, as it is very improbable that fuch an opportunity will occur again to any European, I hope it will not be ungratefully received.

I SHALL only add an anfwer to a very obvious queftion which may occur. Why is it that, in this country, nothing that would make bread will grow? Is it from the ignorance of the inhabitants in not choofing the proper feafons, or is it the imperfection of the foil? To this I anfwer, Certainly the latter. For the inhabitants of Ras el Feel were ufed to plow and fow, and did conftantly eat bread; but the grain was produced ten or fifteen miles off upon the fides

of

---

* This fenfation of the favage in the heart of Africa feems to be unknown to the enemies of the flave-trade; they talk much of heat, without knowing the material fuffering of the negro is from cold.

of the mountains of Abyssinia, where every certain number
of soldiers had small farms allowed them for that purpose
by government; but still they could never bring up a crop
in the Mazaga; and the progress of the miscarriage was
this: Before the month of May all that black earth was rent
into great chasms, trode into dust, and ventilated with hot
winds, so as to be a perfect *caput mortuum*, incapable of any
vegetation.   Upon the first sprinkling of rain the chasms
are filled up, and the whole country resembles dry garden-
mould newly dug up.   As the sun advances the rains increase; there is no time to be lost now; this is the season
for sowing; let us suppose wheat. In one night's time, while
the wheat is swelling in the ground, up grows an immense
quantity of indigenous natural grass, that, having sowed
itself last year, has lain ever since in a natural matrix, ready
to start at the most convenient season.   Before the wheat, or
any grain soever can appear, this grass has shot up so high
and so thick as absolutely to choke it.   Suppose it was possible to hoe or weed it, the grass will again overtop the grain
before it is an inch from the ground. Say it could be again
hoed or cleared, by this time the rains are so continual, the
black earth becomes a perfect mire.   The rain increases,
and the grain rots without producing any crop.

THE same happens to millet, or Indian corn; the rain rots
the plant which is thrown down by the wind.   It is equally
destroyed if sown at the end of the rains; the grass grows
up, wherever the ground is cleared, in a greater proportion,
if possible, than in the beginning of the year; and the rain
ceasing abruptly, and the sun beginning to be intensely hot
the very day it passes the zenith, the earth is reduced to an
impalpable

impalpable powder, whilst the grain and plant die without ever shewing a tendency to germinate.

We left the king, Ouftas, after detecting a conspiracy, ready to fall upon some settlement of Shangalla. This he executed with great success, and surrounded a large part of the nation called Baafa, encamped under the trees suspecting no danger. He put the grown people to the sword, and took a prodigious number of children of both sexes captive. He was intending also to push his conquest farther among these savages, when he was called to Gondar by the death of his prime minister and confident, Ras Fafa Christos.

Besides his attention to hunting and government, the king had a very great taste for architecture, which, in Abyssinia, is a very popular one, though scarcely any thing is built but churches. In the season that did not permit him to be in the field, he bestowed a great deal of leisure and money this way; and he was, at this time, busy erecting a magnificent church to the Nativity, about a mile below Gondar, on the small river Kahha.

But the season of hunting returning before he had finished it, he left it to repair to Bet Malo, a place in the Kolla, where he had built a hunting-seat, not far distant from the Shangalla, called Baafa. Here he had a most successful hunting-match of the buffalo, rhinoceros, and elephant, in which he often put himself in great danger, and distinguished himself in dexterity and horsemanship greatly above any of his court. He returned upon news, that persons, whom he had secretly employed, had apprehended Betwudet Basilé, and his son Claudius, who had escaped

2   when

when the laft confpirators were feized. Both thefe he fentenced immediately to lofe their eyes.

THESE hunting-matches, fo punctually obferved, and fo eagerly followed by a man already paft the flower of his youth, had, in their firft appearance, nothing but found policy. The king's title was avowedly a faulty one; and the many confpiracies that had been formed had fhewn him the nobility were not all of them difpofed to bear his yoke; nothing then was more political than to keep a confiderable number of them employed in field-exercifes, to be informed of their inclinations, and to attach them to his perfon by favours. At the head of this little, but very active army, he was ready in a moment to fall upon the difaffected, before they could collect ftrength fufficient for refiftance. Time, however, fhewed this was not entirely the reafon of thefe continual intervals of abfence for fo long a time in the Kolla.

NOTWITHSTANDING the misfortune that had befallen the French ambaffador, M. du Roule, at Sennaar, in the reign of Yafous I. and Tecla Haimanout his fon, under Baady el Ahmer, there had ftill remained below, in Atbara, fome of thofe miffionaries who had courage and addrefs enough to attempt the journey into Abyffinia, and they fucceeded in it. Ouftas had probably been privy to their arrival in Yafous's time, and had, equally with him, a favourable opinion of the Romifh religion.

THESE miffionaries, though Yafous was now dead, were perfectly well received by Ouftas; he had given them in charge to Ain Egzie, an old and loyal fervant of Yafous, and governor of Walkayt. He had placed alfo with them an Abyffinian prieft, who had been in Jerufalem, and was well-affected to the Romifh faith, to be their interpreter, ftay with them always, and manage their interefts, while he himfelf, ftealing frequently from the hunting-matches, heard mafs, and received the communion, returning back to his camp, as he flattered himfelf, unperceived. Thefe meetings with the priefts were not, however, fo well concealed but that they came to the knowledge of many people about court, both feculars and clergy. But the king's character, for feverity and vigilance, made everybody confine their thoughts, whatever they were, within their own breafts.

The employment of this year was a fhort journey to Ibaba, a large market-town, where there is a royal refidence, below Maitfha, on the weft, or Gojam fide of the Nile, from which it is about three days diftance. From this he returned again, and went to Tcherkin, a fmall village in Kolla, beyond Ras el Feel, in the way to Sennaar, the principal abode of the elephant. But, in the firft day's hunting, Yared, mafter of his houfehold, and a confiderable favourite, being torn to pieces by one of thefe quadrupeds, he gave over the fport, and returned very forrowful to bury him at Gondar, leaving three of his fervants to execute a defign he had formed againft the Baafa in that neighbourhood.

From the conftant interruptions Ouftas had met with in all thefe hunting-matches, and his fuccefs, notwithftanding, whenever he had himfelf attended, the divining monks had prophefied his reign was to be fhort, and attended with much bloodfhed; nor were they for once diftant from the truth; for, in the month of January 1714, while he was over-
look-

looking the workmen building the church of Abba Anto-
nius at Gondar, he was taken fuddenly ill, and, fufpecting
fome unwholfomenefs or *witchcraft* in his palace, he ordered his tent to be pitched without the town till the apartments fhould be fmoaked with gunpowder. But this was
done fo carelefsly by his fervants, that his houfe was
burnt to the ground, which was looked upon as a very bad
omen, and made a great impreffion upon the minds of the
people.

THE 27th of January it was generally underftood that the
king was dangeroufly ill, and that his complaint was every day
increafing. Upon this the principal officers went, according to
the ufual cuftom, to condole with and comfort him. This
was at leaft what they pretended. Their true errand, however, was pretty well known to be an endeavour to afcertain whether the ficknefs was of the kind likely to continue,
till meafures could be adopted with a degree of certainty to
take the reins of government out of his hand.

THE king eafily divined the reafon of their coming. Having had a good night, he ufed the ftrength that he had
thereby acquired to roufe himfelf for a moment, to put on
the appearance of health, and fhew himfelf, as ufual, engaged in his ordinary difpatch of bufinefs. The feeming good
countenance of the king made their condolence premature.
Some excufe, however, for fo formal a vifit, was neceffary ;
but every apology was not fafe. They adopted this, which
they thought unexceptionable, that hearing he was fick,
which they happily found he was not, they came to propofe
to him a thing equally proper whether he was fick or well ;
that he would, in time, fettle the fucceffion upon his fon

4 C 2   Fafil,

Fafil, then in the mountain of Wechnè, as a means of quiet‐ing the minds of his friends, preventing bloodſhed, and ſe‐curing the crown to his family.

Ouſtas did the utmoſt to command himſelf upon this oc‐caſion, and to give them an anſwer ſuch as ſuited a man in health who hoped to live many years. But it was now too late to play ſuch a part; and, in ſpite of his utmoſt diſſimu‐lation, evident ſigns of decay appeared upon him, which his viſitors conjectured would ſoon be paſt diſſembling, and they agreed to ſtay with the king till the evening.

But the ſoldiers on guard, who heard the propoſal of ſending for Ouſtas's ſon, and who really believed that theſe men ſpoke from their heart, and were in earneſt, were vio‐lently diſcontented and angry at this propoſal. They began to be weary of novelty, and longed for a king of the an‐cient royal family. As ſoon, therefore, as it was dark they entered Gondar, and called together the ſeveral regiments, or bodies of ſoldiers, which compoſed the king's houſe‐hold. Having came to a reſolution how they were to act, they returned to their quarters where they were upon guard, and meeting the great officers coming out of Ouſ‐tas's tent, where they, too, had probably agreed upon the ſame meaſure, though it was not known, the ſoldiers drew their ſwords, and flew them all, being ſeven in number. A‐mong theſe were Betwudet Tamerté, and the Acab Saat; the one the principal lay-officer, the other the chief eccle‐ſiaſtic in the king's houſe.

This maſſacre ſeemed to be the ſignal for a general in‐ſurrection, in the courſe of which, part of the town was
ſet

fet on fire. But the foldiers, at their firft meeting in the palace *, had fhut up the coronation-chamber, and the other royal apartments, and poffeffed themfelves of the kettle-drum by which all proclamations were made at the gate, driving away, and rudely treating the multitude on every fide. At laft they brought out the drum, though it was yet night, and made this proclamation :—" David, fon of our late king Yafous, is our king." The tumult and diforder, neverthelefs, ftill continued ; during all which, it was very remarkable no one ever thought of offering an injury to Ouftas.

WHILE thefe things were paffing at Gondar, a violent alarm had feized all the princes upon the mountain of Wechnè. They had been treated with feverity during Ouftas's whole reign. Their revenues had been with-held, or at leaft not regularly paid, and they had been reduced nearly to perifh for want of the neceffaries of life. When, therefore, the accounts of Ouftas's illnefs arrived, and that the princi-pal

---

* There feems here fome contradiction which needs explanation. It is faid that the palace was burnt before Ouftas went to his tent. How then could the foldiers affemble in it afterwards ? The palace confifts of a number of feparate houfes at no great diftance, but detached from one another with one room in each. That where the coronation is performed is called Anbafa Bet ; another, where the king fits in feftivals, is called Zeffan Bet ; another is called Werk Sacala, the gold-houfe; another Gimja Bet, or the brocade-houfe, where the wardrobe and the gold ftuffs ufed for prefents, or received as fuch, are laid. Now, we fuppofe Ouftas in any one of thefe apartments, fay Zeffan Bet, which he left to go to his tent, and it was then burnt ; ftill there remained the coronation-houfe where the regalia was kept, which the foldiers locked up that it might not be ufed to crown Fafil, Ouftas's fon, whom they thought the feven great men they had murdered confpired to place upon the throne after his father.

pal people had propofed to name Fafil his fon, then their fellow-prifoner, to fucceed him, their fears no longer reminded them of the hardfhips of his father's reign, as they expected utter extirpation as the only meafure by which he could provide for his own fecurity. Full of thefe fears, they agreed, with one confent, to let down from the mountain fifty princes of the greateft hopes, all in the prime of life, and therefore moft capable of defending their own right, and fecuring the lives of thofe that remained upon the mountain, from the cruel treatment they muft obvioufly expect if they fell into the hand of an ufurper or ftranger.

THE brother of Betwudet Tamerté, who, with the fix others, had been murdered before Ouftas's tent, was, at this time, guardian of the mountain of Wechné. His brother's death, however, and the unfettled ftate of government, had fo much weakened both his authority and attention, that he either did not choofe, or was not able, to prevent the efcape of thefe princes, all flying for their lives, and for the fake of preferving the ancient conftitution of their country. And that this, and no other was their object, appeared the inftant the danger was removed; for, as foon as the news that David was proclaimed at Gondar arrived at the mountain, all the princes returned of their own accord, excepting Bacuffa, younger brother to the king, who fled to the Galla, and lay concealed among them for a time.

ON David's arrival at Gondar, all the old misfortunes feemed to be forgotten. The joy of having the ancient royal line reftored, got the better of thofe tears which firft occafioned the interruption. The prifons were thrown open,

3   and

and David was crowned the 30th of January 1714, amidst the acclamations of all ranks of people, and every demonstration of festivity and joy.

DAVID was son of Yasous the Great, and consequently brother to the parricide Tecla Haimanout, but by another mother. At his coronation he was just twenty-one years of age, and took for his inauguration name Adebar Segued.

IN all this time, however, Ouftas was alive. Ouftas was, indeed, sick, but still he was king; and yet it is surprising that David had been now nine days at Gondar, and no injury had been offered to Ouftas, nor any escape attempted for him by his friends.

IT was the 6th of February, the day before Lent, when the king sent the Abuna Marcus, Itchegué Za Michael, with some of the great officers of state, to interrogate Ouftas judicially, for form's fake, as to his title to the crown. The questions proposed are very short and simple—" Who are " you? What brought you here?" To these plain interrogatories, Ouftas, then struggling with death, answered, however, as plainly, and without equivocation, " Tell my " king David, that true it is I have made myself king, " as much as one can be that is not of the royal family; " for I am but a private man, son of a subject, Kasmati " Delba Yasous : all I beg of the king is to give me a little " time, and let me die with sickness, as I shortly shall, with- " out putting me to torment or pain."

ON the 10th day of February, that is four days after the interrogation, Ouftas died, but whether of a violent or natural

tural death is not known. The hiftorian of his reign, a cotemporary writer, fays, fome reported that he died of an amputation of his leg by order of the king; others, that he was ftrangled; but that moft people were of opinion that he died of ficknefs; and this I think the moft probable, for had the king been earneftly fet upon his death, he would not have allowed fo much time to pafs, after his coronation, before his rival was interrogated; nor was there any reafon to allow him four days after his confeffion. David's moderation after the death, moreover, feems to render this ftill more credible; for he ordered his body to be buried in the church of the Nativity, which he had himfelf built, with all the honours and public ceremonies due to his rank as a nobleman and fubject, who had been guilty of no crime, inftead of ordering his body to be hewn in pieces, and fcattered along the ground without burial, to be eat by the dogs; the invariable punifhment, unlefs in this one inftance, of high-treafon in this country.

Posterity, regarding his merit more than his title, have, however, kept his name ftill among the lift of kings; and tradition, doing him more juftice ftill than hiftory, has ranked him among the beft that ever reigned in Abyffinia.

1   DAVID

D A V I D IV.

From 1714 to 1719.

Convocation of the Clergy—Catholic Priests executed—A second Convocation—Clergy insult the King—His severe Punishment—King dies of Poison.

THE moderation of the king, both before and after the death of Ouftas, and perhaps some other favourable appearances now unknown to us, set the monks, the constant pryers into futurity, upon prophecying that the reign of this prince was to be equal in length to that of his father Yafous the Great, and that it was to be peaceable, full of justice and moderation, without execution, or effusion of civil blood.

DAVID, immediately upon his accession, appointed Fit-Auraris Agnè, Ozoro Kedufte's brother *, his Betwudet, and

VOL. II.   4 D   Abra

---

* Miftrefs to Yafous, and mother to David.

Abra Hezekias his mafter of the houfehold; and was proceeding to fill up the inferior pofts of government, when he was interrupted by the clamours of a multitude of monks demanding a convocation of the clergy.

THESE affemblies, however often folicited, are never called in the reign of vigorous princes, but by the fpecial order of the fovereign, who grants or refufes them purely from his own free-will. They are, however, particularly expected at the acceffion of a new prince, upon any apprehenfion of herefy, or any novelty or abufe in church-government.

THE arrival of a new Abuna from Egypt is alfo a very principal reafon for the convocation. Thefe affemblies are very numerous. Many of the moft difcreet members of the church abfent themfelves purpofely. On the other hand, the monks, who, by vows, have bound themfelves to the moft painful aufterities and fufferings; thofe that devote themfelves to pafs their lives in the deep and unwholefome valleys of the country; hermits that ftarve on the points of cold rocks; others that live in deferts furrounded with, and perpetually expofed to wild beafts; in a word, the whole tribe of fanatics, falfe prophets, diviners, and dreamers, people who affect to fee and foreknow what is in future to happen, by living in perfect ignorance of what is paffing at the prefent; people in conftant habits of dirt and naftinefs, naked, or covered with hair; in fhort, a collection of monfters, fcarcely to be defcribed or conceived, compofe an ecclefiaftical affembly in Abyffinia, and are the leaders of an ignorant and furious populace, who adore them as faints, and are always ready to fupport them in fome violation of
the

the laws of the country, or of humanity, to which, by their customs and manner of life, their very first appearance shews they have been long strangers.

DAVID, however averse to these assemblies, could not decently refuse them, now a new prince was set on the throne, a new Abuna was come from Egypt, and a complaint was ready to be brought that the church was in danger. The assembly met in the usual place before the palace. The Itchegué, or head of the monks of Debra Libanos, was ready with a complaint, which he preferred to the king. He stated it was notorious, but offered to prove it if denied, that three Romish priests, with an Abyssinian for their interpreter, were then established in Walkayt, and, for several years, had been there maintained, protected, and consulted by the late king Ouftas, who had often assisted at the celebration of mass as solemnized by the church of Rome.

DAVID was a rigid adherent to the church of Alexandria, and educated by his mother in the tenets of the monks of Saint Euftathius, that is, the most declared enemies of every thing approaching to the tenets of the church of Rome. He was consequently, not by inclination, neither was he by duty, obliged to undertake the defence of measures adopted by Ouftas, of which he was besides ignorant, having been confined in the mountain of Wechné. He ordered, therefore, the missionaries, and their interpreter, whose name was Abba Gregorius, to be apprehended.

THESE unfortunate people were accordingly produced before the most prejudiced and partial of all tribunals. Abba Mafmarè and Adug Tesfo were adduced to interrogate and to interpret to them, as they underftood the Arabic, having been at Cairo and Jerufalem. The trial neither was, nor was intended to be long. The firft queftion put was a very direct one; Do you, or do you not, receive the council of Chalcedon as a rule of faith? and, Do you believe that Leo the pope lawfully and regularly prefided at it, and conducted it? To this the prifoners plainly anfwered That they looked upon the council of Chalcedon as the fourth general council, and received it as fuch, and as a rule of faith : that they did believe pope Leo lawfully and regularly prefided at it, as being head of the Catholic church, fucceffor to St Peter, and Chrift's vicar upon earth. Upon this a general fhout was heard from the whole affembly; and the fatal cry, " Stone them."—" Whoever throws not three ftones, he is accurfed, and an enemy to Mary," immediately followed.

ONE prieft only, diftinguifhed for piety and learning among his countrymen, and one of the chief men in the affembly, with great vehemence declared, they were tried partially and unfairly, and condemned unjuftly. But his voice was not heard amidft the clamours of fuch a multitude ; and the monks were accordingly by the judges condemned to die. Ropes were inftantly thrown about their necks, and they were dragged to a place behind the church of Abbo, in the way to Tedda, where they were, according to their fentence, ftoned to death, fuffering with a patience and refignation equal to the firft martyrs.

THE juftice, however, which we owe to the memory of the deceafed M. du Roule, muft always leave a fear in every Chriftian mind, that, fpotted as thefe miffionaries were with the horrid crime of the premeditated, unprovoked murder

of

of that ambaſſador, the indifference they teſtified at the approach, and in the immediate ſuffering of death, had its origin rather in hardneſs of heart than in the quietneſs of their conſciences. Many fanatics have been known to die, glorying in having perpetrated the moſt horrid crimes to which the ſentence of eternal damnation is certainly annexed in the book before them.

I HAVE often, both on purpoſe and by accident, paſſed by this place, where three large, and one ſmall pile of ſtones, cover the bodies of theſe unfortunate ſufferers ; and, with many heavy reflections upon my own danger, I have often wondered how theſe three prieſts, of whatever nation they were, paſſed unnoticed among the number of their fraternity, whoſe memory is honoured with long panegyrics by the Romiſh writers of thoſe times, as deſtined one day to appear in the kalendar. Though thoſe that compoſe the long liſt of Tellez died with piety and reſignation, they were ſurely guilty in the way they almoſt all were engaged, contrary to the laws and conſtitution of the country, in actions and deſigns that can be fairly qualified by no other name than that of treaſon, while no ſuch political meddling out of their profeſſion ever was reproached to theſe three, even by their enemies.

TELLEZ ſays not a word of them ; Le Grande, a zealous Catholic writer of theſe times, but little ; though he publiſhes an Arabic letter to conſul Maillet, which mentions their names, their ſufferings, and other circumſtances attending them. I ſhall, therefore, take the liberty of offering my conjecture, as I think this ſilence, or the ſuppreſſion

of

of a fact, gives me a title to do ; but fhall firft produce the letter of Elias Enoch, upon which I found my judgment.

TRANSLATION *of an* ARABIC LETTER *wrote to* M. DE MAILLET.

" AFTER having affured M. de Maillet, the conful, of my
" refpects, and of the continuation of my prayers for his
" health, as being a gentleman venerable for his merits,
" diftinguifhed by his knowledge and great penetration,
" of a noble birth, always beneficent, and addicted to pious
" actions, (may God preferve his life to that degree of ho-
" nour due to fo refpectable a perfon), I now write you from
" the town of Mocha.   I left Abyffinia in the year 1718, and
" came to this town of Mocha in extreme poverty, or ra-
" ther abfolutely deftitute.   God has affifted me : I give
" praife to him for his bounty, and always remain much o-
" bliged to you.   What follows is all that I can inform you
" as touching the news of Abyffinia.   King Yafous is long
" fince dead: his fon, Tecla Haimanout, having feized upon
" the kingdom by force, caufed his father to be affaffinated.
" This king Yafous, having given me leave to go to Sennaar,
" furnifhed me with a letter addreffed to the king there, in
" which he defired him to put no obftacles in the way of
" du Roule the French ambaffador's journey, but to fuffer
" him to enter Ethiopia.   He alfo gave me another letter
" addreffed to the bafha and officers of Grand Cairo ; and
" another letter to the ambaffador himfelf, by which he fig-
" nified to him that he might enter into Ethiopia without
" fear.   Accordingly I had departed with thefe letters for Sen-
" naar; but king Tecla Haimanout, fon of king Yafous, ha-
" ving taken poffeffion of the kingdom while I was yet in
                                              " Abyffinia,

" Abyffinia, I returned and delivered to him the letters
" which had been given me by his father. It was now
" three months fince Tecla Haimanout had been upon the
" throne; he approved of the letters, and caufed them to
" be tranfcribed in his own name; and ordered me to go
" and join du Roule the ambaffador, and accompany him
" back again to Gondar. King Yafous had already fent an
" officer to meet the ambaffador at Sennaar; and he had
" been gone fix months without my knowledge; but that
" officer, having trifled away his time in trading, did not
" enter Sennaar till that king had caufed the ambaffador
" to be murdered, together with thofe that were with him.
" As for me, not knowing what had happened, I was ad-
" vancing with the orders of Tecla Haimanout, when, being
" now within three days journey of Sennaar, I heard of the
" ambaffador's death, and that of his companions; and
" being terrified at this, I returned into Abyffinia to let
" Tecla Haimanout know what the king of Sennaar had
" done. Immediately upon hearing of this, Tecla Haima-
" nout formed a refolution to declare war againft the king
" of Sennaar, but was foon after flain in a mutiny of the
" foldiers. He reigned two years. Tifilis, brother of Ya-
" fous, fucceeded him, and reigned three years and three
" months. Ouftas, nephew of king Yafous, fucceeded Ti-
" filis, and ufurped the kingdom, of which he was actual-
" ly prime minifter, being fon of a fifter of Yafous. Ouftas
" was dethroned, and died foon after. David, fon of Ya-
" fous, fucceeded him, and reigned five years and five
" months. The *friars*, who arrived in Ethiopia in the reign
" of Ouftas, were ftoned to death, upon the fucceffion of
" David to the throne, by thofe that were of the party of
" David. A fon of *Michael*, whom he had by a flave, aged
" only

" only fix years, was ftoned with him.   It was the *fourth* fon
" he had.   I made Yafous believe that the religion of the
" French was the fame with that of Ethiopia," &c. &c.

FROM this letter, we fee a boy of fix years old, fon of one
of thefe priefts or friars, was ftoned to death with them; and
his heap of ftones appears with thofe of the others.   It was,
indeed, a common teft of the people fufpected to be priefts,
who ftole into Abyffinia, to offer them women, their vows
being known, and that they could not marry.   I apprehend,
to avoid detection, one at leaft of them had broken his vow
of celibacy and chaftity, and that this child was the confequence, but not the only one, as Enoch fays, in his letter,
he had three others ; and this probably was the reafon why
the Catholics of thofe times had configned their merit to
oblivion, rather than record it with their failings.

FOR although we know that there were friars who had
been in Ethiopia fince the time of Ouftas, we fhould not have
been informed who they were, had it not been for a fmall
fheet, publifhed at Rome in the year 1774, by a capuchin
prieft called Theodofius Volpi, fent to me by my learned
and worthy friend the honourable Daines Barrington. From
this we find, that thefe three were, Liberato de Wies, apoftolical prefect in Auftria; Michael Pius of Zerbe, in the
province of Padua ; and Samuel de Beumo, of the Milanefe.
The account of their death is the fame as already given,
though the publifher fuppreffes the ftoning of the child,
and the exiftence of the three other, fruits of the feraphic
miffion, through the endeavours of father Michael Pius of
Zerbe, of the province of Milan.   The child, too, ftoned to
death with his father, was fix years old, and was, as Elias

2   fays,

fays, fourth fon of Michael; and it was in 1714 this cataftrophe happened, fo that this will bring thefe fathers entrance into Nubia about the time of the murder of M. du
Roule: fo confiftent with every crime is fanaticifm and falfe
religion.

THE barbarous monks, gratified in the firft inftance,
would not be contented without extending their vengeance
to Abba Gregorius, the Abyffinian prieft, the interpreter.
But David, who found upon trial that, in going to attend
the priefts in Walkayt, he had only obeyed the exprefs command of Ouftas, then his fovereign, abfolutely refufed to
fuffer him to be either tried or punifhed, but difmiffed him,
without further cenfure or queftion, to his native country.

WHILE David was thus employed at Gondar, news were
brought to him that his brother Bacuffa had left the Galla,
and was then in a fmall town in Begemder, called Wetan.
It was this prince who, together with fifty others of the
royal family, were let down from the mountain of Wechné,
upon Ouftas's fon being propofed, and he alone refufed
to return upon his brother's acceffion to the throne. David
fent Azaleffi, Guebra Mehedin, and Badjerund Welled de
l'Oul, to Wetan, where they apprehended Bacuffa by furprife,
and lodged him in the mountain of Wechné, after having
cut off a very fmall part of the tip of his nofe, which was
fcarcely difcernible when he came to the throne.

Kafmati Georgis, had been banifhed to the mountain in
the reign of the late king, where he had contracted an intimate friendfhip with David. He had alfo married a fifter
of Ozoro Mamet, by whom Yafous had feveral children, par-

ticularly one Welleta Georgis, a prince then of years to govern, and confined to the mountain. David, on his coming to the throne, did not forget his old friendſhip on the mountain; and, paſſing by Emfras, he ſent to Wechné to bring down Kaſmati Georgis to Arringo, one of the king's palaces in Begemder, where he intended to paſs the ſummer. On his return he gave him the government of Gojam; and his favourite Agné, his uncle, dying at this time, very much regretted, Georgis was alſo created Betwudet in his place.

This year Abuna Marcus died; and his ſucceſſor, Abuna Chriſtodulus, arriving the third day of November, this made the calling of another aſſembly of the clergy abſolutely neceſſary, although, from the humour the laſt was in, the whole time of their meeting, the king was very little inclined to it.

The monks in Abyſſinia, as I have often ſaid, are divided into two bodies, thoſe of Debra Libanos and thoſe of Abba Euſtathius. Some have imagined that the difference between theſe two bodies ariſes from a diſpute about two natures in Chriſt. But this is from miſinformation; for, were a diſpute to ariſe about the two natures in Chriſt, each party would declare the other a heretic; but at preſent a few equivocal words, uſed to define the mode and moment of our Saviour's incarnation, though neither opinion is thought heretical *, have the effect to make theſe two ſects enemies all their lives.

The

---

* But there can be no doubt both opinions are abſolute hereſy, in the moſt liberal ſenſe of that word, as expreſsly denying our Saviour's conſubſtantiality

The Abuna is the head of the Abyssinian church; yet, as he is known to be a slave of the Mahometans, upon his first arrival, and permission obtained from the king, the assembly meets in a large outer court, or square, before the palace, where he is interrogated, and where he declares which of the two opinions he adopts. If he has been properly advised, he declares for the ruling and strongest party; though sometimes he is determined, by the address of those about him, to side with the weakest; and very often, if he has had no instruction on his arrival, he does not know what this reference means; for no trace of such dispute exists among his brethren in Cairo, from whence he came. He is, moreover, a stranger to the language, and the words containing either opinion, which, for shortness sake, are made to mean a great deal more than they at first seem to import; and, whether freely or literally translated, are equally unintelligible to a foreigner. After the Abuna has declared his choice, this is announced by beat of drum to the people, and is called *Nagar Haimanout*, or, the Proclamation of the Faith. The only ordinary effect this declaration has, is to make the person who is at the head of one party an adversary to him who is the head of the other, all his life after.

The king at his accession makes his declaration also. The clergy maintain, that he should do this in an assembly called for that purpose, though the king denies that there is any necessity for the clergy to be present; but he considers it as his privilege to choose his own time and place, and announces it to the people, by proclamation, at what time, and in what manner, he thinks most convenient.

Although

ALTHOUGH David had given his permiſſion to aſſemble the clergy to hear the Abuna's declaration, he did not think himſelf bound to aſſiſt at it, and, therefore, he ſent to the monks of Debra Libanos, and thoſe of Abba Euſtathius, to go to the Abuna with Betwudet Georgis, who ſhould interrogate the Abuna, and report the anſwer to the king, who thereupon would order it to be proclaimed to the people. The monks of Debra Libanos refuſed this, as they did not conſider Georgis as indifferent, being known to be a ſtaunch Euſtathian. They declared, therefore, they would neither hear nor regard what the Abuna ſaid, unleſs it was in the king's preſence; and this was juſt what David was reſolved not to humour them in.

BETWUDET GEORGIS, the great officers of ſtate, and moſt of the people of conſideration about Gondar, waited upon the Abuna as the king had commanded; and the Betwudet having deſired him to make his profeſſion, he would only give this evaſive anſwer; That his faith was in all reſpects the ſame as that of Abba Marcos and Abba Sanuda, the ancient and orthodox Abunas.

THIS anſwer left every party at liberty to imagine that the Abuna was their own. But this evaſion did not content the king, who therefore ordered the Betwudet, without taking further notice of the Abuna, to make proclamation in terms of the profeſſion of the monks of Abba Euſtathius. This occaſioned great heats among the monks of Debra Libanos. They ran all with one accord to the Itcheguè's houſe, for he is their general, or chief of their convent, and here they came to the moſt violent reſolutions, declaring that they would die either together, or man by man,

in

in fupport of their privileges and the freedom of their affemblies. From the Itchegué's houfe they ran to the Abuna's, without foliciting or receiving any permiffion from
the king; and, upon interrogation, they fucceeded with the
Abuna to the height of their wifhes; for he anfwered in
the precife words of their profeffion—" One God, of the
Father alone, united to a body perfectly human, confubftan-
tial with ours, and by that union becoming the Meffiah;"
in direct oppofition to what was proclaimed by the king's
order at the gate of the palace the day before—Perfect God
and perfect man, by the union one Chrift, whofe body is
compofed of a precious fubftance, called *Bahery*, not con-
fubftantial with ours, or derived from his mother.

Had they ftopt here it had been well; but the victory
was too great, too unexpected, and complete, to admit of
their fitting quietly down without a triumph. They returned, therefore, from the Abuna's, frantic with joy, fhouting,
and finging, and more peculiarly one kind of fong, or hallelujah, ufed always upon victories obtained over infidels.
As they paffed the door of the king's palace, fome of the
officers of the houfehold, Azage Zakery, Azage Tecla Haimanout, and Badjerund Welleta David, moderate men, lovers
of peace, and inclined to no party, endeavoured to perfuade
them to content themfelves with what they had done, to
difperfe, and each go to his home, before fome mifchief
overtook them. But they were too high-minded. They
redoubled their fongs; and, in this manner, again affembled in the Itchegué's houfe to deliberate on what further
they were to attempt; when one of the monks, a prophet,
or dreamer, declared, " That God had opened his eyes, and
that he then faw a cherub with a flaming fword guarding
the

the Itchegué's gate :" with fuch a centinel they concluded that they were perfectly fafe from any attempts of man.

In the mean time, however, the king was violently affected at the feditious behaviour of the monks ; nor did he hefitate a moment in what manner he was to punifh it. As they had employed the fong which was fung only for victories obtained over infidels, by which they meant to allude particularly to the king, he detached a body of Pagan Galla to punifh them ; having furrounded the Itcheguè's houfe, where the monks were affembled, they forced open the gate, (and the cherub with the flaming fword not interfering) they fell, fword in hand, upon the unarmed priefts, and in an inftant laid above a hundred of the principal of them dead upon the floor. They then fallied out with their bloody weapons into the ftreet, and hewed to pieces thofe that attended the proceffion, and who were ftill diverting themfelves with their fong. Gondar now appeared like a town taken by ftorm ; every ftrcet was covered with the dead, and dying ; and this maffacre continued till next day at noon, when, by proclamation, the king ordered it to ceafe.

David, now fatisfied as to the priefts, thought he owed to the Abuna a mortification for his double-dealing. He fent, therefore, the foldiers to take him out of his houfe, and bring him to the gate of the palace, where the poor wretch, half dead with fear, expected every moment to fall by the bloody hands of the Djawi. Having enjoyed his panic fome time, the king ordered him to be placed clofe befide the kettle-drum, and a profeffion of faith was made in the royal prefence, and announced by beat of drum to the people, agreeing in every refpect to that publifhed the firft day by

3 Betwudet

Betwudet Georgis, and directly contradicting what he had said with his own mouth to the monks of Debra Libanos, which was the occasion of the riot.

THIS bloody, indiscriminate massacre had comprehended too many men of worth and distinction not to occasion great discontent among the principal people both within and without the palace. Conspiracies against the king were now everywhere openly talked of, the fruits of which soon appeared. David fell sick, and those about him endeavoured to persuade him that it was the remains of an injury which he had lately received from a fall off his horse. But, upon the meeting of a council on the 9th of March 1719, it was discovered and proved, that Kafmati Laté and Ras Georgis had employed Kutcho, keeper of the palace, to give a strong poison to the king, which he had taken that morning from the hands of a Mahometan. Ras Georgis was then brought before the council, and scarcely denied the fact; upon which his only son was ordered to be hewn to pieces before his face, and immediately after the father's eyes were pulled out. Kutcho, keeper of the palace, and the Mahometan who gave the poison, were hewn to pieces with swords before the gate of the palace, and their mangled bodies thrown to the dogs. The king died that evening in great agony.

THE king's favourite, Betwudet Georgis, found himself now in a most dangerous situation. David his protector was dead, and he was left now alone to answer for those bloody measures of which he was universally believed to be the adviser. It was absolutely necessary, therefore, if possible, to secure a successor of David's own family, who might

might ftop the profecutions againft him for fteps the king had adopted as his own, and as fuch had carried into execution.

We have already obferved, that, when banifhed to the mountain of Wechné by Ouftas, he had contracted there, firft a friendfhip with David, and, at the fame time, with another prince, Ayto Welled Georgis, who was fon to Yafous by Ozoro Mamet, whofe fifter Georgis had married, and confequently was uncle to Ayto Welleta Georgis, as having married his aunt, fifter to Ozoro Mamet. When this prince now arrived at manhood, he knew himfelf perfectly fecure; and, therefore, a number of the men in power being then affembled at his houfe, he loft no time, but furrounded it with a body of foldiers. He propofed to them Welled Georgis as immediate fucceffor to David. The people prefent, feeing themfelves in the foldiers hands, and convinced from the recent examples, that Georgis was not very tender in the ufe of them, in appearance chearfully, and without hefitation, approved of the Betwudet's choice; and Lika Jonathan, one of the chief civil judges, performed the office of crier, proclaiming with an audible voice, " Ayto Welled Georgis, brother to our late king David, fon of our great king Yafous, he is now our king. Mourn for the king that is dead, but rejoice with the king that is alive." This is the ordinary ftile of the proclamation. Mutual congratulations and promifes paffed among the members of the meeting, but with very different refolutions.

All the company, efcorted by a body of archers, and another of fuzileers, with Betwudet Georgis at their head, repaired to the great place before the palace to make the

I

fame

fame proclamation by beat of drum that they had done in the Betwudet's houfe. They found the drum ready, and the whole body of the king's houfehold troops under arms, and drawn up before it. Upon the fight of their companions, the foldiers left the Betwudet, and fell into a proper place referved vacant for them by their brethren. Without lofs of time the drum was beat, and a proclamation made, " Bacuffa, fon of Yafous, is our king! Mourn for the dead, and rejoice with the living." Loud acclamations from the people were echoed back again by the foldiers, and Bacuffa's name was received with univerfal acclamations. Some of the principal people then went to the council-chamber, and fent proper officers, with a good body of troops, to efcort the king from Wechné.

Upon their arrival they found the fentiments of the princes upon the election were widely different from thofe teftified by the people. They all to a man declared their diffent from that election. They upbraided Bacuffa for his brutal manners; for his violent, unfociable, unrelenting temper, from the which, they faid, they had the crueleft confequences to apprehend; and, indeed, it was not without great reafon that they made thefe remonftrances; for Bacuffa, when he efcaped from the mountain, fled for refuge among the Galla, and received there a very ftrong tincture of the favage manners of that nation, which neither thofe of Gondar nor the army could have an opportunity to judge of. Refolute, active, and politic, he was very well formed to hold the reins of government in unfettled times; but his temper of itfelf exceedingly fufpicious, and the little regard he had for the life of man, made his whole reign (as it was feared) one continued tragedy. So that, notwithftanding the goodnefs of his underftanding, and many acts of wifdom and juftice, he is confidered as a bloody, mercilefs tyrant, and his memory regarded with the greateft deteftation.

On the firft news of the infurrection of the princes on Wechné, Kafmati Amha Yafous, governor of Begemder, marched with his whole force and encamped under the mountain. He then received Bacuffa as king, having refcued him from the hands of his relations; and, in order to obviate, as much as poffible, any future trouble, he obliged the different branches of the royal family to a reconciliation with each other, making Bacuffa, on the one fide, fwear that he was not to remember nor revenge any injury or affront received upon the mountain; and them on the mountain fwear alfo, that they would forget all old difagreements, confider Bacuffa as their king, and not create him any trouble in his reign by efcapes, or other rebellious practices.

As it was then night, Bacuffa ftaid in the houfe of Azage Affarat, and the next morning came to Serbraxos, whence he fent to the monks of Tedda to meet him there. From Tedda he proceeded to Gondar, where he was met by the Abuna and Itchegue amidft the acclamations of a prodigious number of people.

BACUFFA

B A C U F F A.

From 1719 to 1729.

Bloody Reign—Exterminates the Conspirators—Counterfeits Death—Becomes very popular.

HONEST men, who loved their country, saw the dangerous situation it was then in. Every day had produced instances of a growing indifference to that form of government which, from the earliest times, they had looked upon as sacred ; and upon every slight and unreasonable disgust a person of consequence thought he had met with, a party was immediately formed, and nothing less was agreed on than directly imbruing their hands in the blood of their sovereign.

A PRINCE was necessary who had qualities of mind proper to enable him to put a stop to these enormities before they involved the state in one scene of anarchy and ruin.

Bacuffa

Bacuffa was thought to anfwer thefe expectations; and, in the end, he was found to exceed them.. Silent, fecret, and unfathomable in his defigns, furrounded by foldiers who were his own flaves, and by new men of his own creation, he removed thofe tyrants who oppofed their fovereigns upon the fmalleft provocation. Confpiracy followed confpiracy, and rebellion rebellion; but all were defeated, as foon as they had birth, by the fuperior activity and addrefs of the king.

I HAVE faid he was called Bacuffa by the Galla; but, in compliance with the cuftom of Abyffinia, already mentioned, he had affumed ftill two other names, which were, Atzham Georgis, his name of baptifm, and Adebar Segued, which means "reverenced by the towns or inhabited places of the country," given him at his inauguration. As for that of Bacuffa, which meant the *inexorable*, it was the lefs difhonourable from having been given him by impartial ftrangers from their own obfervation while he was yet in private life; his whole conduct afterwards fhewed how juftly.

THE king has near his perfon an officer who is meant to be his hiftoriographer. He is alfo keeper of his feal, and is obliged to make a journal of the king's actions, good or bad, without comment of his own upon them. This, when the king dies, or at leaft foon after, is delivered to the council, who read it over, and erafe every thing falfe in it; whilft they fupply any material fact that may have been omitted, whether purpofely or not.. This would have been a very dangerous book to have been kept in Bacuffa's time; and, accordingly, no perfon chofe ever to run that rifk; and the king's particular behaviour afterwards had ftill the fur-

ther

ther effect, that nobody would supply this deficiency after his death, a general belief prevailing in Abyssinia that he is alive to this day, and will appear again in all his terrors. It is owing to this circumstance that we have nothing complete of this king's reign; only a few anecdotes are preserved, some of them very odd ones. I shall only, for the present, choose such of those as lead me to the subject I have in hand.

BACUFFA was exceedingly fond of divinations, dreams, and prophecies, so are all the Abyssinians; but he imbibed an additional propensity to these, among the Pagans to whom he had fled. One day, when walking alone, he perceived a priest exceedingly attentive in observing the forms that little pieces of straw, cut to certain lengths, made upon a pool of water into which ran a small stream. From the combination of these in letters, or figures, as they chanced to fall, an answer is procured to the doubt proposed, which, if you believe these idlers, is perfectly infallible.

BACUFFA in disguise, dressed like a poor man, is said to have asked the priest after what he was inquiring. The priest answered, He was trying whether the king would have a son, and who should govern the kingdom after him. The king abode the investigation patiently; and the answer was, That he should have a son; but that a Welleta Georgis should govern the kingdom after him for thirty years, though that Welleta Georgis should be neither his son nor any descendant of his. Full of thought at this untoward prediction, he harboured it in his breast without communicating it to any one, and resolved to blast the hopes of every Welleta Georgis that should be so unfortunate as to stand within the

possibility

poffibility of reigning after him. Many innocent people of different parts difappeared from this unknown crime; and eleven princes on the mountain of Wechné, fome fay more, loft their lives for a name that is very common in Abyffinia, without one overt act of treafon, or even a fufpicion of what they were accufed. A panic now ftruck all ranks of people, without terminating in any fcheme of refiftance; which fufficiently fhewed that the king had fucceeded in diffolving all confederacies among his fubjects, and deftroying radically that rebellious fpirit which had operated fo fatally in the laft reigns.

It is a cuftom among the kings of Abyffinia, efpecially in intervals of peace, to difappear for a time, without any warning. Sometimes, indeed, one or two confidential fervants, pretending to be bufied in other affairs, attend at a diftance, and keep their eye upon him, while, difguifed in different manners, he goes like a ftranger to thofe parts he intends to vifit. In one of thefe private journeys, paffing into Kuara, a province on the N. E. of Abyffinia, near the confines of Sennaar, Bacuffa happened, or counterfeited, to be feized by a fever, a common difeafe of that unwholefome country. He was then in a poor village belonging to fervants of a man of diftinction, whofe houfe was on the top of the hill immediately above, in temperate and wholefome air. The hofpitable landlord, upon the firft hearing of the diftrefs of a ftranger, immediately removed him up to his houfe, where every attention that could be fuggefted by a charitable mind was beftowed upon his difeafed gueft, who prefently recovered his former ftate of health, but not till the kind affiftance and unwearied diligence of the beautiful daughter of the

4   houfe

house had made the deepeſt impreſſion upon him, and laid him under the greateſt obligations.

THE family conſiſted of five young men in the flower of their youth, and one daughter, whoſe name was Berhan Magaſs, *the Glory of Grace*, exceedingly beautiful, gentle, mild, and affable ; of great underſtanding and prudence beyond her age ; the darling, not only of her own family, but of all the neighbourhood.

BACUFFA recovering his health, returned ſpeedily to the palace, which he entered privately at night, and appeared early next morning ſitting in judgment, and hearing cauſes, which, with theſe princes, is the firſt public occupation of the day.

A MESSENGER, with guards and attendants, was immediately ſent to Kuara, and Berhan Magaſs hurried from her father's houſe, ſhe knew not why, but her ſurpriſe was carried to the utmoſt, by being preſented and married to the king, no reply, condition, or ſtipulation being ſuffered. She gained, however, and preſerved his confidence as long as he lived : not that Bacuffa valued himſelf upon conſtancy to one wife, more than the reſt of his predeceſſors had done. He had, indeed, many miſtreſſes, but with theſe he obſerved a very ſingular rule ; he never took to his bed any one woman whatever, the fair Berhan Magaſs excepted, without her having been firſt ſo far intoxicated with wine or ſpirits as not to remember any thing that paſſed in converſation.

WHILE

WHILE Bacuffa was on his concealed journey to Kuara, a very dangerous confpiracy was forming at Gondar, under the immediate conduct of Ozoro Welleta Raphael, the king's fifter, a very ambitious woman, and of an unquiet, enter-prifing temper. Difgufted by her brother's refufal of a gift of fome crown lands which were then vacant, and without any owners, fhe thought no vengeance adequate to the af-front, but dethroning Bacuffa. With this view fhe enga-ged feveral men of power in her intereft, and particularly the black fervants of the palace who attend immediately upon the king's perfon, and were to feize upon, or deftroy him, the moment he returned. This plot, in all its parti-culars, was conveyed to the king.

THERE was an old, abandoned houfe of king Yafous, at Bartcho, about a day's journey fouth of Gondar; it ftands on a very extenfive plain. The king intending, as he faid, to repair, or rather clean and prepare this houfe for his im-mediate reception, ordered all the black flaves from Gondar thither for that purpofe, together with fome of their ring-leaders. Kafmati Waragna, in the mean time, was ordered to bring a thoufand horfemen of his Galla Djawi. He arrived at Bartcho nearly at the fame time with the black fervants, who being unarmed, as fufpecting nothing, and on foot, after a fharp reproof from the king, were all furrounded and cut to pieces by the hands of Waragna, and orders were imme-diately fent to Gondar to extirpate the remainder there; and this execution laid a foundation for a feud that endures to this day between the Galla troops and the black horfe, who were then abolifhed, as the Galla have been fince, though both were part of the king's houfehold formerly, before David's or Bacuffa's time. As for Welleta Raphael,

2   fhe

fhe was feized that fame night, and was conveyed to Wal-kayt, to be confined there, with private inftruccions, however, to put her to death fpeedily, which were executed accordingly.

THE queen had a fon within the year, whom the council named Yafous, after his grandfather, whofe memory will ever be dear in Abyffinia; and this again revived the old apprehenfions that Welleta Georgis was to govern the country (as the prophet faid) for thirty years. Tormented with this idea, rather than the havoc it had occafioned, he devifed with himfelf a fcheme which he thought would certainly detect this future ufurper of his crown and dethroner of his child. But firft he directed that the queen fhould be crowned, a ceremony that carries great confequences along with it when folemnized properly, as at that time fhe is made regent, or Iteghè, in all minorities that may happen afterwards.

AFTER he had created his wife Iteghè, Bacuffa pretended to be fick: feveral days paffed without hopes of recovery; but at laft the news of the king's death were publifhed in Gondar. The joy was fo great, and fo univerfal, that nobody attempted to conceal it. Every one found himfelf eafed of a load of fear which had become infupportable. Several princes efcaped from the mountain of Wechné to put themfelves in the way of being chofen; fome were fent to by thofe great men who thought themfelves capable of effecting the nomination, and a fpeedy day was appointed for the burial of the king's corpfe, when Bacuffa appeared, in the ordinary feat of juftice, early in the morning of that day, with the Iteghè, and the infant Yafous, his fon, fitting in a chair below him.

THERE was no occafion to accufe the guilty. The whole court, and all ftrangers attending there upon bufinefs, fled, and fpread an univerfal terror through the whole ftreets of Gondar. All ranks of people were driven to defpair, for all had rejoiced; and much lefs crimes had been before punifhed with death. What this fedition would have ended in, it is hard to know, had it not been for the immediate refolution of the king, who ordered a general pardon and amnefty to be proclaimed at the door of the palace.

THERE are two kettle-drums of a large fize placed one on each fide of the outer gate of the king's houfe. They are called the *lion* and the *lamb*. The lion is beat at the proclamations which regard war, attainders for confpiracies and rebellions, promotions to fupreme commands, and fuchlike high matters. The lamb * is heard only on beneficent, pacific occafions, of gifts from the crown, of general amnefties, of private pardons, and reverfals of penal ordinances. The whole town was in expectation of fome fanguinary decree, when, to their utter furprife, they heard the voice of the lamb, a certain fign of peace and forgivennefs ; and fpeedily followed by a proclamation, forbidding people of all degrees to leave their houfes, that the king's word was pledged for every one's fecurity ; and that all the principal men
fhould

---

* This drum is of beaten filver; the Abyffinians fay, that this metal alone is capable of conveying the fweet found contained in a proclamation of peace. It was carried off by the rebels after the retreat of Serbraxos.

fhould immediately attend him within the palace, in a public place which is called the Afhoa, and that upon pain of rebellion.

THE king appeared cloathed all in white, being the habit of peace; his head was bare, dreffed, anointed, and perfumed, and his face uncovered. He thus advanced to the rail of the gallery, about 10 feet above the heads of the audience, and, in a very graceful, compofed, but refolute manner, began a fhort oration to the people. " He put them in mind " of their wantonnefs in having made Ouftas, a man not of " the royal line of Solomon, king of Abyffinia; of their ha- " ving incited his brother, Tecla Haimanout, to affaffinate " their father Yafous; that they had afterwards murdered " Tecla Haimanout himfelf, one brother, and lately his " other brother David, his own immediate predeceffor: That " he had taken due vengeance upon all the ringleaders of " thofe crimes, as was the duty of his place, and, if much " blood had been fhed, it was becaufe many enormities had " been committed; but that knowing now that order was " eftablifhed, and confpiracies extinguifhed among them, he " had counterfeited death, to fignify an end was put to Ba- " cuffa and his bloody meafures; that he now was rifen " again, and appeared to them by the name of Atzham " Georgis, fon of Yafous the Great; and ordered every man " home to his houfe to rejoice at the acceffion of a new " king, under whom they fhould have juftice, and live " without fear, as long as they refpected the king that God " had anointed over them."

THIS fpeech was followed by the loudeft acclamations, " Long live Bacuffa! Long live Atzham Georgis!" It was

well

well known that this king never failed in his word, or any
way prevaricated in his promifes. Every one, therefore,
went home in as perfect peace as if war had never been a-
mong them; and Bacuffa's delicacy in this refpect was feen
a few days after; for Hannes his brother having been
brought clandeftinely from Wechné by Kafmati Georgis, a
nobleman of great confequence, they were both taken by
the governor of Wechnè and fent in chains to the king.
The ordinary procefs would have been to put them inftantly to death, as being apprehended in the very higheft act of
treafon; nor would this have alarmed any perfon whatever,
or been thought an infraction of the king's late promife.
Bacuffa, however, was of another mind. He fent the criminal judges, who ordinarily fit upon capital crimes, to meet
the two prifoners in their way to Gondar, and carried them
back to the foot of the mountain of Wechnè to have their
crimes proved, and to be tried there out of his prefence and
influence, where they were both condemned, Hannes to
have an arm cut off, Georgis to be fent to prifon to the governor of Walkayt, with private orders to put him to death;
both which fentences were executed; though Hannes fo far
recovered that he was king of Abyffinia in my time, notwithftanding this mutilation; but it was a direct violation
of the laws of the land.

It is faid that a difcovery, which happened in the king's
feigned illnefs, promoted this fudden revolution of manners.
In one of his fecret tours through Begemder, (after Tigrè,
the moft powerful province in Abyffinia, and by much the
moft plentiful) being difguifed like a poor man, dirty and
fatigued with the length of the way and heat of the weather, he came to the houfe of a private perfon, not very rich
indeed,

indeed, but of noble manners and carriage, and who, by the juftice and mildnefs of his behaviour and cuftoms, had acquired a great degree of influence among his neighbours. The father was old and feeble, but the fon in the vigour of his age, who was then ftanding in a large pool of water, at his father's door, wafhing his own cotton cloak, or wrapper, which is their upper garment; an occupation below no young man in Abyffinia.

Bacuffa, as overcome with heat, threw himfelf down under the fhade of a tree, and, in a faint voice and foreign dialect, intreated the young man to wafh his cloak likewife, after having finifhed his own. The young man confented moft willingly; and, throwing by his own garment, fell to wafhing the ftranger's with great diligence and attention. In the mean time, Bacuffa began queftioning him about the king, and what his opinion was of him. The young man anfwered, he had never formed any. Bacuffa, however, ftill plied him with queftions, while he continued wafhing the cloak, without giving him any anfwer at all; at laft, being able to hold out no longer, he gathered Bacuffa's cloak in his arms, wet as it was, and threw it to him : " I thought, fays he, when you prayed me to take your cloak, that I was doing a charitable action to fome poor Galla fainting with fatigue, and perhaps with hunger; but, fince I have had it in my hands, I have found you an inftructor of kings and nobles, a leader of armies and maker of laws. Take your cloak, therefore, and wafh it yourfelf, which is what Providence has ordained to be your bufinefs; it is a fafer trade, and you will have lefs time to cenfure your fuperiors, which can never be a proper or ufeful occupation to a fellow like you."

THE king took his wet cloak, and the rebuke along with it, and, on his return, he sent for the man to Gondar, and raised him in a short time to the first offices in the state. He possessed his entire confidence; and he deserved it. He was the only man to whom the king had confided his fears of the usurper Welleta Georgis. While Bacuffa was supposed to be ill, the queen and this officer only present, he mentioned, for the first time, some surprise that no such person as Welleta Georgis had appeared during so long and so many inquiries, and could not help dropping some words as if he doubted the truth of this prophecy.

BADJERUND WARAGNA, for that was the name of the king's friend, maintained modestly that it might be a temptation of the devil to mislead him to his destruction. He told the king, that, by his own account of it, this Welleta Georgis was to have no power over *him*, as he was only to appear in his son's time. He begged him, therefore, to lay aside all further thoughts of his prophecy, whilst he trusted his son's succession to God's mercy, and to the prayers, the charity, and prudence of the queen. The Iteghé all this time was lost in silence. She desired the king to repeat to her the whole circumstances of the prophecy, which he distinctly did. " I wish," says she laughing, " this Welleta Georgis may not be now nearer us than we imagine; perhaps in the palace." " In the palace!" says the king, with great emotion. " I doubt so," says the queen; " suppose it should be me your own wife; for Welleta Georgis was the name given to me in baptism; and your late coronation of me, should a minority happen in the person of your son, or even a grandson, undoubtedly leaves me regent of the kingdom

kingdom by your own intentions when you made me Iteghè.

Whether the king was convinced or not, is not known; but he, from this time, defifted from his perfecution of Welleta Georgis; and this the queen often told me among feveral anecdotes of that fingular reign. She was my great patronefs while at Gondar, and from her I received conftant protection in the moft difaftrous times. To the credit of the prophet, fhe continued regent full thirty years; till the folly and ambition of her own family gave her a mafter that put an end to all her influence, except what fhe enjoyed from exemplary piety, and the moft extenfive works of charity and mercy.

The king died after a vigorous reign, and after having cut off the greateft part of the ancient nobility near Gondar, who were of age to have been concerned in the tranfactions of the laft reigns. This has rendered his memory odious, though it is univerfally confeffed he faved his country from an ariftocratical or democratical ufurpation; both equally unconftitutional, as they equally ftruck at the root of monarchy.

The queen, with very great prudence, concealed the day of the king's death; nor did any one, after the laft experiment, affect rafhly to believe that his death was real. Thus all were upon their guard againft another refurrection. In that interval, fhe called her brothers from Kuara, and ftrengthened her fon's and her own government, by putting the principal offices of ftate into the hands of perfons attached to her family, fo that, though her fon Yafous was an infant, no attempt was at that time made towards any refo-

3.　　　　　　　　　　　　　　　　lution,

lution. Even after the king's death was known to be real, for many years afterwards there were people of credit at different times found, who faid they had met him at fundry places alive; whether by inftigation, for any particular purpofe, or not, is difficult to fay.

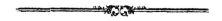

YASOUS II. or, ADIAM SEGUED.

From 1729 to 1753.

Rebellion in the beginning of this Reign—King addicted to hunting—To building, and the Arts of Peace—Attacks Sennaar—Lofes his Army—Takes Samayat—Receives Baady King of Sennaar under his Protection.

BESIDES the queen, mother of Yafous, Bacuffa had feveral other wives and divers children by them; none of them, however, had any degree of intereft, or many followers, owing to the very fingular practice of Bacuffa, already mentioned, in not admitting to his bed, from the time of his coming to the crown, any women except the queen, mother of Yafous, without having firft fo far intoxicated them with liquor as to produce an oblivion of all that paffed at the interview. Some fay this arofe from his own jealous ideas; but the

I   moft

moft general opinion was, that it was a kind of covenant with the queen, by which fhe pardoned him this temporary alienation of his perfon, for this fecurity, that he was to give her no rival in his confidence. Indeed, his own temper led him naturally to eftrange himfelf from every intimate connection, that could pretend to any lawful fhare with him in government. And this had gone fo far, that he fent his wife, favourite as fhe was, and his fon Yafous, to the low, hot, and unwholefome province of Walkayt, the ordinary place to which ftate criminals were banifhed, in order that they might be under the eye of Ain Egzie, a confidential fervant of his, and governor of that province. It is true this was done without any mark of difguft; and the queen returned immediately by his own command; but Yafous ftaid at Walkayt with Ain Egzie, till he was four years old, without the king his father having fhewn any anxiety for his return.

The queen's firft care was to call her brothers to court. The eldeft, Welled de l'Oul, had been a favourite of the late king, and occupied under him a very confiderable poft in the palace. Geta, her fecond brother, was a man of flow parts, but efteemed a good foldier; being covetous, he was not a favourite of the people, and lefs fo of the king. The third was Efhtè, (pronounced in that country Shitti); he was amiable, liberal, affable, and brave, but rather given to indolence and pleafure, which alone hindered him from being a good ftatefman and general. He was a kind friend to ftrangers, a good mafter, and placable enemy; ftedfaft to his promife, and on all occafions a lover of truth; a quality fo very rare in Abyffinia, that it was faid there had not been one in this refpect like him fince the time of Yafous the Great. Notwithftanding this, Bacuffa liked him not, as being too great a favourite of the people, and, for that reafon, never gave him any employment.

THE next brother was Eufebius, a very brave and fkilful foldier, but rafh, avaricious, paffionate, and treacherous, and as great an enemy to truth as his brother Efhtè was a friend to it. Bacuffa, upon fome flight complaint, had refolved to put him to death; and, though he was diffuaded from this, he could never be fo far reconciled to him as ever to releafe him from prifon. The fifth brother was Netcho, whom the defire of living at home, or, perhaps, a want of money to defray his expences at court, kept low and in obfcurity all his life-time. Yet he was a tried, gallant, and fkilful foldier; and in later years, when I was at Gondar, was often praifed as fuch by Ras Michael, the beft judge, becaufe the greateft general of his time, though, by reafon of Netcho's private life, and abfence from court, he never charged him with any important commiffion. Another brother was dead, and had left a fon called Mammo, a good horfeman, the only quality, as far as I know, that he poffeffed to which could juftly be annexed the epithet of Good.

OF thefe brothers, Geta and Netcho were alive in my time. Efhtè was dead, but had left two fons, Ayto Engedan and Ayto Aylo, who were among the moft intimate of my friends, from my entering Ethiopia till my leaving it; both were brave and good, and endowed with excellent qualities. Engedan, without any allowance for his country, and want of education, was, I think, by very much, the moft amiable and complete man that I have ever yet feen.

4

SANUDA,

Sanuda, fon of Welled de l'Oul, played a very confider-able part in the revolution that happened in my time; was of a figure more than ordinary graceful; was brave, and did not want good difpofitions; but thefe were obfcured by de-bauchery in wine and women, to which there were no bounds. Eufebius left two fons, both more worthlefs and profligate than himfelf, and both came to untimely ends: Guebra Mehedin, the eldeft, was flain in a private quarrel at Lebec by a near relation, Kafmati Ayabdar, after having robbed my fervants and plundered my baggage, in Foggo-ra, near the village Dara; and the fecond, Ayto Confu, was killed in rebellion at the battle of Serbraxos, among the Begemder horfe, fighting againft his fovereign.

Mammo we fhall find acting infignificant parts at times, never trufted, nor of confequence to any one. As for the queen herfelf, fhe was reputed the handfomeft woman of her time. She was defcended from Victor, eldeft brother to Menas, and fon of David, who died without coming to the crown. This daughter was married to Robel, governor of Ti-grè, whofe mother was a Portuguefe, and the queen inherit-ed the colour of her European anceftors; indeed was whi-ter than moft Portuguefe. She was very vain of this her defcent; had a warm attachment to the Catholic religion in her heart, as far as fhe could ever learn it; nor did fhe value herfelf lefs upon her beauty, as we may judge by the feveral names fhe took at different times. The firft was Iteghè Mantuab, or *the beautiful queen;* the fecond was Berhan Magwafs, or *the glory of grace;* though her chriftened name was Welleta Georgis, as we have already obferved.

After

After the death of her husband, Bacuffa, she is said to have descended to a variety of attachments of short duration. She married a man of quality, Kasmati Netcho of Kuara, by whom she had three daughters. The first was Ozoro Esther, of whom I shall often speak, being, next to her mother, the greatest friend I had in Abyssinia, and one who had the most frequent opportunities of being so. She was married, in very early life, to Kasmati Netcho of Tcherkin, a man of great personal qualities, and who had a very large territory, reaching down to the Pagan blacks, or Troglodytes, called Shangalla.

This marriage was of very short duration. Netcho left one son, Ayto Confu, my very great and firm, though young friend, who likewise inherited his father's fortune and virtues. She was afterwards married to Ayo Mariam Barea, (excepting Ras Michael) reputed the best general in Abyssinia, but who died before I came into the country. By him she had one son and a daughter, infants. Lastly, she was married to Ras Michael, by whom she had two sons, the favourites of Michael's old age. Rustic and cruel as that old tyrant was, bred up in blood, and delighting in it, she governed him despotically, from the day of her marriage, yet so prudently, as to excite the envy of no one, excepting the murderers of her husband Mariam Barea, who, luckily, were also the constitutional enemies of her country.

The second daughter of the Iteghé was Ozoro Welleta Israel, the most beautiful woman in Abyssinia, with whom I had very little acquaintance, she being at constant war with Ras Michael. She had married a nobleman of the first consideration, to whom half of the large and rich province of

Gojam belonged, by whom fhe had Aylo, one of the lar-geft men that I ever faw, the only particular remarkable in him.

THE third was Ozoro Altafh, married to Welled Hawaryat, Ras Michael's fon, by whom fhe had three children, two fons and one daughter. One of them died of the fmall-pox foon after my arrival at Gondar, as did his father alfo; the other fon and daughter happily recovered.

BACUFFA had provided fufficiently for the fecurity of his provinces, by placing tried and veteran officers in his govern-ments. Elias, indeed, was Ras and Betwudet at Gondar, and he was fufpected of wifhes contrary to his allegiance; but far before any, in the confidence of the late king, was War-agna Shalaka, that is, colonel of a regiment of Djawi Galla, with which he defended the provinces of Damot and Agow againft his countrymen on the other fide of the Nile; for he was a Galla of that nation himfelf, and his name was Ufho, which fignifies *a dog*. But it was more by his inter-eft, which he preferved with thofe people, than by his arms, that he kept thofe barbarians from wafting that country.

THE reader will eafily remember the firft occafion of his coming to Gondar was when Bacuffa faw him wafhing his clothes in a pool of water; and from the reproof, and his behaviour to the king on that occafion, as well as the duty and implicit obedience he paid to his commands afterwards, he was called Waragna, by way of contradiction, that word fignifying a fturdy rebel, or one that ftands up in defiance of the king. That name became much more famous afterwards

wards in the perfon of his fon, Waragna Fafil, to the very great detriment of the country in general.

The firft thing the queen did was to fend Shalaka Waragna, and Billetana Gueta David, with a large body of Mahometan fufileers, Djawi and Toluma Galla, to guard the mountain of Wechné, where the males of the royal family were imprifoned, that no competitor might be releafed from thence. The next ftep was to marry Ozoro Welleta Tecla Haimanout to Ras Elias, to confirm him, if poffible, in his much fufpected allegiance. After which, the Ras, judges, and foldiers of the king's houfehold, made this proclamation—" Bacuffa, king of kings, is dead! Yafous, king of kings, liveth! Mourn for thofe that are dead, and rejoice with thofe that are alive!" Orders were then given for burying Bacuffa with all magnificence poffible.

The firft thing that feemed the beginning of trouble in the new regency, and likely to deftroy the calm that had hitherto fubfifted, was an information given by Azage Georgis againft Tecla Saluce, a great officer at court. Georgis accufed him before the king and council, that he had been heard to fay that king Yafous was dangeroufly ill. Tecla Saluce abfolutely denied this charge, and faid it was an invention of his enemy Georgis, and challenged him to prove it. Evidence being called, he was convicted in the moft direct and fatisfactory manner; was therefore condemned to death, and hewn to pieces at the king's gate that fame day by the common foldiers.

Here is a fpecies of treafon without any overt act. The imagining the king's death, which feems much to refemble
ble

ble the law of England, may be defended from the importance of the cafe, but fcarcely from any principle of juftice
or reafon.

It foon appeared that a confpiracy had been on foot;
feveral great men fled from court, among thefe Johannes,
who had the charge of the king's horfes. But Shalaka Waragna and Billetana Gueta David, being fent immediately
after him, this confpiracy was foon ftifled, and the ringleaders difperfed, moftly into Amhara, where they were taken
prifoners by Woodage governor of the province, and fent to
the king. Johannes, finding it impoffible to efcape, took to
one of thofe papyrus boats ufed in navigating the lake Tzana; and, being driven by the wind, landed in an ifland* belonging to the queen, where he was taken prifoner, with
his wife and family, and delivered up, on condition that he
fhould not be put to death.

Kasmati Cambi, returning from Damot, fell acciden-
tally upon Palambaras Mafmari and feveral others, and
brought them prifoners to Gondar. A council was
thereupon held, and the confpirators put upon their trial,
Palambaras Mafmari, and Abou Barea who was one of the
judges, were condemned to be hanged on the tree before
the palace-gate. Johannes and the reft were committed to
clofe prifon, in the hands of the Betwudet.

It was thought a proper expedient to check thefe diforders,
to haften the coronation of the king, though very young.
The

* Dek.

The judges and all the officers being affembled in the pre-fence-chamber, where the king fits on his throne, (for in the council-chamber he fits in a kind of cage, or clofe balcony) where no part of him is difcovered, Sarach Mafferi Mammo, whofe office it was, ftood up with the Kees Hatzé, or king's almoner; when this laft had anointed him with oil, Mammo placed the crown upon his head; upon which the whole affembly, his mother only excepted, fell down and paid him homage; and at his inauguration he took the name of Adiam Segued.

On a feparate throne, on his right hand, fat the queen-mother. She, too, was crowned, though not anointed; but the fame homage was performed to her that had been done to the king, who fat on the throne with his head covered; nor did the Abuna interfere, nor was his attendance judged any part of the ceremony.

The firft feeds of difcontent had been fown in Damot, where a party of rebels had attacked Kafmati Cambi in the night, cut moft of his army to pieces, and obliged Shalaka Job to fly into Gojam, and then return in hafte to Gondar.

The king found no better remedy againft this rebellion than to appoint Kafmati Waragna governor of Damot, and Sanuda guardian of Wechné, with orders to take with him a fon of the late Ouftas the ufurper, and confine him with the king's fons upon that mountain. At the fame time he appointed Ayo governor of Begemder; both thefe prefer-ments being much to the fatisfaction of the whole nation. Waragna, knowing the neceflities of his province, marched from Gondar with what forces he could collect, and took

up

up his head-quarters at Samseen, where, on the very night after his arrival, he was set upon by Tenfa Mammo at the head of the Agows. However unexpected this was, Waragna, a good soldier, was not to be taken by surprise. He knew the country, and had not a great opinion either of the force or courage of the enemy, or capacity of their general. Presenting, therefore, only one half of his troops, which could not be easily discovered in the dark, he sent Fit-Auraris Tamba to make a small compass, and fall upon their rear with the other half. Mammo's troops, thinking this to be a fresh and separate army, immediately took to flight, and were many of them slain, after leaving behind them their tents, baggage, and the greatest part of their fire-arms, which had been of very little service to them in the dark.

WARAGNA, who knew the consequence of his province was the riches of it, and the dependence the capital had upon it for constant supplies of provisions, was loath to pursue his victory farther, if any means could be fallen upon to bring about a pacification. To effect this, he dispatched messengers to his friends, the Galla, on the other side of the Nile, ordering them to be ready to pass the river on the day he should appoint, and to lay waste the country of the Agow with fire and sword. He then decamped with his army from Samseen, and marched to Sacala, and took up his head-quarters in St Michael's church, where he found the Agows in the utmost terror from apprehension of being over-run with barbarians. But he soon eased them of their fears by a proclamation, in which he told them plainly, that it was owing to the goodness of the country, and not any merit in the people, that the king's palace and capital was so plentifully supplied with provisions from thence;

Vol. II.   4 I   that

that all his purfuit was peace, but that he was refolved to effect that end by every poffible means; therefore the time was now come that they were to make a refolution, and abide by it, to fubmit and behave peaceably as good citizens ought; or, when his army of Galla joined him, he would extirpate them to the laft man. In the mean time, he publifhed an amnefty of all that had paffed.

The Agows knew well that they were in the hands of one who was no trifler, nor in his heart much their friend. They ran to him, ready to make that compofition which he fhould raife from them for their paft tranfgreffions and his future protection. The tribute laid upon them, for both was moderate beyond all expectation, 2000 oxen for the king and queen, and 500 for himfelf; upon which he left Sacala, and entered Goutto, a very fertile country, between Maitfha and the Agows, where he ufed the fame moderation, and by thefe means quieted and reconciled his whole province.

Nothing could have been more advantageous to the king's affairs than the prudent conduct of this wife officer, which left him at liberty to afford him his affiftance; for in the mean time a confpiracy was formed at Gondar, which had taken deep root, and had a powerful faction, Elias, late Ras and Betwudet, Tenfa Mammo, Guebra l'Oul, Matteos and Agnè, all principal men in Gondar, and poffeffed of great riches and dependencies throughout the whole kingdom.

On the 8th of December 1734, being joined by their followers from without, they all rendezvoufed upon the ri-

ver

ver Kahha, below the town. After holding council in the king's houfe which is there, they refolved to proclaim one of the princes upon the mountain Wechné, named Hezekias, king. For this purpofe, furnifhed with a kettledrum, they marched in three divifions, by three different ways, to the palace, avowedly with an intention to force the gates and murder the king and queen. But Fit-Aurarís Ephraim, having intelligence of this tumult, firft fhut up and obftructed all the entrances to the king's houfe, then gave advice to Billetana Gueta, Welled de l'Oul, of the rebellion of Tenfa Mammo, their defign to murder the king, and their having proclaimed Hezekias.

THESE immediately repaired to the king's houfe to take council together what was to be done, and to defend the place if it was neceffary. The rebels were now drawn up, and were beating their kettle-drum to make their proclamation, "Hezekias was king !" while Shalaka Tchinfho, a young nobleman of great hopes, who commanded the troops in the court where was the outer gate, impatient to hear an u-furper proclaimed in the very face of his fovereign, directed the outer-court gate to be opened, and, with two bodies of Galla, Djawi and Toluma, and feveral corps of lances, which compofe the king's houfehold, however inferior in number, he rufhed upon the rebels fo fuddenly, that they were foon obliged to think of other occupation.

THE firft that fell was Afaleffi Lenfa, who ftood by the drum, and was flain by Shalaka Tchinfho with his own hand; his drum taken and fent to the king as the firft fruits of the day. The foldiers, encouraged by the example of their leader, fell fiercely upon the rebels, difperfed and

4 I 2   broke

broke through them wherever they faw the greateft number together; a great flaughter was made, and Tenfa Mammo, with difficulty, efcaped. The victory indeed would have been complete, had not an accidental fhot from a diftance wounded Shalaka Tchinfho mortally. His own people carried him within the gate of the palace, where he glorioufly expired at the feet of his fovereign.

THE rebels, notwithftanding this check, increafed every day in number and refolution, when the news arrived that Waragna had compofed all the differences in Damot, Agow, and Goutto, and, at the head of a numerous army, was waiting the king's orders. This intelligence firft had the effect to difconcert the rebels, who fuddenly left the capital in their way to Wechnè.

THE king, now mafter of Gondar, ordered a proclamation to be made for all perfons whatever holding fiefs of the crown, as alfo all others, to affemble before him on a fhort day, where the Itcheguè and Abuna, holding the picture of our Saviour, with the crown of thorns *, up before the people, did adminifter to them a folemn oath, to live and die with the king and Iteghé; a feeble experiment, often tried by a weak government. The only confequence of this was prefent expence to the crown in a diftribution of beef, honey, butter, wheat, and all kinds of provifions; after which each man returned to his houfe, ready to repeat the perjury ten times a day for the fame emolument, and fame fincerity.

MES-

---

* A relict of the moft precious kind, believed to have come from Jerufalem, and been painted by St Luke.

MESSENGERS were next difpatched to Kafmati Waragna, ordering him to come to Gondar with the greateft force he could raife. The fame day Azage Kyrillos, whom the king had made governor of Wechné, and Azage Newaia Selaffé, went to the mountain, pretending that king Yafous was dead, and that the choice of the principal members of government had fallen upon Hezekias, who thereupon was delivered to him, and faluted king; and, without lofing time, they marched to Kahha, and encamped on that river below Gondar.

IN the mean while, the great men and officers of the court, and in particular thofe who had eftates and houfes in Gondar, began to confider the danger of the town at the fo near approach of the rebels. Several diftricts, or ftreets, fituated on eminences, by fhutting up accefs to them, were made tenable pofts, and, having filled them with good foldiers, they fet about the defence of the town and annoying the enemy. Hezekias had removed to the houfe of Bafha Arkillidas; and it was agreed to fend their whole forces to fee if they could fucceed in forcing the king's houfe. But before this another ftratagem was tried to alienate the minds of the people of Gondar from their fovereign. It was faid that certain Roman Catholic priefts had arrived at Gondar; that they were fhut up privately in the palace with the king and queen; and, upon the Abuna and Itchegué coming to Hezekias to afk him how he happened to be proclaimed king, without making to them fome confeffion of his faith, (a queftion they put to all young or weak princes), Hezekias anfwered, It was becaufe he had heard the Itchegué, and the reft of the clergy, feemed to be carelefs about the true faith, by fuffering Catholic priefts to live with the king in
the

the palace. A great ferment immediately followed; all the monks, priests, and madmen that could be affembled, (and on thefe occafions they gather quickly), with the Itchegue and Abuna at their heads, went to Dippabye, the open place before the palace, and pronounced the Iteghè, Yafous, and all their abettors, accurfed and given up to burn with Dathan and Abiram.

For feveral days and nights attempts were made to fet fire to, and break open the gate. But the loyalifts charged them fo vigoroufly upon all thefe occafions, efpecially Billetana Gueta Welled de l'Oul, and the walls of the palace were fo exceedingly thick and ftrong, that little progrefs was made in proportion to the men thefe attempts coft daily. However, on that fide of the palace called Adenaga, the rebels had lodged themfelves fo near as to fet part of it on fire.

The king's houfe in Gondar ftands in the middle of a fquare court, which may be full an Englifh mile in circumference. In the midft of it is a fquare tower, in which there are many noble apartments. A ftrong double wall furrounds it, and this is joined by a platform roof; loop-holes, and convenience for difcharging miffile weapons, are difpofed all around it. The whole tower and wall is built of ftone and lime; but part of the tower being demolifhed and laid in ruins, and part of it let fall for want of repair, fmall apartments, or houfes of one ftorey, have been built in different parts of the area, or fquare, according to the fancy of the prince then reigning, and thefe go now by the names of the ancient apartments in the palace, which are fallen down.

These

THESE houfes are compofed of the frail materials of the country, wood and clay, thatched with ftraw, though, in the infide, they are all magnificently lined, or furnifhed. They have likewife magnificent names, which we have mentioned already. Thefe people, barbarous as they are, have always had a great tafte for magnificence and expence. All around them was filver, gold, and brocade, before the Adelan war, in which they loft the commerce of that country, by lofing their connection with India.

THE next night the foldiers of Elias made their lodgments fo near the walls, that, with fiery arrows, they fet one of thefe houfes, called " Werk Sacala," within the fquare, in flames ; but Welled de l'Oul, with the Toluma Galla, fallying at that inftant, furprifed Elias's foldiers, not expecting fuch interruption, and put the greateft part of them to the fword, fetting on fire the houfes that were near the palace, till part was entirely burnt to the ground. The next night, an attempt was made upon the gate to blow it up with gunpowder ; but, before it was completed, the two rebels employed in the work were fhot dead from the wall, and their train mifcarried.

ON the 25th of December they burned a new houfe in the town built by the king, called Riggobee Bet. Thefe frequent fires had turned the minds of people in general very much againft Hezekias the rebel. The night after, there was another great fire in the king's houfe ; Zeffan Bet, and another large building, were deftroyed by the rebels, as was the church of St Raphael. Gondar looked like a town that had been taken by an enemy, and battles were every day fought in the ftreets, with no decifive advantage to either

3   party

party. Some part of the town was on fire every night; nobody knew for what reafon, nor what was the quarter that
was next to be burnt.

In the mean time, Azage Georgis arrived in the country
of the Agows at Bafil Bet, where Waragna was, and delivered him the king's order, that he fhould make all poffible
hafte to his affiftance at Gondar, with as large an army as
he could fuddenly bring; and thefe difpatches conferred
upon him, at the fame time, as a mark of favour, the poft
of Ibaba Azage, or governor of Ibaba, together with Elmana and Denfa, two diftricts inhabited by Galla, fubjects to
the king, which pofts were then held by Tenfa Mammo, and
forfeited by his rebellion.

The next morning Waragna left his head-quarters at
Bafil Bet; thence he marched to Gumbali, and thence to
Sima. At Sima he heard, that, the day before, it had been
proclaimed at Ibaba, by orders of Tenfa Mammo, that Yafous was dead, and Hezekias was now king; upon this
intelligence he marched from Sima, and, while it was yet
early in the day, he came to Ibaba.

The firft inquiry was concerning the Shum (or chief of
the town) left there by Tenfa Mammo; and this man, coming readily to him to receive his commands, and offer
him any fervice in his power, was afked by whofe orders
the proclamation of Hezekias was made? Being anfwered,
by Tenfa Mammo's, he directed the Shum and his two fons
to be hanged on three feparate trees in the middle of the
town; the Shum with the nagareet round his neck which
had ferved in the proclamation of Hezekias; he then de-
I   clared

clared Tenfa Mammo a rebel and outlaw, and confifcated his eftate to the king's ufe.

At Ibaba he met Fit-Auraris Tamba, with a large body of Damots and Djawi; then he decamped from Ibaba, and, at the bridge over the Nile, was met by Azage Georgis, with all Maitfha, Elmana, and Denfa following, and thence proceeded to Waira, where he fet Arkillidas at liberty. This officer, after diftinguifhing himfelf before all others in the king's defence, had been taken prifoner by Tenfa Mammo, and fent thither. Advancing into Foggora, with a large army, he halted at Gilda, and fent fome foldiers on the road to Gondar, to fee if he could apprehend any travellers, efpecially thofe going or coming to or from market. But, after three days waiting on the road, the foldiers returned without any perfon or intelligence, by which he judged the town was already in great ftraits. In two days after, he advanced to Wainarab, and thence he fent his Fit-Auraris forward to fet a houfe at Tedda on fire, to fhew to the king at Gondar that he was thus far advanced to his affiftance. This barbarous cuftom of burning a houfe wherever an army encamps, though but for an hour, is invariably practifed, as a fignal by armies, throughout all Abyffinia.

At this time there was a treaty begun between the king and Tenfa Mammo. The rebels, weary of the little advantage they had gained, and hearing Waragna was about to march againft them, offered the queen her own terms, provided fhe publifhed a general amnefty, and that each man fhould be allowed to keep the pofts he had before the rebellion. The queen, weary and terrified with war, readily agreed to this propofal; and this facility, inftead of accelerating the treaty, gave the rebels an opportunity of afking further terms, and a fettlement was fpoken of for the king Hezekias, in fome of the low provinces near Wal-kayt.

WELLED DE L'OUL, the queen's brother, a man in whom: the rebels had truft, feconded his fifter's defire, and carried' on the treaty, but from different motives ; it was his opinion,. that, to make peace with the rebels, leaving their party unbroken, was to fpread the infection of rebellion all over the kingdom ; and to let them keep their pofts, was leaving a fword in their hands to enable them to defend themfelves on any future occafion. He therefore thought, that, as the king had Waragna now at his command, they fhould make ufe of him to pluck up this rebellion by the roots, cut off all the ringleaders, and difperfe the faction ; but, in the mean time, in order to be able to effect this, they fhould keep up the appearance of being anxious for agreeing, in order to lull the enemy afleep, till Waragna made his inftructions. and defigns known to the king.

FROM Wainarab, Waragna fent a meffenger to let the king and queen know of his arrival ; and with him came Arkillidas, that no doubt might remain of the truth of the meffage. This officer told the king, that Waragna fhould advance to Tedda, and offer the rebels battle there ; but if they retired (as he heard they intended) to Abra, he would follow them thither. He defired the king alfo to iffue his orders to the feveral Shums to guard the roads,. that as few of the ringleaders of the rebels might efcape as poffible.

HEZEKIAS,

HEZEKIAS, with his army, decamped, taking the road to Woggora; and Waragna, following him, came up with him at Fenter, on January 20th 1735. The rebels, inferior in number, though they did not wish an engagement at that time, were too high-minded to avoid it when offered. Both armies fought a long time with equal fortune; and though Waragna at the first onset had slain two men with his own hands, and taken two prisoners, the battle was supported with great firmnefs till the evening, when Waragna ordered all his Galla, the men of Maitfha, Elmana, and Denfa, to leave their horfes, and charge the enemy on foot. This confident ftep, unknown and unpractifed by Galla before, had the defired effect. The Galla now fought defperately for life, not for victory, being deprived of their only means of faving themfelves by flight.

MOST of the principal officers among the rebels being killed or wounded, their army at laft was broken, and took to flight. Hezekias was furrounded and taken, fighting bravely; being firft hurt in the leg, and then beat off his horfe with a ftone. The purfuit was prefently ftayed. Tenfa Mammo efcaped fafely through Woggora, a diffaffected province; and had now paffed the Tacazzè, when he was taken by the men of Siré, and brought to the king for the reward that had been offered for his head by Waragna.

HEZEKIAS was brought to his trial before the king, nor did he prefume to deny his guilt. He was therefore fentenced to die, and committed to clofe prifon. Tenfa Mammo was arraigned, and, although he confeffed the treafon, he pleaded the peace he had made with the king before

4 K 2   the

the arrival of Waragna at Gondar. This plea was unanimoufly over-ruled by the judges, becaufe the treaty had not been completed. He was, therefore, fentenced to die, and immediately carried out to the daroo-tree before the palace, and hanged between two of his moft confidential counfellors.

The Abuna and Itcheguè were next ordered to appear, and anfwer for the crime of high treafon in excommunicating the king; they declared they proceeded on no other grounds than an information, that the king and queen were turned Franks, and had two Catholic priefts with them in the palace. The men complained of were produced, and proved to be two Greeks; Petros, a native of Rhodes, and Demetrius. This explanation being given, the Abuna and Itcheguè thereupon afked pardon of the king and queen, and were ordered to make their recantation at Dippabye, which they immediately did, declaring they were wrong, and had proceeded on falfe information.

It was on the 28th of January that Sanuda and Adero were ordered to carry king Hezekias to Wechnè, which they did, and left him there without disfiguring him in any part of his body, as is the cruel, but ufual cuftom in fuch cafes. But both the Iteghè and her fon were of the moft merciful difpofition; and the general reputation they had for this was often the caufe of tumults and rebellions that would not have had birth in feverer reigns.

It was not long after this when there appeared a pretender to the crown, very little expected. He faid he was the old king Bacuffa; that he had given it out that he was
dead;

dead, for political reafons, and was come again to claim his crown and kingdom. Never was refurrection fo little wifhed for as this; a violent fear fell upon part of the multitude for fome time; but his name making no party, whether true or falfe, he was feized upon without bloodfhed, tried, and condemned to die. This punifhment was changed into one of a *fuppofed* gentler kind, the cutting off his leg, and fending him to Wechnè. The operation, always performed in the groffeft manner by an ax, high up the leg, and near the knee, is generally fatal; for there is no one, having either fkill or care, to take up the ends of the veins and arteries feparated by the amputation; they only apply ufelefs ftiptics and bandages, of no effect, till the patient bleeds to death. This is the common cafe, fo that the pretended Bacuffa died, in confequence of the operation, before he came to Wechné, though he was by his fentence reprieved from death.

The king, now arrived at the feventh year of his reign, proclaimed a general hunt, which is a declaration of his near approach to manhood; but he purfued it no length, and again returned to Gondar.

At that time, a great party of the queen's relations was made againft Ayo governor of Begemder. It began by a competition between Kafmati Geta the queen's brother, and Ayo, who fhould have that province. The common voice was for Ayo, not only as a man of the greateft intereft in the province, but in all refpects unexceptionable throughout the kingdom. Welled de l'Oul, (brother to Geta) however, being now Ras and Betwudet, Geta governor of Samen, Eufebius, and all the reft of them in high places at

court,

court, Geta was preferred to the government of Begemder. Ayo, though avowedly a good fubject of the king, was determined not to be made a facrifice to a party. He therefore refufed to refign his government, and prepared to defend himfelf.

Upon this, Adero, governor of Gojam, with the whole forces of that province, paffed the Nile, and entered Begemder; Geta on the fide of Samen, and laft of all Welled de l'Oul marched with a royal army to join the forces that had already begun to lay wafte the country, where unufual exceffes were committed. Ayo's houfe was burned to the ground, fo were all thofe of his party, and their lands deftroyed, greatly to the general damage of the province and capital. Ayo was now obliged to fave himfelf by flight. It was faid, that the king (though his army was ready) refufed to march againft Ayo ; but with a party of his own fet out for Aden, on the frontiers of Sennaar, to hunt there; nor did he return till the executions were over in Begemder.

Adero fell back to Gojam, and Welled de l'Oul to Gondar foon after. The king himfelf appeared very much contented with his own expedition, in which he had fhown great dexterity and bravery, having killed two young elephants, and a gomari, or hippopotamus, with his own hands. Nor did he ftay any time at Gondar, or make any preferments, the ufual confequences of victories, but prepared again for another hunting-expedition, or an attack upon the Shangalla. The queen and Welled de l'Oul oppofed ftrongly his refolution. But Yafous feemed to be weary of being governed. He was faft advancing to manhood, and

of

of a difpofition rather forward for his age. His expedition againft the Shangalla was attended with no accident; and he returned to Gondar on the 3d of June, with a number of flaves, much better pleafed that he had neglected, rather than taken, his mother's advice.

It was on the 23d day of December that Yafous again fet out on another hunting-party, and killed two elephants and a rhinoceros. He then proceeded to Tchelga, and from Tchelga to Waldubba; thence he went to the rivers Gandova and Shimfa. Thefe are two rivers we fhall have occafion frequently to fpeak of in our return through Sennaar, in which kingdom the one is called Dender, the other Rahad. Here he exercifed himfelf at a very violent fpecies of hunting, that of forcing the gieratacachin, which means long-tail; it is otherwife called giraffa in Arabic. It is the talleft of beafts; I never faw it dead, nor, I think, more than twice alive, and then at a diftance. It is, however, often killed by the elephant-hunters. Its fkin is beautifully variegated when young, but turns brown when arrived at any age. It is, I apprehend, the camelopardalis, and is the only animal, they fay, that, in fwiftnefs, will beat a horfe in the fair field.

It was not with a view to hunt only, that Yafous made thefe frequent excurfions towards the frontiers of Sennaar. His refolution was formed (as it appeared foon after) in imitation of his forefather Socinios, to revive his right over the country of the *Shepherds*, his ancient vaffals, who, fince the acceffion of ftrength by uniting with the Arabs, had forgot their ancient tribute and fubjection, as we have already obferved.

THE king in five days marching from Gidara came to a ftation of the Daveina, which is a tribe of fhepherds, by much the ftrongeft of any in Atbara. He fell into their encampments a little before the dawn of day. The firft fhew they made was that of refiftance, till they had got their horfes and camels faddled; they then all fled, after the king had killed three of them with his own hand. Ras Woodage fignalized himfelf likewife by having flain the fame number with the king. The cattle, women, and provifions fell all into the king's hand, and were driven off to Gondar. Their arrival gave the town an entertainment to which they had a long time been ftrangers. Many thoufand camels were affembled in the plain, where ftands the palace of Kahha, (upon a river of that name) large flocks of horned cattle, of extraordinary beauty, were alfo brought from Atbara, which the king ordered to be diftributed among his foldiers, and the priefts of Gondar, and fuch of the officers of ftate as had been neceffarily detained on account of the police, and had not followed the army.

This year, 1736, there happened a total eclipfe of the fun which very much affected the minds of the weaker fort of people. The dreamers and the prophets were everywhere let loofe, full of the lying fpirit which poffeffed them, to foretel that the death of the king, and the downfal of his government were at hand, and deluges of civil blood were then fpeedily to be fpilt both in the capital and provinces. There was not, indeed, at the time any circumftance that warranted fuch a prediction, or any thing likely to be more fatal to the ftate, than the expenditure of the large fums of money that the turn the king had taken fubjected him to.

4   HE

He had built a large and very coftly church at Kofcam, and he was ftill engaged in a more expenfive work in the building of a palace at Gondar. He was alfo rebuilding his houfe at Riggobee-ber, (the north end of the town) which had been demolifhed by the rebels ; and had begun a very large and expenfive villa at Azazo, with extenfive groves, or gardens, planted thick with orange and lemon trees, upon the banks of a beautiful and clear river which divides the palace from the church of Tecla Haimanout, a large edifice which, fome time before, he had alfo built and endowed. Befides all thefe occupations, he was deeply engaged in ornamenting his palace at Gondar. A rebellion, maffacre, or fome fuch misfortune, had happened among the Chriftians of Smyrna ; who, coming to Cairo, and finding that city in a ftill lefs peaceable ftate than the one which they had left, they repaired to Jidda in their way to India ; but miffing the monfoon, and being deftitute of money and neceffaries, they croffed over the Red Sea for Mafuah, and came to Gondar. There were twelve of them filver-fmiths, very excellent in that fine work called filligrane, who were all received very readily by the king, liberally furnifhed both with neceffaries and luxuries, and employed in his palace as their own tafte directed them.

By the hands of thefe, and feveral Abyffinians whom they had taught, fons of Greek artifts whofe fathers were dead, he finifhed his prefence-chamber in a manner truly admirable. The fkirting, which in our country is generally of wood, was finifhed with ivory four feet from the ground. Over this were three rows of mirrors from Venice, all joined together, and fixed in frames of copper, or cornices gilt with gold. The roof, in gaiety and tafte, correfponded perfectly

fectly with the magnificent finiſhing of the room; it was the work of the Falaſha, and conſiſted of painted cane, ſplit and diſpoſed in Moſaic figures, which produces a gayer effect than it is poſſible to conceive. This chamber, indeed, was never perfectly finiſhed, from a want of mirrors. The king died; taſte decayed; the artiſts were neglected, or employed themſelves in ornamenting ſaddles, bridles, ſwords, and other military ornaments, for which they were very ill paid; part of the mirrors fell down; part remained till my time; and I was preſent when the laſt of them were deſtroyed, on a particular occaſion, after the battle of Ser-braxos, as will be hereafter mentioned.

THE king had begun another chamber of equal expence, conſiſting of plates of ivory, with ſtars of all colours ſtained in each plate at proper diſtances. This, too, was going to ruin; little had been done in it but the alcove in which he ſat, and little of it was ſeen, as the throne and perſon of the king concealed it.

YASOUS was charmed with this multiplicity of works and workmen. He gave up himſelf to it entirely; he even wrought with his own hand, and rejoiced at ſeeing the fa-cility with which, by the uſe of a compaſs and a few ſtraight lines, he could produce the figure of a ſtar equally exact with any of his Greeks. Bounty followed bounty. The beſt villages, and thoſe near the town, were given in property to the Greeks that they might recreate themſelves, but at a diſtance, always liable to his call, and with as little loſs of time as poſſible. He now renounced his favourite hunting-matches and incurſions upon the Shangalla and Shepherds of Atbara.

THE.

THE extraordinary manner in which the king employed his time foon made him the object of public cenfure. Pafquinades began to be circulated throughout the capital; one in particular, a large roll of parchment, intituled, " The expeditions of *Yafous the Little*." The king in reality was a man of fhort ftature. The Ethiopic word Tannufh, joined to the king's name Yafous el Tannufh, applied both to his ftature and actions. So Tallac, the name given to another Yafous, his predeceffor, fignified great in capacity and atchievement, as well as that he was of a large and mafculine perfon.

THESE expeditions, though enumerated in a large fheet of parchment, were confined to a very few miles; from Gondar to Kahha, from Kahha to Kofcam, from Kofcam, to Azazo, from Azazo to Gondar, from Gondar to Kofcam, from Kofcam to Azazo, and fo on. It was a fimilar piece of ridicule upon his father Philip, as we are informed, that, in the laft century, coft Don Carlos, prince of Spain, his life.

THIS fatire nettled Yafous exceedingly; and, to wipe off the imputation of inactivity and want of ambition, he prepared for an expedition againft Sennaar. It was not, however, one of thofe inroads into Atbara upon the Arabs and Shepherds, whom the Funge had conquered and made tributary to them; but was a regular compaign with a royal army, aimed directly at the very vitals of the monarchy of Sennaar, the capital of the Funge, and at the conqueft or extirpation of thofe ftrangers entirely from Atbara.

WE have feen, in the courfe of our hiftory, that thefe two kingdoms, Abyffinia and Funge, had been on very bad

terms

terms during feveral of the laft reigns ; and that perfonal affronts and flights had paffed between the cotemporary princes themfelves. Baady, fon of L'Oul, who fucceeded his father in the year 1733, had been diftinguifhed by no exploits worthy of a king, but every day had been ftained with acts of treachery and cruelty unworthy of a man. No intercourfe had paffed between Yafous and Baady during their refpective reigns ; there was no war declared, nor peace eftablifhed, nor any fort of treaty fubfifting between them.

Yasous, without any previous declaration, and without any provocation, at leaft as far as is known, raifed a very numerous and formidable army, and gave the command of it to Ras Welled de l'Oul ; and Kafmati Waragna was appointed his Fit-Auraris. The king commanded a chofen body of troops, feparate from the reft of the army, which was to act as a referve, or as occafion fhould require, in the pitched battle. This he ardently wifhed for, and had figured to himfelf that he was to fight againft Baady in perfon. Yafous, from the moment he entered the territory of Sennaar, gave his foldiers the accuftomed licence he always had indulged them with, when marching through an enemy's country. He knew not, in thefe circumftances, what was meant by mercy; all that had the breath of life was facrificed by the fword, and the fire confumed the reft.

An univerfal terror fpread around him down to the heart of Atbara. The Shepherds and Arabs, as many as could fly, difperfed themfelves in the woods, which, all the way from the frontiers of Abyffinia to the river Dender, are very thick, and in fome places almoft impenetrable. Some of the Arabs,

Arabs, either from affection or fear, joined Yafous in his march ; among thefe was Nile Wed Ageeb, prince of the A-rabs ; others taking courage, gathered, and made a ftand at the Dender, to try their fortune, and give their cattle time to pafs the Nile, and then, if defeated, they were to follow them. Kafmati Waragna, (as Fit-Auraris) joined by the king, no fooner came up with thefe Arabs on the banks of the Dender, than he fell furioufly upon them, broke and dif-perfed them with a confiderable flaughter ; then leaving Ras Welled de l'Oul with the king, and the main body to encamp, taking advantage of the confufion the defeat of the Arabs had occafioned, he advanced by a forced march to the Nile, to take a view of the town of Sennaar.

BAADY had affembled a very large army on the other fide of the river, and was preparing to march out of Sennaar ; but, terrified at the king's approach, the defeat of the Arabs, and the velocity with which the Abyffinians advanced, he was about to change his refolution, abandon Sennaar, and retire north into Atbara.

THERE is a fmall kingdom, or principality, called Dar-Fowr, all inhabited by negroes, far in the defert weft of Sennaar, joining with two other petty negro ftates like itfelf; ftill farther weftward, called Selé and Bagirma, while to the eaftward it joins with Kordofan, formerly a province of Dar Fowr, but conquered from it by the Funge.

HAMIS, prince of Dar Fowr, had been banifhed from his country in a late revolution occafioned by an unfuccefsful war againft Selé and Bagirma, and had fled to Sennaar; where he had been received kindly by Baady, and it was by

his

his affiftance the Funge had fubdued Kordofan. This prince, a gallant foldier, could not bruik to fee the green ftandard of his prophet Mahomet flying before an army of Chriftians; and, being informed of the king's march and fe-paration from the main body nearly as foon as it happened, he propofed to Baady, that, as an allurement to Yafous to pafs the river with only the troops he had with him, he fhould do from prudence what he refolved to do from fear, and fall back behind Sennaar, leaving it to Yafous to en-ter; but, in the mean time, that, he fhould difpatch him with 4000 of his beft horfe, armed with coats of mail, to pafs the Nile at a known place below, on the right of Wel-led de l'Oul, on whom he fhould fall by furprife, and, if lucky enough to defeat him, as was probable, he would then clofe upon Yafous's rear, which would of neceffity either oblige him to furrender, or lofe his life and army in attempting to repafs the river between the two Nubian ar-mies. This counfel, for many reafons was perfectly agree-able to Baady, who inftantly fell back from covering Sen-naar, and then detached Hamis to make a circuit out of fight, and crofs the Nile as propofed.

In the mean time, Yafous advanced to Bafboch, where he found the current too rapid, and the river too deep for his infantry. He difpatched, therefore, a meffenger to Wel-led de l'Oul for a reinforcement of horfe, and gave his in-fantry orders to retire to the main body upon the arrival of the reinforcement of cavalry. This refolution he had taken upon advancing higher up the river from Bafboch, till oppofite to the town of Sennaar, and when divided only from it by the Nile. He there faw the confufion that reign-ed in that large town. No preparation for refiftance being

I   vifible,

vifible, the cries of women at the fight of an enemy fo near them, and the hurry of the men deferting their habitation loaded with the moft valuable of their effects, all increafed the king's impatience to put himfelf in poffeffion of this capital of his enemy.

It happened that an Arab, belonging to Nile Wed Ageeb, had feen the manœuvre of Hamis and his cavalry. This man, croffing the Nile at the neareft ford, came and told his mafter, Wed Ageeb, what he had feen, who informed the king of his danger. Upon interrogating the Arab, it was found that the affair of Welled de l'Oul would certainly be over before the king could poffibly join him; and in that cafe he muft fall in the midft of a victorious army, and his deftruction muft then be inevitable, if he attempted it. It was, therefore, agreed, as the only means poffible to fave the king and that part of the army he had with him, to retreat in the route Shekh Nile fhould indicate to them, marching up with the river Nile clofe on their right hand, and leaving the defert between that and the Dender, which is abfolutely without water, to cover their left. This was executed as foon as refolved.

In the mean time, Hamis had croffed the Nile, and continued his march with the utmoft diligence, and, in the clofe of the evening, had fallen upon Welled de l'Oul as unexpectedly as he could have wifhed. The Abyffinians were everywhere flaughtered and trodden down before they could prepare themfelves for the leaft refiftance. All that could fly fheltered themfelves in the woods: but this refuge was as certain death as the fword of the Funge; for, after leaving the river Dender, all the country behind them was

was perfectly deftitute of water. Ras Welled de l'Oul, and fome other principal officers, under the direction of fome faithful Arabs, efcaped, and, with much difficulty, two days after, joined the king.

Besides thefe, the army, confifting of 18,000 men, either perifhed by the fword, by thirft, or were taken prifoners; all the facred reliques, which the Abyffinians carry about with their armies to enfure victory, and avert misfortune; the picture of the crown of thorns, called *fele quarat rafou;* pieces of the true crofs; a crucifix that had on many occafions fpoke, (which fhould ever after be dumb fince it fpoke not that day); all thefe treafures of prieftcraft were taken by the Funge, and carried in triumph to Sennaar. Great part of thofe Arabs, who had joined the king in his march northward, had now quitted him and attached themfelves to the purfuit of the fugitive remains of Welled de l'Oul's army. As thefe Arabs were thofe that lived neareft the Abyffinian frontier, and to whom the king had done no harm, becaufe they had moftly joined him, no fooner was he informed of their treachery, but juft arrived in their country, and fcarcely out of danger from the purfuit of the Funge, Yafous turned fhort to the left, deftroying with fire and fword all the families of thofe that had forfaken him, and fo continued to do till arrived on the banks of the Tacazzé.

The Arabs and Shepherds there, many of whom had juft returned from the deftruction of Welled de l'Oul's army at Sennaar, and were now rejoicing their families with the news of fo complete a victory, and that all danger from the Chriftian army was over, were aftonifhed to fee Yafous at the head of a frefh and vigorous army, burning and de-

ftroying

ſtroying their country, and committing all ſort of devaſtation, when they thought him long ago dead, or fugitive, and ſkulking half-famiſhed on the banks of the Dender.

The king returned in this manner to Gondar, carrying more the appearance of a conqueror than one who had ſuffered the loſs of a whole army, his ſoldiers being loaded with the ſpoils of the Arabs, and multitudes of cattle driven before them.   It was but too viſible, however, by the countenances of many, how wide a difference there was between the loſs and the acquiſition.

It was, indeed, not from the preſence or behaviour of the king, nor yet from his diſcourſe, that it could be learned any ſuch misfortune had befallen him.   On the contrary, he affected greater gaiety than uſual, when talking of the expedition ; and ſaid publicly, and laughing, one day, as he aroſe from council, " Let all thoſe who were not pleaſed with the ſong of Koſcam ſing that of Sennaar." From this many were of opinion, that he enjoyed a kind of malevolent pleaſure from the misfortune which had befallen his army, who, not content with ſeeing him cultivate and enjoy the arts of peace, had urged him to undertake a war of which there was no need, and for which there was no provocation given, though in it there was every ſort of danger to be expected.

Although Yaſous gave no conſolation to his people, the prieſts and fanatics ſoon endeavoured to prepare them one. Tenſa Mammo arrived from Sennaar with the crown of thorns, the true croſs, and all the reſt of that precious merchandiſe, ſafe and entire, only a little profaned by the bloody hands of the Moors.   Ras Welled de l'Oul's army, confifting of 18,000 of their fellow-citizens, was lying dead upon the Dender.   It was no matter; they had got the fpeaking crucifix, but had paid 8000 ounces of gold for it.   Still it was no matter; they had got the crown of thorns.   The priefts made proceffions from church to church, finging hallelujahs and fongs of thankfgiving, when they fhould have been in fackcloth and afhes, upon their knees deprecating any further chaftifement upon their pride, cruelty, and profanenefs.   All Gondar was drunk with joy; and Yafous himfelf was aftonifhed to fee them finging the fong of Sennaar much more willingly than that of Kofcam.

At this time died Abuna Chriftodulus; and it was cuftomary for the king to advance the money to defray the expence of bringing a fucceffor.   But Yafous's money was all gone to Venice for mirrors ; and, to defray the expence of bringing a new Abuna, as well as of redeeming of the facred reliques, he laid a fmall tax upon the churches, faying merrily, " that the Abuna and the croffes were to be maintained, and repaired by the public ; but it was incumbent upon the church to purchafe new ones when they were worn out."

Theodorus, prieft of Debra Selalo, Likianos of Azazo, and Georgis called Kipti, were configned to the care of three Mahometan merchants and brokers at court, whofe names were Hamet Ali; Abdulla, and Abdelcader, to go to Cairo and fetch a fucceffor for Chriftodulus.   They arrived at Hamazen on April 29th 1743, where the Mahometan guides chofe rather to pafs the winter-feafon than at Mafuah, as at that place they were apprehenfive they would fuffer extortions and

and ill-ufage of every fort.   We know not what came of Georgis Kipti ; but, as foon as the rainy feafon was over, Theodorus and Likianos came ftraight to Mafuah.

As foon as the Naybe got the whole convoy of priefts and Mahometans into his hands, he demanded of them half of the money the king had given them to defray the expences of fetching the Abuna. He pretended alfo, that both Mahometans and Chriftians fhould have paffed the rainy feafon at Mafuah. He declared that this was his perquifite, and that he had prepared great and exquifite provifions for them, which, being fpoiled and become ufelefs, it was but reafonable they fhould pay as if they had confumed them : till this was fettled, he declared that none of them fhould embark or ftir one ftep from Mafuah.

THE news of this detention foon arrived at Gondar ; and Yafous gave orders that Michael Suhul, governor of Tigrè, (afterwards Ras) and the Baharnagafh, fhould with an army blockade Mafuah, fo as to ftarve the Naybe into a more reafonable behaviour. But, before this could be executed, the Naybe had called the priefts before him, and declared, if they did not furrender the money that inftant, he would put them to death ; and, in place of giving them time to refolve, he gave them a very plain hint to obey, by ordering the executioner to ftrike off the heads of two criminals condemned for other crimes, after having brought them into their prefence. The poor wretches, Theodorus and Likianos, did not refemble Portuguefe, who would have braved thefe threats in the purfuit of martyrdom. The fight of blood was the moft convincing of all arguments the Naybe could ufe. They gave up the money, leaving the divifion of it to his own difcretion. He then hurried them on board a veffel, giving Michael and the Baharnagafh notice that they were gone in fafety, and that he had obeyed the king's orders in all refpects. Michael was at that time in the ftricteft friendfhip with the Naybe, who was his principal inftrument in collecting fire-arms' in Arabia to ftrengthen him in the quarrel he was then meditating againft his fovereign.

On the 8th of February 1744 the priefts and their guides failed from Mafuah; and they did not arrive at Jidda till the 14th of April. There they found that the fhips for Cairo were gone, and that they had loft the monfoon; and, as no misfortune comes fingle, the Sherriffe of Mecca made a demand upon them for as much money as they had paid the Naybe; and, upon refufal, he put Abdelcader in prifon, nor was he releafed for a twelvemonth after, when the money was fent from Abyffinia; and it was then agreed, that 75 ounces of gold* fhould in all future times be paid for leave of paffage to thofe who went to Cairo to fetch the Abuna; and 90 ounces a-piece to the Sherriffe, and to the Naybe, for allowing him to pafs when chofen, and furnifhing him with neceffaries during his ftay in their refpective government; and this is the agreement that fubfifts to this day.

In this interim, Likianos of Azazo, one of the priefts, weary of the journey and of his religion, and having quarrelled with Abdulla, renounced the Chriftian faith, and embraced that of Mahomet; and Theodorus, Abdulla, and Hamet Ali, being the only three remaining, hired a veffel at Jidda to carry them to the port of Suez, the bottom of the Arabic

*About one hundred and eighty-fix pounds, an ounce of gold at a medium being 10 crowns.

Arabic Gulf. Before they had been a month at fea, Abdulla died, as did Hamet Ali feven days after they arrived at Suez. They had been on fea three months and fix days from Jidda to that port, becaufe they failed againft the monfoon.

It was the 25th of June that Theodorus arrived at Cairo, delivered the king's prefent, the account of the Abuna's death, and the king's defire of having fpeedily a fucceffor. The patriarch, having called together all his bifhops, priefts, and deacons, conferred the dignity on a monk of the Order of St Anthony, the only Order of monks the Coptic church acknowledges. Thefe pafs a very auftere life in two convents in a dreary defert, never tafting flefh, but living on olives, falt fardines *, wild herbs, and the worft of vegetables. Yet fo attached are they to this folitude, that, when they are called to be ordained to this prelature of Abyffinia, a warrant from the bafha, and a party of Turks, is neceffary to bring this eleft one to Cairo in chains, where he is kept in prifon till he is ordained; guarded afterwards, and then forced on board a veffel which carries him to Abyffinia, whence he is certain never to return.

The Abuna departed from Suez the 20th of September; the beginning of November he arrived at Jidda; in February 1745 he failed from Jidda, taking with him Abdelcader, now freed from prifon; he arrived at Mafuah the 7th of March, and immediately fent an exprefs to notify his arrival to the king and queen, and to Ras Welled de l'Oul. Congratulations

---

* This is a fifh common in the Mediterranean, of the kind of anchovies, the common food of the galley-flaves, and lower fort of people.

gratulations upon the event were returned from each of them; they requested he would immediately come to court; but this the Naybe refused to permit, till he had first received his dues; and Yafous feemed inclined to pay no more for him than what he had coft already.

THE priefts, and devout people in Tigré, were very defi-rous to free the Abuna from his confinement in Mafuah. They faw that the king was not inclined to advance money, and all of them knew perfectly, that, whatever face he put upon the matter, the Ras would not give an ounce of gold to prevent the Abuna from ftaying there all his life. In this exigency they applied to Janni, a Greek, living at Ado-wa, (of whom I fhall hereafter fpeak), a confidential fervant and favourite of Michael, and alfo well acquainted at Ma-fuah, to fee if he could get him releafed by ftratagem. Janni concerted the affair with the monks of the monaftery of Bizan, two of whom conducted the Abuna by night out of the ifland of Mafuah, and landed him fafely in their mona-ftery in the wildernefs, with the *myron*, or confecrated oil, in one hand, and his miffal, or liturgy, in the other. So far the efcape was complete; but unluckily no orders had been gi-ven for Theodorus, who accordingly remained behind at Mafuah.

THE Naybe, exafperated at the Abuna's flight, wrecked his vengeance on poor Theodorus; he put him in irons, and threw him into clofe prifon, where he remained for two months. There was no remedy but paying 80 ounces of gold to the Naybe for his releafe; he might elfe have remained there for ever.

2   THE

THE king, not a little furprifed at thefe frequent info-
lences on the part of the Naybe, began to inquire what
could be the reafon ; for he perfectly knew, not only Suhul
Michael, the governor of Tigrè, but even the Baharnagafh,
could reduce Mafuah to nothing with their little finger; and
he was informed, that a ftrong friendfhip fubfifted between
the Naybe and Suhul Michael, and that it was by relying on
his friendfhip that the Naybe adventured to treat the.
king's fervants, at different times, in the manner he had
done.

YASOUS, defirous to verify this himfelf, and to diffolve the
bands of fo unnatural a friendfhip, marched into Tigrè with
a confiderable army. Paffing by Adowa, the refidence of
Suhul Michael, he was pleafed with the warlike appearance.
of this his feat of government, and the perfect order and
fubordination that reigned there. Certain diforders and tumults were faid to prevail in the neighbouring province of
Enderta where Kafmati Woldo commanded. The favage
people, called Azabo, living at Azab, the low country below.
Enderta and the Dobas, (a nation of *Shepherds* near them, ftill
more favage, if poffible, than them) had laid wafte the diftricts that were next to their frontier, burning the churches,
and flaying the priefts in the daily inroads which they
made into Abyffinia. All thefe things, bad enough indeed,
were at this time aggravated, as was thought, for two reafons ; the firft was to caft an odium upon Kafmati Woldo, Michael's great enemy, as incapable of governing his province ;
the fecond, to prevent the king in his progrefs to Mafuah, as
he openly profeffed his fixed intention was to punifh the
Naybe with the utmoft feverity.

Tнг.

THE protection of his subjects, therefore, from the savages, was represented to the king as the most pressing service; and, marching with his usual diligence straight to Enderta, he was met there by Kasmati Woldo, an old experienced officer, who aiming at no preferment, paying his tribute punctually, and having been constantly occupied in repelling the incursions of the Pagans on the frontier, had not been at court since the reign of Theophilus.

AFTER receiving the necessary information about the country he intended to enter, and taking Kasmati Woldo's two sons with him, the king descended into the low country of Dancali, once a petty Mahometan kingdom, and friendly to Abyssinia, now a mixture of Galla and the natives called Taltal. Without delay he pushed on to Azab, spreading desolation through that little province, always desert enough from its nature, though formerly, from its trade, one of the richest spots in the world.

THE king then turned to the right upon the Dobas, who, not expecting an army of that strength, fled and left their whole cattle a prey to Yasous and his soldiers; a greater number was scarce ever seen in Abyssinia. The king now returned to Enderta, where he confirmed Kasmati Woldo in his government with distinguished marks of favour; and he this year again came back victorious to Gondar, leaving his campaign against the Naybe for another season.

IN passing by Adowa, a fray happened among the king's troops and those of Michael; several were killed on both sides; and, as the dispute was between Tigrè and Amhara, the two great divisions of the country, it threatened to create

4

a party-a party-quarrel between the foldiers of one divifion and thofe of the other. No notice was taken of this when Ya- fous· marched eaftward; but, on his return, Michael begged the king to interfere, and make peace between the two par- ties. To this Yafous anfwered, That he did not think it worth his while, for they would make peace themfelves when they were tired of quarrelling.

Whether this was the motive of fending for Michael to Gondar, or whether it was the ftory of the Naybe, or what elfe was the king's motive, we do not know ; but, fo foon as he was arrived in the capital, he fent Kafmati Ephraim, and Shalaka Kefla, into Tigré, commanding Michael's attendance at Gondar. This Michael abfolutely refufed; he pretended Kafmati Woldo had eftranged the king's affection from him, and that Yafous had called him to Gondar now to put him to death, upon a pretence of his foldiers quarrel with the king's troops. This refufal was repeated to Yafous, with- out any palliation whatever; and he inftantly marched from Gondar, and encamped upon the river Waar, where he was reinforced a few days afterwards by Ras Welled de l'Oul, whofe intention was to perfuade Michael to fubmiffion ; for he had been advifed not to truft the king's oath of forgiven- nefs unlefs he had likewife that of Welled de l'Oul.

The king's readinefs difconcerted Suhul Michael. Tho' well armed and appointed himfelf, as alfo an excellent ge- neral, he did not rifk the prefenting himfelf againft the king on a plain ; for Yafous was much beloved by the foldiers, and always very kind and liberal to them.

THE mountain Samayat, though not the moft inacceffible in Tigrè, was a place of great confequence and ftrength, when poffeffed by an army and officer fuch as Michael. To this natural fortrefs he carried all his valuable effects, occupied and obftructed all the avenues to it, and refolved there to abide his fortune. The king, with his army, fat down at the foot of the mountain; and, encircling it with troops, he ordered it to to be affaulted on four fides at once; on one, by Kafmati Ayo, governor of Begemder; on the fecond, by Kafmati Waragna; the third, by Kafmati Woldo; and the fourth, by Ras Welled de l'Oul. The king himfelf went round about to every place, giving his orders, encouraging his men, and fighting himfelf in the foremoft ranks like a common foldier. The mountain was at length carried, with much bloodfhed on both fides, and Michael was beat from every part of it but one, which, though not ftrong enough to hold out againft the king's army, if well defended could not be carried without great lofs of men.

HERE Michael defired to capitulate. But, before he left the mountain and furrendered to the king, he defired that an officer of truft might be fent to him, becaufe he had then upon the mountain a large collection of treafure, which he defired to keep for the king's ufe, otherwife it would be diffipated and loft in the hands of the common foldiers. The Ras fent two confidential officers, who took from the hands of Michael a prodigious fum of gold, the precife amount of which is not named. He then defcended the mountain, carrying, as is the cuftom of the country for vanquifhed rebels, a ftone upon his head, as confeffing himfelf guilty of a capital crime. A violent ftorm of rain and wind prevented, for that day, his coming into the pre-

fence

fence of the king; and the devil, as the Abyffinians believe, began in that ftorm a correfpondence with him which continued many years; I myfelf have often heard him vaunt of his having maintained, ever fince that time, an intercourfe with St Michael the archangel.

On the morning of the 27th of December, Ras Welled de l'Oul ordered Michael to attend him in the habit of a penitent; and, followed by his companions in misfortune, (that part of his troops which was taken on the mountain) and furrounded by a number of foldiers, with drums beating and colours flying, he was carried into the king's prefence.

Ras Welled de l'Oul had, with difficulty, engaged the king's promife that he was not to put him to death. The good genius of Yafous and his family was labouring by one laft effort to fave him. On feeing Michael upon the ground, Yafous fell into a violent tranfport of rage, fpurned him with his foot, declaring he retracted his promife, and ordered him to be carried out, and put to death before the door of his tent. Ras Welled de l'Oul, Kafmati Waragna, Kafmati Woldo, and all the officers of confideration, either of the court or army, now fell with their faces upon the ground, crying to the king for mercy and forgivenefs. Yafous, if in his heart he did not relent, ftill was obliged to pardon on fuch univerfal folicitation; and this he did, after making the following obfervation, which foon after was looked on as a prophecy: " I have pardoned that traitor at your inftance, becaufe I at all times reward merit more willingly than I punifh crimes; but I call you all to witnefs, that I wafh my hands before God to-day of all that innocent blood Michael fhall

4 N 2   fhed

fhed before he brings about the deftruction of his country, which I know in his heart he has been long meditating."

I CANNOT help mentioning it as an extraordinary circumftance, that at the time I was at Gondar, in the very height of Suhul Michael's tyranny, a man quarrelled with another who was a fcribe, and accufed him before Michael of having recorded this fpeech of the king, as I have now ftated it, in a hiftory that he had written of Yafous's reign. The book was produced, the paffage was found and read; and I certainly expected to have feen it torn to pieces, or hung upon a tree about the author's neck. On the contrary, all the Ras faid was, "If what he writes is true, wherein is the man to blame?" And turning with a grin to Tecla Haimanout, one of the judges, he faid, "Do you remember? I do "believe Yafous did fay fo." The book was reftored to the author, and no more faid of the matter, not even an order was given to erafe the paffage. He had no objection to Yafous and to his whole race being prophets; he had only taken a refolution that they fhould not be kings.

A GENERAL filence followed this fpeech of Yafous, inftead of the acclamations of joy ufual in fuch cafes. The king then ordered Ras Welled de l'Oul to lead the army on to Gondar, which he did with great pomp and military parade, while the king, who could not forget his forebodings, retired to an ifland, there to faft fome days in confequence of a vow that he had made. This being finifhed, Yafous returned to Gondar; and, as he was now in perfect peace throughout his kingdom, he began again to decorate the apartments of his palace. A large number of mirrors had arrived at

I   this

this time, a prefent from the Naybe of Mafuah, who, after what had happened to his friend Michael, began to feel a little uneafy about the fate of his ifland.

WHILE Yafous was thus employed, news were fent him from Kafmati Ayo, governor of Begemder, that he had beat the people of Lafta in a pitched battle in their own country, had forced their ftrong-holds, difperfed their troops, and received the general fubmiffion of the province, which had been in rebellion fince the time of Hatzè Socinios, that is, above 100 years. Immediately after thefe news, came Ayo himfelf to parade and throw his *unclean* trophies of victory before the king, and brought with him many of the principal people of Lafta to take the oaths of allegiance to the king.

YASOUS received the accounts of the fuccefs with great pleafure, and ftill more fo the oaths and fubmiffions made to him. He then added Lafta to the province of Begemder, and cloathed Ayo magnificently, as well as all thofe noblemen that came with him from Lafta. The end of this year was not marked with good fortune like the beginning. A plague of locufts fell upon the country, and confumed every green thing, fo that a famine feemed to be inevitable, becaufe, contrary to their cuftom, they had attached themfelves chiefly to the grain. This plague is not fo frequent in Abyffinia as the Jefuits have reported it to be. Thefe good fathers indeed bring the locufts upon the country, that, by their pretended miracles, they may chace them away.

MICHAEL had continued fome time in prifon, in the cuftody of Ras Welled de l'Oul. But he was afterwards fet at

full

full liberty; and it was now the 17th year of Yafous's reign, when, on the 17th of September 1746, at a great promotion of officers of ftate, Michael, by the nomination of the king himfelf, was reftored to his government of Tigrè; and, a few days after, he returned to that province. All his ancient friends and troops flocked to him as foon as he appeared, to welcome him upon an event looked upon by all as nearly miraculous. Nor did Michael difcourage that idea himfelf, but gave it to be underftood, among his moft intimate friends, that a vifion had affured him that he was thenceforward under the immediate protection of St Michael the archangel, with whom he was to confult on every emergency.

As foon as he had got a fufficient army together, the firft thing he did was to attack Kafmati Woldo, without any provocation whatever; and, after beating him in two battles, he drove him from his province, and forced him to take refuge among the Galla, where, foon after, by employing fmall prefents, he procured him to be murdered; the ordinary fate of thofe who feek protection among thofe faithlefs barbarians.

It will feem extraordinary that the king, who had fuch recent experience of both, the one diftinguifhed for his duty, the other for his obftinate rebellion, fhould yet tamely fuffer his old and faithful fervant to fall before a man whom in his heart he fo much miftrufted. But the truth is, all Michael's danger was paft the moment he got free accefs to the king and queen, though he was defervedly efteemed to be the ableft foldier in Abyffinia of his time, he was infinitely more capable in intrigues, and private negociations

at

at court, than he was in the field, being a pleafant and a-
greeable fpeaker in common converfation; a powerful and
copious orator at council; his language, whether Amharic
or Tigrè, (but above all the latter) correct and elegant above
any man's at court; fteady to the meafures he adopted, but
often appearing to give them up eafily, and without paffion,
when he faw, by the circumftances of the times, he could
not prevail: though violent in the purfuit of riches, when
in his own province, where he fpared no means nor man
to procure them, no fooner had he come to Gondar than
he was lavifh of his money to extreme; and indeed he fet
no value upon it farther than as it ferved to corrupt men
to his ends.

When he furrendered his treafure at the mountain Samayat, he is faid to have divided it into feveral parcels with
his own hand. The greateft fhare fell to the king, who
thought he had got the whole; but the officers who received
it, and faw different quantities deftined for the Iteghé and
Ras Welled de l'Oul, took care to convey them their fhare,
for fear of making powerful enemies. Kafmati Waragna
had his part; and even Kafmati Woldo, though Michael
foon after plundered and flew him. All Gondar were his
friends, becaufe all that capital was bribed on this occafion.
It was gold he only lent them, to refume it, (as he afterwards
did) with great intereft, at a proper time.

It ftill remained in the king's breaft to wipe off his defeat at Sennaar, as he had, upon every other occafion, been
victorious; and even in this, he ftill flattered himfelf he had
not been beat in perfon. He fet out again upon another
expedition to Atbara; inftead of coafting along the Dender,

he

he defcended along the Tacazzé into Atbara, where, finding no refiftance among the Shepherds, he attached himfelf in particular to the tribe called Daveina, which, in the former expedition, had joined Welled de l'Oul's army. Upon the firft news of his approach they had fubmitted ; but, notwith-ftanding all promifes and pretences of peace, he fell upon them unawares, and almoft extirpated the tribe.

Suhul Michael, while the king was thus occupied in the frontier of his province, did every thing that a faithful, active fubject could do. He furnifhed him conftantly with the beft intelligence, fupplied him with the provifions he wanted, and made, from time to time, ftrong detachments of troops to reinforce him, and to fecure fuch pofts as were moft commodious and important in cafe of a retreat beco-ming neceffary.

Yasous, who had fucceeded to his wifh, was fully fen-fible of the value of fuch fervices, and fent, therefore, for Michael, commanding his attendance at Gondar. There was no fear, no hefitation now, as before in the affair of Sama-yat. He decamped upon the firft notice, even before the rainy feafon was over, and arrived at Gondar on Auguft 30th 1747, bringing with him plenty of gold ; few foldiers, in-deed, but thofe picked men, and in better order, than the king had ever yet feen troops.

It was plain now to everybody, that nothing could ftop Michael's growing fortune. He alone feemed not fenfible of this. He was humbler and lefs affuming than before. Thofe whom he had firft bribed he continued ftill to bribe, and added as many new friends to that lift as he thought

could

could ferve him. He pretended to no precedency or pre-eminence at court, not even fuch as was due to the rank of his place, but behaved as a ftranger that had no fixed abode among them.

One day, dining with Kafmati Geta, the queen's brother, who was governor of Samen, and drinking out of a common-glafs decanter called Brulhé, when it is the privilege and cuftom of the governor of Tigré to ufe a gold cup, being afked, Why he did not claim his privilege? he faid, All the gold he had was in heaven, alluding to the name of the mountain Samayat, where his gold was furrendered, which word fignifies Heaven. The king, who liked this kind of jefts, of which Michael was full, on hearing this, fent him a gold cup, with a note written and placed within it, "Happy are they who place their riches in heaven;" which Michael directed immediately to be engraved by one of the Greeks upon the cup itfelf. What became of it I know not; I often wifhed to have found it out, and purchafed it. I faw it the firft day he dined, after coming from council, at his return from Tigré, after the execution of Abba Salama; but I never obferved it at Serbraxos, nor fince. I heard, indeed, a Greek fay he had fent it by Ozoro Efther, as a prefent to a church of St Michael in Tigré.

Enderta was now given him in addition to the province of Tigré, and, foon after, Siré and all the provinces between the Tacazzé and the Red Sea; fo he was now mafter of near half of Abyffinia.

The reft of this king's reign was fpent at home in his ufual amufements and occupations. Several fmall expedi-

tions were made by his command, under Palambaras Se-
laflé, and other officers, to harrafs the Shepherds, whom he
conquered almoft down to Suakem. His ravages, however,
had been confined to the peninfula of Atbara, and had not
ever paffed to the eaftward of the Tacazzé, but he had impoverifhed all that country. After this, by his orders, the
Baharnagafh, and other officers, entered that divifion called
Derkin, between the Mareb and the Atbara, and, ftill further, between the Mareb and the mountains, in a part of it
called Ajam. In this country Haffine Wed Ageeb was defeated by the Baharnagafh with great flaughter; and the
Shekh of Jibbel Mufa, one of the moft powerful of the Shepherds, was taken prifoner by Palambaras Selaffé, without
refiftance, and carried, with his wife, his family, and cattle,
in triumph to Gondar, where, having fworn allegiance to
the king, he was kindly treated, and fent home with prefents, and every thing that had been taken from him.

THIS year, being the 24th of Yafous's reign, he was taken ill, and died on the 21ft day of June 1753, after a very
fhort illnefs. As he was but a young man, and of a ftrong
conftitution, there was fome fufpicion he died by poifon given him by the queen's relations, who were defirous to fecure another minority rather than ferve under a king,
who, by every action, fhewed he was no longer to be led or
governed by any, but leaft of all by them.

YASOUS was married very young to a lady of noble family
in Amhara, by whom he had two fons, Adigo and Aylo.
But their mother pretending to a fhare of her hufband's government, and to introduce her friends at court, fo hurt
Welleta Georgis the Iteghé, or queen-regent, that fhe prevailed

vailed on the king to banish both the mother and fons to the mountain of Wechné.

In order to prevent fuch interference for the future, the Iteghé took a ftep, the like of which had never before been attempted in Abyffinia. It was to bring a wife to Yafous from a race of Galla. Her name was Wobit, daughter of Amitzo, to whom Bacuffa had once fled when he efcaped from the mountain before he was king, and had been kindly entertained there. Her family was of the tribe of Edjow, and the divifion of Toluma, that is, of the fouthern Galla upon the frontiers of Amhara. They were efteemed the politeft, that is, the leaft barbarous of the name. But it was no matter, they were Galla, and that was enough. Between them and Abyffinia, oceans of blood had been fhed, and ftrong prejudices imbibed againft them, never to be effaced by marriages. She was, however, brought to Gondar, chriftened by the name of Beffabée, and married to Yafous: By her he had a fon, named Joas, who fucceeded his father.

J O A S.

From 1753 to 1768.

This Prince a Favourer of the Galla his Relations—Great Diſſentions on bringing them to Court—War of Begemder—Ras Michael brought to Gondar—Defeats Ayo—Mariam Barea refuſes to be acceſſary to his Death—King favours Waragna Faſil—Battle of Azazo—King Aſfaſſinated in his Palace.

UPON the firſt news of the death of king Yaſous, the old officers and ſervants of the crown, remembering the tumults and confuſion that happened in Gondar at his acceſſion, repaired to the palace from their different governments, each with a ſmall well-regulated body of troops, ſufficient to keep order, and ſtrengthen the hands of Ras Welled de l'Oul, whom they all looked upon as the father of his country. The firſt who arrived was Kaſmati Waragna of Damot; then Ayo of Begemder, and very ſoon after, though at much the greateſt diſtance, Suhul Michael, governor of Tigrè. Theſe three entered the palace, with Welled

4   de

de. l'Oul at their head, and received the young king Joas from the hands of the Iteghé his grandmother, and proclaimed him king, with the usual formalities, without any oppofition or tumult whatever.

A NUMBER of promotions immediately followed; but it was obferved with great difcontent by many, that the Iteghé's family and relations were grown now fo numerous, that they were fufficient to occupy all the great offices of ftate without the participation of any of the old families, which were the ftrength of the crown in former reigns ; and that now no preferment was to be expected unlefs through fome relation to the queen-mother.

WELLED HAWARAYAT, fon to Michael governor of Tigré, had married Ozoro Altafh, the queen's third daughter, al-moft a child ; and long before that, Netcho of Tcherkin had married Ozoro Efther, likewife very young; and Ras Michael, old as he was, had made known his pretenfions to Ozoro Welleta Ifrael, the queen's fecond daughter, immediately younger than Ozoro Efther. Thefe propofals, from an old man, had been received with great contempt and derifion by Welleta Ifrael, and fhe perfevered fo long in the derifion of Michael's courtfhip, that it left ftrong impreffions on the hard heart of that old warrior, which fhewed themfelves after in very difagreeable confequences to that lady all the time Michael was in power.

THE firft that broke the peace of this new reign was Nanna Georgis, chief of one of the clans of Agows of Damot. Engaged in old feuds with the Galla on the other fide of the Nile, the natural enemies of his country, he could

not

not fee, but with great difpleafure, a Galla fuch as Kafmati Waragna, however worthy, governor of Damot, and capable, therefore, of over-running the whole province in a moment, by calling his Pagan countrymen from the other fide.

WARAGNA, though this was in his power, knew the meafure was unpopular. Kafmati Efhté was the queen's brother, and governor of Ibaba, a royal refidence, which has a large territory and falary annexed to it. When, therefore, at council, he had complained of the injury done to him by Nanna Georgis, he refufed the taking upon him the redreffing thefe injuries, and punifhing the Agows, unlefs Kafmati Efhté was joined in the commiffion with him.

THE reafon of this was, as I have often before obferved, that, as the Agows are thofe that pay the greateft tribute in gold to the king, and furnifh the capital with all forts of provifions, any calamity happening in their country is feverely felt by the inhabitants of Gondar; and the knowledge of this occafions a degree of prefumption and confidence in the Agows, of which they have been very often the dupes. This, indeed, happened at this very inftant. For Waragna and Efhtè marched from Gondar, and with them a number of veteran troops of the king's houfehold of Maitfha, depending on Ibaba; and this army, without bringing one Galla from the other fide of the Nile, gave Nanna Georgis and his Agows fuch an overthrow that his clan was nearly extirpated, and many of the principal of that nation flain.

NANNA GEORGIS, who chiefly was aimed at as the author of this revolt, efcaped, with great difficulty, wounded, from the field ; and the feud which had long fubfifted between Waragna's family and the race of the Agows, received great addition that day, and came down to their pofterity, as we fhall foon fee by what happened in Waragna's fon's time at the bloody and fatal battle of Banja.

THE next affair that called the attention of government, was a complaint brought by the monks of Magwena, a ridge of rocks of but fmall extent not far from Tcherkin, the eftate of Kafmati Netcho. Thefe mountains, for a great part of the year, almoft calcined under a burning fun, have, in feveral months, violent and copious fhowers of rain, which, received in vaft caves and hollows of the mountain, and out of the reach of evaporation, are means of creating and maintaining all forts of verdure and all fcenes of pleafure, in the hot feafon of the year, when the rains do not fall elfewhere ; and as the rocks have a confiderable elevation above the level of the plain, they are at no feafon infected with thofe feverifh diforders that lay the low country wafte.

NÈTCHO was a man of pleafure, and he thought, fince the monks, by retiring to rocks and deferts, meant thereby to fubject themfelves to hardfhip and mortification, that thefe delightful and flowery fcenes, the groves of Magwena, were much more fuited to the enjoyment of happinefs with the young and beautiful Ozoro Efther, than for any fet of men, who by their aufterities were at conftant war with the flefh. Upon thefe principles, which it would be very difficult for the monks themfelves to refute, he took poffeffion of the mountain Magwena, and of thofe bowers that,

that, though in poffeffion of faints, did not feem to have been made for the folitary pleafures of one fex only. This piece of violence was, by the whole body of monks, called Sacrilege. Violent excommunications, and denunciations of divine vengeance, were thundered out againft Kafmati Netcho. An army was fent againft him ; he was defeated and taken prifoner, and confined upon a mountain in Wal-kayt, where foon after he died, but not before the Iteghè had fhewn her particular mark of difpleafure, by taking her daughter Ozoro Efther, his wife, from him, that fhe, too, and her only fon Confu, might not be involved in the monk's excommunications, and the imputed crime of fa-crilege.

At this time died Kafmati Waragna, full of years and glory, having, though a ftranger, preferved his allegiance to the laft, and more than once faved the ftate by his wifdom, bravery, and activity. He is almoft a fingle example in their hiftory, of a great officer, governor of a province, that never was in rebellion, and a remarkable inftance of Ba-cuffa's penetration, who, from a fingle converfation with him, while engaged in the vileft employment, chofe him as capable of the greateft offices, in which he ufefully ferved both his fon and grandfon.

Soon after, Ayo governor of Begemder, an older officer ftill than Waragna, arrived in Gondar, and refigned his go-vernment into the queen's hands. This refignation was re-ceived, becaufe it was underftood that it was directly to be conferred upon his fon Mariam Barea, by far the moft hope-ful young Abyffinian nobleman of his time. Another mark of favour, foon followed, perhaps was the occafion of this.

Ozoro

Ozoro Efther, the very young widow of Netcho, was married, very much againft her own confent, to the young governor of Begemder, and this marriage was crowned with the univerfal applaufe of court, town, and country; for Mariam Barea poffeffed every virtue that could make a great man popular; and it was impoffible to fee Ozoro Efther, and hear her fpeak, without being attached to her for ever after.

STILL the complaint remained, that there was no promotion, no diftinction of merit, but through fome relation to the queen-mother; and the truth of this was foon fo apparent, and the difcontent it occafioned fo univerfal, that nothing but the great authority Ras Welled de l'Oul, the Iteghé's brother, poffeffed, could hinder this concealed fire from breaking out into a flame.

THE queen, mother to Joas, was Ozoro Wobit, a Galla. Upon Joas's acceffion to the throne, therefore, a large body of Galla, faid to be 1200 horfe, were fent as a prefent to the young king as the portion of his mother. A number of private perfons had accompanied thefe; part from curiofity, part from defire of preferment, and part from attachment to thofe that were already gone before them. Thefe laft were formed into a body of infantry of 600 men, and the command given to a Galla, whofe name was Woofheka; fo that the regency, in the perfon of the queen, feemed to have gained frefh force from the minority of the young king Joas, as yet perfectly fubject to his mother.

THERE were four bodies of houfehold troops abfolutely devoted to the king's will. One of thefe, the Koccob horfe, was commanded by a young Armenian not 30 years of age. He had been left in Abyssinia by his father in Yasous's time, and care had been taken of him by the Greeks. Yasous had distinguished him by several places while a mere youth, and employed him in errands to Masuah and Arabia, by which he became known to Ras Michael. Upon the death of Yasous, the Iteghè put him about her grandson Joas, as Baalomal, which is, *gentleman of the bed-chamber*, or, *companion to the king*. He then became Asaleffa el Camisha, which means *gr om of the stole*, but at last was promoted to the great place of Billetana Gueta Dakakin, *chamberlain*, or *master of the houscholl*, the third post in government, by which he took place of all the governors of provinces while in Gondar.

THERE is no doubt Joas would have made him Ras, if he had reigned as long as his father. Besides his own language, he understood Turkish, Arabic, and Malabar, and was perfect master of the Tigrè. But his great excellence was his knowledge of Amharic, which he was thought to speak as chastely and elegantly as Ras Michael himself. He is reported likewise to have possessed a species of jurisprudence, whence derived I never knew, which so pleased the Abyssinians, that the judges often requested his attendance on the king; at which time he sat at the head of the table, where it is supposed the king would place himself did he appear personally in judgment, (which, as it may be learned from divers places in this history, he never does); certain mornings in the week, therefore, he sat publicly in the market-place, and gave judgment soon after the break of day.

I SAW

I saw this young man with his father at Loheia. He underftood no European language; was juft then returned from India, and had a confiderable quantity of diamonds, and other precious ftones, to fell. He fpoke with tears in his eyes of Abyffinia, from which he was banifhed, and urged that I fhould take him there with me. But I had too much at ftake to charge myfelf with the confequences of anybody's behaviour but my own, and therefore refufed it.

The great favour the Galla were in at court encouraged many of their countrymen to follow them; and, by the king's defire, two of his uncles were fent for, and they not only came, but brought with them a thoufand horfe. Thefe were two young men, brothers of the queen Wobit, juft now dead. The eldeft was named Brulhè, the younger Lubo. In an inftant, nothing was heard in the palace but Galla. The king himfelf affected to fpeak nothing elfe. He had entirely intrufted the care of his perfon to his two uncles; and, both being men of intrigue, they thought themfelves fufficiently capable to make a party, fupport it, and place the king at the head of it; and this they effected as foon as it was conceived, whilft the Abyffinians faw, with the utmoft deteftation and abhorrence, a Gallan and inimical government erected in the very heart or metropolis of their country.

Woodage had been long governor of Amhara. He had fucceeded Palambaras Durè in Bacuffa's time, when he had been promoted to the dignity of Ras.

These

THESE two were heads of the only great families in Amhara, who took that government as it were by rotation. Woodage, in one of the excursions into Atbara, had made an Arab's, or a Shepherd's daughter, prisoner, baptized her, and lived with her as his mistress. The passion Woodage bore to this fair slave was not, however, reciprocal. She had fixed her affections upon his eldest son, and their frequent familiarities at last brought about the discovery. This very much shocked Woodage; but, instead of having recourse to public justice, he called his brothers, and some other heads of his family before him, and examined into the fact with them, desiring his son to defend himself. The crime was clearly proved in all its circumstances. Upon which Woodage, by his own authority, condemned his son to death; and not only so, but caused his sentence to be put in execution, by hanging the young man over a beam in his own house. As for the slave, he released her, as not being bound to any return of affection to him, from whom she had only received evil, and been deprived of her natural liberty.

IT seems this claim of *patria potestas* was new in Abyssinia; and Bacuffa took it so ill, that he deprived Woodage of his office, and banished him to Amhara, then governed by Palambaras Durè. To this loss of influence another circumstance contributed. He was a relation of Yasous's first wife, who, by the Iteghé's intrigues, had been sent with her two sons to the mountain of Wechné, and Joas, a young son of Yasous, preferred in their places.

IT happened that Palambaras Durè died; and as the succession fell regularly upon the unpopular Woodage, the king's uncle, Lubo obtained a promise of the government

of

of Amhara for himfelf. All Gondar was fhocked at this ftrange choice : Amitzo and his Edjow were already upon the fouthern frontiers of that province, domiciled there ; and there was no doubt but this nomination would put Amhara into his poffeffion for ever. All the inhabitants of Gondar were ready to run to their arms to oppofe this appointment of the king ; and it was thought that, underhand, the Iteghè fomented this diffatisfaction. The king, however, terrified by the violent refentment of the populace, at the inftance of Ras Welled dc l'Oul, recalled his nomination.

At this time Michael, who faw the confequence of thefe difputes, but abftained from taking any fhare, becaufe he knew that both parties were promoting his intereft by their mutual animofity, came to Gondar in great pomp, upon an honourable errand.

Baady, fon of l'Oul, king of Funge, or, as they are called in the Abyffinian annals, Noba *, who had defeated Yafous at Sennaar, after a tyrannical and bloody reign of thirty-three years, was depofed in the 1764 by Naffer his fon, whom his minifter Shekh Adelan, with his brother Abou Kalec, governor of Kordofan, had put in his place ; and Baady had fled to Suhul Michael, whofe fame was extended all over Atbara. Michael received him kindly, promifed him his beft fervices with Joas, and that he would march in perfon to Sennaar, and reinftate him with an army, if the king fhould fo command.

Michael

---

* Noba, in the language of Sennaar, fignifies Soldier ; it is probably from this the ancient name of Nubia firft came.

Michael conducted him into the presence of the king, where, in a manner unbecoming a sovereign, and which Joas's successor would not have permitted, he kissed the ground, and declared himself a vassal of Abyssinia. The king assigned him a large revenue, and put him in possession of the government of Ras el Feel upon the frontier of Sennaar, where Ras Welled de l'Oul advised him to wait patiently till the dissensions that then prevailed at court were quieted, when Michael should have orders to reinstate him in his kingdom. This was a wise counsel, but he to whom it was given was not wise, and therefore did not follow it. After some short stay at Ras el Feel he was decoyed from this place of refuge by the intrigues of Adelan, and brought to trust himself in Atbara, where he was betrayed and taken prisoner by Welled Hassen, Shekh of Teawa, and murdered by him in Teawa privately, as we shall hereafter see, two years after his flight from Gondar.

At this time, Ras Welled de l'Oul's death was a signal for all parties to engage. Nothing had withheld them but his prudence and authority; and from that time began a scene of civil blood, which has continued ever since, was in its full vigour at the time when I was in Abyssinia, and without any prospect that it would ever have an end.

The great degree of power to which the brothers and their Galla arrived; the great affection the king shewed to them, owing to their having early infected him with their bloody and faithless principles, gave great alarm to the queen and her relations, whose influence they were every day diminishing. The last stroke, the death of Welled de l'Oul, seemed to be a fatal one, and to threaten the

entire

entire diffolution of her power. In order to counterbalance this, they affociated to their party and council Mariam Barea, who had lately married Ozoro Efther, and was in poffeffion of the fecond province in the flate for riches and for power, and greatly increafed in its importance by the officer that commanded it. Upon the death of Welled de l'Oul, the principal fear the party of the Galla had was, that Mariam Barea fhould be brought to Gondar as Ras.. The union between him and, Kafmati Efhtè, formerly as ftrong by inclination as now it was by blood, put them in terror for their very exiftence, and a ftroke was to be ftruck at all hazards that was to feparate thefe interefts for ever.

Eshte, upon taking poffeffion of the province of Damot,. found the Djawi, eftablifhed upon the frontiers of the province, very much inclined to revolt. Notwithftanding peace had been eftablifhed among the Agows ever fince Nanna· Georgis had been defeated at the laft battle, the Galla had ftill continued to rob and diftrefs them, contrary to the public faith that had been pledged to them..

Eshte was too honeft a man to fuffer this; but the truth was, the Djawi had felt the advantage of having a man like the late Waragna·governor of Damot ; and they wanted, by all means, to reduce the minifters to the neceffity of making that command hereditary in his family, by Fafil his fon. being preferred to fucceed him.

This Fafil, whom I fhall hereafter call Waragna Fafil, a name which was given to diftinguifh him from many other Fafils in the army, was a man then about twenty-two, whom

Efhtè

Efhté had kept about him in a private ftation, and had lately given him a fubaltern command among his own countrymen, the Djawi of Damot. From the fervices that he had then rendered, it was expected a greater preferment was to follow.

The infolence of the Djawi had come to fuch a pitch that they had offered Efhté battle; but they had fled with very little refiftance, and been driven over the Nile to their countrymen whence they came. Efhté, roufed from his indolence, now fhewed himfelf the gallant foldier that he really was. He croffed the Nile at a place never attempted before; and though he loft a confiderable number of men in the paffage, yet that difadvantage was more than compenfated by the advantage it gave him of falling upon the Galla unexpectedly. He therefore deftroyed, or difperfed feveral tribes of them, poffeffed himfelf of their crops, drove off their cattle, wives, and children, and obliged them to fue for peace on his own terms; and then repaffed the Nile, re-eftablifhing the Djawi, after fubmiffion, in their ancient poffeffions.

Upon news of Welled de l'Oul's death, and the known intention of the queen that Efhté fhould fucceed him in the office of Ras, he was muftering his foldiers to march to Gondar: Damot, the Agows, Goutto, and Maitfha, all readily joined him from every quarter; and Waragna Fafil had been fent to bring in the Djawi with the reft. Efhtè had marched by flow journies from Burè, flenderly attended, to arrive at Goutto the place of rendezvous; and, being come to Fagitta, in his way thither, he encamped upon a plain there, near to the church of St George.

It

It was in the evening, when news were brought him that the whole Djawi had come out, to a man, from good-will, to attend him to Gondar. This mark of kindness had very much pleafed him; and he looked upon it as a grate-ful return for his mild treatment of them after they were vanquifhed. A ftool was fet in the fhade, without a fmall houfe where he then was lodged, that he might fee the troops pafs; when Hubna Fafil, a Galla, who commanded them, availing himfelf of the privilege of approaching near, always cuftomary upon thefe occafions, run him through the body with a lance, and threw him dead upon the ground. The reft of the Galla fell immediately upon all his attendants, put them to flight, and proclaimed Wa-ragna Fafil governor of Damot and the Agows.

This intelligence was immediately fent to their country-men, Brulhè and Lubo, at Gondar, who prevailed upon the king to confirm Waragna Fafil in his command, though purchafed with the murder of the worthieft man in his do-minions, who was his own uncle, brother to the Iteghè; and this was thought to more than counterbalance the acceffion of ftrength the queen's party had received from the marriage of Ozoro Efther with Mariam Barea.

In critical times like thefe, the greateft events are pro-duced from the fmalleft accidents. Ayo, father to Mariam Barea, had always been upon bad terms with Michael. It was at firft emulation between two great men; but, after Ayo had affifted the king in taking Michael prifoner at the mountain Samayat, this emulation had degenerated into perfect hatred on the part of Michael.

Just before Kafmati Ayo had refigned Begemder to his fon, and retired to private life, two fervants of Michael had fled with two fwords, which they ufed to carry before him, claiming the protection of Kafmati Ayo. Michael had claimed them before the king, who, loath to determine between the two, not being at that time infligated by Galla, had accepted the propofal of Michael to have the matter of right tried before the judges ; but, upon his refignation of the province, and retiring, the thing had blown over and been forgotten.

Soon after this acceffion of Mariam Barea, Michael intimated to him the order the king had given that the judges fhould try the matter of difference between them. Mariam Barea refufed this, and upbraided Michael with meannefs and proftitution of the dignity he bore, to confent to fubmit himfelf to the venal judgment of weak old men, whofe confciences were hackneyed in prejudice or partiality, and always known to be under the influence of party. He put Suhul Michael in mind alfo, that, being both of them the king's lieutenant-generals, reprefentatives of his perfon in the provinces they governed, noble by birth, and foldiers by profeffion, they had no fuperior but God and their fovereign, therefore it was below them to acknowledge or receive any judgment between them unlefs from God, by an appeal to the fword, or from the king, by a fentence intimated to them by a proper officer; that Suhul Michael might choofe either of thefe manners of deciding the difference as fhould feem beft unto him ; and if he chofe the latter, of abiding by the fentence of the king, he would then reftore him the fwords upon the king's firft command, but he defpifed the judges, and difowned their jurifdiction.

This

This fpirited anfwer was magnified into the crime of difobedience and rebellion. Michael purfued it no further. He knew it was in good hands, which, when once the matter was fet agoing, would never let it drop. Accordingly, to every one's furprife but Michael's, a proclamation was made, that the king had deprived Mariam Barea of his government for difobedience, and had given it to Kafmati Brulhé his uncle, now governor of Begemder.

All Abyffinia was in a ferment at this promotion. The number, power, and vicinity of that race of Galla being confidered, this was but another way of giving the richeft and ftrongeft barrier of Abyffinia into the hands of his hereditary and bloody enemy. There could be no doubt, indeed, but that, as foon as Brulhè fhould have taken poffeffion of his government, it would be inftantly over-run by the united force of that favage and Pagan nation; and there was nothing afterwards to avert danger from the metropolis, for the boundaries of Begemder reach within a very fhort day's journey of Gondar.

Mariam Barea, one of the nobleft in point of birth in the country where he lived, fetting every private confideration afide, was too good a citizen to fuffer a meafure fo pernicious to take place quietly in his time, while the province was under his command. But, befides this, he confidered himfelf as degraded and materially hurt both in honour and in intereft, and very fenfibly felt the affront of being, himfelf and his kindred, fubjected to a race of Pagans whom he had fo often overthrown in the field.

4 Q 2

The king's army marched, under the command of his uncle Brulhè, to take poffeffion of his government; it was with much difficulty, indeed, that Joas could be kept from appearing in perfon, but he was left under the infpection and tuition of his uncle Lubo, at Gondar. Brulhè made very flow advances; his army feveral times affembled, as often difbanded of itfelf; and near a year was fpent before he could move from his camp on the lake Tzana, with a force capable of fhewing or maintaining itfelf in Begemder, from the frontiers of which he was not half a day's journey.

Mariam Barea remained all this time inactive in Begemder, attending to the ordinary duties of his office, with a perfect contempt of Brulhé and his proceedings. But, in the interim, he left no means untried to pacify the king, and diffuade him from a meafure he faw would be ruinous to the ftate in general.

Mariam Barea, though young, had the prudence and behaviour of a man of advanced years. He was efteemed, without comparifon, the braveft foldier and beft general in the kingdom, except old Suhul Michael, his hereditary rival and enemy. But his manners were altogether different from thofe of Michael. He was open, chearful, and unreferved; liberal, even to excefs, but not from any particular view of gaining reputation by it; as moderate in the ufe of victory as indefatigable to obtain it; temperate in all his pleafures; eafily brought to forgive, and that forgivennefs always fincere; a fteady obferver of his word, even in trifles; and diftinguifhed for two things very uncommon in Abyffinia, regularity in his devotions, and conftancy to one wife, which never was impeached. In his laft remonftrance, af-

ter

ter many profeſſions of his duty and obedience, he put
the king in mind, that, at his inveſtiture, " The laws of
" the country impoſed upon him an oath which he took
" in preſence of his majeſty, and, after receiving the holy
" ſacrament, that he was not to ſuffer any Galla in Begem-
" der, but rather, if needful, die with ſword in hand
" to prevent it; that he conſidered the contravening that
" oath as a deliberate breach of the allegiance which he
" owed to God and to his ſovereign, and of the truſt repo-
" ſed in him by his country; that the ſafety of the princes
" of the royal family, ſequeſtered upon the mountain of
" Wechné, depended upon the obſervance of this oath; that
" otherwiſe they would be in conſtant danger of being
" extirpated by Pagans, as they had already nearly been
" in former ages, at two different times, upon the rocks
" Damo and Geſhen; he begged the king, if, unfortunate-
" ly, he could not be reconciled to him, to give his com-
" mand to Kaſmati Geta, Kaſmati Euſebius, or any Abyſ-
" ſinian nobleman, in which caſe he would immediately
" reſign, and retire to private life with his old father."

  He concluded by ſaying, that, " As he had formed a re-
" ſolution, he thought it his duty to ſubmit it to the king;
" that, if his majeſty was reſolved to march and lead the army
" himſelf, he would retire till he was ſtopt by the frontiers of
" the Galla, and the fartheſt limits of Begemder; and, ſo far
" from moleſting the army in their route, the king might
" be aſſured, that, though his own men ſhould be ſtraitened,
" abundance of every kird of proviſion and refreſhment
" ſhould be left in his majeſty's route. But if, contrary to
" his wiſh, troops of Galla, commanded by a Galla, ſhould
" come to take poſſeſſion of his province, he would fight
                                                " them

" them at the well of Fernay*, before one Galla fhould
" drink there, or advance a pike-length into Begemder."

THIS declaration was, by orders of Ras Michael, entered
into the Deftar, and written in letters of gold, after Mariam
Barea's death, no doubt at the inftigation of Ozoro Efther,
jealous for the reputation of her dead hufband.   It is intitled, *the dutiful declaration of the governor of Begemder;* and is
figned by two Umbares, or judges.   Whether the original
was fo or not, I cannot fay.

THE return made to this by the king was of the harfh-
eft kind, full of taunts and fcoffs, and prefumptuous confidence; announcing the fpeedy arrival of *Brulhé*, as to a
certain victory; and, to fhew what further afliftance he
trufted in, he ordered Ras Michael to be proclaimed governor of Samen, the province on the Gondar fide of the Tacazzé, that no obftacle might be left in the way of that general from Tigrè, if it fhould be refolved upon to call him.

IN Abyffinia there is a kind of glafs bottle, very light,
and of the fize, fhape, and ftrength of a Florence wine-
flafk; only the neck is wider, like that of our glafs decan-
ters, twifted for ornament fake, and the lips of it folded
back, fuch as we call cannon-mouthed.   Thefe are made
at Triefte on the Adriatic; and thoufands of packages of
thefe are brought from Arabia to Gondar, where they
are in ufe for all liquors, which are clear enough to
bear the glafs, fuch as wine and fpirits.   They are very
thin

---

* A well near Karoota, immediately on the frontiers of Begemder.

thin and fragil, and are called *brulbè*. Mariam Barea, provoked at being so undervalued as he was in the king's meſſage, returned only for anſwer, " Still the king had bet-
" ter take my advice, and not ſend his *brulhè's* here ; they
" are but weak, and the rocks about Begemder hard ; at
" any rate, they do right to move ſlowly, otherwiſe they
" might break by the way."

As ſoon as this defiance was reported to the king and his counſellors all was in a flame, and orders given to march im-mediately. The whole of the king's houſehold, conſiſting of 8000 veteran troops, were ordered to join the army of Brulhè. This, tho' it added to the diſplay of the army, contributed no-thing to the real ſtrength of it ; for all, excepting the Gal-la, were reſolved neither to ſhed their own blood nor that of their brethren, under the banners of ſo deteſted a leader.

THIS was not unknown to Mariam Barea ; but neither the advantage of the ground, the knowledge of Brulhè's weakneſs, nor any other conſideration, could induce him to take one ſtep, or harraſs his enemy, out of his own pro-vince ; nor did he ſuffer a muſket to be fired, or a horſe to charge, till Brulhè's van was drawn up on the brink of the well Fernay. After he had placed the horſe of the province of Laſta oppoſite to the Edjow Galla, againſt whom his de-ſign was, the armies joined, and the king's troops immediately gave way. The Edjow, however, engaged fiercely and in great earneſt with the horſe of Laſta, an enemy fully as cruel and ſavage as themſelves, but much better horſe-men, better armed, and better ſoldiers. The moment the king's troops turned their backs, the trumpets from Ma-riam Barea's army forbade the purſuit ; while the reſt of the

2 Begemder

Begemder horfe, who knew the intention of their general, furrounded the Edjow, and cut them to pieces, though valiantly fighting to the laft man.

Brulhe fell, among the herd of his countrymen, not diftinguiſhed by any action of valour. Mariam Barea had given the moſt exprefs orders to take him alive; or, if that could not be, to let him efcape; but by no means to kill him. But a menial fervant of his, more willing to revenge his maſter's wrongs than adopt his moderation, forced his way through the crowd of Galla, where he faw Brulhè fighting; and, giving him two wounds through his body with a lance, left him dead upon the field, bringing away his horfe along with him to his maſter as a token of his victory. Mariam Barea, upon hearing that Brulhè was dead, forefaw in a moment what would infallibly be the confequence, and exclaimed in great agitation, " Michael and all the army of Tigrè will march againſt me before autumn."

He was not in this a falfe prophet; for no fooner was Brulhè's defeat and death known, than the king, from refentment, fear the fatal ruler of weak minds, the conſtant inſtigation of Lubo, and the remnant of Brulhè's party, declared there was no fafety but in Ras Michael. An exprefs was therefore immediately fent to him, commanding his attendance, and conferring upon him the office of Ras, by which he became inveſted with fupreme power, both civil and military. This was an event Michael had long wiſhed for. He had nearly as long forefeen that it muſt happen, and would involve both king and queen, and their refpective parties, equally in deſtruction; but he had not fpent his

4   time

time merely in reflection, he had made every preparation possible, and was ready. So soon then as he received the king's orders, he prepared to march from Adowa with 26,000 men, all the best soldiers in Abyssinia, about 10,000 of whom were armed with firelocks.

It happened that two Azages, and several other great officers, were sent to him into Tigré with these orders, and to invest him with the government of Samen. Upon their mentioning the present situation of affairs, Michael sharply reflected upon the king's conduct, and that of those who had counselled him, which must end in the ruin of his family and the state in general. He highly extolled Mariam Barea as the only man in Abyssinia that knew his duty, and had courage to persevere in it. As for himself, being the king's servant, he would obey his commands, whatever they were, faithfully, and to the letter; but, as holding now the first place in council, he must plainly tell him the ruin of Mariam Barea would be speedily and infallibly followed by that of his country.

After this declaration, Michael decamped with his army encumbered by no baggage, not even provisions, women, or tents, nor useless beasts of burden. His soldiers, attentive only to the care of their arms, lived freely and licentiously upon the miserable countries through which they passed, and which they laid wholly waste as if belonging to an enemy.

He advanced, by equal, steady, and convenient marches, in diligence, but not in haste. Not content with the subsistance of his troops, he laid a composition of money upon all thofe diftricts within a day's march of the place through which he paffed; and, upon this not being readily complied with, he burnt the houfes to the ground, and flaughtered the inhabitants. Woggora, the granary of Gondar, full of rich large towns and villages, was all on fire before him; and that capital was filled with the miferable inhabitants, ftript of every thing, flying before Ras Michael as before an army of Pagans. The king's underftanding was now reftored to him for an inftant.; he faw clearly the mifchief his warmth had occafioned, and was truly fenfible of the rafh ftep he had taken by introducing Michael. But the dye was caft; repentance was no longer in feafon; his all was at ftake, and he was tied to abide the iffue.

MICHAEL, with his army in order of battle, approached Gondar with a very warlike appearance. He defcended from the high lands of Woggora into the valleys which furround the capital, and took poffeffion of the rivers Kahha and Angrab, which run through thefe valleys, and which alone fupply Gondar with water. He took poft at every entrance into the town, and every place commanding thofe entrances, as if he intended to befiege it. This conduct ftruck all degrees of people with terror, from the king and queen down to the loweft inhabitant. All Gondar paffed an anxious night, fearing a general maffacre in the morning; or that the town would be plundered, or laid under fome exorbitant ranfom, capitation, or tribute.

BUT this was not the real defign of Michael; he intended to terrify, but to do no more. He entered Gondar early in the morning, and did homage to the king in the moft refpectful manner. He was invefted with the charge of Ras by

x   Joas

Joas himself; and from the palace, attended by two hundred soldiers, and all the people of note in the town, he went straight to take possession of the house which is particularly appropriated to his office, and sat down in judgment with the doors open.

MARAUDING parties of soldiers had entered at several parts of the town, and begun to use that licence they had been accustomed to on their march, pilfering and plundering houses, or persons that seemed without protection. Upon the first complaints, as he rode through the town, he caused twelve of the delinquents to be apprehended, and hanged upon trees in the streets, sitting upon his mule till he saw the execution performed. After he had arrived at his house, and was seated, these executions were followed by above fifty others in different quarters of Gondar. That same day he established four excellent officers in four quarters of the town. The first was Kefla Yasous, a man of the greatest worth, whom I shall frequently mention as a friend in the course of my history; the second, Billetana Gueta Welleta Michael, that is, first master of the household to the king. He had given that old officer that office, upon superseding Lubo the king's uncle, without any consent asked or given. He was a man of a very morose turn, with whom I was never connected. The third was Billetana Gueta Tecla, his sister's son, a man of very great worth and merit, who had the soft and gentle manners of Amhara joined to the determined courage of the Tigran.

MICHAEL took upon himself the charge of the fourth district. He did not pretend by this to erect a military go-

vernment

vernment in Gondar; on the contrary, thefe officers were only appointed to give force to the fentences and proceedings of the civil judges, and had not deliberation in any caufe out of the camp. But two Umbares, or judges, of the twelve were obliged to attend each of the three diftricts; two were left in the king's houfe, and four had their chamber of judicature in his.

The citizens, upon this fair afpect of government, where juftice and power united to protect them, difmiffed all their fears, became calm and reconciled to Michael the fecond day after his arrival, and only regretted that they had been in anarchy, and ftrangers to his government fo long.

The third day after his arrival he held a full council in prefence of the king. He fharply rebuked both parties in a fpeech of confiderable length, in which he expreffed much furprife, that both king and queen, after the experience of fo many years, had not difcovered that they were equally unfit to govern a kingdom, and that it was impoffible to keep diftant provinces in order, when they paid fuch inattention to the police of the metropolis. Great part of this fpeech applied to the king, who, with the Iteghè and Galla, were in a balcony as ufual, in the fame room, though at fome diftance, and above the table where the council fat, but within convenient hearing.

The troubled ftate, the deftruction of Woggora, and the infecurity of the roads from Damot, had made a famine in Gondar. The army poffeffed both the rivers, and fuffered no fupply of water to be brought into the town, but allow-

ed

ed two jars for each family twice a-day, and broke them when they returned for more

RAS MICHAEL, at his rifing from council, ordered a loaf of bread, a brulhè of water, and an ounce of gold, all articles portable enough to be expofed in the market-place, upon the head of a drum, without any apparent watching. But tho' the Abyffinians are thieves of the firft rate, tho' meat and drink were very fcarce in the town, and gold ftill fcarcer, though a number of ftrangers came into it with the army, and the nights were almoft conftantly twelve hours long, nobody ventured to attempt the removing any of the three articles that, from the Monday to the Friday, had been expofed night and day in the market-place unguarded.

ALL the citizens, now furrounded with an army, found the fecurity and peace they before had been ftrangers to, and every one deprecated the time when the government fhould pafs out of fuch powerful hands. All violent oppreffors, all thofe that valued themfelves as leaders of parties, faw, with an indignation which they durft not fuffer to appear, that they were now at laft dwindled into abfolute infignificance.

HAVING fettled things upon this bafis, Ras Michael next prepared to march out for the war of Begemder; and he fummoned, under the fevereft penalties, all the great officers to attend him with all the forces they could raife. He
infifted

---

* This is commonly done in times of trouble, to keep the townfmen in awe, as if fire was intended, which would not be in their power to quench.

infifted likewife that the king himfelf fhould march, and refufed to let a fingle foldier ftay behind him in Gondar; not that he wanted the affiftance of thofe troops, or trufted to them, but he faw the deftruction of Mariam Barea was refolved on, and he wifhed to throw the odium of it on the king. He affected to fay of himfelf, that he was but the inftrument of the king and his party, and had no end of his own to attain. He expatiated, upon all occafions, upon the civil and military virtues of Mariam Barea; faid, that he himfelf was old, and that the king fhould walk coolly and cautioufly, and confider the value that officer would be of to his pofterity and to the nation when he fhould be no more.

Upon the firft news of the king's marching, Mariam Barea, who was encamped upon the frontiers near where he defeated Brulhé, fell back to Garraggara the middle of Begemder. The king followed with apparent intention of coming to a battle without lofs of time; and Mariam Barea, by his behaviour, fhewed in what different lights he viewed an army, at the head of which was his fovereign, and one commanded by a Galla.

No fuch moderation was fhewn on the king's part. His army burnt and deftroyed the whole country through which they paffed. It was plain that it was Joas's intention to revenge the death of Brulhé upon the province itfelf, as well as upon Mariam Barea. As for Ras Michael, the behaviour of the king's army had nothing in it new, or that could either furprife or difpleafe him. Friend as he was to peace and good order at home, his invariable rule was to indulge

his

his foldiers in every licence that the moft profligate mind could wifh to commit when marching againft an enemy.

It was known the armies were to engage at Nefas Mufa, becaufe Mariam Barea had faid he would fight Brulhé, to prevent him entering the province, but retreat before the king till he could no longer avoid going out of it. The king then marched upon the tract of Mariam Barea, burning and deftroying on each fide of him, as wide as poffible, by detachments and fcouring parties. Allo Fafil, an officer of the king's houfehold, a man of low birth, of very moderate parts, and one who ufed to divert the king as a kind of buffoon, otherwife a good foldier, had, as a favour, obtained a fmall party of horfe, with which he ravaged the low coun-try of Begemder.

The reader will remember, in the beginning of this hif-tory, that a fingular revolution happened, in as fingular a manner, the ufurper of the houfe of Zaguè having volunta-rily refigned the throne to the kings of the line of Solomon, who for feveral hundred years had been banifhed to Shoa. Tecla Haimanout, founder of the monaftery of Debra Liba-nos, a faint, and the laft Abyffinian that enjoyed the dignity of Abuna, had the addrefs and influence to bring about this revolution, or refignation, and to reftore the ancient line of kings. A treaty was made under guarantee of the Abuna, that large portions of Lafta fhould be given to this prince of the houfe of Zaguè, free from all tribute, tax, or fervice whatever, and that he fhould be regarded as an indepen-dent prince. The treaty being concluded, the prince of Za-gué was put in poffeffion of his lands, and was called Y'Laf-ta Hatzè, which fignifies, not the king of Lafta, but *the king*

at

at or in Lafta*.   He refigned the throne, and Icon Amlac of the line of Solomon, by the queen of Saba, continued the fucceffion of princes of that houfe.

THAT treaty, greatly to the honour of the contracting parties, made towards the end of the 13th century, had remained inviolate till the middle of the 18th; no affront or injuftice had been offered to the prince of Zagué, and in the number of rebellions which had happened, by princes fetting up their claims to the crown, none had ever proceeded, or in any fhape been abetted, by the houfe of Zagué, even though Lafta had been fo frequently in rebellion.

As Joas was a young prince, now for the firft time in the province of Begemder and paffing not far from his domains, the prince of Zaguè thought it a proper civility and duty to falute the king in his paffage, and congratulate him upon his acceffion to the throne of his father. He accordingly prefented himfelf to Joas in the habit of peace, while, according to treaty, his kettle-drums, or nagareets, were filver, and the points of his guard's fpears of that metal alfo. The king received him with great cordiality and kindnefs; treated him with the utmoft refpect and magnificence ; refufed to allow him to proftrate himfelf on the ground, and forced him to fit in his prefence. Michael went ftill farther ; upon his entering his tent he uncovered himfelf to his waift, in the fame manner as he would have done in prefence of Joas. He received him ftanding, obliged him to fit in his

own

---

* Nearly the fame diftinction as the filly one made in Britain between the French king and king of France.

own chair, and excufed himfelf for ufing the fame liberty of fitting, only on account of his own lamenefs.

The king halted one entire day to feaft this royal gueft. He was an old man of few words, but thofe very inoffenfive, lively, and pleafant ; in fhort, Ras Michael, not often accuftomed to fix on favourites at firft fight, was very much taken with this Lafta fovereign. Magnificent prefents were made on all fides ; the prince of Zagué took his leave and returned ; and the whole army was very much pleafed and entertained at this fpecimen of the good faith and integrity of their kings.

He had now confiderably advanced through his own country, Lafta, which was in the rear, when he was met by Allo Fafil returning from his plundering the low country, who, without provocation, from motives of pride or avarice, fell unawares upon the innocent, old man, whofe attendants, fecure, as they thought, under public faith, and accoutred for parade and not for defence, became an eafy facrifice, the prince being the firft killed by Allo Fafil's own hand.

Fasil continued his march to join the king, beating his filver kettle-drums as in triumph. The day after, Ras Michael, uninformed of what had paffed, inquired who that was marching with a nagareet in his rear? as it is not allowed to any other perfon but governors of provinces to ufe that inftrument ; and they had already reached the camp. The truth was prefently told ; at which the Ras fhewed the deepeft compunction. The tents were already pitched when Fafil arrived, who, riding into Michael's

tent,

tent, as is ufual with officers returning from an expedition, began to brag of his own deeds, and upbraided Michael, in a ftrain of mockery, that he was old, lame, and impotent.

This raillery, though very common on fuch occafions, was not then in feafon; and the laft part of the charge againft him was the moft offenfive, for there was no man more fond of the fex than Michael was. The Ras, therefore, ordered his attendants to pull Fafil off his horfe, who, feeing that he was fallen into a fcrape, fled to the king's tent for refuge, with violent complaints againft Michael. The king undertook to reconcile him to the Ras, and fent the young Armenian, commander of the black horfe, to defire Michael to forgive Allo Fafil. This he abfolutely refufed to do, alledging, that the paffing over Fafil's infolence to himfelf would be of no ufe, as his life was forfeited for the death of the prince of Zagué.

The king renewed his requeft by another meffenger; for the Armenian excufed himfelf from going, by faying boldly to the king, That, by the law of all nations, the murderer fhould die. To the fecond requeft the king added, that he required only his forgivenefs of his infolence to him, not of the death of the prince of Zagué, as he would direct what fhould be done when the neareft of kin claimed the fatisfaction of retaliation. To this Ras Michael fhortly replied, " I am here to do juftice to every one, and will do it without any confideration or refpect of perfons." And it was now, for the firft time, Abyffinia ever faw a king folicit the life of a fubject of his own from one of his fervants, and be refufed.

The

THE king, upon this, ordered Allo Fafil to defend himfelf; and things were upon this footing, the affair likely to
end in oblivion, though not by forgivennefs. But, a very
fhort time after, the prince of Zaguè's eldeft fon came privately to Michael's tent in the night; and, the next morning, when the judges were in his tent, Michael fent his
door-keeper (Hagos) reckoned the braveft and moft fortunate in combat of any private man in the army, and to
whom he trufted the keeping of his tent-door, to order Allo
Fafil to anfwer at the inftance of the prince of Zaguè, then
waiting him in court, Why he had murdered the prince his
father? Fafil was aftonifhed, and refufed to come: being a-
gain cited in a regular manner by Hagos, he feemed defirous to avail himfelf of the king's permiffion to defend
himfelf, and call together his friends. Hagos, without giving him time, thruft him through with a lance; then cut
off his head, and carried it to Michael's tent, repeating what
paffed, and the reafon of his killing him.

As a refufal in all fuch inftances is rebellion, this had
paffed according to rule: a party of Tigrans was ordered
to plunder his tent; and all the ill-got fpoils which he had
gained from the poor inhabitants of Begemder were abandoned to the foldiers. Fafil's head was given to the prince
of Zaguè, as a reparation for the treaty being violated; the
filver nagareet and fpears were returned; and, highly as this
affair had been carried by Ras Michael, the king never after
mentioned a word of it. But this was univerfally allowed
to be the firft caufe of their difagreement.

MARIAM BAREA, feeing no other way to fave his province
from ruin but by bringing the affair to a fhort iffue, re-

folved

folved likewife to keep his promife. He retired to Nefas Mufa, and encamped in the fartheft limits of his province : behind this are the Woollo Galla, relations of Amitzo the king's parents. Joas and Ras Michael followed him without delay, and, having called in all the out-pofts, both fides prepared for an engagement.

ABOUT nine in the morning, Mariam Barea prefented his army in order of battle. Michael had given orders to Kefla Yafous and Welleta Michael how to form his. He then mounted his mule, and with fome of his officers rode out to view Mariam Barea's difpofition. The king, anxious about the fortune of the day, and terrified at fome reports that had been made him, by timid or unfkilful people, of the warlike countenance of Mariam Barea's army, fent to the Ras, whom he faw reconnoitring, to know his opinion of what was likely to happen. " Tell the king," fays the veteran, " that a young man like him, fighting with a fub-ject fo infinitely below him, with an army double his number, fhould give him fair play for his life and reputation. He fhould fend to Mariam Barea to encreafe the ftrength of his center by placing the troops of Lafta there, or we fhall beat him in half an hour, without either honour to him or to ourfelves." The king, however, did not underftand that fort of gallantry ; he thought half an hour in fufpence was long enough, and he ordered immediately a large body of mufquetry to reinforce Fafil, who commanded the center, and thereby he weakened his own right wing.

MICHAEL, who commanded the right of the royal army, had placed himfelf and his fire-arms in very rough ground, where cavalry could not approach him, and where he fired

as

as from a citadel, and foon obliged the left wing of the
rebels to retreat. But the king, Kefla Yafous, and Lubo
on the right, were roughly handled by the horfe of Lafta,
and would have been totally defeated, the king and Lubo
having already left the field, had not Kefla Yafous brought
up reinforcement of the men of Sirè and Temben, and retrieved the day, at leaft brought things upon an equal
footing.

Fasil, with the horfe of Foggora and Damot, and a
prodigious body of the Djawi and Pagan Galla, defirous to
fhew his confequence, and confirm himfelf in his ill-got
government by his perfonal behaviour, attacked the Begemder horfe in the center fo irrefiftibly, that he not only
broke through them in feveral places, but threw the whole
body into a fhameful flight. Mariam Barea himfelf was
wounded in endeavouring to ftop them, and hurried away,
in fpite of his inclination, crying out in great agony, " Is
there not one in my army that will ftay and fee me die
like the fon of Kafmati Ayo?" It was all in vain; Powuffen,
and a number of his own officers, furrounding him, dragged
him as it were by force out of the field. The country behind Nefas Mufa is wild, and cut with deep gullies, and the
woods almoft impenetrable; they were therefore quickly
out of the enemy's purfuit, and fafe, as they thought, under
the protection of the Woollo Galla. The whole army of
Begemder was difperfed, and Michael early forbade further
purfuit.

The account of this battle, and what preceded it, from the
mouth of the prince of Zaguè, is not in the annals or hiftory of Abyffinia, which I have hitherto followed; at leaft it

has

has not appeared yet, probably out of delicacy to Ozoro Efther, fear of Ras Michael, and refpect to the character of Mariam Barea, whofe memory is ftill dear to his country. But the whole was often, at my defire, repeated to me by Kefla Yafous, and his officers who were there, whom he ufed to queftion about any circumftance he did not himfelf remember, or was abfent from ; for he was a fcrupulous lover of truth; and nothing pleafed him fo much as the thought that I was writing his hiftory to be read in my country, although he had not the fmalleft idea of England or its fituation.

As for the converfation before the battle, it was often told me by Ayto Aylo and Ayto Engedan, fons of Kafmati Efhté, who were with the Ras when he delivered the meffage to the king, and were kept by him from engaging that day in refpect to Mariam Barea, who was married to their aunt Ozoro Efther.

The king and Lubo fent Woofheka to their friends among the Woollo, who delivered up the unfortunate Mariam Barea, with twelve of his officers who had taken refuge with him. Mariam Barea was brought before the king in his tent, covered with blood that had flowed from his wound ; his hands tied behind his back, and thus thrown violently with his face to the ground. A general murmur which followed fhewed the fentiments of the fpectators at fo woful a fight; and the horror of it feemed to have feized the king fo entirely as to deprive him of all other fentiments.

I HAVE

I HAVE often faid, the Mofaical law, or law of retaliation, is conftantly obferved over all Abyffinia as the criminal law of the country, fo that, when any perfon is flain wrongfully by another, it does not belong to the king to punifh that offence, but the judges deliver the offender to the neareft relation of the party murdered, who has the full power of putting him to death, felling him to flavery, or pardoning him without any fatisfaction.

LUBO faw the king relenting, and that the greateft crime, that of rebellion, was already forgiven. He ftood up, there- fore, and, in violent rage, laid claim to Mariam Barea as the murderer of his brother: the king ftill faying nothing, he and his other Galla hurried Mariam Barea to his tent, where he was killed, according to report, with fundry circumftan- ces of private cruelty, afterwards looked upon as great ag- gravations. Lubo, with his own hand, is faid to have cut his throat in the manner they kill fheep. His body was af- terwards disfigured with many wounds, and his head feve- red and carried to Michael, who forbade uncovering it in his tent. It was then fent to Brulhé's family in their own country, as a proof of the fatisfaction his friends had ob- tained; and this gave more univerfal umbrage than did even the cruelty of the execution.

SEVERAL officers of the king's army, feeing the bloody intentions of the Galla, advifed Powuffen, and the eleven other officers that were taken prifoners, to make the beft ufe of the prefent opportunity, and fly to the tent of Mi- chael and implore his protection. This they moft will- ingly did, with the connivance of Woofheka, who had been intrufted with the care of them, and Lubo having finifhed Mariam Barea, came to the king's tent to feek the unhappy prifoners, whom he intended as victims to the memory of Brulhè likewife. Hearing, however, that they were fled to Michael's tent, he fent Woofheka to demand them; but that officer had fcarce opened his errand, in the gentleft manner poffible, when Michael, in a fury, cried out, Cut him in pieces before the tent-door. Woofheka was indeed lucky enough to efcape; but we fhall find this was not forgot, for his punifhment was more than doubled foon afterwards.

At feeing Mariam Barea's head in the hands of a Galla, after forbidding him to expofe it in his tent, Michael is faid to have made the following obfervation: " Weak and cowardly people are always in proportion cruel and unmerciful. If Brulhè's wife had done this, I could have forgiven her; but for Joas, a young man and a king, whofe heart fhould be opened and elated with a firft victory, to be partaker with the Galla, the enemies of his country, in the murder of a nobleman fuch as Mariam Barea, it is a prodigy, and can be followed by no good to himfelf or the ftate; and I am much deceived if the day is not at hand when he fhall curfe the moment that ever Galla croffed the Nile, and look for a man fuch as Mariam Barea, but he fhall not find him." And, indeed, Michael was very well entitled to make this prophecy, for he knew his own heart, and the defigns he had now ready to put in execution.

It is no wonder that thefe free communications gave the king reafon to diftruft Michael. And it was obferved that Waragna Fafil had infinuated himfelf far into his favour: his late behaviour at the battle of Nefas Mufa had

3   greatly

greatly increafed his importance with the king; and the number of troops he had now with him made Joas think himfelf independent of the Ras. Fafil had brought with him near 30,000 men, about 20,000 of whom were horfe-men, wild Pagan Galla, from Bizamo and other nations fouth of the Nile. The terror the favages occafioned in the countries through which they paffed, and the great difor-ders they committed, gave Ras Michael a pretence to infift that all thofe wild Galla fhould be fent back to their own country. I fay this was a pretence, becaufe Michael's fol-diers were really more cruel and licentious, becaufe more confident and better countenanced than thefe ftrangers were. But the war was over, the armies to be difbanded, thefe Pagans were confequently to return home; and they were all fent back accordingly, excepting 12,000 Djawi, men of Fafil's own tribe, and fome of the beft horfe of Maitfha, A-gow, and Damot.

This was the firft appearance of quarrel between Fafil and Ras Michael. But other accidents followed faft that blew up the flame betwixt them; of which the following was by much the moft remarkable, and the moft unex-pected.

At Nefas Mufa, near to the field of battle, was a houfe of Mariam Barea, which he ufed to remove to when he was bufy in wars with the neighbouring Galla. It was fur-rounded with meadows perfectly well-watered, and full of luxuriant grafs. Fafil, for the fake of his cavalry, had en-camped in thefe meadows; or, if he had other views, they are not known; and though all the doors and entrances of the houfe were fhut, yet within was the unfortunate

Ozoro Efther, by this time informed of her hufband's death, and with her was Ayto Aylo, a nobleman of great credit, riches, and influence. He had been at the campaign of Sennaar, and was fo terrified at the defeat, that, on his return, he had renounced the world, and turned monk. He was a man of no party, and refufed all pofts or employments; but was fo eminent for wifdom, that all fides confulted him, and were in fome meafure governed by him.

This perfon, a relation of the Iteghé's, had, at her defire, attended Ozoro Efther to Nefas Mufa, but, adhering to his vow, went not to battle with her hufband. Hearing, however, of the bad difpofition of the king, the cruelty of the Galla, and the power and ambition of Fafil, whofe foldiers were encamped round the houfe, he told her that there was only one refolution which fhe could take to avoid fudden ruin, and being made a facrifice to one of the murderers of her hufband.

This princefs, under the faireft form, had the courage and decifion of a Roman matron, worthy the wife of Mariam Barea, to whom fhe had born two fons. Inftructed by Aylo, early in the morning, all covered from head to foot, accompanied by himfelf, and many attendants and friends, their heads bare, and without appearance of difguife, they prefented themfelves at the door of Michael's tent, and were immediately admitted. Aylo announced the princefs to the Ras, and fhe immediately threw herfelf at his feet on the ground.

As Michael was lame, tho' in all other refpects healthy and vigorous, and unprepared for fo extraordinary an interview,

it was fome time before he could get upon his feet and un-
cover himfelf before his fuperior. This being at laft accomplifhed, and Ozoro Efther refufing to rife, Aylo, in a
few words, told the Ras her refolution was to give him inftantly her hand, and throw herfelf under his protection, as
that of the only man not guilty of Mariam Barea's death, who
could fave her and her children from the bloody cruelty
and infolence of the Galla that furrounded her. Michael,
fanguine as he was in his expectations of the fruit he was
to reap from his victory, did not expect fo foon fo fair a
fample of what was to follow.

To decide well, inftantly upon the firft view of things, was
a talent Michael poffeffed fuperior to any man in the kingdom. Tho' Ozoro Efther had never been part of his fchemes,
he immediately faw the great advantage which would ac-
crue to him by making her fo, and he feized it ; and he was
certain alfo that the king, in his prefent difpofition, would
foon interfere. He lifted Ozoro Efther, and placed her upon his feat ; fent for Kefla Yafous and his other officers, and
ordered them, with the utmoft expedition, to draw up his army in order of battle, as if for a review to afcertain his lofs.
At the fame time he fent for a prieft, and ordered feparate
tents to be pitched for Ozoro Efther and her houfehold.
All this was performed quickly ; then meeting her with
the prieft, he was married to her at the door of his own tent
in midft of the acclamations of his whole army. The occafion of thefe loud fhouts was foon carried to the king,
and was the firft account he had of this marriage. He recci-
ved the information with violent difpleafure, which he could
not ftifle, or refrain from expreffing it in the fevereft
terms, all of which were carried to Ras Michael by officious

perfons,

perfons, almoſt as ſoon as they were uttered, nothing ſof-tened.

THE conſequences of the marriage of Ozoro Eſther were very ſoon ſeen in the inveterate and determined hatred againſt the Galla. Eſther, who could not ſave Mariam Barea, ſacri-ficed herſelf that ſhe might avenge his death, and live to ſee the loſs of her huſband expiated by numberleſs heca-tombs of his enemies and murderers. Mild, gentle, and compaſſionate as, from my own knowledge, ſhe certain-ly was, her nature was totally changed when ſhe caſt back her eyes upon the ſufferings of her huſband; nor could ſhe be ever ſatiated with vengeance for thoſe ſufferings, but conſtantly ſtimulated Ras Michael, of himſelf much in-clined to bloodſhed, to extirpate, by every poſſible means, that odious nation of Galla, by whom ſhe had fallen from all her hopes of happineſs.

FASIL, as being a Galla, the firſt man that broke thro' the horſe of Begemder, and wounded and put to flight her huſ-band Mariam Barea, was in conſequence among the black liſt of her enemies. Faſil, too, had murdered Kaſmati Eſhté, who was her favourite uncle, faſt friend to Mariam Barea, and the man that had promoted her marriage with him.

THE great credit of Faſil with the king had now given Ras Michael violent jealouſy. Theſe cauſes of hatred accu-mulated every day, ſo that Michael had already formed a reſolution to deſtroy Faſil, even though the king ſhould periſh with him. In theſe ſentiments, too, was Guſho of Amhara, a man of great perſonal merit, of whoſe father, Ras Woodage, we have already ſpoken, who had filled ſucceſſive-

4   ly

ly all the great offices in the laſt reign. He was immenſely
rich; had married a daughter of Ras Michael, and afterwards ſix or ſeven other women, being much addicted to the
fair ſex, and was lately married to Ozoro Welleta Iſrael, the
Iteghé's daughter. Nor was he in any ſhape an enemy to
wine; but very engaging, and plauſible in diſcourſe and behaviour; in many reſpects a good officer, careful of his
men, but ſaid to be little ſolicitous about his word or promiſe to men of any other profeſſion but that of a ſoldier.

An accident of the moſt trifling kind brought about an
open breach between the king and the Ras, which never after was healed. The weather was very hot while the army
was marching. One day, a little before their arrival at Gondar, in paſſing over the vaſt plain between the mountains
and the lake Tzana, (afterwards the ſcene of much bloodſhed) Ras Michael, being a little indiſpoſed with the heat,
and the ſun at the ſame time affecting his eyes, which were
weak, without other deſign than that of ſhading them, had
thrown a white cloth or handkerchief over his head. This
was told the king, then with Faſil in the center, who immediately ſent to the Ras to inquire what was the meaning
of that novelty, and upon what account he preſumed to
cover his head in his preſence? The white handkerchief
was immediately taken off, but the affront was thought ſo
heinous as never after to admit of atonement.

It muſt be here obſerved, that, when the army is in the
field, it is a diſtinction the king uſes, to bind a broad fillet
of fine muſlin round his head, which is tied in a double
knot, and hangs in two long ends behind. This, too, is worn
by the governor of a province when he is firſt introduced
into

into it; and, in abfence of the king, is the mark of fupreme power, either direct or delegated, in the perfon that wears it.

UNLESS on fuch occafions, no one covers his head in prefence of the king, nor in fight of the houfe or palace where the king refides: But it was not thought, that, being at fuch a diftance in the rear, he was in the king's prefence, nor that what was caufed by infirmity was to be conftrued into prefumption, or weighed by the nice fcale of jealous prerogative.

THE armies returned to the valleys below Gondar, and encamped feparately there, Fafil upon the river Kahha, and Ras Michael on the Angrab. Gufho was on the right of Michael and left of Fafil, a little higher up the Kahha, near Kofcam, the Iteghè's palace; but he was on the oppofite fide of the river from Fafil, where he had a houfe of his own, and feveral large meadows adjoining. Gufho's fervants and foldiers now began cutting their mafter's grafs, and were foon joined by a number of Fafil's people, who fell, without ceremony, to the fame employment. An interruption was immediately attempted, a fray enfued, and feveral were killed or wounded on both fides, but at laft Fafil's people were beat back to their quarters.

GUSHO complained to Ras Michael of this violation of his property; and he being now in Gondar, and holding the office of Ras, was, without doubt, the fuperior and regular judge of both, as they were both out of their provinces, and immediately in Michael's. Upon citation, Fafil declared that he would fubmit to no fuch jurifdiction; and,

and, the cafe being referred to the judges next day, it was found unanimoufly in council, that Ras Michael was in the right, and that Fafil was guilty of rebellion. A proclamation in confequence was made at the palace-gate, fuperfeding Fafil in his government of Damot, and in every other office which he held under the king, and appointing Boro de Gago in his place, a man of great intereft in Damot and Gojam, and with the Galla on both. fides of the Nile, and married to a fifter of Kafmati Efhté's, by another mother, otherwife a man of fmall capacity.

FASIL, after a long and private audience of the king in the night, decamped early in the morning with his army, and fat down at Azazo, the high road between Damot and Gondar, and there he intercepted all the provifions coming from the fouthward to the capital.

IT happened that the houfe in Gondar, where Ras Michael lived, was but a fmall diftance from the palace, a window of which opened fo directly into it, that Michael, when fitting in judgment, could be diftinctly feen from thence. One day, when moft of his fervants had left him, a fhot was fired' into the room from this window of the palace, which, though it miffed Michael, wounded a dwarf, who was ftanding before him fanning the flies from off his face, fo grievoufly, that the page fell and expired at the foot of his mafter. This was confidered as the beginning of the hoftilities. Nobody knew from whofe hand the fhot came; but the window from which it was aimed fufficiently fhewed, that if it was not by direction, it muft at leaft have been fired with the knowledge of the king.

JOAS

Joas loft no time, but removed and encamped at Tedda, and fent Woofheka to Michael with orders to return to Tigrè, and not to fee his face; and, at the fame time, declared Lubo governor of Begemder and Amhara. The Ras fcarcely could be brought to fee Woofheka; but did not deign to give any further anfwer than this, " That the king " fhould know, that the proper perfons to correfpond with " him as Ras, upon the affairs of the kingdom, were the " judges of the town, or of the palace; not a flave like " Woofheka, whofe life, as well as that of all the Gallas in " the king's prefence, was forfeited by the laws of the " land. He cautioned him from appearing again in his " prefence, for if he did, that he fhould furely die."

The next day a meffage came from the king, by four judges, forbidding the Ras again to drink of either the Angrab or the Kahha, but to ftrike his tents and return to Tigré upon pain of incurring his higheft difpleafure.—To this Michael anfwered, " That, true it was, his province was " Tigrè, but that he was now governor of the whole realm; " that he was an extraordinary officer, called to prevent the " ruin of the country, becaufe, confeffedly, the king could " not do it; that the reafon of his coming exifted to that " day; and he was very willing to fubmit it to the judges " for their folemn opinion, whether the kingdom, at pre- " fent in the hands of the Galla, was not in more danger " from the power of thofe Galla than it was from the con- " ftitutional influence of Mariam Larea. He added, that he " expected the king fhould be ready to march againft Fafil, " for which purpofe he was to decamp on the morrow." The king returned an abfolute refufal to march: The Ras thereupon made proclamation for all the Galla, of every denomination,

mination to leave the capital, the next day, upon pain of death, declaring them outlawed, and liable to be slain by the first that met them, if, after twenty-four hours, they were found in Gondar or its neighbourhood, or, after ten days, in any part of the kingdom. After this, accompanied by Gusho, he decamped to dislodge Fasil from the strong post which he held at Azazo.

By the king's refusal to march with Ras Michael in person, it was supposed that his houfehold troops would not join, but remain with him to garrison his palace. Joas, however, was too far decided in favour of Fasil to remain neuter. Michael had encamped the 21st of April in the evening, on the side of the hill above Azazo, in very rough and rocky ground, as unfavourable for Fasil's horse as the slope it had was favourable for Michael's musquetry.

The battle was fought on the 22d in the morning, and there was much blood shed for the time that it lafted. A nephew of Michael, and his old Fit-Auraris, Netcho, were both slain, and Fasil was totally defeated. The Galla, who had come from the other side of the Nile, were very much terrified at Michael's fire-arms, which contained what they called the zibib, or grape, meaning thereby the ball. Fasil retired quickly to Damot, to increase and collect another army again, and to try his fortune after the rains.

It happened, unfortunately, that among the prisoners taken at Azazo were some of the king's black horse. These being his slaves, and subject only to his commands, sufficiently shewed by whose authority they came there. They were, therefore, all called before Michael; two of them were firſt interrogated, whether the king had ſent them or not? and, upon their denying or refuſing to give an anſwer, their throats were cut before their companions. The next queſtioned was a page of the king, who ſeeing, from the fate of his friends, what was to follow his denial, frankly told the Ras, that it was by the king's ſpecial orders they, and a conſiderable body of the houſehold troops, had joined Faſil the night before; and further, that it was the Armenian, who, by the king's order, had fired at him, and killed the dwarf who was fanning the flies from him.

Upon this information all the priſoners were difmiſſed. The army returned the ſame night to Gondar, and, though they had been faſting all day, a council was held, which ſat till very late, at the riſing of which a meſſenger was diſpatched to Wechné for Hatzé Hannes, who was brought to the foot of the mountain the next day. In the ſame night Shalaka Becro, Nebrit Teola and his two ſons, Lika Netcho and his two ſons, and a monk of Tigrè, called Welleta Chriſtos, were ſent to the palace to murder the king, which they eaſily accompliſhed, having found him alone. They buried him in the church of St Raphael, as we ſhall find from the regicide's own confeſſion, when he was apprehended, when we ſhall relate the particulars.

At the ſame time Michael exhibited a ſtrange contraſt in his behaviour to the Armenian, who had fled to the houſe of the Abuna for refuge. He ſent and took him thence, and baniſhed him from Abyſſinia, but ſo conſiderately, that he diſpatched a ſervant with him to Maſuah to furniſh him with neceſſaries, to ſee him embark, and ſave him from the cruelty and extortions of the Naybe.

HANNES

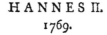

HANNES II.
1769.

Hannes, Brother to Bacuffa, chosen King---Is brought from Wechné---Crowned at Gondar---Refuses to march against Fasil---Is poisoned by Order of Ras Michael.

HANNES, a man past seventy years of age, made his entry into Gondar the 3d of May 1769. He was brother to Bacuffa, and having in his time escaped from the mountain, and being afterwards taken, his hand was cut off by order of the king his brother, and he was sent back to the place of his confinement.

IT is a law of Abyssinia, as we have already observed, derived from that of Moses, that no man can be capable either of the throne or priesthood, unless he be perfect in all his limbs; the want of a hand, therefore, certainly disqualified Hannes, and it was with that intent it had been cut off. When this was objected to him in council, Michael laughed violently, and turned it into ridicule; " What is it that a " king has to do with his hands? Are you afraid he shall " not be able to saddle his own mule, or load his own bag-

v. ii.   4 U 2   " gage?

" gage? Never fear that; when he is under any fuch diffi-
" culty, he has only to call upon me *, and I will help
"; him."

HANNES, befides his age, was very feeble in body; and
having had no converfation but with monks and priefts,,
this had debilitated his mind as much as age had done his.
body. He could not be perfuaded to take any fhare in government. The whole day was fpent in pfalms and prayers;
but Ras Michael had brought from the mountain with him
two fons, Tecla Ha'manout the eldeft, a prince of fifteen
years of age, and the younger, called George, about thirteen.

GUEBRA DENGHEL, a nobleman of the firft family in
Tigré had married a daughter of Michael by one of his
wives in that province. By her he had one daughter, Welleta Selaffé, whom Michael in the beginning, while Joas
and he were yet friends, had deftined to be queen, and to
be married to him. Hannes was of the age only to need a
Shunnamite; and Welleta Selaffé, young and beautiful, and
who merited to be fomething more, was deftined as this
facrifice to the ambition of her grandfather. A kind of
marriage, I believe, was therefore made, but never confum-
mated. She lived with Hannes fome months in the palace,
but never took any ftate upon her. She was a wife and a
queen merely in name and idea. Love had in that frozen
compofition as little fhare as ambition, and thofe two great
temptations,

---

* What made the ridicule here was, Michael was older than the king, and could not
ftand alone.

temptations, a crown and a beautiful miftrefs, could not a-
nimate Harzé Hannes to take the field to defend them.
Every poffible method was taken by Michael to overcome
his reluctance, and do away his fears. All was vain; he
wept, hid himfelf, turned monk, demanded to be fent a-
gain to Wechné, but abfolutely refufed marching with the
army.

MICHAEL, who had already feen the danger of leaving a
king behind him while he was in the field, and finding
Hannes inexorable, had recourfe to poifon, which was
given him in his breakfaft; and the Ras, by this means, in
lefs than fix months became the deliberate murderer of two
kings.

TECLA HAIMANOUT II.
1769.

TECLA HAIMANOUT fucceeded his father. He was a
prince of a moft graceful figure, tall for his age, rather
thin, and of the whiteft fhade of Abyffinian colour, fuch are
all

all thofe princes that are born in the mountain. He was not
fo dark in complexion as a Neapolitan or Portugueze, had a
remarkably fine forehead, large black eyes, but which had
fomething very ftern in them, a ftraight nofe, rather of the
largeft, thin lips, and fmall mouth, very white teeth and long
hair. His features, even in Europe, would have been thought
fine. He was particularly careful of his hair, which he dreffed
in a hundred different ways. Though he had been abfent but
a very few months from his native mountain, his manners
and carriage were thofe of a prince, that from his infancy
had fat upon an hereditary throne. He had an excellent
underftanding, and prudence beyond his years. He was
faid to be naturally of a very warm temper, but this he had
fo perfectly fubdued as fcarcely ever to have given an inftance of it in public. He entered into Ras Michael's views
entirely, and was as forward to march out againft Fafil, as
his father had been averfe to it.

From the time of Hannes's acceffion to the throne, Tecla
Haimanout called Michael by the name of Father, and during the few flight ficknelfes the Ras had, he laid by all his
ftate, and attended him with an anxiety well becoming a
fon. At this time I entered Abyffinia, and arrived in Mafuah, where there was a rumour only of Hatzé Hannes's illnefs.

The army marched out of Gondar on the 10th of November
1769, taking the route of Azazo and Dingleber. Fafil was at
Buré, and had affembled a large army from Damot, Agow,
and Maitfha. But Welleta Yafous, his principal officer, had
brought together a ftill larger one, from the wild nations of

Galla beyond the Nile, and this not without fome difficulty. The zibib, or bullet, which had deftroyed fo many
of them at Azazo, had made an impreffion on their minds,
and been reported to their countrymen as a circumftance
very unpleafing. Thefe wild Pagans, therefore, had, for the
firft time, found a reluctance to invade their ancient enemies
the Abyffinians.

FASIL, to overcome this fear of the zibib, had loaded fome
guns with powder, and fired them very near at fome of his
friends, which of courfe had hurt nobody. Again he had
put ball in his gun, and fired at cattle afar off; and thefe being for the moft part flightly wounded, he inferred from
thence that the zibib was fatal only at a diftance, but that
if they galloped refolutely to the mouth of the gun, the grape
could do no more than the firft gun he fired with powder
had done to thofe he had aimed at.

As foon as Fafil heard that Michael was on his march, he
left Burè and advanced to meet him, his wifh being to fight
him if poffible, before he fhould enter into thofe rich provinces of the Agows, from whence he drew the maintenance of
his army, and expected tribute. Michael's conduct warranted
this precaution. For no fooner had he entered Fafil's government, than he laid wafte all Maitfha, deftroying every
thing with fire and fword. The old general indeed being perfectly acquainted with the country, and with the
enemy he was to engage, had already fixed upon his field
of battle, and meafured the ftations that would conduct
him thither.

INSTEAD of taking up the time with spreading the desolation he had begun, after the first two days, by forced marches he came to Fagitta, confiderably earlier than Fasil expected. This field that Michael had chosen, was rocky, uneven, and full of ravines in one part, and of plain smooth turf on the other, which divisions were separated by a brook full of large stones.

THE Nile was on Ras Michael's left, and in this rugged ground he stationed his lances and musquetry; for he never made great account of his horse.   Two large churches, St Michael and St George, planted thick **with** cedars, and about half a mile distant from each other, were on his right and left flanks, or rather advanced farther before his front. A deep valley communicated with the most level of these plains, descending gently all the way from the celebrated sources of the Nile, which were not more than half a day's journey distant.   Michael drew up his army behind the two churches, which were advanced on his right and left flanks, and among the cedars of these he planted 500 musqueteers before each church, whom the trees perfectly concealed; he formed his horse in front, knowing them to be an object the Galla did not fear, and likely to lead them on to charge rashly.   These he gave the command of to a very active and capable officer, Powuffen of Begemder, one of those eleven fervants of Mariam Barea, whose lives Michael faved, by protecting them in his tent after the battle of Nefas Mufa. He had directed this officer, with a few horse, to scour the small plain, as soon as he saw the Galla advancing into it from the valley.

3

As foon as the fun became hot, Fafil's wild Galla poured into the plain, and they had now occupied the greateſt part of it, which was not large enough to contain his whole army, when their ſkirmiſhing began by their driving Powuſſen before them, who fled apparently in great confuſion, croſſed the brook, and joined the horſe, and formed nearly between the churches. The Galla, deſirous to purſue, were impeded by the great ſtones, ſo that they were in a crowd at the paſſage of the brook.

Ayto Welleta Gabriel, factor to Ozoro Eſther, was intoxicated with liquor, but he was a brave man, very active and ſtrong, and of a good underſtanding, though, according to a cuſtom among them, he, at times, to divert the Ras, played the part of a buffoon. In this character, with his muſquet only in his hand, he, though on foot, ſkirmiſhed in the middle of a party of Powuſſen's horſe. When they turned to fly, Welleta Gabriel found it convenient to do ſo likewiſe, and he croſſed the brook without looking behind him. Upon turning round, he ſaw the Galla halt, as if in council, in the bed of the rivulet, and taking up his gun as a bravado, he levelled at the crowd, and had the fortune to hit the principal man among them, who fell dead among the feet of the horſes.

A small pauſe enſued; the cry of the Zibib! the Zibib! immediately began, and a downright confuſion and flight followed. The Galla, already upon the plain, turned upon thoſe coming out of the valley, and theſe again upon their companions behind them. The cry of Zibib Ali*! Zibib Ali!

Vol. II.   4 X

---

* They have the grape along with them.

Ali! was repeated through the whole, fpreading terror and difmay wherever it was heard. Nobody knew what was the misfortune that had befallen them. Welleta Yafous, who commanded the van, was carried away by the multitude flying: Fafil, who was at the head of the Damot and Agows, had not entered the valley, nor could any one tell him what was the accident in the plain.

Even Michael himfelf, (as I have heard him fay) when, fitting upon his mule on a fmall eminence, he faw this extraordinary confufion and retreat, was not able to affign any caufe for it. Though no man on thefe occafions had more prefence of mind, he remained for a time motionlefs, without giving any orders. The troops, however, that lay hid in the groves of cedars before the churches, who had been filent and attentive, and Powuffen, who commanded the horfe which had been fkirmifhing, faw diftinctly the operation of Welleta Gabriel, and the confufion that had followed it; without lofs of time they attacked the Galla in the valley, and were foon joined by Gufho and the reft of the army.

Fasil, in defpair at a defeat of which he knew not the caufe, came down among the Galla, fighting very bravely, often facing about upon thofe that preffed them, and endeavouring at leaft to retreat in fome fort of order; but the mufqueteers from the church, commanded by Hezekias, inftead of entering the valley, had advanced and afcended the hills, fo that from the fides of them, in the utmoft fecurity, they poured down fhot upon the fliers beneath them.

FASIL here loft a great part of his army; but feeing a place in one of the hills acceffible, he left the valley, and afcended the fide of the mountain, leading a large body of his own troops; and, having gained the fmooth ground behind the mufqueteers, he came up with them, whilft intent only upon annoying the Galla, and cut 300 to pieces. Content with this advantage, and finding his army entirely difperfed, he paffed the fources of the Nile at Gcefh, defcended into the plain of Affoa, and encamped near Gooderoo, a fmall lake there, intending to pafs the night, and collect his fcattered forces.

MICHAEL's army had given over purfuit, but Powuffen, with fome chofen horfe of Lafta and Begemder, followed Fafil upon his track, and came up with him a little before the dufk of the evening, on the fide of the lake. Here a great flaughter of wounded and weary men enfued : Fafil fled, and no refiftance was attempted, and the foldiers, fatiated with blood, at laft returned, and purfued the enemy no further.

IT was the next day in the evening before Powuffen joined the camp, having put to the fword, without mercy, all the ftragglers that fell in the way upon his return. The appearance of this man and his behaviour made Michael's joy complete, who already had begun to entertain fears that fome untoward accident had befallen him.

THIS was the battle of Fagitta, fought on the 9th of December 1769, on the very ground in which Fafil, juft five years before, had murdered Kafmati Efhté. Thofe philofophers, who difclaim the direction of a divine Providence,

will

will calculate how many chances there were, that, in a kingdom as big as Great Britain, the commiffion of a crime and its punifhment fhould both happen in one place, on one day, in the fhort fpace of five years, and in the life of one man.

The extraordinary feverity exercifed upon the army of the Galla, after the battle, was ftill as apparent as it had been in t e flight. Woofheka, of whom we have had already occafion to fpeak, fell in among the horfe of Powuffen and Gufho, and being known, his life was fpared. He was coufin-german to Lubo, but a better man and foldier than his relation, and, in all the intrigues of the Galla at Gondar, was confidered as an undefigning man, of harmlefs and inoffenfive manners. He had been companion of Gufho, and many of the principal commanders in the army, and, after the defeat at Nefas Mufa, had the guard of Powuffen and the eleven officers, whom he fuffered to efcape into Michael's tent, as I have already faid, while Lubo was murdering Mariam Barea. He had been, for a time, well known and well efteemed by Ras Michael, nor was he ever fuppofed perfonally to have offended him, or given umbrage to any one. As he was a man of fome fortune and fubftance, it was thought the forfeiture of all that he had might more than atone for any fault that he had ever committed.

It was therefore agreed on the morning after Powuffen's return from the purfuit, that Gufho and he, when they furrendered this prifoner, fhould afk his life and pardon from the Ras, and this they did, proftrating themfelves in the humbleft manner with their foreheads on the earth. Ras
Michael,

M'chael, at once forgetting his own intereft, and the quality
a'd confequence of the officers before him, fell into a violent and outrageous paffion againft the fupplicants, and,
after a very fhort reproof, ordered each of them to their
tents in a kind of difgrace.

He then fternly interrogated Woofheka, whether he did
not remember that, at Tedda, he had ordered him out of
the country in ten days? then, in his own language of Tigré,
he afked, if there was any one among the foldiers that
could make a leather bottle? and being anfwered in the af-
firmative, he ordered one to be made of Woofheka's fkin,
but firft to carry him to the king. The foldiers underftood the command, though the miferable victim did not,
and he was brought to the king, who would not fuffer him
to fpeak, but waved with his hand to remove him; and
they accordingly carried him to the river fide, where they
flayed him alive, and brought his fkin ftuffed with ftraw to
Ras Michael.

It was not doubted that Ozoro Efther, then in the camp,
had fealed the fate of this wretched victim. She appeared
that night in the king's tent dreffed in the habit of a bride,
which fhe had never before done fince the death of Mariam
Barea. Two days after, having obtained her end, fhe returned triumphant to Gondar, where Providence vifited her
with diftrefs in her own family, for the hardnefs of her
heart to the fufferings of others.

During this time I was at Mafuah, where, by reafon of
the great diftance and interruption in the roads, thefe tranfactions

1

actions were not yet known. Hatzé Hannes was still supposed alive, and my errand from Metical Aga that of being
his Physician. I shall now begin an account of what passed at
Masuah, and thence continue my journey to Gondar till
my meeting with the king there.

END OF THE SECOND VOLUME.

83299